D1221695

FROM CREATION TO SINAI

Published by the Religious Studies Center, Brigham Young University, Provo, Utah, in cooperation with Deseret Book Company, Salt Lake City, Utah.
Visit us at rsc.byu.edu.

Printed in the United States of America by Sheridan Books, Inc.

Deseret Book is a registered trademark of Deseret Book Company.
Visit us at DeseretBook.com.

Cover and interior design by Emily V. Rogers

ISBN: 978-1-9503-0419-6

Library of Congress Cataloging-in-Publication Data

Names: Belnap, Daniel, editor. | Schade, Aaron, editor.
Title: From creation to Sinai : the Old Testament through the lens of the Restoration / edited by Daniel L. Belnap and Aaron P. Schade.
Description: Provo, Utah : Religious Studies Center, Brigham Young University ; Salt Lake City, Utah : Deseret Book, [2021] | Includes index. | Summary: "Admittedly, the Old Testament is a difficult volume to read, much less understand. The language, symbolism, and history depicted within it can be challenging and at times frustrating. Modern biblical research and the methodologies used in that research have opened up this book of scripture to greater understanding. So too have the restoration of the priesthood and continuing revelation, which have revealed that the Old Testament patriarchs are not simply literary examples of righteous behavior in the past but living beings who have engaged with the Saints in this dispensation. This volume incorporates both academic insights and restoration revelation, thus demonstrating the way in which both can be used to gain greater insight into these pivotal narratives"-- Provided by publisher.
Identifiers: LCCN 2021028754 | ISBN 9781950304196 (hardcover)
Subjects: LCSH: Bible. Genesis--Criticism, interpretation, etc. | Bible. Exodus--Criticism, interpretation, etc. | Church of Jesus Christ of Latter-day Saints--Doctrines. | Mormon Church--Doctrines.
Classification: LCC BS1235.52 .F765 2021 | DDC 222/.1106--dc23
LC record available at https://lccn.loc.gov/2021028754

FROM CREATION TO SINAI

THE OLD TESTAMENT THROUGH THE LENS OF THE RESTORATION

DANIEL L. BELNAP AND **AARON P. SCHADE**, EDS.

CONTENTS

SECTION 3: THE PATRIARCHAL NARRATIVES

SECTION 4: THE EXODUS AND SINAI

INTRODUCTION

The Church of Jesus Christ of Latter-day Saints embraces a canon of scripture that comprises the Old and New Testaments, the Book of Mormon, the Pearl of Great Price, the Doctrine and Covenants, and the words of living prophets and apostles. It seems, at times, that these scriptures hold different priorities in the eyes of individuals, with the Old Testament tending to find itself at the bottom of the scriptural totem pole. For example, while attending a stake priesthood meeting, one of the speakers spoke about the importance of scripture study and their own growth in developing a productive scripture study habit. In the course of his presentation, the speaker spoke of some advice that he had received by one of his ecclesiastical leaders. According to the individual, he was instructed, "Go ahead and skip the Old Testament, as it has no real value, and go straight into the Book of Mormon." Undoubtedly, the leader's counsel to skip the Old Testament had good intentions, encouraging the listeners to focus on what they felt was the most important for them at that time. Yet the outcome of such an attitude toward the Old Testament prevents one from enjoying all that it has to offer. Certainly not everyone feels apathetic about the Old Testament, but what seems fairly common in our encounters with fellow churchgoers is a bit of an intimidation factor in regard to the Old Testament due to difficulties in trying to understand it.

Admittedly, the Old Testament is a difficult volume to read, much less understand. The language, symbolism, and history depicted within it can be challenging, and at times frustrating. Old Testament books present us with an entirely different social and cultural environment, separating us, the modern readers, from them, the ancient writers and peoples living in that distant day and age. This is further complicated when one recognizes that the Old Testament is made up of a number of texts from different periods, resulting in shifting symbolism or meaning from one text to another.

Biblical scholars, clergymen, and laypeople have attempted to elucidate these interpretive difficulties and provide a coherent exegesis, or internal meaning of the texts. They have done so by applying a wide array of methodologies to the narratives and teachings of the Old Testament, including efforts to provide a historical, linguistic, and theological context to each of the stories. Such methodologies have included applying the documentary hypothesis, source criticism, redaction history of the texts, form criticism, literary and comparative studies with cognate languages, and discussions of the texts in relation to their final form. The strength of these approaches is that they allow the Old Testament to be read on its own terms and appreciated for the lessons or principles the authors themselves presented, rather than solely trying to read one's own meaning into the text, an approach known as eisegesis.

Eisegesis is a favorite methodology employed by Latter-day Saints reflecting an approach to scripture often attributed to the Book of Mormon in that we "liken all scriptures unto us" (1 Nephi 19:23). This approach can be deeply personal and meaningful and can bring in much personal revelation that we seek in our lives. However, if left to itself, we fall short of enjoying all that God has revealed. Additionally, if approached solely from an eisegetical approach, it is possible to create an application that is independent of the text itself. Thus, putting in the work to try our best to understand some of the difficulties presented in our studies of the Old Testament can lead to scriptural literacy that is liberating, enlightening, and inspiring.

Yet the exegetical methodologies listed above are not sufficient to produce a definitive understanding of the Old Testament either. While they do allow for a greater understanding of a given text and its place within the larger textual body, their objective basis means that divine revelation and prophetic authority are often not recognized as legitimate avenues for understanding.[1] It thus seems of value to synthesize the insights from revelation with what academic exegesis can produce through strenuous work. The result can be that we fully engage with scriptural canon in a way that is meaningful and uplifting, offering clarity to the past, present, and future. Thanks to the restoration of the priesthood and continuing revelation, the Old Testament patriarchs are not simply literary examples of righteous behavior but contemporary beings that have engaged, and continue to engage, with the Saints in this dispensation. The Joseph Smith Translation of the Bible, the Book of Mormon, and the texts contained in the Pearl of Great Price, by virtue of their inception via divine authority, allow for insights and interpretations to biblical narratives that are not always acceptable to modern exegetical analysis. In our eyes, they continue and build on those narratives in ways that may not always be possible to authenticate by modern scholarship, but that are nevertheless realities and that can be confirmed by faith and revelation.

The genesis (pun intended) of this volume finds its origins in the desires of the editors to bring together a collection of essays on the Old Testament, which have attempted to implement multiple approaches to the texts. We have tried to accomplish this by introducing a unique approach to biblical exegesis that would resonate with adherers to the theology, teachings, and doctrines of The Church of Jesus Christ of Latter-day Saints.

The purpose of the volume, then, is to provide perspectives using sound academic methodologies, while simultaneously drawing upon insights gained through prophets, apostles, and Restoration scripture.

1. While the methodologies purport to be objective, the authors and scholars who engage the methodologies rarely are and therefore bring their own biases to the text. We need to be aware of these preconceived notions when studying any scholarly report or work.

In terms of the volume's organization, the chapters have been arranged into four sections. The first engages with the antediluvian (preflood) narratives. Dan Belnap begins the volume by addressing the creation narrative depicted in Genesis 1–3 and applying a social-critical and anthropological lens to the text, as well as intersecting it with Restoration scripture through which modern application can be made. Andrew Skinner follows with his approach to the Cain and Abel narrative, noting the role of modern scripture in the Book of Moses to help us understand this difficult narrative, while Jared Ludlow provides an overview to Enoch, a figure mentioned once in the Old Testament and yet, who plays a pivotal role in the Book of Moses and later apocryphal writings. Aaron P. Schade engages with the flood narrative, using modern prophetic teachings to provide greater meaning to the narrative in question.

Section 2 of the book includes four chapters surveying the historical context of the patriarchal period. George Pierce begins by providing an overview of the second millennium BC period of Syro-Palestine, the time period of the patriarchs, demonstrating the value, and challenges, of applying archaeological and historical methodologies to the biblical text. He is followed by Kerry Muhlestein, whose focus is on Egypt during the same period. The next chapter is by Shon Hopkin, who discusses the concepts of covenants and covenant making, particularly in regard to Abraham. John Gee rounds out these chapters by reviewing historical elements related to Abraham's journeys.

The actual narratives are explored in section 3 of the volume. Avram Shannon discusses the patriarchal narrative while RoseAnn Benson examines the often overlooked narrative of Abraham's nephew, Lot, and the surprising Latter-day Saint insights that give greater glimpses into this patriarch. We hear again from Aaron P. Schade, who explores those narratives associated with Isaac and Jacob, particularly examining the difficult narrative of Jacob's perceived deception of his father. Camille Fronk Olson discusses the other side of the patriarchal narratives—namely, the significant role of the patriarchs' wives—and in so doing, outlines a greater understanding as to the role of women within the Church today. Finally, John Gee examines the narrative of Joseph through the lens of material culture.

The last section concerns itself with the events of the Exodus. Kerry Muhlestein places the Exodus account within its Egyptian context, as Andrews Skinner and Dan Belnap address the concept of the provocation and the temple in the Sinai events, while Matt Bowen outlines the components of the law of Moses. The volume concludes with Dana Pike, who provides insight into the conquest of Israel as depicted in Numbers, with particular emphasis on the unique narrative of Balaam.

As with any volume, we recognize that we must work within certain limits and page constraints. Thus, we want to be clear that this book is not an exhaustive study of the early biblical narratives but comprises selections of passages or topics that can be difficult to understand. We have had to make judgment calls on what that included. Second, we understand that some may recognize that we are not always trying to break new ground in terms of exegesis, but are rather attempting to synthesize material that may not generally or easily be readily available to many readers. Finally, while we have tried to address some of the more well-known narratives of the early history of Israel, we recognize that there are many other narratives and approaches to those narratives that we have excluded. With that said, we feel that the chapters contained within this volume represent a way to productively integrate academic scholarship into scripture study in a meaningful and uplifting way. In so doing, it is our hope that the volume provides the means by which an audience comprising adherents to The Church of Jesus Christ of Latter-day Saints may recognize the value and importance of the Old Testament, even understanding how this volume of difficult scripture indeed still speaks to us today. Indeed, our hope is that through this volume all may develop a love of the Old Testament leading to a lifetime of study and the fulfillment of Joseph Smith's exclamation: "he who reads it oftenest will like it best!"[2]

—Daniel L. Belnap and Aaron P. Schade

2. From a discourse given by Joseph Smith on July 2, 1839, in Montrose, Iowa; reported by Wilford Woodruff and Willard Richards. The Elders of the Church encouraged their brethren abroad to continue studying the scriptures and to recognize the omniscience of God in them, for "he that can mark the power of Omnipotence inscribed upon the heavens, can also see His own hand-writing in the sacred volume; and he who reads it oftenest will like it best." "Letter to the Church, circa March 1834," p. 142, The Joseph Smith Papers.

— 1 —

IN THE BEGINNING

GENESIS 1–3 AND ITS SIGNIFICANCE TO THE LATTER-DAY SAINTS

DANIEL L. BELNAP

This volume begins with the same event the Bible itself does—the Creation. The Creation narrative and the Garden of Eden narrative that immediately follows have been the subject of much study throughout the years. Over the past century, particular attention has been given to the similarities between it and other ancient Near Eastern Creation narratives. For Latter-day Saints, the Creation and Garden of Eden narratives play central roles in their worship practices, the narratives themselves laying down the plan of salvation God ordained for all his children. In this first chapter, Dan Belnap describes what creation meant to those of the ancient Near East and how that understanding continues to provide a template of salvation for God's family. —DB & AS

The Creation narratives of Genesis 1–3 are arguably the most well-known Old Testament narratives. They make up the first six pages of the Bible, and they describe God bringing everything into existence. But beyond their location in the text, the narratives may also be used to set up an important but perhaps overlooked concept: the election of Israel and their foundational role in Christianity's understanding of salvation.[1] For Latter-day Saints, these narratives are a primary component of our religious experience, while our additional scriptures (The Book of Moses and the Book of Abraham) provide unique insights into the significance and purpose of these events. And because we understand scripture to be more than historical documents, the principles of creation, the establishment of community, and the responsibilities given to Adam and Eve speak to us and our own place within the cosmos.

"THE EARTH WAS WITHOUT FORM, AND VOID": THE CREATION OF THE PHYSICAL COSMOS

Genesis 1 begins with a setting familiar to those who know ancient Near Eastern cosmology. According to verse 2, the precreative state (Hebrew *tohû wābohû*)[2] was one which had no distinctive shape or purpose yet. Translated in English as "without form, and void", *tohû wābohû* does not

---

1. C. John Collins, *Genesis 1–4: A Linguistic, Literary, and Theological Commentary* (Phillipsburg, NJ: P&R, 2006), 35: "Genesis 1–11 sets the stage for the mission of Israel to live as God's treasured people and thereby to be the vehicle of blessing to the rest of the world." Similarly, Bernhard W. Anderson, *From Creation to New Creation: Old Testament Perspectives* (Minneapolis: Fortress Press, 1994), 25: "In the book of Genesis creation does not stand by itself. . . . Rather, as indicated by the position of the creation stories at the opening of the Bible, creation is a prologue to history. . . . Creation provides the background and setting for the vocation of God's people." See also Seth D. Postell, *Adam as Israel: Genesis 1–3 as the Introduction to the Torah and Tanakh* (Cambridge, MA: James Clarke and Co., 2012), 97: "A confirmation that Gen 1:2 anticipates redemptive themes, such as the crossing of the Red Sea, is found in Deuteronomy 32, a song about the 'last days.'"
2. This study employs transliteration diacriticals and spellings of Hebrew and Greek. While the author will be consistent in his usage, when directly quoting other sources he will revert to the cited author's usage or format.

mean "nothing" or indicate an absence, but instead refers to a state in which material was present, but in an unorganized, unformed, state.[3] The *tohû wābohû* is paralleled with "the deep" (*tᵉhōm* in Hebrew, *abussos* in Greek), reflecting the common ancient Near Eastern association of the sea or ocean with the unorganized material of this precreative state. Thus the Creation event opens with a sense of potential or expectation, a sense strengthened by what appears to be divine preparatory action: "and the spirit of God moved [brooded] over the waters."[4]

---

3. John H. Walton, *The Lost World of Adam and Eve: Genesis 2–3 and the Human Origins Debate* (Downers Grove, IL: InterVarsity Press, 2015), 29: "In [*tohu*'s] twenty occurrences (more than half in Isaiah), we find that it often describes a wilderness or wasteland (e.g., Deut. 32:10; Job 6:18, 12:24; Ps. 107:40). It can describe the results of destruction (Jer. 4:23). It is used to convey things that have no purpose or meaning (e.g., idols, Isa. 41:29, and those who make them, Isa. 44:9). All its uses can be consolidated in the notion of things that are of no purpose or worth. They lack order and function. It now becomes clear that the starting condition in Genesis 1:2, the pre-creation situation that describes nonexistence, is a condition that is not lacking material. Rather, it is a situation that is lacking order and purpose." Also, John Day, *From Creation to Babel: Studies in Genesis 1–11* (London: Bloomsbury, 2013), 8–9: "It is clear that the word's connotations in Biblical Hebrew range from the concrete 'desert' to the abstract 'non-entity,' the central meaning uniting these being that of 'empty' or 'nothing.' 'Empty' seems to be the meaning we have in Gen. 1:2. . . . Of course the world was not completely empty, since it was covered in water. What is meant is that the earth existed only in an inchoate state and was devoid of all its familiar features and inhabitants which are subsequently created in Genesis 1. D. T. Tsumura and Terry Fenton are right in saying that *tohû wābohû* in Gen. 1:2 has sometimes been wrongly understood as chaos. However, the term *chaos* is surely not inappropriately used of the raging waters that God has to do battle with in some parts of the Old Testament at the time of creation (e.g., Ps. 104:6–9) and which ultimately lies behind the waters of the deep in Gen. 1:2."
4. David Tsumura, *Creation and Destruction: A Reappraisal of the Chaoskampf Theory in the Old Testament* (Winona Lake, IN: Eisenbrauns, 2005), 33: "The author's intention in describing the earth in its initial state as *tohu wabohu* was not to present the earth as 'the terrible, eerie, deserted wilderness' but to introduce the earth as being 'not yet' normal. . . . This interpretation of *tohu wabohu* (lit. 'desert-like and empty') as describing a bare state, a 'desolate and uninhabited' state, of the earth fits the literary structure of the entire chapter." Seth D. Postell, *Adam as Israel: Genesis 1–3 as the Introduction to the Torah and Tanakh* (Cambridge, MA: James Clarke and Co., 2012), 97: "A confirmation that Gen

The actual creative process involving the shaping or organizing of the preexisting material begins as God speaks light into existence, thereby delineating the elemental states of light and dark, an act that typifies the creation process as God takes the undifferentiated and unformed precreation material and organizes or arranges the material via separation.[5] The

---

1:2 anticipates redemptive themes, such as the crossing of the Red Sea, is found in Deuteronomy 32, a song about the "last days." There, a cluster of terms from the Creation account—a cluster appearing nowhere else in the entire Hebrew Bible—describes Israel's redemption using the same terms: "He found him in a desert land and in an uninhabitable (*tohu*) howling wasteland, he surrounded him, he attentively considered him, he protected him as the apple of his eye. As an eagle stirs up its nest, brooding (*yarakhef*) over its chicks, he carries him upon his pinions (Deut. 32:10–11)." See Michael DeRoche, "The *rûaḥ ʾelōhîm* in Gen 1:2c: Creation or Chaos?," in *Ascribe to the Lord: Biblical and Other Studies in Memory of Peter C. Craigie*, ed. Lyle Eslinger and Glen Taylor, Journal for the Study of the Old Testament Supplement Series 67 (Sheffield, MA: JSOT Press, 1988), 303–18, who compares Genesis 1:2 and the *ruach*, or "spirit," of God stirring the waters to the role of the *rûach* in Genesis 8:1 and the drying of the waters following the flood and the dry land appearing in the Exodus 14:21., suggesting that one role of the *rûach* is annunciatory in function, effectively indicating that the work of creation is about to commence: "The *rûaḥ ʾelōhîm* of Gen 1:2c refers to the impending creative activity of the deity. . . . It expresses Elohim's control over the cosmos and his ability to impose his will upon it" (318).

5. Walton, *Lost World*, 30: "To bārāʾ something brings it into existence by giving it a role and function in an ordered system. . . . In this view, the result of bara is order. The roles and functions are established by separating and naming. These are the acts of creation." See also Don Michael Hudson, "From Chaos to Cosmos: Sacred Space in Genesis," in *Zeitschrift für die alttestamentliche Wissenschaft* 108 (1996): 87–97: "Sacred space, according to Eliade and others, is space that is separated from the sameness of the creative order by differentiating a place that is symbolically or ritually different from any place like it. . . . The introduction of sacred space into a predominantly profane world reflects the possibility for orientation. . . . Without a divinely appointed reference point in the profane world of relativity and sameness, humankind is left with no possibility of orienting himself or herself around that which is 'wholly other' and that which has the potential of transcending himself or herself in the mundane world of existence" and "differentiation and orientation provided humankind with the symbolic means to distinguish in the midst of sameness, orient himself or herself in the midst of potential wastelands, and thereby communicate ritually with the sacred world in which the gods resided" (90–91).

general concept of separation during creation seems clear with the broad function of establishing a sacred space wherein God and his creations will dwell in order to fulfill his purposes. While this broad differentiation is clear, the significance or function of this specific first, separating process is less clear. Some have suggested that this first separation or distinction with light and dark highlights the creation of time via alternating states of darkness and light. While this may be the case, the actual measurements of time are created later with the establishment of the heavenly bodies (such as the sun and the moon). If this first separation is not the presence of time, it is possible that the establishing of light reflects another purpose. Throughout the ancient Near East and the Bible, the presence of light indicates the presence of Deity. Moreover, the role of light in ritual processes throughout the ancient Near East suggest that light was understood as an energizing or vitalizing agent as well as a purifying one. These associations suggest that the creation of light can indicate direct, divine activity or the creation of an environment in which the divine may be directly and always present, an aspect of the cosmos necessary for the fulfilment of the plan of salvation.[6]

6. In this paper, the term *cosmos*, derived from the Greek *kosmos*, is meant to refer to the organized state that is the result of creative labor, not necessarily the fully articulated ancient Greek usage. See Bernhard W. Anderson, *From Creation to New Creation: Old Testament Perspectives* (Minneapolis: Fortress Press, 1994), 27–8: "The Hebrew Bible does not have the equivalent of the Greek term *kosmos*, which suggests the view of the universe as a rationally constituted and self-sustaining structure of reality. Instead, it speaks of the relationship between the Creator and the creation, a relationship that is essentially that of the covenant. . . . The covenant, rather than a rational principle, is the ground of the unity of the creation. Hence psalmists exclaim that divine *ḥeṣed* or covenant loyalty embraces all God's works." The theological nature of the biblical cosmos may be reflected in the principles outlined in Doctrine and Covenants 88:7–11, in which the relationship between the cosmos and Christ is outlined: "This is the light of Christ. As also he is in the sun, and the light of the sun, and the power thereof by which it was made. As also he is in the moon, and is the light of the moon, and the power thereof by which it was made; as also the light of the stars, and the power thereof by which they were made; and the earth also, and the power thereof, even the earth upon which you stand. And the light which shineth, which giveth you light, is through him who enlighteneth your eyes, which is the same light that quickeneth your understandings; the light

With images of the divine presence in place, we are then told that God separated the precreation water and sustained that separation via the firmament. This act created a space in which the rest of the earth could be established, with land emerging and the seas gathered and bound in their place. Following the establishing of the boundaries of land, sea, and sky, God then named these physical locales earth, sea, and heaven. This act of naming may be understood as much a part of the creation process as the physical separation, because defining and naming provides order and meaning, assigning purpose in individualizing each aspect from the others. This twofold process of separating or distinguishing followed by the naming or identification of the object is repeated throughout the creative process and is often concluded with God's declaration that the Creation to this point is "good."[7] More than merely an acknowledgment of what has happened, the declaration that the aspects of the Creation are

---

which is in all things, which giveth life to all things, which is the law by which all things are governed, even the power of God who sitteth upon his throne."

7. Norman Habel has pointed out the similarity between this sequence and the birth process. See Norman Habel, *The Birth, the Curse and the Greening of the Earth: An Ecological Reading of Genesis 1–11*, Earth Bible Series 1 (Sheffield, MA: Sheffield Phoenix Press, 2011), 31–33: "The implication of this reading that a womb/birth metaphor lies behind the imagery for the setting and appearance of Erets [earth] on day three may seem surprising, given the tendency of many interpreters to view *tehom* and the waters as evidence of primal chaos. That Erets has been viewed as a mother in some biblical passages is well known (Ps. 139:13–15). Job cries out, 'Naked I came from my mother's womb and naked I shall return there' (Job 1:21). A primal birth image is explicit in passages such as Job 38:8 where sea comes forth from a primal womb to be clothed and contained by God. Immediately relevant is the imagery of Ps. 90:2 where the psalmist asserts that El, the creator God, was present before the mountains were born (*yld*) and before Erets and the inhabited world came to birth and was brought forth in labour (*chwl*). This passage quite explicitly speaks of the origin of Erets at the hands of the maker/midwife in terms of a birthing process—a tradition that I suggest is also reflected in Genesis 1. . . . If we recognize the validity of the birth metaphor, the progression from Gen. 1:2–10 becomes clear. A form, like an embryo, is located in the waters of the deep. These waters suggest a placid womb rather than a raging sea. Light and space are created so this form can be revealed. At the 'birth' moment, the waters separate/burst and—at the invitation of Elohim—the form appears/emerges out of the waters as a newborn child. God names the form Erets, looks at her and responds with

good represents a fundamental and crucial observation that the objects noted are fulfilling their divine purpose and function.[8] It represents the intrinsic integrity making up the cosmic entities and thereby the underlying order and organization of the cosmos as a whole.[9]

---

delight." We thus see God portrayed in terms of Father and giver of life in the creation.

8. Thus, this process (differentiating, naming, and declaring as good) may also be understood as a revelatory one. As Habel points out that the verb "to appear" in the clause "cause dry land to appear" may also be translated "be revealed." "The Niphal form of this verb used here is used elsewhere when God or an angel of God is revealed or 'appears.' In Gen. 18:1, 'Yhwh appeared to Abraham (cf. Gen 12:7; 35:1). The language of God's theophanic appearances to humans is here, in Gen. 1:9–10, associated with the appearance of Erets, highlighting the climactic significance of the event . . ." Habel, *The Birth*, 31–32. In creation, God is revealing his purposes.
9. Rolf Knierim, "Cosmos and History in Israel's Theology," in *Horizons in Biblical Theology 3* (1981): 59–124, particularly 87: "The created world-order has certain qualitative notions which explicate Yahweh's relationship to and presence in it. The fact of creation out of chaos alone represents more than a merely quantitative event. It is a good event. The priestly formulation according to which the whole creation is 'very good' in God's judgment (Gen. 1:31) is not superficial because the word 'good' is a common word. It is the most profound formulation which in essence includes all else that can be said. It cannot be said better. And it is a fundamental theological statement about the world. This is goodness is not only true for the order of creation in the beginning. It is also true for all the time throughout which this order exists in accordance with its beginning." Similarly, John H. Walton, *Genesis 1 as Ancient Cosmology* (Winona Lake, IN: Eisenbrauns, 2011), 169: "The recurring formula in Genesis 1—'it was good'—offers this same assessment of the creative acts that brought order to the cosmos: the cosmos now functioned well. The evidence that this is the nuance of the Hebrew word *tob* (which admittedly has a wide semantic range) comes from the context. Contextually, it is useful to consider the nuance that the word has by asking what it would look like for something not to be good. Fortunately, the context does indicate something that is not good: 'It is not good for man to be alone' (Gen. 2:18). The word *tob* in this good concerns proper functioning: it is not a negative assessment of craftsmanship or moral purity. We can therefore infer that the recurring assessment that things were good in Genesis 1 does not refer to the absence of corruption or flaw. It instead it is an affirmation that the functions were set to operate according to their design." Habel suggests a more intimate aspect as well, see Habel, *The Birth*, 32: "The 'good' that Elohim sees in Erets is not 'good' in some dualistic or moral sense. 'Good' is Elohim's response

At this point, what may be deemed the first stage of the Creation, the formation and ordering of the basic physical environment of land, sea, and sky, is completed. As noted earlier, the Creation narrative describes not just the material organization but the establishment of their function as well. It is this aspect that now comes to the fore with the beginning of the second stage of the Creation, the ordering of life. Just as in the first stage, this one too begins with differentiation and delineation as vegetation is divided into three categories: grass, herbs, and fruit trees. Further differentiation and complexity are made by the injunction that each is to produce seed after its own kind, meaning that while all three may be the same type (i.e., plant life in general as opposed to other creations), each plant could be differentiated from others, thereby rendering the nascent cosmos incapable of returning to its undifferentiated, precosmic state. In this, the command "after its own kind" serves a similar function as the naming did in the first stage, and, as in the first stage, this level of differentiation is also recognized by God that it was "good," highlighting the order and purpose of the Creation with its attendant limitations, prescriptions, designs, and given creative powers in each respective sphere and function.

Though the next aspect of the Creation process, the formation and placement of the astronomical bodies, may appear to be a backward step from the physical, material organization, the Creation narrative is not concerned with our modern concept of the universe as cosmos where earth is but a small and seemingly insignificant piece of the equation. Instead, all focus is on the creation of this earth within the larger cosmos. The earth is the focus and thus the establishment of the other astronomical bodies is not meant to place the earth within a larger cosmic context of galaxies and so forth, but to define the earth's temporal cosmos or the ordering of time on the earth. The triad of sun, moon, and stars, the reader is told, would be used to designate night and day, as opposed to light and dark, as well as seasons, days, and years. Complementing their function as time measures, the astronomical objects also function as "signs." What is meant exactly

---

to what is seen, experienced in the moment of its appearance. A similar idiom is used to describe the response of Moses' mother when he is born. When she first bonds with the child 'she sees he is good' (Ex. 2:1). Elohim beholds Earth emerge from the waters below and 'sees Earth is good.'"

is not clear, but it hints of a function useful primarily to humankind and highlights the anthropocentric purpose of the cosmos within this narrative. Humans will thus constitute the main purpose behind God's creations. Just as the vegetation all reflects types useful to humanity, so too the astronomical bodies as signs, or semiotic devices representing other concepts, find meaning in their relationship to humankind. If there is any independent meaning of the stars and planets outside of human comprehension, it is simply not indicated in the text. And it is this function, when performing properly, that God declares is "good."

With both space and time now sufficiently differentiated, life is created in the sea and in the air, the text further differentiating this life into (1) the 'great *tannīm*', (2) all living things which the waters bring forth, and (3) all winged life (specifically avian forms).[10] Immediately following the emergence of this original triad of moving life, another triad is described

---

10. The great *tannīm*, translated here as "whales," is translated elsewhere in the Old Testament as "dragon (twenty-one times), "serpent" (three times), "whale" (three times), and "sea monster" (one time), these other translations reflecting another creation tradition, often found in the poetic and prophetic material of the biblical text, that depicts the cosmos as a result of a battle between God and a monster representing the unorganized material. In this tradition, the carcass of the monster-as-unorganized-material is used to construct the cosmos. This tradition is conspicuously missing from the Genesis version, though this most likely reflects the writer(s) or editor(s) desire to emphasize God as one who transcends all aspects of the cosmos, who is not constantly threatened by existential disorder. Thus, the *tannīm*, the personification of unorganization elsewhere, is here rendered as simply another type of living animal. See Mary K. Wakeman, *God's Battle with the Monster: A Study in Biblical Imagery* (Leiden: Brill, 1973); also Patrick D. Miller Jr., *The Divine Warrior in Early Israel* (Cambridge, MA: Harvard University Press, 1973); Millard Lind, *Yahweh Is a Warrior: The Theology of Warfare in the Ancient Israel* (Scottsdale, PA: Herald Press, 1980); John Day, *God's Conflict with the Dragon and the Sea: Echoes of a Canaanite Myth in the Old Testament* (Cambridge, MA: Cambridge University Press, 1985). For both an excellent review of this imagery and material on the influence of this imagery beyond the Hebrew Bible, see Michael A. Fishbane, *Biblical Myth and Rabbinic Mythmaking* (Oxford: Oxford University Press, 2003). For a Book of Mormon usage, see Daniel Belnap, "'I Will Contend with Them That Contendeth with Thee': The Divine Warrior in Jacob's Speech of 2 Nephi 6–10," in *Journal of Book of Mormon & Restoration Scripture 17*, nos. 1–2 (2008): 20–39.

consisting of the "beasts of the field," cattle, and nonmammals that walk on land (reptiles, amphibians, and so forth). While "creeping things," or the nonmammals that walk on land, suggests differentiation of type, the other two suggest differentiation by function—namely, nondomesticated versus domesticated—again highlighting the anthropocentric purpose of the Creation. With these two orderings, life is now present in the three environments of the cosmos: the earth, the sea, the sky, and all of it is functioning properly and differentiated one from another, thereby receiving the divine acknowledgment that it is "good."

The final ordering is the making of man. This ordering differs from the earlier ones as the instruction is now collaborative, with the inclusion of the first-person plural "let us" rather than singular God (Genesis 1:26). Though it may be tempting to read this as an indication that Israel worshipped more than one deity, it appears to reflect their understanding of the function of the divine assembly that was led by God and is attested throughout the Old Testament, particularly in its role in the calling of a prophet.[11] In this final ordering, the unique position of humankind is noted by the inclusion of other divine beings in this assembly. Stress is placed on the form of humankind, "let us make man in our own likeness and in our own image." While the exact nature of these clauses has been discussed for literally millennia, the meaning is relatively straightforward. The first term, *ṣelem*, or image, denotes an actual, physical representation and is used elsewhere to designate an idol. In Genesis 5:3, the term is used to describe the similarity between Adam and his son Seth, highlighting the usage of the term to denote similarity in physical form.[12] Thus, both terms

11. See Jeremiah 23:16–22; Isaiah 6:8; 1 Kings 22:19–21. Amos 3:7 in the original Hebrew states clearly that God does nothing except he reveals his *sōd* (i.e., divine council, translated in KJV as "secret") to his prophets. The literature of this concept is extensive, but an excellent introduction is E. Theodore Mullen Jr., *The Assembly of the Gods: The Divine Council in Canaanite and Early Hebrew Literature*, Harvard Semitic Monographs 24 (Chico, CA: Scholars' Press, 1980).

12. Day, *From Creation to Babel*, 13–14: "Traditionally, for many centuries in Christian theology it was believed that the image implied a spiritual likeness between God and humanity. However, the word *ṣelem*, 'image,' is characteristically used of physical images in the Old Testament. . . . The Hebrew word for 'image' is also employed by P of Seth's likeness to Adam (Gen. 5:3), following a

indicate that ancient Israel understood God to have at least looked like man, but the greater ontological implication, that similarity of form indicates similarity of type (i.e., that God is the same type of being as humankind) is often a more contentious implication for students of the bible. For Latter-day Saints, though, this ontological relationship lies at the center of our identity as children of God. And, as we shall see, it informs our reading of both the Creation narrative and the Garden of Eden narrative.

As equally important was the function or responsibility that humanity was to have: "let them have dominion over the flesh of the sea, and over the fowl of the air, and over the cattle, and over all the earth, and over every creeping thing that creepeth upon the earth" (Genesis 1:26). This function is reinforced in God's blessing over the primordial pair: "Be fruitful, and multiply, and replenish the earth, and subdue it: and have dominion over the fish of the sea, and over the fowl of the air, and over every living thing that moveth upon the earth" (Genesis 1:28). As noted earlier, the blessing, be fruitful and multiply, was associated with entities that moved of their own volition (i.e., animal life), but the additional instruction to subdue and have dominion separates humankind from animal, suggesting that humankind would have not only the ability to move under their own power, but to be aware of one's decisions and choose knowingly. It also further reinforces the divine similarities between humankind and God, as

---

repetition of Genesis 1's statement that humanity was created in the likeness of God (Gen. 5:1), which further supports the notion that a physical likeness was included in P's concept." See also Anderson, *From Creation to New Creation*, 14: "One should take the word translated 'image' (*ṣelem*) much more concretely than is often done by those who attenuate its meaning the 'spiritual' part of human nature, or, in Greek fashion, to the 'soul' as distinguished from the 'body.' Elsewhere the Hebrew word refers to something concrete and visible, . . . but the main import of the statement about the imago Dei is not just to define human nature in relation to God but to accent the special function that God has assigned human beings in the creation. Human beings, male and female, are designed to be God's representatives, for they are created and commissioned to represent or 'image' God's rule on earth. To be made in the image of God is to be endowed with a special task."

humanity is given authority akin to that of the Creator himself, as well as acting upon that authority as God did during the earlier creative periods.[13]

Difficult for some is the meaning of the verbs "subdue" and "have dominion over" (Genesis 1:28). While the two are used elsewhere to describe the total power of one over another, at least one reference uses the same designation to describe construction overseers, which suggests the terms did not necessarily mean tyrannical domination, but were used to describe one who was placed over another to monitor work progress. This perspective allows for these verbs to be seen through a lens of compassionate authority, a characteristic of leadership Israel was expected to demonstrate both in their relationships with their fellow humans and in their relationship with the earth itself.[14] Regardless, it does not appear that humankind was simply given carte blanche over the rest of creation, but instead God gave humanity heavy responsibilities similar to his own and, having done so, he then declares that the Creation to this point was "very good" (Genesis 1:31).[15]

---

13. Moreover, the blessing to be fruitful and multiply and its attendant responsibilities to subdue and have dominion over the earth are repeated later in the covenant established between God and the patriarchs and their descendants, Israel (Genesis 13:14–17, 15:4–5; see also Numbers 32:22, 29; Joshua 18:1). These in turn suggest that just as humankind was to have dominion over the earth, so Israel was expected to continue the purposes of the work of creation, having responsible stewardship over the rest of humankind.
14. Perhaps related to this responsibility was the recognition by Israel that the land was God's over which Israel was to be the steward. It is also possible that the blessing or responsibility reflects an aspect of conflict creation imagery, but instead of God as divine warrior, it is humankind who must subdue and exercise dominion over the remaining chaotic forces and thereby continue to maintain the cosmos.
15. Day, *From Creation to Babel*, 15: "The verbs used here, *kabash*, 'subdue,' and *rada*, 'have dominion over,' may at first sound rather harsh; . . . however, immediately afterwards in Genesis God commands both humans and animals to exist on a vegetarian diet (Gen. 1:29–30), so it is clear that no ruthless dominion is intended at all but rather a benign rule over the natural order, what we should nowadays refer to as a stewardship over creation." It would appear that this responsibility is for both male and female, see Habel, *The Birth*, 38–39: "The implementation of the joint decision to 'make' humans in the tselem of Elohim is described in poetic language. The new dimension of this divine act is the

One last differentiation concludes this first period of creation—the designation of the Sabbath over other time delineations and one in which God rests from his earlier activities. Though it is often assumed that the mention of God's rest reflects divine inactivity, the narrative suggests that there is not so much a cessation of work as there is a change in the type of work or purpose of the work as God now blesses and sanctifies, acts that not only apply to the specific time of the Sabbath, but presumably to the entire creation up to this point.[16]

The act of sanctification, based on the term *qdš*, is often understood as a "setting apart" as objects sanctified are assigned a new position or function apart from similar objects. Yet the adjectival form is often translated as "holy" and reflects a divine status in the given object. Thus, the act of sanctification is the moving of an object or item to a divine state. Moreover, the English word *holy* carries with it the sense of completeness or wholeness; therefore sanctification can be understood as the process by which a thing enters into a divine state by being whole or complete. Thus it could be understood that the Creation was not truly complete until it had been sanctified, a process similar to that of a temple dedication. Scholars have long noted the relationship between the Creation and its culminating

designation of both male and female as bearers of the tselem. Both male and female humans bear this royal image and have the mandate to rule all other living creatures. There is no indication of male rulers being superior in any way to female rulers; they are separated by sex but both bear the tselem that gives them the capacity to dominate."

16. S. D. McBride, "Divine Protocol: Genesis 1:1–2:3 as Prologue to the Pentateuch," in *God Who Creates: Essays in Honor of W. Sibley Towner* (Grand Rapids, MI: Eerdmans, 2000), 3–41: "This day of silent divine rest is a consummation of all that has gone before because it inaugurates God's residence within the cosmic temple." This implies that God's creation is now not only a fit habitation for his children, but also for himself. Habel suggests that the Sabbath marks the transition from preparation to performance. Habel, *The Birth*, 34: "At this point in the narrative [the blessing over the Creation] a divine blessing is introduced, a key factor in sustaining the creation process. To bless (*barak*) is to impart power. In this instance, that power activates a capacity to procreate and 'multiply on Erets.'" Whether his conclusion is accurate in terms of ability to reproduce, his observation that God's blessing on the Sabbath was a crucial, necessary next step in the creation process appears to be correct.

Sabbath, and the construction and subsequent dedication of the tabernacle/temple. In a similar manner, the Creation may be understood as a priestly activity enacted by God as priest.[17]

The verb used to describe the act of dividing or separating the different creation constituencies (light from dark, waters from waters, and so forth), *hibdîl*, is also used to describe the dividing up of the sacrificial animals following their slaughter; thus God and priest performed the same creative, cosmic act, albeit in different settings. But it wasn't just priests who reflect God as creator/sanctifier. Throughout Leviticus and Deuteronomy, Israel was exhorted to be holy even as God was holy. As noted above, the Hebrew term for holy is *qdš*, but the meaning or usage of the term in any particular scriptural passage depended upon which version of *qdš* was used. The most common form is the adjective *qodeš*, yet a select number of objects are designated as *qādôš*, used to describe objects or individuals who are not just holy but have the dynamic quality to move objects into a divine

17. Much has been written about this relationship. In particular, see Gordon Wenham, "Sanctuary Symbolism in the Garden of Eden Story," in *I Studied Inscriptions from before the Flood*, ed. R. Hess and D. T. Tsumura, Sources for Biblical and Theological Study 4 (Winona Lake, IN: Eisenbrauns, 1994), 399–404. See also Moshe Weinfeld, "Sabbath, Temple and the Enthronement of the Lord: The Problem of the Sitz im Leben of Genesis 1:1–2:3," in *Melanges bibliques et orientaux en l'honneur de M. Henri Cazelles*, ed. A. Caquot and M. Delcor, AOAT (Kevelaer: Verlag Butzon & Bercker Kevelaer / Neukirchener Verlag Neukirchen-Vluyn, 1981), 501–12. As for God as priest, see Robert B. Coote and David Robert Ord, *In the Beginning: Creation and the Priestly History* (Minneapolis: Fortress Press, 1991), 57: "A main function of the priesthood was, as Leviticus 10:10 expresses it, to 'distinguish between the holy and the common, and between the clean and the unclean.' The centrality of this function could hardly be overstated. 'Distinguish' is exactly what God did in the first act of Creation: in Hebrew, God 'distinguished' light and darkness. The priestly tradition understood this distinguishing, this separating, to be integral to the inceptive divine act." See also J. Levenson, *Creation and the Persistence of Evil* (Princeton: Princeton University Press 1988), 127: "God functions like an Israelite priest, making distinctions, assigning things to their proper category, and assessing their fitness and hallowing the Sabbath. . . . As a result, the creative ordering of the world has become something that humanity can not only witness and celebrate, but something in which it can also take part." The apparent priestly orientation to Genesis 1 has led many to believe that the chapter represents a text written by a priestly source (see more below).

state. Not surprisingly, God is the number one entity described as *qādôš*, but Israel too is expected to be *qādôš*, like their God.[18] Certainly Israel's observance of the Sabbath reflected these creation activities. Just as God was not inactive, so too Israel participated in sanctioned activities associated only with the Sabbath. For instance, on the Sabbath burnt offerings were doubled and the bread of the presence, which would have lain on a table inside the sanctuary all week, was consumed and replaced. These, of course, were priestly activities, but the general congregation also participated in Creation activities; namely, the activity of assembly.

This particular activity does not appear at first glance to be referenced in the Creation narrative, yet it seems to be present in the first verse of Genesis 2, which sums up the creative process so far by stating that heaven and earth were finished, "and all the host of them." While the idea that heaven and earth are finished or completed makes sense, the last subject, the "host" and its relationship to the verb is less so, as the term itself is used almost exclusively to describe a gathered convocation or assembly. It is possible that it refers to a final organizing act in which the entire host of heaven and earth was established into a social/ecclesiastical structure. Such an event is recorded in Doctrine and Covenants 121 when the council of God assembled and "ordained" the set functions of the cosmos.

This particular event may be what is alluded to in Job 38 among the rhetorical questions God asked of Job: "Where wast thou when I laid the foundations of the earth. . . . Who hath laid the measures thereof . . . or who hath stretched the line upon it? Whereupon are the foundations thereof fastened? Or who laid the cornerstone thereof; When the morning stars sang together, and all the sons of God shouted for joy?" (Job 38:4–7). In this reference, the divine assembly is described as singing and praising as God organizes the earth, which, coupled with the rest of the sanctification, again may suggest that the establishment of the Sabbath reflects a

18. E. Jan Wilson, *"Holiness" and "Purity" in Mesopotamia*, Alter Orient und Altes Testament 237 (Kevelaer: Butzon & Bercker; Neukirchen-Vluyn; Neukirchener, 1994), 87–88. For more discussion on the distinction of these terms, see Gaye Strathearn, "'Holiness to the Lord' and Personal Temple Worship," in *The Gospel of Jesus Christ in the Old Testament*, ed. D. Kelly Ogden, Jared W. Ludlow, and Kerry Muhlestein (Provo, UT: Religious Studies Center, Brigham Young University; Salt Lake City: Deseret Book, 2009), 219–32.

dedicatory event.[19] If this reading is correct, the Sabbath was meant to be a recognized period that harmonized the divine and mortal communities both at the time of creation and in later historical time.[20] Either way, the

---

19. Day, *From Creation to Babel*, 12–13: "The dominant view nowadays is that there is a reference to the heavenly court which God addressed (cf. Job 38:7, where 'all the sons of God shouted for joy' at the time of the creation, though admittedly it does not say that God consulted them. . . . It might be objected that in Gen. 1:28 it was only God, not the heavenly court, who actually created humanity. However, it is arguable that the momentous decision to create humanity is envisaged as a joint act between God and his heavenly council, even if was only God himself who finally enacted the decision." Lorenzo Snow suggested that this event was the dedication of the earth and the shout was in fact the Hosanna Shout. See Jacob W. Olmstead, "From Pentecost to Administration: A Reappraisal of the History of the Hosanna Shout," in *Mormon Historical Studies* 2, no. 2 (2001): 28: "On 2 July 1899, during a solemn assembly in the Salt Lake Temple, the Prophet Lorenzo Snow was the first to teach that the shout was linked with Old Testament concepts. He stated that at the creation of the world when 'all the sons of God shouted for joy,' Job was describing the first shout of 'Hosanna' (see Job 38:107)."
20. Weinfeld, "Sabbath," 502–3: "The fact that with the completion of the instructions for the building the Tabernacle in P. there appears a commandment on the Sabbath (Ex. 31:12–17), shows also the connection which existed between Creation and the Building of the Temple. Indeed, this connection is well expressed in the congruence which is found between the description of the completion of the Tabernacle in Exodus. Gen. 1:1–2:3 and Ex. 39:1–40:33 are typologically identical. Both describe the satisfactory completion of the enterprise commanded by God, its inspection and approval, the blessing and the sanctification which are connected with it." See also Postell, *Adam as Israel*, 113: "In one real sense, the garden serves as the prototypical reality of which the tabernacle serves only as a copy or a type. The tabernacle and its operation are permeated with an aroma of Eden. A link is forged between God's creation's purposes and the construction of the tabernacle, whereby the Mosaic tabernacle and its priesthood perpetuate, albeit imperfectly, the 'sanctuary' in Eden and its 'priesthood.'" See also Walton, *Lost World*, 50: "Solomon spent seven years building the house to be used as the temple of God in Jerusalem. When the house was complete, however, all that existed was a structure, not a temple. It was ready to be a temple, but it was not yet functioning like a temple, and God was not dwelling in it. . . . What constituted the transition from a structure that was ready to be a temple to an actual functioning temple? How did the house become a home? This is an important question because there is a comparison to be drawn if Genesis 1 is indeed a temple text. We find that in

establishment of the Sabbath was not a period of inactivity but a period of sanctifying, completing events that made it possible for the next stage of the cosmos to begin.[21]

---

both the Bible and the ancient Near East there is an inauguration ceremony that formally and ceremonially marks the transition from physical structure to functioning temple. . . . In that inauguration ceremony, the functions of the temple are proclaimed, the functionaries are installed and rituals are begun as God comes down to inhabit the place that has been prepared by his instruction. It is thus no surprise that in Genesis 1 we find the proclamation of functions and the installation of functionaries."

21. Carol L. Meyers, *The Tabernacle Menorah,* ASOR diss 2 (Missoula, MT: Scholars Press, 1975), 179–80: "What is the nature of divine rest in the Hebrew Bible? In the ancient Near Eastern literature, we have noted a range of activities (and inactivity) that were involved in rest: from peaceful sleep, to leisure time for entertainment and banquets, to sovereign rule. Some have interpreted the rest in Genesis 1 as representing disengagement and the enjoyment of relaxation. Thus, Levenson comments that the text 'leaves us with an impression of the deity in a state of mellow euphoria, benignly fading out the world that he has finished and pronounced "very good."' J. Levenson, *Creation and the Persistence of Evil,* 109. It should be noted, however, that the 'disengagement' form of rest in the ancient Near East is consistently based either in polytheism (e.g., social activities among and entertainment with other gods) or in the belief that the gods had humanlike needs and desires (e.g., sleep or sexual activity). . . . In fact, however, although the idea of divine rest in the ancient Near Eastern [*sic*] includes retirement as one possibility, other texts examined above showed rest as the freedom to rule. In the Hebrew Bible, Psalm 132 provides a key passage, in which not only is the temple identified as the resting place of Yahweh but we also find rest identified with rue, for in the temple he sits enthroned. In this sense, divine rest is not primarily an act of disengagement but an act of engagement. No other divine rest occurs in the Hebrew Bible than the rest that is associated with his presence in his temple." See also, Habel, *From Creation,* 41: "The cosmos is now complete and Elohim can rest (*shabat*) with creation. But that rest apparently does not mean inaction or taking a vacation: the use of bara' in Gen. 2:3 indicates continued divine action. And, as van Wolde suggests, this verse means that God made the seventh day by 'separating' it and setting it apart of the other days." Ellen van Wolde, "Why the Verb Bara' Does Not Mean 'To Create' in Genesis 1.1–2.41," in *Journal for the Study of the Old Testament* 34, no.1 (2009): 22: "Elohim also blesses and sanctifies the day that celebrates completion—Elohim invests that day with a power comparable to the power of procreation given to living creatures of Erets. . . . Prior to that day, blessing has been dispensed to activate life as such. Now time is blessed with the inherent

"THERE WAS NOT A MAN TO TILL THE GROUND": GENESIS 2–3 AND THE CREATION OF THE SOCIAL COSMOS

This next stage of the creative process is described in Genesis 2–3 and focuses on the localized events experienced in the Garden of Eden. Because of differences in narrative, setting, and even terminology—all particularly highlighting the direct, personal interaction between God and man—it has been presumed that chapters 2 and 3 have been written by another author or redactor representing a different Creation narrative (known as J because of the preponderance of the title Jehovah).[22] For Latter-day Saints, the differences between the two narratives has been understood to reflect two different temporal periods of the Creation, a premortal organization by which the spiritual reality and relationship of all things was established before their physical creation and arrangement.

Whether or not this explanation is the correct one as to the origin of these two different narratives, it does highlight the intended relationship between them, for, even if they are two separate narrative traditions, at some point someone(s) believed them to be complementary rather than contrasting. And, in fact, the narrative elements mentioned above do not so much highlight a different physical creation as much as they highlight the creation of the "social" cosmos.[23]

---

capacity to initiate, sustain and restore life." We thus seem to witness the transition to a functioning holy place (earth) where God's children will act on his behalf.

22. As noted earlier, it is commonly assumed that Genesis 1 was written under priestly influence and reflects priestly concepts and thus is known as "P" source.

23. Eckart Otto, "Paradieserzählung Genesis 2–3, Eine nachpriesterschriftliche Lehrerzählung in ihrem religionshistorischen Kontext," in *Jedes Ding hat seine Zeit*, ed. Otto Kaiser, BZAW 241 (Berlin: de Gruyter, 1996), 167–92: "Not only is Genesis 2:7 terminologically tied to Genesis 1, Genesis 1:27 contains the 'fact' of the creation of man, whereas following up on Genesis 2:7 the 'how' is developed" (183–84). Postell, *Adam as Israel*, 18: "Otto's words point to overriding compositional intentions that go beyond any putative and contradictory sources. Moreover, the fact that Genesis 2–3 is aware of the 'priestly' materials and even includes vocabulary classically assigned to 'P' undermines Wellhausen's theory both in terms of his understanding of the chronological relationship of 'J' to 'P'

J begins in Genesis 2:5, where the reader is told that no plant life yet existed because "the Lord God (Jehovah Elohim) had not caused it to rain upon the earth and there was not a man to till the ground." The requirement of both God and mortal action to bring forth this aspect of creation marks a new stage of the creation, one in which male and female are necessary participants in the further completion of the cosmos, a requirement that was implied, but not explicit, in Genesis 1.[24] In light of this new significance to humankind, it is not surprising to find the description of Adam's physical emergence as first and foremost in this second creation narrative. His creation consisted of two parts: that which came from the earth, and the vitality or living essence—namely, the breath of life, which is received directly from God himself, an understanding of man which builds upon the relationship between man and God established first in Genesis 1. Whereas there the reader is told that man was in the image and likeness of God, now the reader finds that man's physical makeup is infused by the divine breath of God.

Differentiation continues in this narrative as the earth itself is divided into geographical areas, beginning with Eden, the garden of God. Further

---

and in terms of the notion of clearly identifiable and distinguishable literary criteria used to distinguish one hypothetical source from another." Similarly, Walton, *Lost World*, 69: "In Genesis 1:2, an inchoate cosmos is described, whereas an inchoate earth is described in Genesis 2:5–6. . . . Genesis 2 explains how humans function in sacred space and on its behalf (in contrast to Genesis 1, which addressed how sacred space functioned for humanity)"; and Day, *From Creation to Babel*, 24–25: "The account in Gen. 2:4b–3:24 is often spoken of as the second Creation account in Genesis, following on that of P in Gen. 1:1–2:4a. This is true, but the second account very much centers on the Garden of Eden and the first man and woman, and apart from that there is very little on the creation of the world." In all of these cases, there is an awareness that Genesis 2 is not merely another tradition, but describes the next stage of the creation event, the creation of society.

24. David Tsumura, *Creation and Destruction: A Reappraisal of the Chaoskampf Theory in the Old Testament* (Winona Lake, IN: Eisenbrauns, 2005), 127: "The situation in 2:5–6 as a whole is simply this: Because of the lack of rain, there was no plant life on the earth, while the *ed*-water [precosmic water] was flooding out of the earth to water, that is, inundate, the entire surface of the land, which was only part of the earth. The problem here was not the lack of water, but the lack of adequate control of water by man for the purpose of agriculture."

geographical areas are designated by the four rivers that flow from Eden, the rivers themselves presumably associated with rivers in the ancient Near East. But unlike the earlier differentiations, these do not signify new physical objects or states. Instead, they represent what could be called social space, or space that indicates their social function—in this case, inhabited areas of the ancient Near East.[25] The designation of a garden in Eden suggests that it too may be understood as social space, in that gardens are planned environments to indicate prestige or other social dynamics.

Further delineation of social space follows with the introduction of two particular trees whose functions are socially oriented: the tree of life and the tree of the knowledge of good and evil. The function of these trees lay at the center of the Garden of Eden narrative, acting as the catalyst to the next stage of the cosmos. With man's placement within the garden and the instruction given concerning his responsibilities regarding the garden, Adam is told that the fruit of all the trees may be eaten, except for the fruit of the tree of knowledge of good and evil, the reason being that Adam would die from doing so:

> 16b. Of every tree of the garden thou mayest freely eat:
>
> 17. But of the tree of the knowledge of good and evil, thou shalt not eat of it: for in the day that thou eatest thereof thou shalt surely die.

This injunction scene has been most commonly understood as the narrative device by which evil is introduced. For Christians, it creates the tension

25. The focus on socially recognized spaces has led some to note the relationship between the Genesis 2–3 narrative and those of the patriarchs. See Postell, *Adam as Israel*, 90–91: "Scholars have noticed inner-textual parallels between Adam and Abraham. Not only does the text thematically link Abram to Adam, but Genesis 15–16 appears to be an intentional recapitulation of Adam's story in Genesis 2–3. . . . First, in both passages the central figure undergoes a deep and divinely induced slumber. Second, both passages provide homogenous geographical information regarding the boundaries of a divinely provided land. Third, while Genesis 2 does not mention a covenant as does Genesis 15, it is clearly covenantal in nature." Interestingly, in the Book of Abraham, no nomenclature is mentioned (see Abraham 5:10), perhaps reflecting its earlier, pre-Israelite origin.

by which the Fall begins, as Adam's hubris will lead him to eat of the fruit and therefore no longer be able to remain in the garden. For Latter-day Saints, the passage creates difficulty as it appears to contradict the earlier instructions to multiply and replenish the earth. This is a unique perspective in two ways. First, it requires a reading in which the primordial couple are not able to bear children while in the garden. Second, it implies that humankind was not meant to be in the garden permanently under these conditions. While these two perspectives are particularly influenced by latter-day scripture, the Book of Mormon and the Book of Moses in the Pearl of Great Price (both of which will later be discussed in greater detail), at least the latter may also have grounding in the Hebrew text itself.[26]

Though often understood as merely prohibitive, the divine injunction is our first indication that humankind possesses individual agency. Syntactically the formation of the commandment is similar to that of conditional oaths in which an individual declares what will happen if they engage in

---

26. Though not discussed earlier because of the approximate similarities between the Genesis version and the Moses account found in the Pearl of Great Price, in fact the Moses version has reflected a number of differences. First, the inclusion of Moses 1 and Moses's three encounters with supernatural entities changed the function of the Creation narrative. Though the narrative itself remained approximately the same (physical creation followed by social creation), the purpose of the narrative is one which emphasizes the calling of Moses and his work similar to that of the creators rather than the further cosmological ordering through the emergence of Israel. The Moses account has also suggested a unified source, rather than the two sources noted among biblical scholars. One particular element that the Moses account adds is a Christological meaning to the Creation. In Moses 1 we find that Moses's work will be similar to the work of God's Only Begotten, through whom God created the biblical cosmos. Fronting the introduction of the serpent to the Garden of Eden, the Moses account recounts the premortal rebellion of the adversary in which Satan sought to overthrow the preeminent position of Christ while simultaneously doing away with individual agency, at least for those other than himself. Moses's version of the injunction is also different from the biblical version, though not thematically. Instead, the Moses version emphasizes even more the role of agency in the injunction: "But of the tree of knowledge of good and evil, thou shalt not eat, *nevertheless, thou mayest choose for thyself, for it is given unto thee; but remember that I forbid it,* for in the day thou eatest thereof thou shalt surely die" (Moses 3:17; emphasis added).

the behavior either allowed or disallowed (covenant language). Such formations are more than simple injunctions, and recognize the agency of the individual (but counting on fidelity, or the covenant breaker will die). Similarly, here, while Adam is told not to eat the fruit, he is also told what will happen if he does, which emphasizes the role of Adam's agency rather than merely restricting his behavior. Moreover, the conditional nature of the instruction gives Adam knowledge that allows his choice to have efficacy. Such instruction allows for Adam to disregard the instruction if he is willing to die and the fact that Adam does make this choice later suggests that he had weighed the consequences and decided that death is preferable, perhaps even valued, rather than remaining alone.

Yet the consequences of Adam's act in this regard are preceded by a number of events that both develop Adam's and Eve's awareness and exercising of agency and accentuate their roles as beings like God who bring about cosmos.[27] The first such act is Adam's naming the animals. According to verse 19, God has them brought before Adam "to see what [Adam] would call them." Like God who had named the components of the physical cosmos, thus differentiating and giving meaning to the components, so now Adam differentiated each creature from one another, thereby establishing their place in the nascent cosmos.[28] The act also reinforced Adam's responsibilities to care for the cosmos given both in Genesis 1 and earlier

27. Walton, *Lost World*, 106–7: "I would propose the following line of logic: Since there are a couple of contexts in which *šmr* here favors sacred service, and *'ibd* is likely to refer to sacred service as to agricultural tasks. . . . If the priestly vocabulary in Genesis 2:15 indicates the same kind of thinking, the point of caring for sacred space should be seen as much more than landscaping or even priestly duties. Maintaining order made one a participant with God in the ongoing task of sustaining the equilibrium God had established in the cosmos. . . . This combines the subduing and ruling of Genesis 1 with the *'bd* and *šmr* of this chapter."

28. Ziony Zevit, *What Really Happened in the Garden of Eden?* (New Haven, CT: Yale University Press, 2013), 131: "This episode about the formation and naming of animals is significant for a number of reasons. . . . Practically speaking, this involved the man's being able to sort out the animals and to create logical categories into which they would fit, to distinguish monkeys from himself, and dogs from cats, from camels, from horses, from donkeys. The ability to create categories under which everything that existed could be filed was considered

in chapter 2 by establishing a relationship between Adam and the animals. Finally, the event also provides Adam the opportunity to recognize that the cosmos is incomplete. Before his bringing the animals before Adam, God states that it is not good that Adam be alone, yet the organization of Eve takes place only after the animals are named and the deficiency is made obvious.[29] In other words, it is not enough for God to pronounce that Adam alone is 'not good,' Adam himself needs to know and recognize his incompleteness, implying that this stage of creation is not completely "good" without Eve.[30]

---

an important type of knowledge in ancient Mesopotamia and underlies analytic thought, ancient and modern."

29. Habel, *The Birth*, 54: "It is perhaps significant that this partner is called a 'helper,' a term also used of God in the Hebrew Scriptures (Exod. 18:4; Deut. 33:7; Ps. 70:5). This lack of a suitable partner and 'helper' represents the final absence in the primordial world that needs to be rectified. The fulfillment of this lacuna will bring the primordial world to completion . . . the 'helper' will be the culmination of this creation process in Eden."

30. Zevit, *What Really Happened*, 129–30: "Freedman argues that *ʿ-z-r*, the three-consonant root of *ʿēzer* reflects two original, distinctive roots. The first, most frequently attested in biblical Hebrew, is *ʿ-z-r*, with an original *ʿayyin*, meaning 'rescue/save/help.' The second, with an original ghayyin, is *ġ-z-r*, meaning 'be strong.' The second root, *g-z-r*, is attested in Ugaritic. . . . On the basis of this evidence, Freedman suggests that the Hebrew expression *ezer kenegdow* be translated as 'a power equal to him.' Drawing on the philological insights of Freedman and Fox, translators may render the expression *ezer kenegdow* ['an helpmeet'] as a 'powerful counterpart.' Not only is this linguistically possible, but it is appropriate in context." Later, Zevit provides another, alternative etymological understanding. Zevit, *What Really Happened*, 135–36: "In the Hebrew text of both verses where it appears, Genesis 2:18, 20, a disjunctive accent mark called a ṭipḥāh . . . is found under the first word, separating it from the second one. . . . The disjunctive tiphah instructs readers to pause after the marked word, as if after an English comma, so that a sliver of silence separates it from the following word: *ezer* [helper] + disjunctive accent + *ke* [like] + *neged* + *ow* [his]. . . . Accordingly, verse 18b may be translated: 'I will make for him a helper, like his *neged*.' This only leaves *neged* in need of clarification. . . . Ancient Ethiopic, Ge'ez, a language distantly related to Hebrew, provides an etymological cognate that fits the semantic bill: *nagad*, a word meaning 'tribe, clan, kin.' The Ge'ez word is also cognate to Hebrew *neked*, whose meaning as determined by context is 'progeny' or 'descendant' (Gen. 21:23; Isa. 14:22; Job 18:19). I propose that in its two occurrences in the Garden story, *neged* is

This incompleteness is resolved with the formation of the woman: "And the Lord God caused a deep sleep to fall upon Adam, and he slept: and he took one of his ribs, and closed up the flesh instead thereof; and the rib, which the Lord God had taken from man, made he a woman, and brought her unto the man. And Adam said, This is now bone of my bones and flesh of my flesh: and she shall be called Woman, because she was taken out of Man"[31] (Genesis 2:21–23).

This event parallels the naming of the animals in that God brings her before Adam and Adam recognizes his relationship to her by giving her an ontological title that denotes both the sameness and difference of Adam to Eve. Yet the ritualized nature of this event suggests that the event is more than a mere presentation, especially when coupled with Adam's words that the woman is "bone of my bones and flesh of my flesh," which reflects a covenantal usage elsewhere in the Old Testament.[32] In Genesis

---

not the common preposition but, like its cognate in Ge'ez, a kinship term. . . . Recognizing neged in the Garden story as a noun belonging to the sphere of kinship terminology explains why it does not provide information about positional relationships as in the other 149 attestations of the word in the Bible. It is not a preposition. Applying this conclusion to verse 18b yields: 'I will make for him a helper like his kin.' . . . This interpretation is less dramatic than 'a powerful counterpart,' but it accounts for the use of the preposition *ke*, "like," and rests on a more solid philological base as well."

31. Walton, *Lost World*, 80: Pertaining to the word for Adam's sleep: "This sleep blocks all perception in the human realm. In each [usage of the term] there is either danger in the human realm of which the sleeper is unaware, or there is insight in the visionary realm to be gained. Pertaining to the latter possibility, it is of interest that the Septuagint translators chose to use the Greek word *ekstasis* in Genesis 2:21. This word is the same as the one they used in Genesis 15:12, suggesting an understanding related to visions, trances and ecstasy (cf. the use of this Greek word in Acts 10:10; 11:5; 22:17). . . . From these data it is easy to conclude that Adam's sleep has prepared him for a visionary experience rather than for a surgical procedure. . . . The vision would concern her identity as ontologically related to man."

32. While this is possible, it is possible that the mention of the rib was meant as a wordplay. As noted earlier, one of the terms to describe the creation of Adam and Eve in the priestly version was image, or *ṣelem*. The Hebrew word for rib here is *ṣēlāʿ* rather than the more common term for bone, *ʿeṣem*. *ṣēlāʿ* is found elsewhere referring to boards or planks that are used as supports in a number of edifices including the tabernacle, thus it is possible that the usage of the term

29:14, Jacob is accepted by Laban, his future father-in-law, by the declaration "Surely thou art my bone and my flesh." While this may reflect the actual genetic relationship between Jacob and Laban, who is his uncle on his mother's side, it also foreshadows the family relationship that will exist between Jacob and Laban following Jacob's marriages to Laban's daughters.

Similarly, in Judges 9:1–2, Abimelech seeks to establish legitimacy among the inhabitants of Shechem, who were related to him through his maternal uncle, by stating, "I am your bone and your flesh." In 2 Samuel 5:1, the acceptance of David's regency by the tribes of Israel at Hebron is noted by their declaration, "Behold, we are thy bone and thy flesh." Following Absalom's rebellion, David uses the same terminology to remind the tribal elders and Amasa of his legitimate claim to the throne (2 Samuel 19:12–13). In all these cases, whether the individuals are directly related or not, the terminology is used to either establish or maintain a legitimately recognized relationship that demonstrated acceptance of the individual within the community. In the case of the last two, the terminology suggests a covenant between David and the rest of Israel with their recognition of him as family. And if this is in fact what the terminology implies, then Adam's declaration is one which recognizes the covenantal relationship between himself and the woman, a relationship institutionalized in marriage.

Whether the modern reader reads the account as one indicating marriage, it is clear that the ancient redactor(s) viewed this event as one that instituted marriage: "Therefore shall a man leave his father and his mother, and shall cleave unto his wife: and they shall be one flesh" (Genesis 2:24). The mention of the couple as "one flesh" reflects the covenantal usage of "bone of my bone and flesh of my flesh" declared by Adam and reflects the social meaning as noted elsewhere in the Old Testament in which these

---

is a pun reflecting the woman as foundational support to Adam as well as his image. A rare usage of the term is that of essence, presumably the bone represents the essence or foundation of the body and thus may stand as representative of the essence of the individual. In light of this, it is possible that the use of *ṣēlāʿ* here carries multivalent meaning, which may include the essence nuance, thus rendering a reading in which Adam's very essence is unfinished without Eve.

refer to the concept of "family."[33] Here, the individual is to leave a family of "one flesh" (the primary unit of mother-father-child) to become another family of "one flesh" (husband-wife and potential mother-father).[34] The verb "cleave" is also suggestive of the marriage covenant as it is found elsewhere in a covenantal sense to describe the relationship one is to have with God (Deuteronomy 10:20; Joshua 22:5).[35]

For Latter-day Saints, this designation takes on even greater meaning because Zion is also characterized by its oneness of "flesh," or one heart and one mind, thus suggesting that not only is the social institution of

---

33. It is possible that it also highlights the action taken above. Just as the rib was removed from Adam's side, so Adam removes himself from the side of his parents. Now she is his *k*ᵉ*negdô*, "his power/his helper/his kin," not his parents.

34. Another interpretation is as follows, Zevit, *What Really Happened*, 156–57: "verbs from the root ʿ-z-b ['leave'] are attested 216 times in the Hebrew Bible. In three passages where a meaning such as 'leave' or 'abandon' is inappropriate they are translated differently . . . not until the twentieth century did scholars posit the existence of another root, identified as ʿ-z-b II, and recognize that it has cognate verbs in Ugaritic, Epigraphic South Arabian, and Ge'ez. On the basis of these cognates, the posited means of the newly discovered Hebrew root are "to help, fix, make whole, set right." . . . The verse now supports the following translation: "Therefore a man strengthens/supports/helps his father and his mother and clings to his woman/wife and they become one flesh." . . . In this context . . . 'therefore' makes a conclusion that humans behave differently from animals that do not care or even recognize their mother and father after they mature, that mate (more or less) indiscriminately and casually, and that are unaware of their own offspring after they mature. The verse implies that since parents birth sons and (may) provide those sons with wives, every son is obliged to care for his father and his mother and to cling to his wife simultaneously. Understood this way, the verse also alludes to the formation of extended families embracing three generations in a single household that were typical of Israelite society."

35. Mettinger, *The Eden Narrative*, 72: "Validation of social values may also be involved in the motif of the woman as created from the rib of the man. Though 2:23–24, in which a man must leave his father and mother and cling to his wife, hardly reflects established marriage customs in Israel, one should not disregard the possibility that these verses with the formula "bones of my bones and flesh of my flesh" may nevertheless validate marriage as a fundamental social institution." See W. Reiser, "Die Verwandtschaftsformel in Gen 2:23," in *Theologische Zeitschrift* 16 (1960); 1–4, see also Genesis 29:14; Judges 9:2–3; 2 Samuel 5:1; 19:13–14.

marriage created in the garden, but the highest form of social communion, a Zion society, was also present via the institution of marriage. Thus, the institution of marriage and the recognition by both Adam and Eve as to its importance for their own identity is a major event in the continuing process of making the cosmos.[36] And yet it is not the completion of the cosmos. That required a fall.

WHEN THE WOMAN SAW THE FRUIT WAS GOOD: THE FALL AS A COSMOS-MAKING EVENT

The first indication following the Creation and the marriage of Adam and Eve that the cosmos is still incomplete is the observation that "they were both naked, the man and his wife, and were not ashamed" (Genesis 2:25). Though it might seem that this phrase simply points out that Adam and Eve are unaware that they lack clothing, nakedness is more than a synonym for nudity; it is often associated with the social experiences of shame and humiliation.[37] In fact, this is the only place in the scriptures where nakedness does not bring about negative social consequences. Yet the negative experiences associated with nakedness are in fact constructive to the functioning of society as they provide a clear delineation

---

36. Walton, *Lost World*, 80–81: "Genesis 2:24 is responding to the question of why a person would leave the closest biological relationship (parents to children) in order to forge a relationship with a biological outsider. The answer offered is that marriage goes beyond biology to recover an original state, for humanity is ontologically gendered. Ontology trumps biology. This has shown Adam that the woman is not just a reproductive mating partner. Her identity is that she is his ally, his other half. We can now see that Genesis 2:24 makes more of a statement than we had envisioned. Becoming one flesh is not just a reference to the sexual act. The sexual act may be the one that rejoins them, but it is the rejoining that is the focus. When Man and Woman become one flesh, they are returning to their original state."

37. See Isaiah 20:2–4; 58:7; Ezekiel 18:7, 16; Amos 2:16; Job 1:21; 22:6; 24:7, 10; Ecclesiastes 5:14; Alma 18:14–22.

between what is proper and what is not, particularly in the dynamics between male and female.[38]

Adam's and Eve's unawareness of their state, therefore, is striking and suggests that further cosmic differentiation is necessary. This differentiation would entail the moral principles by which a society could be sustained such as right/wrong, obedience/disobedience, innocence/guilt, correct/incorrect, and so forth. Each of these polarities are at the foundation of a socio-legal tradition and are essential to a functioning society as they provide meaning, structure, and limitations by which identity and purpose can be established. Thus, Adam and Eve's lack of awareness concerning their nakedness may serve as the indicator that these binaries have not been enacted and that therefore the cosmos is not yet fully complete.

The Book of Mormon—Lehi's discourse in 2 Nephi 2 in particular—highlights the negative aspects of this undifferentiation: "Behold, if Adam had not transgressed, he would not have fallen, but he would have remained in the garden of Eden. And all things which were created must have remained in the same state in which they were after they were created, . . . having no joy, for they knew no misery; doing no good, for they knew no sin" (2 Nephi 2:22–23). This last clause is particularly indicting as the pronouncements or recognitions of the creation as "good" demonstrates the divine awareness that they are functioning correctly. That Adam and Eve were unable to do good while in the garden, arising from their lack of awareness concerning the polarities of good/bad, joy/misery, and so forth, suggests that remaining in such a state would be "not good," or incomplete, similar to the state of Adam alone in the garden. This would necessitate their leaving the garden to fulfill their purpose. Thus, while it is true that leaving the garden would result in death, life and death now became a

38. Zevit, *What Really Happened*, 172–73: "Although their rush to make loincloths is sometimes presented as a demonstration of their guilt, it is actually about the rush of knowledge that follows a blush of shame. Shame is tied to understanding cultural values and to changeable individual behavior; guilt is tied to juridic, forensic contexts and can sometimes be expiated. For individuals to experience shame, they must know social codes and must be aware they committed or were subjected to an impropriety related to a particular value or norm. They also must know what is required to rectify the situation."

differentiation both cognitively and experientially that was necessary for Adam and Eve to do good and continue toward the ultimate creation of exaltation.[39]

At this point in the narrative, the reader is introduced to the serpent, which is the antagonist to the conflict in which the differentiations mentioned will be experienced. Because this figure is never explicitly identified in either the Old or New Testaments, modern scholarship has treated the serpent as a trickster, a character often found in folklore who is morally and ethically ambiguous but is instrumental in the acquisition or innovation of social goods. Yet by the intertestamental period, it appears that a number of extrabiblical texts had begun to associate the serpent with Satan, an individual of premortal, divine origin who had rebelled from God and was thrust down to earth. As early as the mid-second century, Christians have assumed the same.[40]

Like other Christians, Latter-day Saints also understand the figure to be Satan, but this understanding emerges from more than common Christian interpretation; it includes material concerning the Creation and the Garden of Eden from latter-day scripture as well. Moses 4, in particular, interrupts the narrative of the garden to include a brief excursus

---

39. Mettinger, *The Eden Narrative*, 4: "An interpretation that increasingly attracts attention is the Eden Narrative as a story about human maturation. In her semiotic analysis, Ellen van Wolde argues that this is in fact the central thematic aspect of the story. She sees Gen. 2:24 (the man leaving his father and mother) as presenting 'man's process of development in a nutshell' [Ellen van Wolde, *A Semiotic Analysis of Genesis 2–3*, SSN 25 (Assen: Van Gorcum, 1989), 217]. Van Wolde takes the four narrative episodes as referring the subsequent stages of 'before birth' (2:4b–6), 'childhood' (2:7–25), 'adolescence' (3:1–7), and 'maturity' (3:8–24). The tree is the knowledge of good and evil. The same type of knowledge is mentioned in connection with children in Deut. 1:39, 'your children, who this day have no knowledge of good or evil' (RSV)."

40. Elaine A. Phillip, "Serpent Intertexts: Tantalizing Twists in the Tales," in *Bulletin for Biblical Research* 10, no. 2 (2000): 233–345. "By the first centuries BCE and CE, the serpent had become linked with the malevolent figure of Satan, the devil, the great dragon. This connection is most comprehensively articulated for the Christian community in Rev 12:9 and 20:1, but some aspects of the identification are evident in extracanonical texts as well. See *Apoc.* Mos. 15–21; *Life of Adam and Eve* 12–16; 2 *Enoch* 31:3–6; Wis 2:23–24; *Apoc. Abr:* 23., 238."

concerning Satan's rebellion in the premortal realm. While the excursus outlines Satan's attempt to become the Redeemer, it also highlights the reasons as to why he wanted to become such: "Wherefore, because that Satan rebelled against me, and sought to destroy the agency of man, which I, the Lord God, had given him, and also, that I should give unto him mine own power . . . I caused that he should be cast down; and he became Satan, yea, even the devil" (Moses 4:3–4).

Though the text is relatively straightforward, there is ambiguity, particularly regarding the referent to the pronoun "him" in the two instances. While the common reading assumes that the first pronoun refers to man (thus Satan sought to destroy the agency given by God to all humankind), with the second referring to the adversary (thus suggesting that Satan's reception of God's power at this point could only happen through the destruction of humankind's agency), it is possible the two pronouns refer either to humankind or Satan in both instances. If the second of these other options reflects the reading, it appears to highlight the nature of agency, as Satan, who seeks to destroy the agency of others, possesses his own. The other alternative reading suggests that the adversary struggles with man possessing both agency and God's own power.[41] Regardless, if

41. Intriguingly, while Satan's refusal to accept Adam's selection over himself is not found within the Latter-day Saint scriptural canon, it is a narrative found in a number of extrabiblical texts, perhaps reflecting later changes made in the scriptural texts, as we've noted earlier elsewhere. See B. Surah 7:11–18, *Life of Adam and Eve*, *Slavonic III Baruch*, *The Revolt of Satan, and the Battle in Heaven*, *Cave of Treasures*, St. Ephrem, *De Ecclesia* 47, *Discourse of Abaddon*. In these texts, Satan, who is leader of the divine host, is asked to give obeisance to Michael, who had been chosen to have preeminence and authority over the host. Satan refuses to do so and thus rebels. Though not found explicitly anywhere in the scriptures, this narrative may be alluded to in Hebrews 1:6, as part of Paul's scriptural references to Christ's preeminence: "And again, when he bringeth in the firstbegotten into the world, he saith, and let all the angels of God worship him." This follows Paul's use of two Old Testament references, neither of which, in its original context, is about Christ specifically (Psalm 2, which can be messianic, but refers to the Davidic covenant specifically, and 2 Samuel 7:14, which again is the covenant established with David) and reflects the common rhetorical practice of using material out of its original context to make a new point. In these cases, though the verses are about David and the covenant established with him, they are used by Paul to describe Christ's election. Verse

the verse reflects the second reading, again we find God accentuating the ontological relationship between humankind and the divine, as they too will have agency and divine power.

Following the excursus, the reader is back in familiar biblical territory as we are told that the serpent is "more subtle" or clever than any other animal (Moses 4:5). But this is then followed by another crucial addition: "And Satan put it into the heart of the serpent . . . and he sought also to beguile Eve, for he knew not the mind of God, wherefore he sought to destroy the world" (Moses 4:6). With this addition, the trickster nature of the serpent figure is gone and the beguiling of Eve is given a teleological dimension as it reflects the apparent antipathy of the adversary for the progression of humankind, as noted in the earlier excursus. Yet it also suggests that the act will not, in fact, have the devastating consequences Satan believes will result as the beguiling of Eve will not lead to the destruction of the world.

This lack of understanding strengthens a pun long recognized in the Garden of Eden narrative. The Hebrew terms for "naked" and "subtle," terms describing the states of Adam and Eve, and the serpent, respectively, are *ʿarûmmîm* (naked, plural) and *ʿārûm* (subtle). The narrative irony is that while Adam and Eve are physically naked and unaware, they will not remain in this state because they become aware and will progress and experience the cognitive differentiation necessary for the ongoing cosmic process. Satan, on the other hand, who knows not the mind of God, will never progress beyond his current state, unaware that he is, in fact, naked before God.

What exactly Satan does not know regarding the mind of God is not made explicit. But because this insight is associated with the beguiling of Eve, it suggests the adversary believes that the casting of Adam and Eve out of the garden will go contrary to the will of God. The beguiling scene begins with the serpent's query: "Hath God said—Ye shall not eat of every tree of the garden?" (Moses 4:7). The intent of the question is to get Eve to partake of the fruit; that required her perceiving the fruit differently

---

6 appears to also be a quote from another text, but nowhere is this text to be found. In light of its language, it is possible that we have here a known biblical text speaking of the second type of fall narrative.

than she had before. Her response is a repetition of the original injunction, which suggests that she has in fact never really considered the differences between the trees. The serpent retorts by saying that death will not be the result, instead the partaker will be like the gods, recognizing the difference between good and evil, a state referred to as "eyes . . . opened," thus implying the ability to see or discern truly (Moses 4:8 –13).

The result of the dialogue is a paradigm shift in which Eve now sees the tree and its fruit in a completely different light, one in which the tree is aesthetically attractive and, more importantly, good. As noted earlier, the declaration of a thing or state as good indicates that it is functioning properly and has been associated solely as a divine responsibility. With her recognition that the tree is good, Eve, like Adam before, demonstrates her divine nature, even her specific responsibility in the creation process. In this case, that which makes the fruit good is the potential it has to make one wise. The Hebrew verb *sākal* translated as "to make wise," perhaps may more accurately be translated as "to understand or to have insight," even "to act prudently." Thus, eating the fruit may be understood as revelatory as it is the mechanism by which Eve may now understand or comprehend the polarities mentioned above and in so doing actually do good, or fully function to her purpose, as Lehi explained.[42]

With these newly acquired insights, it appears that according to the narrative, Eve ate the fruit, gave some to Adam, who, as her husband, also ate the fruit, presumably in response to the same insights that Eve had. With both sets of eyes now open, the primal couple now realized their nakedness and organized their first creation together—clothing. Elsewhere in the ancient Near East, the acquisition of clothing highlights the boundary between the wild/undifferentiated and civilization/cosmos.[43] As

42. Zevit, *What Really Happened*, 170: "The conversation with the snake is often labeled 'the Temptation of Eve' or 'The Seduction of Eve.' Such loaded terms are inappropriate, since most of what took place occurred within Hawwa's [Eve's] head as she processed cognitive information."

43. Bernard F. Batto, *Slaying the Dragon: Mythmaking in the Biblical Tradition* (Louisville, KY: Westminster/John Knox Press, 1992), 55–57: "In Mesopotamia the ancient bards had long since used the nakedness of the first humans to symbolize that these primitives, without benefit of the divinely bestowed gifts of civilization, were little better than animals. . . . In Mesopotamian tradition the

for the clothing itself, though some have suggested symbolic significance in the fig leaves, it is most likely that the narrative employs these leaves for a more prosaic reason—its maximum coverage. Functionally, the new clothing acts as camouflage as the reader is told that the newly dressed Adam and Eve hid themselves among the flora of the Garden from the presence of God.[44]

While the camouflage does not ultimately work, as Adam and Eve both respond to the inquiries of God, it does highlight the social separation that Adam and Eve now recognize as present between themselves and the divine.[45] Whereas before there appears to have been no social distinction between God and the couple, now the couple deliberately separate themselves from the divine, feeling shame and believing that they are no longer worthy to be in his presence. The ensuing dialogue between God and the couple confirms their guilt as they both admit to eating the fruit. In both instances, the two individuals take responsibility for their own agency, noting that whatever the circumstances were at the moment of decision, the decision made was theirs alone. As with the production of the clothing, the acceptance of responsibility for one's choices highlights the increasing cosmic social order as this too is necessary for a competent society. Yet, while Adam and Eve are now socially aware and responsible, the consequences outlined by God earlier must still be met.

---

humans' donning of clothes was accomplished with the good graces of the gods. Clothes were one of the gifts of civilization, along with knowledge of irrigation, agriculture, and the building of cities, which the gods bestowed upon humankind for their advancement. . . . Whereas it was the nature of animals to go without clothes, gods wore clothing. . . . Accordingly, clothes were an effective metaphor of the dignity of humanity, beings closer in nature to the gods than to the animals."

44. For more on the role of clothing as social signifier see Daniel Belnap, "Clothed with Salvation: The Garden, the Veil, Tabitha and Christ," in *Studies in Antiquity* 4 (2012): 43–70.

45. While the significance of this act is not explained in the Creation narrative, clothing generally, whether in an ancient context or a modern one, has a primary function of defining an individual within the larger social setting. Clothing often denoted one's social status (married, class affiliation, trade, and so forth) and the acts of investiture or divestiture indicated one's movement from one social level to another.

However, expulsion and death aren't the only consequences given; two specific ones are given to Eve: the difficulty and pain associated with bearing and delivering children, and the establishment of Adam as the hierarchical head of the relationship. While the latter of the two may sound inappropriate today, this describes the most common power dynamic in marriage arrangements of ancient Israel. It may also reflect the tradition in which the woman leaves her family to follow after her husband, as the word for desire *tešûqāh* is derived from *šûq*, which carries the nuance of "follow" or "run after." In at least one verb form, it carries with it the sense of "abundance" and "overflowing," suggesting that her fortunes are now tied to those of her husband. Yet this dependence is not necessarily one-sided and may be viewed as complementary with the earlier editorial comment that the husband was to leave his family to cleave to his wife, a recognition that the wife was much more than property but, in fact, kin and to be treated as such.

As for the first consequence, the experience of sorrow via childbearing and -rearing, it reflects a similar consequence given to Adam. In his case, sorrow would be experienced through his efforts to bring forth produce from the earth itself. The Hebrew nominative form, translated as "sorrow," is rare and does not necessarily carry the emotional nuance that the English term "sorrow" does (though the verbal form does). Instead, it is found within the context of the difficulty in the production of a thing; thus, its use in terms of childbirth refers to the difficulty and pain associated with the process of childbirth or childrearing and its usage regarding Adam's sorrow with the difficulty of agricultural work.

For many, the promise of sorrow is a negative experience, and indeed the term is often used to denote the suffering and adversity that afflict Israel, and by extension, all humankind that followed the expulsion from the Garden of Eden. Yet throughout the scriptures the experience of grief has manifold functions, a consequence of wrongdoing being only one. Though grief is not mentioned by name, the law of Moses emphasized again and again the expectation that Israel have empathy for the marginalized and less fortunate. Such empathy was to arise out of Israel's recognition that they too had once been in similar straits. In the writings of Isaiah, the servant, explicitly identified as Israel elsewhere, is described as one who, having experienced grief and sorrow, bears grief and carries sorrow (see Isaiah 53:3–5). Perhaps reflecting their common Israelite background, the faithful of Alma are told that if they desire to enter "into the fold of God," they must demonstrate a willingness to bear one another's burdens and "mourn with those who mourn" (Mosiah 18:8–9), characteristics that Jesus Christ would later encapsulate in his Beatitudes, including the declaration "blessed are they that mourn" (Matthew 5:4).

Perhaps the most significant, from a Latter-day Saint view, is Alma's teaching that grief was an essential component of Christ's ability to succor humankind. According to the prophet, Christ suffered all pain, including sorrow and grief, so that he could succor all in redemption. This sentiment was reflected in the Christian text of Hebrews in which the writer noted that those who were given the priesthood had the responsibility to "show compassion upon the ignorant and those that are out of the way; for he himself also is compassed about with infirmity," suggesting that at least one later tradition understood that sorrow was a primary component of priestly duties (see Hebrews 5:1–2). In each of these instances, sorrow appears to provide for differentiation of experience, becoming a foundational element of memory by which individuals, through empathy, could participate in a cooperative community. In this manner, the promise of sorrow may be recognized as a cosmos-making act as much as the dividing of the waters, the naming of the animals, and the institution of marriage.

Two last events conclude the narrative. The first of these is Adam's naming of the woman as Eve. The placement of this event seems odd and much later in the narrative then one would assume, yet it works within the context. Like other naming events, the naming of Eve has to do with identity and relationship, but unlike the earlier events, which emphasize the type of the object, in this case it is her actual name that is given, which suggests that it is meant to recognize Eve as an individualized being, separate and distinct from Adam, who could act independently and as significantly as Adam himself.

The name itself is *ḥavvāh*, or "life," and reflects Eve's crucial and fundamental role in the presence, maintenance, and expression of life. Adam's further identification of her as the "mother of all living" (Genesis 3:20) highlights both her sociological and cosmological responsibilities.[46] As such, she not only is necessary for the continuation of humankind and society but also, as the one who noted the fruit was good and partook of it first, created the conditions by which all life had the opportunity to progress. Again, this is expressed best in the Book of Mormon, where the reader is informed that without a fall, "all things which were created must have remained in the same state in which they were after they were created" (2 Nephi 2:22). In this decision, Eve complemented the role of God as creator, and the designation of mother reflects the larger, cosmological scope as well as the more particular, physical aspects of motherhood. Indeed, one could make the case that the designation demonstrates an ecclesiastical, even priestly, dimension to motherhood generally, and Eve specifically.[47]

Yet the narrative is not merely an etiology to the name of Eve, it also highlights the importance of Adam's recognition of its meaning. This

---

46. Ziony Zevit has suggested that the root stems instead from an Arabic cognate meaning "kin." See *What Really Happened*, 229: "The word *ḥay* in this expression is cognate to Arabic noun hayya, meaning 'kin, related members of a clan, descendants of a father or ancestor.' . . . The proposed etymology clarifies not only the explanation provided for the name but also the name itself. Hawwa's name, ḥawwāh, is derived from h-w-y also cognate to h-y-y and refers to related people. Its translation should reflect that fact, and verse 20a, paraphrased expansively, reads: 'And he called her Hawwa, that is, Kin-maker, because she was the mother of all kinfolk.'"
47. Walton, *Lost World*, 112–13: "In Genesis 2 the woman is seen as the ally to man in service in sacred space. As an ally, she would not have to have the same roles as man, but little more can be said given the lack of information provided in the text. . . . Returning to the priestly roles of Adam and Eve, we will gain more insight if we look to the larger paradigm offered by the identification of Israel as a 'kingdom of priests.' Israel's priestly role is found neither in the offering of rituals on behalf of the rest of the nations nor in servicing sacred space for them. Their role is to mediate knowledge of God, and their end goal is ultimately not to restrict access to the presence of God but to mediate access through instruction. The role of Adam and Eve in the garden, I would propose, has less to do with how the priests operated within Israel and more to do with Israel's role as priests to the world. In such a view, we need not be concerned about a lack of women priests in Israel."

reflects another important differentiation, this time of Adam and Eve as separate, unique individuals who may act according to their own will. Like the naming of the animals revealed to Adam what was lacking in the nascent cosmos—namely, a partner—so it is now that Adam acknowledges that the partner is something other than himself but complementary, that possesses her own ideas and approaches which are also creative, cosmic, and divine in scope. Whereas before Eve was "woman" and "helpmeet," now she is an actualized individual named Eve. Though subtler than other differentiations, this one is just as important in the creation of the social cosmos as society is made up of individuals bound together, yet it could not have occurred until Eve had exercised her own agency, thus its placement so late in the narrative.

The final event before their expulsion is the investiture of Adam and Eve in clothing made by God. The investiture of Adam and Eve with clothing that God himself made is highly significant when viewed through the earlier lens concerning the social function of clothing. If the earlier construction and wearing of clothing represented Adam and Eve's definition of self and a recognition of the perceived changes in social status, it suggested that these definitions and recognitions were their own, independent of God's consideration. In other words, while the clothing has functioned properly, the definitions themselves are faulty because Adam and Eve made the clothing under the assumption that God is disappointed, angry, vengeful, and so forth. These are faulty assumptions and may reflect some of the deception of the adversary, who, by suggesting that God was hiding truth from Adam and Eve, had set up an antagonistic relationship between the couple and God. Thus their clothing reflects their belief, not necessarily God's perspective. God's investiture resets the relationship. Yes, they are to experience the consequences of eating the fruit, but the antagonistic relationship they assumed was in place, because of the adversary's words, was not correct. Importantly, the clothing represented God's definition as to where they stood in his esteem while his actual investing them in the clothing suggested that they were indeed worthy to be a part of the divine community, even if they were to be physically separated for a time.[48]

---

48. Jung Hoon Kim, *The Significance of Clothing Imagery in the Pauline Corpus* (London: Clark International, 2004), 17: "The garment of skin also connotes

The act itself is also reminiscent of other divine investitures, namely of the priests, as well as the righteous at judgment, and reflects the eschatological nature of the creation.[49] As for the new identity specifically, while no new designation is given, it is telling that it is only after the second investiture that God now declared that "man is now become as one of us."

Thus, Adam and Eve have now become like the Gods and can now create cosmos. Their expulsion is not so much a punishment, but the opportunity to put the creative cosmos-making skills, inherent as the same type of being as God and given to them in their interaction with the same, to use. That the book of Genesis ends with the creation of Israel suggests that to the writers or redactors, the creation process was understood as continuing still through the presence of Israel as God's chosen people. Like their forebears, who themselves reflected priestly, even divine, responsibilities, Israel was chosen to bless all nations of the earth, becoming a kingdom of priests themselves.

Yet, for all of the significant insights into the very nature and relationship of God and man, and their apparent reflection in the later purposes of Israel, it is not until the New Testament that the Creation narratives of Genesis 1–3 are explicitly alluded to in the biblical text. But the

---

reconciliation with God. While Adam wore his own fig-leaves apron, he was afraid of God, but when he was clothed in a garment of skin provided by God, he did not panic before him. In short, the clothing image in Gen. 3:21 signifies that Adam's restoration to his original life and glory, to peace with God, and to kingship over the other creatures has started." It is possible that the clothing also reflected another important aspect of the Creation narrative, the necessity of the Atonement. While the Fall was necessary for human exaltation, Adam and Eve needed to learn that this was not going to be possible on their own; thus, the investitures and divestitures present in the narrative become the mechanism by which this knowledge is gained.

49. See 2 Nephi 9:14; Doctrine and Covenants 29:13. Though he references Genesis 1 specifically, Anderson also notes the eschatological nature of the creation narratives: "It is significant that the Priestly creation story is articulated in the time sequence of a week. The week is governed not by an abstract principle of Time but by the will of God, which gives each day its meaningful content. In Israel's faith time does not move in a circle; it moves toward the culmination of the Creator's intention, just as the week of creation moves toward the Sabbath rest. Thus the creation faith is eschatological. The affirmation "in the beginning" is incomplete without the related affirmation "in the end." *From Creation*, 16.

prominence of these narratives in the Book of Mormon suggests that the narratives continued to have meaning to ancient Israel. We have already seen the value of 2 Nephi 2 in understanding the incomplete nature of the Garden of Eden. In fact, the entire chapter appears to be structured on the principle of differentiation, demonstrating its vital function in the fulfilling of universal salvation.

Noting that there must be opposition in all things, Lehi points out that such a state provides for the presence of choice, a factor that is necessary to "bring about [God's] eternal purposes in the end of man" (2 Nephi 2:15). Lack of agency, or the ability to act on or create differentiation, keeps an object or entity as "one body, . . . having no life neither death, nor corruption nor incorruption, happiness nor misery, neither sense nor sensibility. Wherefore it must needs have been created for a thing of naught; wherefore there would have been no purpose in the end of its creation" (verses 11–12). It is this state of nonexperience that Lehi later intimates was the Garden of Eden: "And now . . . if Adam had not transgressed, . . . he would have remained in the garden of Eden. And all things which were created must have remained in the same state in which they were after they were created . . . they would have remained in a state of innocence . . . doing no good, for they knew no sin" (verses 22–23). Thus the Fall of Adam and Eve, in which the primordial couple chose so that humankind "might have joy" (verse 25), or the ability to differentiate or act on differentiation, becomes fundamental to the continuing progression and salvation of all. That differentiation continues to play this role throughout an individual's existence is noted by Lehi as he tied the creative principle of differentiation to one's eschatological state: Humankind has "become free forever, knowing good from evil; to act for themselves. . . . And they are free to choose liberty and eternal life . . . or to choose captivity and death" (verses 26–27).[50]

50. Five hundred years later, Alma uses the garden narrative to highlight the fundamental nature of the law of justice and its relationship to the law of mercy. In two instances, once before the people of Ammonihah and once in a personal conversation with his son Corianton, Alma follows the perspective of God and his agency, noting that if God had let Adam and Eve experience the negative consequences of death and expulsion following their disobedience, then "the plan of redemption would have been frustrated, and the word of God would

Besides the application of the Creation principles to existences at every stage, the Creation narratives appear to have been used as models for Book of Mormon experiences. For instance, the account of Lehi's seminal dream in 1 Nephi 8 may best be understood as a Creation narrative similar to the ones found in Genesis 1–3. Like the undifferentiated precosmos, Lehi begins his dream in a "dark and dreary" waste, until the appearance of a being dressed in a white robe who provides a contrast to the dark and dreary state. His appearance gives Lehi a meaningful direction and a choice to either follow or remain in the state now defined in opposition to the being. Choosing to follow, Lehi eventually encounters a field characterized by a tree whose fruit was so white it exceeded "all the whiteness that [he] had ever seen" (1 Nephi 8:11), of which he partakes. Though he is not expelled from the environment of the tree for doing so, he does take on the role of the guide by leading others to the tree, a role that is intimated to be possible only after eating the fruit.

Nephi, Lehi's son, will later see this highly symbolic narrative through a very historical lens by which the future of his people is viewed through the prism of Lehi's creation narrative. Indeed, the culminating event of the Book of Mormon, the appearance and ministry of Christ to Lehi's and Nephi's descendants approximately six hundred years later, may be profitably be read as the physical analogue of the dream and thus as another creation narrative. According to the text in 3 Nephi, with the death of Christ in the Old World, the New World experienced three days of physical upheaval that completely reconfigured the local geography and which included "a mist of darkness" that no light could penetrate (1 Nephi 12:4), characteristics that are similar to the precosmic state described in Genesis 1.[51] That Christ came as a glorious, light-filled being to the temple in the land of Bountiful is almost expected when the event is viewed

have been void," (Alma 12:26) leading to a situation in which "God would cease to be God" (Alma 42:13).

51. For more on the relationship between the creation narratives, Lehi's Dream, Nephi's Vision, and the physical ministry of Christ in the New World, see Daniel Belnap, "'There Arose a Mist of Darkness': The Narrative of Lehi's Dream in Christ's Theophany," in *Third Nephi: An Incomparable Scripture*, ed. Andrew C. Skinner, Gaye Strathearn (Salt Lake City: Neal A. Maxwell Institute and Deseret Book, 2012), 75–106.

through the Creation narrative; that he then empowers the present congregation who go out among the greater population reflects the expulsion and the true purpose of Adam and Eve.

CONCLUSION

For millennia, the creation narratives of Genesis 1–3 have informed communities on the principles of differentiation, reflecting humankind's, and Israel's in particular, responsibility to continue the process of cosmos construction.[52] Thanks to these narratives, the reader could recognize that the work of Adam and Eve was no different from their own responsibility to be holy and establish holiness. This is no less true for the Latter-day Saints, who also recognize that the narratives highlight the ontological similarities that lie at the heart of our salvation. As such, the creative narratives hold a special place in Latter-day Saint religious experience, being the narrative to the temple endowment. There members experience these narratives as if they were actually present and through the process realize their own role in the continuation and further work necessary to the social cosmos with Zion and exaltation as the culmination of the Creation. Thus, the Creation narratives are much more than simple tales, but are rich, complex accounts that have as much meaning today as they did when first crafted thousands of years ago. And this meaning is what provides one of its more important lessons: that the Bible overall still has a message for us.

52. Jon D. Levenson, *Creation and the Persistence of Evil: The Jewish Drama of Divine Omnipotence* (Princeton: Princeton University Press, 1988), 119: "Genesis 1:1–2:3, the priestly cosmogony, presents creation as an event ordered toward the rest of God, with which it closes, a rest that signifies an act of redemption and social reform and an opportunity for human participation in the sublime quietude of the unopposed creator God." Anderson, *From Creation*, 6–7: "The redemptive word, by which Israel was created as the people of God, is none other than the creative word, by which the heavens were made. The point bears reemphasis that in the Bible creation is not an independent doctrine but is inseparably related to the basic story of the people in which Yahweh is presented as the actor and redeemer. Salvation and creation belong together."

CAIN AND ABEL (GENESIS 4 AND MOSES 5)

ANDREW C. SKINNER

The narrative of Cain and Abel is often recognized as one of the more difficult narratives in the Bible. Introducing as it does the first instances of interpersonal violence, it is never referenced or alluded to again explicitly anywhere in the Old Testament; thus, the purpose of this narrative within the larger context of the book of Genesis is not altogether clear. Because of this, it is often relegated to the genre of "folklore." Restoration scripture though, as Andrew Skinner demonstrates in this chapter, adds new understanding to the narrative, noting the role of Cain in the institution of those societies similar to, yet diametrically opposed to, the concept of Zion. —DB and AS

The story of Cain and Abel is one of the most famous in our biblical repertoire, rousing us to a sense of our social responsibility with the immortal line "Am I my brother's keeper?" (Genesis 4:9). It is situated in that earliest portion of the Bible (Genesis 1–11) that modern scholars generally label "primeval history,"[1] pointing out that this section has significant parallels in the literature of the ancient Near East. Since a good deal of this literature is shown to be older than the usually accepted dates for the book of Genesis, it is sometimes assumed that portions of Genesis are dependent on the older ancient Near Eastern material.[2] Such an assumption "implies that the primeval history is actually only primeval mythology."[3] Thus, the story of Cain and Abel in Genesis is often classified as "folkloric" material, like the Garden of Eden narrative (Genesis 2:4–3:24) and the rest of Genesis 4–11.[4] As a prime example, the Cain and Abel episode is discounted as a real occurrence because it is truncated, lacking important details, and it appears (to some) to be based on an ancient Sumerian tale of the contest between Dumuzi, the shepherd-god, and Enkimdu, the farmer-god.[5] However, other scholars have shown that the equation of Cain and Abel with Dumuzi and Enkimdu is flimsy[6] and that the biblical story "must once have existed as an independent, full-bodied tale."[7]

---

1. Michael D. Coogan, *The Old Testament: A Historical and Literary Introduction to the Hebrew Scriptures* (New York: Oxford University Press, 2006), 31; Stephen L. Harris and Robert L. Platzner, *The Old Testament: An Introduction to the Hebrew Bible* (Boston: McGraw Hill, 2003), 106.
2. Genesis chapters 1–11 "freely borrow and adopt" preexisting "parallel materials from the ancient Near East." Coogan, *Old Testament*, 31.
3. Andrew E. Hill and John H. Walton, *A Survey of the Old Testament*, 3rd ed. (Grand Rapids, MI: Zondervan, 2009), 80; Douglas A. Knight and Amy-Jill Levine, *The Meaning of the Bible: What the Jewish Scriptures and Christian Old Testament Can Teach Us* (New York: HarperCollins Publishers, 2011), 128, refer to the Cain and Abel story as "part of the mythic prehistory of Genesis 1–11."
4. Coogan, *Old Testament*, 31.
5. Walter C. Kaiser, *The Old Testament Documents: Are They Reliable and Relevant?* (Downers Grove, IL: InterVarsity Press, 2001), 59–60. Samuel Noah Kramer, Sumerian Myths, rev. ed. (New York: Harper Torchbooks, 1961), 101–3.
6. Kaiser, *Old Testament Documents*, 60.
7. Nahum M. Sarna, *Understanding Genesis* (New York: Schocken Books, 1966), 29.

In contrast to the shortage of details in the Genesis 4 account, Latter-day Saints possess a greatly expanded version of the Cain and Abel episode in the Joseph Smith Translation of Genesis, which provides information too specific, detailed, and context-appropriate to dismiss as fiction. In addition, Cain and Abel are presented in other passages of the standard works as authentic figures, including in the Book of Mormon, and by living prophets (see below). All of this persuades us of the reality of the characters and the story's overall veracity. In this chapter we will examine the Hebrew text of Genesis 4:1–17, compare it with Joseph Smith's revised version of the Cain and Abel story in the Book of Moses, and consider the importance of the episode for modern readers.

CHARACTERISTICS OF THE STORY

The Hebrew Bible (Christian Old Testament) presents the story of Cain and Abel in seventeen succinct verses and assumes several "firsts" in the earth's temporal history, or history after the Fall of Adam and Eve:

- the first act of mortal procreation (Genesis 4:1)
- the first son (Cain) born to Eve and Adam (4:1)
- the first set of brothers (4:2)
- the first clear differentiation of vocations (4:2)
- the first mention of offerings or sacrifice in the Hebrew Bible (4:3)
- the first rejection, by God, of an offering made to him (4:5)
- the first of many examples of God favoring the youngest son over the eldest, even though the rule of primogeniture was established early on (4:5)
- the first case of family antagonism (4:6)
- the first murder in human history (4:8)
- the first case of trying to deceive God (4:9)
- the first fugitive (4:14)

- the first sign or mark of identification placed on a mortal by Deity (4:15)
- the first grandchild of Adam and Eve (4:17)
- the first construction of a city (4:17)

This list of firsts is impressive. However, Nahum Sarna has described the Hebrew text of this periscope as "tantalizingly incomplete," even obscure in places,[8] leading several modern commentators to label portions of the text as corrupted.[9] It certainly raises many questions. For example, why does the text omit crucial details? Why does Jehovah (Yahweh) accept Abel's offering and not Cain's? Why does God favor the younger son over the elder? Where does Cain's murderous impulse come from? How do two brothers, born of the exact same righteous parentage into the same environment uncorrupted by an as yet nonexistent society, turn out with such differing views and behavior? As the firstborn, where did Cain get a wife? With the building of the first city, doesn't this assume a large population already in existence? How does the Masoretic text of the story differ from other versions: Greek or Septuagint (LXX hereafter), Latin Vulgate, Syriac, and Samaritan Pentateuch? We will explore some of these issues in the following discussion.

HEBREW TEXT

The story begins with Eve's conception and birthing of Cain (4:1). The name Cain (Hebrew, *qayin*) probably derives from a root word meaning, "metal worker, artificer."[10] Cain's descendant, Tubal-cain, became a metal-worker, forging tools out of bronze and iron (4:22), which scholars associate with the etymology of the name Cain because (*qayin*) is the identical

8. Sarna, *Understanding Genesis*, 28.
9. George Arthur Buttrick, commentary editor, *The Interpreter's Bible*, 12 vols. (Nashville: Abingdon, 1978), 1:518; Richard S. Hess, "Cain," *Anchor Bible Dictionary*, ed. David Noel Freedman, 6 vols. (New York: Doubleday, 1992), 1:807.
10. Francis Brown, S. R. Driver, and Charles Briggs, *A Hebrew and English Lexicon of the Old Testament* (Oxford: Clarendon Press, 1976), 883–84.

word for "smith." It is also the probable root of the name of a nomadic group called the Kenites who interacted with the Israelites and whose activities included metallurgy.[11]

The name Cain also sounds like the Hebrew word for "acquired" (*qanah*)[12] and is likely a purposeful play on words, "I have gotten a man from the Lord" or "With the help of the Lord I have brought forth a man" (Genesis 4:1 NIV).[13] This last phrase conveys thanksgiving for God's providence in providing a son. This sentiment underpins a fundamental value of Old Testament society reflected later in the Psalmist's expression of God's involvement in providing the blessing of posterity: "Children are an heritage of the Lord" (Psalm 127:3). The opposite condition, the curse of barrenness, was also ascribed to the Lord. For example, "the Lord had shut up [Hannah's] womb" (1 Samuel 1:5).

Another son was born to Adam and Eve, how long after Cain we do not know. His Hebrew name, Abel (*hāvel*), is a form of the Hebrew root *hevel*, meaning "breath, vapour."[14] One interpretation infers his name was a play on words because a "breath" is short, like Abel's tragic life.[15] The Assyrian cognate, *ablu*, simply means "son," and may be the etymology of Abel's name.[16] Without any discussion of his or Cain's upbringing, an immediate differentiation of vocations is made: Abel is a *ro ʿēh tso ʾn*, shepherd of sheep and goats,[17] while Cain is a *ʿobēd ʾadāmāh*, worker or tiller of the ground (Genesis 4:2). Throughout the Bible, God often shows a preference for the lifestyle of the shepherd over the farmer, and two of the most

11. Richard S. Hess, "Cain," 1:806; Coogan, *Old Testament*, 32.
12. Brown et al., *Hebrew and English Lexicon of the Old Testament*, 888.
13. The NIV translation attempts to acknowledge more directly God's role as the one responsible for giving all life and breath, as mentioned by the Apostle Paul in Acts 17:25.
14. Brown et. al., *Hebrew and English Lexicon of the Old Testament*, 211.
15. J. H. Hertz, ed. *The Pentateuch and Haftorahs, Hebrew Text, English Translation and Commentary*, 2nd ed. (London: Soncino Press, 1967), 14.
16. Brown et al., *Hebrew and English Lexicon of the Old Testament*, 211.
17. Literally, "small cattle."

notable leaders chosen by the Lord were shepherds: Moses (Exodus 3:1) and David (1 Samuel 16:11; 2 Samuel 7:8).[18]

In the course of time, Cain brought an offering (Hebrew, *minkhah*) from the fruit of the ground to the Lord. And Abel also brought an offering from the firstlings (first born sheep) of his herd as well as their fat, which Jehovah regarded with favor or acceptance (4:3–4). But Jehovah did not look favorably or with acceptance on Cain and his offering. Therefore, Cain's anger burned greatly (*wayyihar leqayin me'od*) and his countenance (literally "face") fell (4:5).

No reason is given in the Hebrew text as to why Cain's offering was rejected and Abel's accepted, nor even a comment as to why sacrificial offerings were instituted at that time. Specific regulations governing offerings are absent here. Later sections in the Bible tell us that firstlings of the flock were the most valuable and important. Only the firstlings of the flocks should be dedicated to Jehovah (Leviticus 27:26). Deuteronomy 15:19 is unequivocal: "All the firstling males that come of thy herd and of thy flock thou shalt sanctify unto the Lord thy God: thou shalt do no work with the firstling of thy bullock, nor shear the firstling of thy sheep." Based on these criteria, it might be implied that because Abel offered firstlings of his flock, while Cain offered only the fruit of the ground, the latter was rejected. The fat of sacrificial animals is also attested as the highly prized portion of the sacrifice, in Jehovah's view (1 Samuel 15:22), and this awareness seems to be missing in Cain's consciousness.

By New Testament times, Abel's acceptance and Cain's rejection by the Lord had become illustrations of faith or lack of it. The author of the book of Hebrews wrote, "By faith Abel offered unto God a more excellent sacrifice than Cain, by which he obtained witness that he was righteous, God testifying of his gifts: and by it he being dead yet speaketh" (Hebrews 11:4). Jude 1:11 pronounces strong judgment upon those who "have gone in the way of Cain," leading others into sin or even murder.

After Cain became angry, the Lord spoke directly and personally to him and asked why he was angry and why his face was fallen or downcast, referring, as we suppose, to either disappointment or offense taken because he was being snubbed by Jehovah (4:6). The text does not make

18. Coogan, *Old Testament*, 32.

this clear. Cain was told that if he did well (or better) his countenance would be lifted. But if he did not do well, sin was lying, stretching out, or couching (Hebrew, *rovēts*) at the door.[19] And, in an even more difficult Hebrew passage to make complete sense of, Cain was further told, "To you is its desire, and you will rule over it" (4:7, author's translation).

Something seems to be missing in this passage, creating a translation problem of some "complexity."[20] In this pericope, sin is spoken of as desiring to have or possess Cain, to control him. Sin seems to possess complete volition, with feelings of desire and the ability to act. While there is no doubt that sin is a powerful influence among mortals and operates in all our lives, sin is not an independent agent or a sentient entity. As implied by God's early commands to Adam and Eve, mortals do have agency, the power to choose, and to control sinful impulses (Genesis 2:16; compare Moses 3:17; 7:32). We get some interpretive help with this passage from an Akkadian cognate. The Hebrew word translated as "lieth" (KJV) or "crouching" (NIV) at the door "is the same as an ancient Babylonian [Akkadian] word used to describe a demon lurking behind a door, threatening the people inside."[21] Thus sin is not the volitional agent, but a demon promoting sin, which, as we will see, comports better with the story as told in the Pearl of Great Price, Moses 5:23, where Satan is the controlling agent. Significantly, and of great interest to Latter-day Saints, E. A. Speiser translates Genesis 4:7 as "Surely if you act right, it should mean exaltation. But if you do not, sin is the demon at the door, whose urge is toward you; yet you can be his master."[22] Therefore, the most important meaning of the passage, as Jehovah tells Cain, is that he can do better and be exalted by

19. See E. A. Speiser, *The Anchor Bible: Genesis—Introduction, Translation, and Notes* (Garden City, NY: Doubleday, 1964), 33.

20. Speiser, *Anchor Bible: Genesis—Introduction, Translation, and Notes*, 32.

21. Study note to Genesis 4:7 of the *New International Version Archaeological Study Bible* (Grand Rapids, MI: Zondervan, 2001), 9. The Old Babylonian or Akkadian word is *rabitsum*. Speiser, *Anchor Bible: Genesis—Introduction, Translation, and Notes*, 33.

22. Speiser, *Anchor Bible: Genesis—Introduction, Translation, and Notes*, 29.

God if he chooses to do right ethically (Hebrew, *hêtib*),[23] implying that he had not done so.

In the Masoretic text, the scene immediately changes. "Cain spoke to Abel his brother and while they were in the field Cain rose up against Abel his brother and he killed him" (4:8). An expanded reading is provided in the Septuagint, Vulgate, Syriac, and Samaritan Pentateuch version: "And Cain said to Abel his brother, *Let us go out into the plain;* and it came to pass that when they were in the plain Cain rose up against Abel his brother, and slew him."[24] This addition lends an air of premeditation to Cain's act of murder, whereas its absence from the Masoretic text leaves open the possibility that Cain's action was spur of the moment.

After Cain's deed, the Lord asked him the whereabouts of his brother, Abel. Because the Lord knows all things (Moses 1:6), it seems the question was intended to elicit a confession of guilt. This also was the judgment of the great medieval Jewish biblical exegete Rashi.[25] Cain's answer is the origin of the world-famous brush-off, "I know not; am I my brother's keeper?" (4:9). Of course, Cain's response, to answer the Great Jehovah so insolently and at the same time renounce any sense of family connectedness, is not only dishonest but disrespectful.

The Lord responded to Cain with an exclamation of shock, not a question, "What have you done! The voice of your brother's blood cries out to me from the ground" (4:10, author's translation). The word "blood" in the Hebrew is plural, "bloods," which is sometimes interpreted to mean that Cain also slew Abel's unborn descendants.[26] The book of Hebrews takes a different approach to the Lord's words, saying that Abel (not mentioning his blood) continues to speak, though he is dead, through his example of offering his sacrifice in faith. "By faith Abel offered unto God a more excellent sacrifice than Cain, by which [faith] he obtained witness that he was

---

23. Brown et al. *Hebrew and English Lexicon of the Old Testament*, 406.

24. Sir Lancelot C. L. Brenton, ed., *The Septuagint with Apocrypha: Greek and English*, reprint (Peabody, MA: Hendrickson Publishers, 1995), 5.

25. J. H. Hertz, ed. *The Pentateuch and Haftorahs, Hebrew Text, English Translation and Commentary* (London: Oxford University Press, 1951), 14.

26. Hertz, ed. *Pentateuch and Haftorahs*, 14.

righteous, God testifying of his gifts: and by it he being dead yet speaketh" (Hebrews 11:4).

As also recorded in the New Testament, Jesus Christ used the image of Abel's spilled blood to chastise the Pharisees for their hypocrisy, especially their antagonism toward him and their personal private disloyalty to prophetic messages. As he was speaking to these Jewish leaders during the last week of his mortal life, he referred to them repeatedly as hypocrites, and then declared they would have a lot to answer for: "Ye serpents, ye generation of vipers, how can ye escape the damnation of hell? Wherefore, behold, I send unto you prophets, and wise men, and scribes: and some of them ye shall kill and crucify; and some of them shall ye scourge in your synagogues, and persecute them from city to city: that upon you may come all the righteous blood shed upon the earth, from the blood of righteous Abel unto the blood of Zacharias son of Barachias, whom ye slew between the temple and the altar" (Matthew 23:33–35; also Luke 11:50–51). Jesus uses the memory of Abel as a symbol here to summarize something of the history of martyrdom in the Old Testament, Abel being the first whose life was taken in innocence and righteousness.

Abel's death had actually become a powerful symbol in much earlier Old Testament times as recounted in the Joseph Smith Translation (JST) of Genesis 17. In describing the covenant Jehovah made with the patriarch Abraham, the JST adds a fascinating insight about Abel's memory among those of Abraham's generation: "And God talked with him, saying, My people have gone astray from my precepts, and have not kept mine ordinances, which I gave unto their fathers; and they have not observed mine anointing, and the burial, or baptism wherewith I commanded them; but have turned from the commandment, and taken unto themselves the washing of children, and the blood of sprinkling; and have said that the blood of the righteous Abel was shed for sins; and have not known wherein they are accountable before me" (JST Genesis 17:4–7). Apparently, those who had not kept God's laws in Abraham's day, and labored in ignorance regarding the true nature of Messianic redemption, began to believe that Abel was a messianic figure, whose shed blood was a propitiatory offering for sin. A profound human similitude of the Messiah, Abel, began to be looked upon as though he were the real Savior. Abel's mistaken identity is a remarkable witness to the power of similitudes to teach as well as to mislead when viewed without the Lord's Spirit to provide correct interpretation. Furthermore, we see that Cain's act of shedding his brother's blood influenced several future dispensations, and Abel's blood continued to speak from the ground, so to speak, as mentioned in Genesis 4:11.[27]

As the story of Cain continued in Genesis 4, the Lord placed a curse on him for his murderous deed, a curse involving the ground: "And now you are cursed from the earth (*min ha-ʾadamah*), which has opened her mouth to receive the blood of your brother from your hand. When you till the earth it will not give to you her strength; you will be a fugitive and a wanderer on the earth" (4:11–12). It appears that Cain was cursed by Jehovah in terms of the amount of produce the earth would yield for him specifically. Perhaps it is implied that Cain's curse associated with the land was greater than the curse over the land previously pronounced upon Adam and Eve, because that curse was for their sakes (Genesis 3:17), whereas there is no hint of Cain's curse being for his sake. Whenever and wherever Cain tilled the ground it would not yield anything for him. Cain was also condemned to be a fugitive, wandering the earth, the underlying Hebrew terms implying a homeless, wandering soul.[28]

It has been argued that this description was "not a description of nomadism, for the nomad was no fugitive or aimless wanderer. Rather, it describes a completely cultureless existence from which Cain's descendants began to rise again only some generations later."[29] One is not quite sure what this means, exactly. Culture may be defined in its simplest aspect as learned behavior. Thus, every person possesses a personal culture. Perhaps it would be more helpful to describe Cain's life after the curse was pronounced as a *rootless* existence, socially and materially, out of which he began to rise only sometime later as he married and had children.

In response to the curse, Cain told the Lord that his punishment was greater than he could bear. "Behold, You have driven me out today from

27. For further discussion, see Andrew C. Skinner, *Prophets, Priests, and Kings: Old Testament Figures Who Symbolize Christ* (Salt Lake City: Deseret Book, 2005), 15–20.

28. Brown et al., *Hebrew and English Lexicon of the Old Testament*, 627.

29. Buttrick, *Interpreter's Bible*, 1:520.

upon the face of the earth; and from Your face I will hide myself, and I will be a fugitive and a wanderer on the earth, and it will happen that all who find me will kill me" (4:13–14). The Targum renders verse 13 as "mine iniquity is too great to be pardoned."[30] The *niphal* form of the Hebrew verb *ʾasāthēr* (from the root meaning "to hide") is reflexive,[31] suggesting that Cain *hid himself* from God's face precisely because he recognized his culpability in an act of *premeditated* murder. In other words, Abel's death was not accidental, but thought out ahead of time. This further fits with the earlier phrase that Cain spoke to Abel, "Let us go out to the field," omitted in the Masoretic text, but included in the Septuagint, Vulgate, Syriac, and Samaritan Pentateuch. Cain planned for his brother's death; therefore, he hid himself from the face of God, implying he cut himself off from God, thus seeking to forfeit divine acknowledgement, interaction, and protection from that time forth. And it is clear that Cain feared death at the hands of some blood avengers on the earth, saying, "Whoever finds me will kill me" (4:14). This statement also presumes that there are already people on the earth even though the Hebrew text implies that Cain was the firstborn of Adam and Eve. This inconsistency is resolved in the Book of Moses version, as we will see below.

In answer to Cain's complaint, Jehovah declared that for any who killed Cain, vengeance would be taken on him sevenfold. Therefore, "the Lord put on Cain a sign [or mark] lest any finding him would smite him" (4:15). The number seven is highly symbolic, indicating a large number or amount. Thus Cain's killer would incur God's wrath and experience a punishment much greater than Cain's (see Leviticus 26:28; Proverbs 24:16). The sign put on Cain was unspecified. According to rabbinic interpretation, it was a sign of a repentant sinner,[32] but this does not seem likely for reasons explained below. So Cain went forth from the presence (literally "face") of the Lord in the neighborhood of Eden and dwelt in the land of Nod, east of Eden (4:16). Nod is derived from the same Hebrew root for

30. Translation in Hertz, *Pentateuch and Haftorahs*, 15.
31. Brown et al., *Hebrew and English Lexicon of the Old Testament*, 711.
32. Translation in Hertz, *Pentateuch and Haftorahs*, 15.

"wanderer," means "wandering," and is undoubtedly symbolic, an etiology playing off of Cain's declared punishment.[33]

At this juncture in the narrative Cain's wife is introduced, but she remains nameless in the text. She conceived and bore Enoch. Cain is described as "building a city," which he called after his son, Enoch (4:17). Perhaps Cain did not complete the city, but he is nonetheless depicted as the first city builder and originator of urban civilization, according to interpreters of the Masoretic text.[34] Cain's wife would also had to have been a descendant of Adam and Eve, perhaps even a sister of Cain's, such marriages being common and acceptable in very early biblical times.[35] After the Exodus, however, such practices became expressly forbidden under the Mosaic Code (Leviticus 18:9). One of Cain's direct descendants, Lamech, introduced polygamy by marrying two women who gave rise, on the one hand, to a generation of those who lived in tents and raised livestock, and, on the other hand, a line of metalworkers—the meaning of the name "Cain" in Hebrew being, as we have said, "smith" or "metalworker"—thus, tying Cain's descendants back to him (Genesis 4:19–22). With that the Masoretic version of the story of Cain and Abel comes to an end but sets the stage for the rest of Genesis's focus on the ancestors of the nation of Israel.[36]

In terms of the compositional history of the Cain and Abel story in Genesis 4, premodern Judeo-Christian tradition considered the prophet Moses to be the author of everything in the first five books of the Hebrew Bible or Old Testament, Genesis through Deuteronomy, also called the books of Moses, the Torah, or the Pentateuch. However, during the Middle Ages, problems began to be recognized with this strict notion. For example, did Moses write about his own death and burial in Deuteronomy 34:5–12? Then, beginning in about the seventeenth century, new, more

---

33. David Noel Freedman, ed., *Eerdman's Dictionary of the Bible* (Grand Rapids, MI: William B. Eerdmans, 2000), 971, s.v. "Nod."

34. Buttrick, *Interpreter's Bible*, 1:521; Hertz, *Pentateuch and Haftorahs*, 15.

35. Hertz, *Pentateuch and Haftorahs*, 15. Moses 5:3 makes it quite clear that the sons and daughters of Adam and Eve paired off and "begat sons and daughters" of their own.

36. Harris and Platzner, *Old Testament*, 113.

thought-critical ways of approaching the biblical text became acceptable. Over time, different theories challenged the traditional view of strict Mosaic authorship of the Pentateuch in dramatic ways until a German professor, Julius Wellhausen, was able to summarize the conclusions of his predecessors in what came to be the classic statement of the "Documentary Hypothesis" of Pentateuchal authorship.

Wellhausen argued that the Pentateuch is composed of four independent, relatively intact, sources or compositions or documents, whatever one chooses to call them, that were woven together by ancient editors or redactors. The original basis for recognizing or separating out these different sources was the different names used for God in each source. Thus, biblical exegetes ascribed Genesis 4 to a strand of authorship labeled J, because of the consistent use of the term LORD or Jehovah (Yahweh) throughout that portion of Genesis. The Documentary Hypothesis was refined and today holds that the four originally independent compositions are labeled J, E, D, and P. The first or earliest of these documents was the Yahwist or Jahwist (J) source, followed by the Elohist (E) because that name of Deity (Elohim) is used, then the Deuteronomist (D) source used almost entirely in the Book of Deuteronomy, and the Priestly (P) composition, which emphasizes religious observance and rituals.[37] The J source has been dated to the mid-tenth century BC,[38] which means, according to the Documentary Hypothesis or model, that Genesis 4 cannot be dated any earlier than that.

Challenges to the Documentary Hypothesis arose almost from its inception for a variety of reasons. One is the perceived attack that the documentary model levels against the divine authority and composition of scripture. Another is the way scholars have further divided the sources into "a bewildering variety" of more sources.[39] Yet another type of challenge is the dating of the sources, and on and on. Such debates make us all the more grateful for living prophets and divine revelation in modern times.

---

37. See the excellent summaries in Coogan, *Old Testament*, 21–27; and Harris and Platzner, *Old Testament*, 90.

38. Richard D. Draper, S. Kent Brown, Michael D. Rhodes, *The Pearl of Great Price, A Verse-by-Verse Commentary* (Salt Lake City: Deseret Book, 2005), 413–14.

39. Coogan, *Old Testament*, 28.

JOSEPH SMITH TRANSLATION

The Book of Moses is part of the Joseph Smith Translation of the Bible. It comprises an introduction to Genesis under the heading of Moses 1, followed by a revision of the first six chapters of Genesis, under the headings Moses 2–8. The Book of Moses was put with other selected documents by Elder Franklin D. Richards of the Quorum of the Twelve Apostles to produce the first edition of the Pearl of Great Price in 1851.[40] The narrative in which the Cain and Abel story sits (Moses 5) was completed, except for later editorial details, by the Prophet Joseph Smith between June and October, 1830. In June 1830, Oliver Cowdery became Joseph Smith's scribe for a second time, writing dictation for what would become known as Moses 1:1 to Moses 5:43. Then a new scribe was called—John Whitmer. Between October 21 and November 30, 1830, Joseph Smith dictated from Moses 5:43 through Moses 6:18.[41] In a revelation given to Joseph Smith and Sidney Rigdon in December 1830, the Lord said of the Prophet's efforts to produce the new inspired version or revision of the Bible, "the scriptures shall be given, even as they are in mine own bosom, to the salvation of mine elect" (Doctrine and Covenants 35:20).[42] This endorsement is significant as we consider the placement of the Cain and Abel narrative in the Prophet's inspired revision of the Bible: the Lord wanted it in the scriptures for our benefit—to learn the lessons to be gleaned from orthodox doctrine. It also invites us to consider its authenticity—the narrative constitutes part of the scriptures "as they are in [the Lord's] own bosom."

Of course, the Joseph Smith Translation did not have just one purpose, but attempted to do several things. Perhaps three of the most important, emphasized generally by the Prophet Joseph himself, include (1) correcting false doctrine and inaccurate information, (2) restoring original texts that had been lost or taken from the earliest editions of the Bible, and (3) revealing texts or concepts that never made it into the Bible, perhaps

40. For a fuller explanation, see "Introductory Note" of the Pearl of Great Price of the Church's standard works (Bible, Book of Mormon, Doctrine and Covenants, and Pearl of Great Price).

41. Draper et al., *Pearl of Great Price*, 13.

42. Earlier in the Doctrine and Covenants, the Lord had defined his "elect" as those who "hear my voice and harden not their hearts" (29:7).

even oral traditions that may have circulated for a time, but which the Lord wanted his sons and daughters to have in written form for the benefit of their salvation.[43] The Cain and Abel narrative presented in Moses 5:16–42 probably contains all three of these types of additions and corrections. Indeed, the much more detailed story of Cain and Abel in Moses 5, compared with the one found in the Masoretic text or King James Version, argues for a richer, more expansive, original narrative of the episode.

As we have seen, our current Hebrew version raises questions because of the probable omissions and corruptions it contains. Moses 5:16–42 answers these questions because it is a superior reading, constituting material coming directly from a prophet. Something Joseph Smith said seems to fit here: "I believe the Bible as it read when it came from the pen of the original writers. Ignorant translators, careless transcribers, or designing and corrupt priests have committed many errors."[44] Earlier translators such as Latin Church Father and producer of the Vulgate, St. Jerome recognized the inherent problems with their current editions of the Bible. In AD 382 he became secretary to Pope Damasus and formulated a plan to produce a more trustworthy version of the Bible, correcting problems in the existing Old Latin manuscripts of the Bible. In 383 he sent a letter to the pope: "For if we are to pin our faith to the Latin texts, it is for our opponents to tell us which; for there are almost as many forms of texts as there are copies. If, on the other hand, we are to glean the truth from a comparison of many, why not go back . . . and correct the mistakes introduced by inaccurate translators, and the blundering alterations of confident but ignorant critics, and further all that has been inserted or changed by copyists more asleep than awake?"[45] The JST would change and rectify this condition.

By comparing the King James Version (KJV) with the JST, we can gain tremendous illumination that helps clarify obscure passages in the King

---

43. Robert J. Matthews, *A Plainer Translation: Joseph Smith's Translation of the Bible, a History and Commentary* (Provo, UT: Brigham Young University Press, 1985), 12.

44. *Teachings of Presidents of the Church: Joseph Smith* (Salt Lake City: The Church of Jesus Christ of Latter-day Saints, 2007), 207.

45. James Stevenson, ed., *Creeds, Councils, and Controversies: Documents Illustrating the History of the Church, A.D. 337–461* (London: SPCK, 1989), 183.

James narrative and teaches significant theological and doctrinal lessons for the benefit of our salvation—as the Lord intended. At the beginning of Moses 5, readers immediately notice that, unlike the KJV, the JST provides a detailed context for the Cain and Abel story. Adam and Eve labored together, tilling the earth and caring for the beasts of the field. Cain and Abel had a model before them. Eve gave birth to sons and daughters and began to replenish or "fill" (Hebrew, *male'*) the earth. The Hebrew used in KJV (Genesis 1:28) supports the substantially enhanced version of the story in the JST. These "sons and daughters of Adam began to divide two and two in the land, to till the land and tend flocks, and beget sons and daughters" (Moses 5:3). Thus, we see that Cain was not the first child nor the first son born to Adam and Eve. There were others populating the earth and establishing families before Cain and Abel appeared on the scene. Marriage between Adam's and Eve's descendants was approved by God.[46]

We also learn that the practice of offering animal sacrifices to the Lord was first revealed to Adam and Eve before Cain and Abel participated in this important ordinance (Moses 5:5–9). The brothers were *not* the first to make offerings, as the Masoretic text implies. Again, they had a template to follow—the commandment that was obeyed by our first parents to "offer the firstlings of their flocks, for an offering unto the Lord" (5:5). The Book of Moses makes clear that Adam and Eve "made all things known unto their sons and their daughters" (5:12). All the children of Adam and Eve were raised in an environment of righteousness. They were oriented by their parents toward the Lord but given agency to choose what they would do.

With that as backdrop to subsequent events, Satan came among them trying to persuade them to renounce their faith, "and *he* commanded them, saying: Believe it not; and they believed it not, and they loved Satan more

---

46. Marriage between Adam's and Eve's children should not offend modern sensibilities, though such a practice today is forbidden. As Joseph Smith once taught in a letter to Nancy Rigdon, "That which is wrong under one circumstance, may be and often is, right under another. . . . This is the principle on which the government of heaven is conducted—by revelation adapted to the circumstances in which the children of the kingdom are placed. Whatever God requires is right, no matter what it is, although we may not see the reason thereof till [*sic*] long after the events transpire." See "Discourse, [January 5, 1841] A," page 1, The Joseph Smith Papers.

than God. And men began from that time forth to be carnal, sensual, and devilish" (5:13; emphasis added). This background is significant because it helps us to understand the environment in which Adam's and Eve's children made their decision to follow the Lord or Satan, and the influences that affected their interactions with each other, including Cain and Abel. It is this kind of contextual information that answers questions raised in the Masoretic text, fills in gaps, and revises the details of the biblical record.

The phrase used to describe those who love and follow Satan—"carnal, sensual, and devilish"—is an extraordinarily descriptive one that is not found in the Masoretic text. It summarizes the essence of a person under Satan's influence, not inclined to follow the Spirit of God but the spirit of worldliness, not inclined to seek the will of God but the instincts of self. This pattern developed in Moses 5. Such a person, said President Spencer W. Kimball, lives without divine refinement, but "is the 'earthly man' who has allowed rude animal passions to overshadow his spiritual inclinations."[47] This became the natural state of many of Adam's and Eve's posterity after Satan came among them early on, according to the modern revealed text of the JST. This brings us to the actual story, comparing the verses of the KJV and JST in parallel columns, which immediately highlights the amount of additional material revealed through the Prophet Joseph Smith as well as its theological profundity.

Genesis 4	Moses 5
1 And Adam knew Eve his wife; and she conceived, and bare Cain, and said, I have gotten a man from the Lord.	16 And Adam and Eve, his wife, ceased not to call upon God. And Adam knew Eve his wife, and she conceived and bare Cain, and said: I have gotten a man from the Lord; wherefore he may not reject his words. But behold, Cain hearkened not, saying: Who is the Lord that I should know him?

47. Spencer W. Kimball, "Ocean Currents and Family Influences," *Ensign*, November 1974, 112.

Genesis 4	Moses 5
2 And she again bare his brother Abel. And Abel was a keeper of sheep, but Cain was a tiller of the ground.	17 And she again conceived and bare his brother Abel. And Abel hearkened unto the voice of the Lord. And Abel was a keeper of sheep, but Cain was a tiller of the ground.
3 And in process of time it came to pass, that Cain brought of the fruit of the ground an offering unto the Lord.	18 And Cain loved Satan more than God. And Satan commanded him, saying: Make an offering unto the Lord. 19 And in process of time it came to pass that Cain brought of the fruit of the ground an offering unto the Lord.
4 And Abel, he also brought of the firstlings of his flock and of the fat thereof. And the Lord had respect unto Abel and to his offering: 5 But unto Cain and to his offering he had not respect. And Cain was very wroth, and his countenance fell.	20 And Abel, he also brought of the firstlings of his flock, and of the fat thereof. And the Lord had respect unto Abel, and to his offering; 21 But unto Cain, and to his offering, he had not respect. Now Satan knew this, and it pleased him. And Cain was very wroth, and his countenance fell.
6 And the Lord said unto Cain, Why art thou wroth? and why is thy countenance fallen? 7 If thou doest well, shalt thou not be accepted? and if thou doest not well, sin lieth at the door. And unto thee shall be his desire, and thou shalt rule over him.	22 And the Lord said unto Cain: Why art thou wroth? Why is thy countenance fallen? 23 If thou doest well, thou shalt be accepted. And if thou doest not well, sin lieth at the door, and Satan desireth to have thee; and except thou shalt hearken unto my commandments, I will deliver thee up, and it shall be unto thee according to his desire. And thou shalt rule over him; 24 For from this time forth thou shalt be the father of his lies; thou shalt be called Perdition; for thou wast also before the world. 25 And it shall be said in time to come—That these abominations were had from Cain; for he rejected the greater counsel which was had from God; and this is a cursing which I will put upon thee, except thou repent. 26 And Cain was wroth, and listened not any more to the voice of the Lord, neither to Abel, his brother, who walked in holiness before the Lord.

Genesis 4	Moses 5
	27 And Adam and his wife mourned before the Lord, because of Cain and his brethren.
	28 And it came to pass that Cain took one of his brothers' daughters to wife, and they loved Satan more than God.
	29 And Satan said unto Cain: Swear unto me by thy throat, and if thou tell it thou shalt die; and swear thy brethren by their heads, and by the living God, that they tell it not; for if they tell it, they shall surely die; and this that thy father may not know it; and this day I will deliver thy brother Abel into thine hands.
	30 And Satan sware unto Cain that he would do according to his commands. And all these things were done in secret.
	31 And Cain said: Truly I am Mahan, the master of this great secret, that I may murder and get gain. Wherefore Cain was called Master Mahan, and he gloried in his wickedness.
8 And Cain talked with Abel his brother: and it came to pass, when they were in the field, that Cain rose up against Abel his brother, and slew him.	32 And Cain went into the field, and Cain talked with Abel, his brother. And it came to pass that while they were in the field, Cain rose up against Abel, his brother, and slew him.
	33 And Cain gloried in that which he had done, saying: I am free; surely the flocks of my brother falleth into my hands.
9 And the Lord said unto Cain, Where is Abel thy brother? And he said, I know not: Am I my brother's keeper?	34 And the Lord said unto Cain: Where is Abel, thy brother? And he said: I know not. Am I my brother's keeper?
10 And he said, What hast thou done? the voice of thy brother's blood crieth unto me from the ground.	35 And the Lord said: What hast thou done? The voice of thy brother's blood cries unto me from the ground
11 And now art thou cursed from the earth, which hath opened her mouth to receive thy brother's blood from thy hand;	36 And now thou shalt be cursed from the earth which hath opened her mouth to receive thy brother's blood from thy hand.

Genesis 4	Moses 5
12 When thou tillest the ground, it shall not henceforth yield unto thee her strength; a fugitive and a vagabond shalt thou be in the earth.	37 When thou tillest the ground it shall not henceforth yield unto thee her strength. A fugitive and a vagabond shalt thou be in the earth.
13 And Cain said unto the Lord, My punishment is greater than I can bear.	38 And Cain said unto the Lord: Satan tempted me because of my brother's flocks. And I was wroth also; for his offering thou didst accept and not mine; my punishment is greater than I can bear.
14 Behold, thou hast driven me out this day from the face of the earth; and from thy face shall I be hid; and I shall be a fugitive and a vagabond in the earth; and it shall come to pass, that every one that findeth me shall slay me.	39 Behold thou hast driven me out this day from the face of the Lord, and from thy face shall I be hid; and I shall be a fugitive and a vagabond in the earth; and it shall come to pass, that he that findeth me will slay me, because of mine iniquities, for these things are not hid from the Lord.
15 And the Lord said unto him, Therefore whosoever slayeth Cain, vengeance shall be taken on him sevenfold. And the Lord set a mark upon Cain, lest any finding him should kill him.	40 And I the Lord said unto him: Whosoever slayeth thee, vengeance shall be taken on him sevenfold. And I the Lord set a mark upon Cain, lest any finding him should kill him.
16 And Cain went out from the presence of the Lord, and dwelt in the land of Nod, on the east of Eden.	41 And Cain was shut out from the presence of the Lord, and with his wife and many of his brethren dwelt in the land of Nod, on the east of Eden.
17 And Cain knew his wife; and she conceived, and bare Enoch: and he builded a city, and called the name of the city, after the name of his son, Enoch. . . .	42 And Cain knew his wife, and she conceived and bare Enoch, and he also begat many sons and daughters. And he builded a city, and he called the name of the city after the name of his son, Enoch. . . .
23 And Lamech said unto his wives, Adah and Zillah, Hear my voice; ye wives of Lamech, hearken unto my speech: for I have slain a man to my wounding, and a young man to my hurt.	47 And Lamech said unto his wives, Adah and Zillah: Hear my voice, ye wives of Lamech, hearken unto my speech; for I have slain a man to my wounding, and a young man to my hurt.
24 If Cain shall be avenged sevenfold, truly Lamech seventy and sevenfold.	48 If Cain shall be avenged sevenfold, truly Lamech shall be seventy and seven fold;
25 And Adam knew his wife again; and she bare a son, and called his name Seth: For God, said she, hath appointed me another seed instead of Abel, whom Cain slew.	49 For Lamech having entered into a covenant with Satan, after the manner of Cain, wherein he became Master Mahan, master of that great secret which was

Genesis 4	Moses 5
	administered unto Cain by Satan; and Irad, the son of Enoch, having known their secret, began to reveal it unto the sons of Adam; 50 Wherefore Lamech, being angry, slew him, not like unto Cain, his brother Abel, for the sake of getting gain, but he slew him for the oath's sake. 51 For, from the days of Cain, there was a secret combination, and their works were in the dark, and they knew every man his brother. 52 Wherefore the Lord cursed Lamech, and his house, and all them that had covenanted with Satan; for they kept not the commandments of God, and it displeased God, and he ministered not unto them, and their works were abominations, and began to spread among all the sons of men. And it was among the sons of men. 53 And among the daughters of men these things were not spoken, because that Lamech had spoken the secret unto his wives, and they rebelled against him, and declared these things abroad, and had not compassion; 54 Wherefore Lamech was despised, and cast out, and came not among the sons of men, lest he should die. 55 And thus the works of darkness began to prevail among all the sons of men.

The story of Cain's birth in the JST is different from the KJV from the start. In a phrase not attested in the Hebrew Bible, we learn that Adam and Eve had "ceased not to call upon God" before Cain's conception. This was undoubtedly because of Satan's influence among their other children, as Moses 5:13 indicates. For after Cain's birth and Eve's expression of joy over a new son from God, she pronounces a kind of hopeful maternal blessing upon Cain, "wherefore he may not reject his words" (5:16). However, Cain's rebellious nature was soon frightfully manifest in direct opposition to his mother's hope and blessing, as the wording makes clear: "But behold, Cain hearkened not [to his mother], saying: Who is the Lord that I should know him?" (5:16).[48] This statement, not found in the KJV, greatly enhances our understanding of Cain's orientation. It would be roughly repeated centuries later during the Exodus by Pharoah, a man who possessed the same kind of arrogance as Cain (Exodus 5:2). Fortunately, Eve bore another son, Abel, who "hearkened unto the voice of the Lord" (Moses 5:17). This phrase, again absent in the Bible, sets forth another fundamental difference between the brothers, in addition to their vocations. Their vocations influence their spiritual orientations. "As a keeper of sheep, Abel seems to see the earth as a source for his animals, a source that can be influenced by God for good or ill. Cain, however, believes that he owns the land and that God, though the creator of the land, has nothing more to do with it."[49]

The KJV describes how, in the course of time, Cain brought an offering to Jehovah of the produce of the earth. Arrestingly, Moses 5 prefaces its similar report of this offering by describing Cain's real reason for making his offering in the first place, and the true object of his loyalty—Satan. Cain offered his sacrifice because Satan commanded him to do so, thereby entering into an implied covenant with the adversary and not the Lord. In this odd twist in the story, we are presented with Cain's motivation for all he will do—to please Satan (5:18–19). The narrative that follows in both the KJV and the JST, a description of Abel's offering of the firstlings of his flock and the fat thereof, declares that the Lord looked favorably upon Abel's offering (Genesis 4:4; Moses 5:20). But the text describing the Lord's rejection of Cain's offering shows a significant variant, noting that Satan knew of the Lord's rejection of Cain's offering and that it pleased him! Satan could then exploit the wedge developing between Cain and the Lord.

In the ensuing dialogue, the Lord reminded Cain that he could be accepted if he did well, as both the KJV and the JST report. But at this point, the text of the KJV becomes confusing. If Cain does not do well, sin lies at the door, "And unto thee shall be his desire, and thou shalt rule over him." Whose desire is being spoken of here, sin's desire? And was Cain being told that if he did not do well, he would rule over sin? Only the JST

48. Draper et al., *Pearl of Great Price*, 65.

49. Draper et al., *Pearl of Great Price*, 65–66.

provides the clarification that makes theological sense out of the whole story. The antagonist is clearly Satan; he desires to have Cain as a follower, it will be to Cain according to Satan's desire, and ironically Cain will come to rule over Satan, demonstrating that a person possessing a physical body holds power over one who does not possess a body (5:23).[50]

Everything from Moses 5:24 through 5:31 is narrative material revealed through the Prophet Joseph Smith, not found in the Masoretic Text, Septuagint, Vulgate, Syriac, or Samaritan Pentateuch. The theological treasures contained therein include Cain's designation by the Lord from that time forth as the father of Satan's lies, as Perdition (from the Latin *perditus*, meaning "lost" or "destruction"), and as the inaugurator of the "abominations" (Moses 5:24–25). Cain's designation as Perdition followed Lucifer's path (Doctrine and Covenants 76:26). Just as Lucifer had basked in the heights of the divine presence as an angel in authority (Doctrine and Covenants 76:25) and had subsequently descended to the depths and lost all, so had Cain.

From this point on, Cain's anger moved him to cease listening anymore to the voice of the Lord, which caused his parents to mourn—an authentic, realistic, and empathy-evoking comment. Unlike the Masoretic biblical text, the JST provides background information for Cain's marriage to his niece as well as her own mindset—she also loved Satan more than God (5:28).

Moses 5:29–31 describe the origins of secret combinations, which were created and administered by Satan. They were established through oath taking to "murder and get gain" (Moses 5:31). Though Satan initiated the first of these agreements by having his partner Cain swear by his life (represented by the throat, a vulnerable part of the body to the ancients), and ensured Cain's secrecy by threatening death if he did not keep the great secrets, Cain quickly took control of these secret conspiracies and exulted in his newfound leadership: "Truly I am Mahan, the master of this great secret, that I may murder and get gain. Wherefore Cain was called Master Mahan, and he gloried in his wickedness" (Moses 5:31). At that moment the Lord's warning was fulfilled that if Cain did not do well Satan would have control and that Cain would end up ruling over Satan! (5:23). The meaning of Cain's new title, Master Mahan, is unknown. Presumably,

50. "Discourse [January 5, 1841] A," The Joseph Smith Papers.

the language being spoken at that time was the Adamic language, which "was pure and undefiled" (Moses 6:6, 46). Hugh Nibley proposed that *Mahan* might have meant "great" and that *Master* may have meant "keeper (of secrets)," and thus Master Mahan meant "great secret keeper."[51] But the etymology remains uncertain.

At that point it was also a foregone conclusion that when Cain went into the field with Abel, the latter would be murdered. Satan had pledged to Cain to deliver his brother, Abel, into his hands in exchange for Cain's sworn loyalty as well as those who followed him, including his wife who, remember, loved Satan more than God (5:28). Immediately afterward, "Cain gloried in that which he had done, saying: I am free; surely the flocks of my brother falleth into my hands" (5:33). How wrong Cain was! Free he was not, on a number of levels. Certainly, his bondage to Satan was now unbreakably cemented and his eternal destiny irrevocably determined by his actions of embracing Satan, ignoring the Lord, and murdering to get gain. Cain's entire experience was filled with irony. In addition to never being free, though he declared himself to be, Cain became controlled by commandments—he bridled against the Lord's but kept Satan's (5:18). Cain was required by Satan to swear unto him (Satan) that he would keep the great secret but, in an odd twist, was commanded by Satan to swear by the living God (5:29). "Irony brims in these words, for 'the living God' is invoked as a witness of these deadly, satanic pledges. It seems plain that Satan's oaths gain credibility not through *his* name but only through the *divine* name and, possibly, by mimicking genuinely sacred covenants made in God's name."[52]

All these issues highlight the contrast between the KJV and the JST. They illustrate the challenges of interpretation that arise when working with a text that has suffered losses and deletions over time, such as the KJV.[53] Because they have been working with a deficient biblical text, some

---

51. Hugh Nibley, "Lecture 19, Adam and Eve," *Ancient Documents and the Pearl of Great Price* (Provo, UT: FARMS, 1986), 12.

52. Draper et al., *Pearl of Great Price*, 68.

53. E. A. Speiser's work can be used as an example of such omissions and deletions when he asserts, "The original text [of Genesi 4:8] must have contained Cain's original statement, but text was accidentally omitted in MT [Masoretic text].

exegetes have promoted skewed interpretations, asserting, for example, that Cain was not a "wholly bad" man or that "there is no indication that Cain intended to commit murder" or that he was "a repentant sinner."[54] The JST adds much to our understanding, and, in this context, it would be hard to overstate the corrective value of the Book of Moses.

Many verses in the KJV and JST that describe events after Abel's murder, especially the verbal exchange between Cain and the Lord, closely parallel each other. Moses 5:38 reports a portion of Cain's response not found in the biblical record: "Satan tempted me because of my brother's flocks." This demonstrates again the fundamental principle of Satan's secret combinations—murder to get gain. The KJV implies that Cain went out from the Lord's presence of his own volition and dwelt in the land of Nod, whereas the JST states he was "shut out from the presence of the Lord, and with his wife and many of his brethren dwelt in the land of Nod" (compare Genesis 4:16 and Moses 5:41). Moses 5:42 discloses that before Cain built the city that he named after his son, Enoch, he fathered "many [other] sons and daughters," which is a detail the biblical record does not contain.

Finally, both the biblical record and the JST describe how the lives of one of Cain's descendants, Lamech, and Cain himself each parallel the other. Lamech killed a man, and "if Cain shall be avenged sevenfold, truly Lamech seventy and sevenfold" (Genesis 4:24). However, it is the JST again that fills in a huge gap left in the KJV by linking Lamech with the same Satanic covenant entered into by Cain. "For Lamech having entered into a covenant with Satan, after the manner of Cain, wherein he became Master Mahan, master of that great secret which was administered unto Cain by Satan; and Irad, the son of Enoch, having known their secret, began to reveal it unto the sons of Adam" (Moses 5:49). It was after Lamech entered into this covenant that he murdered a man, but not to get gain like Cain.

The Anchor Bible: Genesis—Introduction, Translation, and Notes, 30; or when the commentary to Genesis 4:1–17 in the *Interpreter's Bible* repeatedly makes such references as the material of Genesis 4:1–26 being "not in its original order," or "The text is corrupt," or "the verse is truncated," and so forth. Buttrick, *Interpreter's Bible*, 1:516, 518, 519.

54. Hertz, *Pentateuch and Haftorahs*, 15; John Skinner, *A Critical and Exegetical Commentary on Genesis*, rev. ed. New York: Charles Scribner's Sons, 1925), 108; Buttrick, *Interpreter's Bible*, 1:516.

Rather, he committed the atrocity solely "for the oath's sake" (5:50), having sworn to Satan by his own life to maintain secrecy because, like Cain, he loved Satan more than he loved God. Secrecy was such a powerful cornerstone of the Satanic covenant that it would remain so throughout the earth's temporal history.

REFLECTIONS ON THE CAIN AND ABEL STORY

The story of Cain and Abel is an invaluable part of the "primeval history" presented in Genesis. Cain and Abel represent an eternal archetype, going all the way back to our premortal existence when two spirit brothers also clashed with each other (Moses 4:1–4; Abraham 3:27–28; Doctrine and Covenants 76:26–29). They were born into the same environment, but one remained righteous, while the other rebelled and turned thoroughly wicked. Both had agency and both made their own choices. One was accepted of God; the other was not. One remained in God's presence; the other was driven out. The wicked brother was lost, and heaven wept over him. The righteous brother became the Messiah, and heaven rejoiced over him (Doctrine and Covenants 76:26–29). In truth, Cain and Abel represent in several ways the story of Jesus Christ and Lucifer. Cain was wicked just as Lucifer was wicked. Cain chose Satan over the Lord and was irretrievably lost. Cain was cast out of his father's presence just as Lucifer was cast out of his Father's presence for rebellion. Abel carried out his father's will just as Jesus Christ carried out his Father's will. The parallels are powerful didactic models.[55]

The story of Cain and Abel we have examined is told in two textual traditions, the second based on the first, but diverging from it in the main with the appearance and extensive involvement of Satan and his efforts to take Adam's and Eve's posterity away from God. "The entire story exhibits dissimilarities with Genesis because of Satan's interfering allure, particularly on Cain, whom he will come to serve (see Moses 5:23, 30)."[56] This element of Satan becoming the second major moving force in human

55. Skinner, *Prophets, Priests, and Kings*, 15–20.

56. Draper, et al., *Pearl of Great Price*, 70.

history, God being the first, is largely absent in the KJV account of Cain and Abel. An examination of some of the early Church fathers of Christianity (down to AD 325) indicates that they may have possessed a version of the story closer to the JST than the KJV or may have had more interpretive material to draw from. For example, Theophilus writes a letter to one Autolycus, saying, "Satan, . . . being carried away with spite, . . . wrought upon the heart of [Abel's] brother Cain, and caused him to kill his brother Abel."[57] In addition, it seems that the Church fathers usually followed the Septuagint reading, which in some cases added text, as in the case of the First Epistle of Clement adding to Genesis 4:8, "Let us go into the field," which does not appear in the Hebrew.[58]

Perhaps the greatest theological contribution of the Book of Moses version of the story to our understanding of the Father's plan of salvation is its discussion of the origin and perpetuation of secret combinations—Satan's major work. A secret combination (Moses 5:51) is one bound together by oaths made with Satan, who first commanded Cain to make an oath of secrecy to murder to get gain. Lamech made such an oath, and others besides him and Cain were part of this secret work of evil (Moses 5:52). However, "among the daughters of men these things were not spoken," because after Lamech "had spoken the secret unto his wives, . . . they rebelled against him, and declared these things abroad, and had not compassion" (Moses 5:53).

The Book of Mormon is another witness to the accuracy of the JST record regarding the origin and perpetuation of secret combinations:

> Now behold, those secret oaths and covenants did not come forth unto Gadianton from the records which were delivered unto Helaman; but behold, they were put into the heart of Gadianton by that same being who did entice our first parents to partake of the forbidden fruit—

57. Alexander Roberts and James Donaldson, eds., *The Ante-Nicene Fathers, The Writings of the Fathers Down to A.D. 325*, vol. 2: *The Fathers of the Second Century* (Grand Rapids MI: Eerdmans, repr., 1986), 2:105.
58. Alexander Roberts and James Donaldson, eds., *The Ante-Nicene Fathers, The Writings of the Fathers Down to A.D. 325*, vol. 1, 1:6.

> Yea, that same being who did plot with Cain, that if he would murder his brother Abel it should not be known unto the world. And he did plot with Cain and his followers from that time forth. . . .
>
> And behold, it is he who is the author of all sin. And behold, he doth carry on his works of darkness and secret murder, and doth hand down their plots, and their oaths, and their covenants, and their plans of awful wickedness, from generation to generation according as he can get hold upon the hearts of the children of men. (Helaman 6:26–27, 30)

Third Nephi and the book of Ether are other witnesses to the origins of the covenant "which was given by them of old, which covenant was given and administered by the devil, to combine against all righteousness" (3 Nephi 6:28; Ether 8:15). Many scriptural witnesses attest to the authenticity, accuracy, and superiority of the Book of Moses as a textual witness to the veracity of the Cain and Abel story.

Value in the Cain and Abel story is also found in its presentation of the origins of the decline of moral resolve among the human family. Cain's killing Abel was an example of that declining moral resolve that should not have accompanied the offering of sacrifice. Just the opposite should have prevailed. As Elder Jeffrey R. Holland notes, "The moral resolve that should have accompanied [sacrifice] didn't last long enough for the blood to dry upon the stones. In any case, it didn't last long enough to preclude fratricide, with Cain killing his brother Abel in the first generation."[59] It strikes me that the Cain and Abel story tells us why we're in the situation we're experiencing today and points to the future. "Once the shedding of human blood has begun, . . . humanity's condition deteriorates rapidly, . . . establishing a culture of violence that leads to humanity's destruction."[60]

In one sense, the story of Cain and Abel revolved around the offering of animal sacrifice, which foreshadowed the coming of Jesus Christ. This doctrine is at the heart of Cain's animosity. The Prophet Joseph Smith taught this with clarity:

---

59. Jeffrey R. Holland, "Behold the Lamb of God," *Ensign*, May 2019, 45.
60. Harris and Platzner, *Old Testament*, 112.

> By faith in this atonement or plan of redemption, Abel offered to God a sacrifice that was accepted, which was the firstlings of the flock. Cain offered of the fruit of the ground, and was not accepted, because he could not do it in faith; he could have no faith, or could not exercise faith contrary to the plan of heaven. It must be shedding the blood of the Only Begotten to atone for man, for this was the plan of redemption, and without the shedding of blood was no remission. And as the sacrifice was instituted for a type by which man was to discern the great Sacrifice which God had prepared, to offer a sacrifice contrary to that, no faith could be exercised, because redemption was not purchased in that way, nor the power of atonement instituted after that order; consequently Cain could have no faith; and whatsoever is not of faith, is sin. But Abel offered an acceptable sacrifice, by which he obtained witness that he was righteous, God Himself testifying of his gifts.[61]

The story of Cain and Abel may serve as a template as well as something of a little salve to comfort parents who torture themselves with questions about what more they could have done for wayward children. Sometimes no matter what righteous parents do, they cannot change the course of children who exercise their agency in heartbreaking ways. Cain caused great anguish to Adam and Eve, as any like-minded son would do to faithful parents. Cain spoke directly with God yet was guilty of premeditated murder, was in league with Satan, suffered spiritual death, and was a son of perdition. He held the patriarchal priesthood. He was not ignorant. It is impossible to imagine a more horrific situation, except for the one Satan himself lives in.

What must Adam and Eve have felt, knowing with certainty their son was lost? Yet, our first parents provide for us an example in working through their sorrow, as "Adam and his wife mourned before the Lord" (Moses 5:27), but "ceased not to call upon God" (5:16). Adam is the great patriarch and head of all dispensations; Eve the great mother of all living and the nurturer of her faithful daughters (Doctrine and Covenants 138:38–39). From them we take strength.

---

61. *Teachings of Presidents of the Church: Joseph Smith*, 48.

Additionally, Abel provides a thought-provoking model of the way mortality sometimes treats the righteous—the very most righteous. Though he "walked in holiness before the Lord" (Moses 5:26), he had to face the brutality of his brother, becoming "the first martyr" in the world of spirits but possessing the reward of the righteous (Doctrine and Covenants 138:40).

ENOCH IN THE OLD TESTAMENT AND BEYOND

JARED W. LUDLOW

Despite the brevity of the Enoch narrative in the Old Testament, later traditions about Enoch highlight the importance he held in religious communities that were attempting to create a religious environment wherein heaven could be obtained. Yet many may not be aware of these rich Enoch traditions or understand their relationship to the Latter-day Saint canon. With this in mind, Jared Ludlow outlines these traditions by reviewing them throughout the different literature in which they appear. He then explores the insights provided by Joseph Smith and recorded in Joseph's translations of the Bible and the Book of Moses. In exploring these insights, Ludlow notes the pivotal role Enoch plays in our understanding of the accountability of human action, from the Creation to the "end of days," wherein all will stand accountable before God. —DB and AS

"And Enoch walked with God: and he was not; for God took him" (Genesis 5:24). This brief yet rich passage of Old Testament scripture has puzzled and fascinated Bible readers and interpreters for millennia. Despite having such a cursory role in the Old Testament, Enoch went on to be a popular figure in Jewish, Christian, and Muslim literature well into late antiquity.[1] What does it mean to say that Enoch walked with God? How and where did God take him? Turning to the Old Testament will not provide much assistance to these questions since there are only four verses that discuss Enoch's life and mission. However, later texts, prophets, and apostles—particularly those from the Restoration—shed light on Enoch, this significant Old Testament prophet. These later sources highlight the increased and glorious roles that Enoch played within his own society on earth as well as his elevated functions in the heavenly courts above.

OLD TESTAMENT

The Old Testament is brief about Enoch's mission on earth. "And Enoch lived sixty and five years, and begat Methuselah: And Enoch walked with God after he begat Methuselah three hundred years, and begat sons and daughters: And all the days of Enoch were three hundred sixty and five years: And Enoch walked with God: and he was not; for God took him" (Genesis 5:21–24). This passage's most important contribution is that it twice states that Enoch walked with God (Genesis 5:22, 24; *yithallek et-ha'elohim*). The phrase "walk with God" shows up in additional Old Testament passages in relation to other prophetic figures. Genesis 6:9

---

1. James VanderKam, a scholar of Enochic literature, dates the earliest extrabiblical Enochic literature (what is now found in 1 Enoch 72–82) to the third century BC. James VanderKam, *Enoch and the Growth of an Apocalyptic Tradition* (Washington, DC: The Catholic Biblical Association of America, 1984), 17. This text likely relied on traditions surrounding Enoch that had existed previously, though it is impossible to state when such stories began. Later writings expanded on Genesis's cryptic portrait of Enoch and often described him receiving "esoteric revelation about the nature of the universe and about the end time." George W. E. Nickelsburg, *Jewish Literature between the Bible and the Mishnah*, 2nd ed. (Minneapolis: Fortress Press, 2005), 44.

describes Noah as a just man—perfect (or blameless) in his generations—and as one who "walked with God," a description indicating that Enoch was Noah's forerunner.[2] Abraham was commanded by God to "walk before [him]" and be perfect (Genesis 17:1; *halak* [or *yithallek*] *lipne* in various Old Testament passages).[3] Abraham's servant tried to convince Laban that Rebekah should marry Isaac. The servant quotes from his master's instructions, saying, "The Lord, *before whom I walk*, will send his angel with thee" (Genesis 24:40; emphasis added).[4] When Jacob blessed his son Joseph, Jacob referred to his own father and grandfather as fathers who did walk before God (Genesis 48:15). "A bit more intimacy seems to be suggested by 'walking with' as over against 'walking before.' 'Walk with' captures an emphasis on communion and fellowship. In a number of passages, all addressed to a king or his dynasty, 'to walk with God' strongly suggests obedience and subordination (1 K. 2:4; 3:6; 8:23, 25; 9:4), rather than worship and communion."[5] Walking with God seems to denote not only obedience but also a close relationship with God that may have

---

2. Moses 8:27, which is the Joseph Smith Translation equivalent of Genesis 6:9, states that Noah's sons Shem, Ham, and Japheth also walked with God. The phrase *walk with God* indicates the "moral conduct of life which finds favor in the eyes of God and has as consequence his intimate, protective friendship." Benno Jacob, *The First Book of The Bible: Genesis*, ed. Ernest I. Jacob and Walter Jacob (New York: KTAV Publishing House, 1974), 42. One commentator interprets the phrase as implying that "Enoch stood in a direct and immediate relationship to God . . . and so was entrusted with God's plans and intentions." Claus Westermann, *Genesis 1–11: A Commentary* (Minneapolis: Augsburg Publishing House, 1984), 358.
3. This expression "indicates the service of a loyal servant, who goes before his [or her] master (sometimes human but mostly divine), paving the way, or who stands before his [or her] master ready to serve. Thus, Hezekiah walked before God (2 K. 20:3 par. Isa. 38:3), as did the patriarchs (Gen. 17:1; 24:40; 48:15)." Victor P. Hamilton, *The Book of Genesis: Chapters 1–17*, NICOT (Grand Rapids, MI: Eerdmans, 1990), 258.
4. It may be noteworthy that the phrase "before whom I walk" is not found in Abraham's own direct words of instruction to his servant (Genesis 24:7), of which this later passage is a retelling, perhaps because of Abraham's humility in not stating himself that he is righteously walking before the Lord. Yet the servant feels that this is a worthy description of Abraham.
5. Hamilton, *Book of Genesis*, 258.

included walking (literally) in God's presence, such as what Adam and Eve did and seemed to enjoy in the Garden of Eden before their expulsion.[6] The later parts of the Old Testament seem to replace the idea of *walking with*[7] or *before*[8] God with walking *in* God's paths and laws (e.g., Exodus 16:4; 18:20).[9] God stated that his purpose in giving commandments to the Israelites was so that he could walk among them and be their God (Leviticus 26:12), but this is not fulfilled to all the congregation as it had been for the earlier patriarchs.

The other Old Testament phrase about Enoch that has led to even more speculation about this prophet is found in Genesis 5:24: "And he was not; for God took him." There is no explanation given in the Genesis text for what this phrase means.[10] Although the Hebrew verb *laqach* has a variety

6. "The *hitpael* of *halak* occurs more than 60 times in the Hebrew Bible and is often used to indicate habitual or ongoing association. F. J. Helfmeyer writes that the phrase in question means '"intimate companionship" . . . with God, like that expressed in the divine revelations of Noah and perhaps to Enoch.' As it does elsewhere, the verb denotes that two parties are in continual contact (cf. 1 Sam 25:15 where the same verb and preposition appear but *God* is not the object of the preposition)." VanderKam, *Enoch and the Growth*, 31.
7. This is derived from the *hitpa'el* verb form with a direct object marker.
8. This is derived from the *hitpa'el* verb form with the preposition *lipne*. This construction is found in the injunction and promise to the members of the high priestly family that they would have walked before the Lord forever had they not honored their sons more than God (1 Samuel 2:30). With another verb form, but the same preposition, David is held up as a model of one who walked before God (2 Chronicles 7:17).
9. Menahem Haran has argued that "any cultic activity to which the biblical text applies the formula 'before the Lord' can be considered an indication of the existence of a temple at the site, since this expression stems from the basic conception of the temple as a divine dwelling-place and actually belongs to the temple's technical terminology." Menahem Haran, *Temples and Temple-Service in Ancient Israel: An Inquiry into Biblical Cult Phenomena and the Historical Setting of the Priestly School* (Winona Lake, IN: Eisenbrauns, 1995), 26. Some passages come close to saying something similar to the earlier meaning of *walking with God* when commanding that the Israelites should walk *after* the Lord, but the next phrase shows that it has the later meaning: "And keep his commandments" (Deuteronomy 13:4 [verse 5 in Hebrew]).
10. For ancient interpretations of these enigmatic verses, see John Bowker, *The Targums and Rabbinic Literature: An Introduction to Jewish Interpretations of*

of meanings—including taking things (stealing), taking a wife (marrying), and taking a life (killing)—*laqach* has usually been interpreted in this verse as God taking up Enoch in his body from the earth (in Latter-day Saint terms, God made Enoch a translated being).[11] This interpretation is in direct opposition to how the other ancestors in the genealogical list are described as they faced the reality of the Fall and tasted death.[12] There is another Old Testament example of God taking up (*laqach*) another living human, Elijah, from the earth. In this later passage, more description of the process by which Elijah was taken up into the heavens from the earth is given as Elijah conversed with his successor, Elisha: "Thou hast asked a hard thing: nevertheless, if thou see me when I am *taken* from thee, it shall be so unto thee; but if not, it shall not be so. And it came to pass, as

---

Scripture (Cambridge: Cambridge University Press, 1969), 142–50. Craig R. Koester notes that "the OT does not explain what it meant for God to 'take' Enoch, but most took it to mean that Enoch did not die (Philo, *Change* 38; *QG* 1.86; Josephus, *Ant.* 1.85; *Jub.* 4:23), not that he was taken by death (*Tg. Onq.* Gen 5:24; *Gen. Rab.* 25.1; Rose, *Wolke*, 182)." *Hebrews: A New Translation with Introduction and Commentary by Craig R. Koester*, The Anchor Yale Bible Commentary (New York: Doubleday, 2001), 476.

11. "The negative particle *ayin* with suffix and the explanatory clause *ki laqah oto elohim* (note that there is no article on *elohim*) are too brief and enigmatic to be comprehensible in and of themselves. In view of the preceding *wayyithallek hanok et haelohim* it seems unlikely that *enennu* expresses an absolute denial of his existence; rather, the meaning is that 'he was not there, was not present.' The words which follow also support the interpretation that Enoch was removed to another location; they explain why he was not found in the customary places. The clause as it stands is marvelously laconic and open-ended, leaving questions such as the location of Enoch's new home unanswered, but the verb *laqah* can in some contexts express more than the simple notion of taking. In some passages it is employed to describe removal to the divine presence: there are two instances in the story of Elijah's removal (2 Kgs 2:9 [*ellaqah*] and v 10 [*luqqah*])." VanderKam, *Enoch and the Growth*, 33.

12. These other descriptions (Genesis 5:5, 8, 11, 14, 17, 20, 27, 31) end with phrases like "and he died." For a good discussion of the many ways in which the description of Enoch breaks the pattern for the biographical summaries in Genesis 5, see James C. VanderKam, *Enoch: A Man for All Generations* (Columbia: University of South Carolina Press, 1995), 4–6. The story of Enoch thus offers hope of life and overcoming death through God's saving grace and obedience to his laws.

they still went on, and talked, that, behold, there appeared a chariot of fire, and horses of fire, and parted them both asunder; and Elijah went up by a whirlwind into heaven" (2 Kings 2:10–11; emphasis added). Genesis's description of Enoch seems to be in this sense: a living body being taken up to heaven (translated) by God.[13] As will be shown next, the New Testament helps explain this passage in this sense also.

NEW TESTAMENT

The New Testament is also very brief in its treatment of Enoch. He is first mentioned in the New Testament in the Gospel of Luke's genealogy of Jesus. In this genealogical line, Enoch is listed as the seventh patriarch after Adam, just as the Old Testament states. Yet nothing else is revealed except that Enoch was the son of Jared and the father of Methuselah (Luke 3:37).

Hebrews 11:5 is the key passage for understanding more about Enoch's departure from the earth. In this great chapter on faith, Enoch is held up as a role model of faith along with two other antediluvian figures: Abel and Noah. The verse specifically says that because of Enoch's faith, he was "translated that he should not see death" (Hebrews 11:5). The Greek term *μετατίθημι* is the same term that is used in the Septuagint to describe what God did to Enoch in Genesis 5:24. The phrase "that he should not see death" is not present in the Septuagint: its presence here makes explicit the fact that God's "taking" of Enoch meant that he left earth without death.[14] The verse continues to explain that Enoch was no longer found on the earth because (1) God had translated Enoch and (2) God had translated Enoch

---

13. J. Edward Wright notes that the Greek translation of Genesis 5:24 and its use of *μετατίθημι* (which can mean "to bring to another place," "to set in another place," "to conduct across," or "to transform") implies that Enoch did ascend into heaven. See J. Edward Wright, "Whither Elijah? The Ascension of Elijah in Biblical and Extrabiblical Traditions," in *Things Revealed: Studies in Early Jewish and Christian Literature in Honor of Michael E. Stone*, ed. Esther G. Chazon, David Satran, and Ruth A. Clements (Leiden: Brill, 2004), 124.
14. Harold W. Attridge, *The Epistle to the Hebrews*, Hermeneia Series: A Critical and Historical Commentary on the Bible (Philadelphia: Fortress Press, 1989), 317.

to show him "that he [had] pleased God" (Hebrews 11:5).[15] The Greek sense of that phrase—"that he pleased God"—is that Enoch's translation demonstrated to him (in the past perfect tense: had witness borne to him) that he had pleased God and that Enoch's testimony, or witness, continues to stand for others to see. It is worth noting that the Hebrew text of Genesis 5:22, 24 focuses on Enoch "walking with God," while the Septuagint emphasizes that "he [Enoch] pleased God." The author of Hebrews draws on this Septuagint description.

The next crucial verse (Hebrews 11:6) states that without faith it is impossible to please God, so Enoch is held up as the example of one who did please God through faith and faithfulness.[16] Perhaps part of the purpose for Enoch's translation was to show a faithless generation that what he had been teaching was true (see discussion below on Moses 7:20–28 and 8:2, which explains that a "residue" remained because the people were cursed and because Noah needed to come from Enoch's posterity).

One other passage of New Testament scripture is important in reference to Enoch. In this case, Enoch is not only mentioned, but he is quoted.[17] Jude 1:14–15 once again acknowledges that Enoch is the seventh

---

15. "The order of statements in Gn. 5:24 is doubtless assumed to reflect the order of events: first Enoch pleased God (cf. Gn. 5:22), then he was 'removed.' The implication of v.6c is that his 'removal' was a reward for his faithful life, and evidence that it had pleased God." Paul Ellingworth, *The Epistle to the Hebrews: A Commentary on the Greek Text* (Grand Rapids, MI: Eerdmans, 1993), 576.

16. "The argument unfolds in this way: If Enoch pleased God, then Enoch was a person of faith, because 'without faith it is impossible to please God' (v.6). Both the reference to what is impossible (6:4, 18; 10:4) and the form of the argument (6:16; 7:12; 9:22) are familiar in Hebrews." Fred B. Craddock, *The Letter to the Hebrews: Introduction, Commentary, and Reflections*, New Interpreter's Bible: A Commentary in Twelve Volumes (Nashville: Abingdon Press, 1998), 12:133.

17. "Jude's use of *1 Enoch* became problematic for the later use of Jude's letter in churches and for its acceptance as a canonical authority. Writing in the early to mid-third century, Origen attests to debates about Jude's authority (*Commentary on John* 19.6). Jude was not included in the Syriac version of the New Testament (the *Peshitta*) until the sixth century. Jude was, however, listed as Scripture in the Muratorian canon (second or fourth century CE) and in Athanasius's Festival Letter of 367 CE. Jerome specifically mentions Jude's use of *1 Enoch* as a mark against it, though he himself affirmed its authority as Scripture (*Lives of Illustrious Men* 4). *Enoch*, a book whose authorship could not

descendant from Adam and then Jude quotes from Enoch's prophecy: "Behold, the Lord cometh with ten thousands of his saints, to execute judgment upon all, and to convince all that are ungodly among them of all their ungodly deeds which they have ungodly committed, and of all their hard speeches which ungodly sinners have spoken against him." Besides highlighting the extreme wickedness of the people during Enoch's day, this passage foresees the great coming of the Lord with thousands of his saints. Other passages of scripture also prophesy of the great multitudes of saints/angels who will accompany Jesus's glorious Second Coming (e.g., Deuteronomy 33:2; Daniel 7:10; Zechariah 14:5; Matthew 25:31; Hebrews 12:22).[18] But where does this prophecy of Enoch come from? It is not found in Genesis, which only gives the brief description of his ministry discussed above. Many scholars have turned to noncanonical texts related to Enoch in attempts to answer this question.

---

be verified and which contained 'incredible things about giants, who had angels instead of men as fathers, and which are clearly lies' (*On Jude*, PL 93:129). Bede argued, however, that since the verse that Jude actually recites is consonant with Christian teaching, Jude ought not itself to be dismissed (*On Jude*, PL 93:129). Of course, the opposite argument could also be made, as in fact Tertullian did: since Jude regarded *1 Enoch* so highly as to quote it, the church should accord *1 Enoch* canonical authority (*On the Dress of Women* 3.3)!" David A. deSilva, *The Jewish Teachers of Jesus, James and Jude: What Earliest Christianity Learned from the Apocrypha and Pseudepigrapha* (Oxford: Oxford University Press, 2012), 109–10.

18. "Traditional Jewish scenarios depict the great parousia of God like the state visit of a monarch, whose honor and status are expressed by the number and bearing of his attendants and courtiers (Deut 33:2; Zech 14:5). Hence, myriads of heavenly, powerful, glorious angels attend the great God, who is often depicted as a warrior in triumphant procession (VanderKam, "The Theophany of Enoch I 3b–7, 9," 148–50). When the coming of Jesus came to be described, the honorable trappings of a monarch's parousia were transferred from God to him (Mark 8:38; Matt 25:31–33; 2 Thess 1:7). But the scenario here is more of a great assize than a warrior's progress, for the myriads of angels will separate the good from the wicked. Jude stresses that this parousia is 'to pass judgment' and 'convict' the wicked." *2 Peter, Jude: A New Translation with Introduction and Commentary by Jerome H. Neyrey*, The Anchor Yale Bible Commentary (New York: Doubleday, 1993), 81–82.

OTHER SECOND TEMPLE JEWISH TEXTS

The Second Temple period—roughly from the Israelites' return from the Babylon Exile until the destruction of the Jerusalem Temple by the Romans (450 BC–AD 70)—is replete with texts related to the Old Testament.[19] This is the time period of great copying and translating of the Hebrew Bible, a period that produced the Septuagint (the Greek version of the Hebrew Bible), Targums (or Targumim (pl.); Aramaic translations of the Hebrew Bible), and the Dead Sea Scrolls. In addition to these manuscripts of biblical texts, many additional texts related to Old Testament figures and events were produced. Most of these texts were deemed noncanonical and are now categorized as Pseudepigrapha, which is a collection of texts falsely ascribed to Old Testament figures and most likely not written by them or from their actual time period.[20] For the modern reader, some texts may appear to be filled with fanciful tales that have no basis in the actual historical lives of these figures.[21] Yet the modern view of the Pseudepigrapha as noncanonical was not always in line with the ancient readers' view of the collection. Some of these pseudepigraphal texts were read and copied by ancient Jewish and Christian congregations who probably accepted the texts as either part of their authoritative canon or, at

---

19. For a good overview of these texts, see Nickelsburg, *Jewish Literature between the Bible and the Mishnah*. At the end of each chapter is a useful bibliography that lists good translations and commentaries for each text.
20. The process of canonization of religious texts is a complicated process and varies from religious group to religious group. The mere copying of a religious text usually meant that it had some value or authority within a group, hence the need to produce another copy of it for reading or preservation. Some of the different Jewish and Christian sects recognized different books as part of their "scripture." Councils were sometimes held to determine which books should be included in their respective canons.
21. Latter-day Saint readers have often combed these pseudepigraphal texts for remnants of true stories and teachings from these Old Testament figures. While it is possible that some oral traditions from the time period of these individuals could have been passed down and written in these later texts, there is no way to prove this transmission. We should approach these texts with healthy skepticism since more than likely the later authors created stories around these earlier figures to boost the authority of their own writings.

least, as having some teachings worthy of the congregations' attention.[22] It is from one such text, *1 Enoch* 1:9, that this New Testament prophecy of Enoch is found and copied. Besides this quotation of a passage from a Second Temple text, several other texts discuss similar issues and events that expand Enoch's role in ancient Jewish and Christian thought.

First Enoch is probably the most well-known Second Temple text related to Enoch.[23] It is an apocalypse (a heavenly journey account) that has only been found in its complete form in Ethiopic. *First Enoch* is most likely a composite text of five originally independent texts[24] that are

---

22. "Certain writers in the second and third centuries accepted at least parts of the Enochic corpus as Sacred Scripture authored by the prophet Enoch. The appeal to Enochic authority is explicit in Jude, Barnabas, Irenaeus, Tertullian, Clement of Alexandria, and Origen. Other authors, although they do not invoke Enoch's name, employ material of Enochic provenance to provide an authoritative explanation for the presence of evil in the world. Some of them cite a form of the tradition that is alluded to but not explicated in 1 Enoch, viz., the idea that the angels were sent to earth for the benefit of humanity and only subsequently sinned with the women (Papias, Justin, Athenagoras, Lactantius, Commodianus, Rufinus, and Pseudo-Clement). . . . These authors recount or allude to the [Enochic] stories as accurate explanations of how things are and how they came to be." George A. Nickelsburg, *1 Enoch 1: A Commentary on the Book of 1 Enoch, Chapters 1–36; 81–108*, ed. Klaus Baltzer, Hermeneia Series: A Critical and Historical Commentary on the Bible (Minneapolis: Fortress Press, 2001), 101.

23. For an excellent translation of this text, see George W. E. Nickelsburg and James C. VanderKam, *1 Enoch: A New Translation* (Minneapolis: Fortress Press, 2004).

24. "Thanks largely to the pioneering research of R. H. Charles (1855–1931), it was established that *1 Enoch* is a collection of at least five separate writings. . . . Speculations about the date, provenance, and original language of these books varied until the discovery of Aramaic fragments of *1 Enoch* among the Dead Sea Scrolls and their publication by J. T. Milik from 1951 to 1976. The distribution of material in the eleven fragments confirmed Charles' theory that *1 Enoch* is a collection of originally distinct documents. In addition, the paleographical evidence of the earliest fragments suggested that two of these documents, the *Astronomical Book* (*1 En.* 72–82) and the *Book of the Watchers* (*1 En.* 1–36), date from the third century BCE, making them our oldest known apocalypses and among our most ancient nonbiblical examples of Jewish literature." Annette Yoshiko Reed, *Fallen Angels and the History of Judaism and Christianity: The Reception of Enochic Literature* (New York: Cambridge University Press, 2005), 3.

usually broken down by chapters as follows: *Book of the Watchers* (1–36), the *Book of Parables* or *Similitudes* (37–71), the *Astronomical Book* or *Book of the Luminaries* (72–82), the *Book of Dreams* (83–90), and the *Epistle of Enoch* (91–108).[25] The order of these sections is not chronological, with the earliest sections having been written in Palestine in the third century BC and the last before or during the first century AD. *First Enoch* was probably originally written in Aramaic, then translated into Greek and other languages, including the text's only complete form in Ethiopic.[26] The Ethiopian church canonized the text, and more than ninety Ethiopic manuscripts of *1 Enoch* have been found—the oldest one has been dated back to around the fifteenth century.[27] Fragments from most of the sections of *1 Enoch* have been found among the Aramaic Dead Sea Scrolls in Cave 4 and in some Greek texts found at places like Oxyrhynchus and Cairo (and

---

25. See *The Eerdmans Dictionary of Early Judaism*, ed. John J. Collins and Daniel C. Harlow (Grand Rapids, MI: Eerdmans, 2010) for this breakdown of the text and information in some of the subsequent summaries of *1 Enoch*.
26. "The components of 1 Enoch were composed in Aramaic and then translated into Greek, and from Greek into ancient Ethiopic (*Ge'ez*). The entire collection is extant only in manuscripts of the Ethiopic Bible, of which this text is a part. Approximately fifty such manuscripts from the fifteenth to the nineteenth centuries are available in the [W]est. Roughly twenty-five percent of 1 Enoch has survived in two Greek manuscripts from the fourth and fifth/sixth centuries (chaps 1:1—32:6; 97:6—107:3) and two and perhaps three fragments of other parts. Eleven manuscripts from Qumran contain substantial as well as tiny fragments of the Aramaic of parts of chapters 1–36, 72–82, 85–90, and 91–107. A fragment of a sixth/seventh century Coptic manuscript (93:3–8), an extract in a ninth-century Latin manuscript (106:1–18), and a twelfth-century Syriac excerpt (6:1–6) have also survived." Nickelsburg and VanderKam, *1 Enoch*, 13.
27. Reasons for the popularity and eventual canonization of 1 Enoch in the Ethiopian Orthodox church are matters of scholarly debate. For a good discussion of the history and issues, see Nickelsburg, *1 Enoch 1*, 104–8. "In short, 1 Enoch took root in Ethiopia because: (a) it was brought there by missionaries who came from an environment that had long cherished the book; (b) its worldview spoke to the Ethiopians' worldview, and the environment it imaginatively portrayed resonated with their environment; and (c) Ethiopian Christianity [did not focus on the same theological debates] that led to the book's rejection in Mediterranean Christianity."

possibly Qumran Cave 7). A brief discussion of each of the sections of *1 Enoch* will follow.

The first section of *1 Enoch* (chaps. 1–36) is commonly called the *Book of the Watchers.* It gets it title from the story at the beginning of Genesis 6 about the "sons of God" watching the "daughters of man" and taking them to wife. The sons' actions initiated a period of great wickedness and eventually led to the Flood and its attendant destruction. Some later texts from the Second Temple period view this story as being about angelic or heavenly beings (the sons of God) leaving their heavenly abode and cohabitating with human women.[28] Their union resulted in "mighty men" or "men of renown" who were also known as "giants" (Genesis 6:4), which led to the conceptions associated with Greek mythological characters. In the midst of this peculiar society, Enoch came and preached repentance. The first part of the *Book of the Watchers* includes a strong oracle of eschatological judgment from the mouth of Enoch as he warns the people that God will appear with his heavenly army to destroy the wicked. In *1 Enoch* 1:4–5, Enoch says, "He [God] will appear with his host, and will appear in the strength of his power from heaven. And all will be afraid, and the Watchers will shake, and fear and great trembling will seize them unto the ends of the earth."[29] Yet amid the wicked exist some of the elect that Enoch also speaks to and encourages. The second part of the *Book of the Watchers* delves into more detail about the Watchers and their illicit plans. This section ends while Enoch serves as a mediator figure (a scribe of righteousness) between heaven and the Watchers and upholds the warning of

---

28. "The *Book of the Watchers* provides our earliest extant evidence for the exegesis and expansion of [Genesis 6:1–4]. . . . The apocalypse describes the descent of angelic Watchers from heaven, their impure relations with human women, and the bloodthirsty violence of their progeny. Throughout these chapters, the biblically based theme of sexual mingling is interwoven with an extrabiblical tradition that levels a far more dire accusation against Asael and other Watchers: according to the *Book of the Watchers*, their revelation of secret knowledge caused 'all manner of wickedness' to be adopted by humankind, thereby accounting for the antediluvian proliferation of sin." Reed, *Fallen Angels*, 6.

29. Quotations of *1 Enoch* are taken from Miryam T. Brand, "1 Enoch," in *Outside the Bible: Ancient Jewish Writings Related to Scripture*, ed. Louis H. Feldman, James L. Kugel, and Lawrence H. Schiffman (Philadelphia: The Jewish Publication Society, 2013), 1339–1452.

punishment that they received. The last section of the *Book of the Watchers* (chapters 17–36) gives a great description of Enoch's journeys to the ends of the earth and the cosmos, including his travels to the mountain of God and the tree of life, to the Garden of Eden and the tree of wisdom, and through Sheol (the world of the spirits), where the dead were held. The *Book of Watchers* ends with Enoch's praise of God's creations and his great deeds.

The second section of *1 Enoch* (chapters 37–71) can be termed the *Book of Parables* or *Book of Similitudes* because of the text's description of the instructions and parables that were given to Enoch (*1 Enoch* 68:1). Chronologically, it is probably the latest of all the sections of *1 Enoch* and dates to roughly the late first century AD. The second section of *1 Enoch* consists of three individual parables, or figurative discourses, bound together by an account of an otherworldly journey by Enoch. Central to this journey is Enoch's view of the divine throne room, replete with the Son of Man enthroned. Upon seeing the judgment scene, Enoch relates the following in *1 Enoch* 46:1–3:

> And there I saw one who had a head of days,
>   and his head [was] white like wool;
> And with him [there was] another, whose face had the appearance of a man,
>   and his face [was] full of grace, like one of the holy angels.
> And I asked one of the holy angels who went with me, and showed me all the secrets, about that Son of Man, who he was, and whence he was, [and] why he went with the Head of Days.
> And he answered me and said to me:
> "This is the Son of Man who has righteousness,
>   and with whom righteousness dwells;
> he will reveal all the treasuries of that which is secret,
>   for the Lord of Spirits has chosen him,
>   and through uprightness his lot has surpassed all before the Lord of Spirits forever."

This passage's greatest importance may be in how it interprets the Son of Man traditions of Daniel 7 and how it depicts Final Judgment.[30] The judgment (the flood) at the time of Noah functions as a prototype of the Final Judgment. The righteous who currently suffer at the hands of the wicked—the wicked who are often rulers—will enjoy life on a restored earth with the Son of Man while the sinners are destroyed by fire. Thus, throughout this section, Enoch is the figure who asks questions and receives answers from his angelic escorts to describe all the heavenly scenes and future events.

The next section of *1 Enoch* (chapters 72–82) discusses astronomical knowledge, so it is called the *Book of the Luminaries* or the *Astronomical Book*. One of the heavenly archangels, Uriel, has leadership over the celestial objects, and, in this section, he transmits that knowledge to Enoch, who then shares it with his son Methuselah.[31] In *1 Enoch* 82:1–2 Enoch tells Methuselah, "And now, my son Methuselah, all these things I recount to you and write down for you; I have revealed everything to you and have given you books about all these things. Keep, my son Methuselah, the books from the hand of your father, that you may pass [them] on to the

30. "The major and unique component in these chapters, however, is a series of heavenly tableaux that portray the judgment and the events leading up to it. Presiding over the judgment is a heavenly figure known variously as Righteous One, Elect One, Anointed One, and Son of Man. This vice-regent of God, whose description is a composite of features drawn from Daniel 7 and from biblical texts about the Davidic king and the Servant of the Lord, was a prototype for NT speculation about the Son of Man, although the precise relationship between the Gospel texts and the Parables is uncertain." Nickelsburg, *1 Enoch 1*, 7.

31. "It is also worth noting that the [Astrological Book], from its inception, may have had both a theological and eschatological element. First, it presents itself as the holy angel Uriel's disclosure to Enoch of information not accessible to any others. In other words, what Enoch sees, hears, and relates to his children has the stamp of divine authenticity. It should also be recalled that the opening verse, 72:1, claims that Uriel showed Enoch 'all their regulations exactly as they are, for each year of the world and for ever, until the new creation shall be made which shall last for ever.' The revealed laws will be operative until the new creation. The writer therefore knows of a theory by which time is divided into eras. Moreover, all of the laws are revealed by an angel, and indeed, nature is governed and run by angels on behalf of God (cf. 80:1)." VanderKam, *Enoch: A Man*, 25.

generations of eternity. I have given wisdom to you and to your children, and to those who will be your children, that they may give [it] to their children for all the generations forever—this wisdom [which is] beyond their thoughts." The calendar system presented follows a 364-day calendar—unlike the lunar calendar, which has 354 days, or the common Mesopotamian calendar, which has 360 days—probably as an effort to maintain the Jewish festivals happening in their proper season (since the lunar calendar falls behind each year, and without any adjustment, harvest festivals would find themselves in the time of planting, and so forth).[32] Enoch's knowledge of astronomy is found in other Second Temple texts, including in the Book of Jubilees, which was found among the Dead Sea Scrolls. The Dead Sea Scrolls also contain at least four Aramaic fragmentary copies of the third section of *1 Enoch*, which were all found in Qumran Cave 4. The astronomical knowledge said to have been passed down through Enoch in these texts had a modest impact on Jewish, Christian, and Ethiopian astronomy and especially on the Ethiopian calendar, which has 364 days per year.

The fourth section of *1 Enoch* (chapters 83–90) is the *Book of Dreams*. The first two chapters are a dream vision, and then the next six chapters form the so-called *Animal Apocalypse*.[33] Both visions occur in Enoch's

---

32. "It is extremely important for our author to validate the fact that there are precisely 364 days in the year and that this has been the case from creation and will last until the new creation (cf. *1 En.* 72:1). And why should this be thought so crucial? . . . In [1 Enoch] 74–75 the author informs us that the number of days for the moon to fulfill its yearly cycle 'falls behind' that of the sun. Thus the lunar calendar has 360 days, as compared to the solar calendar of 364. . . . It appears that our author is in dispute with an unnamed group or custom that follows a lunar calendar. According to our author and the community he represents, this is an error of grave proportions. For pious Jews, who are committed to the entire keeping of the pentateuchal legislation, performing ritual worship on the prescribed days is absolutely essential. But if the proper calendar is not observed, then the ritual is performed on the wrong day and it is presumably ineffectual at best and sacrilegious at worst." Larry R. Helyer, *Exploring Jewish Literature of the Second Temple Period: A Guide for New Testament Students* (Downers Grove, IL: IVP Academic, 2002), 79–80.

33. "With respect to form and content, the generic and peculiar features of this text are evident from a comparison with the visions in Daniel 2, 7, 8, and 10–12.

grandfather's home, although the first vision, about the imminent flood, comes when Enoch is learning literacy, and the second vision, about the end of days, came before he got married. In both cases, Enoch attempts to intercede, first for the earth/humankind, and secondly for the people of Israel. (Compare with the instances of Enoch intervening with God on behalf of others in Moses 7, discussed below). The *Animal Apocalypse* provides a sweep of religious history in the style of a fable, with animals representing different characters (e.g., bull=Adam; heifer=Eve) and different species representing different nationalities (e.g., Israelites=sheep; Egyptians=wolves). Perhaps the fable uses animals as symbolic imagery to veil the true meaning of the destructive events that would take place to the Israelites' surrounding neighbors. The fable begins with Adam and ends with the final battle after which Jerusalem is rebuilt (with a new temple), and all have become righteous. Enoch beholds the world's events unfold from a celestial temple. The final verses of this section record Enoch's reaction to the vision: "But after this I wept bitterly, and my tears did not stop until I could not endure it; when I looked, they ran down on account of that which I saw; for everything will come to pass and be fulfilled; and all the deeds of men in their order were shown to me. That night I remembered my first dream, and because of it I wept and was disturbed, because I had seen that vision" (*1 Enoch* 90:41–42).[34]

The final section of *1 Enoch* (chapters 91–108) is often called the *Epistle of Enoch* or *The Two Ways of the Righteous and the Sinner*. This section's discourses on ethical behavior are similar to Near Eastern wisdom literature, which has an emphasis on the two ways or two choices in life (good and evil). This section compiles various accounts such as a description of Noah's miraculous birth and various exhortations tied into the period

In common with the Danielic texts, 1 Enoch 85–90 is a pseudonymous dream vision (cf. Dan 2:1; 7:1–2, 7, 13; 8:1–2, 17–18), which recounts a sequence of historical events up to the eschaton (cf. Dan 2:31–45; 7:1–27; 8:3–26; 11:2–12:4), using animals to symbolize human beings or nations (cf. Daniel 7, 8) and viewing these events in the context of related events in heaven (Dan 7:9–10, 13–14; 8:10–12; 10:20–21)." Nickelsburg, *1 Enoch 1*, 357.

34. Compare the times in the Book of Moses where Enoch wept in response to visions (Moses 7:41, 44, 49, 58), as well as the comment in Moses 7:67 that "the Lord showed Enoch all things, even unto the end of the world."

of the flood and of the last days. Part of this final section reviews history like the *Animal Apocalypse* but does so in a schema of ten-week periods that represent eras of unequal lengths. Enoch is born in the first week, while the tenth week describes the time when a new heaven arises.[35] In between, the review of history covers figures like Noah, Abraham, and Moses and also covers important future events, including the destruction of the wicked and the blessing of the righteous. Throughout this section the exhortations from Enoch to the people are often set up in testamentary fashion. That is, Enoch gathers his children and others around him to give his last counsel before his departure from the earth (usually testaments are given before one's death, but this is not the case with Enoch). The admonitions are pretty straightforward: to love righteousness (with promises of blessings) and to reject evil (with warnings of punishment and stern woes). He warns the wicked in *1 Enoch* 103:7–8 with this somber imagery:

> Know that their souls will be made to go down into Sheol, and they will be wretched,
> and their distress [will be] great;
> and in darkness and in chains and in burning flames
> your spirits will come to the great judgment,
> and the great judgment will last for all generations forever.
> Woe to you, for you will not have peace.

Enoch sorrows over the people's wickedness and laments that his eyes may become like a cloud of waters to weep over the people. Throughout this section Enoch plays a central role in instructing others and being the writer of all the signs of wisdom, wisdom that he gained by reading the "tablets of heaven" (e.g., *1 Enoch* 93:2)

35. "Human history from creation to the emergence of the new heavens and new earth is divided into ten periods, each of which is referred to as a 'week.' The scheme itself carries a message: God has carefully measured out human history in advance, and it unfolds in an orderly fashion according to God's determination. Such schematizations of history are frequent in apocalyptic literature, reminding their audiences that when things seem most out of control, the course of history is never out of *God's* control." deSilva, *The Jewish Teachers*, 120.

Second Enoch is another Enochic text compiled in the Pseudepigrapha, although it is not directly related to *1 Enoch*. A major difference with *2 Enoch* and its transmission with *1 Enoch* is that rather than becoming a major part of the Ethiopic tradition, *2 Enoch* became part of the Slavonic (eastern European) tradition (many Pseudepigrapha texts became popular in eastern Europe and were preserved and transmitted in the region's liturgical codices and compendia). The full text of *2 Enoch* has only been found in Slavonic, although some transcriptions and photographs of Coptic fragments of *2 Enoch* were recently found among the stored finds of British excavations in Nubia that had focused on the Nubian kingdom's Christian phase (during the fifth to fifteenth centuries AD). The dating of the Coptic fragments is uncertain. Although the twenty or so Slavonic manuscripts date from the Middle Ages (from the fourteenth to the eighteenth centuries AD), *2 Enoch* was most likely written in the first century AD as a Jewish text, probably in Alexandria, and was then picked up and transmitted by Christians.[36] *Second Enoch*'s major theme is the ascent of Enoch through the heavens as he is initiated into the heavenly mysteries. "[There was] a wise man and a great artisan whom the Lord took away. And he

36. While some scholars in the past have regarded *2 Enoch* as a text composed by Christians, most now believe that it was originally a Jewish text. "In spite of its biblical style, there is no point at which it can be shown to depend on the text of the New Testament, barring obvious Christian glosses, whose extraneous character is betrayed by their presence in only one manuscript or at most in manuscripts of one family. There is not a distinctively Christian idea in the book. Alleged use of it in the New Testament (evidence that it is a pre-Christian Jewish work) is in passing phrases of a very general kind; either 2 Enoch and the New Testament are drawing on a common background, or else a later author is vaguely influenced by such expressions." F. I. Andersen, "2 (Slavonic Apocalypse of) Enoch," in *Old Testament Pseudepigrapha*, vol. 1: *Apocalyptic Literature and Testaments*, ed. James H. Charlesworth (Garden City, NY: Doubleday, 1983), 95. "Michael Stone and George Nickelsburg, while acknowledging the complexities and enigmas of *2 Enoch*, nonetheless hold that there are no compelling arguments for rejecting a date as early as the first century A.D. Anderson and Stone prefer a Palestinian provenance, whereas Nickelsburg and Collins opt for a Diaspora setting, most likely Egypt. There is no consensus, but a majority holds that the original was in Greek and was later translated into Slavonic. One cannot, however, rule out completely the possibility that there was a Semitic original." Helyer, *Exploring Jewish Literature,* 380.

[the Lord] loved him so that he might see the highest realms; and of the most wise and great and inconceivable and unchanging kingdom of God almighty, and of the most marvelous and glorious and shining and many-eyed station of the Lord's servants, and of the Lord's immovable throne" (2 Enoch 1:1–4).[37] As such, *2 Enoch*'s form is both an apocalypse (heavenly journey) and a testament (last instruction) since Enoch shares with his children on earth his newfound heavenly knowledge from God and angels, including the secrets of creation: "Before anything existed at all, from the very beginning, whatever exists I [God] created from the non-existent, and from the invisible the visible. Listen, Enoch, and pay attention to these words of mine! For not even to my angels have I explained my secrets, nor related to them their origin, nor my endlessness [and inconceivableness], as I devise the creatures, as I am making them known to you today" (24:2–3). The later part of the text continues the line of Enoch's family and their priestly role among the people.[38] This text is important in Enochic tradition because it represents a development in the depiction of Enoch as not simply "a human taken to heaven and transformed into an angel, but as a celestial being exalted above the angelic world."[39] This depiction is an intermediate stage leading to later mystical rabbinic sources that describe a supreme angel Metatron or "the Prince of the Presence" that is sometimes identified with Enoch.[40]

---

37. Quotations of *2 Enoch* are taken from Andersen, "2 (Slavonic Apocalypse of) Enoch," 102–221 [longer recension-J].
38. The latter part of the text also has a discussion on Melchizedek. In this case, Melchizedek is Noah's miraculously born nephew who would escape the Flood and ascend to heaven to be "the priest to all holy priests" and "the head of the priests of the future" (2 Enoch 71:29). This Melchizedek would return later to find and instruct another Melchizedek who would then become "the first priest and king in the city Salim in the style of this Melkisedek, the originator of the priests" (72:6). This second Melchizedek refers to the Melchizedek associated with Abraham in Genesis.
39. Andrei Orlov, *The Eerdmans Dictionary of Early Judaism*, 589.
40. "According to the initial story in the early Enochic tradition, Enoch had a vision in his sleep. He rose up to the skies where he saw a crystal wall, then a crystal palace surrounded by flames and ultimately a fiery palace bathed in an unbearable brilliance, in which he saw God's Throne. It is generally considered that this vision of the celestial temple actually corresponds to the image of the

Third Enoch, also known as *Sefer Hekhalot*, differs from the other Enochic texts not only in its later date (likely from the fifth or sixth century AD)[41] but also in its main character. Rather than Enoch being the protagonist character whose exploits move the text forward, *3 Enoch* tells the story of Rabbi Ishmael, a character who takes a heavenly journey that includes seeing the archangel Metatron and learning that Metatron's real identity was, in fact, Enoch. Thus the text elaborates on Enoch but does so as a heavenly being seen by someone else on his heavenly journey. *Third Enoch* also explains how Enoch achieved his lofty status as a "youth" by becoming the youngest of the angels and how he fulfills his scribal and judicial roles.[42] Perhaps the most surprising thing about Metatron is his exalted

---

Temple in Jerusalem. There Enoch contemplated God's majesty and received instructions on the secret doctrines concerning the past and future. For his righteousness God turned him into an angel under the name of Metatron and appointed him a mediator between himself and man." Felicia Waldman, "Some Considerations on Enoch/Metatron in the Jewish Mystical Tradition," in *In the Second Degree: Paratextual Literature in Ancient Near Eastern and Ancient Mediterranean Culture and Its Reflections in Medieval Literature*, ed. Philip S. Alexander, Armin Lange, and Renate J. Pillinger (Boston: Brill, 2010), 207–8.

41. "It is impossible to reach a very firm conclusion as to the date of 3 Enoch. The main problem is the literary character of the work: it is not the total product of a single author at a particular point in time, but the deposit of a 'school tradition' which incorporates elements from widely different periods. Certain rough chronological limits can, however, be established. . . . [T]hough 3 Enoch contains some very old traditions and stands in direct line with developments which had already begun in the Maccabean era, a date for its final redaction in the fifth or sixth century A.D. cannot be far from the truth." P. Alexander, "3 (Hebrew Apocalypse of) Enoch," in *Old Testament Pseudepigrapha*, 228–29.

42. "[Enoch/Metatron] develops from being a simple angelic scribe appointed to record both the Jews' evil doings before the flood (thus justifying it), and also their merits, to being a heavenly judge with a prominent place in the scheme of divine judgment; from a recipient and sharer of celestial and earthly secrets (concerning both creation and man) to their embodiment (as they are written on his crown by the Lord himself); from an intercessor before God for various creatures of the lower realms to Israel's attorney in the celestial court and even a redeemer who takes upon himself Israel's sins; from a witness of Israel's deeds to God's secretary, mediator of knowledge, divine judgement, and God's presence and authority." Waldman, "Some Considerations on Enoch/Metatron in the Jewish Mystical Tradition," 210.

role as a vice-regent to God and his title as the "lesser YHWH."[43] Metatron/Enoch is a new figure associated with the Godhead, and he plays a powerful role in later Jewish mysticism.

The Testament of Abraham is another Second Temple Jewish text that mentions Enoch and his heavenly role. It is specifically its shorter recension (version), Recension B, that identifies Enoch by name as one of the figures at the heavenly judgment setting.[44] Within this judgment setting Enoch is described as a man of great stature with three crowns on his head—called the crowns of witness—and a golden pen in his hand.[45] As

43. "After having been installed as ruler over the angels, Metatron was given a new distinctive name: 'the lesser YHWH.' . . . [The name used] in ch. 12 and 48:7 [is] indicative of Metatron's character of or representative, *vicarius*, of the Godhead; it expresses a sublimation of his vice-regency into a second manifestation of the Deity in the name YHWH. The special features that accompany and symbolize Metatron's elevation into a lesser manifestation of the 'Divine Name' are, besides his being enthroned, the *conferment upon him of (part of) the Divine Glory*, 'honour, majesty and splendor' (ch. 48:7), 'a garment of glory, robe of honour," but especially a 'crown of kingship' (10:1–4) on which the mystical 'letters,' representing cosmic and celestial agencies, are engraved—after the pattern of the Crown of the Holy One—and lastly *knowledge of all the secrets of Creation, and of 'Torah,' otherwise in possession of the Most High alone.*" Hugo Odeberg, *3 Enoch or The Hebrew Book of Enoch* (New York: Ktav Publishing House, 1973), 82.

44. The longer version, Recension A, has many figures associated with the heavenly judgment setting that are similar to Recension B, but Recension A does not mention Enoch by name and actually has two angelic beings fulfilling the same roles assigned to Enoch in Recension B. This is a common difference between the two recensions, where Recension B usually makes direct ties to biblical figures while Recension A does so much less, which may be an indication that Recension B came later and tried to strengthen the connections with the Bible and the traditional stories about these figures. See Jared W. Ludlow, *Abraham Meets Death: Narrative Humor in the Testament of Abraham* (Sheffield, UK: Sheffield Academic Press, 2002), 137–38, 182–83.

45. "[Enoch's] exalted status in Judaism is well-attested, and his features in [Testament of Abraham] are paralleled in Jewish writings—his giant size (*3 En.* 9:2; 48C:5 [Schafer, *Synopse* 12 = 893, 73]), his being crowned (*3 En.* 12:3–5; 13:1; 48C:7 [Schafer, *Synopse* 15–16 = 896–97, 73]), and his scribal office (*Jub.* 4:17–24; *1 En.* 12:3–4; 15:1; 4Q203; 4Q227; Tg. Ps.-Jn. on Gen 5:25; *Jub.* 4:23 says that he is now in Eden, 'writing condemnation and judgment of the world'; cf. 10:17: he will 'report every deed of each generation in the day of judgment').

the "scribe of righteousness" and "teacher of heaven and earth," Enoch not only records the sins and righteousness of each soul but also reads from the book of heavenly records when requested by the judge (Abel). In the particular case portrayed in chapter 10 of *The Testament of Abraham*, a female soul tried to deny charges of serious sin waged against her by the judge, but Enoch brings forward evidence against her.

> And the judge [Abel] said to him [Enoch], "Give proof of the sin of this soul." And that man opened one of the books which the cherubim had and sought out the sin of the woman's soul, and he found (it). And the judge said, "O wretched soul, how can you say that you have not committed murder? Did you not, after your husband's death, go and commit adultery with your daughter's husband and kill her?" And he charged her also with her other sins, including whatever she had done from her childhood. When the woman heard these things, she cried aloud, saying, "Woe is me, woe is me! Because I forgot all my sins which I committed in the world, but here they were not forgotten." (*Testament of Abraham*, Rec B, 10:10–15)[46]

When the archangel Michael, Abraham's escort in this text, described Enoch's role in the judgment setting in chapter 11, Abraham asked how Enoch could bear the weight of the souls, seeing that he had never tasted of death. Abraham also asked how Enoch could give sentence to all the souls. Michael quickly corrected Abraham's question and stated that it was not permitted for Enoch to give sentence to the souls—it is the Lord who does so. Enoch only has to worry about recording. According to Michael

---

Perhaps Enoch the scribe was replaced by two recording angels. The demotion could carry forward an impulse that VanderKam detects in [Testament of Abraham], in which Enoch is only an assistant. VanderKam views this as an implicit criticism of 'devotees of Enoch who saw him as the son of man, the judge of the last days' (cf. *1 Enoch* 70–71)." Dale C. Allison Jr., *Testament of Abraham*, ed. Loren T Stuckenbruck et al., Commentaries on Early Jewish Literature (New York: Walter de Gruyter, 2003), 259–60.

46. The English translations of *The Testament of Abraham* are from E. P. Sanders, "Testament of Abraham," in Charleworth, *The Old Testament Pseudepigrapha*, 871–902.

this role was directly requested by Enoch: "Lord, I do not want to give the sentence of the souls, lest I become oppressive to someone." The Lord replied: "I shall command you to write the sins of a soul that makes atonement, and it will enter into life. And if the soul has not made atonement and repented, you will find its sins (already) written, and it will be cast into punishment" (11:8–10). Through this interaction, we see Enoch becoming the heavenly scribe and participant at the judgment scene, roles that are found in other texts related to Enoch.

The Dead Sea Scrolls include not only fragments of texts like *1 Enoch*, but they also include other Old Testament retellings that expand on Enoch and other Old Testament figures. The book of *Jubilees*, for example, discusses Enoch's visions of the future, including the final judgment day, his knowledge of the heavens gained from living an extended period with the angels of God, and his exalted role as heavenly scribe and priest, during which he wrote many books and mediated for the people. Jubilees 4:17–19 enumerates several of the traditions surrounding Enoch.

> This one was the first who learned writing and knowledge and wisdom, from (among) the sons of men, from (among) those who were born upon earth. And who wrote in a book the signs of the heaven according to the order of their months, so that the sons of men might know the (appointed) times of the years according to their order, with respect to each of their months. This one was the first (who) wrote a testimony and testified to the children of men throughout the generations of the earth. And their weeks according to jubilees he recounted; and the days of years he made known. And the months he set in order, and the sabbaths of the years he recounted, just as we made it known to him. And he saw what was and what will be in a vision of his sleep as it will happen among the children of men in their generations until the day of judgment. He saw and knew everything and wrote his testimony and deposited the testimony upon the earth against all the children of men and their generations.[47]

47. The English translations of *Jubilees* are from O. S. Wintermute, "Jubilees," in *The Old Testament Pseudepigrapha*, vol. 2, ed. James H. Charlesworth (New York: Doubleday, 1985), 35–142.

On the topic of writing, Enoch is said to have been the first patriarch who learned writing and wisdom among the sons of men (Moses 6:5–6 attributes this feat to Adam and his family).[48] Enoch wrote about astronomy and related issues so that mortals would know the appointed times of the years, which was an important concern in the book of *Jubilees*. Enoch also wrote his testimony and testified to the people and had stern warnings against the Watchers. A difference with this text from others is that rather than Enoch being translated from the earth, he was taken to the Garden of Eden to function as a scribe of the sins of humanity and to protect Eden from the floodwaters. "And we led him to the garden of Eden for greatness and honor. And behold, he is there writing condemnation and judgment of the world, and all of the evils of the children of men. And because of him none of the water of the Flood came upon the whole land of Eden, for he was put there for a sign and so that he might bear witness against all of the children of men so that he might relate all of the deeds of the generations until the day of judgment" (Jubilees 4:23–24).

The *Book of the Giants* was another Dead Sea Scroll text that included significant stories about Enoch. Several fragmentary manuscripts of this anthology of Enoch stories were uncovered among the scrolls. As the title suggests, this text revolves around the story of the Watchers at the

48. "In his expansion of the biblical text the writer of *Jubilees* is impressed with Enoch's being first in various categories, just as Pseudo-Eupolemus found him to be the first astrologer/astronomer. He was the first human to learn how to write. The source of this motif is not supplied, but the older Enochic booklets mention his ability to write, and they would not have existed if he had been unable to use a pen. . . . *1 Enoch* 82:1 has Enoch address Methuselah and tell him, among other things, that he has written a book for him. The next verse may identify that book with wisdom, a subject that *Jubilees* adduces in the same phrase as Enoch's skill at writing. The [Book of the Watchers] presents Enoch as a scribe of righteousness (12:4, 15:1) who records the petition of the watchers and the divine reply to it (see 14:4, 7). The journey sections of the BW (chaps. 17–19, 20–36) also note his writing (33:3) . . . [as does] and the [Book of Dreams], in which Enoch dates his first dream vision to the time when he was beginning to learn how to write (83:2; see 83:3). In his notice about Enoch as the pioneer author, then, the writer of *Jubilees* was not drawing on Genesis, which never mentions this about him, but probably on the information contained in the Enochic booklets." VanderKam, *Enoch: A Man*, 113.

beginning of Genesis 6 and their subsequent offspring who were "giants." Enoch serves in his familiar mediatorial role as he interprets the giants' ominous dreams and tries to intercede with God on the giants' behalf. As the great scribe, Enoch returns with a tablet that foretells harsh judgment but still holds out an invitation for repentance.

The *Testaments of the Twelve Patriarchs* includes the last counsel and teachings of Jacob's sons to their descendants. Seven of these twelve testaments refer to a book (or books) of Enoch. Most of the references are warnings about the sins of the people that are leading them astray, but these warnings had been foretold in the writings of Enoch (e.g., *Testament of Simeon* 5.4).[49] The *Testament of Dan* 5.6 goes so far as to say that Satan has become their leader: "For I read in the Book of Enoch the Righteous that your prince is Satan and that all the spirits of sexual promiscuity and of arrogance devote attention to the sons of Levi in the attempt to observe them closely and cause them to commit sin before the Lord."[50] The *Testament of Levi* says the people's sins will become so bad and disgraceful that Jerusalem will not bear their presence, the curtain of the temple will be torn, and they will be scattered. "For the house which the Lord shall choose shall be called Jerusalem, as the book of Enoch the Righteous maintains" (*Testament of Levi* 10.5). Throughout these texts, it is righteous Enoch who has written the warnings and prophecies about their descendants.

When reviewing these Second Temple Jewish texts, we can learn how later Jews and Christians viewed Enoch and his roles. Enoch becomes primarily known as a scribe (often in judgment settings), a teacher of wisdom, a mediator between mortals and heaven, and an elevated celestial figure. Enoch received many sweeping visions of God's creations and the unfolding of his salvation history among his children. Thus, Enoch's importance and status was greatly expanded from the Genesis account, although the sources for these expansions are usually unknown. Similar to the Apocrypha, perhaps we can approach these texts as counseled in Doctrine and Covenants 91, when the Lord proclaimed that "there are many things contained therein that are true, . . . [and] there are many things contained

---

49. See also TLevi 14.1, 16.1; TJudah 18.1; TNaphthali 4.1; TBenjamin 9.1

50. The English translations are from H. C. Kee, "Testaments of the Twelve Patriarchs," in Charlesworth, *Old Testament Pseudepigrapha*, vol. 1, 776–828.

therein that are not true, which are interpolations by the hands of man" (91:1–2). Whether truths or interpolations, however, these depictions are primarily *later* Jewish and Christian interpretations of Enoch; thus the depictions highlight the significant roles Enoch played in each religion's interpretations. When turning to Restoration scripture, on the other hand, we are told the source of the expanded stories of Enoch: revelatory experiences through the Prophet Joseph Smith, most notably during the process of the new translation of the Bible (the JST). When compared to the material discussed above, some parallels and significant differences become noticeable.[51]

RESTORATION SCRIPTURE

Our understanding about Enoch is greatly enriched because of the additional accounts about Enoch and his ministry that were revealed through the prophet Joseph Smith and now contained in the Pearl of Great Price, the Doctrine and Covenants, and other sources. The account of Enoch in the Book of Moses[52] came as part of Joseph Smith's translation of the Bible and extended the discussion (in Genesis) on Enoch's ministry from around 5 verses to 114 verses.[53] Below we will highlight some of the key

51. For a concise list of the many parallels between the Book of Moses's account of Enoch with scattered elements related to Enoch found in other Enochic literature, see Andrew C. Skinner, "Joseph Smith Vindicated Again: Enoch, Moses 7:48, and Apocryphal Sources," in *Revelation, Reason, and Faith: Essays in Honor of Truman G. Madsen*, ed. Donald W. Parry, Daniel C. Peterson, and Stephen D. Ricks (Provo, UT: Foundation for Ancient Research and Mormon Studies, Brigham Young University, 2002), 370–71.
52. For an excellent overview of the modern translation and publication of the Book of Moses (including transcriptions of the original manuscript texts), see Kent P. Jackson, *The Book of Moses and the Joseph Smith Translation Manuscripts* (Provo, UT: Religious Studies Center, Brigham Young University, 2005).
53. Church history scholar Richard Bushman has commented on how the Enoch material was a shift from Joseph's previous augmentation of the biblical narrative. "In redoing the early chapters of Genesis, the stories of Creation, of Adam and Eve, and [of] the Fall were modified, but with less extensive interpolations than in the revelation to Moses. Joseph wove Christian doctrine into the text without altering the basic story. But with the appearance of Enoch in

aspects of this JST account as well as look at what other Restoration scripture says about this great prophet.

Moses 6:26–27 gives a detailed description of Enoch's commission as a prophet. The Spirit of God descended out of heaven and abode upon Enoch, whereupon he heard a voice from heaven declaring that he should prophesy and preach repentance to the people with a warning of God's anger against their deep wickedness.[54] Enoch's role as preacher to the wicked is similar to what we saw in the Jewish and Christian literature discussed above. Enoch's meek, reluctant response in Moses 6:31 focused on his youthful age,[55] his self-perceived slowness of speech, and the fact that

---

the seventh generation from Adam, the text expanded far beyond the biblical version. In Genesis, Enoch is summed up in 5 verses; in Joseph Smith's revision, Enoch's story extends to 110 verses." Richard Lyman Bushman, *Joseph Smith: Rough Stone Rolling* (New York: Alfred A. Knopf, 2006), 138.

54. "Curiously, the closest biblical parallel to the wording of these opening verses is not to be found in the call of any Old Testament prophet but rather in John the Evangelist's description of events following Jesus' baptism in which, like Enoch, [John] saw 'the Spirit descending from heaven' and it 'abode on him' (i.e. Jesus). Two additional parallels with Jesus' baptism follow: first in the specific mention of a 'voice from heaven,' then in the proclamation of divine sonship by the Father. The connection between Enoch's divine encounter and the baptism of Jesus becomes intelligible when one regards the latter event, as do Margaret Barker and Gaetano Lettieri, as an 'ascent experience' consistent with the idea of baptism as a figurative death and resurrection. From this perspective, Enoch's prophetic commission may be seen as given him in the context of a heavenly ascent." Jeffery M. Bradshaw and David J. Larsen, *In God's Image and Likeness 2: Enoch, Noah, and the Tower of Babel* (Salt Lake City: Interpreter Foundation and Eborn Books, 2014), 35.

55. Several Enochic texts give Enoch the title of "lad" or "youth." In the pseudepigraphal books of Enoch, this is explained "as due to the fact that Enoch was taken up to heaven during the era of the flood and elevated to a status over that of the angels. This elevation bothered the angels and they made accusations against the person of Enoch, though the specific nature of these accusations have fallen out of the present form of the text. This leads God to asseverate that Enoch is to be prince and ruler over all the angels. At this point the angels relent, prostrate before Enoch, and acclaim him 'Lad.' . . . In any event, the reason our text supplies for this title is deceptively simple and straightforward: 'And because I was the *youngest* among them and a "lad" amongst them with respect to days, months, and years, therefore they called me "lad."'" Gary A. Anderson,

the people hated him. The Lord reassured Enoch in verse 32 that he would be protected in his ministry, his mouth would be filled, and God would give him utterance. God went on to say in verse 34 that not only would he justify Enoch's words, but Enoch's speech would be so powerful it would move mountains and change rivers' courses. God finished his instructions to Enoch with the invitation to "walk with me."[56] The Pearl of Great Price seems to use the term "walking with God" to emphasize Enoch's lengthy life of righteousness, and the Book of Moses repeats it several times throughout Enoch's ministry, whereas in Genesis the phrase is mentioned right as Enoch is taken to God.

Enoch's divine experience continued with God's invitation to Enoch to anoint his eyes with clay and wash them, which he did (Moses 6:35). Enoch's experience is similar to other prophets, like Jeremiah and Isaiah, who had their lips touched to prepare them for prophetic service. "However, in the case of both Joseph Smith's revelations and pseudepigrapha, Enoch's *eyes* 'were opened by God' to enable 'the vision of the Holy One and of heaven.' The words of a divinely given song recorded in Joseph Smith's Revelation Book 2 are in remarkable agreement with *1 Enoch*: '[God] touched [Enoch's] eyes and he saw heaven.' This divine action would have had special meaning to Joseph Smith, who alluded elsewhere to instances in which God touched his own [Joseph's] eyes before he received a heavenly vision."[57] Enoch then beheld all the spirits that God had created and many things not visible to the natural eye (Moses 6:36). As a result of those experiences, Enoch gained the reputation among the people as a seer. These visions of God's vastness agree with texts discussed above in which Enoch came to know all of God's creations. With his newly gained knowledge and experience, Enoch went forth and preached against the wickedness of the people—doing so offended some but produced curiosity in others (6:37–38). But none dared apprehend him for fear of God because Enoch walked with God (6:39). However, a man named Mahijah stepped forward

---

"The Exaltation of Adam and the Fall of Satan," in *Literature on Adam and Eve: Collected Essays,* ed. Gary A. Anderson, Michael E. Stone, and Johannes Tromp (Boston: Brill, 2000), 107.

56. Recall the earlier discussion of Enoch and other patriarchs "walking" with God.

57. Bradshaw and Larsen, *In God's Image*, 40–41.

and asked Enoch who he was and where he had come from (6:40).[58] Enoch gave a lengthy response that shared his commission from God to come among the people and teach them God's word revealed through visions to him (6:41–44). Enoch then shared the fact that a book of remembrance had been preserved from their ancestors, allowing Enoch's people to know their ancestors ever since Adam (6:45–46).[59] Enoch's sharing of written knowledge is similar to times when Enoch in other texts taught his son Methuselah or when others later read Enoch's words to learn their history and wisdom. The people here responded with trembling and could not stand in his presence (6:47). Enoch then taught about the plan of salvation, some of the first principles and ordinances of the gospel, and the atoning role of Jesus Christ (6:48–7:1), which are clear gospel principles certainly not found in earlier Enochic texts (although some do expound on the figure and purpose of the Son of Man).

---

58. "There are intriguing similarities not only in the name but also in the role of the Mahijah/Mahujah character in Joseph Smith's book of Moses and the role of a character named Mahujah (MHWY) in the *Book of the Giants*. . . . In the *Book of the Giants*, we read the report of a series of dreams that troubled the *gibborim*. The dreams 'symbolize the destruction of all but Noah and his sons by the Flood.' In an impressive correspondence to the questioning of Enoch by Mahijah in the book of Moses, the *gibborim* send one of their fellows named Mahujah to 'consult Enoch in order to receive an authoritative interpretation of the visions.' In the *Book of the Giants*, we read: '[Then] all the [*gibborim* and the *nephilim*] . . . called to [Mahujah,] and he came to them. They implored him and sent him to Enoch, the celebrated scribe and they said to him: "Go . . . and tell him to [explain to you] and interpret the dream."'" Bradshaw and Larsen, *In God's Image*, 45.
59. "In the book of Moses, Enoch says the book is written 'according to the pattern given by the finger of God.' This may allude to the idea that a similar record of their wickedness is kept in heaven as attested in *1 Enoch*: "Do not suppose to yourself nor say in your heart, that they do not know nor are your unrighteous deeds seen in heaven, nor are they written down before the Most High. Henceforth know that all your unrighteous deeds are written down day by day, until the end of your judgment.' As Enoch is linked with the book of remembrance in the book of Moses, so he is described in the *Testament of Abraham* as the heavenly being who is responsible for recording the deeds of [hu]mankind so that they can be brought into remembrance." Bradshaw and Larsen, *In God's Image*, 47.

Enoch proceeded to share his very powerful experience on Mount Simeon in which the heavens were opened, he was clothed with glory, and he saw and talked with the Lord (Moses 7:2–4). Similar to other ascension narratives in Enochic texts, here Enoch beholds the Lord and learns directly from him. The Lord granted a vision of the world for the space of many generations, which included the conquest of the people of Canaan over the land (7:4–9).[60] The Lord then commanded Enoch to preach repentance and baptize the people, which Enoch did, except among the people of Canaan (7:10–12). There is no reason given for why the Canaanites were excluded, but perhaps it was because of their violence and conquest (7:7). The narrative then shifts to the conflict between the people of God who were led by Enoch and their enemies. Through Enoch's faith and the power of language that God had granted him, Enoch was able to work mighty changes throughout nature, such that all nations feared greatly (7:13).[61] After the enemies of the people of God fled to a newly raised up piece of land and both they and the giants of the land stood afar off, they were greatly cursed such that there would be wars and bloodshed among them (7:14–16). The righteous, however, saw great blessings as the Lord came and dwelt with them. The glory of the Lord came upon them, they flourished, and they were blessed upon the mountains and high places (meaning that Enoch's people received power, rituals, and maybe even something we might equate with today's endowments. See 7:16–17).[62] The

---

60. While the content of the visions shares little in common, the pseudepigraphal accounts of Enoch describe him receiving several visions of future events and secrets known only by heaven. (See, particularly, Enoch's dream visions in *1 Enoch* 83–90.)

61. "Of special note is a puzzling phrase in Martinez'[s] translation of the *Book of the Giants* that immediately follows the description of the battle: ' . . . the roar of the wild beasts has come and they bellowed a feral roar.' Remarkably the [B]ook of Moses account has a similar phrase following the battle description, recording that 'the roar of the lions was heard out of the wilderness.'" Bradshaw and Larsen, *In God's Image*, 49.

62. According to Doctrine and Covenants 76:67, the righteous will join "the general assembly and church of Enoch, and of the Firstborn." The Church of the Firstborn usually refers to those who have had their calling and election made sure. "[Mountains and high places] were the sites of sanctuaries. These places of worship became the locus for receiving divine blessings such as revelation and

people were united in righteousness without poor among them, so the Lord called them Zion (7:18). A significant difference between the Book of Moses and other Enochic texts is its emphasis on Enoch's *earthly* ministry. Most of the other texts focus on Enoch's *heavenly* ministry. In the Book of Moses, Enoch was not merely a mediator between heaven and earth, but he actively ministered among his people and prepared them for their own translations as well. The parallels between Restoration scripture and ancient sources seem to point to the existence of more accounts of Enoch than what has been transmitted through canonical sources, and the Latter-day Saint belief in the existence and knowledge of the gospel and the plan of salvation from the foundation of the world certainly comes through strongly in the Enoch material from Restoration scripture.

The next section of the text focuses on the dialogue between the Lord and Enoch, which leads into more of a heavenly ministry for Enoch. In the course of this dialogue Enoch sees all the nations of the earth and eventually Zion being taken up into heaven (Moses 7:19–23). Enoch was now "high and lifted up,[63] even in the bosom of the Father, and of the Son of Man," and from his glorious vantage point, he saw the generations of man and the contest for the souls between heavenly angels sent to earth and Satan's efforts among the wicked (7:24–27). Those who accepted the angels' message were lifted into Zion by the powers of heaven (7:27), but the residue fell under Satan's power and were the object of God's weeping (7:28).[64] God's weeping led Enoch to question how God could weep over

---

sacred ordinances." Richard D. Draper, S. Kent Brown, and Michael D. Rhodes, *The Pearl of Great Price: A Verse-by-Verse Commentary* (Salt Lake City: Deseret Book, 2005), 120.

63. "The parallel between Enoch being lifted up in this verse and the Son of Man being 'lifted up on the cross, after the manner of man' in Moses 7:55 is noteworthy. In addition, there may be some connection between the idea of being 'lifted up' and initiation into the heavenly mysteries. In the *Book of Parables* 71:3 Enoch recounts: 'And the angel Michael, one of the archangels, took me by my right hand, and *raised me up*, and brought me out to all the secrets; and he showed me all the secrets of mercy.'" Bradshaw and Larsen, *In God's Image*, 140.

64. In contrast to God's tears of compassion in the Book of Moses, Jed L. Woodworth notes that "The God in [*1 Enoch*] seems to show some remorse, but only after it becomes obvious the floods did not have the desired effect: 'Afterwards the Ancient of days repented, and said; In vain have I destroyed all the inhabitants of

such a seemingly insignificant portion of his creations. God responded that these people were the workmanship of his hands, and he had given them all the conditions and commandments needed to choose him to be their Father; but they had rejected him and now faced his indignation, which included facing the floods and being turned over to Satan to be their father (7:29–38). Yet, even despite their wicked state, God had prepared a place and plan for them, wherein his chosen one could deliver them (7:38–39).

As Enoch began feeling godly compassion and sorrow for the scene unfolded before him, he "wept and stretched forth his arms, and his heart swelled wide as eternity; and his bowels yearned; and all eternity shook" (Moses 7:41; compare with 1 Enoch 90:39–42 mentioned above, when Enoch "wept bitterly" after God showed him a symbolic vision of the future). Yet even when beholding the terrible destruction of the floods, Enoch saw the temporal deliverance of Noah, his family, and their descendants, who were all spreading forth to fill the earth again, which comforted and gladdened Enoch's heart (7:41–45). When Enoch asked about the timing of the day of the Lord, Enoch saw in vision the great day, and his soul rejoiced (7:45–47). Enoch's attention then turned to the voice of the earth: "He heard a voice from the bowels [of the earth], saying: Wo, wo is me, the mother of men; I am pained, I am weary, because of the wickedness of my children.[65] When shall I rest, and be cleansed from the

---

the earth' (54:1). When wickedness returns, the God in [*1 Enoch*], like the God of the Biblical narrative, seems to second-guess himself for ever having sent the flood." Jed L. Woodworth, "Extra-Biblical Enoch Texts in Early American Culture," in *Archive of Restoration Culture: Summer Fellows' Papers, 1997–1999* (Provo, UT: Joseph Fielding Smith Institute for Latter-day Saint History, 2000), 193n44.

65. Rampant wickedness on the earth is one of the central themes of the Book of the Watchers (*1 Enoch* 1–36) and a source of consternation for God throughout much of Enochic literature. However, unlike in the Book of Moses, the root of this evil is identified not as the wickedness of men but rather as the actions of the angelic Watchers. "[The Book of the Watchers] is much absorbed with the problem of the origin of evil, . . . [which] is traced back to an angelic rebellion. This is a major burden of [Book of Watchers]. For our author, evil is of such magnitude that it cannot be attributed to a misuse of human freedom alone—there must be a more cosmic and sinister explanation. . . . This is a keynote of

filthiness which is gone forth out of me? When will my Creator sanctify me, that I may rest, and righteousness for a season abide upon my face?" (Moses 7:48).

The Mother Earth figure may not be commonly presented in Latter-day Saint theology, but it is a common feature in many ancient religions. Not surprisingly, she appears in other Enochic literature where she cries out for the wickedness upon her (*1 Enoch* 7:4–6; 8:4; 9:2, 10; *4QEnGiants* 8, lines 3–4, 6–12).[66] In the Book of Moses, Enoch turned to his familiar role as mediator when pleading to God in the name of Christ for rest and sanctification on behalf of the earth and also for the children of Noah (Moses 7:49–50). Making a covenant with Enoch, the Lord promised that he would stay the floods and call upon the children of Noah so that a remnant of Enoch's seed would always be found on the face of the earth (7:51–52).[67] Enoch continued to be concerned about the earth and asked if she would receive her rest at the time of the coming of the Son of Man (7:54).[68] Enoch

---

the apocalyptic movement. Evil is bigger than humanity and has consequences beyond one's comprehension. Evil has invaded the earth from the heavenly realms." Helyer, *Exploring Jewish Literature*, 84.

66. For a discussion of the similarities and differences of these texts (which mention the earth crying out) with Moses 7:48, see Skinner, "Joseph Smith Vindicated Again," 374–80.

67. Enoch mentions similar promises in 1 Enoch 65:12, where he appears in a vision to Noah. Enoch says, "[God] has confirmed your name among the holy ones, and he will preserve you among those who dwell on the earth, and he has confirmed your righteous descendants to be kings and for great honors. And from your descendants there will flow a fountain of the righteous and the holy, and they will be without number forever."

68. Many scholars have examined *1 Enoch*'s use of the title "Son of Man," particularly in relation to how the term is used by Jesus in the New Testament. "The role and person of the Son of Man, who is also referred to as 'the Chosen One,' 'the Righteous One,' and, once, the 'Messiah,' are significantly developed in *1 Enoch* in comparison with Daniel. The Son of Man predates creation itself, hidden in God's presence and revealed only to the chosen until the time of his decisive visitation (see *1 Enoch* 48:2–7; 62:7). While he still exercises rule in an eschatological kingdom as in Daniel 7:13–14 (see *1 Enoch* 45:4–6; 51:5; 62:14–16), ushering in 'the house of his congregation' after the 'kings and the powerful of this earth' are dragged off by the angels of punishment and destroyed (*1 Enoch* 53:5–6), the Son of Man/Chosen One also plays a direct role in the

then beheld the crucifixion of Christ and the subsequent resurrection of the just (7:55–57), but it would still not be the time for the earth to rest. The earth's rest would only occur when Christ returned in the last days (7:59–61). As part of the last days, a Holy City would be established for the elect, a New Jerusalem (7:62). A grand reunion would then occur as the Lord and Enoch would welcome the elect into their bosom, fall upon their necks, and kiss them, thus ushering in a thousand-year period of righteousness (7:63–64). In sum, Enoch saw the day of the coming of the Son of Man and all the great tribulations that would precede it, and as the Lord showed Enoch all things, Enoch received a fullness of joy (7:65–67).[69]

The Pearl of Great Price's account of Enoch ends with some events that parallel some of the Genesis account but changes the events to affect a corporate body (Zion) rather than simply affecting Enoch as an individual. All the days of Zion, in the days of Enoch, were 365 years (rather than Enoch's lifespan alone) (Moses 7:68). Enoch *and all his people* walked with God as he dwelt in the midst of Zion until Zion was received into God's own bosom (7:69). Enoch lived upon the earth four hundred and thirty years (8:1),[70] and the Pearl of Great Price specifically points out that

---

judgment of the nations, a role previously executed by the ancient of days (Dan 7:9; contrast *1 Enoch* 45:2–3; 46:4–8; 51:1–5; 61:8–9; 69:26–29). The Son of Man sits 'on the throne of his glory' in judgment (*1 Enoch* 61:8; 62:5; 69:26–29), and even at one point sits on the throne of glory of the Head of Days (*1 Enoch* 55:4), testing the works of human beings and executing judgment upon angels. The author of the Parables of Enoch weaves together Danielic imagery with Isaiah's prophecies of a coming ruler upon whom God's manifold Spirit would rest (cf. Isa 11:1–2 with *1 Enoch* 49:3) and of a servant who would be 'the light of the nations' (cf. Isa 42:6; 49:6, with *1 Enoch* 48:4), as well as expectations concerning the Davidic king's righteous character (cf. Isa 11:5 and Jer 23:5–6 with *1 Enoch* 38:2; 46:3) and ascendancy over the nations (cf. Ps 2:7–11 with *1 Enoch* 46:4–6)." deSilva, *The Jewish Teachers*, 133–34.

69. In *2 Enoch* 40:1, there is a telling comment from Enoch to his children: "Now therefore, my children, I know everything; some from the lips of the Lord, others my eyes have seen from the beginning even to the end."

70. "One reaches this figure by adding Enoch's age at the time of Methuselah's birth, sixty-five—evidently Enoch's age when he was called (see Moses 6:25–26)—to the number of years that Zion existed under Enoch's leadership, 365 (see Moses 7:68). In contrast, the Bible reckons Enoch's earthly age to have been 365 years,

Enoch's son Methuselah was not taken up with the rest so that the Lord's covenant that Noah would come from the fruit of his loins could be fulfilled (8:2). This explains how Enoch's posterity would continue and what the fate of the residue left behind would be, as discussed in other Enochic texts. The order of the priesthood and the commission to declare the gospel are also continued from Enoch to Noah: "And the Lord ordained Noah after his own order, and commanded him that he should go forth and declare his Gospel unto the children of men, *even as it was given unto Enoch*" (8:19; emphasis added).

Other parts of Joseph Smith's translation of the Bible address Enoch. More emphasis seems to be placed in these passages on earlier covenants made with Enoch, which is not a significant theme in other Enochic literature. JST Genesis 9:15 first promises that God would establish his covenant with Noah, the same one "which I [God] made unto your father Enoch, concerning your seed after you" (see the following chapter in this volume). Shortly thereafter JST Genesis 9:21 describes the rainbow that would be shown to Noah as a sign of the covenant. The Lord says that when he sees the rainbow, he will be reminded of the everlasting covenant he made with Noah's forefather, Enoch, "When men should keep all my commandments, Zion should again come on the earth, the city of Enoch which I have caught up unto myself" (JST Genesis 9:21). A covenant with Enoch is also mentioned in relation to Melchizedek's ordination to the priesthood when it is said that "he was ordained an high priest after the order of the covenant which God made with Enoch" (14:27). This order was after the order of the Son of God, which did not come from earthly origins but from God, and thus the order had no beginning or end (14:28).[71] God's covenant with Enoch was further described in the next verses in which it is explained that God swore unto Enoch and his seed that they would have power, by faith, to do many mighty works (many of which Enoch demonstrated in the Pearl of Great Price account). And those with this faith and

---

counting 300 years from the birth of Methuselah (see Genesis 5:21–23)." Draper, Jackson, and Rhodes, *The Pearl of Great Price*, 155.

71. This clarifies the somewhat cryptic statement in Hebrews 7:3, which says that the venerable Melchizedek was "without father, without mother, without descent, having neither beginning of days, nor end of life."

with the priesthood "were translated and taken up into heaven" (14:32). Melchizedek and his righteous people had this faith and priesthood, thus they "sought for the city of Enoch which God had before taken, separating it from the earth, having reserved it unto the latter days, or the end of the world" (14:34).

Doctrine and Covenants section 107 offers more insight on Enoch, especially in relation to priesthood authority.[72] Section 107:48 states that Enoch was 25 years old when Adam ordained him to the Melchizedek Priesthood, and Enoch was blessed by Adam again at age 65.[73] The next verse (107:49) reiterates Enoch's experience with walking with the Lord but also emphasizes the frequent nature of it: "He saw the Lord, and he walked with him, and was before his face *continually*; and he walked with God three hundred and sixty-five years." The last part of the verse differs from the Genesis account, which seems to imply that Enoch was translated at the age of 365, but in Doctrine and Covenants 107:49, 365 years is how long he walked with the Lord on the earth, which is then added to Enoch's age (65) when he was given a second blessing from Adam. Thus according to Doctrine and Covenants 107:49 Enoch was 430 years old when he was translated, which agrees with the age given in Moses 8:1. Section 107 goes on to describe a great gathering of high priests and other righteous people that happened three years before Adam's death. Enoch was among these antediluvian patriarchs who met at Adam-ondi-Ahman, where the Lord appeared and where they all rose up to bless Adam. Then Adam gave his final counsel, blessings, and prophecies (Doctrine and Covenants 107:53–56), and all these things were recorded in a book of Enoch (107:57).[74]

---

72. For excellent information on the origin, content, and results of Doctrine and Covenants 107, see Stephen C. Harper, *Making Sense of the Doctrine and Covenants: A Guided Tour through Modern Revelations* (Salt Lake City: Deseret Book, 2008), 395–99.

73. This was the same time that Enoch's son Methuselah was born. The blessing that Adam gave to Enoch when he was 65 may also relate to Enoch's prophetic call when, as mentioned in Moses 6:25–27, the Spirit of God descended upon Enoch.

74. "The book of Enoch is one of the ancient writings that Latter-day Saints anticipate receiving sometime in the future. This is not to be confused with the pseudepigraphic books of Enoch, which nevertheless have garnered the

Besides canonized Latter-day Saint scripture, there are a few other references to Enoch from early Church leaders. Joseph Smith taught that Enoch was reserved by God unto himself, explaining that Enoch "should not die at that time and [that God] appointed unto him a ministry unto terrestrial bodies of whom there have been but little revealed. He is reserved also unto the Presidency of a dispensation. . . . He is a ministering Angel, to minister to those who shall be heirs of salvation, and appeared unto Jude as Abel did unto Paul, therefore Jude spoke of him 14 & 15 v."[75] Brigham Young connected Enoch with temple worship: "Enoch had temples and officiated therein, but we have no account of it."[76]

SIGNIFICANCE OF ENOCH

Despite Enoch's brief mention in the Old Testament, the figure of Enoch played a very significant role in early Judaism and Christianity. He is one of the dominant figures of the Second Temple period, perhaps precisely

---

interest of some Latter-day Saints since at least 1840. In Doctrine and Covenants 107:53–57, reference is made to a meeting of Adam's righteous posterity [that was] held at Adam-ondi-Ahman three years before Adam's death. The influence of the Holy Spirit was manifested powerfully in prophecy as Adam blessed his posterity. While these verses give a précis of what happened, many more things were 'written in the book of Enoch, and are to be testified of in due time' (D&C 107:57). Speaking of this book in December 1877, Elder Orson Pratt said, 'When we get that, I think we shall know a great deal about the ante-diluvians of whom at present we know so little' (*JD* 19:218)." Lewis R. Church, "Enoch: Book of Enoch," in *Encyclopedia of Mormonism*, ed. Daniel H. Ludlow (New York: Macmillan, 1992), 2:460.

75. "History, 1838–1856, volume C-1 [2 November 1838–31 July 1842] [addenda], p. 17 [addenda], The Joseph Smith Papers.

76. Brigham Young, in *Journal of Discourses* (London: Latter-day Saints' Book Depot, 1877), 18:303. Hugh Nibley argued that today we do have such accounts of Enoch and temples (within the apocryphal sources of Enoch). See Hugh Nibley, *Enoch the Prophet*, ed. Stephen D. Ricks (Salt Lake City: Deseret Book, 1986), 20. Some of these accounts refer to heavenly temples, the Jerusalem temple, or the future temple in a New Jerusalem (for the heavenly temple, see 1 Enoch 14:8–15:4; 87:4; 89:59–90:31; for the Jerusalem temple, see 1 Enoch 89:50, 54, 66–67, 73–74; for the eschatological temple in New Jerusalem, see *1 Enoch* 90:28–29, 35–36).

because so little was written about him in the Old Testament and because what was in the text seemed to beg for exploration and expansion. One prominent scholar went so far as to state that "the influence of Enoch in the New Testament has been greater than that of all the other apocryphal and pseudepigraphical books taken together."[77] The rich transmission history of Enochic texts, from the Dead Sea Scrolls to medieval manuscripts, stands as a testament to the importance of Enoch and the texts associated with him. Some scholars have even argued in favor of the existence of a particular strand of Judaism in the first centuries BC—Enochic Judaism—which was similar to the development of Jewish sects like the Essenes and Pharisees.[78] Citations from Enoch texts are found in the Jewish apocalyptic writings of Jubilees, the Testament of the Twelve Patriarchs, the Assumption of Moses, 2 Baruch, and 4 Ezra. In later Jewish mystical texts, Enoch is raised to the highest levels of the heavenly courts, becoming a priest and vice-regent to God.[79]

The early Christian fathers and apologists treated some Enoch texts, particularly *1 Enoch*, as a canonical text.[80] In this case, more than thirty

77. R. H. Charles, *The Apocrypha and Pseudepigrapha of the Old Testament* (Oxford: Clarendon Press, 1966), 2:180. For discussions of how Enochic writings affect New Testament texts, see deSilva, *The Jewish Teachers*, 101–140; Helyer, *Exploring Jewish Literature*, 77–92, 136–39, 379–88.

78. For example, see John W. Rogerson, Judith Lieu, *The Oxford Handbook of Biblical Studies* (Oxford: Oxford University Press, 2006), 106. See also Gabriele Boccaccini, *Roots of Rabbinic Judaism: An Intellectual History, from Ezekiel to Daniel* (Grand Rapids, MI: Eerdmans, 2002), 89–102; Margaret Barker, *The Lost Prophet: The Book of Enoch and Its Influence on Christianity* (1998; repr., Sheffield: Phoenix Press, 2005), 19.

79. For a comprehensive examination of how the figure of Enoch/Metatron evolves in Jewish thought over the centuries, see Andrei A. Orlov, *The Enoch-Metatron Tradition*, Texts and Studies in Ancient Judaism, 107 (Tübingen: Mohr-Siebeck, 2005).

80. For a comprehensive discussion of both the Jewish and Christian reception of Enochic writings, see Reed, *Fallen Angels and the History of Judaism and Christianity*. George Nickelsburg provides a thorough overview of the influence of *1 Enoch* on the Son of Man concept in Christian thought in *1 Enoch* 1, 82–108.

patristic writers include quotations from Enoch.[81] Irenaeus and Clement of Alexandria both cited *1 Enoch* without questioning whether its character was sacred.[82] Tertullian acknowledged that some do not accept the genuineness of the prophecy of Enoch because it was no longer part of the Jewish canon or because it would have been lost in the flood, but Tertullian argued that either Noah had taken a copy on the ark with him, or he had reproduced it later through inspiration. In either case, Tertullian felt that the content in the prophecy of Enoch deemed it worthy of inclusion, especially because Enoch preached about the Lord and because part of Enoch's testimony is preserved in Jude.[83] Irenaeus described the common view of Enoch as the following: "Enoch too, pleasing God, without circumcision, discharged the office of God's legate to the angels although he was a man, and was translated, and is preserved until now as a witness of the just judgment of God, because the angels when they had transgressed fell to the earth for judgment, but the man who pleased [God] was translated

81. R. H. Charles, *The Book of Enoch* (London: Oxford University Press, 1913), lxxxi–xci.

82. "In the late second century, Athenagoras and Irenaeus both demonstrate knowledge of *1 Enoch*, and particularly the Watchers story, and appear to accord it prophetic authority. In the same period, Clement of Alexandria refers to *1 Enoch* in *Selections from the Prophets* 2.1 and 53.4, seeing it as a source of accurate information. He also mentions the Watchers story in *Stromata* 5.1.10; here he is dependent on *1 Enoch*, but its status is less clear: it may well be distinguished from Moses and the prophets, but remains at least a reliable source." Nicholas J. Moore, "Is Enoch Also among the Prophets? The Impact of Jude's Citation of *1 Enoch* on the Reception of both Texts in the Early Church," *Journal of Theological Studies* 64, no. 2 (2013): 498–515.

83. "Since Enoch in the same book tells us of our Lord, we must not reject anything at all which genuinely pertains to us. Do we not read that every word of Scripture useful for edification is divinely inspired? As you very well know, Enoch was later rejected by the Jews for the same reason that prompted them to reject almost everything which prophesied about Christ. It is not at all surprising that they rejected certain Scriptures which spoke of him, considering that they were destined not to receive him when he spoke to them himself. But we have a witness to Enoch in the epistle of Jude the apostle." Tertullian, *On the Apparel of Women*, book 1, chapter 3.

for salvation."[84] However, Enoch's importance in Christianity, especially western Christianity, began to wane around the fourth century AD as writers like Hilary, Jerome, and Augustine condemned his writings and rejected the mystical and apocalyptic strands associated with his literature. For example, Augustine wondered, "Does not the canonical epistle of Jude the apostle openly declare that Enoch spoke as a prophet? It is true that his alleged writings have never been accepted as authoritative, [n]either by Jews or Christians, but that is because their extreme antiquity makes us afraid of handing out as authentic works [that] may be forgeries."[85]

CONCLUSION

When looking at all these examples of references to Enoch in the Old Testament and the Second Temple period, we see the rising importance of Enoch far beyond the brief mention of him in Genesis. He becomes a glorious personage who has special connections with the heavens but who still maintains contact with earthly inhabitants, often acting as a mediator for them. He is closely connected with the story of the Watchers because he tries to thwart the wickedness that eventually leads to the Flood. Enoch is the scribe *par excellence* whose writings, visions, and prophecies not only have been transmitted through the ages among his descendants but have also played a role in the heavenly judgment scene. Enoch's rising prominence even leads some Jewish groups to see him as another power in heaven, a lesser YHWH. Among early Christians, Enoch was also a prominent figure, although his prestige declined in western Christianity after the fourth century AD. However, among eastern Christians, especially Ethiopic Christianity, Enoch maintained his special status as they used these texts to teach about judgment and mystical traditions in order to connect with God.

When we compare the Latter-day Saint Restoration scriptures about Enoch with these other texts, we see that they also amplify the role of

84. Iranaeus, *Against Heresies*, book IV, chapter 16.2. The Latin word used by Irenaeus for "translated" is *translatus* and is probably derived from the Greek *μετετέθη*.

85. Augustine, *City of God*, 18.38.

Enoch among his people. We get much more detail about his great ministry here on earth as a prophet and seer and more about his heavenly duties. Enoch was a man of visions, which led him to preach repentance and see the future events of the world. Like the other texts, the Pearl of Great Price highlights Enoch's conflict with the giants, his translated state, his intimate knowledge of the heavenly court, his role as mediator for others, his visions of the future Son of Man, and his scribal role of writing down his prophecies for his descendants. Restoration scriptures go on to emphasize Enoch's connection with priesthood—the order of the priesthood was even called after Enoch (Doctrine and Covenants 76:57)—and the attendant powers associated with the priesthood. Covenants, priesthood, and commissions were granted to Enoch and transmitted to his posterity, most notably to Noah. In the end, Enoch is held up as the righteous model that all should aspire to be in order to create Zion societies here on earth that can be accepted by God in heaven. Enoch was successful in raising up a corporate body to the Lord, which was the original intention of God's commandments—so the Lord could walk among the people and be their God. Likewise, we are all encouraged to walk with God and prepare for the last days, when the righteous will be gathered in one heart and one mind. May we heed Joseph Smith's admonition to follow the example of our great ancestor, Enoch:

> Let the Saints remember, that great things depend on their individual exertion, and that they are called to be coworkers with us and the Holy Spirit, in accomplishing the great work of the last days, and in consideration of the extent, the blessings and glories of the same, let every selfish feeling, be not only buried, but annihilated; and let love to God and man, predominate and reign triumphant in every mind, *that their hearts may become like unto Enoch's of old*, and comprehend all things, present, past, and future, and come behind in no gift waiting for the coming of the Lord Jesus Christ.[86]

Thanks to revelation received through the Prophet Joseph Smith, we once again enjoy the teachings of Enoch and the prominence that other

86. "History, 1838–1856, volume C-1," p. 1118; emphasis added.

communities ascribed to him as reflected in their literatures. But beyond commonalities and certain similarities existing between the literatures through time, the Lord has helped us understand Enoch's ancient connection to the priesthood, the veracity of his life in ancient times and his relevance to future times, the influence covenants and obedience can have on communities that obtained heaven anciently, and the inspiration their experiences can have on developing such communities in the present. We learn of templates of salvation and God's work in the past, present, and future in order to develop individuals who can obtain heaven and who can, once again, "walk with God."

THE RAINBOW AS A TOKEN IN GENESIS

COVENANTS AND PROMISES IN THE FLOOD STORY

AARON P. SCHADE

Though most readers are probably familiar with the story of Noah and the flood, they may not know that flood stories circulated throughout the ancient Near East, which resulted in a body of literature discussing a great deluge. Moreover, Restoration scripture and prophetic commentary offer further insights into the purposes of the biblical narrative as well as the symbols used throughout that narrative. In particular, the Latter-day Saint material reveals the relationship between the flood account and the Enoch narrative that preceded it. The result is the fulfillment of a covenant that preserves and binds God's children and family within the template of salvation. —DB and AS

If you were to ask the question "What is the meaning of the rainbow in the flood story?," a common response would be the following: "The rainbow represented a promise from the Lord assuring his people that he would never again send a flood to destroy the earth." This response is, of course, correct; however, such an explanation only constitutes part of the story. Many Bible scholars recognize the role that flood narratives have in constructing a universal theme of salvation,[1] and Restoration scripture also contributes to this theme by defining the relationship between Noah and the flood and the stories of Enoch. Defining this relationship also explicitly highlights the continuity of the priesthood and the covenant from the preflood community up to Abraham and his seed and beyond. As such, the flood narratives are more than a resetting of human history—they are a narrative in which humans' covenantal relationship with God is firmly established.[2] With this covenantal focus in mind, this chapter

---

1. See, for example, Bruce K. Waltke, *Genesis: A Commentary* (Grand Rapids, MI: Zondervan, 2001), 156; R. W. Moberly, *Old Testament Theology: The Theology of the Book of Genesis* (New York: Cambridge University Press, 2009), 110, 120; Gordon J. Wenham, *Genesis 1–15*, Word Biblical Commentary 1 (Dallas: Word Publishing, 1987), 156–57, 206–7; John E. Hartley, *Genesis*, New International Biblical Commentary (Peabody, MA: Hendrickson, 2000), 100; Bill T. Arnold, *Genesis*, New Cambridge Bible Commentary (New York: Cambridge University Press, 2009), 104.
2. Bible scholarship generally speaks of multiple flood accounts in Genesis, often labeled P (Priestly) or J (Yahwistic), that preserve various details of the flood that are not always complementary. For example, Genesis 6:19–20 and 7:15–16 speak of taking two animals of every kind into the ark, and Genesis 7:2–3 requires Noah to take seven pairs of clean animals and one pair of unclean animals with them. Genesis 7:24 and 8:3 talk of it taking 150 days for the flood waters to rise and another 150 for them to recede, along with a drying period that takes even more time, over a year, to complete. Genesis 7:4 describes seven days of waiting, followed by forty days of flooding. Bible scholars generally attribute such differences to the agendas of various writers, details of the story that were particularly important to each writer, and what they wanted the reader to know about a given episode. Apparent discrepancies need not throw us into testimonial panic, as they do not invalidate the underlying purposes of the stories. In fact, sometimes the discrepancies help us comprehend significant details that we would not otherwise perceive had we only been working with a single description. In contrast to a focus on multiple authorship, rather than assigning disunity, many studies now focus on the unity of the biblical flood

explores the flood in relation to ancient Near Eastern literature, to biblical scholarship, and, most importantly, with the unique insights provided by Restoration scripture. This chapter then concludes that the story of Noah and the flood offers a covenantal picture of salvation that would bridge heaven and earth and link generations of people to the presence of God, as symbolized within the token of the rainbow.

Comparative analyses of ancient Near Eastern flood accounts with the Bible have been conducted, among other things, for exegetical purposes that examine the influence that one source may have had upon another.[3]

---

account, highlighting that it has deliberately been worked and situated to effectively convey the message of salvation that has been aligned in chiastic fashion. See G. J. Wenham, "The Coherence of the Flood Narrative," *Vetus Testamentum* 28 (1978): 336–48; see also Wenham, *Genesis 1–15*, 155–58; Bruce W. Waltke, *Genesis: A Commentary* (Grand Rapids, MI: Zondervan, 2001), 125–26. Thus, the multiplicity of elements used to tell the flood story highlights important features of the message (often paralleling accounts of creation), the construction of the tabernacle, and the deliverance of the covenant codes on Mount Sinai. Despite the various proposals as to the central events that are used to form these chiastic structures, what is almost universally agreed upon is that God and salvation are the focal points of the story. See John H. Walton, *Genesis: The NIV Application Commentary* (Grand Rapids, MI: Zondervan Academic, 2001), 315. In the words of a prominent Bible scholar, who discusses the variations in storyline, "While it may seem odd to us at first that an editor retained such discrepancies, we may assume that the sources or traditions underlying the whole had already attained authoritative status, and the editor valued the traditions enough to retain the inconsistencies, which were not problematic in ancient literature." Bill T. Arnold, *Genesis*, The New Cambridge Bible Commentary (Cambridge: Cambridge University Press, 2009), 97. It is probably unrealistic of us to believe that the oral and written traditions that have been circulating for thousands of years would exist without any internal variations, and if the text were formed to execute a chiasm, the variations would serve a deliberate theological purpose. As canonized scripture, the stories we find in the Bible are accepted as the word of God with applications and relevance not only for ancient cultures but also for us today. Restoration scripture adds an additional testimony to the truthfulness of these events.

3. For a description of how Mesopotamian flood accounts may have affected the development of Babylonian flood stories, see Y. S. Chen, "Major Literary Traditions Involved in the Making of Mesopotamian Flood Traditions," in *Opening Heaven's Floodgates: The Genesis Flood Narrative, Its Context, and Reception*, ed. Jason Silverman, Biblical Intersections 12 (Piscataway, NJ:

One purpose of this paper is to examine the biblical flood through the lens of another source: the Restoration and its scripture. In taking this approach, I acknowledge that I am deviating from conventional scholarly consensus and practice in approaching the flood narratives. I am deliberately drawing upon Restoration scripture, such as the Book of Moses, the Doctrine and Covenants, and modern-day texts from prophets and apostles that are admittedly not a part of the standard academic repertoire. Nonetheless, these texts constitute scripture and canonized sources that have been legitimized by The Church of Jesus Christ of Latter-day Saints and are thus used as significant sources throughout this study in conjunction with the Bible.

Gorgias Press, 2013), 141–90. There have been many scholarly debates as to the source and composition of the flood stories contained in the Bible. For example, as mentioned above, the two similar but differing stories we encounter in Genesis, which each seem to have different focal points and concerns, are sometimes attributed to a Priestly source (P) and a Yahwistic (J) source, thus each story derives from separate authors. For a discussion on theories surrounding these sources, see John Day, *From Creation to Babel: Studies in Genesis 1–11* (New York: Bloomsbury, 2013), 102–12. On the other hand, other studies conclude, partially as a result of chiastic structures extant in the accounts mentioned above, that the apparent separate stories form a literary coherence, bound together to form a literary whole, and thus they discuss a *final form* of the text with a deliberate theological purpose. See, for example, J. A. Emerton, "An Examination of Some Attempts to Defend the Unity of the Flood Narrative in Genesis, Part I," *Vetus Testamentum* 37, no. 1 (1987): 402; Gordon J. Wenham, "Coherence of the Flood Narrative," *Vetus Testamentum* 28 (1978): 342–45; Kenneth A. Mathews, *Genesis 1–11:26*, The New American Commentary 1A, ed. E. Ray Clendenen (Nashville: Broadman & Holman, 1996), 354–55; Gordon J. Wenham, *Genesis 1–15* Word Biblical Commentary 1 (Dallas: Word, 1987), 167. In describing the elements used to compose the final form of the flood story, Wenham, *Genesis 1–15*, 157, speaks of the story falling into natural halves, framed by Noah entering and exiting the ark and the rising and falling of the flood waters. Again, the theme is God's salvation and deliverance, not an ad-hoc mishmash of sources that have magically come together with such coherency. We thus find deliberate "'epic repetition' and 'chiastic coordination.' Thus, far from being a haphazard mixture of two divergent accounts of the flood, the end result of the narrative composition 'looks as if it has been made out of whole cloth.'" John H. Sailhamer, *Genesis*, The Expositor's Bible Commentary, (Grand Rapids, MI: Zondervan Academic, 2008), locs. 4519–20 of 10676, Kindle. See also Wenham, *Genesis 1–15*, 168–69.

ANCIENT FLOOD STORIES

Flood stories began emerging in the ancient Near East as early as the twentieth to the seventeenth centuries BC.[4] Sumerian and Old Babylonian versions of flood stories, in the form of *The Tale of Ziusudra* (ca. 2000 BC), the *Epic of Gilgamesh* (ca. thirteenth and seventh centuries BC), and *Atrahasis* (ca. 1700 BC), were in circulation before the time of Moses.[5] Because of the circulation of these stories throughout the region, it is possible that while Moses was recording his revelations of the biblical record of the flood, a process possibly derived from both written and revelatory communication, he might have had at least some exposure to oral or written traditions of other Near Eastern flood stories from around the region in which he was raised.[6] This does not mean that Moses drew upon those sources for the composing and recording of the biblical flood account, but it simply implies that floods and flood stories constituted historical realities in various forms that numerous civilizations recorded and from which they found meaning.[7] Regardless of the similarities or differences between

---

4. See, for example, John Collins, *Introduction to the Hebrew Bible* (Minneapolis, MN: Augsburg Fortress, 2004), 30–36; Stephanie Dalley, trans., *Myths from Mesopotamia: Creation, the Flood, Gilgamesh, and Others* (Oxford: Oxford University Press, 1989), 3.
5. For a convenient translation of some of these stories, see W. W. Hallo and K. L. Younger, eds., *Canonical Compositions from the Biblical World*, The Context of Scripture 1 (Leiden: Brill, 2003).
6. The Book of Moses describes such revelatory knowledge of the events of the flood. Therein we witness Enoch (who beholds the impending flood and the ministry of Noah), his story that Moses was then recording, and, subsequently, the story that the Prophet Joseph Smith received by revelation.
7. There are "minimalist" and "maximalist" views that either trace the parallels between the biblical flood stories and the Mesopotamian accounts back to a common tradition or attempt to describe the Genesis account as a "deliberate rewriting of the Mesopotamian versions of the flood story" (Wenham, *Genesis 1–15*, 168). Such a genetic relationship of the ancient accounts seems improbable due to "the obvious similarities and the clear differences between the Mesopotamian and biblical stories of the flood. We do believe the origin of these stories is in an actual devastating flood, and this fits with our understanding of Genesis 6–9 being theological history. This event embedded itself in the minds of the people who lived through the experience." Tremper Longman III and

these accounts (and there are many differences between the extrabiblical and biblical texts), the various versions (including the biblical one) preserve and establish the relevance of flood stories in these ancient cultures' religious conceptions by describing gods who act, react, and interact with

---

John H. Walton, *The Lost World of the Flood*, The Lost World Series (Downers Grove, IL: InterVarsity Press, 2018), 86. Attempting to claim that all the ancient accounts originate from one another is problematic, since "the differences are too extensive to allow confident claims that they must be narrative reflections of the same event." Walton, *Genesis: The NIV Application Commentary*, 319. Traditions of floods were widespread throughout the region. "Excerpts from the *Gilgamesh* flood tradition have been recovered at Megiddo (modern Tell al-Mutasallim) in Canaan (fourteenth century) and at Emar (modern Meskene) in Syria (thirteenth century)." Brian B. Schmidt, "Flood Narratives of Ancient Western Asia," in *Civilizations of the Ancient Near East*, ed. Jack Sasson (Peabody, MA: Hendrickson, 2000), 3:2343. Despite all the differences in transmission of flood narratives from society to society, their predominance suggests that a flood or multiple floods of enormous magnitude at some point affected their worlds and were a part of these ancient cultures' experiences, and they describe the various ways in which these floods may have manifested themselves from region to region. See discussion in Longman and Walton, *Lost World of the Flood*, 145ff. These flood stories convey different messages and were written to serve different purposes; however, there seems to have been a common theme of a divinely sent deluge with the purpose of destruction, as well as the re-creation and regeneration of life. The distribution of the accounts indicates that such flood stories were circulating in the region by the time of Moses. This is not to imply that Moses copied these verbatim but simply that such flood traditions were widespread and that Moses obtained, through revelation, details that God intended for him to understand about the nature and purpose of the biblical flood. "The flood stories from the ancient Near East and from around the world offer persuasive evidence that a flood of significant magnitude occurred and was remembered. The accounts from [the] ancient Near East are closest to the biblical account and help us to see how the Israelites would have understood the whole event differently from their neighbors." John H. Walton, *Genesis*, Zondervan Illustrated Bible Backgrounds Commentary (Grand Rapids, MI: Zondervan Academic, 2016), loc. 2326 of 10396, Kindle. It is these differences that highlight the salvation in the biblical flood account and the specific redemptive purposes of God that contrast other ancient flood stories. Additional revelation given to the Prophet Joseph Smith also helps clarify the matter.

humankind.[8] Depending on the audience and purpose of the writer, the stories highlight societal conceptions of deity and humankind's relationship to it, and the stories also describe mortals' quest for immortality, their ability to be saved from the destructions that were coming upon the earth, and mortals' potential to become deified. In the Bible, these themes revolve around obedience, repentance, covenant, and sacrifice, and the themes focus on God's attempts to save—not destroy. There are differences that set the biblical flood story apart from other Near Eastern literature that involve flood stories. The following analysis accepts the historicity and reality of the events of a great flood.

The contributions of modern-day revelation and Restoration scripture provide brilliant insights into the meaning and purposes of the biblical flood by augmenting and accentuating the specifics provided in the Genesis account, specifically with the reference to the rainbow as a token of the Noahic covenant. The rainbow, this celestial symbol in the heavens, has become a focal point in the story, a token of the covenant established between God and his creations. Further, the "[rain]bow and the signs of other biblical covenants consecrate already common events and invest them with new sacred significance."[9] Restoration scripture and prophetic commentary inform us that the rainbow became a token of the same covenant that can be traced back to Adam through Enoch and from Noah to the present.[10] It is thus imperative to understand the antediluvian cove-

---

8. For a comparison of the similarities and differences between biblical and Near Eastern flood stories, see John H. Walton, "Flood," in *Dictionary of the Old Testament: Pentateuch*, ed. T. Desmond Alexander and David W. Baker (Downers Grove, IL: InterVarsity Press, 2002), 315.

9. Waltke, *Genesis*, 146.

10. Some scholars have demonstrated a close association between creation and the flood. "The flood is the counterpart, the alternative to creation," and "God's covenant with Noah and his descendants, including the post-Flood generation . . . renews basic confidence in the regulation of creation that had been breached." Othmar Keel and Silvia Schroer, *Creation: Biblical Theologies in the Context of the Ancient Near East* (Winona Lake, IN: Eisenbrauns, 2015), 154–55. The flood story was a re-creation with Noah and his family, a continuation of the covenant. As one scholar put it, "If in fact this theme of the covenant between God and Noah (in promise, Genesis 6:18, and in realization, 9:8–17) was originally part of Israel's ancient priestly traditions, it has been given new theological

nant that Enoch entered into in order to understand how it plays a crucial role in the covenant established with Noah. We get no better glimpse of this role than through Restoration scripture. As will be seen, the Book of Moses includes an additional focus on Enoch's future role and return with the Lord at his Second Coming (Moses 7:63).[11] With the covenant

---

significance by its present location in the canon. The final editors of the book of Genesis have retained the theme, no doubt because Noah's covenantal righteousness resulted in salvation for him, his family, and the animals, and probably also because this theme was already widely accepted and venerated as an authoritative explanation of the events. But the editors have also amplified the covenant theme by including it soon after the narratives of human origins (sin in the Garden of Eden, and Cain's murder of Abel, Genesis 2:4–4:16) and after the descriptions of the sinful human condition (6:5 and 6:11–12). By means of contrast with the unrighteousness of humanity at large, Noah's covenant with God is given fuller meaning. Covenant living is not only the means of survival (i.e., salvation) from the flood, but also the Bible's answer to humanity's sinful nature more generally. In this, and in other ways, Noah's covenant anticipates and previews the covenant between God and Abraham, as we shall see. Righteous covenant-living will be highlighted as Israel's hope for salvation, nationally and individually." Arnold, *Genesis*, 100–101. This covenant has also been described to form the backbone of the Sinai experience with Moses, the construction of the tabernacle, and the covenants the Israelites received. Additionally, Noah's covenant with God also became the backbone of stories in the New Testament, where themes of covenant and the ordinances of baptism are rooted in stories of the flood (compare 1 Peter 3: 21). See discussion in Sailhamer, *Genesis*, loc. 4430 of 10676, Kindle.

11. Additionally, "In later post-Persian works Enoch becomes the example of a prophet of the quasi-eschatology of the flood (cf. 1 En 106–7; Gen Apoc col. 1–2). He forecasts not just the deluge but all future history, especially in the Animal Apocalypse (1 En 85–90). Significantly, late Second Temple interpreters considered this ancestor from the *beginning* of Israel's story to be the logical recipient of revelation about the *end* of Israel's story. Lying in the background is the ancient conviction that the primordial past holds the key to the present and the future; Enochic *ex eventu* prophecies review history in order to order current life and point to the end." Jonathan Huddleston, *Eschatology in Genesis* (Tübingen: Mohr Siebeck, 2012), 190–91. Enoch's connection with his near and distant future helps to contextualize the visions and teachings he receives, as presented in the Book of Moses, and to find some conceptual parallels in the Enochian literature composed in the post-Persian period. See chapter 3 in this volume.

Noah received through Enoch and with Enoch's appearance at the Second Coming, the description of this covenant holds a quintessential position in understanding the gospel during the patriarchal age and acts as a bridge to the current dispensation in its covenantal context—Enoch being a key figure in the equation as well as in our understanding of Noah and the flood.[12]

---

12. In describing the logistics of the dating of the flood, very little may be said with certainty. Some have theorized that "the flood tradition owes its start to the cataclysmic events in the Neolithic Period (5500 BCE), when, with the melting of the polar ice caps, the Mediterranean Sea rose to catapult water across the Bosporus, turning a freshwater lake into the Black Sea. The population displaced by that catastrophe is presumed to have carried memories of this flood to the wider ANE and beyond." J. David Pleins, "Flood," in *The New Interpreter's Dictionary of the Bible*, volume 2: *D–H* (Nashville: Abingdon Press, 2007), 465. Sumerians divided their history into periods that occurred before and after the "Great Flood," and, based on the records, some Assyriologists reckon such an event as occurring around 2900 BC. See K. A. Kitchen, *On the Reliability of the Old Testament* (Grand Rapids, MI: Eerdmans, 2003), 426. "Some modern scholars believe this division reflects the memory of an inundation that occurred some 10,000 years ago at the end of the Ice Age, when huge portions of land were covered by what are now the waters of the Persian Gulf. It was this cataclysmic event, they believe, that later became transfigured in myth." Stephen Bertman, *Handbook to Life in Ancient Mesopotamia* (New York: Oxford University Press, 2003), 316. According to some Bible chronologies, the Creation occurred around 4000 BC, with the flood around 2400 BC. See Collins, *Introduction*, 11. The Bible Chronology in the appendix of the current Latter-day Saint edition notes "that many dates cannot be fixed with certainty," that "much work has still to be done in this direction," and that "the dates found at the top of many printed English Bibles . . . have been shown to be incorrect." I do not present these theories of Bible chronology as definitive, merely as theories. The so-called dilemma of dating the flood does not have to be a source of irritation but rather can be seen as the result of insufficient evidence that would speak conclusively one way or the other. Neither should the geographical, geological, or archaeological strata of the flood push us into minimalist or maximalist corners. We simply do not know how the surface of the earth changed or to what degree it was exposed subsequent to the flood (in relation to pre-flood conditions), and working without sufficient data, we should not jump to conclusions or revert to testimony panic. The fact of the matter is, answering these questions in scientific terms is a modern application of science. Ancient civilizations would most likely have not found significance in the question and would have viewed the events through a different lens,

PRELUDE TO THE FLOOD—THE STATE OF AFFAIRS

The Bible and the Book of Moses describe the people of Noah's day in the following manner:

Genesis 6:5–7, 13	Moses 8:22–26, 30
5 And God saw that the wickedness of man was great in the earth, and that every imagination of the thoughts of his heart was only evil continually.	22 And God saw that the wickedness of men had become great in the earth; and every man was lifted up in the imagination of the thoughts of his heart, being only evil continually. *23 And it came to pass that Noah continued his preaching unto the people, saying: Hearken, and give heed unto my words;* *24 Believe and repent of your sins and be baptized in the name of Jesus Christ, the Son of God, even as our fathers, and ye shall receive the Holy Ghost, that ye may have all things made manifest; and if ye do not this, the floods will come in upon you; nevertheless they hearkened not.*
6 And it repented the *Lord* that he had made man on the earth, and it grieved him at his heart.	25 And it repented *Noah*, and his heart was pained that the Lord had made man on the earth, and it grieved him at the heart.
7 And the Lord said, I will destroy man whom I have created from the face of the earth; both man, and beast, and the creeping thing, and the fowls of the air; for it repenteth me that I have made them.	26 And the Lord said: I will destroy man whom I have created, from the face of the earth, both man and beast, and the creeping things, and the fowls of the air; for it repenteth *Noah* that I have created them, and that I have made them; and he hath called upon me; for they have sought his life.

attempting to understand why it had happened and what purpose it served (i.e., the ontological meaning). See Longman and Walton, *Lost World of the Flood*, 321ff. The issue does have theological implications and has led to numerous interpretations. The scriptures attest to a flood with its attendant cause and purpose, without providing the specific details of the history or science behind it. This paper works in accordance with the scriptural and prophetic records that state that a flood did indeed happen.

Genesis 6:5–7, 13	Moses 8:22–26, 30
13 And God said unto Noah, The end of all flesh is come before me; for the earth is filled with violence *through them*; and, behold, I will destroy them *with the earth.*	30 And God said unto Noah: The end of all flesh is come before me, for the earth is filled with violence, and behold I will destroy all flesh *from off the earth.*[13]

Both accounts describe an awful scene of wickedness, violence, and the continually evil state of the thoughts and hearts of the people. Such behavior might suggest that the actions of the people had undone the Creation and its purpose in bringing to pass the "immortality and eternal life" (Moses 1:39) that God had designed for them. "Indeed, what God decided to 'destroy' (13) had been virtually self-destroyed already."[14] Genesis 6:13 describes that the violence came "through" the people, not from God. In

13. Italics here emphasize important differences and contributions made between Genesis and Restoration scripture of these passages.
14. David Clines, "Noah's Flood I: The Theology of the Flood Narrative," *Faith and Thought* 100, no. 2 (1972–73): 135. It is commonly accepted in biblical studies that the flood constitutes a re-creation of life, paralleling the context and language of the creation stories in Genesis. See, for example, Sailhamer, *Genesis*, loc. 4282 of 10676, Kindle, who discusses the flood story with the reversal of creation as given in its Edenic state but also with its immediate connections with the conditions of the Fall in Genesis 3. "The Flood defaces the original creation headed by Adam and cleanses the earth for its re-creation headed by Noah. Warren Gage notes striking parallels between the prediluvian and postdiluvian worlds, making Adam the father of humanity and Noah its father in the postdiluvian world." Waltke, *Genesis*, 127. The flood's preoccupation is with hope, salvation, and covenantal responsibility, rather than a total concentration on judgment and destruction. Later prophets in the Bible drew on language of the flood (such as *polluting* and *violence*) to foreshadow and describe Judah's impending destruction and exile, but they also used the story to highlight hope for a new start and "a 'new order,' introducing a 'radical change in the mechanism of sin.' Gen. 8:15–9:17 thus parallels prophetic descriptions of a new solution to the sin-punishment cycle that caused Judah's destruction." Huddleston, *Eschatology*, 141. "The creation has refused to be God's creation. That essential fracture between creator and creation is the premise and agenda of the flood narrative. This text provides a way to reflect on the meaning and cost of that fracture and upon the future that is yet in prospect between God and God's world." Walter Brueggemann, *Genesis*, Interpretation: A Bible Commentary

fact, the Moses account portrays Noah as God's messenger preaching repentance, baptism, and the reception of the Holy Ghost as a means to avert the flood waters that were to bring destruction as a result of the wickedness of the people, but "they hearkened not" (Moses 8:24). The Pearl of Great Price further describes the Lord's displeasure with this apostasy.[15]

---

for Teaching and Preaching (Louisville, KY: Presbyterian Publishing, 2010), 74. The story is about loss but also about gain.

15. Moses 6:28–29 seems to imply the possibility of this interpretation of an apostasy, and "Genesis documents the downward slide of humanity from the idyllic garden to the chaotic anarchy that introduces the Flood story. Violence has become an incorrigible way of life, and the waters are sent as an act of justice." Walton, *Genesis*, Zondervan Illustrated Bible Backgrounds Commentary, loc. 2307 of 10396, Kindle. Clines, "Theology," 133, concluded that "the 'violence' (*ḥamas*) 6:11, 13 . . . has religious overtones, for it is the violation of an order laid down or guaranteed by God." The Hebrew word translated as "violence" refers elsewhere to a broad range of crimes, including unjust treatment (Genesis 16:5; Amos 3:10), injurious legal testimony (Deuteronomy 19:16), deadly assault (Genesis 49:5), murder (Judges 9:24), and rape (Jeremiah 13:22). All of these would later be articulated in covenantal, priestly, and social codes of conduct. Later traditions and religious writings did indeed attribute the behavior of the people to apostasy, and this seems consistent with that which is presented in the Book of Moses. "[Fourth] Ezra (3:9–12) cites the pre-flood conditions as a stage of apostasy." Jack P. Lewis, "Flood," in *The Anchor Bible Dictionary*, ed. David Noel Freedman (New York: Doubleday, 1992), 801 and the Damascus Document from Qumran also seem to imply a form of apostasy: "For having walked on the stubbornness of their hearts the Watchers of the heavens fell; on account of it they were caught, for they did not follow the precepts of God. And their sons, whose height was like cedars and whose bodies were like mountains, fell. All flesh which there was in the dry earth decayed and became as if it had never been, for having realized their desires and failing to keep their creator's precepts, until his wrath flared up against them." Florentino García Martínez, "Interpretations of the Flood in the DSS," in *Interpretations of the Flood*, ed. Florentino García Martínez and Gerardus Petrus Luttikhuizen (Leiden, Netherlands: Brill, 1998), 87. There are also several ties with creation accounts, the Garden of Eden, and the flood story—stories tying obedience to God with the contrast of disobedience to him. "Throughout this story there are numerous ties to the creation account in Genesis 1. The intent is apparently to depict the great flood as a reversal of God's work of creation. In ch. 1 God prepared the good land for the man and his family. In the account of the flood, God takes back the good land because humankind acted corruptly and did not walk in God's way. The central themes introduced in these opening verses are divine

Subsequently, this text is filled with warnings against such a turning-away from the things of God and is filled with passionate, loving, and concerned pleas allowing us to comprehend that God, through his prophet, was calling the people to repentance and wanted to save his children from the course they were pursuing and the consequences it was bringing upon them:

Genesis 6:3–4	Moses 8:17–21
3 And the Lord said, My spirit shall not always strive with man, for that he also is flesh: yet his days shall be an hundred and twenty years.	17 And the Lord said unto Noah: My Spirit shall not always strive with man, for he shall know that all flesh shall die; yet his days shall be an hundred and twenty years; and if men do not repent, I will send in the floods upon them.
4 There were giants in the earth in those days; and also after that, when the sons of God came in unto the daughters of men, and they bare children to them, the same became mighty men which were of old, men of renown.[16]	18 And in those days there were giants on the earth, and they sought Noah to take away his life; but the Lord was with Noah, and the power of the Lord was upon him. 19 And the Lord ordained Noah after his own order,[17] and commanded him that he should go forth and declare his Gospel unto the children of men, even as it was *given unto Enoch.* 20 And it came to pass that Noah called upon the children of men that they should repent; but they hearkened not unto his words; 21 And also, after that they had heard him, they came up before him, saying: Behold, we are the sons of God; have we not taken unto ourselves the daughters of men? And are we not eating and drinking, and marrying and giving in marriage? And our wives bear unto us children, and the same are mighty men, which are like unto men of old, men of great renown. And they hearkened not unto the words of Noah.

judgment and God's gracious salvation." Sailhamer, *Genesis*, locs. 4279–82 of 10676, Kindle.

16. The mention of sons of God and daughters of men has led to theories paralleling Greek mythology and its unions between divine beings and human beings.

In the Moses account, we read of the warnings and calls to repentance and the declaration that the flood could be averted by turning back to the covenant. Perhaps this is highlighted in the term *giants*, which may not

---

See, for example, Barry L. Bandstra, *Reading the Old Testament: An Introduction to the Hebrew Bible* (Belmont, CA: Wadsworth Publishing, 1999), 74. It is clear from biblical studies that this view is commonly forwarded as a legitimate interpretation. Others seem to look at a symbolic interpretation. Simon B. Parker, "Sons of (the) God(s)," in *Dictionary of Deities and Demons in the Bible*, 2nd ed., ed. Karel van der Toorn, Bob Becking, and Pieter W. van der Horst (Grand Rapids, MI: Eerdmans, 1999), 796 stated, "It is clear that the author is summarizing traditional mythical material about divine-human unions as an illustration of the disorder that prevailed immediately before the flood." A recent study has examined the phrase "sons of gods," along with similar phrases in the Bible, and concluded that the expression could also be describing an attitude that envisages "having God as their father." Day, *Genesis 1–11*, 80. Keeping in line with the mode of thinking and links to an apostasy, it may be a possible solution to put this phrase within the realms of individuals who are designated and associated with keeping (sons or daughters *of God*) and breaking (sons or daughters of *men*) their covenants with God. See Moses 8:13–15 and the contrast used in these designations that describe hearkening and not hearkening to the voice of God. Although the text is fragmentary, the *DSS* "Genesis Apocryphon" (I QapGen, IQ20) VI line 20 uses the term "holy ones" in contrast with the "daughters of man" in the account about Noah. See Geza Vermes, *The Complete Dead Sea Scrolls in English*, rev. ed. (London: Penguin, 2004), 482. Although others have attempted to argue that these polar terms are about "believers" versus "unbelievers," this is not a generally accepted interpretation in biblical scholarship based on the phraseology present in the Old Testament and how it tends to be understood. Debates on the matter are not conclusive. Later Rabbinic and Christian interpretations viewed these groups in humanly fashion in efforts to avoid the implication of sexual relationships between angels and divine beings or humans. See Day, *Genesis 1–11*, 78. In the Old Testament these designated individuals, peoples whose specific characteristics are unknown in the few environments in which they are described, are generally described in negative terms as great people (kings and warriors) who are doing bad things and in opposition to God or his people. See Walton, *Genesis: The NIV Application Commentary*, 297ff. These verses appear to describe a situation based on obedience/disobedience to the laws of God. See the discussion in John E. Hartley, Genesis, New International Biblical Commentary (Peabody, MA: Hendrickson, 2000), 95–96; Day, *Genesis 1–11*, 77–80.

17. "The Lord ordained Noah after his own order. In other words, the Lord ordained Noah to 'the Holy Priesthood, after the Order of the Son of God.'"

have reference to tall people but rather to *apostates* who had fallen from the truth (i.e., the "lapsed") and who were then violently seeking Noah's life.[18] The word used in the Genesis text to mean "giants" (נפל *npl*)—a root meaning "to fall," perhaps as in "fallen one"—describes the behavior of apostasy that resulted in the people disobeying the precepts of God and thus falling. Nevertheless, the etymology of the word and the interpretation used in this context is uncertain, but, as described in the previous note, the interpretation generally refers to these individuals negatively.[19]

Jeffrey M. Bradshaw and David J. Larsen, *In God's Image and Likeness 2: Enoch, Noah, and the Tower of Babel* (Salt Lake City: The Interpreter Foundation and Eborn Books, 2014), 228.

18. The translation of this word has been notoriously problematic and is charged with mythological meaning. See the discussion in D. Mangum, M. Custis, and W. Widder, *Genesis 1–11* (Gen. 6:1–22) (Bellingham, WA: Lexham Press, (2012). The Hebrew and Greek words נְפִלִים and γίγαντες, respectively, are generally translated as the word "giants" (see F. Brown, S. R. Driver, and C. A. Briggs, *Enhanced Brown-Driver-Briggs Hebrew and English Lexicon* [Oxford: Clarendon Press, 1977], 658) and are often interpreted in light of traditions associated with Greek mythology and a race of giant warriors or even semi-gods who were lost in major battles and imprisoned in the region of the dead. However, "giants—The term in *Hebrew* implies not so much the idea of great stature as of reckless ferocity, impious and daring characters, who spread devastation and carnage far and wide." R. Jamieson, A. R. Fausset, and D. Brown, *Commentary Critical and Explanatory on the Whole Bible* (Oak Harbor, WA: Logos Research Systems, 1997), 1:21. The interpretation of the *Nephalim* as "fallen ones" seems to work in terms of individuals who had "fallen and were no more," in this case, ones who have fallen spiritually. See Day, *Genesis*, 83. Whatever the etymology, the description of the term in the flood story implies that the *Nephalim* "contributed to the increasing state of wickedness." Hartley, *Genesis*, 97.

19. The mention of Enoch in these passages and the gospel given to him, which was then being preached to the people of Noah, provides an interesting clue to interpreting the story: "Enoch's escape from death is tied directly to the fact that he 'walked with God.' This phrase 'walked with God' describes a life of faithfulness and obedience to God. Noah too 'walked with God' and was 'a righteous man, blameless among the people of his time' (6:9). Abraham and Isaac, as faithful servants of God, also walked with God (24:40; 48:15). The repetition of the phrase in vv. 22 and 24 suggests it is the author's way of explaining why Enoch did not die. By means of subtle selectivity the author's purpose begins to emerge. Enoch found life and escaped the curse, death. In this brief episode the author uncovers a fundamental truth: Death is not the last word. In the face

In light of the rampant wickedness displayed by the people, what Moses 8:19–20 reveals is that God and his prophet Noah sought every means in their power to lead people to safety and righteousness.[20] God is not at fault, and through the passive use of the verb *šḥt* (the Niphal form) in Genesis 6:11–12, God is distanced from the cause of the flood (meaning that it is the wickedness of the people who brought this upon themselves). In contrast, by using the Hiphil causative verbal form from the same root (*šḥt*), God is highlighted as the cause of reversing and cleansing the corruption, just as the people are highlighted for being responsible for causing that corruption. The following parallel is taken from the Hebrew Bible:

> "The earth *was corrupt* in God's sight" (*šḥt*, in the Niphal, v. 11)
> "God saw that the earth *was corrupt*" (*šḥt*, in the Niphal, v. 12)
> "all flesh *had corrupted* its way" (*šḥt*, in the Hiphil, v. 12)
> "I am *going to destroy* them" (*šḥt*, in the Hiphil, v. 13)

"In a way difficult to express in English, the use of this Hebrew verb [*šḥt*] illustrates that God's actions are both unavoidable and just. Humanity has corrupted itself and therefore God declares humanity corrupt (i.e., 'destroyed')."[21]

---

of death one can, like Enoch, find life by 'walking with God.' In his focus on Enoch's fate (and faith), the author has found a door leading back to the tree of life (3:24). The door is faith and obedience, or, as later illustrated in the life of Abraham, to trust and obey. For Enoch the door opened because he 'walked with God. . . . For the author of Genesis, 'walking with God' is the way to life." Sailhamer, *Genesis*, locs. 3994–4003 of 10676, Kindle. The premise of the flood story is the contrast between obedience and disobedience and salvation and death.

20. "The text has built strong moral grounds for the flood based on the wickedness of humans and pathos of a just God. But again, it is the 'grace' (Hebrew *ḥēn*, NRSV's "favor") of Yahweh that intervenes. . . . Noah does not somehow limit God's plan but rather becomes the excuse God is seeking in order to avoid the disaster. Yahweh's approval of Noah turns the tide of evil and destruction. The one who is grieved at heart before the inevitable obliteration is the one with whom the single human being finds favor." Arnold, *Genesis*, 91. God is attempting to save in the story.

21. Arnold, *Genesis*, 99. Concerning the wickedness and violence that prevailed, and the impossibility "to deny the need for punitive action," Arnold, *Genesis*, 98

When one reviews chapters 6–8 of the Book of Moses, it is hard to overlook the efforts that were taken (by God and through Noah) to help the people repent and avoid the destruction of the flood. An example that highlights such efforts is in Moses chapter 7, wherein Noah's great-grandfather Enoch is described as being overcome by his vision of the people's eventual wickedness, followed by his desire to change their situation:

> And it came to pass that the God of heaven looked upon the residue of the people, and he wept; and Enoch bore record of it, saying: How is it that the heavens weep, and shed forth their tears as the rain upon the mountains?
>
> And Enoch said unto the Lord: How is it that thou canst weep, seeing thou art holy, and from all eternity to all eternity? . . .
>
> The Lord said unto Enoch: Behold these thy brethren; they are the workmanship of mine own hands, and I gave unto them their knowledge, in the day I created them; and in the Garden of Eden, gave I unto man his agency;
>
> And unto thy brethren have I said, and also given commandment, that they should love one another, and that they should choose me, their Father; but behold, they are without affection, and they hate their own blood; . . .
>
> But behold, their sins shall be upon the heads of their fathers; Satan shall be their father, and misery shall be their doom; and the whole heavens shall weep over them, even all the workmanship of mine hands; wherefore should not the heavens weep, seeing these shall suffer? (Moses 7:28–29, 32–33, 37)

God is heartbroken over his children, and Genesis 6:6 and Moses 8:25 depict both God and Noah being filled with pity toward the wicked state

---

explains, "On the one hand, Noah stands before God as one who brings a smile to God's face and fulfills the purpose for humanity's existence. On the other hand, the inevitability of the flood is not to be denied. . . . Noah's righteous presence changes everything and nothing; that is, it changes *nothing* about the need for an expression of God's justice, but it changes *everything* about our understanding of God's mercy. The justice of God demands that a flood occur, but the grace of God allows for an escape for Noah."

of the people (the KJV states "it repented the Lord"), underscoring the compassion that they possessed toward humankind.[22] With this in mind,

22. The verb used in expressing repenting ("it *repented* the Lord that he had made man on earth") is from the root נחם: see Brown, Driver, and Briggs, *Enhanced Brown-Driver-Briggs Hebrew and English Lexicon*, 636.2, which, besides repenting, has meanings such as to "be sorry," "be moved to pity," "have compassion (for others)," or "suffer grief or distress." See also J. Swanson, *Dictionary of Biblical Languages with Semantic Domains: Hebrew (Old Testament)* (Oak Harbor, WA: Logos Research Systems, 1997). The Arabic term نَحَمَ (*naḥama*) can mean to *breathe pantingly* and may help describe the exasperated anguish of both God and Noah, highlighting the compassion being depicted in the account where repentance is the desired outcome. The Lord is not repenting for creating his children; rather, he is about to have compassion on them and the state that they have created for themselves through their own wickedness. Genesis 6:6 uses parallel verbs pertaining to the fact that the Lord "was grieved to his heart" and was experiencing "emotional pain." *The NET Bible First Edition Notes* (Biblical Studies Press, 2006), Genesis 6:6. It is appropriate that Noah, whose name means, *to rest, give rest, settle, provide quiet, appease*, or possibly the nuance of *to comfort*, is called to cry repentance to the people. Jon D. Levenson, "Genesis," in *The Jewish Study Bible*, ed. Adele Berlin and Marc Brettler (Oxford: Oxford University Press, 2004), 21 states, "The sudden mention of Noah (v. 8)—whose Heb name ("*n-ḥ*") is "favor" ("*ḥ-n*") spelled backwards—indicates that human perversion and divine grief will not be the last word." Noah's father had given him the name because "this same shall comfort us concerning our work" (Genesis 5:29), and Noah's great-grandfather, Enoch, after viewing the flood that would come upon Noah's generation and who "refused to be comforted" (Moses 7:44), did indeed find some comfort witnessing the day of the Lord and the redemption of the world. Then Enoch received the following promise:

> And it came to pass that Enoch continued his cry unto the Lord, saying: I ask thee, O Lord, in the name of thine Only Begotten, even Jesus Christ, that thou wilt have mercy upon Noah and his seed, that the earth might never more be covered by the floods.
>
> And the Lord could not withhold; and he *covenanted with Enoch*, and sware unto him with an oath, that he would stay the floods; that he would call upon the children of Noah;
>
> And he sent forth an unalterable decree, that a *remnant of his seed* should always be found among all nations, while the earth should stand;
>
> And the Lord said: Blessed is he through whose seed Messiah shall come; for he saith—I am Messiah, the King of Zion, the Rock of Heaven, which is broad as eternity; whoso cometh in at the gate and

Genesis 6:7 and Moses 8:26 set the stage for covenantal restoration as they employ the language of Creation (*man*, *beast*, *creeping things*, and *fowls of the air*), which were about to be destroyed but not completely. In so doing, the story becomes one of salvation and creation rather than destruction and futility.[23]

PURPOSES OF THE FLOOD

Despite the significant nature of the flood and its abundance in other ancient Near Eastern texts, direct references to the flood of Noah's day in the Old Testament (and not just references to floodwater) do not abound with frequency.[24] Isaiah 54:9, Ezekiel 14:14, 20, Matthew 24:37–39, and

---

> climbeth up by me shall never fall; wherefore, blessed are they of whom I have spoken, for they shall come forth with songs of everlasting joy. (Moses 7:50–53)

Noah would indeed become a source of comfort and rest to his descendants (compare Moses 8:9). On the thematic wordplay on Noah evident in terms like *comfort* and *rest* in Moses 7-8, see Matthew L. Bowen, "'This Son Shall Comfort Us': An Onomastic Tale of Two Noahs," *Interpreter: A Journal of Mormon Scripture* 23 (2017): 266, where Bowen explains, "In the context of the narrative, Enoch's declaration '*I will refuse <u>to be comforted</u>*' clearly anticipates the formal etiology subsequently proffered in Genesis 5:29/Moses 8:9: 'And he called his name Noah, saying: This [son] *<u>shall comfort us</u>* [Hebrew *yĕnaḥămēnû*] concerning our work and toil of our hands, because of the ground which the Lord hath cursed.' . . . Enoch's 'refus[al] to be comforted' thus frames Noah's story in an entirely new way and helps us understand the 'comfort' which Lamech foresees (and which the Lord shows Enoch) [that] Noah will bring. Noah and his posterity—specifically his descendant Jesus Christ—will eventually bring 'comfort' and 'rest.'"

23. Moses 8:30 clarifies that the Lord would destroy all flesh "from off the earth" not "with the earth" (as Genesis 6:13 reads). The preservation of the earth, the covenant, and a family of covenant keepers provides the undergirding of the story.
24. Schmidt, "Flood Narratives," 2343 lists Ezekiel 14:14, 20 and Isaiah 54:9 as the only three references. For an overview of Flood references in biblical, Targumic, pseudepigraphic, and rabbinic sources, see Lewis, "Flood," 800–803. There it states, "Outside Genesis, biblical texts advert to a primordial flood and to isolated details of the Genesis narrative. . . . The word *mabbûl* occurs outside of

Luke 17:26, 27 discuss the flood in relation to wickedness and eventual salvation, and passages such as 2 Peter 2:5 and Hebrews 11:7 describe Noah as a preacher and heir of righteousness.[25] In this vein, however, recent scholarship and studies are noticing parallel nuances and phraseology between the flood account in Genesis and the prophetic prophecies pertaining to the destruction and restoration of ancient Israel and Judah.[26] Such studies are indicating that, despite the paucity of direct references to the flood in the Bible, the theology of the flood may be more prominent from an Old Testament perspective as a template of destruction and salvation than has previously been believed.

Genesis only in Ps 29:10, but the flood motif may be reflected in later sections of the Isaianic prophetic corpus." Schmidt, "Flood Narratives," 800.

25. See Lewis, "Flood," 801 for the prolific mention of Noah the person—rather than mentioning the flood—in biblical, apocryphal, rabbinic, and Christian traditions.

26. More and more, flood theology is postulated in modern scholarship through studies seeking similarities in phraseology and covenantal contexts identified in the book of Genesis. Parallels are being identified in Creation references in relation to impending destruction as a result of the breaking of covenants in books such as Amos, Jeremiah, Ezekiel, Habakkuk, and Isaiah. See, for example, Huddleston, *Eschatology*, 140–43; Gavin Cox, "The 'Hymn' of Amos: An Ancient Flood Narrative," *Journal for the Study of the Old Testament* 38, no. 1 (2013): 81–108. While not all the examples cited in these studies are, in my opinion, directly connected with the flood in Genesis, it is clear that a flood theology is becoming more recognized as existing in the Bible. Given the covenantal magnitude of what the original story represented in Genesis and in conjunction with its implications for the future, it seems that these studies are worthy of our consideration and attention. It is clear that the flood story was viewed with a present judgment, but the story also carried eschatological undertones related to the future, end of days, and restoration. Interestingly, the layout and language of the flood story, particularly in relation to the construction of the ark, has also been compared to the layout and terminology used in both the Creation account as well as in the construction of the tabernacle. These stories appear to form a thematic link with each other and highlight God's designs in providing deliverance and salvation through the covenant. See Sailhamer, *Genesis*, loc. 4345 of 10676, Kindle; Waltke, *Genesis*, 127–28, 152; Nicolas Wyatt, "'Water, Water Everywhere . . . ': Musings on the Aqueous Myths of the Near East," in *The Mythic Mind: Essays on Cosmology and Religion in Ugaritic and Old Testament Literature*, ed. Nicholas Wyatt (London: Equinox, 2005), 189–237.

Furthermore, recent scholarship has been challenging the conception that Abraham is the originator of the promises made from God to his children. Recent claims assert that Noah and the flood, not Abraham, are actually the point of a major break in the Bible (Genesis 1–11) and that we should be looking there for tracing the covenants that God made to his people.[27] The covenants made between God and Noah and his family will play a major role in this process: "Noah's righteousness resulted in a covenant with God that saved him and his family during the flood, and now God extends that salvation-covenant to all the living as a second chance for the world. These themes are forward looking, since all of this will recur in a crucial text of the Abrahamic narrative (Gen 17), including specific terminology. Just as covenant defines God's relationship with post-flood humanity generally, so covenant will define God's relationship with Israel's ancestors, and by extension, with Israel. . . . Noah's covenant anticipates and previews the covenant between God and Abraham."[28]

---

27. Thematic and stylistic similarities between the flood and covenant theology in the Bible "show that God's covenant at Sinai did not signal a new act of God. The covenant at Sinai was a return to God's original promises in creation. At Sinai, as in the past, God restored fellowship with humankind and called them back. The covenant with Noah plays an important role in the author's understanding of the restoration of divine blessing. It lies midway between God's original blessing of humankind at creation (1:28) and God's promise to bless 'all peoples on the earth' through Abraham (12:1–3). What all of these covenants have in common is a focus on the universal scope of the divine blessing (1:28; 9:10; 12:1–3)." Sailhamer, *Genesis*, locs. 4733–37 of 10676, Kindle. See also Arnold, *Genesis*, 1; Brueggemann, *Genesis*, 11; Theodore Hiebert, "Dividing Genesis: The Role of the Flood in Biblical History and the Shape of Israelite Identity" (address at SBL annual meeting, 25 November 2013). It has also been stated that the human family was "in unity growing out of its descent from Noah." John H. Tullock and Mark McEntire, *The Old Testament Story*, 7th ed. (Upper Saddle River, NJ: Pearson Education, 2006), 46. Also, "the covenant with Noah is the foundation for rather than a prefiguration of the subsequent, sanctifying covenant begun with Abraham, given full form on Sinai, and completed on Golgotha. 'Be still before the Lord,' the covenant with Noah would seem to signal, 'and wait patiently for him' (Ps. 37:7)." R. R. Reno, *Genesis*, Brazos Theological Commentary on the Bible (Grand Rapids, MI: Brazos Press; Baker Publishing Group, 2010), 127.
28. Arnold, *Genesis*, 91, 101, 111.

The purposes of the flood are thus underscored by the hope in a redemptive God who is using the mechanism of the flood to paradoxically deliver salvation to the generations who had been built upon wickedness and who were the recipients of Noah's preaching. From the Fall in the Garden of Eden to the murder of Abel by Cain and to the wickedness and violence that prevailed through secret combinations and apostasy by the time of the flood, repentance was not being pursued, and the people were ripening for destruction (despite Noah's efforts to turn them back to the Lord's covenant). All that had been declared "good" by God in creation was now reversed and undone through wickedness.

> "The Lord saw" is a reversal of the positive evaluation of everything God created ([Genesis] 1:31): "God saw everything that he had made, and indeed, it was very good." Reference to the human "heart" (lēb, lēbāb) denotes more than one's emotions, as is often asserted, since the heart is also the seat of one's intellect and will.
>
> Humanity's heart is evil, and Yahweh's heart is broken (v. 6). The narrator exposes Yahweh's inner life as painfully grief-stricken and deeply distressed. "Pain" has become the common experience of all humans in this world (iṣṣābôn in 3:16, 17 and 5:29) and is paralleled by the anguish of God (the verb ʿṣb, "it grieved him," v. 6). The Bible's emotive language portrays no Aristotelian unmoved Mover, but a passionate and zealous Yahweh moved by his pathos into action. NRSV's "so the Lord said" might be better translated, "so the Lord decided" (v. 7), thus introducing his measured decree. Specific terms and themes of v. 7 combine the creation account of Gen 1 with the "man"-"ground" emphases of the Eden narrative, in order to show that all has been undone. The result is a divine decree that is both devastating and undeniably just. God's magnificent creation has been irrevocably ruined, and his passion and sorrow drive God into action.[29]

29. Arnold, *Genesis*, 91. "God is aware that something is deeply amiss in creation, so that God's own dream has no prospect of fulfillment. With that perverted imagination, God's world has begun to conjure its own future quite apart from the future willed by God (cf. 11:6). As a result, verse 6 shows us the deep pathos of God. God is not angered but grieved. He is not enraged but saddened. God does

Through the events leading up to the flood, God had been emotionally devastated by the behavior of his children, and, in an act of mercy and compassion, he decided to intervene with the intent to save through the waters of the flood. John Taylor insightfully remarked, "God destroyed the wicked of that generation with a flood. Why did He destroy them? He destroyed them for their benefit, if you can comprehend it."[30] The flood

---

not stand over against but with his creation. Tellingly, the pain he bequeathed to the woman in 3:16 is now felt by God. Ironically, the word for 'grieve' ('asaʋ) is not only the same as the sentence on the woman ('pain' 3:16), but it is also used for the state of toil from which Noah will deliver humanity (5:29). The evil heart of humankind (v. 5) troubles the heart of God (v. 6). This is indeed 'heart to heart' between humankind and God. How it is between humankind and God touches both parties. As Ernst Wiirthwein suggests, it is God who must say, 'I am undone.'" Brueggemann, *Genesis*, 77.

30. John Taylor, in *Journal of Discourses* (London: Latter-day Saints' Book Depot, 1854–86), 24:291. The flood as an element of compassion was also addressed in rabbinic literature: "Noah's story becomes the occasion for the rabbis to highlight God's compassion. Taking 120 years to build the ark, Noah has ample time to warn his hard–hearted compatriots of their doom. In hopes they would repent, God even tacks on an additional week at the end to give one last chance for repentance." Pleins, "Flood," 467. Elder Neal A. Maxwell stated that God intervened "when corruption had reached an agency-destroying point that spirits could not, in justice, be sent here." Neal A. Maxwell, *We Will Prove Them Herewith* (Salt Lake City: Deseret Book, 1982), 58; see also "The Flood Was an Act of Love," in *Old Testament Student Manual: Genesis–2 Samuel* (Salt Lake City: The Church of Jesus Christ of Latter-day Saints, 2003), 55–56. As difficult as the act may be to comprehend, John Taylor summarized what this calculated act of compassion in the form of the flood accomplished: "By taking away their earthly existence he [God] prevented them from entailing their sins upon their posterity and degenerating them, and also prevented them from committing further acts of wickedness." John Taylor, in *Journal of Discourses*, 19:158–59. Chrysostom, a fourth–fifth-century AD archbishop of Constantinople, referred to the destruction of the flood as "a strange form of loving kindness." R. W. L. Moberly, *Old Testament Theology: The Theology of the Book of Genesis* (New York: Cambridge, 2009), 111. Other Christian writings (like *Homilies on Gen. 28:4*), described the flood as an act of love that prevented further wickedness. According to Chrysostom, God said, "I brought on the deluge out of love, so as to put a stop to their wickedness and prevent their going to further extremes." Andrew Louth, ed., *Genesis 1–11*, in *Ancient Christian Commentary on Scripture: Old Testament*, ed. Thomas C. Oden (Downers Grove, IL: InterVarsity Press,

will become a powerful image of salvation and will be viewed through the lens of ordinances and associations with baptism and cleansing.

By 1835 some Church publications[31] began to portray the flood in terms of the baptism of the earth, reflecting and amplifying nineteenth-century Protestant teachings.[32] While some statements implied a sentient

2001), 1:154. The early Jewish retelling of the flood story (*1 Enoch* 1–36, *The Book of the Watchers*), "consistently presents the flood not primarily as a means of punishing the wicked, as in Genesis, but as an act accomplished by God on behalf of the righteous." Ryan E. Stokes, "Flood Stories in 1 Enoch," in *Opening Heaven's Floodgates: The Genesis Flood Narrative, Its Context, and Reception*, ed. Jason Silverman, Biblical Intersections 12 (Piscataway, NJ: Gorgias Press, 2013), 231.

31. W. W. Phelps, "Letter No. 9," *Latter Day Saints' Messenger and Advocate*, July 1835, 146. "Here Phelps mentions both a baptism and a cleansing of the earth from "her sins." While these may have been merely rhetorical moves, Phelps can also be seen as introducing, however preliminarily and unintentionally, an ambiguity into the discussion that still besets Mormon discourse. That is, though by "her sins" he likely referred to sins committed by mortals living on the earth, subsequent developments make his usage notable because it can be read as positing a sentient earth. This ambiguity, it turns out, would continue throughout the twentieth century in much of the Latter-day Saint discourse about the Flood." Hoskisson and Smoot, "Noah's Flood," 136–63.

32. By the nineteenth century, Protestant groups, for example, viewed the flood story through of lens of baptism. "C. F. Keil and F. Delitzsch, two highly influential German Protestant scholars of the second half of the nineteenth century, in a sophisticated analysis of 1 Peter 3, opined that the flood of Noah contained dual symbolism. On the one hand, according to Keil and Delitzsch, the flood represented 'a judgment of such universality and violence as will only be seen again in the judgment at the end of the world,' yet on the other, the flood was also an act of mercy which made the flood itself a flood of grace, and in that respect a type of baptism (1 Pet. iii. 21), and of life rising out of death. . . . As would be expected, there is considerable overlap between nineteenth-century Latter-day Saint and Protestant understandings of the flood as a cleansing of the earth of wickedness and therefore a symbolic prefiguring of Christian baptism. Yet Latter-day Saints seemed much more invested than Protestants in interpreting the flood as a literal ordinance, perhaps because the Restoration presents stronger forms of sacramentalism than Protestantism does." Paul Y. Hoskisson and Stephen O. Smoot, "Was Noah's Flood the Baptism of the Earth?," in *Let Us Reason Together: Essays in Honor of the Life's Work of Robert L. Millet*, ed. J. Spencer Fluhman and Brent L. Top (Provo, UT: Religious Studies Center and Neal A. Maxwell Institute for Religious Scholarship, 2016), 136–63.

earth, others simply made the connection between the flood and the concept of baptism.[33] By 1851 Elder Orson Pratt described a major purpose of the flood, connecting it with cleansing: "The first ordinance instituted for the cleansing of the earth, was that of immersion in water; it was buried in the liquid element, and all things sinful upon the face of the earth were washed away. As it came forth from the ocean floor, like the new-born child, it was innocent; it rose to newness of life. It was its second birth from the womb of mighty waters—a new world issuing from the ruins of the old, clothed with all the innocence of this first creation."[34]

From this perspective, the earth is seen as a living thing, and it was necessary for it to be baptized and move forward in its progression and preparations to receive its paradisiacal glory, and eventually, its celestial glory. Furthermore, in the Book of Moses, Enoch beheld the following, encompassing the baptism of the earth by water ("cleansed"), fire ("sanctify me"), and the millennial reign that would come upon it for "a season": "And it came to pass that Enoch looked upon the earth; and he heard a voice from the bowels thereof, saying: Wo, wo is me, the mother of men; I am pained, I am weary, because of the wickedness of my children. When

33. "The destruction of the Antediluvian world, by water, was typical of receiving remission of sins through baptism. The earth had become clothed with sin as with a garment; the righteous were brought out and saved from the world of sin, even by water; the like figure, even baptism, doth now *save* us, says Peter (1 Peter iii. 21). . . . Noah and family were removed, and disconnected from sins and pollutions, by *means* of water; so baptism, the like figure, doth now remove our souls from sins and pollutions, through faith on the *great* atonement made upon Calvary." Lorenzo Snow, *The Only Way to Be Saved* (London: D. Chalmers, 1841), 3–4.

34. Orson Pratt, in *Journal of Discourses*, 1:331; Joseph Fielding Smith, *Answers to Gospel Questions* (Salt Lake City: Deseret Book, 1980), 4:20. For a discussion on the argumentation in favor of the universality of the flood based on the language of the text, see Richard M. Davidson, "Biblical Evidence for the Universality of the Genesis Flood," *Origins* 22, no. 2 (1995): 58–73; "The Genesis Flood Narrative: Crucial Issues in the Current Debate," *Andrews University Seminary Studies* 42, no. 1 (2004): 49–77. For a brief summary of academic arguments for and against a universal flood, see J. C. Kuo, "Flood," in *The Lexham Bible Dictionary*, ed. J. D. Barry et al., (Bellingham: Lexham Press, 2012, 2013, 2014). Concerning the issue of the universality of the flood, the text seems to imply it, aligning with the representation of a baptism.

shall I rest, and be cleansed from the filthiness which is gone forth out of me? When will my Creator sanctify me that I may rest, and righteousness for a season abide upon my face?" (Moses 7:48).

In the end, an interpretation seems to imply that the template of baptism refers to the people on the earth rather than necessitating that the earth was a sinner and required baptism and that the comparisons and symbols between earth and people form an archetypal paradigm of progression.[35] Whether the flood was global or local, the earth will be cleansed and will eventually be prepared to become an abode for the righteous.

A NEW PERSPECTIVE

Interestingly, as we view the above verses through a salvific lens, we are here introduced to a different perspective.[36] Up to this point, we have witnessed the flood through the eyes of God and Noah. Now the earth is portrayed as speaking. These portrayals offer powerful symbols of salvation as Noah was coming before the flood to warn and call God's children to repentance, an effort of salvation and compassion on both his and God's part. The cleansing of the earth by water and fire would become necessary components leading up to its eventual celestialization, a preparation to become the abode of God's celestial family, and here the earth is depicted as calling for it. Interestingly, the apocryphal book of *1 Enoch* 7:6 and 9:2 also depict the earth bringing forth accusations against lawless ones and crying out up to the gates of heaven. Similarly, the Dead Sea Scrolls speak of the earth complaining and raising accusations to the heavens against

35. Hoskisson and Smoot, "Noah's Flood," 136–63. See Aaron P. Schade and Matthew Bowen, "Moses 8: Noah and the Flood," in *The Book of Moses: From the Ancient of Days to the Latter Days* (Provo, UT: Religious Studies Center, Brigham Young University; Salt Lake City: Deseret Book, 2021).

36. Restoration scripture gives us unique glimpses into the flood story through various eyes: God's, Enoch's, and Noah's. In Genesis, "the reader views the events solely from the perspective of the main characters. This means that we see the story only as those inside the ark saw it. Or, to say it differently, we don't see what they also don't see. There is no neutral corner from which the reader may safely view the events." Sailhamer, *Genesis*, locs. 4251–53 of 10676, Kindle. The Book of Moses sheds immense light on the flood story from various perspectives.

the people of the earth who have corrupted it.[37] From the earth's perspective, the flood is viewed through a salvific lens; the imagery of the destroying and cleansing nature of the flood waters along with the representation of the ark being taken to safety, provides a backdrop of salvation and covenantal rescue.[38]

The links of holy images attached to an ark are postulated in the early flood stories from Mesopotamia,[39] are in the Bible[40] and are developed in early Christian writings.[41] The ark is often viewed as a template of a temple,

---

37. See Richard D. Draper, S. Kent Brown, and Michael D. Rhodes, *The Pearl of Great Price: A Verse-by-Verse Commentary* (Salt Lake City: Deseret Book, 2005), 140. For a discussion on *1 Enoch* and the context of the earth's cries, see Stokes, "Flood Stories in Enoch," 235. See also chapter 3 in this volume.
38. See Cox, "Hymn," 97, 101–2 for the interpretation that later biblical writers such as Isaiah and Amos used the flood to project a theme of destruction and salvation through the development of a flood theology, and where the conclusion is reached that "the Noachian covenant involved salvation within the Ark of a faithful remnant." Cox, "Hymn," 97.
39. In Mesopotamian flood accounts, the boat is sometimes portrayed as being constructed by material from a holy shrine and constructed in the shape of a Ziggurat (a holy place of worship—possibly depicting the concept of divine deliverance). See Walton, "Flood," 316.
40. The word used for *ark* in the Old Testament occurs only in the flood story and for the container in which Moses was placed by his mother when she sent him down the Nile River in efforts of divinely rescuing him from death. The ark has also been interpreted as a functioning sanctuary. See Walton, "Flood," 322.
41. Early Christian traditions viewed Noah as a template of Christ, as well as another Adam, and the ark became symbolic of Christ's Church. See Louth, *Ancient Christian Commentary*, 131–35, and H. S. Benjamins, "Noah, the Ark, and the Flood in Early Christian Theology: The Ship of the Church in the Making," in *Interpretations of the Flood*, ed. Florentino García Martínez and Gerardus Petrus Luttikhuizen (Leiden, Netherlands: Brill, 1998), 131–35. These became powerful symbols of Christ's redemptive power and the necessity of entering his church clean (just as clean animals and righteous Noah entered the ark), which enabled a process of salvation. Subsequently, early Christian fathers, such as Justin, viewed the flood in line with 1 Peter 3:18–21 and the cleansing power of baptism. See Benjamins, "Ark," 136–40. The process entails coming to Christ, being cleansed through the waters of baptism, and entering his church in holiness. The description of clean animals has also been situated within priestly language and covenantal contexts. See Waltke, *Genesis*, 138.

and the "author of the Pentateuch uses the ark in the flood narrative to foreshadow the salvation that comes through the tabernacle and the covenant. Such a reading of this material reflects a similar understanding of this passage in 1 Peter 3:21. The ark prefigures the saving work of Christ as pictured in NT baptism."[42] In this view of salvation, "it is possible that the earth, in like manner and in preparation for eventual celestialization, was physically washed and symbolically cleansed so that it could become free from the blood and sins of the mortals who polluted its surface. So might the earth, like King Benjamin, metaphorically sing the praises of a just God for the flood of Noah that washed away the blood and sins of the generations who inhabited or will inhabit this earth,"[43] and part of the equation is that "the flood is interpreted primarily as an act of judgment meant to purify the earth."[44]

COVENANT RENEWAL

In conjunction with the paradigm of salvation, another important purpose of the flood was to fulfill and continue the covenants of the fathers:

> And it came to pass that Methuselah, the son of Enoch, was not taken, that the *covenants of the Lord might be fulfilled*, which he made to Enoch; for he truly covenanted with Enoch that Noah should be of the fruit of his loins.
>
> And it came to pass that Methuselah prophesied that from his loins should spring all the kingdoms of the earth (through Noah), and he took glory unto himself. (Moses 8:1–3; emphasis added)

42. Sailhamer, *Genesis*, locs. 4425–30 of 10676, Kindle. "Like the Tabernacle, Noah's Ark 'was designed as a temple,' and the Ark's three decks suggest both the three divisions of the Tabernacle and the threefold layout of the Garden of Eden. . . . Indeed, each of the decks of Noah's Ark was exactly 'the same height as the Tabernacle and three times the area of the Tabernacle court.'" Bradshaw and Larsen, *In God's Image and Likeness 2*, 126–28.
43. Hoskisson and Smoot, "Noah's Flood," 136–63.
44. Longman and Walton, *Lost World of the Flood*, 97.

The flood was foreseen as coming to cleanse the earth of its wickedness; and Methuselah was not translated (compare Moses 7:27) and taken to heaven with other righteous individuals so that the promises made to Enoch might be fulfilled and the covenant might be preserved, brought through the flood, and perpetuated by subsequent generations, rather than coming to an end with the flood. The relationship between the flood narrative and the continuity of the priesthood is strengthened further by JST Genesis 6:18: "But with thee will I establish *my covenant, even as I have sworn unto thy father, Enoch, that of thy posterity shall come all nations; and thou* shalt come into the ark, thou, and thy sons, and thy wife, and thy sons' wives with thee." It is within this framework that Noah is given the token of the rainbow to contextualize and place meaning to the covenant with reference to the flood that was coming: "Among the things revealed to Enoch was the knowledge of the flood, which was to take place. And the Lord made a covenant with Enoch, that He would set his bow in the cloud—just as it afterwards was given to Noah—not as a mere token alone that the Lord would no more drown the world, but as a token of the new and everlasting covenant that the Lord made with Enoch."[45] According to Orson Pratt in this interpretation, the rainbow became a token of the new and everlasting covenant (Genesis 9:16 states that it was a *bĕrît ʿôlām*—an everlasting covenant). How or why it is a suitable token is discussed next.

THE COVENANT AND THE TOKEN OF THE RAINBOW

The biblical account describes what happened subsequent to the flood in the following manner: "And God blessed Noah and his sons, and said unto them, Be fruitful, and multiply, and replenish the earth" (Genesis 9:1–3). Here we have allusions to the covenant language found in the Garden of Eden—specifically, references to the commandments pertaining to marriage (multiply and replenish the earth, followed by the concept of dominion over the other creations; Genesis 9:2–3). The details of the covenant continue as follows:

---

45. Pratt, in *Journal of Discourses*, 16:49.

> And I, behold, I establish my covenant with you, and with your seed after you;
>
> And with every living creature that *is* with you, of the fowl, of the cattle, and of every beast of the earth with you; from all that go out of the ark, to every beast of the earth.
>
> And I will establish my covenant with you; neither shall all flesh be cut off any more by the waters of a flood; neither shall there any more be a flood to destroy the earth.
>
> And God said, This *is* the token of the covenant which I make between me and you and every living creature that *is* with you, for perpetual generations:
>
> I do set my bow in the cloud, and it shall be for a token of a covenant between me and the earth.
>
> And it shall come to pass, when I bring a cloud over the earth, that the bow shall be seen in the cloud:
>
> And I will remember my covenant, which *is* between me and you and every living creature of all flesh; and the waters shall no more become a flood to destroy all flesh.
>
> And the bow shall be in the cloud; and I will look upon it, that I may remember the everlasting covenant between God and every living creature of all flesh that *is* upon the earth.
>
> And God said unto Noah, This *is* the token of the covenant, which I have established between me and all flesh that *is* upon the earth. (Genesis 9:9–17)

Several elements highlight the covenantal nature of these scriptural passages, of which the rainbow became a token.[46] First, the word "covenant" (*berit*) is repeated seven times in Genesis 9:8–17.[47] Second, in the

---

46. The covenant protects three fundamental issues explained in Genesis 9:1–7: "(1) the propagation of life (9:1, 7), (2) the protection of life, from both animals and humans (9:2a, 4–6), and (3) the sustenance of life (9:2b–3)." Waltke, *Genesis*, 143.

47. See Nahum M. Sarna, *The JPS Torah Commentary: Genesis* (Philadelphia: The Jewish Publication Society, 1989), 62. The number seven and its meaning may be associated with covenantal activities and the swearing of oaths. The Hebrew verb שָׁבַע "*swear, take an oath*," seems to derive from the word "seven,"

English translations of these verses, we have a variety of phrases describing "establishing" and "maintaining" covenants (9:9, 11). The Hebrew uses the root/form הקים (*hqym*) to convey this concept, which means to confirm or ratify pre-existing promises, oaths, vows, or covenants, and suggests that Noah is already in a covenant relationship with God and is thus not entering into a totally new one.[48] This highlights that Noah has brought a set of covenants through the flood that will link him to the fulfillment of covenants made between God and his great grandfather Enoch,[49] a continuity of the covenant that the Prophet Joseph Smith declared:

---

meaning "*seven oneself*, or *bind oneself by seven things*." Brown, Driver, and Briggs, *Brown-Driver-Briggs Hebrew and English Lexicon*; Swanson, *Dictionary of Biblical Languages*. A few possible examples of this may be found in Genesis 21:27–34; Numbers 22:37–23:3; 2 Kings 5:10–15. Thus, although such an etymology for swearing is not certain, it falls within the semantic domain of the word and appears to be a focal point in the story.

48. See Wenham, *Genesis 1–15*, 175. See also Arnold, *Genesis*, 110, who points out the use of *qwm*, instead of *kārat*, which is the verb usually employed in initiating a new covenant rather than ratifying a previously existing one (the duty of *qwm*). For a discussion on some of the complex issues surrounding the interpretation of the phraseology of covenants, as well as some pros and cons of the interpretation followed above, see Day, *Creation to Babel*, 123–36. For a possible link and development of a flood theology and applied phraseology in relation to covenant renewal in ancient Israel, see John H. Sailhamer, "Genesis," in *The Expositor's Bible Commentary: Genesis–Leviticus*, rev. ed, ed. Tremper Longman III and David E. Garland (Grand Rapids, MI: Zondervan, 2008), 131, where Genesis 8–9 is compared with Exodus 24:4–18 against the backdrop of Creation, salvation, deliverance, blessings, signs, and covenant renewal within the framework of the Israelites' exodus and reception of law codes in the desert.

49. Wenham, *Genesis 1–15*, 170, offers another interesting link between Enoch and Noah; they both "walked with God" (Genesis 5:22, 24; 6:9). "This phrase puts Noah on a par with Enoch (5:22, 24), the only other named individual to have walked with (התהלך את) God. . . . He walked with God like Enoch, the only man in Genesis to have been translated to heaven. Utnapishtim [Mesopotamian flood story] went to dwell with the gods after the flood, but Noah enjoyed God's close presence beforehand." Arnold, *Genesis*, 88, explains that the terminology "describes Noah as a an especially righteous individual (6:9), and connotes a life of consistent fellowship with God." Moses 8:27 states that Noah's sons also walked with God.

> Thus we behold the keys of this Priesthood consisted in obtaining the voice of Jehovah that He talked with him [Noah] in a familiar and friendly manner, that He *continued* to him the keys, the covenants, the power and the glory, with which He blessed Adam at the beginning. . . . The Priesthood was first given to Adam; he obtained the First Presidency, and held the keys of it from generation to generation. . . . He had dominion given him over every living creature. He is Michael the Archangel, spoken of in the Scriptures. Then to Noah, who is Gabriel; he stands next in authority to Adam in the Priesthood; he was called of God to this office, and was the father of all living in his day, and to him was given the dominion. These men held keys first on earth, and then in heaven.[50]

Part of that covenant revolved around never sending a destructive flood again, and this promise is explicitly connected to the token of the rainbow. "As a sign and guarantee of this covenant God placed a rainbow (*qeshet*, three times) in the clouds (*be'anan*, three times). The interweaving of these pivotal terms evokes the image of a beautiful tapestry of God's desire that all humans have confidence in divine mercy as they populate the earth. Moreover, in this way God fulfills the promise made to Noah before the deluge ([Genesis] 6:18)."[51] In its ancient Near Eastern context, the *bow* could be associated with war and devastation; however, "against this background, the rainbow in our narrative takes on added significance as a departure from Near Eastern notions. The symbol of divine bellicosity and hostility has been transformed into a token of reconciliation between God and man."[52] "The covenant with Noah in Genesis means that Yahweh sets aside His bow and hangs it up in the clouds as a sign that His anger has

---

50. "History, 1838–1856, volume C-1 [2 November 1838–31 July 1842] [addenda]," p. 18 [addenda], The Joseph Smith Papers; "Instruction on Priesthood, circa 5 October 1840," p. 8, The Joseph Smith Papers. As discussed, some scholars have also proposed the covenant made with Noah originated with Adam. See discussion in Day, *Genesis 1–11*, 123–36.

51. Hartley, *Genesis*, 110.

52. Nahum M. Sarna, Chaim Potok, Jacob Milgrom, and Jeffrey H. Tigay, *The JPS Torah Commentary: Genesis* (Philadelphia: Jewish Publication Society, 1989), 63.

subsided. When [people] gaze upon this rainbow, they feel assured that the storm has passed and no flood will come again; cf. Sir 43:11, 50:7."[53] In this light, the bow represents a reconciliation between God and his children's unrighteous state and establishes an environment of restitution before him. The rainbow is displayed for everyone to see and "provides a key to understanding many subsequent signs. A sign points to something larger and beyond itself. The rainbow, a divine covenant sign, joins other covenant signs like circumcision, Sabbath, baptism and the Lord's Supper, which are God-initiated."[54] In fact, the Hebrew word used for "sign" here (אוֹת [*ʾôṯ*] "sign," "token," or "pledge")—described as "a non-verbal symbol or signal which has meaning"[55]—can represent promises made between two parties in the form of pledges and seems to constitute and highlight that the biblical flood episode has covenant as a focal point between God and his creations, particularly with Enoch and Noah.[56] Significantly, here, אוֹת is a token that people will see but that also acts as a reminder to God that he will keep his covenants with the people (Genesis 9:15–16).[57]

---

53. J. Massyngberde Ford, *Revelation* (Garden City: Doubleday, 1975), 71. "It is true that Noah's flood is the only mabbul that the Bible acknowledges, but the use in Psalm 29 compared to the broader cultural usage suggests that the word may have had broader currency as a cosmic water-weapon wielded by deity." Walton, *Genesis: The NIV Application Commentary*, 313.
54. R. G. Branch, "Rainbow," in *Dictionary of the Old Testament: Pentateuch*, ed. T. Desmond Alexander and David W. Baker (Downers Grove, IL: InterVarsity Press, 2002), 667.
55. Swanson, *Dictionary of Biblical Languages*.
56. For a few examples of *ʾôṯ* in a pledge-covenantal context, see Genesis 9:12–13, 17; 17:11; Exodus 31:13, 31:17; Ezekiel 20:12, 20. "In Genesis the visible "sign" of the covenant is a rainbow in the "clouds" (*beʿānān*, 9:13–17); in Exodus the covenant is marked by the appearance of the glory of God in the "cloud" (*heʿānān*, 24:15) that covered the mountain." Sailhamer, *Genesis*, locs. 4728–30 of 10676, Kindle. "Thus, when the rainbow is viewed in light of the preceding Flood narrative, its appearance at the very moment when one can see both darkness and light in the sky comes to symbolize God's commitment to light over darkness, to beauty over chaos, to life over death." Moberly, *Theology*, 110–11.
57. Michael V. Fox, "The Sign of the Covenant: Circumcision in Light of the Priestly ʾôṯ Etiologies," *Revue biblique* 81 (1974): 557–96. "Because this covenant is the first one explicitly mentioned in Scripture, the rainbow is the first sign of a covenant. Later we will see that circumcision is the sign of the Abrahamic covenant

Viewing the bow as directly connected with war and reconciliation is not the only possible interpretation. For example, some scholars see the bow as a sign of the separation of the waters above from the waters below, a preventive act taken to ensure that the waters will not converge upon the earth again in a massive, all-encompassing deluge that destroys all creations: "A number of scholars have seen the deficiencies in the argument that the rainbow in Gen. ix represents God's war bow. . . . The rainbow is an appropriate sign of the covenant that God will not again cause the *mabbŭl* [flood] to destroy the earth. First, it is seen in the clouds after rain and thus recalls the occasion when the waters covered the earth. Secondly, it represents the *rāqîa*ʿ (firmament) which has been established to keep these waters at bay."[58]

Still other explanations of the origin of the bow link "a natural phenomenon after rain or thunderstorm" with the figurative use of the bow in parallel with God's "glory" or "splendor and appearance of God's glory" (Isaiah 21:16–17; Job 29:20; Ezekiel 1:1–3:15).[59] However one chooses to interpret the etymology and specific meaning attached to the bow, the text is clear that the rainbow has become a token of the covenant between God and Noah, God's creations, and power and salvation at the hand of

(Gen 17: 9–14), the sabbath is the sign of the Mosaic covenant (Ex 31:12–18), and the Lord's Supper is the sign of the new covenant (Lk 22: 20). These signs serve as reminders to the covenant partners of the relationship established between them. In the case of the rainbow, God says the sign will especially remind God of his commitment to his creatures, human and all other living creatures, to allow for continuity of creation by not bringing a flood again." Longman and Walton, *Lost World of the Flood*, 105–6.

58. Laurence A. Turner, *Vetus Testamentum* 43, Fasc. 1 (January 1993): 119–24. The word *rāqîa*ʿ, sometimes translated as "firmament," is also a term used in the Creation account, accentuating a re-creation to a state of innocence through the mechanism of the flood.

59. קֶשֶׁת, *Theological Dictionary of the Old Testament*, ed. G. Johannes Botterweck, Helmer Ringgren, and Heinz-Josef Fabry (Grand Rapids, MI: Eerdmans, 2011), 13:206–7. "The designation of the rainbow as a sign of the covenant does not suggest that this was the first rainbow ever seen. The function of a sign is connected to the significance attached to it. In like manner, circumcision is designated as a sign of the covenant with Abraham, yet that was an ancient practice, not new with Abraham and his family." Walton, *The IVP Bible Background*, 39.

God in the form of both destruction and deliverance.[60] "Nothing about the Flood is narrated for the sake of sensationalism but [rather] in order to assure the audience that there had been another salvation and that with this episode the last truly great crisis between gods and [humankind] was overcome."[61] The rainbow thus marked a positive outcome to the flood and symbolized a source of salvation via a pledge made between God and his creations. Noah has trusted and obeyed God, and he has been brought through the waters into life and salvation—against a backdrop of death and sin—a meaning that would be associated with cleansing and the concept of cleansing through baptism.

Joseph Smith's translation of Genesis 9 brings new insights into the significance of the rainbow's covenantal token, highlighting its association with gaining the presence of God: "And I will establish my covenant with you, which I made unto Enoch, concerning the remnants of your posterity."[62]

> And the bow shall be in the cloud; and I will look upon it, that I may remember the everlasting covenant, *which I made unto thy father Enoch; that, when men should keep all my commandments, Zion should again come on the earth, the city of Enoch which I have caught up unto myself.*
>
> *And this is mine everlasting covenant, that when thy posterity shall embrace the truth, and look upward, then shall Zion look downward, and all the heavens shall shake with gladness, and the earth shall tremble with joy;*
>
> *And the general assembly of the church of the firstborn shall come down out of heaven, and possess the earth, and shall have place*

60. "An eleventh-century Assyrian relief shows two hands reaching out of the clouds, one hand offering blessing, the other holding a bow. Since the word for rainbow is the same word as that used for the weapon, this is an interesting image." Walton, *The IVP Bible Background*, 39; Walton, *Genesis: The NIV Application Commentary*, 345.
61. Keel and Schroer, *Creation*, 154.
62. "Old Testament Revision 1," p. 24, The Joseph Smith Papers.

> *until the end come. And this is mine everlasting covenant, which I made with thy father Enoch.*
>
> *And the bow shall be in the cloud, and I will establish my covenant unto thee, which I have made* between *me* and *thee,* for every living creature of all flesh that *shall be* upon the earth.
>
> And God said unto Noah, This is the token of the covenant which I have established between me and *thee; for* all flesh that *shall be* upon the earth. (JST Genesis 9:17, 21–25)

Here Noah learned that as part of the fulfillment of the covenant, generations both in heaven and on earth would be reunited together. Just as Enoch and his city had been taken up into heaven, so would they return in the latter days to fulfill that covenant (possibly depicted in the ascending and descending arch at each end of the rainbow).[63] This understanding is also striking because it gives us glimpses into the covenantal meaning of the rainbow for God himself. The passage describing God's perspective, "And the bow shall be in the cloud and I will look upon it" (JST Genesis 9:17), seems to parallel the reunification of Zion and the Saints in his presence—the ultimate goal accomplished by and through the covenant. In essence, "God tells Noah he is . . . reaffirming the 'everlasting covenant' already established with Enoch and his predecessors. And that covenant,

63. We may not know all the reasons why the bow was chosen as the token, but perhaps the shape indicated an exit and a return, stretching "from earth to heaven and extend(ing) from horizon to horizon," demonstrating a totality and bridge between heaven and earth. Waltke, *Genesis*, 146. Some scholars have interpreted the rainbow to form a bridge between heaven and earth. See Moberly, *Old Testament Theology*, 110; Branch, "Rainbow," 668. Although on the periphery of the current point, it is interesting that Cox, "Ancient Flood Narrative," 89, while examining the development of a flood theology in the book of Amos, finds similarities in flood phraseology between biblical and Egyptian texts, which parallel "Egyptian temple—throne allusions," "inundations ascending up to the sky," and language that "describes ascent into the sky, then descent back to earth." The bow is used elsewhere to depict humans who had entered God's presence. "The rainbow was thought to typify the ancient connection between the world of the gods and the world of [humankind]. . . . The later Rabbis carried this thought further in their warning not to look at the rainbow." G. Kittel and W. G. Bromiley, eds., *Theological Dictionary of the New Testament* (Grand Rapids, MI: Eerdmans, 1966, repr. 1999), 3:340.

rooted in antiquity, anticipates the future merging of the celestial city (the general assembly of the church of the firstborn) with the earthly Zion, which is later developed into the concept of an eternal heavenly family bound together by temple covenants and the priesthood power of sealing."[64]

Just like the intersecting perspectives of God and humans, God looking down as his children look up emphasizes the reunification between God and his people through the instrumentality of the covenant and its salvific effects, a covenant portrayed by the token of the rainbow that spans heaven and earth.[65]

The Doctrine and Covenants describes the millennial descent of the city of Enoch with the Lord and its reunification with the Zion on earth:

> The Lord hath brought again Zion; The Lord hath redeemed his people, Israel, According to the election of grace, Which was brought to pass by the faith and covenant of their fathers.
>
> The Lord hath redeemed his people; And Satan is bound and time is no longer. The Lord hath gathered all things in one. The Lord hath brought down Zion from above. The Lord hath brought up Zion from beneath.
>
> The earth hath travailed and brought forth her strength; And truth is established in her bowels; And the heavens have smiled upon her; And she is clothed with the glory of her God; For he stands in the midst of his people. (Doctrine and Covenants 84:99–101)

---

64. Givens, *Pearl of Greatest Price*, 75–76. Schade and Bowen, "Moses 8: Noah and the Flood."
65. It may also be of interest that scholars identify a turning point of pre- and post-flood activities as hinging upon God "remembering" Noah, which is displayed in a chiastic pattern: a series and its inversion. The story highlights a "de-creation" and a "re-creation." See Gordon J. Wenham, "Genesis," in *Eerdmans Commentary on the Bible*, ed. James D. G. Dunn (Grand Rapids, MI: Eerdmans, 2003), 44. God's activities are characterized by bridging heaven and earth, and the deliverance of Noah foreshadows the eschatological nuances applied to the text and the Second coming of Christ as the Savior and Redeemer of the covenant.

The token of the rainbow highlights the successful reunification of God's children through the fulfillment of covenants and provides the eschatological backdrop of Enoch's mission in relation to the covenant.

While receiving important promises from the Lord, Enoch saw the preparations necessary for this reunification in the latter days:

> And righteousness will I send down out of heaven; and truth will I send forth out of the earth, to bear testimony of mine Only Begotten; his resurrection from the dead; yea, and also the resurrection of all men; and righteousness and truth will I cause to sweep the earth as with a flood, to gather out mine elect from the four quarters of the earth, unto a place which I shall prepare, an Holy City, that my people may gird up their loins, and be looking forth for the time of my coming; for there shall be my tabernacle, and it shall be called Zion, a New Jerusalem. (Moses 7:62)

The New Jerusalem (among which is situated the Lord's tabernacle) will be built, and the city of Enoch will dwell in its midst.[66]

> And the Lord said unto Enoch: Then shalt thou and all thy city meet them there, and we will receive them into our bosom, and they shall see us; and we will fall upon their necks, and they shall fall upon our necks, and we will kiss each other;
>
> And there shall be mine abode, and it shall be Zion, which shall come forth out of all the creations which I have made; and for the space of a thousand years the earth shall rest. (Moses 7:63–64)

When all is prepared and the signs and pledges are fulfilled, the Lord will come. These are major components of the sacred promises given to Enoch in the form of covenants and perpetuated through Noah and the flood. According to Restoration scripture, the token of the rainbow thus goes much further beyond a promise of never again sending the floods upon the earth; the rainbow additionally represented the covenantal promises

66. For the effects of Moses 7 on the early Church and its pursuit of Zion, a New Jerusalem, see the chapter on Zion in Schade and Bowen, *Book of Moses*.

that would result in gaining the presence of God, as depicted in the symbol of the token of the rainbow.

SALVATION FOR THE DEAD

Restoration scripture contributes yet another dimension of God's mercy in relation to the story of the flood: the work and salvation for the dead. Enoch witnessed the following pertaining to those who would die by the waters of the flood, defining the significance and scope of God's work and glory to bring to pass the immortality and eternal life of his children:

> But behold, these which thine eyes are upon shall perish in the floods; and behold, I will shut them up; a prison have I prepared for them.
>
> And that which I have chosen hath pled before my face. Wherefore, he suffereth for their sins; inasmuch as they will repent in the day that my Chosen shall return unto me, and until that day they shall be in torment. (Moses 7:38–39)

Enoch gets a glimpse of the redemptive power of the Atonement of Christ and how it would reach those shut up in a spirit prison.[67] Thus,

---

67. Although the context is not identical with Enoch's experience presented in the Book of Moses, *1 Enoch* preserves a tradition that associates the wicked of Noah's day being imprisoned to preserve righteous Noah. 1 Enoch 17–36 also describe Enoch's purported experiences and narrate, "Enoch's journey to the end of the earth, in which the patriarch visits various sites of eschatological import, such as the garden of Eden, the holding chambers of the dead, and the prison in which the rebellious Watchers [wicked] are being held until the day of judgment. Enoch's eyewitness account assures the reader that these places do indeed exist and, thus, that a day is coming in which the righteous and wicked will be rewarded according to their deeds." Stokes, "Flood Stories in Enoch," 235. Day, *Genesis 1–11*, 83 also postulates that a parallel term used in the flood account exists between *Nephilim*, discussed earlier as potentially representing "fallen ones," and a word describing and being associated with "the dead." Wenham, *Genesis 1–15*, 143 also discusses some interesting connections with the Nephilim as they appear in the Bible: "If Ezek 32:20–28 is alluding [to] Gen 6:1–4, it seems likely that he [Ezekiel] connected the Nephilim with נפל "to fall." There he repeatedly speaks of גבורים "the warriors," the same term as here,

rather than all being lost through the flood, all could be gained through the redemptive power of Christ and the cleansing power of the Atonement with its attendant ordinances. Sin and death could be bridged and life, given, as reflected in the reunification motif inherent in the token of the rainbow. First Peter 3:19–21 speaks of the Savior's visit to the spirit world prior to his resurrection, "By which also he went and preached unto the spirits in prison; Which sometime were disobedient, when once the longsuffering of God waited in the days of Noah, while the ark was a preparing, wherein few, that is, eight souls were saved by water. The like figure whereunto even baptism doth also now save us (not the putting away of the filth of the flesh, but the answer of a good conscience toward God,) by the resurrection of Jesus Christ" (see also Doctrine and Covenants 138); and "The flood becomes a typological figure of baptism. . . . Beyond baptism is newness of life (cf. Rom 6:4)."[68] Enoch receives revelation into the purposes of the spirit prison and the work of salvation to be accomplished on behalf of the dead who would be destroyed by the flood and who would remain there until after the resurrection of Christ. The implications of this component of the work of salvation for subsequent generations—including our own—are staggering, and Enoch witnessed at least some portion of it. Joseph Fielding Smith taught: "What was the promise made to the fathers that was to be fulfilled in the latter-days by the turning of the hearts of the children to their fathers? It was the promise of the Lord made through Enoch, Isaiah, and the prophets, to the nations of the earth, that the time should come when the dead should be redeemed. And the turning of the hearts of the children is fulfilled in the performing of the vicarious temple work and in the preparation of their genealogies."[69]

This redemptive work of the dead began taking shape in New Testament times:

---

who have fallen in battle and who now inhabit Sheol. Similarly, the *gigantes* of Greek mythology were defeated and imprisoned in the earth." Origen, a third-century Christian theologian, believed the three decks of the ark were symbolic of heaven, earth, and the underworld, and the decks constituted individual progress within God's Church. Benjamins, "Ark," 148.

68. Lewis, "Flood," 801.

69. Joseph Fielding Smith, *Doctrines of Salvation: Sermons and Writings of Joseph Fielding Smith* (Salt Lake City: Bookcraft, 1954), 2:154.

> Jesus preached to the dead. The apostle Peter taught this in his day, saying that after the death of the Savior, and while his body lay in the tomb, the Lord, as a Spirit, went to the realm of the dead and there preached to the spirits of the people who previously had lived on the earth. (1 Pet. 3:18–20.) Then he gives us the reason for this preaching: "For this cause was the gospel preached also to them that are dead, that they might be judged according to men in the flesh, but live according to God in the spirit." (1 Pet. 4:6.) Having heard the gospel, they might accept it or reject it and thus be "judged according to men in the flesh." As they did accept it, they could then "live according to God in the spirit" just as the scripture indicated.[70]

From a Restoration perspective, Enoch appeared to be no stranger to this doctrine that would materialize in the meridian of time, and it brought him great comfort when nothing else would. After weeping for those whose lives would be lost in the flood, and after witnessing this component of salvation for the dead in the plan of God, "The Lord showed Enoch all things, even unto the end of the world; and he saw the day of the righteous, the hour of their redemption, and received a fulness of joy" (Moses 7:67). The flood and its token of the rainbow thus become appropriate and powerful symbols of covenantal promises and the redemptive power of Christ and help us view the story of the flood through the lens of salvation, not death—the beginning, not the end. These symbols encapsulate the salvation that comes through ordinances and that bridges the gap between heaven and earth and life and spiritual or physical death. The covenant made with Noah at the time of the flood—symbolized by the token of the rainbow and the covenantal pledges of God—plays a significant part to be fulfilled in these latter days. In an 1842 publication in the *Times and Seasons*, the following observation was made on the topic of salvation for the dead:

> When speaking about the blessings pertaining to the gospel, and the consequences connected with disobedience to its requirements, we

70. Petersen, *Noah and the Flood*, 62–63. See also Wilford Woodruff, in *Journal of Discourses*, 13:163.

> are frequently asked the question, what has become of our [ancestors]? will they all be damned for not obeying the gospel, when they never heard it? certainly not. But they will possess the same privilege that we here enjoy, through the medium of the *everlasting* priesthood, which not only administers on earth but in heaven, and the wise dispensations of the great Jehovah; hence those characters referred to by Isaiah will be visited by this priesthood, and come out of their prison, upon the same principle as those who were disobedient in the days of Noah, were visited by our Saviour,—[who possessed the everlasting, Melchizedec priesthood,]—and had the gospel preached to them, by him.[71]

The covenant revolves around salvation being made possible to the living and the dead. How appropriate that these teachings would be revealed to Enoch, the one whose ministry has been described as follows, "Enoch's fate was not the stinging 'and he died.' . . . Death is not the last word after all. Enoch offers a solution to the transgression and violence that had marred God's creation[s]; that is, a life with God that somehow transcends life and death itself."[72]

SACRIFICE AS A SYMBOL OF SALVATION

As the flood story concludes in the book of Genesis, the covenantal nature of the flood comes to an apex. After the floodwater recedes, Noah offers a sacrifice to God.

> Noah, the priest, and his burnt offering are prototypes of Israel's priests and their sacrifices (cf. Job 1:5 42:8) and prefigure Jesus Christ, the High Priest, and his sacrifice. Matthews astutely observes, "The manifestation of Christ has taken away these shadows." The value God places upon the sacrifice of Christ can be inferred from his reaction to Noah's offering. His atoning sacrifice so assuages God's heart . . . that God resolves never again to destroy

71. "*Times and Seasons*, 15 April 1842," p. 760, The Joseph Smith Papers.
72. Arnold, *Genesis*, 88.

> the earth (8:21). For the covenant people of God, Christ's sacrifice secures their cleansing from all sin and secures for them eternal life with God (Heb. 10:11–24).[73]

Describing the sacred sacrificial offering brought forth by Noah after the flood, we read, "Thus, we discover that the first act after the destruction of the world by a flood was a recognition of the great expiatory principle of the atonement, which was to be made by the Only Begotten Son of God, as revealed by the angel to Adam. And as God recognized Adam's and Abel's offerings, so He also recognized that of Noah: and as a result, the Patriarch obtained great promises, in which the people of all ages, then to come, would be interested."[74] The covenant given to Noah and traced back to the days of Adam and Eve through Enoch, was the source of salvation for Noah and his family in his day. So also, it became the source of salvation for future days and, now, our day. The context and meaning of the sacrifice Noah offered seem to speak to components of holiness, ritual, and redemption through the symbols and meanings of the sacrificial offerings that lay upon the altar:

> And Noah builded an altar unto the Lord; and took of every clean beast, and of every clean fowl, and offered burnt offerings on the altar.[75]

---

73. Waltke, *Genesis*, 159.
74. John Taylor, *Mediation and Atonement* (Salt Lake City: Deseret News, 1972), 83.
75. JST Genesis 9:4–6 has Noah offering burnt offerings, giving thanks, and rejoicing in his heart. Giving thanks may constitute a Peace Offering/Thank Offering, although the Genesis text does not designate other categories of sacrifice offered by Noah. The sacrifice is simply described as עֹלָה, "burnt offering." In light of the priestly code presented in Leviticus and the sequence in which sacrifices were to be offered (Sin/Transgress, Burnt, and Peace offerings being three major categories with subsets within each), some interesting things may be happening here with Noah's sacrifice. "There is no indication that the sacrifice was a sin offering—the sin of the earth (6:5) had already been judged by the flood. The sacrifice more likely symbolized a restoration of harmony between God, creation, and humanity." See Genesis 8:20 in J. D. Barry, M. S. Heiser, M. Custis, D. Mangum, and M. M. Whitehead, *Faithlife Study Bible* (Bellingham, WA: Logos Bible Software, 2012). Noah may thus be offering a burnt offering (Leviticus 1; 6:9–13), in "similitude of the sacrifice of the Only

> And the Lord smelled a sweet savour; and the Lord said in his heart, I will not again curse the ground any more for man's sake; for the imagination of man's heart is evil from his youth; neither will I again smite any more every thing living, as I have done.
>
> While the earth remaineth, seedtime and harvest, and cold and heat, and summer and winter, and day and night shall not cease. (Genesis 8:20–22)

God was pleased with the sacrifices and the offerings upon an altar on a mountain peak, along with the renewal of the covenant, seems to put this into a sacred sacrificial context of covenant renewal and fulfillment.[76] The

---

Begotten of the Father" (Moses 5:7), and as insinuated in the JST mentioned above, offering a category of Peace offerings which may have included a Thank Offering, or even a Vow or Freewill Offering in covenant renewal (Leviticus 22:18–21). "It is noteworthy that when the three offerings were offered together, the sin always preceded the burnt, and the burnt the peace offerings. Thus, the order of the symbolizing sacrifices was the order of atonement, sanctification, and fellowship with the Lord." Latter-day Saint Bible Dictionary, s.v. "sacrifices." Individuals have attempted to provide symbolic connections between the dove Noah sends out (a raven is also listed) and the dove that appears at Jesus's baptism (Matthew 3:16; Mark 1:10; Luke 3:22; John 1:32). Early Christian writer Maximus connected the two and wrote, "'The very dove that once hastened to Noah's ark in the flood now comes to Christ's church in baptism' (64.2; cf. 50.2 on the flood). As was true with regard to Noah, 'baptism is a flood to the sinner and a consecration to the faithful'; 'by the Lord's washing, righteousness is preserved and unrighteousness is destroyed' (50.2)." Everett Ferguson, *Baptism in the Early Church* (Grand Rapids, MI: Eerdmans, 2009), 653. The symbol of a dove may help create a descriptive environment of postbaptismal sanctification, working in conjunction with the personal and eschatological roles the flood story plays in Bible theology. Following the flood, the dove, and the coming forth to the mountain peak to offer sacrifice, in JST Genesis 9:5 we read, "And the Lord spake unto Noah, and he blessed him."

76. "God accepted his sacrifice, indicating that now deity and humanity were reconciled." Bandstra, *Reading the Old Testament*, 78. The comparison of a mountain peak and a temple is quite common, and it is used in the Epic of Gilgamesh story of the flood. Ziggurat temple towers are sometimes referred to as "house of the foundation of heaven and earth," "house of the bond between heaven and earth," and "house of the mountain" Ziggurat can also simply mean "mountain." In Gilgamesh, Utnapishtim pours out a libation to the gods on the Ziggurat (the top of the mountain) after the flood. See Othmar Keel, *The Symbolism of*

righteousness of Noah qualified him for the covenant, and God blessed him through it in the picture of salvation on a mountain peak following the waters of destruction and re-creation (an image of coming forth from death and communing with God, as symbolized in the covenant and ordinance of baptism). "Perhaps the most important detail in the Priestly account of the flood is the covenant that God concludes with Noah at its end. God undertakes not to destroy the earth by flood again, and sets the rainbow in the sky as a sign of this promise."[77] The token of the rainbow represented various aspects of this covenant and epitomized the very

---

the Biblical World (Winona Lake, IN: Eisenbrauns, 1997), 113. In similar fashion, so does Noah in the midst of a covenant renewal in a sacred precinct and with a sacred offering. This underscores that God is responsible for the rescue and that he has led Noah to the mountain peak or holy place of salvation, and it is to remind Noah of the sacred nature of covenants, the necessity to renew them, and the significance of recognizing God as the source of salvation through those covenants. We return to holy places to remember what God has done in delivering us and to renew promises to continue his work of salvation while life is granted to us. "After the waters abated, the ark came to rest on the mountains of Ararat (8:4). The picture of the ark resting creates an interesting word play, since the verb used here ("rest" *nwḥ*) is the same from which Noah's name is derived. In a similar play on his name, he brings 'relief' to humanity (*yĕnaḥămēnû*, 5:29), and now Noah, whose name itself means 'rest,' rides the ark to its resting place. Noah's righteousness blesses humanity with relief and preserves its remnant, along with the animals, in the resting ark in Ararat." Arnold, *Genesis*, 104. "At the close of the flood account, the author makes a direct reference to the sacrificial importance of these "clean animals." They were taken into the ark to be used as offerings (8:20–21). The Lord's acceptance of these offerings (*wayyāraḥ yhwh ʾet -rêaḥ hannîḥōaḥ*, "the pleasing aroma," 8:21) is cast in the terminology of Leviticus 1:17 (*rêaḥ nîḥōaḥ layhwh*, "an aroma pleasing to the Lord"). As we might expect, these same events at the end of the flood are tied specifically to the notion of a covenant (9:8, 11). The author of the Pentateuch uses the ark in the flood narrative to foreshadow the salvation that comes through the tabernacle and the covenant." Sailhamer, *Genesis*, locs. 4424–29 of 10676, Kindle. The ark has also been compared to temples and temple worship. S. W. Holloway, "What Ship Goes There: The Flood Narratives in the Gilgamesh Epic and Genesis Considered in Light of Ancient Near Eastern Temple Ideology," *Zeitschrift für die alttestamentliche Wissenschaft* 103 (1991): 328–55.

77. Collins, *Introduction*, 80.

essence of regaining the presence of God.[78] As Noah and his family rested safely on the mountain peak, having been delivered from the cleansing flood waters of both life and death, we get a visual picture of the saving power of God through covenants as Noah offers the sacrifice in remembrance of the salvation brought forth by God.

CONCLUSION

Themes running throughout ancient Near Eastern flood stories, in conjunction with the developing flood theology found within the Bible, revolve around the concepts of destruction and salvation. These, along with insights gained from extrabiblical religious literature, shed light on how we understand the covenantal implications of the flood and on the token associated with the rainbow. They connect the past with the future within a template of divine deliverance, creation, and salvation. The biblical account expresses both "humanity's moral culpability" and "divine compassion and concern for human perpetuity."[79] Covenantal significance is further highlighted when viewed through the lens of Restoration scripture, as we comprehend the eschatological views forward from the perspective of God, Enoch, Noah, and the earth. Elements of salvation and covenant become clear and are present throughout the flood narrative. These elements are portrayed and conveyed through tokens highlighting God's power and desire to save and preserve (rather than to destroy and eliminate) and highlighting his willingness to do so by covenant.

Through the images of floodwaters and arks, we witness a loving God who preserves covenants and saves through ordinances.[80] The flood story

---

78. Revelation 4:3 describes a rainbow "round about" the throne of God, and Ezekiel 1:28 also portrays Ezekiel witnessing God and a "bow" surrounding him.

79. Schmidt, "Flood Narratives," 2348.

80. Parallels have been drawn between the ark and the priestly images surrounding the tabernacle, and it has been noted that the "author of the Pentateuch uses the ark in the flood narrative to foreshadow the salvation that comes through the tabernacle and the covenant." Sailhamer, *Genesis*, locs. 4428–30 of 10676, Kindle.

is thus about the preaching of prophets and God's efforts to rescue his children. In relation to the rainbow, it becomes a token representing both a pledge from God and a symbol of the bridging of the gulf between heaven and earth, a promise of hope, restitution, and salvation. The rainbow also constitutes a representation of overcoming spiritual and physical death within the context of the flood, demonstrating God's love and mercy within the framework of creation and salvation. As described by Elder Howard W. Hunter, "The Lord made a covenant with Noah, and the rainbow became the token of that eternal covenant with all [hu]mankind."[81] Such are the covenantal and salvific implications of the sign of the rainbow given as a token of the covenant to Noah at the time of the flood, and such are the far-reaching eschatological implications that extend to us today. Through the lens of the Restoration, we see the mercy, love, and ever-protective care of God who makes and keeps covenants. We see the redemptive power of God through an eternal perspective spanning heaven and earth to save and redeem those who were lost and reclaim them through the covenant. The token of the covenant reminds us of the bridge between heaven and earth and allows us to see God in his overarching work to bring to pass the salvation of his children from beginning to end.

81. Howard W. Hunter, "Commitment to God," *Ensign*, November 1982, 57.

— 5 —

THE ANCESTORS OF ISRAEL AND THE ENVIRONMENT OF CANAAN IN THE EARLY SECOND MILLENNIUM BC

GEORGE A. PIERCE

One challenge for any reader of the Old Testament is trying to understand the historical context for the people and narratives found in the text, since readers are separated from those events by thousands of years. What the daily life of these individuals would have been like can be hard to imagine. Yet the more one knows of the historical context, the more one can relate to the given individual. In this chapter, George A. Pierce provides such a context to the ancestral narratives of Genesis 12–50, those narratives concerned with the families of Abraham, Isaac, Jacob, and Joseph. While the author does not discuss the narratives themselves in detail, he does provide a scaffolding to recognize the world they lived in and, in so doing, gain an appreciation of their experience

The narrative of Genesis 11:31–32 declares that Terah and his family—comprising Abram (later Abraham), Sarai (later Sarah), Lot, and other retainers—left their homeland bound for Canaan and dwelt in Haran for a period during which Terah passed away.[1] While in Haran, Abraham received the initial covenant call to leave his family group and sojourn in a land that the Lord would show him (Genesis 12:1).[2] From this point forward, the literary narrative of Genesis focuses its attention on this man and his promised offspring who would become the ancestors of the covenant people of Israel. An awareness of the historical, environmental, sociocultural, archaeological, and economic contexts underlying the ancestral narratives of Genesis 12–50 should help readers to develop a deeper appreciation for the theological message of the biblical record; that is, knowing about the trials and lives of Abraham, Isaac, and Jacob may provide us instruction and guidance in our modern world. Unpacking the complete context of the ancestral narratives would entail a greater space than allotted here. Thus, this paper presents an archaeological and historical overview of Canaan in the second millennium BC during the period known as the Middle Bronze Age (ca. 1950–1550 BC), situating Abraham and his family members in their geographic and cultural contexts and examining the economic interactions between the ancestors of Israel and the land of Canaan and its inhabitants.[3] Combined, these efforts suggest

1. Despite the biblical text using the name "Abram" from Genesis 11:27–17:5, the name "Abraham" is used within this paper for this ancestor of Israel due to its familiarity for the reader. This is not to downplay the significance of the name changes for Abram and Sarai by divine decree in Genesis 17.
2. The order of events related in Abraham 2 are slightly reversed, in that the Lord first caused a famine and then called Abraham to leave Ur and go to a land that God would show to Abraham, after which his family travels to Haran (Abraham 2:1–4).
3. The date of Abraham's birth as discussed by scholars in the twentieth century ranges between 2100 and 1800 BC. Assuming the years for lifespans in the biblical text as literal and accurate and adhering to the lower date, the scholar and archaeologist William F. Albright surmised that Abraham lived well into the eighteenth century BC, which would place the death of Jacob near the end of the sixteenth century and situate the ancestors within the Middle Bronze Age and the transition to the Late Bronze Age. William F. Albright, "From the Patriarchs to Moses: From Abraham to Joseph," *Biblical Archaeologist* 36 (1973): 16. While

an archaeological signature for the ancestors and reshape modern expectations in terms of extant material culture versus received literary legacy.

Alan Millard relates that "the discussion of Genesis cannot stay in the literary sphere; it reaches out into history and religion, and cannot expect to reach anything approaching a full appreciation of the book without doing so, just as a full appreciation of Shakespeare's plays includes [an] understanding of the Elizabethan theatre and audience."[4] Therefore, a study of the ancestors of Israel should include an understanding of the natural and cultural environment of Canaan, the stage upon which the ancestral narratives unfolded. While many aspects of the land of Canaan during this period are lost to the ages, scientific data derived from climate studies and archaeological excavations, coupled with historical data interpreted from ancient texts and the Bible, can greatly inform the student of the Old Testament about the land in which Abraham and his descendants sojourned.[5]

---

modern scholars have dismissed the historical veracity of the ancestral narratives and early attempts to situate them within a historical period, some biblical scholars now view these passages as cultural memories that include traditions that predate major biblical authors and the formation of Israel but do include some editorial updating for their intended ancient audience. Ronald S. Hendel, Remembering Abraham: Culture, Memory, and History in the Hebrew Bible (Oxford: Oxford University Press, 2005), 45–47.

4. Alan R. Millard, "Methods of Studying the Patriarchal Narratives as Ancient Texts," in *Essays on the Patriarchal Narratives*, ed. A. R. Millard and D. J. Wiseman (Leicester, UK: InterVarsity Press, 1980), 45.

5. Concerning the use of ancient texts as data sources, surviving Canaanite material from the Middle Bronze Age is scarce, and many of the textual sources are presented from an elite or royal perspective and lack individuality. To mitigate these textual problems, a familiarity with the regional settlement history and material culture gained from the archaeological record aids in appreciating the lifeways of the Canaanites while ancient, extrabiblical texts play a supporting, albeit important, role in illuminating certain cultural aspects of the period. Ancient Near Eastern texts from Egypt and various Syrian and Mesopotamian cities like Nuzi, Mari, Emar, and Alalakh do not provide direct parallels but illustrate that the ancestral narratives reflect common practices of the Near East in the second millennium BC. See Bill T. Arnold and Bryan E. Beyer, *Readings from the Ancient Near East: Primary Sources for Old Testament Study* (Grand

CANAAN IN THE SECOND MILLENNIUM BC

The beginning of the Middle Bronze Age in Canaan is marked by the establishment of palatial and fortified centers, monumental architecture, and international trade.[6] Although outside the chronological scope of this study, the preceding Early Bronze Age (ca. 3400–1950 BC) was a formative period in the settlement history of Canaan in which an initial phase of urbanization and the formation of territorial states occurred. Bronze Age settlement patterns took advantage of elements needed for the establishment of permanent sites concentrated on aspects of agriculture and pastoralism such as being in close proximity to a permanent source of water and having land cleared or ready for agriculture.[7] During this period, Egypt established trade relations with inland sites in Canaan and with coastal centers, both of which supplied the Egyptian courts with items not found in Egypt like timber, bitumen, copper, and turquoise. Collapse of this urban culture occurred abruptly about 2200 BC as sites across the Near East were abandoned or destroyed. Climate data indicate that a shift to a warmer and drier climate led to the abandonment of cities in Canaan and Syria, events that coincided with the demise of Egypt's Old Kingdom and the downfall of the Akkadian Empire in Mesopotamia. Climatic phenomena such as famines would later play an important role in the story of Abraham.

The reurbanization of Canaan at the beginning of the Middle Bronze Age was a process whose whole was greater than the sum of its various parts. Canaan transformed from a largely rural population with ephemeral archaeological remains into an urban society with settlement hierarchies and extensive trade networks that were of a greater diversity in size, function, and distribution of sites and that had expanded into previously unexploited environmental niches. The Middle Bronze Age material culture

---

Rapids, MI: Baker Academic, 2002), 72; John H. Walton, *Ancient Israelite Literature in Its Cultural Context* (Grand Rapids, MI: Zondervan, 1989), 49–58.

6. David Ilan, "The Dawn of Internationalism: The Middle Bronze Age," in *The Archaeology of Society in the Holy Land*, ed. T. E. Levy (London: Leicester University Press, 1995), 297.

7. Ram Gophna, "Early Bronze Age Canaan: Some Spatial and Demographic Observations," in Levy, *Archaeology of Society*, 269.

was the result of multiple internal and external factors such as population movements, trade, and communication, in addition to cultural continuity. A study of the Canaanites provides the cultural background of the people among whom the ancestors sojourned (Genesis 12:6) and against whom the Israelites would later fight to conquer the land promised to Abraham and to struggle to resist spiritual corruption and idolatry.

THE NATURAL ENVIRONMENT: A RECONSTRUCTION OF CANAAN'S CLIMATE

Understanding Canaan as Abraham experienced it includes a reconstruction of the climate of Canaan in the early second millennium BC. Such efforts are necessary given the shifts in global climate, changes in local topography and hydrology, presence of intrusive vegetation, and decrease or disappearance of animal ranges. Reconstructing paleoclimates and past landscapes can be accomplished through a variety of scientific avenues.[8] Determining the effects of climatic shifts on the population of Canaan requires reconstructing the ancient climate of the eastern Mediterranean basin, which can be accomplished in a number of ways, including oxygen isotope analysis and the use of ice and sediment cores, lithology, and palynology.[9] Despite uncertainties when analyzing these proxies and relating them to natural processes or climatic events, the approaches treated here form the best information to propose the environmental and climatic conditions of Canaan in the Middle Bronze Age.[10] While the temptation exists to apply the specific information provided by specialist studies for

8. Site catchment analysis, soil quality (or potential), archaeobotany, pollen and mollusk studies, geomorphology, and archaeozoology all contribute to an overall perception of the paleoenvironment. See Kevin Walsh, "Mediterranean Landscape Archaeology and Environmental Reconstruction," in *Environmental Reconstruction in Mediterranean Landscape Archaeology*, ed. P. Leveau et al. (Oxford: Oxbow Books, 1999), 1–3.
9. Raymond S. Bradley, *Paleoclimatology: Reconstructing Climates of the Quaternary* (San Diego: Academic Press, 1999), 5.
10. Fatima F. Abrantes et al., "Paleoclimate Variability in the Mediterranean Region," in *The Climate of the Mediterranean Region: From Past to Future*, ed. Piero Lionello (Amsterdam: Elsevier, 2012), 4–17.

a wider area than originally intended or to employ extraregional data by analogy, careful synthesis of all the information can present a fuller picture of a region's past landscape and climate as well as the social, political, and economic strategies employed by its inhabitants.

Employing various methods permits a synthetic overview of climate for the Levant for the period before the arrival of Abraham and his household and the duration of the ancestors' sojourn in Canaan before Jacob moved his family to Egypt (Genesis 46:5–27). Toward the end of the third millennium BC, climatic warming resulted in lake levels dropping, rivers becoming seasonal, and deserts expanding. Aridification of the Near East resulted from lower rainfall related to cooling of subpolar and subtropical surface waters of the North Atlantic.[11] This major crisis, lasting about a century from 2200 to 2100 BC, included a drop in the Dead Sea water level of nearly 100 meters and the drying up of the southern basin, a rise of oceanic levels of 1.5 meters, and a decrease in olive pollen and a rise in oak and pistachio pollen around the Sea of Galilee, indicating a decline in olive cultivation and in the permanent settlements' abilities to maintain such olive groves.[12] The beginning of the Middle Bronze Age witnessed a reversal of these trends as the climate became cooler and more humid through about 1800 BC, when wetter events are recorded.[13] Increased rainfall, the growth of cypress and willow trees in wetter environments along river banks, the renewed cultivation of olives, and a decrease in oak forests are all indicated by various environmental data; thus, the land of Canaan was not an entirely hot, dry, and foreboding landscape wherein Abraham's family would have struggled to survive, but it was a cooler

---

11. Peter B. de Menocal, "Cultural Responses to Climate Change during the Late Holocene," *Science* 292 (2001): 670.

12. Arie S. Issar and Mattanyah Zohar, *Climate Change—Environment and History of the Near East* (Berlin: Springer, 2007), 135.

13. Arie S. Issar, *Climate Changes during the Holocene and Their Impact on Hydrological Systems* (Cambridge: Cambridge University Press, 2003), 21; Issar and Zohar, *Climate Change*, 150. Stable isotope analysis of speleothems in the Soreq Cave provides substantiation for a drier climate after 2000 BC; see Miriam Bar-Matthews, Avner Ayalon, and Aaron Kaufman, "Late Quaternary Paleoclimate in the Eastern Mediterranean Region from Stable Isotope Analysis of Speleothems at Soreq Cave, Israel," *Quaternary Research* 47 (1997): 155–68.

region with higher rainfall and more lush vegetation that allowed settlements to flourish in marginal areas like the biblical Negev and the location of Beersheba and Gerar (see Genesis 20; 21:22–32), locations that are very dry and barren today.

THE SOCIOCULTURAL ENVIRONMENT OF CANAAN

Limited religious, administrative, and personal documents from ancient Canaan have been found archaeologically. Indeed, the Canaanites did not leave behind textual records clearly defining who they were and what it meant to be a Canaanite. Archaeology indicates that the Canaanites have a shared cultural heritage with other groups in the Near East (ranging from Mesopotamia to Egypt) termed "Amorite," a group name that also appears in the Old Testament. Scholars have suggested that certain aspects of Canaanite society, including architecture, crafts, and language, originated in eastern Syria with the Amorites and that the Amorite peoples or culture spread throughout the Near East during the Middle Bronze Age.[14] This can especially be seen in Amorite names for rulers and sites in Syria and Canaan—names found in the Execration Texts, a set of Middle Kingdom Egyptian ritual texts meant to magically bind and break the power of Egypt's foreign enemies.[15] Personal names in an administrative document from Hebron reflect a mixture of Amorite and Hurrian names,

---

14. William F. Albright, *The Archaeology of Palestine* (Harmondsworth, UK: Penguin, 1960); Albright, "Abraham the Hebrew: A New Archaeological Interpretation," *Bulletin of the American Schools of Oriental Research* 163 (1961): 36–54; Kathleen Kenyon, *Amorites and Canaanites* (London: Oxford University Press, 1966); William G. Dever, "The Beginning of the Middle Bronze Age in Palestine," in *Magnalia Dei, The Mighty Acts of God: Essays on the Bible and Archaeology in Memory of G. Ernest Wright*, ed. F. M. Cross, W. E. Lemke, and P. D. Miller (Garden City, NY: Doubleday, 1976), 3–38.

15. Kurt Sethe, *Die Ächtung feindlicher Fürsten, Volker, und Dinge auf altägyptischen Tongefäßcherben des Mittleren Reiches* (Berlin: Verlag der Akademie der Wissenschaft, 1926); Georges Posener, *Princes et Pays d'Asie et de Nubie: Textes Hiératiques sur des Figurines d'Envoûtement du Moyen Empire* (Brussels: Fondation Égyptologique Reine Élisabeth, 1940); Anson F. Rainey and R. Steven

suggesting that Abraham would have interacted with a mixed population while he dwelt near Hebron and may have been integrated into a diverse community as a nonnative inhabitant of Canaan.[16] These suggestions help paint the ethnically diverse backdrop of Abraham's purchase of the cave of Machpelah as a burial place for his family (Genesis 23). In addition to Amorite names, other features such as defensive works, entombments beneath houses and palaces, temple architecture, donkey burials, and pottery also indicate either a transmission of knowledge or a migration of people from a core area in eastern Syrian and northern Mesopotamia to places like Canaan.[17] Abraham and his family may have found themselves in the midst of these waves of migrations of diverse peoples throughout the region. While the archaeological record shows that the Amorite culture was clearly dominant in Canaan, it should be noted that the Canaanites were a multicultural amalgamation of people who shared many traits in common. This accords well with the statement by the Lord through the prophet Ezekiel, who reminded the city of Jerusalem of its Canaanite roots: "Your origin and your birth were in the land of the Canaanites; your father was an Amorite, and your mother a Hittite" (Ezekiel 16:3 NRSV).

To assume that the Canaanites were a single group of people would be incorrect, and the Bible and the Book of Abraham portray Abraham amid diverse communities of people. Extrabiblical texts from Canaan suggest that most people during the Bronze Age would not have considered themselves "Canaanite" but would have identified with a tribal ancestor or with a city or territory in which they lived. The biblical table of nations in Genesis 10:15–18 NRSV suggests that a patchwork of peoples and places comprised the Canaanites, including Sidon (presumably the eponymous ancestor of the Phoenician city bearing that name), Heth, "the Jebusites, the Amorites, the Girgashites, the Hivites, the Arkites, the Sinites, the Arvadites, the Zemarites, and the Hamathites." Genesis 15:19–21 lists "the

---

Notley, *The Sacred Bridge: Carta's Atlas of the Biblical World* (Jerusalem: Carta, 2006), 100–102.

16. Moshe Anbar and Nadav Na'aman, "An Account Tablet of Sheep from Ancient Hebron," *Tel Aviv* 13–14 (1986): 3–12.

17. Aaron A. Burke, "Entanglement, the Amorite *koiné*, and Amorite Cultures in the Levant," *ARAM* 26 (2014): 360–62.

Kenites, and the Kenizzites, and the Kadmonites, and the Hittites, and the Perizzites, and the Rephaims, and the Amorites, and the Canaanites, and the Girgashites, and the Jebusites" as the inhabitants of the land promised to the would-be patriarch Abraham.

The few Egyptian texts dated to this period that concern Canaan offer some tantalizing evidence about the natural environment and social organization of the Levant in the Middle Bronze Age. The *Tale of Sinuhe* is a Middle Egyptian tale detailing the experiences of an Egyptian courtier who, for reasons unexplained, flees to Canaan upon the death of the pharaoh Amenemhet I, the first king of Dynasty 12 (1938–1908 BC).[18] Although prosperous in Canaan, Sinuhe later realizes the necessity of returning to Egypt to effect a reconciliation with the new king, Senusret I, and receive proper funerary rituals and burial rites on Egyptian soil. Sinuhe describes the natural environment of the area in which he lived—Canaan, Sinai, and the inhabitants of these lands—and provides perspective on the social organization and cultural traits of the Canaanites at his time. He describes the natural environment and fertility of Canaan: "It was a wonderful land called Yaa. There were cultivated figs in it and grapes, and more wine than water. Its honey was abundant, and its olive trees numerous. On its trees were all varieties of fruit. There were barley and emmer [wheat], and there was no end to all varieties of cattle (i.e., small livestock)."[19]

Game animals that were hunted in the "desert," or wilderness areas, also comprised part of Sinuhe's daily food. In addition to cultivation and herding, Sinuhe also acted as the commander of his patron's forces, conducting raids against disruptive nomadic groups on the fringe of society and directing warfare against neighboring kingdoms.[20] Thus, within the

18. Explaining the reason for his flight later to a Canaanite ruler, Sinuhe states, "I do not know what brought me to this land. It was like the plan of a god." William K. Simpson, ed., *The Literature of Ancient Egypt: An Anthology of Stories, Instructions, Stelae, Autobiographies, and Poetry* (New Haven, CT: Yale University Press, 2003): 54–66.
19. Simpson, *Literature of Ancient Egypt*, 58.
20. Anson F. Rainey, "The World of Sinuhe," *Israel Oriental Studies* 2 (1972): 378–79. Rainey interpreted these aspects of Sinuhe's activities in Canaan, together with the organization needed to conduct horticulture and pastoral endeavors and the mention of Sinuhe entertaining Egyptian dignitaries, as signs that the land of

story, we encounter diverse communities within Canaan, wherein a multifarious range of ethnicities interacted and integrated indigenous cultural and religious elements pertaining to their individual cultural identities found outside the boundaries of Canaan.

THE BUILT ENVIRONMENT: CANAANITE CENTERS

Middle Bronze Age sites are typically found along the margins of good soil types to maximize the amount of ground available for agriculture and are situated on natural hills with at least one good permanent source of water.[21] Such conditions led to the growth of urban centers with fortifications, religious precincts, and palatial architecture, and the preeminent sites of this period included Jerusalem, Shechem, and other locations discussed below (see figure 1). In addition to cities with massive fortifications complete with gates and ramparts, smaller unwalled villages and farmsteads were located in the countryside between larger urban centers. As Abraham journeyed southward from Haran into Canaan, he would have enjoyed a cooler climate with more precipitation and vegetation in which both established settlements and nomadic groups existed. As a pastoralist, he and his household would have been on the margins of Canaanite society, interacting with large, fortified centers and smaller hamlets when necessary but dwelling outside of the agricultural zones surrounding these sites in order to pasture the flocks. The fortified sites must have presented a visually formidable obstacle to the realization of the promise given to Abraham (and his descendants) by God regarding the possession of the land (Genesis 12:7, 15:7).

Sinuhe's sojourn was a developed society with elements of settled and nomadic groups. Interestingly, the Book of Abraham also describes Egyptianized societies among whom Abraham lived.

21. For a discussion of this settlement pattern in the western Galilee during the Middle Bronze Age, see Assaf Yasur-Landau, Eric H. Cline, and George A. Pierce, "Middle Bronze Age Settlement Patterns in the Western Galilee, Israel," *Journal of Field Archaeology* 33 (2008): 59–83. This provides the backdrop for farming and the raising of cattle in the Isaac and Jacob stories.

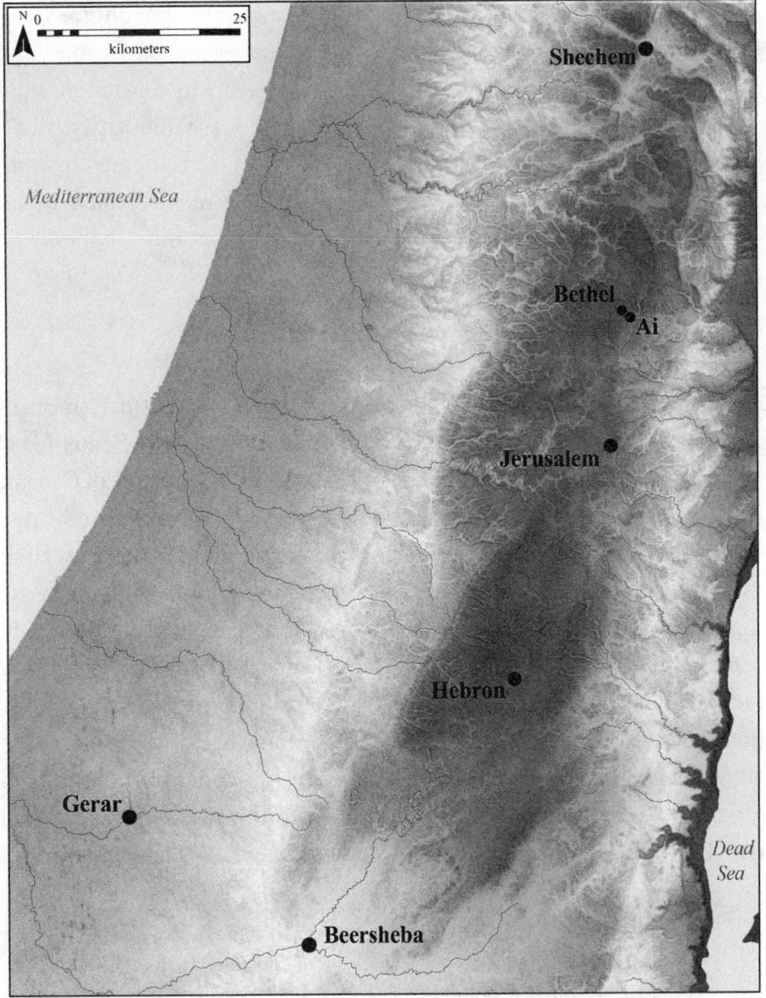

Figure 1. Middle Bronze Age Canaanite centers associated with the ancestral narratives. Map by the author.

Although large portions of Middle Bronze Age cities have not been exposed by archaeology, the remains that have come to light, such as paved streets, public courtyards, and large palatial buildings with stone foundations, mud-brick walls, central courtyards, and plaster floors, exhibit a degree of town planning. However, while some streets followed straight lines, most residential areas grew organically with little thought for street layout, so lanes run along irregular lines with narrow passages and blind alleys.[22] The cyclical travels of the ancestors of Israel in Canaan brought Abraham and his descendants into contact with Canaanite cities, and a survey of these sites provides an understanding of the settlement picture during the ancestral age and the relationship between fortified urban centers and ephemeral sites associated with campsites and seminomadic activities.

SHECHEM

Abraham traveled from Haran in northern Mesopotamia to Hebron in Canaan via Shechem (spelled *Sichem* in Genesis 12:6) and Bethel likely using a route that followed the ridges of the central hill country of Canaan. Excavations at Shechem revealed multiple phases of Middle Bronze Age occupation, most with monumental architecture and large fortification walls.[23] In the eighteenth century, an earthen rampart was built to enclose the city surmounted by a mud-brick wall and was abutted by a series of courtyard and building complexes, part of which has been interpreted as a sacred precinct.[24] In the later phases of the Middle Bronze Age, a fortification wall of large boulders, called the "Cyclopean wall," became part of the city's defenses, and a large fortress-temple was first constructed. Although Abraham did not have much interaction with the site, Jacob purchased land from the territory of Shechem where he pitched his tent and built an

22. Sites with Middle Bronze Age palaces reveal that the palace of the city was usually located close to a temple. Palaces were decorated with orthostats, large stones placed along the bottom of a wall for support and decoration. Both the use of orthostats and the general layout and characteristics of Middle Bronze Age palaces in Canaan show direct influence from larger Syrian palaces that predate those in Canaan, again showing shared culture thought to be Amorite in origin.

23. Edward F. Campbell, "Shechem: Tell Balâtah," in *The New Encyclopedia of Archaeological Excavations in the Holy Land*, ed. Ephraim Stern (New York: Simon and Schuster, 1993), 4:1347; see also G. Ernest Wright, *Shechem: The Biography of a Biblical City* (New York: Doubleday, 1965); Dan P. Cole, *Shechem I: The Middle Bronze IIB Pottery* (Winona Lake, IN: Eisenbrauns, 1984).

24. Campbell, "Shechem," 1349.

altar for religious worship (Genesis 33:18–20). This landscape presents an interesting scenario of local Canaanite religious practices within the city of Shechem, as evinced by the large, archaeologically excavated temple and the personal religious experiences Jacob enjoys on the outskirts of town. Throughout the ancestral narratives, Abraham and his descendants are on the outskirts of Canaanite society yet have profound experiences with the divine away from such urban centers.

BETHEL

The site of Bethel is mentioned once in connection with Abraham in which the patriarch built an altar between this site and Hai ('Ai; Genesis 12:8) and was the site of Jacob's dream, a reiteration of the Abrahamic covenant, and the construction of another altar (Genesis 28:10–22; 35:3–7). Originally named Luz by the Canaanites (Genesis 28:19), Bethel witnessed habitation since the Early Bronze Age when it served as a campground for shepherds before a permanent settlement was established.[25] During the Middle Bronze Age, some building activity occurred near the spring at the site with a fortification wall and gates in a subsequent phase of occupation. Inside the walled area of the city was a sanctuary marked by large quantities of animal bones and cultic vessels, although the precise dating for this sacred precinct is difficult since pottery vessels from multiple periods were found in excavations attesting to the persistence of cultic rituals in that location. Again, in contrast to the Canaanite religious worship in the city proper, the ancestors found religious significance with the God of Israel on the outskirts of town.

HEBRON

Hebron and the plain of Mamre are recorded as places frequented by Abraham and Jacob (Genesis 13:18; 14:13; 18:1; 23:2, 19; 35:27), and as the location of the only parcel of the promised land that Abraham legally owned through purchase. In addition to a fortification wall, which has

---

25. James L. Kelso, *The Excavation of Bethel (1934–1960)* (Cambridge: American Schools of Oriental Research, 1968); James L. Kelso, "Bethel," in Stern, *New Encyclopedia*, 1:193.

survived with a height of more than two meters faced with a stone rampart, excavations have also exposed a tower adjoined to the city wall.[26] Near this wall inside the city, fieldwork revealed a room with a great quantity of animal bones, ceramic sherds, and ash. Part of the debris from this room yielded a fragmentary cuneiform tablet that listed several animals and named four individuals.[27]

Philip Hammond, an excavator of Hebron, also found burial caves on the southeastern portion of the mound, one of which evinced a continuity of use from the Middle Bronze Age to the Iron Age I.[28] Such extensive use corresponds well with the use of the Cave of Machpelah as a burial place for the ancestors of Israel. Operating within the cultural norms, Abraham acquired the natural cave that would serve as the family tomb after Sarah's death (Genesis 23:3–20).[29] The dialogue with Ephron the Hethite began with the polite rhetoric of offering Abraham the cave freely, which Abraham knew to refuse, and then ended with Abraham weighing out the four hundred shekels of silver to Ephron. No mention is made of a written land deed, but parallels from Mari and Emar in Syria suggest that Abraham received a tablet with the details of the transaction that was witnessed by both parties.

Canaanites in the Middle and Late Bronze Ages laid their dead to rest in various ways, and the deposition of the dead and the various accompanying grave goods inform us about Canaanite views on death and family.[30] In the Middle Bronze Age, the use of burial caves for an extended period of time indicates the desire of families to bury several generations of deceased family members together. A body would be laid out in the center

---

26. Avi Ofer, "Hebron," in Stern, *New Encyclopedia*, 2:608.
27. Anbar and Na'aman, "An Account Tablet of Sheep"; a *bulla* (a lump of clay used to seal documents, jars, or rooms) bearing an Egyptian scarab impression was also found in the room, and a socketed ax head was found in an adjacent room. Both items could be indicators that the resident was of high status within Canaanite society.
28. Ofer, "Hebron," 608.
29. Joseph A. Callaway, "Burials in Ancient Palestine: From the Stone Age to Abraham," *Biblical Archaeologist* 26 (1963): 90.
30. Rachel S. Hallote, "Real and Ideal Identities in Middle Bronze Age Tombs," *Near Eastern Archaeology* 65 (2002): 105–11.

of the cave, often on a wooden bed, and surrounding the deceased were various gifts consisting of storage jars with food or wine, containers for various other goods, weapons, and items of personal adornment.[31]

Alternatively used as the place-name for a cave and field (Genesis 23:9, 25:9; Genesis 49:30), the name Machpelah may have been derived from the Hebrew root *kpl*, meaning "double"; thus, the cave may have originally had two caverns suited for the burial of successive family generations.[32] Although the biblical text is silent on the details, Sarah may have been laid to rest with scarabs and other jewelry in addition to grave goods consisting of luxury items such as ivory inlaid boxes or ceramics containing oils or perfumes. When the cave was needed for later family members, her remains would have been moved aside to make way for the newly deceased. The continued use of the burial cave would have been seen as the family's staking a claim on the property and renewing their rights of ownership.[33]

Additionally, archaeological surveys have recorded eight additional Middle Bronze Age sites within the region around Hebron. According to the surveyors, these sites were fortified during this period and located along routes through the hill country and the Shephelah.[34] Thus, Abraham and his progeny would not have wandered in a barren land devoid of settlement as they moved their flocks to different seasonal pastures. Rather, they probably moved from one site's territory to another's, using the fortified settlements and permanent water sources as waystations and trading posts.

31. Kenyon, *Amorites and Canaanites*, 74–76; The presence of individual graves for persons who were buried with spears, daggers, and bronze belts as well as accompanying equid burials in Syria, Canaan, and the Nile Delta led scholars to associate these "warrior burials" with a common Amorite background.

32. Victor P. Hamilton, *The Book of Genesis: Chapters 18–50* (Grand Rapids, MI: Eerdmans, 1995), 125.

33. Hallote, "Real and Ideal Identities," 109.

34. Moshe Kochavi, "The Land of Judah," in *Judaea, Samaria, and the Golan: Archaeological Survey, 1967–1968*, ed. Moshe Kochavi (Jerusalem: Carta and Archaeological Survey of Israel, 1972), 20.

JERUSALEM

While the specific place-name *Jerusalem* does not appear as such in the ancestral narratives in Genesis, scholars have equated the Holy City with Salem, the city of the priest-king Melchizedek (Genesis 14:18; see also Alma 13:17–18).[35] This association is based on the clear link between Salem and the rendering of Jerusalem as *(U)rusalimum* in the Execration Texts.[36] Excavations at Jerusalem have revealed that the area around the southeastern spur of the Eastern Hill, or the City of David, was settled long before the Middle Bronze Age. In addition to the city wall and fort surmounting the southeastern spur,[37] additional fortified towers dubbed the Pool Tower and the Spring Tower were exposed near the Gihon Spring. Both towers were built using large boulders weighing 3–4 tons each. Construction efforts near the water source also included digging a large pool (16 x 10 m, 14 m deep) as a reservoir for water and digging channels to divert some of the water for irrigation in the Kidron Valley.[38] The complexity of the water system that included two large fortification towers, channels, a reservoir cut into bedrock, and the incorporation of natural fissures indicates a certain level of labor organization in Jerusalem during the Middle Bronze Age required for these construction efforts to have been completed and for the sole water source of the city to have been protected. Such may have been the setting of Abraham's visit with Melchizedek (Genesis 14:17–20).

---

35. William F. Albright discounted the association between Salem and Jerusalem and emended the text of Genesis 14:18 to read, "And Melchizedek, a king allied to him [Abram] brought out bread and wine," removing any association between Melchizedek and Jerusalem and Abraham and Jerusalem. Driving this emendation was Albright's understanding of the archaeology of Jerusalem current with his time. See Albright, "Abraham the Hebrew," 52.
36. Rainey, "World of Sinuhe," 407.
37. This fortress is most likely the "stronghold of Zion" captured by David in 2 Samuel 5:6–9.
38. Ronny Reich and Eli Shukron, "Jerusalem: Excavations within the Ancient City, the Gihon Spring and Eastern Slope of the City of David," in *Stern, New Encyclopedia*, 5:1801–1805.

MORIAH

Jerusalem has also been linked to the binding and near sacrifice of Isaac in Genesis 22. God instructed Abraham to go "into the land of Moriah; and offer him there for a burnt offering upon one of the mountains which I will tell thee of" (Genesis 22:2). No further details are given about Moriah except that it was three days' journey from Beersheba and that Abraham named the place "Jehovah-jireh" after the episode was complete (Genesis 22:3–4, 14). Moriah was equated with Jerusalem later when the Chronicler tied the land of Moriah/Jehovah-jireh and the mountain where Abraham bound Isaac to the Temple Mount in Jerusalem (2 Chronicles 3:1), thereby linking the hierophany that occurred in Genesis 22 to the hierophany at the threshing floor of Araunah the Jebusite, where David had built an altar and offered sacrifice to stop the plague caused by his census of Israel (2 Samuel 24:10–25) and, ultimately, the construction of the First Temple, the supreme sacred space for biblical Israel and Judah. Thus, the sacrifice of Isaac may have occurred just to the north of the city of David at a place now associated with the First and Second Temples and the current Temple Mount in Jerusalem.

GERAR

Both Abraham and Isaac lived in the region of Gerar during droughts, and both had encounters with a ruler, or successive rulers, in the area named Abimelech (Genesis 20:1, 26:6). Concerning Abraham's activity in the region of Gerar and Beersheba, a place under the control of Gerar, the biblical record does not explicitly claim that he sacrificed in this area, but it is likely that he and Isaac both did so. Also, Abraham devoted some of his flock to establish a covenant with Abimelech. The fortifications at biblical Gerar in the western Negev date to the Middle Bronze Age and enclose an area of forty acres, making the site one of the largest in southern Canaan.[39] The site was surrounded by a defensive ditch and an earthen rampart with a stone facing. Within the fortifications, excavations encountered an extensive cultic complex consisting of a courtyard and various structures and installations. The remains of offerings, including sheep and goat bones

39. Eliezer D. Oren, "Haror, Tel," in Stern, *New Encyclopedia*, 2:580.

(62 percent of the collection), were found throughout the complex and in *favissae*, pits dug to dispose of ritual offerings or votive items. Excavators uncovered a palace or large patrician house, and pottery imported from Cyprus attests the site's prestige and commercial ties. Abimelech may have been a person of considerable relevance at the time, and a covenantal contract with Abraham seems to be reflected in religious relevance with the sacrifices offered between them. The favor Abraham gains in Abimelech's sight seems significant given his kingly status.

BEERSHEBA

No Middle Bronze Age remains were found in excavations of Tel Sheva, yet the excavator associated the well that had been dug near the gate of the site with the Abraham and Isaac traditions (Genesis 21:15; 26:25).[40] However, it can be seen that this theory is built on the faulty assumption that the well near the later Iron Age gate at Tel Sheva should be equated with the wells dug by Abraham and Isaac, although wells were usually dug closer to riverbeds to access groundwater during the Middle Bronze Age. Also, the location of any settlement called Beersheba during this ancestral period could be anywhere along the Nahal Beersheba and covered by alluvium from the seasonal stream, or the settlement's location was so ephemeral that no traces of habitation would be visible. However, there are locations in this region that could have fit the narrative of the ancestral stories.

SETTLEMENT PATTERNS IN THE NEGEV

The sites discussed above are named within the Genesis accounts of Abraham, Isaac, and Jacob. Additional sites in the Negev, unnamed in the biblical text but extant in the Middle Bronze Age, provide additional data about the experiences of Abraham and Isaac as they moved throughout the region (see figure 2). From west to east along the watercourses of the Nahal Besor, Nahal Beersheba, and Nahal Malhata, fortified centers and smaller sites that lack architecture in most cases testify to the nature of settlement along the southern frontier of Canaan. Two sites along the

40. Yohanan Aharoni, "Nothing Early and Nothing Late: Re-Writing Israel's Conquest," *Biblical Archaeologist* 39 (1976): 63.

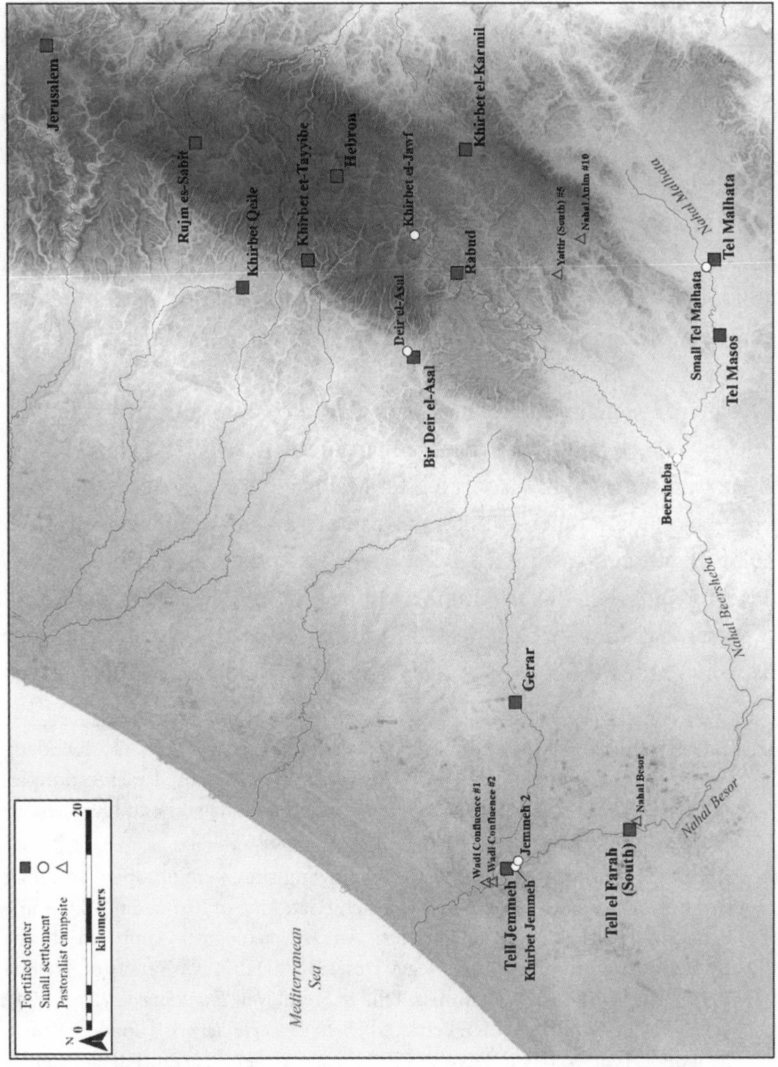

Figure 2. Middle Bronze Age fortified and unfortified settlements and campsites in the hill country and biblical Negev. Map by the author.

Nahal Besor are examples of sites with impermanent habitation.[41] In the absence of any trace of architecture, it is likely that these sites were

41. Amnon Gat, *Archaeological Survey of Israel: Map of Nirim (112)* (Jerusalem: Israel Antiquities Authority, 2012), sites 13 and 14.

campsites for nomadic or seminomadic groups that discarded broken items or left behind items that did not need to be transported to another site. In the region between Tel Masos and Hebron, an intensive survey was conducted around Horvat Yattir, and two Middle Bronze sites were likely satellites of a larger site yet to be discovered or were temporary settlements for seminomadic groups.[42] Inside the remains of an elliptical building made of fieldstones, a stone installation probably served as a hearth, and flint tools were found near the structure. It is possible that Isaac and Jacob may have lived in such structures during their extended habitation in the areas of Gerar or Shechem.

The permanent settlements were likely a chain of fortified sites comprising Tell el-Ajjul near the Mediterranean coast, Tell Jemmeh, Tell el-Farah (South), Tel Masos, and Tel Malhata. These fortified sites functioned not only as defensive sites but also as waystations for caravans from points south and east that headed overland to the Mediterranean ports or to Egypt via the Sinai.[43] Imported pottery from Cyprus at these sites suggests that they were connected to the larger Mediterranean exchange network of the Middle Bronze Age and were well situated on the overland

42. Yattir (South) and Nahal Anim; see Ya'akov Baumgarten and Hillel Silberklang, *Archaeological Survey of Israel: Map of Yattir (136)* (Jerusalem: Israel Antiquities Authority, 2015), sites 165 and 229; Hanan Eshel, Jodi Magness, and Eli Shenhav, "Yattir, Khirbet," in Stern, *New Encyclopedia*, 5:2069.

43. Archaeological data suggests that the following sites were occupied and fortified during the same period: Tell Jemmeh (Gat, *Map of Nirim*, Site 10; Jerome Schaefer, "The Ecology of Empires: An Archaeological Approach to the Byzantine Communities of the Negev Desert" [PhD diss., University of Arizona, 1979]; Gus W. Van Beek, "Jemmeh, Tell," in Stern, *New Encyclopedia*, 2:667–74); Tell el-Far'ah (South) (W. M. F. Petrie, ed., *Beth-Pelet I (Tell Fara)* [London: British School of Archaeology in Egypt, 1930]; Yigael Yisraeli, "Far'ah, Tell el- (South)," in Stern, *New Encyclopedia*, 2:441–44; Dan Gazit, *Archaeological Survey of Israel: Map of Urim (125)* [Jerusalem: Israel Antiquities Authority, 1996]); Tel Masos (Volkmar Fritz and Aharon Kempinski, eds., *Ergebnisse der Ausgrabungen auf der Hirbet el-Msas (Tel Masos), 1972–1975* [Wiesbaden: Harrassowitz, 1983]; Aharon Kempinski, "Masos, Tel," in Stern, *New Encyclopedia*, 3: 986–989); and Tel Malhata (Ruth Amiran and Carmela Arnon, "Notes and News: Small Tel Malhata," *Israel Exploration Journal* 29 [1979]: 255–56; Ruth Amiran and Ornit Ilan, "Malhata, Tel (Small)," in Stern, *New Encyclopedia*, 3:937–39; Moshe Kochavi, "Malhata, Tel," in Stern, *New Encyclopedia*, 3:934–36).

route connecting Egypt and Canaan.[44] For most of these sites, smaller, less permanent satellite sites were found in close vicinity. These smaller sites lacking architecture may be considered campsites or areas where herds and flocks were kept and were dependent on the larger settlements for stable food and water supplies.[45] The ancestral narratives may have occurred in such settings as they traveled extensively across the region. Smaller structures may have also been used by those engaged in pastoral nomadism, or transhumance, as a temporary dwelling for those accompanying flocks to pasture areas, an example of "indigenous hardiness structures" in which people adapt to being sedentary or nomadic through a cycle of dwellings from buildings to caves to tents.[46] The archaeology of these sites provides a window into the seminomadic life of the Middle Bronze Age and may indicate the types of artifacts left behind by Abraham, Isaac, and their households as they moved from Hebron through the Negev to Beersheba, Gerar, Kadesh, and other sites in the western Negev.

PASTORAL ELEMENTS OF NEAR EASTERN SOCIETY

It is clear from the accounts in Genesis that the ancestors focused much of their efforts on pastoral pursuits, although herding was only part of their group economy.[47] From the division of the livestock of Abraham and

---

44. Celia Bergoffen, "Imported Cypriot and Mycenaean Wares and Derivative Wares," in *The Smithsonian Institution Excavation at Tell Jemmeh, Israel, 1970–1990*, ed. Gus W. Van Beek and David Ben-Shlomo (Washington, DC: Smithsonian Institution Scholarly Press, 2014), 657–61; David Ben-Shlomo, "Synthesis and Conclusions: The Significance of Tell Jemmeh," in Van Beek and Ben-Shlomo, *Tell Jemmeh*, 1054.
45. Nelson Glueck, "The Age of Abraham in the Negeb," *Biblical Archaeologist* 18 (1955): 4.
46. Øystein LaBianca, *Hesban 1, Sedentarization and Nomadization: Food System Cycles at Hesban and Vicinity in Transjordan* (Berrien Springs, MI: Andrews University Press, 1992).
47. Victor H. Matthews, "Pastoralists and Patriarchs," *Biblical Archaeologist* 44 (1981): 215. Additionally, Albright argued that Abraham was a donkey caravaneer in the nineteenth century BC based on an understanding that verbs

Lot (Genesis 13:5–12) to Jacob's perception about flock watering (Genesis 29:1–10) and a perception about animal genetics (Genesis 30:41–42), the biblical record indicates that the ancestors of the Israelites were highly engaged with pastoralism. Transhumance, moving pastures seasonally with a herd or flock, is highlighted in the ancestral narratives once a stable base of operations was established, such as Isaac's dwelling near Gerar or Jacob's dwelling near Hebron.[48]

In the ancient Near East, both Palestine and most of northern Syria and Mesopotamia accommodated a mixed economy of pastoral nomadic and agricultural activity.[49] Environmental conditions in the hill country of Canaan and the Negev prompted the development of a society in which farmers and pastoralists would have had a natural symbiosis to better

---

stemming from the root *sḥr* meaning "to trade (in), trader" applied directly to Abraham (Genesis 23:16) and later Jacob and his sons (Genesis 34:10, 21; 37:28; 42:34). See Albright, "Abraham the Hebrew," 44–52; Albright, "From the Patriarchs to Moses," 12. However, applying this term to Abraham and his descendants based on these scriptural references is problematic because the verses do not directly refer to activities conducted by the ancestors. In Genesis 23:16, the passage refers to the weighing of silver according to the merchant standards of the day as Abraham purchased the Cave of Machpelah from Ephron the Hethite without clearly stating that Abraham or Ephron were merchants: "Abraham weighed to Ephron the silver, which he had named in the audience of the sons of Heth, four hundred shekels of silver, current *money* with the merchant" (italics in KJV). In the later uses, E. A. Speiser preferred to interpret the forms of *sḥr* as "to move about (freely)" so that both Genesis 34:10, 21 and Genesis 37:28 can be seen as encouragements from the ruler of Shechem to the household of Jacob to stay within the territory of Shechem with the understanding that as pastoral nomads, Jacob and his family would interact with the members of the settled population and provide products such as wool, hair, milk, other dairy products, and even animals for cultic practices. Ephraim A. Speiser, *Genesis: Introduction, Translation, and Notes* (New York: Doubleday, 1964). The final occurrence in Genesis 42:34 would also draw in this meaning of free movement as Joseph instructs his brothers to return to Egypt with Benjamin to secure safe travel in the land.

48. Matthews, "Pastoralists and Patriarchs," 217.

49. Pastoralism is an adaptation to environmental and political conditions and is an economic mode of production not indicative or exclusively tied to a permanent habitation within a region. Victor H. Matthews, "The Wells of Gerar," *Biblical Archaeologist* 49 (1986): 119.

exploit the region's limited natural resources.[50] However, local pastoralists who were living in villages and migratory pastoralists would have interacted and even come into conflict with each other. Grazing and water rights would have been shared between members of the same kinship group or their allies, prompting outside groups to move their flocks elsewhere in search of pastures without tribal claims.[51] Engaging in pastoralism mixed with other economic endeavors would have been considered the norm for marginal regions such as the hill country and Negev.

Faunal remains from archaeological excavations and ancient textual records illustrate the importance of pastoralism and pastoral products within the economy of Canaan. The age at death in the faunal remains at Canaanite sites indicates a primacy on dairy production.[52] Further, a cuneiform tablet found during excavations at Hebron records numbers of sheep, "small cattle," and lambs collected by female tax collectors and mentions a king, possibly the king of Hebron.[53] Some of the sheep and goats may be described as "shorn," indicating that wool and hair were collected from these animals prior to their transfer to the tax collectors.[54] Seventy-seven of the sheep or goats were destined for sacrifice or covenant rituals. This accords with the ancestral narratives in that pastoralists were an acknowledged component of Canaanite society and were valued for the products of their flocks and herds. It is also possible that Abraham and Isaac may have also been taxed in such materials in exchange for grazing rights.

The number of sheep and goat bones from pits and cultic contexts at biblical Gerar and Shechem show the importance of these animals in religious rites. The practice of slaughtering an animal in sealing a covenant

---

50. Michael B. Rowton, "Dimorphic Structure and Topology," *Oriens Antiquus* 15 (1976): 20.

51. Matthews, "The Wells of Gerar," 121.

52. Edward Maher, "Temporal Trends in Animal Exploitation: Faunal Analysis from Tell Jemmeh," in Van Beek and Shlomo, *Tell Jemmeh*, 1038–53.

53. Anbar and Na'aman, "An Account Tablet of Sheep," 10–11.

54. Wayne Horowitz and Takayoshi Oshima, *Cuneiform in Canaan: Cuneiform Sources from the Land of Israel in Ancient Times* (Jerusalem: Israel Exploration Society, 2006), 90.

was widespread in the Near East and attested in several texts. This portrays such rituals as witnessed between Abraham and the Lord (Genesis 15:8–17) and Abimelech (Genesis 21:22–34). A tablet found at the ancient site of Alalakh in Turkey relates the details of a covenant between an imperial vizier and a local ruler in which the local ruler received the city of Alalakh in exchange for another town destroyed in the process of suppressing a rebellion.[55] As part of the covenant ritual, the vizier "placed himself under oath to [the local ruler] and had cut the neck of a sheep (saying): '(Let me so die) if I take back that which I gave you.'"[56] The local ruler was required to maintain allegiance to his overlord lest he forfeit the territory granted to him. Among the twenty thousand cuneiform tablets found at the ancient site of Mari on the Euphrates River, several references are made concerning the establishment of covenants and the animals sacrificed.[57] Parallels between these rituals and the establishment of the covenant between Abraham and the Lord in Genesis 15:9–17, in which Abraham slaughters a young heifer, a she-goat, a dove, and a pigeon, are clear since these bisected animals represent the penalty if the covenant is forfeited.

Anthropological concepts of pastoralism, ancient texts, and the archaeological record illustrate the pastoral economies of the ancestors in the biblical record. Conflict between herding groups competing for resources is exemplified in Genesis 13:6, in which "the land was not able to bear them," causing Abraham and Lot to separate and causing a reassurance of the covenant blessing of property given to Abraham (Genesis 13:14–17). Isaac is depicted engaging in both agriculture and pastoralism in the region of Gerar (Genesis 26:12, 14), but his group soon comes into conflict with the herders from the sedentary population over access to water, suggesting that the wells were nearer to grazing areas than the agricultural fields or urban center (Genesis 26:14–33). The seizure and defense of wells mentioned in the *Tale of Sinuhe* also finds parallels in the lives of

---

55. Donald J. Wiseman, *The Alalakh Tablets* (London: The British Museum, 1953), AT 1 and AT 456.
56. Donald J. Wiseman, "Abban and Alalah," *Journal of Cuneiform Studies* 12 (1958): 129.
57. Moshe Held, "Philological Notes on the Mari Covenant Rituals," *Bulletin of the American Schools of Oriental Research* 200 (1970): 33, 40.

Abraham and Isaac in the Negev (Genesis 21:25; 26:15, 20).[58] Yet it must be noted that the ancestors were not outcasts or shunned by society but were economically integrated into the larger economies of the Canaanite kingdoms by providing wool, hair, hides, dairy products, meat, and even live animals to the settled centers. As Matthews observes, "The patriarchal narratives simply point out to the reader how crucial the maintenance of good relations with the indigenous inhabitants of the land actually were."[59]

THE ANCESTRAL NARRATIVES AS A COGNITIVE MAP

Landscape is more than a flat backdrop for events through time or a container for actions. Equally, it is more than a playing board for a complex geopolitical chess game between historical figures, warring tribes, or conquering empires. Regardless of geographical or temporal location, every feature of landscape is enriched with people's stories and beliefs, and these associated meanings give those places significance. A deeper investigation into the sites and regions associated with the ancestors of Israel gives possible insight into the collective consciousness of Israel as a people later in history. The ancestral narratives within the book of Genesis function as a cognitive map informing audiences, ancient and modern, about the places associated with these accounts.

The concept of a cognitive map, and its associated layers of meanings for locales and for guiding of actions, is employed by anthropologists intent on discovering the thought processes of ancient peoples. People navigate by landmarks—things that can be seen—and along paths, choosing the correct route whilst at a node, a connection, or intersection of paths. Because mental maps represent a shared worldview with other members of society and because those maps bind society together, they are part of a person's cultural makeup.[60] Being able to construct a cognitive

58. Simpson, *Literature of Ancient Egypt*, 59.

59. Matthews, "The Wells of Gerar," 124.

60. John J. Chiodo, "Improving the Cognitive Development of Students' Mental Maps of the World," *Journal of Geography* 96 (1997): 154.

map requires composing a complex image of locations and their spatial relationship, drawing on layers of meaning for each locale.

Traditional homelands form part of the cultural reality of the cognized landscape, and multiperiod settlements hold spiritual and secular values.[61] It is the site from which the ancestors came and the place where the descendants will return. A sense of place is fundamental to the formation of biographies and the establishment of identities for groups and individuals.[62] This sense of place marks the fundamental concept underlying a reading of Genesis as a cognitive map for its Israelite audience. The ancestors sojourned and built altars to their deity throughout Canaan, the setting of their biographies as related in Genesis, and their chosen descendants are thereby entitled to inherit the land under the terms of the Abrahamic covenant (Genesis 12:7; 15:7, 18–21; 17:8, 22:7; 26:3; 28:13; 35:12).

A cognitive map is not simply an abstract coordinate system of the mind, but a setting loaded with historic references, mythic tales, and past experiences that bridge the gap between the physical and imagined landscape. This study should encourage a new reading of the text, seeking elements that would connect the Israelites with the ancestors and illuminate what the Israelites thought of certain locales. If naming a spot is an act of construction of landscape (constituting an origin point for it), then narratives make locales markers of individual and group experiences. Thus, the ancestral narratives function as a cognitive map, revealing the positive and negative feelings toward various sites and regions within the promised land. Places and movements of people are related to the formation of biographies, and places acquire layers of meaning as people interact with those places throughout time. The locales related in Genesis, such as Hebron, Machpelah, Beersheba, and Shechem, are stratified with the memories of the ancestors. A brief discussion of a few of these places allows one to see the values the Israelites would have associated with them.

---

61. Ezra B. W. Zubrow, "Knowledge Representation and Archaeology: A Cognitive Example Using GIS," in *The Ancient Mind: Elements of Cognitive Archaeology*, ed. Colin Renfrew and E. B. W. Zubrow (Cambridge: Cambridge University Press, 1994), 112.

62. Christopher Tilley, *A Phenomenology of Landscape: Places, Paths, and Monuments* (Oxford: Berg, 1994), 18.

In Genesis 13:17, God commanded Abraham to walk the length and breadth of the land promised to him; therefore, the place-names associated with his journeys would feature in the developing sense of place within the Israelites' minds. Abraham's rescue of Lot and the specific mention of Dan (Genesis 14:14) helped to give boundaries to the later Israelite territory, despite the anachronistic use of the place-name rather than its Canaanite name, Laish (Judges 18:29). Abraham's treaty with Abimelech over watering rights led to the establishment of the "Well of the Oath," or Beersheba (Genesis 21:22–33). Abraham was not the only patriarch to dwell at Beersheba, since Isaac also included Beersheba (Genesis 26:20–32), as well as Hebron (Genesis 35:27–28), Gerar (Genesis 26:1, 7), and Beer-lahai-roi (Genesis 24:62; 25:11), in his nomadic journeys, adding another layer of meaning and history to each place. Later, the prophet Amos (8:14) intimated that Beersheba was a place for pilgrimage and oracles. Taken together, two sites form the all-inclusive boundary for biblical Israel, "from Dan to Beersheba" (Judges 20:1; 2 Samuel 17:11, 24:2, 15; 1 Kings 4:25). Abraham's presence at both sites allowed Israel to know that both sites fell within the land promised to them.

Landscape allows for an observer to investigate and organize reality in a particular way that may be different from others. The narratives surrounding Shechem are an example of the biblical authors having marked differences of opinion about Shechem. The picture of Shechem presented in Genesis is not pleasant. Except for God's revelation to Abraham of the land grant and Abraham's construction of an altar (Genesis 12:6–7), the exploits of Jacob's children in Shechem were unfavorable. The incident between Dinah and Shechem, as well as the revenge taken by Simeon and Levi at the expense of the Shechemites, gave Jacob cause to fear the Canaanites. The honor of Jacob's entire family was at stake, and Jacob's response to his sons' actions (Genesis 34:30) indicates that their recourse was less than honorable as well, even if it was culturally appropriate. Coupled with the actions of Jacob's sons to sell Joseph into slavery in the Dothan region (Genesis 37:17ff), the impression given by the biblical author of the region of Shechem is one of wickedness and bloody revenge, both real and potential. Later, Abimelech, the son of Gideon, failed in his bid to become king during the period of the Judges, and emphasis is made in the story concerning the treachery of the men of Shechem (Judges 9). In a turn of events, Shechem became the first capital of the northern kingdom of Israel under Jeroboam following the division of the kingdom after Rehoboam, Solomon's son, attempted to be recognized as king in Shechem (1 Kings 12:1, 25). Clearly, the role of a refuge city in Joshua 21 contrasts with the pictures of Shechem related in Genesis and Judges, and the perception of Shechem had changed from the powerful Canaanite kingdom to a wicked region during Jacob's lifetime to a city of refuge during the early Israelite settlement to a treacherous city and rival to Jerusalem during the reign of the Judges and early years of the divided monarchy. Landscape archaeologist Christopher Tilley posits that landscape allows for "mnemonic pegs on which moral teachings hang," and the moral lessons of Genesis 34 and 37 probably echoed in the minds of Israelites who knew the story well.[63]

CONCLUSION: LESSONS FROM THE ANCESTORS

Canaan was situated as a "land between" greater political powers of Egypt to the south and Syro-Mesopotamia to the north and east. Certain pottery forms and decoration, metal weapons, and imagery from seals show direct relations with Mesopotamia and northern Syria. Other cultural features such as fortification types, building techniques, architectural styles, burial customs, and artistic motifs appear to be derived from Amorite culture and subsequently shared across the Near East, with Canaan having some developments unique to itself in each of these areas. While some Egyptian texts focus on the destruction of Egypt's enemies in Canaan and elsewhere, other evidence, such as tomb paintings and Egyptian artifacts found at Levantine sites, points to less hostile diplomatic and commercial interactions between Egyptians and Canaanites in the Middle Bronze Age, providing a context for the events of Genesis and the Book of Abraham. The same Egyptian tomb paintings also give a contemporary glimpse into the appearance and lifestyle of the Canaanite population, among whom the ancestors lived their seminomadic existence while leaving little archaeological evidence behind regarding their pastoral pursuits. Canaan as the

63. Tilley, *Phenomenology of Landscape*, 33.

"land between" the powers of Mesopotamia and Egypt was the stage for the ancestral narratives following the obedience of Abraham to the covenant call to leave his family group in Haran and sojourn in a land that the Lord would show to Abraham.

Urban theorist Kevin A. Lynch wrote that "striking landscape is the skeleton upon which many primitive races erect their socially important myths."[64] While one would hesitate to call the ancestral narratives myths from a primitive race, the importance of landscape, both physical and mental, is evident. Although this paper only treated a few of the place-names mentioned in the Genesis text, the ancestral activity at each place tied their descendants to the land. The future Israelites, upon establishing themselves in Canaan, could hardly look to Shechem and not think of Dinah or look to Beersheba and not be mindful of the sheep and watering rights secured by Abraham and Isaac with the local polity. Hebron, with its affiliation as Abraham's home and the ancestral burial place, bears great significance. The conquest narratives end after Kiriath-arba (Hebron) is apportioned to Caleb, thus securing the family burial ground as part of the birthright inheritance of Judah (Joshua 14.15). Only then could the land have rest from war, and only then could the Israelites begin the tasks associated with subsistence and establishment of civil order. With each passing generation since Abraham, the ancestors and their offspring added more and more meaning to the locales.

The stories of ancestors of Israel, their subsistence in Canaan, and their interactions with the local populace provided and continue to provide valuable lessons for the audiences of Genesis. Part of Abraham's test of faith is placing him in a land where he needs to rely on divine providence. He was not placed in a land empty of inhabitants and replete with natural resources and easy conditions for success. Abraham and his descendants, through Jacob and his sons, would effectively be resident aliens on the margins of society in the land promised to them by divine covenant. Part of the test of faith for Abraham and his family involved them looking to God for protection and fulfillment of the covenantal blessings rather than relying on their own intuition, cunning, adept political maneuvering

64. Kevin A. Lynch, *The Image of the City* (Cambridge, MA: Massachusetts Institute of Technology Press, 1960), 4.

when negotiating pastoral rights, or the strength of the fortified centers with which they interacted. Even the wayward Egyptian Sinuhe noted that "God acts in such a way to be merciful to one . . . whom He led astray to another land."[65] The message for the modern reader is clear: in assessing one's faith, God places one in circumstances that will necessitate a decision to look to him for guidance and providence or to rely on the arm of flesh—the perceived strength of the world. Hebrews 11:8–10 relates that Abraham, Isaac, and Jacob hearkened to their divine calls and lived lives of faith, thus providing the example of faithful living to the house of Israel and all the nations of the earth who are and will be blessed through Abraham and his seed.

---

65. Simpson, *Literature of Ancient Egypt*, 60.

ISRAEL, EGYPT, AND CANAAN

KERRY MUHLESTEIN

Valuable to any student of the Bible is an understanding of the geographical and political entities that engaged with ancient Israel. In the previous chapter, George Pierce provided insight into the immediate surroundings of ancient Canaan during the time of the patriarchs and matriarchs. In this chapter, Kerry Muhlestein follows a similar approach but focuses instead on Israel's arguably most important neighbor during the time period we are discussing: Egypt. Delving into the social and cultural world of Egypt and this superpower's influence throughout the known world, this chapter sheds light on the difficulties the ancient Israelites might have encountered and the unique challenges they experienced while engaging with their neighbors to the southwest. —DB and AS

In our attempts to better understand the stories of the Bible, we must come to more fully understand the world of the Bible. An important element of life for biblical characters was the way their culture interacted with the peoples and cultures around them. Egyptian culture was one of the most influential cultures in the era of the Old Testament, especially in the early parts of it. The military and political clout that sprang from the Nile Valley—and the prestige that accompanied the Egyptian culture and its achievements—played a larger role in biblical stories than we often realize. If we truly desire to understand the world of the Bible, then we have to explore the interactions that the people of the Bible had with their powerful southwestern neighbor. As we detail some of these interactions, we can more fully picture familiar biblical stories. As a result, these oft-read stories should then become fuller and more vibrant and, in a way, can then become a new story.

Egypt's relations with the land and peoples of Canaan varied a great deal between the life of Abraham and the conquest of Canaan by the Israelites. During this span we see a continuum of contact that ranges from minor associations between these areas to complete domination of them by Egypt. While we do not know as much about these relations as we would like, analyzing them can help to explain how Egypt and Canaan affected biblical characters and events.

PLACING BIBLICAL EVENTS HISTORICALLY

To explore these interactions, we must first determine which eras of Egyptian history we should consider. Determining a date for the patriarchs and matriarchs is a difficult task. The lack of biblical uniformity in dating schemes, as well as a comparable paucity of biblical information about the world around Abraham and Sarah—which could be synchronized with established chronologies—makes the task of dating the lives of Abraham and Sarah somewhat speculative. For the purposes of this chapter, we will use the dating scheme proposed by John M. Lundquist in the *Studies in Scripture* series.[1] Lundquist posits that Abraham was born in about 1943

1. John M. Lundquist, "The Exodus," in *Studies in Scripture*, vol. 3: *Genesis to 2 Samuel*, ed. Kent P. Jackson and Robert L. Millet (Salt Lake City: Deseret

BC, which would place his long adult life right in the middle of Egypt's Middle Kingdom. While it may seem that the Middle Kingdom's more than two hundred years of existence provides only a very rough date range, we must also remember that Abraham himself lived for almost two hundred years, most of which must have overlapped with Egypt's Twelfth Dynasty (ca. 1950–1750 BC). John Gee has looked further into Egyptian evidence and compared it with the story of the Book of Abraham in order to further refine the date and has confirmed that the Twelfth Dynasty is the era we should be looking at.[2] Accordingly, we turn to the time of the Middle Kingdom to examine its *zeitgeist* (a German term scholars use to describe the unique spirit, circumstances, or climate of the time) of Egypt's relations with its northern neighbors during Abraham's life.

Dating the Israelite conquest of Canaan hinges on the date of the Exodus. There are many theories as to when the Exodus occurred, but we cannot ascertain with any certainty which pharaoh interacted with Moses. We can be sure that it had at least happened by the reign of Merneptah, the son of Ramses the Great, because Merneptah, in the first extrabiblical attestation of Israel,[3] mentions battle with Israelites in the land of Canaan early in his reign.[4] Thus, the conquest should have happened before 1200

Book, 1989), 112. Many historical studies also use this approximate date. See also the discussion by Pierce in this volume.

2. John Gee, "Overlooked Evidence for Sesotris III's Foreign Policy," *Journal of the American Research Center in Egypt* (2004): 23–31.

3. In this reference Merneptah mentions a series of locations, each followed by an Egyptian hieroglyph that indicates that these locations were geographical places. The word *Israel* is followed not by the glyph that indicates a geographic location but by a glyph that indicates a group of people.

4. See Dan'el Kahn, "A Geo-Political and Historical Perspective of Mernephtah's Policy in Canan," in *The Ancient Near East in the 12th–10th Centuries BCE: Culture and History*, ed. Gershon Galil et al., Alter Orient und Altes Testament 392 (Munster, Germany: Ugarit-Verlag, 2012), 255–68; M. G. Hasel, "Israel in the Merneptah Stele," *Bulletin of the American Schools of Oriental Research* 296 (1994): 45–61; Kenneth A. Kitchen, "The Physical Text of Merenptah's Victory Hymn (The 'Israel Stela')," *Journal of the Society for the Study of Egyptian Antiquities* 29 (1994): 71–76. Kahn's article contains a good summary of the scholarship on this important stela.

BC, toward the end of the New Kingdom of Egypt.[5] As a result, we will explore the relations between Egypt and Canaan from 2000 BC until 1200 BC, spanning from Egypt's Middle Kingdom to nearly the end of the New Kingdom.

EGYPT IN CANAAN UNDER ABRAHAM, ISAAC, AND JACOB

Opinions about the extent of Egypt's interrelationship with Canaan and the surrounding area during the Middle Kingdom have shifted substantially over the past fifty years. As we continue to garner more evidence, our understanding becomes more and more nuanced. Currently it seems that while there was no Egyptian empire in Canaan during the lives of Abraham, Sarah, Rebekah, Isaac, Rachel, and Jacob, there was an organic, healthy, and lively exchange between the two areas,[6] though the amount of contact Egypt had with Canaan, especially southern Canaan, is much smaller than Egypt had with Canaan's northern neighbors in modern

5. See Shmuel Ahituv, "The Exodus—Survey of the Theories of the Last Fifty Years," in *Jerusalem Studies in Egyptology*, ed. Irene Shirun-Grumach (Wiesbaden, Germany: Harrassowitz Verlag, 1998), 132; Manfred Bietak, "Comments on the 'Exodus,'" in *Egypt, Israel, Sinai*, ed. Anson F. Rainey (Tel Aviv: Tel Aviv University, 1987); Sarah I. Groll, "The Egyptian Background of the Exodus and the Crossing of the Red Sea: A New Reading of Papyrus Anastasi VIII," in Shirun-Grumach, *Jerusalem Studies in Egyptology*, 189–92. See also Frank J. Yurco, "Merenptah's Canaanite Campaign and Israel's Origins," in *Exodus: the Egyptian Evidence*, ed. Ernest S. Frerichs and Leonard H. Lesko (Winona Lake, In: Eisenbrauns, 1997), 50, who uses the Merenptah Stela, Exodus 15, Judges 5, and "the milieu of Ramesses II's Egypt," to date "the root of the Exodus story to the Ramesside era."
6. See Kerry Muhlestein, "Levantine Thinking in Egypt," in *Egypt, Canaan and Israel: History, Imperialism, Ideology and Literature*, ed. S. Bar, D. Kahn, and J. J. Shirley, Culture and History of the Ancient Near East 52 (Leiden: Brill, 2011), 190–235. See also Donald B. Redford, *Egypt, Canaan, and Israel in Ancient Times* (Princeton: Princeton University Press, 1992), 81.

Lebanon and Syria.[7] Even in the Southern Levant during this period, there were various times and sometimes specific places where and when Egypt demonstrated a strong dominance.[8]

There were undoubtedly cities, such as Megiddo, where Egypt maintained some kind of trading presence that included officials residing in Syria and Canaan for a lengthy period.[9] Egyptian representatives obtained Canaanite levies that included cattle, wine, vessels, oil, metals, food, weapons, semiprecious stones, and people.[10] This was true of areas north

---

7. Susan L. Cohen, "Synchronisms and Significance: Reevaluating Interconnections Between Middle Kingdom Egypt and the Southern Levant," *Journal of Ancient Egyptian Interconnections* 4, no. 3 (2012): 1–8.
8. See Gee, "Overlooked Evidence for Sesotris III's Foreign Policy," 23–31. See also Susan L. Cohen, *Canaanites, Chronologies, and Connections: The Relationship of Middle Bronze IIA Canaan to Middle Kingdom Egypt* (Winona Lake, IN: Eisenbrauns, 2002), 50, 139.
9. See Aylward M. Blackman, *The Rock-Tombs of Meir* (London: Egypt Exploration Society, 1915), pl. 4; Amihai Mazar, *Archaeology of the Land of the Bible*, The Anchor Bible Reference Library (New York: Doubleday, 1990), 187; Manfred Bietak, "Canaanites in the Eastern Nile Delta," in Rainey, *Egypt, Israel, Sinai*, 50; Sami Farag, "Un insciption memphite de la XIIe dynastie," *Revue d'Égyptologie* 32 (1980): 75–82, pls. 3–5; H. Altenmüller and A. M. Moussa, "Die Inschrift Amenemhets II aus dem Ptah-Tempel von Memphis. Ein Vorbericht" *SAK* 18 (1991): 1–48; John Gee and Stephen D. Ricks, "Historical Plausibility: The Historicity of the Book of Abraham as a Case Study," in *Historicity and the Latter-day Saint Scriptures*, ed. Paul Y. Hoskisson (Provo, UT: Religious Studies Center, Brigham Young University, 2001), 77; Georges Posener, "Fragment littéraire de Moscou," *Mitteilungen des Deutschen Archäologischen Instituts* 25 (1969): 101–6; Redford, *Egypt, Canaan, and Israel*, 77–78.
10. See Farag, "Un insciption memphite de la XIIe dynastie," 75–82, pls. 3–5; H. Altenmüller and A. M. Moussa, "Die Inschrift Amenemhets II aus dem Ptah-Tempel von Memphis. Ein Vorbericht," 1–48; Gee and Ricks, "Historical Plausibility" in Hoskisson, *Historicity and the Latter-day Saint Scriptures*, 77. Regarding Egyptian trade routes, see Wolfgang Helck, *Die Beziehungen Ägyptens zu Vorderasien in 3. und 2. Jahrtausend v. Chr.* (Wiesbaden, Germany: Harrasowitz, 1962), 63.

and east of Canaan as well,[11] especially Byblos,[12] and, to a lesser degree, areas such as Ebla.[13] Trade relations are witnessed by the presence of Syro-Canaanite goods in Egypt, such as cedar, which is attested both textually and archaeologically.[14] We cannot always tell which of these goods

---

11. See, for example, Gabriella Matthiae, "The Relations between Ebla and Egypt," in *The Hyksos: New Historical and Archaeological Perspectives,* ed. E. D. Oren (Philadelphia: The University Museum, 1997), 420–21. See also H. A. Liebowitz, "Bone and Ivory Inlay from Syria and Palestine," *Israel Exploration Journal* 27 (1977): 89–97; J. Von Beckerath, *Unterschungen zur politischen Gesichte der zweiten Zwischenzeit in Ägypten* (Glückstadt: Augistin, 1956), 250; Mazar, *Archaeology of the Land of the Bible*, 187; Biri Fay, *The Louvre Sphinx and Royal Sculpture from the Reign of Amenenhat II* (Mainz: Philipp von Zabern, 1006), 64, 68, pl. 94; R. Giveon "The Impact of Egypt on Canaan in the Middle Bronze Age," *Israel, Egypt, Sinai,* A. F. Rainey, ed. (Tel Aviv: Tel Aviv University, 1987), 27; Matthiae, "The Relations between Ebla and Egypt," 422; Redford, *Egypt, Canaan, and Israel,* 81; Kurt Bittel, *Hattusha, the Capital of the Hittites* (New York: Oxford University Press, 1970), 114–15; Rachael Sparks, "Egyptian Stone Vessels in Syro–Palestine During the Second Millennium B.C. and Their Impact on the Local Stone Vessel Industry," in *Cultural Interaction in the Ancient Near East: Papers Read at a Symposium Held at the University of Melbourne, Department of Classics and Archaeology (29–30 September 1994)*, ed. Guy Bunnens (Louvain: Peeters, 1996), 66.
12. See Pierre Montet, *Byblos et l'Egypte: Quatre compagnes de fouilles a Gebeil 1921–1922–1923–1924* (Paris: Geuthnerr, 1929), 127–39; Mazar, *Archaeology of the Land of the Bible*, 187; William Ward, *Egypt and the East Mediterranean World, 2200–1900 B.C.: Studies in Egyptian Foreign Relations during the First Intermediate Period* (Beirut: American University of Beirut, 1971), 62–63; Barry J. Kemp, "Old Kingdom, Middle Kingdom and Second Intermediate Period," in *Ancient Egypt: A Social History*, ed. B. G. Trigger, et al. (New York: Cambridge University Press, 1998), 145–46; Mazar, *Archaeology of the Land of the Bible*, 187; Giveon, *[Title]*, 24; James Allen, "The Historical Inscription of Khnumhotep at Dashur: Preliminary Report," *Bulletin of the American Schools of Oriental Research* 352 (2008): 29–39; Muhlestein, "Levantine Thinking," 190–99.
13. See Muhlestein, "Levantine Thinking," 194–95.
14. See William C. Hayes, "Career of the Great Steward Henenu under Nebhetpetre Mentuhotpe," *Journal of Egyptian Archaeology* 35 (1949): 43–49; James P. Allen, "Some Theban Officials of the Early Middle Kingdom," in *Studies in Honor of William Kelly Simpson*, ed. Peter der Manuelian (Boston: Museum of Fine Arts, 1996), 1:18–21; Gregory Mumford, "Syria-Palestine," in *Oxford Encyclopedia of Ancient Egypt*, ed. Donald B. Redford (Oxford: Oxford University Press, 2001), 338.

came to Egypt via economic trade as opposed to arriving through coerced levies, but certainly both took place.

The fact that the ancient Egyptians felt like they had obtained some kind of hegemony over many parts of Canaan is illustrated by two groups of texts from this time period[15] that were designed to keep down rebellion, or even magically cut off rebellious thinking, in Canaanite cities such as Jerusalem, Ashkelon, Rehob, Akko, Mishal, Achshaf, Valley of Akko, Iyon, Laish, Hazor, Qedesh, and Shechem.[16] Certainly Egypt maintained at least some kind of influence or even dominance in these places if the ancient Egyptians felt that there was potential for rebellion against them in such places. This idea is augmented in a number of ways, especially since there are several texts that describe fighting against the people of Canaan and its neighbors[17] and texts that inform us that Egyptian kings such as

---

15. On the applicability of these texts to this period, see Muhlestein, "Levantine Thinking," 195–97.

16. See Georges Posener and Baudouin van de Walle, *Princes et pays d'Asie et de Nubie: Textes hiératiques sur des figurines d'envoûtement du moyen empire suivis de Remarques paléographiques sur lest textes similaires de Berlin, par B. van de Walle* (Brussels: Fondation égyptologique rein Élisabeth, 1940); Kurt Sethe, *Die Ächtung feindlicher Fürsten, Völker und Dinge auf altägyptischen Tongefässcherben des mittleren Reiches, nach den Originalen im Berliner Museum*, ed. Berlin Deutsche Akademie der Wissenschaften zu, Abhandlungen, Jahrg. 1926, Nr. 5 (Berlin: Verlag der Akademie der Wissenschaften in Kommission bei Walter de Gruyter, 1926); Andre Vila, "Un Depot de Textes D'Envoûtement au Moyen Empire," *Journal des Savants* 41 (1963), 135-60; Yvan Koenig, "Les textes d'envoûtement de Mirgissa," *Revue d'Égyptologie* (1990): 101–28; Amnon Ben-Tor, "Do the Execration Texts Reflect an Accurate Picture of the Contemporary Settlement Map of Palestine?," in *Essays on Ancient Israel in its Near Eastern Context: A Tribute to Nadav Na'aman*, ed. Y. Amit et al. (Winona Lake, IN: Eisenbrauns, 2006), 63–87; Redford, *Egypt, Canaan, and Israel*, 88; and Mazar, *Archaeology of the Land of the Bible*, 186.

17. See Wolfgang Helck, *Die Beziehungen Ägyptens zu Vorderasien im 3. und 2. Jahrtausend v. Chr.*, 2nd ed. (Wiesbaden: Harrasowitz, 1971), 39d–40; Ward, *Egypt and the East Mediterranean*, 62; Redford, *Egypt, Canaan, and Israel*, 82–90; Mumford, "Syria–Palestine," 338.

Mentuhotep II,[18] Senusret I,[19] Amenemhat II,[20] and Senusret III[21] all made military expeditions in the area, spanning from about 2000–1800 BC. It is quite possible that kings before and after this did the same and that we are merely missing the records made of it.

With these records, we can develop a picture of Egypt's relations with Canaan during this era. Due to their relative strategic unimportance, large parts of Canaan would have remained outside the attention of Egypt. Yet key sites along crucial trade routes were frequently the target of Egyptian control. Egypt seems to have developed a strategically selective plan of interaction and control that allowed it to gain the most from the Levant's resources while investing the smallest necessary amount of Egypt's own resources. Egypt seems to have exerted influence in some areas via trade and diplomatic methods, but in other areas Egypt used military occupancy and raids to exert influence. The form of contact with Egypt was not even nor homogenous but rather reflected whatever would best serve Egypt's interests; thus these forms of contact would vary by place and time.

LIFE WITH THE EGYPTIANS FOR THE PATRIARCHS AND MATRIARCHS IN CANAAN

So what did this Egyptian presence in Canaan look like for someone like Abraham, Sarah, Rachel or Jacob? Because the text does not specifically address this, we are left with informed and well-thought-out guesswork as

18. See Ward, *Egypt and the East Mediterranean*, 59–60.
19. See Kemp, "Old Kingdom, Middle Kingdom and Second Intermediate Period," 143; Mumford, "Syria–Palestine," 337.
20. See Farag, "Un insciption memphite de la XIIe dynastie," 75–82, pls. 3–5; Ian Shaw, "Egypt and the Outside World," in *The Oxford History of Ancient Egypt*, ed. Ian Shaw (Oxford: Oxford University Press, 2000), 325. We know of one expedition that brought back 1554 prisoners. See J. Malek and S. Quirke, "Memphis, 1991: Epigraphy," *Journal of Egyptian Archaeology* 78 (1992): 14.
21. See Gee, "Overlooked Evidence," 30. One of his soldiers mentions specifically fighting in *skmm*, which is probably Shechem, thus confirming the indications of the Execration Texts mentioned earlier. See John Garstand, *El Arábah* (London: B. Quaritch, 1900), pls. IV–V; Mumford, "Syria–Palestine," 338; and Kemp, "Old Kingdom, Middle Kingdom and Second Intermediate Period," 143.

our only avenue of investigation. Yet we are derelict in our research duties if we do not at least consider how contact with Egypt would have affected the life of the great biblical patriarchs and matriarchs, for it surely did. We have enough information available to us that even though we cannot point to specific textual examples, we can still better understand the scriptural setting if we address the questions that Abraham, Sarah, Isaac, Rebekah, Jacob, Rachel, and Leah would have asked about life in an area that was so near to Egypt. Let us begin by looking at how Abraham's early life may have been influenced by Egypt.

The influence of Egyptian religion, and probably Egyptian political influence, is spoken of in Abraham's account of his near sacrifice by a priest of Pharaoh (Abraham 1:6–13). Abraham was probably particularly sensitive about the seductiveness of Egyptian religion, having seen his father and relatives, heavily influenced by Egypt, turn to idolatry (Abraham 1:5–7, 16–17). This influence was so seductive that even after Abraham's father repented of his idolatry after Abraham's miraculous deliverance, Abraham's father soon returned to it (Abraham 2:5). All of this gave reason for Abraham to try to have his household avoid contact with Egyptian culture, which was so present in the land of his nativity. Further, Pharaoh's court mourned the destruction that Abraham's delivering angel wrought upon the Egyptian priest (Abraham 1:20). We do not know if this caused Abraham to, for some time, avoid sites that had an Egyptian presence, but it seems likely.

In fact, one bit of inscriptional evidence creates a possible scenario for understanding Abraham's journeys. Two inscriptions, from just before Abraham and contemporary to him, attest to an "Ulishem" west of Ebla, somewhat north of coastal Byblos.[22] As was mentioned above, Byblos experienced heavy Egyptian influence, while Ebla felt a lighter amount.

---

22. "Inscription of Naram-Sin, the Campaign against Armanu and Ebla," in *Monumental Inscriptions from the Biblical World*, ed. William W. Hallo and K. Lawson Younger Jr., The Context of Scripture (Boston: Brill, 2003), 2:245. The line reads, "From the Bank of the Euphrates until Ulisum." See also Benjamin R. Foster, *Before the Muses: An Anthology of Akkadian Literature* (Bethesda, MD: CDL, 1993), 1:53. See also Hans Hirsch, "Die Inschriften der Könige von Agade," *Archiv für Orientforschung* 20 (1963): 74; Benjamin R. Foster, "The Siege of Armanum," *Journal of Ancient Near Eastern Studies* 14 (1982): 29.

Towns that were geographically in between these two cities, such as Ulaza, also found themselves in between them in regard to their amount of contact with Egypt.[23] While most people think of Ur as a city in southern Mesopotamia, the Book of Abraham may cast some more light on this issue.[24] While we cannot tell whether Ur is indeed in southern Mesopotamia, a possible and tentative scenario could arise from comparing the text of the Book of Abraham and some recent archaeological finds. A group of archaeologists have been excavating an area they think may be Ulishem. *If* this purported site for Ulishem—which is being excavated in Turkey, just west of Ebla—is the "Olishem" of Abraham 1:10, where Abraham was nearly sacrificed,[25] it would be in a place that was experiencing just the kind of influence described in the Book of Abraham. As Abraham sought to flee from such life-threatening semi-Egyptianized culture, it would make sense for him to travel east to Haran, where the Egyptians had little or no presence. Then, as the Egyptian presence in Canaan lessened, a phenomenon demonstrated by John Gee, Abraham would have been freer to move to Canaan. While this itinerary is only speculation, it is an interesting possibility.

After Abraham and Sarah moved to Canaan, they spent most of their time in the southern areas between Hebron and Beersheba. Of the places

---

23. See James P. Allen, "The Historical Inscription of Khnumhotep at Dashur: Preliminary Report," *Bulletin of the American Schools of Oriental Research* 352 (2008): 29–39.

24. See the discussion in Stephen O. Smoot, "'In the Land of the Chaldeans': The Search for Abraham's Homeland Revisited," *BYU Studies Quarterly* 56, no. 3 (2017): 7–37, esp. 33–34.

25. See J. R. Kupper, "Uršu," *Revue d'assyriologie* 43 (1949): 80–82; Albrecht Goetze, "An Old Babylonian Itenerary," *Journal of Cuneiform Studies* 7 (1953): 69–70; John Gee, "Has Olishem been Discovered?," in *The Journal of Book of Mormon and Other Restoration Scripture* 22, no. 2 (2013): 104–7; John Lundquist, "Was Abraham in Ebla?," in *Studies in Scripture*, vol. 2: *The Pearl of Great Price*, ed. Robert L. Millet and Kent P. Jackson (Salt Lake City: Randall, 1985), 234–35; Paul Y. Hoskisson, "Where Was Ur of the Chaldees?," in *The Pearl of Great Price: Revelations from God*, ed. H. Donl Peterson and Charles W. Tate Jr. (Provo, UT: Religious Studies Center, Brigham Young University, 1989), 136n44; John Gee, "Abracadabra, Isaac and Jacob," in *Review of Books on the Book of Mormon* 7, no. 1 (1995): 26–27.

they stayed, these locations would have experienced the least amount of contact with Egypt because Egypt's interactions with its northern neighbors were concentrated primarily around those areas with important ports, though Egypt would have maintained some minimal interest in the overland routes that these two sites lay on. Still, the interactions were heavier in the north and west and waned toward the southern and central areas of Canaan and Syria, making Hebron and Beersheba the patriarchal and matriarchal places of abode with the least Egyptian contact.[26] It is interesting that these seem to be the two places where these matriarchs and patriarchs spent the most time.

These founding families spent much of their lives in Canaan in a nomadic lifestyle, moving from place to place as they took their substantial herds to the best grazing areas of the season,[27] and they spent significant amounts of time with their families and flocks in the areas of Beersheba, Gerar, and Hebron, as well as frequenting more northern locations such as Shechem. The Egyptian presence was likely greater during Abraham and Sarah's day than during their children's or grandchildren's. While we cannot tell for certain, it seems probable that the patriarchs and matriarchs would have preferred to avoid any contact with Egypt. There may have been some misgivings because of the problems Abraham had experienced with an Egyptian priest earlier in life (Abraham 1:10–20), though such misgivings could have been somewhat overcome during Abraham's sojourn in Egypt, where Abraham had some positive interactions with the Egyptians. Yet most small groups would want to avoid contact with an entity that occasionally became a large and invading presence that would at times forcibly take people and resources for its own benefit. Thus, we can surmise that unless the founding families were looking for a group with whom they could trade large amounts of their herds, the patriarchs and matriarchs probably tried to "fly below the radar" of the Egyptians.

Because the patriarchs and matriarchs did not live in large established cities (see George Pierce's chapter in this volume), these families were likely able to largely avoid substantial contact with the Egyptians in Canaan.

26. See Cohen, "Synchronisms and Significance," 1–8.

27. See Genesis 20:1, 21:32, 23:2, 24:62, 26:17, 26:22, 26:23, 33:18, 35:1, 35:16, 37:14, etc.

However, these families did have dealings with many of the local leaders who undoubtedly interacted with their powerful southern neighbor, probably often in the form of regular tribute of goods and people sent to the Egyptians. For example, the patriarchs and matriarchs had somewhat regular dealings with the leaders of the Canaanite communities in Beer Sheba, Hebron, and Shechem. These cities lay along minor, yet substantial, trade routes. While it was not the main focus of the Egyptian's foreign presence in Canaan, it is very probable that they passed along these routes from time to time—especially Shechem, which was at a juncture between two small trade routes. They would probably have had some interest in maintaining a form of influence or relation with these regions. Some of the Canaanite leaders of these sites may have even been forced into some degree of subservience to or military conflict with the Egyptians.

Exactly how that would have influenced the families of the patriarchs and matriarchs is unknown, though it is likely that the movements of Egyptian troops and the collection of Canaanite tribute affected where Abraham, Sarah and their family stayed and the people with whom they would trade and interact. It is easy to picture Rebekah keeping her children near her in out-of-the-way places when they knew that Egyptian armies were marching through the countryside. We can imagine Jacob worrying about what would happen to his wives or daughters or granddaughters if the family was unexpectedly overtaken by such an army while in the spirit of claiming booty. This is not to suggest that marauding Egyptian armies were an everyday occurrence, but rather that the armies' presence away from established outposts was rare. At the same time, we know that several Egyptian military expeditions were sent into the land of Canaan during the life of each of the patriarchs and matriarchs. Whether they ever came into contact with Egyptian military expeditions or not, it seems inevitable that Egyptian armies had some impact on the lives of the families of Genesis.

In one circumstance, we know that Abraham was willing to interfere in larger politics in a way that could have raised Egyptian ire. He rescued his nephew Lot from the area of Laish, which would later be named Dan (Genesis 14). The town of Laish straddled a junction of trade routes between Tyre and Damascus and seems to have had regular contact with

Egypt.[28] Interfering with such a site could have raised the attention, and perhaps the military action, of Egyptian kings in the midst of attempting to rescue Lot from the site. Yet Abraham was willing to risk this in order to regain the freedom of Lot and his family.

Along these lines, the fairly regular Egyptian trade during much of this period probably also affected Abraham, Sarah, and their descendants as they sought to turn their numerous flocks into a viable family economy. The biblical narrative does not indicate that they themselves mounted expeditions to Egypt except in the most trying of circumstances (such as when Jacob's sons or Abraham went to Egypt during a famine), but they may have sold their goods to traveling caravans who then sold the goods in Egypt (which is the setting of the Joseph's story in Egypt). This is the only biblical example we know of with surety of participation in human trafficking: when some of Jacob's children sold their brother Joseph to others of Abraham's descendants who were on a trade expedition heading to Egypt (Genesis 37:27–36). Jacob's children's familiarity with this kind of a caravan suggests that they were not strangers to the act of selling things to such merchants.

Additionally, the patriarchs and matriarchs may have thought it wise to refrain from affiliating with those whom the Egyptians may have viewed as enemies, lest their families become guilty by association. Yet these founding families would have had to balance this with their need for trading their flocks and with the importance of maintaining good relations with the peoples who lived in the lands they moved through. The economic benefit that could come from seeking out either Egyptians or those with Egyptian connections as the patriarchs and matriarchs participated in an economic world where Egypt was a major player probably created a tension with their desire to avoid entanglements with Egypt, its allies, or its potential enemies. While we do not know exactly how these competing desires affected the families in the Bible, we can be sure that they did.

As noted, there was an ebb and flow to the amount of contact and control that Egypt had with its Semitic neighbors. Some of these changes may have influenced Abraham and Sarah's movements in the land of

28. For example, it is a town listed in the Execration Texts noted above.

Canaan and into Egypt, and to a lesser extent, Isaac's and Jacob's and their families' movements as well. Regardless, we can be sure that during Abraham and Sarah's tenure in Syria/Turkey, Canaan, and Egypt, those localities experienced a great deal of interaction between the Egyptians and the peoples in the lands where Abraham and Sarah lived. For example, we know of Egyptian officials who brought herds of cattle from Megiddo into Egypt, we know of officials that brought wine and other produce from the area into Egypt, we are aware of cedar coming from Lebanon into Egypt fairly regularly, we know of several officials who record having been on invasions in the region, and we know of several kings who record the same thing.[29] While many of these references are to fairly general areas, some include specifics that overlap with known biblical sites. For example, Sebek-Khu, who lived toward the end of Abraham's life, records that he mounted a very successful invasion of Shechem,[30] a city whose surrounding regions were sometimes a place where Abraham, Jacob, and Jacob's sons fed their flocks. Surely Abraham, Sarah, Jacob, Rachel, Leah, Bilhah, Zilpah, and their children would wish to avoid being present when such plunder-oriented activities were taking place. Thus, it is likely that Abraham, Sarah, and many of their descendants did an interesting dance around the Egyptian presence in Canaan. As a seminomadic family, however, it would have been easier for them to do so than for their urban neighbors.

Another Egyptian influence that Abraham and his posterity dealt with were the polytheistic religions that typically adopted many of the religious practices and gods of neighboring cultures with whom they come in contact. The Book of Abraham makes it clear that aspects of the Egyptian religion were adopted by other groups, possibly including the local Syro-Canaanites (Abraham 1:6–13). This rings an according note with archaeological evidence that demonstrates religious integration of some of the Egyptian pantheon by the inhabitants of the eastern Mediterranean

---

29. See Muhlestein, "Levantine Thinking," 190–99 for a summary of this activity.
30. Garstand, *El Arábah*, pls. IV–V; Mumford, "Syria-Palestine," 338, Kemp, "Old Kingdom, Middle Kingdom and Second Intermediate Period," 143.

areas, such as Ugarit and Ebla.[31] Earlier we noted that Abraham in particular may have been wary of the potential of his family's being seduced by Egyptian religion since he had seen his father and other members of his family turn to the Egyptians' idolatrous practices in a way that proved to be hard to leave behind (Abraham 1:5–7, 16–17; 2:5). This negative family legacy likely made the patriarchs and matriarchs uneasy about contact with Egyptian culture. As Abraham, Sarah, Jacob, and possibly Isaac and Rebekah struggled to get their families to worship Jehovah only (Genesis 35:2), they almost certainly would have been wary of settlement centers that exhibited a strong Egyptian religious influence (Genesis 31:19; 24:3–6; Abraham 1:6–13 cited above and below). We know the patriarchs and matriarchs also struggled with avoiding Canaanite religious influence, as is attested by Rebekah's sorrow over Esau marrying a daughter of the local Canaanites (Genesis 26:34–35). Isaac, Rebekah, Jacob, Rachel, and Leah, who spent most of their time in the south-central part of the region where Egyptian influence seems to have been the smallest, probably attempted to avoid areas of heavy Egyptian influence not just because of the physical danger being in the area could effect but also as part of an effort to try to keep their families away from Egyptian religious influence.

ABRAHAM AND SARAH IN EGYPT

When we consider Abraham and Sarah's trip to Egypt, we must more fully examine the Semitic presence there. Evidence indicates that many Semitic people came to Egypt for a variety of reasons, including Canaanites who

---

31. See O. Negbi and S. Moskowitz, "The 'Foundation Deposits' or 'Offering Deposits' of Byblos," Bulletin of the Schools of Oriental Research, 184 (1966): 21–26; William Stevenson Smith, "Influence of the Middle Kingdom of Egypt in Western Asia, especially in Byblos," *American Journal of Archaeology* 73, no. 3 (1969): 279–80; Harvey Weiss, ed., *Ebla to Damascus: Art and Archaeology of Ancient Syria, a catalogue of an exhibition from the Directorate-General of Antiquities and Museums Syrian Arab Republic* (Seattle: University of Washington Press, 1985), 239–40, objects 112–13; Liebowitz, "Bone and Ivory Inlay from Syria and Palestine," 89–97; G. Scandone Matthiae, "Egyptianizing Ivory Inlays from Palace P at Ebla," *Annales Archeologiques Arabes Syriennes* 40 (1990): 146–60.

came to Egypt to take advantage of the opportunity to trade with this land of plenty.[32] Texts from within Egypt mention a military officer "in charge of the Asiatic troops" and a "scribe of the Asiatics."[33] From other sources we know of male Semites achieving roles such as craftsmen, butler, or even chancellor.[34] Additionally, Egypt was full of Semites who were enslaved through Egypt's wars and outposts in Syro-Canaan.[35]

The most important element of Syro-Canaanite influence in Egypt during Abraham and Sarah's lifetimes was the building up of a largely Semitic city on the northeastern edge of the Nile Delta. Just as Abraham's and Sarah's lives were beginning, the city of Avaris experienced a huge influx of people from northeast Syria.[36] These people would eventually become known as the Hyksos. During the middle part of Abraham and Sarah's lives, this already-large city tripled in size, becoming a thriving port with substantial economic means.[37] The Semitic people there maintained

---

32. See Percy E. Newberry, *Beni Hasan*, 4 vols. (London, 1893–1900); Dietrich Wildung, *Sesostris und Amenemhet:* Ägyten *im Mittleren Reich* (Munich: Hirmer, 1984), 185–86; Hans Goedicke, "Abi-Sha(i)'s Representation in Beni Hasan," in *Journal of the American Research Center in Egypt*, 21 (1984): 203–10; Steven Feldman, "Not as Simple as A-B-C," *Biblical Archaeology Review* 26, no. 1 (2000): 12.
33. Kemp, "Old Kingdom, Middle Kingdom and Second Intermediate Period," 155.
34. See Posener, "Les Asiatiques," 154–55; Kenneth A. Kitchen, "Early Canaanites in Rio de Janeiro and a 'Corrupt' Ramesside Land-Sale," in *Studies in Egyptology Presented to Miriam Lichtheim*, ed. Sarah Israelit-Groll (Jerusalem: Magnes Press, 1990), 2:635–45; G. T. Martin, *Egyptian Administrative and Private-Name Seals* (Oxford: Griffith Institute, 1971), 78–85.
35. Posener, "Les Asiatiques," 145–63; William F. Albright, "Northwest-Semitic Names in a List of Egyptian Slaves from the Eighteenth Century B.C.," *Journal of the American Oriental Society* 74 (1954): 222–33; William C. Hayes, *A Papyrus of the Late Middle Kingdom in the Brooklyn Museum* (New York: The Brooklyn Museum, 1955); Erik Hornung, *History of Ancient Egypt, an Introduction*, trans. David Lorton (Ithaca, NY: Cornell University Press, 1999), 61; Hayes, *A Papyrus of the Late Middle Kingdom*, 99.
36. This is well attested by the sudden buildup of "middle-hall" houses and Semitic burials. See Manfred Bietak, "The Center of Hyksos Rule: Avaris 'Tel el-Dab'a,'" in *The Hyksos: New Historical and Archaeological Perspectives*, ed. E. Oren (Philadelphia: University Museum Press, 1997), 97–99.
37. Bietak, "The Center of Hyksos Rule," 103.

much of their Syrian roots and culture, but they became largely Egyptianized.[38] This unique culture subsequently spread to a number of cities.[39] As this happened, more inhabitants from southern Canaan became part of the Hyksos presence.[40] The Hyksos adopted much of Egyptian religion, but they also mixed it with their own religious practices and beliefs. It is difficult to tell if such a mix would have been more or less of a concern to Abraham and Sarah than a group of people practicing purely Egyptian religion. Either way, because of their conflict with an Egyptian priest earlier in their lives, Abraham and Sarah would almost certainly have deep misgivings about travel to Egypt. Yet when God commanded, they went. It may be that they took some comfort in knowing that they could at least find a portion of Egypt in which being Semitic was not entirely foreign.

During this geographic and economic boom in Avaris, Egypt's strong central government started to slowly collapse. Various regional groups in Egypt broke from central leadership and crowned their own leaders as kings of Egypt,[41] though in reality they were only kings of their parts of Egypt. The Hyksos did this as well; thus, a group of Egyptianized Semites ruled the eastern part of the Nile Delta as Egyptian kings. Their influence spread, and they came to rule more and more of the country until they eventually controlled all of Egypt by about 1650 BC.

When Abraham and Sarah journeyed to Egypt, as is recorded in both Genesis and the Book of Abraham, the first part of the country they would have encountered was the eastern Nile Delta. It is possible that they came to that area while it was a small kingdom ruled by a Semitic kinglet who stylized himself as an Egyptian king and who proclaimed himself king of Egypt. We cannot tell whether Sarah's marriage to and Abraham's interactions with an Egyptian king were with the ruler of a strong, centralized

---

38. Bietak, "Egypt and Canaan During the Middle Bronze Age," 89; Holladay, "Tell el-Maskhuta," 63; Hoffmeir, *Israel in Egypt, The Evidence for the Authenticity of the Exodus Tradition* (New York: Oxford University Press, 1996), 63–64.

39. See Holladay, "Tell el-Maskhuta," 63; Holladay, "The Eastern Nile Delta," 201–9; Bietak, "Canaanites in the Eastern Nile Delta," 43; and Hoffmeir, *Israel in Egypt,* 63–66.

40. See Muhlestein, "Levantine Thinking," 201–4; Bietak, "Center of Hyksos Rule," 113.

41. For example, see Bietak, "Center of Hyksos Rule," 108–9.

Egypt, or with the very beginnings of the Hyksos kings of Egypt, possibly around 1750 BC. While both are possible, I lean slightly toward the latter.

JOSEPH IN EGYPT

Understanding the Hyksos presence may be key to understanding the Joseph in Egypt narrative. Again, we cannot date Joseph precisely, but the most likely setting for Joseph is when the Hyksos began to take control of all of Egypt, in about 1650 BC. We know that a brisk Semitic slave trade was happening in Egypt during the era of the founding families.[42] In some ways, Joseph was just one more of the many enslaved people (Genesis 37:36). However, if he was sold into the household of an Egyptianized Semitic official, it seems all the more likely that Joseph was made the chief steward of the house. Once he was raised to power by the Egyptian king (presumably to the office known as vizier), much of the story works quite well in a Hyksos setting. The Hyksos seem to have gained control of Egypt at least partially, if not largely, through economic means.[43]

The story of Joseph accepting all kinds of payments, including land, from the Egyptians in exchange for grain may very well be an account of how the Hyksos came to power (Genesis 47:13–26). If Joseph were serving under a Semitic king, then the priest of On was likely a relative of that king, making the daughter whom Joseph married (Genesis 41:45) a fellow Semite through whose children the priesthood line and covenant would continue. Many other elements of the Joseph in Egypt story work well if we posit an Egyptian court with many Egyptians that is ultimately controlled by a Semitic group. Such tension between the Semites and Egyptians is evident when Joseph's brothers dined with the Egyptians (Genesis 47). However, while the setting fits the story, we must be clear that we have no way of proving or disproving this hypothesis.

---

42. See Hornung, *History of Ancient Egypt*, 61; Hayes, *A Papyrus of the Late Middle Kingdom*, 99.

43. See John Van Seters, *The Hyksos, A New Investigation* (New Haven, CT: Wipf and Stock, 1966).

MOSES AND THE EXODUS

Eventually, around 1550 BC, in the southern city of Thebes, the local rulers gained enough power to throw off Hyksos control. Their newly developed ability to replicate chariot technology probably put them on an equal enough footing with the Hyksos to find success in battle. These Theban princes slowly pushed the Hyksos north, gaining the support of other Egyptians as they went, until they not only forced their foreign rulers out of the country but also pursued them into Canaan.[44] The Egyptians absolutely detested having been dominated by foreigners and took steps toward never letting it happen again, including making continual military forays into Canaan,[45] starting a more strict control of and physical presence in Canaan, and building forts along Egypt's northeastern border to protect it from foreign incursions from Canaan.

The new Theban dynasty, which founded what is known as the "New Kingdom" in Egyptian history, despised any groups related to the Hyksos, especially if there were some notion that they had aided these rulers. Thus the Exodus reference to a pharaoh arising who "knew not Joseph" (Exodus 1:9) most likely does not mean that he had never heard of Joseph, but instead means that this pharaoh had no respect for Joseph or anything he did. This phrase may be a way of referring to the expulsion of the Hyksos and the establishment of dominance by Theban rulers over all of Egypt that took place in the mid-sixteenth century BC. The enslavement of the Israelite generations before Moses's day is not surprising. The fear of another Hyksos invasion and any known connection between the Israelites and the Hyksos would also explain why these new Egyptian kings wanted to enslave the Israelites in order to avoid their aiding any potential invaders (Exodus 1:10). The frequent campaigns in the Syro-Canaanite area brought back large groups of enslaved Semites as part of the spoils, which made the idea of submitting Semitic groups to slavery a common practice. Regardless of exactly how the Hyksos and the Israelites align historically, we can be sure that the Israelites were enslaved in Egypt during

---

44. See the Kamose Stela; Redford, *Egypt, Canaan, and Israel*, 126–29.
45. See Kurt Sethe, *Urkunden des aegytischen Altertums IV: der 18. Dynastie* (Leipzig, 1906), 1695–97.

the height of Egypt's power during the New Kingdom. While from the biblical point of view, everything in the Israelites' lives during slavery was centered on the building projects they were forced to work on (Exodus 1:11), from the Egyptian vantage, the Israelites would have been one small cog in the machinery that kept the kingdom prosperous and expanding. Israelites would later use artisan skills as they built bronze snakes, an ark, the tabernacle, and homes in Canaan.[46] In fact, it is clear that the long sojourn in Egypt had a cultural influence on the Israelites.[47]

The Bible places the Israelites near the northeastern delta of the Nile, a place with little stone, dictating that almost all building was done with mud bricks. Egyptian records bear witness to the forced mining and brick-making activities of various groups in Egypt, including other Semites.[48] Scenes from Egyptian tombs record that taskmasters insured that those they oversaw made their quota of bricks, which were made using

46. See Scott B. Noegel, "The Egyptian Origin of the Ark of the Covenant," *Israel's Exodus in Transdisciplinary Perspective: Text, Archaeology, Culture, and Geoscience*, ed. Thomas E. Levy, Thomas Schneider, William H. C. Propp (New York: Springer International Publishing, 2013), 223–42; John D. Currid, *Ancient Egypt and the Old Testament* (Grand Rapids, MI: Baker Books, 1997), 142–51; Kenneth A. Kitchen, "The Tabernacle—a Bronze Age Artifact," *Eretz-Israel, Archaeological, Historical and Geographical Studies* 24 (1993): 119–29. Benjamin J. Noonan, "Egyptian Loanwords as Evidence for the Authenticity of the Exodus Tradition," in *"Did I Not Bring Israel Out of Egypt?" Biblical, Archaeological, and Egyptological Perspectives on the Exodus Narratives*, ed. James K. Hoffmeier, Alan R. Millard, and Gary A. Rendsburg (Winona Lake, IN: Eisenbrauns, 2016), 49–67, demonstrates that many of the words used for the tabernacle and its accoutrements are loanwords from Egypt, suggesting that they were also accoutrements known to the Israelites from their time in Egypt.

47. James K. Hoffmeier, "Egyptian Religious Influences on the Early Hebrews," in Hoffmeier, Millard, and Rendsburg, *"Did I Not Bring Israel Out of Egypt?,"* 4–7, argues for overall influence, and the specifically outlines influence seen in names, 18–27, and in narratives concerning the priesthood, 27–34. Similarly, Richard S. Hess, "Onomastics of the Exodus Generation in the Book of Exodus," in in Hoffmeier, Millard, and Rendsburg, *"Did I Not Bring Israel Out of Egypt?,"* 37–48, demonstrates the presence of Egyptian names among the Israelites that come from the correct time period for the Exodus.

48. See Kenneth A. Kitchen, "From the Brickfields of Egypt," *Tyndale Bulletin* 27 (1967): 143–44; Jonathan Kirsch, *Moses: A Life* (New York: Ballantine Books, 1998), 76.

straw, mud, and the sun.[49] Sadly, mud-brick structures do not last the way stone structures do, and we cannot hope to find remains of Israelite settlements in an area with a high water table, such as this area found in this branch of the Nile Delta. Fortunately for the Israelites, they were far north and east, near the frontier. And though the frontier was fortified and guarded,[50] they were not geographically far away from escape. However, in terms of ability, such escape was impossibly distant for them.

We cannot know with any degree of certainty when the story of Moses would have taken place.[51] However, our best indicators are probably the names of the cities the enslaved Israelites helped build: Pithom and Raamses (Exodus 1:11).[52] These cities are, respectively, most likely modern tell el-Retabeh, which is near Wadi Tumilat, and nearby Qantir, which is adjacent to Avaris.[53] Knowing when these cities were built allows us to postulate that the most likely setting for the story of Moses is in the early Ramesside era, under the kings Seti I and Rameses II (or Rameses the Great).[54] If we operate under this assumption, a nice, round date for the

---

49. Kirsch, *Moses: A Life*, 76.

50. See James K. Hoffmeier, "The 'Walls of the Ruler' in Egyptian Literature and the Archaeological Record: Investigating Egypt's Eastern Frontier in the Bronze Age," *Bulletin of the American Schools of Oriental Research*, 343 (2006): 1–20.

51. On this, see Lawrence T. Geraty, "Exodus Dates and Theories," in Levy, Schneider, and Propp, *Israel's Exodus in Transdisciplinary Perspective*, 55–64.

52. This next section is very similar to something that I published as part of a textbook. See Kerry Muhlestein, "The Exodus," in *A Bible Reader's History of the Ancient World*, ed. Kent P. Jackson (Provo, UT: Jerusalem Center for Near Eastern Studies, Brigham Young University, 2016), 119–32. The material was first written for this book, but when I thought that this book may not come about, I used, for this section, portions of what I had written for the chapter of the textbook. The two publications have grown organic differences, but portions of them are very similar.

53. See James K. Hoffmeier, "The Exodus and Wilderness Narratives," in *Ancient Israel's History, an Introduction to Issues and Sources*, ed. Bill T. Arnold and Richard S. Hess (Grand Rapids, MI: Baker Academic, 2014), 59–63; Manfred Bietak, "On the Historicity of the Exodus: What Egyptology Today Can Contribute to Assessing the Biblical Account of the Sojourn in Egypt," in Levy, Schneider, and Propp, *Israel's Exodus in Transdisciplinary Perspective*, 26–31.

54. See James K. Hoffmeier, "What Is the Biblical Date for the Exodus? A Response to Bryant Wood," *Journal of the Evangelical Theological Society* 50, no. 2

Exodus would be 1250 BC. We must keep in mind that this date is speculative; it is based on analyzed information to be sure, but it is still speculative. Nevertheless, it is still our most profitable point of culture to examine as we try to paint a picture of what life may have been like for young Moses and what he may have dealt with as he interacted with Pharaoh while trying to free the Israelites from bondage.

Moses was nursed by his own mother until the age of weaning, which was probably around three years old.[55] It is quite likely that at her knee he learned something of his heritage and their family's religious beliefs. Still, Moses would have spent most of his growing years in the royal harem, the institution where Pharaoh ensured that his family members were raised and educated properly (Exodus 2:10). It is also informative to realize that this was a period when foreign princes were brought to Pharaoh's court and educated along with the elite of Egypt. It is probable that Moses's foreign origins were not hidden. If so, he likely would have been viewed in a manner similar to these foreign princes, and he probably received the same excellent academic and cultural education. We know he was "learned in all the wisdom of the Egyptians" (Acts 7:22). Moreover, it seems quite possible that those with a knowledge of anything Semitic would have been used in the Sinai mining expeditions. If this is the case, Moses may have became familiar with the Sinai area in his youth under Egyptian tutelage, which gave him some experience in a region he would later use as an escape for the Israelites.

During this era, Egypt was in many ways at its empire's apogee. Continuing the post-Hyksos expansion into Canaan and Syria, the empire

---

(2007): 225–47; Kenneth A. Kitchen, *Pharaoh Triumphant: The Life and Times of Ramesses II* (Warminster, PA: Aris and Phillips, 1982), 70–71; James K. Hoffmeier, *Israel in Egypt, the Evidence for the Authenticity of the Exodus Tradition* (Oxford: Oxford University Press, 1996), 116–21. Richard C. Steiner, "The Practices of the Land of Egypt (Leviticus 18:3): Incest ᶜAnat, and Israel in the Egypt of Ramesses the Great," in Hoffmeier, Millard, and Rendsburg, *"Did I Not Bring Israel Out of Egypt?,"* 79–91, uses evidence for incest and worship of Anat in the days of Ramesesses II to argue for dating the Exodus to the era of Ramesses.

55. See Rosalind M. and Jac. J. Janssen, *Growing Up and Getting Old in Ancient Egypt* (London: Golden House, 2007), 13–19.

attained its geographic and military height under Thutmosis III,[56] who gained dominance in the area over impinging empires such as the Hittites and Mitanni, as well as over local rulers. The years of dominance in the area could not last forever, and after several powerful Egyptian rulers, various conditions created a situation in which Egypt's power in the area waned. The Amarna Letters, a set of diplomatic correspondence found in Egypt, help to illustrate the control Egypt once had as well as the wavering and shifting in political alliances toward the end of the Eighteenth Dynasty that were part of the loss of some of that control.

At the beginning of the Nineteenth Dynasty under Seti I (ca. 1290–1280 BC), Egypt resurged in both its ability to control the area and in the perception of Egypt's power in the minds of those in the area. If our posited dating of the Exodus is correct, this is the precise time Moses was being raised in the court. Moses probably came of age in an Egyptian court that was experiencing a real revival of empire, power, and cultural pride. Seti and his son and successor, Rameses II, brought Egypt back to nearly its largest geographic and military extent, and they helped Egypt reach new heights in building, appearance, and pomp. In particular for our purposes, Rameses II conquered and, at least briefly, controlled the Galilean area; the Phoenician and Canaanite coasts, including cities such as Akko, Tyre, Sidon, and Byblos; and areas farther south such as Jerusalem, Jericho, and the plains and towns of Moab, such as Dibon.[57] While Rameses II may not have maintained full presence or control in this area, he made it clear that Egypt was again the superpower in charge, and all took note.

If this is the right period, then as Moses grew up, he witnessed Egypt reasserting itself and intentionally striving to reach its unparalleled dominant status that had slipped away for a few generations. The might and prestige of Egypt was propagandized at home as well as abroad. The court Moses was raised in was one of sumptuous prestige. Members of the royal harem stayed in any of a number of lavish palaces that dotted the Nile. These buildings incorporated pools and gardens, were decorated in

56. On the height of Thutmosis III's power, see Yosef Mizrachy, "The Eighth Campaign of Thutmose III Revisited," *Journal of Ancient Egyptian Interconnections* 4, no. 2 (2012): 24–52.

57. See Kitchen, *Pharaoh Triumphant,* 67–68.

precious stones such as lapis lazuli and green malachite, and housed staff that prepared exquisite food. The palace at the new capital of Pi-Rameses, which the Israelites seem to have been forced to help build, was known for its stunning architecture, airy rooms, and extravagant atmosphere.[58] The military Moses witnessed was efficient but was fond of glorious display.

Moses's Ethiopian wife (Numbers 12:1) perhaps attests the fact that he was at least partially involved in Egypt's foreign diplomacy and would have had firsthand knowledge of Egypt's vast holdings abroad and the enviable position it held in the eyes of its foreign neighbors. He probably witnessed the building of some of the most amazing structures the world has ever seen. He would have seen the regal ceremonies that were a regular part of royal life and must have been schooled, probably starting at age five, not just in subjects such as writing, math, and architecture but also in the religious ideas that portrayed the king as semidivine. Because we know that some of Moses's contemporaries, were taught of the already old and grand history of Egypt, we can presume that Moses was also taught of Egypt's history. He likely studied sites such as the pyramids, which were already a thousand years old. He would have been taught that the Egyptian court was heir to an ancient and glorious past, encompassing kings of untold wonder and numerous gods of unimaginable power, and that all the glory of ancient Egypt was recaptured in their day. Even if he was the least among the harem, which is possible, Moses was part of a privileged and elegant upbringing. No wonder he had never supposed that man was "nothing" in comparison with God (Moses 1:10).

WILDERNESS AND CONQUEST

As the Israelites left Egypt,[59] the route of the Exodus kept them from encountering the major forts and encounters with the forces of the

---

58. See Mark A. Simpkins and Susan Taylor, *Ramses II* (Salt Lake City: Simpkins, 1985), 31.

59. On the role of the plagues in the ability of the Israelites to leave Egypt, see the article on the plagues in this volume. For some time now many scholars have doubted whether the Israelites came from Egypt at all, and instead propose that an indigenous group of Canaanites became what would be known as

Egyptians,[60] including the way of the Philistines and the way of Shur, the shortest and most direct routes to Canaan. The Exodus most likely began near Avaris/Raameses, an area that preserves many linguistic remnants of Semitic place-names, including a likely name and location for biblical Goshen.[61] While we cannot trace the route specifically from there, we know they avoided the more traveled and well-garrisoned route and instead went largely east and a little south.[62] Despite that fact that they were pursued and miraculously delivered, the Israelites' journey largely kept them out of the way of sites with a strong Egyptian presence.[63]

Similarly, their forty-year sojourn in the wilderness most likely kept them out of Canaan and in obscure and unoccupied places as Egypt's interest and presence in Canaan waned,[64] though at times they certainly

---

the Israelites. K. Lawson Younger Jr., "Recent Developments in Understanding the Origins of the Arameans. Possible Contributions and Implications for Understanding Israelite Origins," in *"Did I Not Bring Israel Out of Egypt?"*, 199–222, demonstrates the flaws with the ways this has been proposed thus far.

60. See Kenneth A. Kitchen, *On the Reliability of the Old Testament* (Grand Rapids, MI: Eerdmans, 2006), 268–69; James K. Hoffmeier, "Tell el-Borg on Egypt's Eastern Frontier," *Journal of the American Research Center in Egypt* 41 (2004): 85–111; Orly Goldwasser and Eliezer Oren, "Marine Unites on the 'Ways of Horus' in the Days of Seti I," *Journal of Ancient Egyptian Interconnections* 7, no. 1 (2015): 25–38; Gregory Mumford, "The Sinai Peninsula and Its Environs: Our Changing Perceptions of a Pivotal Land Bridge Between Egypt, the Levant, and Arabia," *Journal of Ancient Egyptian Interconnections* 7, no. 1 (2015): 1–24.

61. See Bietak, "On the Historicity of the Exodus," 21–22; Groll, "The Egyptian Background of the Exodus," in Shirun-Grumach, *Jerusalem Studies in Egyptology* (Wiesbaden: Otto Harrassowitz, 1998), 190.

62. See Stephen O. Moshier and James K. Hoffmeier, "Which Way Out of Egypt? Physical Geography Related to the Exodus Itinerary," in Levy, Schneider, and Propp, *Israel's Exodus in Transdisciplinary Perspective*, 105–7; Bietak, "On the Historicity of the Exodus," 27–31; Hoffmeier, "The Exodus and Wilderness Narratives," 65–81.

63. See Muhlestein, "The Exodus," 119–32.

64. Unfortunately, a nomadic presence leaves little to nothing in the way of archaeological remains, which makes difficult to impossible to use archaeology to trace the route. See Thomas W. Davis, "Exodus on the Ground: The Elusive Signature of Nomads in Sinai," in Hoffmeier, Millard, and Rendsburg, *"Did I Not Bring Israel Out of Egypt?,"* 223–27. Davis hopes to be able to trace contact

did travel through areas that were part of the Egyptian routes of trade and control. For example, the Israelites camped at Dibon, a city that a few Egyptian kings, including Ramses II, had conquered.[65] In fact, part of the Israelite route on the east side of Jordan seems to have followed an Egyptian military route.[66]

Yet, as Joshua took the Israelites into the promised land as he encountered kings of cities and their coalitions, he mentioned nothing about Egypt. This does not mean that the Israelites did not deal with Egypt's presence. We may be able to subtly detect Egypt's weakening influence as we look at lists of towns Joshua occupied but did not maintain control over. It is possible that at least some of the cities that Joshua and the children of Israel chose not to occupy were those that they knew could host Egyptian officials and troops at some point. While we cannot know, it is worth considering. For example, Joshua and the Israelites conquered the inhabitants of Jerusalem, but they did not occupy the city, and later we find that it was still inhabited by Canaanites. This is probably because conquest does not mean either annihilation or occupation, and the Israelites were too pastoral and too small to occupy every city they conquered. While the inhabitants of Jerusalem were beaten in battle by Joshua, at this same time some records indicate that Jerusalem was under Egypt's influence.[67] The choice to occupy some areas but not Jerusalem, though it had been defeated, may have been made because of the known possibility of the return of an Egyptian force to that city.

The Egyptians controlled little of the area between Megiddo and Jerusalem,[68] making this an area that would have been very attractive for early Israelite settlement. Subsequently, since around the beginning of the thirteenth century, the region was in a power vacuum, caught between

---

with nomads at Egyptian sites (228–39), but since the Exodus route seems to have specifically avoided such contact, it is unlikely that this will do much to help refine the route.

65. Charles R. Krahmalkov, "Exodus Itinerary Confirmed by Egyptian Evidence," *Biblical Archaeology Review* 20, no. 4 (1994): 54–62.

66. Krahmalkov, "Exodus Itinerary Confirmed by Egyptian Evidence," 45–62.

67. See Yurco, "Merenptah's Canaanite Campaign and Israel's Origins," 30.

68. See Yurco, "Merenptah's Canaanite Campaign and Israel's Origins," 30.

a military stalemate between Egypt and the Hittites, and was prime for takeover and a new occupation by smaller communities and developing city-states. The hill country of Ephraim, some of the first Israelite areas to flourish according to the biblical record, is matched by the archaeological discovery of some of the Israelites' earliest settlements in this same area.[69] Many think this is exactly the area the Merneptah Stele places the Israelite tribes that Merneptah battles, though some have speculated that it refers to an area in the northernmost parts of Galilee.[70]

After the Israelite conquest of Canaan, the aforementioned Merneptah record is the only evidence we have of the Israelites' contact with Egypt during this era. The confrontation described in the stela is not mentioned in the Bible—which does not make a record of every event the Israelites were part of, just the ones necessary for teaching the theological message the book is created for. However, knowledge of Merneptah's successful raid against the Israelites (who are mentioned by name in the inscription—the first time any extrabiblical writings mention them) in Canaan demonstrates that Egypt still had a presence there and that the Israelites may have dealt with the Egyptians more than we often think.[71]

Egypt maintained good control over some areas, such as the Phoenician coast,[72] central Syria,[73] and southern Canaanite towns such as Gezer,[74]

69. See Lawrence Stager, "The Archeology of the Family in Ancient Israel," *Bulletin of the American Schools of Oriental Research* 260 (November 1985), 1–35.

70. See Dan'el Kahn, "A Geo-Political and Historical Perspective of Mernephtah's Policy in Canan," in *The Ancient Near East in the 12th – 10th Centuries BCE*, 260. Some have speculated that Israel was actually still east of the Jordan when Merneptah found them. See Bietak, "On the Historicity of the Exodus," 30.

71. See Yurco, "Merenptah's Canaanite Campaign and Israel's Origins," 30–31.

72. Kahn, "Geo-Political and Historical View," 258–60.

73. Edward Lipinski, *The Aramaeans: Their Ancient History, Culture, Religion* (Louvain: Peeters, 2000), 32–33; Itamar Singer, "A Political History of Ugarit," in *Handbook of Ugaritic Studies*, ed. W. G. E. Watson and N. Wyatt (Leiden: Brill, 1999), 708–12.

74. E. J. Piltcher, "Portable Sundial from Gezer," *Palestine Exploration Fund Quarterly Statement* 55 (1923): 85–89.

Lachish[75] and Jerusalem.[76] Only a few northern Canaanite sites seem to exhibit significant Egyptian presence, and these sites, such as Megiddo and Beth-Shean,[77] sat at the crossroads of trade routes. The polities Merneptah fought against were in between areas the Egyptians controlled well.

While the rebellions may be an expression of the typical case of countries believing that the death of a powerful king was a good time to assert independence,[78] some have speculated that the war resulted from a failure to send tribute to Egypt, which could have been caused by the destruction of armies and crops brought about by the invading Israelites.[79] Thus, Merneptah's campaign may have been to procure the needed tribute, and upon learning of the reason for the disruption, to then turn to punishing the Israelite (and other) raiders causing the problems. This is an appealing scenario because it harmonizes biblical and political narratives provided from a variety of sources. It is also possible that the battles against these Canaanite entities were part of a plan of making an overland trade route between Egypt and Syria secure.[80]

Whatever the cause of Merneptah's campaign, it is clear that Egypt still had a vested interest in and some ability to control Canaan as the Israelites were settling there. Still, their entrance into Canaan took place as Egypt's claim to that part of the world was waning. There would be a very brief resurgence during the period of the judges, which would mark the end

75. Kenneth A. Kitchen, *Rammesside Inscriptions, Historical and Biographical*, vol. 4 (Oxford: Blackwell Press, 1982), 4:39.

76. Gary Rendsburg, "Merneptah in Canaan," *Journal of the Society for the Study of Egyptian Antiquities* 11 (1981): 171–72; Gabriel Barkay, "A Late Bronze Age Egyptian Temple in Jerusalem?," *Israel Exploration Journal* 46 (1996): 23–43; Kenneth A. Kitchen, "Jerusalem in Ancient Egyptian Documents," in *Jerusalem before Islam*, ed. Z. Kafafi and R. Schick (Oxford: British Archaeological Reports, 2007), 32–34.

77. Kahn, "Geo-Political and Historical View," 260.

78. See Kenneth A. Kitchen, "The Victories of Merenptah, and the Nature of their Record," *Journal for the Study of the Old Testament* 28 (2004): 265–66.

79. See Kitchen, *Reliability of the Old Testament*, 228–29. Contra this view, see Kahn, "Geo-Political and Historical View," 260–61.

80. See Itamar Singer, "Merneptah's Campaign to Canaan and the Egyptian Occupation of the Southern Coastal Plain of Palestine in the Ramesside Period," *Bulletin of the Schools of Oriental Research* 269 (1988): 1–10.

of Egypt's real control in the area. The invasion of the Sea Peoples—the Philistines—and Rameses III's battle against them[81] heralded the effectual beginning of the end of Egyptian control of the Syrian and Canaanite areas for many years. This is about the same time period that Deborah and Barak found success against the Canaanites, success that carried them all the way to Megiddo, a place that had been a former Egyptian stronghold. Megiddo had probably just become something of a power vacuum as the Egyptians shrank back to their native land while the Philistines grew in power but had not yet encroached on Israelite or Canaanite lands that were far away from the coast. The Egyptian abandonment of the coastal areas of Canaan to the Philistines creates a conflict that will mark much of the Israelites' early history. It is the Israelites and the Philistines that step into the power vacuum created by Egypt's substantial withdrawal from the region.

CONCLUSION

It seems that the first part of Israelite history is marked by interaction with Egypt interspersed with careful avoidance. From Abraham and Sarah into the beginning of the period of the judges, the characters of the Bible experienced uneven relations with Egypt. They were welcomed, enriched, educated, and saved by the Egyptians. The Israelites were also enslaved, almost annihilated, nearly sacrificed, and purchased by the Egyptians. While these events are so important they are reported in our biblical text, the quiet norm seems to have been that of the Israelites keeping a healthy distance from Egypt. This may have been the most common and prudent course for Abraham, Sarah, and their descendants most of the time; still there is no doubt that both the encounters and the nonencounters between the Israelites and the Egyptians shaped much of the early Israelite history.

Knowing some of these specifics allows us to picture the lives of biblical characters in a more concrete way. Being able to visualize their lives makes the stories more real to us. Both picturing the lives of the biblical

81. See Harold Hayden Nelson, *Reliefs and Inscriptions at Karnak*, vol. 4 (Chicago: University of Chicago Press, 1936).

characters and appreciating the reality of their lives allows us to better apply their stories and teachings to our own lives. While it is worthwhile to examine the details of the biblical historico-cultural environment, it becomes much more meaningful if we allow such an exploration to cause us to think more deeply about the lives of the people we are studying.

THE COVENANT AMONG COVENANTS

THE ABRAHAMIC COVENANT AND BIBLICAL COVENANT MAKING

SHON D. HOPKIN

Central to one's understanding of Israel, in any dispensation, will be that of covenant and covenant making. In fact, the centrality of covenants has been present in almost every chapter of this volume. In this chapter, Shon D. Hopkin presents the four primary covenants covering the period of the patriarchs and matriarchs down to the Exodus. For each covenant, Hopkin notes their distinctive feature while at the same time noting the similarities that suggest each covenant was representative of a greater covenant made between God and his children, which is represented today in "the new and everlasting covenant." —DB and AS

As stated by one biblical scholar, "It is recognized by all serious students of the Bible that the covenant with Abraham is one of the important and determinative revelations of Scripture. It furnishes the key to the entire Old Testament."[1] Many Christians believe that the Old Testament covenant was superseded with the coming of Christ. Joseph Smith, however, taught that God is always the same, that his plan of salvation does not change, and that his promises in ancient times remain in effect.[2] Thus, for Latter-day Saints, the Restoration of the gospel hinges on "the new and everlasting covenant" (Doctrine and Covenants 132:6), a relationship with God made "new" and alive in modern times, but existing "everlastingly" and introduced in the Hebrew Bible (or Old Testament). Understanding the way that the theme of covenant runs through the Hebrew Bible not only unlocks an understanding of God's relationship with humankind in ancient times but also provides the key for understanding that relationship through the New Testament and into the last days. This chapter will focus on covenants and covenant-making as found in the Old Testament, with additional attention given to the Joseph Smith Translation, but will not discuss all aspects of Latter-day Saint understandings of covenant as found in the Book of Mormon, Doctrine and Covenants, and the teachings of latter-day prophets.

COVENANT IN THE HEBREW BIBLE

In the Hebrew Bible, the word for covenant—*bĕrit*—describes various types of agreements made between two parties in which one or both commit to fulfill stipulations of the agreement. The term emphasizes relationship, connection, and obligation between the two parties.[3] The Greek

1. Keith H. Essex, "The Abrahamic Covenant," *Master's Seminary Journal* 10, no. 2 (1999): 191. Paul House stated it this way: "Simply stated, then, it is hard to overstate its importance in biblical literature and thus biblical theology." Paul R. House, *Old Testament Theology* (Downers Grove, IL: InterVarsity, 1998), 76.
2. "History, 1838–1856, volume C-1 [2 November 1838–31 July 1842]," The Joseph Smith Papers.
3. Numerous etymologies have been proposed for *bĕrit*, including "bond/fetters," "between," or a connection with food or eating, as in a covenantal meal between

word used to translate *bĕrit* in the Septuagint is *diathēkē*, creating a foundation for the way the word is used in the Greek of the New Testament. In its New Testament expressions, *covenant* is often translated as "testament," at times conveying the nuance of a formal will agreement or legal bequest, which is something promised by one party to another. Readers of both the Old and New Testaments (or the Old and New "Covenants") need to remain aware of the Hebrew context that provides meaning for the New Testament understanding and should also understand that the New Testament expression is at times nuanced toward the concept of a legal will or "testament" provided by God.[4] For Latter-day Saints, both Old Testament covenants and New Testament testaments are centered in Christ and are bequeathed by God upon his children. Moreover, Latter-day Saints teach that the "new testament" or covenant discussed by the New Testament writers was a renewal of the ancient covenants that existed throughout the history of the Old Testament.

ELEMENTS OF COVENANT MAKING IN THE BIBLE

Before discussing specific covenants in the Hebrew Bible, it may be helpful to Latter-day Saint readers to recognize elements of covenant making that have been identified by scholars in the Hebrew Bible.[5] Each biblical instance of covenant making does not include all the elements listed below,

---

two parties. See Wolfram von Soden, ed., *Akkadisches Handworterbuch* (Wiesbaden, Germany: Harrassowitz, 1959), 129–30; J. J. Mitchell, "Abram's Understanding of the Lord's Covenant," *Westminster Theological Journal* 32 (1970): 45; M. Noth, *The Laws in the Pentateuch* (Philadelphia: Fortress, 1967), 112–17; Elmer B. Smick, "ברית," in *Theological Wordbook of the Old Testament* (*TWOT*), ed. R. Laird Harris (Chicago: Moody Bible Institute, 1980), 1:128; Moshe Weinfeld, "בְּרִית," in *Theological Dictionary of the Old Testament* (*TDOT*), ed. G Johannes Botterweck, Helmer Ringgren, and Heinz-Josef Fabry (Grand Rapids, MI: Eerdmans, 2011), 2:253.

4. P. R. Williamson, "Covenant," in *Dictionary of Biblical Theology*, ed. T. Desmond Alexander and Brian S. Rosner (Downer's Grove, IL: InterVarsity Press, 2000), 420.

5. See P. R. Williamson, "Covenant," in *Dictionary of the Old Testament: Pentateuch*, ed. Mark J. Boda and J. Gordon McConville (Downers Grove, IL: InterVarsity Press, 2012), 146–47; George E. Mendenhall and Gary A. Herion, "Covenant,"

but these elements do form a basic backbone, both in the Bible and in ancient documents from the time of the Bible.[6]

1. Identification of God as the establisher of the covenant and identification of the recipient of the covenant. This often includes, especially in ancient Near Eastern treaties, a prologue that presents the historical relationship of the two parties and that describes the deeds that the establisher of the covenant has performed in the past on behalf of the recipient.[7] In many covenant settings, it is also preceded by a preamble that introduces the covenant with words such as those found in Genesis 9:8: "And God spake unto Noah, and to his sons with him, saying . . ." In the Noahic covenant, God's role as the initiator receives a repeated emphasis, and the recipients of the covenant are clearly stated: "And God spake unto Noah and to his sons with him, saying, And I, behold, I establish my covenant with you, and with your seed after you; And with every living creature that is with you . . . every beast of the earth" (Genesis 9:8–10). From this view, the Creation and Fall accounts in Genesis serve to prepare the reader for the covenants that follow, because these accounts introduce God and his creations, demonstrating the human need for God (due to the Fall) that can be resolved through covenants. In the Creation account, God is showing the Israelites who he is and what he has done for them; he is introducing himself. He is showing their relationship with him and their need to make covenants with him because of the Fall. He is presenting himself as their Creator-God who has power to create order and life out

---

in *Anchor Bible Dictionary*, ed. David Noel Freedman (New York: Doubleday, 1992), 1:1190–98.

6. These elements, first found in Hittite treaties from the Late Bronze Age, were described in Viktor Korosec, *Hethitische Staatsvertrage* (Leipzig, Germany: Theodor Weicher, 1931). Although these elements are most frequently used to describe the Mosaic covenant, the close connection between the form of these Hittite treaties and that of biblical covenants was first detailed in George E. Mendenhall, "Covenant Forms in Ancient Israelite Tradition," *Biblical Archaeologist* 17 (1954): 50–76. See also Mendenhall and Herion, "Covenant," 1:1190–98. For a Latter-day Saint treatment of the topic, see Victor L. Ludlow, *Isaiah: Prophet, Seer, and Poet* (Salt Lake City: Deseret Book, 1982), 400–406.

7. See McCarthy, *Treaty and Covenant*, 1–5; F. Charles Fensham, "Treaty," in *International Standard Bible Encyclopedia, Fully Revised*, ed. Geoffrey Bromiley (Grand Rapids, MI: Eerdmans, 1988), 4:900–901.

of the chaos and death of the fallen world, if they will enter into covenants with him.

2a. Ritual or ceremonial enactment: Covenant oaths or pledges. Although this element of covenant making is not found in all biblical covenants, one or both parties often made pledges or oaths that served as a physical confirmation or ratification of the covenant. Jonathan gave David his armor, weaponry, and pieces of clothing to cement their covenant relationship (1 Samuel 18:4). In Ezekiel 17:18, Zedekiah gave his hand to the Lord, thus pledging allegiance to him. Oaths or solemn promises were often given as pledges to be faithful to the covenant, such as in 2 Kings 11:4, thereby providing a vocal act that could be heard and witnessed by others. Sometimes, as in the previous example, these oaths were required of the recipient of the covenant, and other times the initiator of the covenant gave these oaths. In both God's reiteration of the Mosaic covenant in Deuteronomy 29:12 and 14 and in God's covenant with David (see Psalm 89:3, 34–37, 49), God cemented his commitment to the covenant by swearing an oath to the recipient. Latter-day Saints are familiar with the "oath and covenant of the priesthood," which is found in Doctrine and Covenants 84:33–45. In the stating of his covenantal promises, God provides an oath that they will be fulfilled.

2b. Ritual or ceremonial enactment: signs. This element of biblical covenant making is similar to the element of oaths and pledges and demonstrates that the understanding of a covenant relationship between two parties must always be acted out or performed in some type of physically witnessed behavior.[8] The main difference between oaths and signs is that signs are physical acts that continue to be repeated in subsequent generations to confirm the existence of the covenant. One example of a sign of a covenant is the rainbow provided by God in Genesis 9:12–16, translated as a "token" (אות/*'ot*) in the King James Version (KJV). The sign that God enjoined Abraham and his descendants to make is that of circumcision (Genesis 17:9–10, 13–14), while the sign of the Mosaic covenant was the keeping of the Sabbath day (Exodus 31:31; Ezekiel 20:12, 20). The biblical

8. See description of the oath process in the preceding section, as demonstrated in Deuteronomy 29:12, 14 and in Psalm 89:3, 34–37, 49. See also Mendenhall and Herion, "Covenant," *Anchor Bible Dictionary*, 1:1183.

text often shows God or individuals repeating similar pledges when God reestablishes the covenant with them. For example, although Isaac and Jacob apparently do not replicate Abraham's passing "among the pieces," they do offer sacrifice or provide some type of unique witness that they will obey God's command when God reinitiates the Abrahamic covenant with them. As with pledges and oaths, signs again testify to the voluntary, conditional aspect of the covenant. For Latter-day Saints, the ordinance of the sacrament has come to be understood as a sign demonstrating renewed acceptance of baptismal covenants and commitment to Christ.[9] Anciently, sacred meals, including the Passover meal, peace offerings, and meals in other settings, were often a part of the covenant-making or covenant-renewal process.[10]

3. *Stipulations*. The Noahic covenant in Genesis 9 demonstrates that even when certain parts of the covenant should be considered unconditional, as in the case of God's promise to never destroy the earth by flood again, other aspects of the covenant remain conditional (see Genesis 9:4–7). The very act of stating requirements of a covenant indicates the ability of the recipient to choose whether to obey those requirements or not. In this sense, when signs are required of the recipient of a covenant, they could also be included under the category of stipulations. Genesis 9:4–7 indicates that God's requirements in connection with the Noahic covenant were to (a) be fruitful and multiply and replenish the earth, (b) not eat the flesh of animals with the blood still in it, and (c) not shed the blood of humankind. The Mosaic covenant provided numerous stipulations as a sign of the covenant, such as honoring the Sabbath day, following the rest of the Ten Commandments, and following the Holiness Code provided in Leviticus 18–25. For Latter-day Saints, the baptismal covenant brings the recipient into a relationship with God and God's community that obligates the recipient to support that community, to stand as a witness of Christ, and to remember Christ always (see Mosiah 18:8–10; Doctrine and Covenants 20:77, 79).

---

9. See Ugo A. Perego, "The Changing Forms of the Latter-day Saint Sacrament," *Interpreter: A Journal of Mormon Scripture* 22 (2016): 1–16.

10. See Dennis E. Smith, "Meal Customs," *Anchor Bible Dictionary*, 4:653–55; see also Mendenhall and Herion, "Covenant," *Anchor Bible Dictionary*, 1:1195.

4. Consequences: blessings and punishments. Another evidence of the conditional, bilateral nature of covenants is that specific blessings or negative consequences are typically provided for faithfulness to or betrayal of the covenant. Such is the case in the Noahic covenant, in which the above stipulations carry a penalty if they are ignored: "And surely your blood of your lives will I require; at the hand of every beast will I require it, and at the hand of man. . . . Whoso sheddeth man's blood, by man shall his blood be shed" (Genesis 9:5–6). The consequences associated with covenants are even more clearly stated regarding the Mosaic law, with entire chapters dedicated to showing the blessings or cursings connected to obedience or disobedience to the covenant (see, for example, Deuteronomy 27–30). Under Joshua the Israelites were to ritually restate those consequences: half of the community would stand on Mount Ebal at one side of a valley to recount the cursings, and the other half would stand on Mount Gerizim to recount the blessings; this ritual created powerful imagery of the Israelites' ability to choose (see Deuteronomy 27–29). Leviticus 26 also contains a lengthy list of blessings and cursings that will come upon God's people if they reject the covenant, including both the future scattering and gathering of Israel. Modern readers are often less comfortable with the idea of punishments proceeding from the hand of God than with the concept of the blessings that flow from God in connection with covenant faithfulness. It is important to recognize the reality that any loss of blessings due to a lack of covenant faithfulness is, in one sense, indistinguishable from a punishment.

5. Witnesses. One of the reasons why covenant making included physical acts, signs, or verbal oaths was so that it could be witnessed by others and so that those witnesses could be called to testify of the reality of the promises made on both sides.[11] The Mosaic covenant provides excellent examples of the importance of witnesses to verify obedience to or betrayal of the covenant. Deuteronomy 4:26, for example, states that if the Israelites do evil in the sight of God, then, "I call heaven and earth to witness against you this day, that ye shall soon utterly perish." Deuteronomy 30:19 offers similar imagery: "I call heaven and earth to record this day against

11. See Stephen D. Renn, "Witness," in *Expository Dictionary of Bible Words* (Peabody, MA: Hendrickson Publishers, 2005), 743.

you, that I have set before you life and death, blessing and cursing." These examples also indicate that heavenly beings and the earth itself, as seen in Genesis 9, are commonly called upon as witnesses in biblical covenants. Latter-day Saints are familiar with the importance of witnesses during the ordinances of sacrament and baptism and during ordinances performed in the temple. Interestingly, ancient Near Eastern treaties almost always provided long lists of witnesses to the treaty, and these witnesses were often divine beings or elements of the natural world that represented the beliefs of both sides in the treaty relationship.[12]

6. *Provisions for the maintenance of the covenant terms.* Provisions made so that the terms of the covenant would be written down or transmitted orally over the course of generations are very clear in ancient Near Eastern treaties and can also be seen in other biblical examples.[13] Jeremiah 32:6–13 demonstrates an ancient tradition of maintaining two copies of the terms of an agreement, one sealed and stored away so that its text cannot be altered, the other left open and publicly available so that it can be reviewed. Deuteronomy 32:9–13 indicates that Moses wrote the law down and then required the Israelites to listen as the priests read the law aloud every seven years during the Feast of Tabernacles, while Joshua 8:32 describes Joshua writing the law down on the stones of an altar. One of the primary purposes of scripture recording and scripture study is to remind the reader of the covenants made and the provisions of those covenants. That awareness is demonstrated on the title page of the Book of Mormon: "Which is to show unto the remnant of the house of Israel what great things the Lord hath done for their fathers; and that they may know the covenants of the Lord, that they are not cast off forever." This brief statement includes God's statement of who he is, who Israel is, and what relationship he has had with them. The reading of that relationship as expressed in the Book of Mormon prepares the reader to enter into sacred covenants with him, indicating the importance of a record to demonstrate God's covenant promises.

---

12. See Mendenhall and Herion, "Covenant," *Anchor Bible Dictionary*, 1:1182.
13. See Bruce K. Waltke with Charles Yu, *An Old Testament Theology* (Grand Rapids, MI: Zondervan, 2007), 176.

BIBLICAL COVENANTS

Numerous covenant relationships designated by God are expressed throughout the Old Testament. Whether these relationships should be seen as threads of one, overarching relationship, or whether they are separate covenants that should carefully be distinguished from each other continues to be disputed today. Biblical scholars typically identify a number of important biblical covenants: the Noahic, the Abrahamic, the Mosaic, the priestly (closely connected to the Mosaic), and the new covenant (mentioned by Jeremiah but mostly emphasized by Christian scholars).[14] While differences between these covenants certainly exist, they also form a unified witness of God's willingness to make covenants with his people, and they build upon and connect to each other.[15] Although this chapter will begin by analyzing the Noahic covenant, since it represents the first time that the word *covenant* is explicitly used in the Old Testament, the Joseph Smith Translation confirms that the Noahic covenant was a renewal of earlier covenants, as will be demonstrated.

1. The Noahic covenant. As the first of the covenants explicitly discussed in the Bible (see Genesis 6:18 for the first instance of the Hebrew word *bĕrit* ["covenant"]), the Noahic covenant of Genesis 6:18 and 8:20–9:18 serves as a foundation for understanding all other covenants and further covenant making in the Old Testament. The covenant is described as "everlasting" (Genesis 9:16), designed to last as long as "the earth remaineth" (Genesis 8:22). As will be discussed later in this section, and as clearly indicated in the Joseph Smith Translation, the Noahic covenant as found in the Bible was a renewal of a covenantal relationship with Adam and Eve and, later, with others, such as Enoch. Thus, this covenant could be understood as "new," meaning, renewed.[16] Furthermore, using terminology from the Doctrine and Covenants, the covenant of Noah could

---

14. See, for one example, Stephen B. Cowan, "Covenant," in *Holman Illustrated Bible Dictionary*, ed. Chad Brand and Charles Draper (Nashville: Holman Bible Publishers, 2003), 143–45.

15. See, for example, William J. Dumbrell, *Covenant and Creation: An Old Testament Covenant Theology* (Milton Keynes, UK: Paternoster, 2013), 1–3; Mendenhall and Herion, "Covenant," 1:1189–90.

16. See Aaron Schade's discussion of Noah in chapter 4 of this volume.

appropriately be called a "new and everlasting covenant" (Doctrine and Covenants 132:6).

This Noahic covenant was universal, meaning that it reflected a new relationship between God and every living thing upon the earth. Indeed, Genesis 9:13 states that the covenant is between God "and the earth." The wording of the covenant appears to reaffirm God's creational intent for the earth in a way that was disrupted by the flood, promising that the ability of humankind and the earth to regenerate and create will never again be stopped (see Genesis 8:22; 9:15).[17] Noah and his family are given obligations to be fruitful, to multiply, and to replenish the earth (Genesis 9:1, 3); to have dominion over the creations of the earth (Genesis 9:2); and to give proper respect to living things (Genesis 9:4–6). These obligations both repeat commandments given to Adam, Eve, and the living creatures at the time of the Creation (Genesis 1:22, 28), as well as show Noah that the destruction of the earth he had just witnessed should not be misinterpreted as meaning that life is not precious. Although God is placing obligations upon Noah and his seed, their faithfulness is not tied to God's promise to never flood the earth again. God offers this promise unilaterally, without any conditions placed upon it, in part to teach Noah and his seed the kind of being that God is. The Noahic covenant, then, had both a unilateral and a bilateral nature, leading some scholars to describe it as a "grant" or a "charter." In the ancient Near East, these types of agreements often existed between a deity, powerful emperor, or king on one side and, on the other side, a subservient leader (such as Noah, Abraham, or David in the biblical accounts) appointed to have rule or dominion. Grants or charters included the expectation of loyalty from the one appointed

---

17. See David VanDrunen, *Divine Covenants and Moral Order: A Biblical Theology of Natural Law* (Grand Rapids, MI: Eerdmans, 2014), 39–41, 95–100; Steven D. Mason, *"Eternal Covenant" in the Pentateuch: The Contours of an Elusive Phrase* (New York: T&T Clark, 2008), 47–50; William J. Dumbrell, *Creation and Covenant: An Old Testament Covenantal Theology* (Flemington Markets, Australia: Paternoster and Lancer Books, 1984), 4–6; John Goldingay, "Covenant, OT and NT," in *New Interpreter's Dictionary of the Bible*, ed. Katherine Doob Sakenfield and Samuel E. Balentine (Nashville: Abingdon Press, 2006), 1:767–78; J. B. Payne, "Covenant (OT)," in *Zondervan Encyclopedia of the Bible* (Grand Rapids, MI: Zondervan, 2009), 1:1054.

and thus had an implied bilateral nature but primarily emphasized the rights of the appointed leader, binding the powerful party who granted the appointment to follow certain stipulations (such as never flooding the earth again). They thus highlighted the benevolence of the powerful party, rather than detailing the many obligations that will be expected of one appointed (as would be the case in a suzerainty or vassal treaty).[18]

Elements of the covenant-making process can be seen in this first of the explicit biblical covenants. The elements are as follows: a ceremony or ritual that includes a sacrificial offering, promises from God, expectations or commandments placed upon Noah, and a sign between God and humankind (the rainbow provided by God). Joseph Smith provided a lengthy expansion or restoration of the Noahic covenant in JST Genesis 9:21–25. This passage adds additional meaning to the sign of the rainbow, indicating that it is also set to remind Noah's posterity that Enoch's city of Zion will return in the last days, thereby demonstrating that the covenant with Noah was a renewal of an earlier covenant relationship with Enoch, as demonstrated in Joseph Smith's Enochic expansion found in Moses 6–7.[19]

The Noahic covenant as a renewal of an earlier covenant with Adam and Eve and others. Although not typically listed with the main biblical covenants, some biblical scholars (even without the benefit of the Joseph Smith Translation) have understood the Noahic covenant as the renewal of a covenant relationship first instituted with Adam and Eve.[20] They suggest that the way the covenant is introduced in Genesis 6:18—"But with thee will I establish my covenant"—reads as if a previously established covenant ("my [God's] covenant") is already understood and is being renewed. This reading is strengthened by the repetition of the expectation first given to Adam and Eve (Genesis 1:28) to multiply and replenish the earth in its

18. Moshe Weinfeld, "The Covenant of Grant in the Old Testament and in the Ancient Near East," *Journal of the American Oriental Society* 90 (1970): 185; Dennis J. McCarthy, *Treaty and Covenant: A Study in Form in the Ancient Oriental Documents and in The Old Testament* (Rome: Biblical Institute Press, 1978), 1–24.

19. For more on the flood story, see Aaron's Schade's chapter 4 in this volume.

20. Mason, "*Eternal Covenant*", 48–56; Jacob Milgrom, *Leviticus 23–27*, Anchor Bible Commentary 3B (New York: Doubleday, 2000), 2243–46; William J. Dumbrell, *Creation and Covenant*, 25–33; J. B. Payne, "Covenant (OT)," 1:1059.

covenantal context: "And God blessed Noah and his sons, and said unto them, Be fruitful, and multiply, and replenish the earth" (Genesis 9:1).[21] These scholars have typically read Genesis 1–3 as representing a general covenantal framework, even though the word *covenant* is not explicitly used.

Jeremiah 33:20, 25 is also used by some biblical scholars to support a covenantal reading of Genesis 1–3.[22] These verses refer to a "covenant with day and night" and have been used to postulate a "covenant of [or with] creation" in the Creation account. These scholars expand the view of the Adamic covenant to include all of creation, with Adam standing at the head, much as the whole earth appears to be included in the Noahic covenant. This view has special interest for Latter-day Saints in light of statements in the Book of Abraham that portray God as commanding his creations and waiting for them to obey (for example, see Abraham 4:18), a description that could imply some type of covenantal relationship between God and his creations. Thus, not only is God making a covenant with Adam, but the entire earth and all other creations are participating in that covenant relationship, supporting and fulfilling God's purposes each in their own designated way.

For Latter-day Saints, the covenantal nature of God's relationship with Adam and Eve, and God's subsequent covenantal relationship with their descendants prior to Noah (particularly with Enoch), is clearly taught in the JST as found in the Pearl of Great Price (Moses 5–7) and in JST Genesis 8:23–24 and 9:10–25. JST Genesis 9:23 explicitly states, "And this is mine everlasting covenant, which I made with thy father Enoch." Due to these Restoration scriptures, Latter-day Saints understand that God has been working through covenants from the beginning of the earth (and before). That God made a covenant with Adam is made fully clear in the Pearl of Great Price at the time of Adam's baptism (Moses 6:64–65).

The additions provided by the Joseph Smith Translation do not only serve to confirm that the Noahic covenant was a renewal of earlier

21. See Schade's analysis in chapter 4 of this volume.

22. See chapter 1 in this volume. VanDrunen, *Divine Covenants and Moral Order*, 39–94; Dumbrell, *Creation and Covenant*, 4–61; Williamson, "Covenant," in Boda and McConville, *Dictionary of the Old Testament*, 421.

covenants but they also provide insight into the nature of the covenant, particularly with regard to the preservation of Noah's descendants. God had made promises to Enoch, which were renewed with Noah, that Noah's seed would not perish—an important concern considering the flood—and that God would continue to "call upon" them (Moses 7:51). According to the JST for Genesis 6:18 (the first instance of the word *covenant* in the Old Testament), God states that "with thee will I establish my covenant, even as I have sworn unto thy father, Enoch, that of thy posterity shall come all nations" (JST Genesis 8:23–24). The obligations of these descendants who will be preserved is to bless all nations of the earth by preaching the truth of God's word. This obligation is made clear in Moses 6:23, which discusses the role of the descendants of Adam: "And they were preachers of righteousness, and spake and prophesied, and called upon all men, everywhere, to repent; and faith was taught unto the children of men." The connections made in the JST between the covenants made with Adam, Enoch, and Noah prepare Latter-day Saint biblical readers to understand the Abrahamic covenant more fully and accurately. No matter the reader's understanding of the existence of an Adamic and Enochic covenant, however, the clarity of language in the Noahic covenant of Genesis 8–9 paves the way for a discussion of the biblical covenant par excellence, the covenant made with Abraham.

2. The Abrahamic covenant. The next covenant relationship in the Bible is the Abrahamic covenant, found primarily in Genesis 12, 15, 17, and 22. Some biblical scholars believe that the separate records of the Abrahamic covenant in these chapters point to different traditions of the same event that were later compiled into one account (a concept generally known as the Documentary Hypothesis).[23] Others read the repetitive accounts as

23. The Documentary Hypothesis continues to dominate many fields of biblical scholarship, although it has received decreasing scholarly support from some in the past few decades. Put in simple terms, it posits the Bible (and particularly the first five books, or the Pentateuch) as a collection of numerous sources created at different points in history to fit certain needs that were then combined by later editors to create a composite whole. Repeated stories, conflicting viewpoints, and varying grammar and language are some of the arguments used to support this theory. One significant challenge to the theory is its risk of circularity: the existence of differing sources is taken as assumed, and then support

God's efforts to reinforce, renew, and progress his covenant relationship with Abraham following important testing events in Abraham's life. In Genesis 12:1–3, God promises a covenantal relationship with Abraham after he leaves Ur and travels to the land of Canaan. He formally initiates that relationship in Genesis 15, promising Abraham that he will become a great nation in the land of Canaan that God gives him. In Genesis 17, he expands on a second promise provided in Genesis 12, a promise that Abraham's royal seed would bless all nations of the earth. That promise is formally confirmed in Genesis 22.

Latter-day Saints find all of these promises—a divinely designated land and the continuation of the covenant relationship in and through Abraham's numerous descendants, who would bless all nations of the earth—expanded upon in the Joseph Smith Translation additions to the biblical passages listed above and also find the promises interwoven in one text in the Pearl of Great Price: Abraham 2:6–12. Additionally, Latter-day Saint scripture (building upon New Testament statements) affirms that the promises of the Abrahamic covenant are still available today, both to the scattered descendants of Abraham—many of whom have lost the memory of their genealogical identity—who are willing to enter into covenants with God and to nondescendants who can be adopted as children of Abraham through the making of covenants (John 8:37–39; Romans 8:14–15; Galatians 3:7–9; Book of Mormon title page; Doctrine and Covenants 84:33–34). For Paul and for Latter-day Saints, covenants—particularly the Abrahamic covenant—have always received their power and vitality through faith in God or Christ in Old Testament times (Genesis

---

for the scholar's assumptions is found, even though other valid arguments could also explain many of the differences. See Joel S. Baden, *The Composition of the Pentateuch: Renewing the Documentary Hypothesis* (New Haven, CT: Yale University Press, 2012), 13–44; Pauline A. Viviano, "Documentary Hypothesis," in *The New Interpreter's Dictionary of the Bible*, 2:131. With regard to the Abrahamic covenant, some biblical scholars posit that the different moments in which God institutes his covenant with Abraham all represent the same real or mythical event as conceived by different authors in different times. As the most prominent example of this type of thinking, see George E. Mendenhall, "The Nature and Purpose of the Abrahamic Tradition," in *Ancient Israelite Religion: Essays in Honor of Frank Moore Cross*, ed. P. D. Miller, P. D. Hanson, and S. D. McBride (Philadelphia: Fortress Press, 1987), 337–56.

15:7; Moses 6:52), New Testament times (Galatians 3:7), and modern times (Doctrine and Covenants 20:25). God's plan has always been formally accepted by his children through covenant making that allows them to enter into an explicitly stated relationship with him. As Joseph Smith stated, "Being born again comes by the Spirit of God through ordinances [or in other words, through covenants that are formalized by the ritual act known as ordinances]."[24] God's children are thus brought into the relationship of firstborn with the Father (Romans 8:14–15) through covenant making (and covenant keeping) with God and are transformed by that relationship, which is made possible and given power by the atoning sacrifice of Christ.[25] Paul connected this process with the Abrahamic covenant, and Latter-day Saints recognize that the Abrahamic covenant itself reflects earlier, cosmic, premortal covenants. As discussed in the section about the Adamic, Enochic, and Noahic covenants, accepting this covenant includes an obligation to bless all nations of the earth by calling on all humankind to repent (see Moses 6:23).

Common elements of biblical covenant making are again found and expanded upon in the various biblical and Restoration texts that provide the Abrahamic covenant. In Genesis 15, God formally introduces himself to Abraham and promises him specific blessings, offering the stars in the heavens as a visual demonstration or sign of the promise of progeny (Genesis 15:5; Abraham 2:8). God then requires Abraham to participate in a sacrificial ceremony or ritual known as "the covenant between the parts," a covenant of obligation with an implied punishment—that Abraham and his family would be torn asunder if they betrayed the covenant (Genesis 15:8–17)—an interpretation strengthened by similar connotations in Jeremiah 34 and in the ancient Near Eastern Sefire Treaties.[26] Interestingly,

24. "Report of Instructions, between 26 June and 4 August 1839–A, as Reported by Willard Richards," p. 72, The Joseph Smith Papers. See also Doctrine and Covenants 84.

25. For a clear demonstration of this Latter-day Saint understanding as found in the Book of Mormon, see Mosiah 5:5–8.

26. Jeremiah 34:18–20 appears to make a similar connection: "And I will give the men that have transgressed my covenant, which have not performed the words of the covenant which they had made before me, when they cut the calf in twain, and passed between the parts thereof. . . . I will even give them into the

God himself participated in the ceremony by passing between the pieces of the sacrifice, indicating his own commitment to the covenant (from a Christian viewpoint, God is possibly implying that he himself would be willing to be "torn asunder," suffering the effects of the broken covenant). This process introduces the phrase "to cut a covenant" that elsewhere became common in the biblical texts. The phrase was used to designate the covenant-making process that, in this case, included cutting an animal into pieces (Genesis 15:8–17).[27] In Genesis 17 circumcision was also part of the covenant-making process in addition to animal sacrifice and was likely included in the concept of "cutting a covenant."[28] "To cut a covenant" is therefore to engage in physical actions designated by God that formalize the covenantal relationship.

Genesis 17 and 22 contain other common biblical elements of covenant making. God places clear expectations or commandments upon Abraham. He also gives Abraham, the "father of a great people" (up until this point, he was "Abram," meaning "exalted father"),[29] a new name, signifying his new life and identity under the covenant. Circumcision is

---

hands of their enemies." See Mitchell, "Abram's Understanding of the Lord's Covenant," 28, 39. See also Moshe Weinfield, "berith," in *Theological Dictionary of the Old Testament*, ed. G. Johannes Botterweck, Helmer Ringgren, and Heinz Josef Fabry (Grand Rapids, MI: Eerdmans, 1964), 2:277. For a discussion of implications connected to the Sefire Treaties, see Joseph A. Fitzmyer, *The Aramaic Inscriptions of Sefîre*, Biblica et Orientalia 19 (Rome: Biblical Institute Press, 1967); see also Michael L. Barré, "Treaties," in Freedman, *Anchor Bible Dictionary*, 6:656.

27. Although many today are uncomfortable with the concept of punishments from God, in antiquity, covenant relationships were connected to both blessings and punishments depending on the receiving party's faithfulness in fulfilling them; a covenant relationship that allows either party to betray the covenant with impunity would create an unhealthy imbalance in the relationship and would signify that one party is obligated to respect the covenant while the other is not.

28. E. Isaac, "Circumcision as Covenant Rite," *Anthropos* 59 (1965): 444–56; Eugene Carpenter, "כרת," in *New International Dictionary of Old Testament Exegesis: Second Edition* (*NIDOTTE*), ed. Moises Silva (Grand Rapids, MI: Zondervan, 2014), 2:723.

29. See P. A. Verhoef, "אברהם," in *NIDOTTE*, 4:351.

introduced as part of the covenant-making process,[30] apparently connected to the idea of marriage and progeny. Abraham was told he would have numerous descendants and was then enjoined to mark that part of his body that allowed physical intimacy, placing the act of sexual intimacy in the realm of the sacred, thus marking sexual intimacy as not just a physical experience but an experience that is part of the covenantal relationship with God, including God's promises of descendants to the married couple. Interestingly, not until Abraham was circumcised was Sarah able to become pregnant.[31] That Abraham was required to provide the sign or act of circumcision as a demonstration of his loyalty to the covenant also indicates that this is a covenant of obligations, in which Abraham will need to faithfully participate, rather than a covenant of entitlement in which Abraham simply receives blessings from God without needing to respond.

The ritual behavior of sacrifice, offering one's own possessions up to the Lord as a sign or symbol of loyalty (and especially the sacrificial animal offering of a living being to represent the making of covenant), was already demonstrated in connection with Noah's covenant (Genesis 8:20) as well as with Abraham's (in Genesis 15:17). The purpose of animal sacrifices has been debated among biblical scholars without definite conclusions. Some have seen the death of animals as a warning of consequences for violation of the covenant. Some have understood the act as turning over something to God (a gift offering) that cannot be returned (due to the death of the animal) and that thereby forges a connection with between the person and God. Others have believed that it represents the submission of one's own will—the animal represents the individual's willingness to give her- or himself over to God's will.[32]

---

30. Robert G. Hall, "Circumcision," in Freedman, *Anchor Bible Dictionary*, 1:1025.

31. As Hall states simply, "Circumcision was a marriage or fertility rite." Hall, "Circumcision," in Freedman, *Anchor Bible Dictionary*, 1:1026. In a connected suggestion, others have indicated that it marks the participant as part of God's community. See P. D. Woodbridge, "Circumcision," in *Dictionary of Biblical Theology*, ed. T. Desmond Alexander and Brian S. Rosner (Downers Grove, IL: InterVarsity Press, 2000), 411.

32. For a good overview of various proposals, see Gary Anderson, "Sacrifice and Sacrificial Offerings," in Freedman, *Anchor Bible Dictionary*, 5:870–73. For

Whichever of these purposes (or all of them) may be intended, Genesis 22 again connects covenant making with a sacrificial offering—but with a shocking twist. The story of Abraham's near sacrifice of his son serves as a supreme example of the type of obedience required of those with whom God will maintain his covenant relationship. Even with the supreme sacrifice of Abraham's desires for offspring and with God's request for the life of Abraham's son, God, in the end, does not require Abraham to offer an animal sacrifice from his own herds at all. In this case, the offering God himself provided was that of a ram in the place of Isaac. There is some similarity in this account with the "covenant between the pieces" of Genesis 15, in which the stronger party, God, performs the role often required of the weaker party. In the New Testament, this moment provides a supreme example that Paul used to demonstrate Abraham's faith (Romans 4:1–16).

John Taylor, in explaining that he overheard a statement from Joseph Smith, attaches a modern-day application to Abraham's near-sacrifice of his son: "You will have all kinds of trials to pass through. And it is quite as necessary for you to be tried as it was for Abraham and other [people] of God. . . . God will feel after you, and he will take hold of you and wrench your very heart strings, and if you cannot stand it you will not be fit for an inheritance in the Celestial Kingdom of God."[33] At another time, relying on the biblical importance of sacrifice in the making of covenants, Joseph Smith and his associates stated, "A religion that does not require the sacrifice of all things never has power sufficient to produce the faith necessary unto life and salvation."[34] Although Latter-Saint ordinances require little in the way of monetary sacrifice in the enacting of the rituals, a willingness to sacrifice is expected as a necessary component of the covenant relationship (Doctrine and Covenants 97:8) and highlights the nature of the purpose of sacrifice.

---

recent proposals, see Daniel Ullucci, "Contesting the Meaning of Animal Sacrifice," in *Ancient Mediterranean Sacrifice*, ed. Jennifer Wright Knust and Zsuzsanna Varhelyi (Oxford: Oxford University Press, 2011), 57–75; William K. Gilders, "Jewish Sacrifice: Its Nature and Function (According to Philo)," in Knust and Varhelyi, *Ancient Mediterranean Sacrifice*, 94–105.

33. John Taylor, in *Journal of Discourses* (London: Latter-day Saints' Book Depot, 1884), 24:264.

34. "Doctrine and Covenants, 1835," p. 60, The Joseph Smith Papers.

As with the Noahic covenant, scholars debate whether or not the Abrahamic covenant should be seen as truly bilateral or not.[35] In other words, is the covenant provided by the sovereign, immutable will of God irrespective of the actions of the human participant, or is the faithfulness of the human participant a crucial part of the covenant relationship? The importance of Abraham's participation in the covenant relationship is clear throughout Genesis 12, 15, 17, and 22, but the promises that accrue to his offspring appear to be granted unilaterally and unconditionally by God: the promises will remain whether or not Abraham's offspring are faithful to the covenant. For Latter-day Saints, the Book of Abraham confirms that the promises will remain with Abraham's seed (Abraham 2:11) but also indicates that the promised blessings must be accepted by those who follow Abraham's example of faith and commitment to God (Abraham 2:11). In other words, God grants Abraham's posterity agency (or free will) to accept or reject their covenantal status that has been offered through the will of God and accepted by faith in Christ, actions that move them to "obedience to the laws and ordinances of the gospel" (Article of Faith 1:3). The Abrahamic covenant thus is both unilateral and bilateral, serving as another example of the ancient "grant" or "charter," as mentioned above with the Noahic covenant.[36]

Before proceeding to a discussion of the Mosaic covenant, it is important to reiterate just how strongly Latter-day Saints rely on and identify with the Abrahamic covenant. Although most modern Jews would prioritize the Mosaic covenant over the Abrahamic covenant in their self-understanding, Latter-day Saints believe that the Abrahamic covenant provided the demarcating outlines for later biblical covenants and that

35. VanDrunen, *Divine Covenants and Moral Order*, 39–41, 95–100; Mason, *"Eternal Covenant" in the Pentateuch*, 47–50; Dumbrell, *Creation and Covenant*, 62–70; Mendenhall and Herion, "Covenant," in Freedman, *Anchor Bible Dictionary*, 1:1189–90.

36. Bruce K. Waltke, *An Old Testament Theology: An Exegetical, Canonical, and Thematic Approach* (Grand Rapids, MI: Zondervan, 2007), 386–87; Walter C. Kaiser Jr., *A History of Israel from the Bronze Age through the Jewish Wars* (Nashville: Broadman & Holman Publishers, 1998), 119–20; Weinfield, "The Covenant of Grant in the Old Testament and in the Ancient Near East," 185.

other covenants (such as the Mosaic covenant) are subsumed within it, as will be described in the next section.

3a. The Mosaic covenant.[37] If the Noahic covenant (itself a reiteration of the Adamic and Enochic covenants, as made clear in the JST), served as a foundation for biblical covenant making in the Old Testament, and if the Abrahamic covenant was the covenant that would continue and provide the identity for the patriarchs, matriarchs, and the house of Israel (including in New Testament times and in Restoration scriptures), then the Mosaic covenant was the covenant relationship that spanned the vast majority of the Hebrew Bible, from Exodus 20 to the end of Malachi (and continuing into the New Testament). The Noahic and Abrahamic covenants set up expectations for biblical covenant making that are found fully described in the Mosaic covenant, including sacrificial offerings in ceremonies or rituals, bilateral obligations between God and his people, and the "sign" of the Sabbath day (Exodus 31:16–17). According to Paul R. Williamson, "The fact that the stipulated covenant sign [of the Sabbath] is identified as such only after the instructions concerning the tabernacle and the priesthood are given (Exodus 25:1–31:11) may suggest that the latter elements [of the tabernacle and the priesthood] were also intrinsically related to the Mosaic covenant (*cf.* 24:12; 31:18)."[38] Under this covenant, the nation of Israel was guaranteed prosperity, land, and protection by God as a confirmation of the Abrahamic covenant, and the obligation was placed upon the Israelites, as a continuation of earlier covenants, to be a light and blessing to all nations.

These guarantees and blessings, however, were conditioned on the Israelites' continued obedience to the terms of the covenant. Because this covenant is bilateral in nature, including the reality that it can be canceled or abrogated by the offerer of the covenant (unlike certain aspects of the Abrahamic and Noahic covenants, such as the promise to never flood the earth again or that the covenant will remain with Abraham's

37. For a more detailed treatment of some of the peculiarities of the Mosaic law, see Bowen in this volume. In forthcoming volumes, the legal, moral, and priestly codes that entailed the Mosaic law will be treated in greater detail.

38. Paul R. Williamson, "Covenant," in *Dictionary of the Old Testament*, 420.

seed), biblical scholars, at times, describe it as more similar to a suzerainty treaty.[39] Anciently, vassal or suzerainty treaties, which set forth detailed stipulations of obedience upon a people or nation that would pay tribute, were often more conditional in nature than grants or charters provided by a monarch to the people (which typically emphasized the rights and blessings that the monarch would bestow rather than the obligations of the people). In suzerainty treaties, the attention was focused on the faithfulness of the recipient and provided very detailed conditions for the treaty relationship to continue.[40] This potential distinction highlights one reason why Paul, Christians, and Latter-day Saints view the Mosaic covenant differently than the Abrahamic covenant.

Latter-day Saints have a relatively unique approach to the Mosaic covenant, which has been influenced by Restoration scriptures such as Doctrine and Covenants 84:23–27. Here and elsewhere, Joseph Smith taught that the Mosaic law was a renewal of the covenant status that had existed between God and his people from the beginning. As taught by Paul and reinforced by Joseph Smith, the Mosaic law differed from earlier covenants because of the refusal of Moses's people—known as the "provocation" (Hebrews 3:8, Hebrews 3:15, Jacob 1:7, Alma 12:36)—to fully participate in the covenant-making experience that was designed to bring them into the presence of God on Mount Sinai (JST Exodus 34:1–2).[41] As stated by Joseph, further describing events in Exodus 19 and Exodus 32–34, "Moses sought to bring the children of Israel into the presence of God, through the power of the Priesthood, but he could not."[42] Due to that transgression (Galatians 3:19), God instituted a more complex system of laws, offerings, and sacrifices. God did not intend this more complex system to be permanent but rather intended a return to the type of law that existed under the Abrahamic covenant. Although it might seem a minor point to some, this

39. See Mendenhall and Herion, "Covenant," *Anchor Bible Dictionary*, 1:1184.

40. See Waltke, *An Old Testament Theology*, 386–87; Kaiser, *History of Israel from the Bronze Age through the Jewish Wars*, 119–20; Weinfield, "The Covenant of Grant in the Old Testament and in the Ancient Near East," 185.

41. See Andrew Skinner and Dan Belnap's chapter in this volume.

42. "History, 1838–1856, volume C-1 [2 November 1838–31 July 1842] [addenda]," p. 12 [addenda], The Joseph Smith Papers.

approach encourages Latter-day Saints to read the Bible differently than some other Christians, who often view the entirety of the Old Testament and its laws (from Adam to John the Baptist) as a lesser preparation for the gospel of Christ that was instituted when Jesus was resurrected.[43]

Instead, Latter-day Saints believe that the gospel existed and was taught as part of God's covenant relationship from the beginning of the Old Testament (Moses 6:48–68). Although the Mosaic law was a modified approach to those gospel teachings and expectations, Old Testament peoples and covenants are seen as fitting perfectly into God's covenantal plan for his people in all times, rather than simply as a preparation for that which would come. Covenants had their power through Christ from the beginning of the world. The Mosaic law was fulfilled with the resurrection of Christ (in the form of the paschal Lamb slain from the foundation of the earth), but Jesus's teachings had existed on the earth in some form from the beginning.[44] The Mosaic covenant was designed to help the house of Israel to be a light and a blessing to all nations of the earth.

3b. The priestly covenant. The priestly covenant was closely related to the Mosaic covenant. It was a covenant relationship established between God and the Levites, who were dedicated for priesthood service and priesthood responsibility in place of the firstborn male from each family in each tribe. Numbers 25:10–13 designates it a "covenant of peace" and a "covenant of perpetual priesthood." At the end of the Old Testament, Malachi 2:8 refers to the priestly covenant, indicating that the people had "corrupted the covenant of Levi" (the tribe designated to hold priestly authority under the Mosaic covenant). As with other covenant relationships, this relationship was signified by sacrificial ceremonies and bilateral

---

43. This is known as replacement theology or, from a critical viewpoint, as supercessionism. See Calvin L. Smith, *The Jews, Modern Israel, and the New Supercessionism* (Lampeter, UK: King's Divinity, 2009), 5–8.

44. According to Joseph Smith, "Some say the kingdom of God was not set up on the earth until the day of Pentecost. . . . ; but I say, in the name of the Lord, that the kingdom of God was set up on the earth from the days of Adam to the present time. . . . Where there is a prophet, a priest, or a righteous man unto whom God gives His oracles, there is the kingdom of God." "History, 1838–1856, volume D-1 [1 August 1842–1 July 1843] [addenda]," p. 5 [addenda], The Joseph Smith Papers.

commitments between God and the priests. Under the Mosaic covenant, the levitical priests wore special ceremonial clothing to officiate in the temple and were consecrated or ordained through special ceremonies that included washing, anointing, and "the filling of the hand."[45]

According to a Latter-day Saint approach, the Mosaic priestly covenant found in the Old Testament can be understood as confirming God's desire to give his priesthood authority to humankind. Priesthood authority was and is given to help prepare God's people to enter into his presence (Doctrine and Covenants 84:20–23). Latter-day Saint scripture confirms that "the sons of Levi [will] offer again an offering unto the Lord in righteousness" (Doctrine and Covenants 13:1). Thus, God's promise to give priesthood authority to the descendants of Levi is not abrogated or superseded in the last days but is confirmed. Additionally, those granted the Aaronic priesthood in the restored church today are designated as "sons of Aaron" (Doctrine and Covenants 84:31; because Aaron was the descendant of Levi who was given the highest level of Levitical, priestly authority), whether or not they are physically descended from Aaron and Levi. All who receive the priesthood in modern times accept the "oath and covenant" of the priesthood as presented in Doctrine and Covenants 84:33–45.

---

45. When the Old Testament states that a priest was ordained or consecrated to office in such locations as Exodus 29:22–25; 28:41; 29:9; 32:29 and elsewhere, the Hebrew literally states that the hand of the priest was filled. (In other words, his hand was filled as a sign or symbol of his ordination.) According to E. W. Bulliger, "This means to fill the hand, especially with that which is the sign and symbol of office, i.e. to fill the hand with a scepter was to consecrate to the office of king. To fill the hand with certain parts of sacrifices was to set apart for the office of priest, and to confirm their right to offer both gifts and sacrifices to God. A ram of 'consecration' (or of filling) was a ram with parts of which the hands of the priests were filled when they were set apart to their office. Whenever the word refers to official appointment, or separation to a work or dignity, it is the sovereign act of God, and the accompanying symbolic act was the filling of the hand of the person so appointed with the sign which marked his office." E. W. Bulliger, *Number in Scripture* (Whitefish, MT: Kessinger Publishing, 2003), 145. Latter-day Saints, who are "set apart" for callings or responsibilities in the Church through the formal ordinance of the laying on of hands, might appropriately see that moment as God "filling" their upturned hand with blessings and authority. The hand would then be turned over in the fulfilling of the ordained duty to pour out those blessings upon others.

In these verses, God promises those who accept his priesthood that they will be renewed and sanctified and that accepting the priesthood is equivalent to accepting him. God swears with an oath that all who accept the covenant of the priesthood will receive "all that [the] Father hath" (Doctrine and Covenants 84:38).

Moreover, building on Psalm 110:4, Hebrews 7 reasons that if Abraham was greater than Aaron or Levi, and if Abraham himself paid tithes to Melchizedek, then there must be a higher priesthood authority than that exercised by the Levites under the priestly covenant of the Mosaic law (Hebrews 7:1–11). That reasoning points to Christ but also points to Abraham and the other patriarchs before the priestly covenant as priests after the order of Melchizedek. Thus, most Latter-day Saints would view the priestly covenant as an additional witness that God works with his covenant people through priesthood authority throughout history, even as they view the priesthood authority provided in this covenant, along with the Mosaic covenant, as being subsumed within the broader priesthood authority of the Abrahamic covenant.

4. *The new covenant.* A new covenant is described in Jeremiah 31:31–34:

> Behold, the days come, saith the Lord, that I will make a new covenant with the house of Israel, and with the house of Judah:
>
> Not according to the covenant that I made with their fathers in the day that I took them by the hand to bring them out of the land of Egypt [in other words, the Mosaic covenant]; which my covenant they brake, although I was an husband unto them, saith the Lord:
>
> But this shall be the covenant that I will make with the house of Israel; After those days, saith the Lord, I will put my law in their inward parts, and write it in their hearts; and will be their God, and they shall be my people.
>
> And they shall teach no more every man his neighbour, and every man his brother, saying, Know the Lord: for they shall all know me, from the least of them unto the greatest of them, saith the Lord: for I will forgive their iniquity, and I will remember their sin no more.

Since the "new covenant" supersedes the Mosaic covenant and describes a future covenant focused more on the heart, many Christian scholars have connected it with the gospel covenant found in Christ.[46] These scholars claim that the gospel covenant of the New Testament supersedes all other covenants and that the others, including the Abrahamic covenant, should be seen through the light of this covenant. Latter-day Saints instead see it as the promise of a restoration of the Abrahamic covenant that is made new and alive again through Christ in New Testament times and again through Christ among his Latter-day Saints. Latter-day Saints know this new covenant as "the new and everlasting covenant" (Doctrine and Covenants 132:6). For Latter-day Saints, then, Jeremiah's prophecy of the new covenant is viewed as anticipating all that Jesus Christ would bring.

THE PREEMINENCE OF THE ABRAHAMIC COVENANT

If the Noahic (the first explicit covenant), Mosaic (the covenant spanning the majority of the Hebrew Bible), and new (the covenant viewed by some as superseding all other covenants) covenants all have at least some claim as the central or preeminent biblical covenant, why do most biblical scholars emphasize the Abrahamic covenant? Simply put, the Israelites were brought out of Egypt and toward Sinai on the basis of the Abrahamic covenant, not on the basis of the Mosaic covenant that would be instituted

---

46. Waltke, *Old Testament Theology*, 43–44; Larry D. Pettegrew, "The New Covenant," *The Master Seminary Journal* 10, no. 2 (1999): 251–70; Andrew Murray, *The Believer's New Covenant* (Minneapolis: Bethany House, 1984), 61–62; O. Palmer Robertson, *The Christ of the Covenants* (Grand Rapids, MI: Baker, 1980), 271–300. As an example, John Davis stated that "all Christians must begin their reading of the Bible with the New Testament, without which there is no Christianity. Consequently, as they read the New Testament Christians become aware that the coming of Jesus introduces a fundamental change in regard to how the Old Testament is understood. This is especially true in regard to the Abrahamic covenant." John P. Davis, "Who Are the Heirs of the Abrahamic Covenant?," *Evangelical Review of Theology* 29, no. 2 (2005): 149.

there.[47] The promises of the Abrahamic covenant—not necessarily the Mosaic covenant that would be broken by the Israelites over and over again—seem to lie beneath the Lord's oft-repeated statements in Deuteronomy, Isaiah, and elsewhere that explain that the Lord would gather the descendants of Israel in the last days. In other words, it is because of the Abrahamic covenant that the Lord chose to initiate the Mosaic covenant with the Israelites, and it is the Abrahamic covenant that defines the boundaries of the Mosaic covenant. The Noahic covenant with its promises to all flesh does not provide the specific, limited people with whom God would make his Mosaic covenant, and the Noahic covenant is rarely referred to by name again throughout the rest of the Hebrew Bible.[48] Finally, while the new covenant certainly could be seen as the preeminent covenant under Christianity—and many Christian theologians do therefore interpret all other covenants through the lens of that covenant rather than through the lens of the Abrahamic covenant—even the authors of the New Testament chose to discuss the gospel covenant in terms of the Abrahamic covenant, and they gave effort to explain the connection between faith in Christ and the Abrahamic covenant (Galatians 3, Romans 4, and Hebrews 7). In Galatians 3, for example, Paul points to the Mosaic covenant as a lesser covenant "added because of transgressions" and as a "schoolmaster to bring us unto Christ" (Galatians 3:19, 24). In the same passages, Paul reinforces the importance of the Abrahamic covenant: "Now to Abraham and his seed were the promises made" (3:16), "God gave [the land] to Abraham by promise" (3:18), and "If ye be Christ's, then are ye Abraham's seed, and heirs according to the promise" (3:29). Thus, the Latter-day Saint emphasis on the Abrahamic covenant follows a New Testament emphasis. Following biblical antecedents, Latter-day Saints view the Abrahamic covenant as God's promise to which they point and as a promise that is still in effect for God's people.

47. The reasoning that the Abrahamic covenant provides the meaning and structure for the Mosaic covenant, not the other way around, is provided in Hebrews 7, Romans 4, and Galatians 3.

48. See chapter 4 of this volume.

CONCLUSION

The primary purpose of this paper is to demonstrate the interconnected nature of biblical covenants. Although the Noahic, Abrahamic, Mosaic, and other covenants do demonstrate unique features, based on God's purposes and the needs of the time, they also interconnect with and build upon each other. That interconnectedness continues through the New Testament texts and into the modern day in The Church of Jesus Christ of Latter-day Saints. A secondary purpose, flowing from the primary purpose, is to show the features of covenant making that are observable in the Old Testament in order to help modern readers recognize similar elements in their own covenant making. A final purpose has been to emphasize the preeminent nature of the Abrahamic covenant in Old Testament, New Testament, and Restoration thought and scripture. The Abrahamic covenant is designed to bless all people who are willing to exercise faith in Christ and to bring all who are willing to come into a covenantal relationship with God. It is God's gracious love, wisdom, and power—received by humankind through faith in Christ—that give covenants (particularly the Abrahamic covenant) their force and power. In Joseph Smith's view, the blessings that we gain through the gospel are gained through faith in Christ and through the restoration of the covenants of old (which are contained in the "new and everlasting" covenant of the restored gospel of Christ). God's plan is designed for all the inhabitants of the earth. It is a plan designed to provide his power—through the atoning love of Jesus Christ—to his children, particularly as they choose to enter into and maintain their covenant relationship with him through faith.

— 8 —

THE WANDERINGS OF ABRAHAM

JOHN GEE

While Pierce and Muhlestein surveyed the general historical context of the patriarchal narratives, setting the stage for the Israelites and their interactions within the greater ancient Near Eastern setting, John Gee focuses instead on the immediate historical settings in the narrative of Abraham. From Ur to Canaan to Egypt to Moriah, Abraham's life was one of the nomad, and that is reflected in the texts describing his life.
—DB and AS

Abraham was a real person who lived in and traveled between real places. He lived, however, so long ago that the world he lived in is completely foreign to most of those who live now, almost four millennia later. Both Abraham and his world seem unreal to us. Understanding something about his world can make it more real to those of us who are still benefiting from the covenants that he made and who are still inheritors of the promises God made to him. While space will not allow a thorough examination of Abraham's world, in this essay we will look at the real world in which Abraham lived and traveled and the real places that he visited.

SOURCES

Latter-day Saints know about the life of Abraham from two sources: the Bible and the Book of Abraham. The book of Genesis in the Bible provides a brief biography of Abraham, while the Book of Abraham provides an incomplete autobiography of Abraham. Based on the covenantal form of the Abrahamic narrative, the sources from which the biblical text was compiled can be dated during the late second millennium BC,[1] although there are indications of editorial tampering with the text later (1 Nephi 13:23–27).[2] The earliest manuscripts of the biblical text date many centuries after the text. With the Book of Abraham we have a different transmission history, much of which is conjectural: it may have been transmitted through Abraham's descendants until it passed into Egypt. A now missing papyrus manuscript was translated by the Prophet Joseph Smith and published in 1842. These two sources provide the basis for reconstructing the life of Abraham, which we will supplement with other contemporary archaeological and epigraphic sources to provide a fuller setting for Abraham's life. The material is far greater than can be covered in this essay, so

1. See Kenneth A. Kitchen and Paul J. N. Lawrence, *Treaty, Law and Covenant in the Ancient Near East* (Wiesbaden: Harrassowitz, 2012), 3:255–61.
2. The fragmentary state of the Dead Sea Scrolls means that most of the Abraham story is missing. There are, however, a few textual variants; see Eugene Ulrich, *The Biblical Qumran Scrolls* (Leiden: E. J. Brill, 2013), 1:8–10.

we will confine ourselves to a description of the places visited by Abraham in his various travels.

THE SETTING

In order to set the life of Abraham among contemporary sources, we must know what is contemporary. If all we had were the Bible, starting from the fall of Jerusalem in 586 BC and kept track of the cumulative error factors,[3] we would only be able to say that Abraham lived from about 2170 to 1995 BC, ± 158 years.[4] Thus, on the low end, Abraham's life would have been

3. Various manuscripts give the number of years in a king's reign differently. Therefore, each variant will add an error factor of the largest difference between the variants. Also, most kings will not reign exactly a certain number of years to the day, but their reign will be counted in a whole number of years. Depending on the numbering system of a given country at a given time, we could have the following situation (which would admittedly be the worst-case scenario): Suppose King Dingsbums takes over the country during the last half of the last month of the year that is counted as his first regnal year, with the next month counting as his second regnal year; after two full years, he dies in the first half of the first month of the subsequent year (his fourth regnal year). How long did King Dingsbums reign? The total time of his reign is two years and about a month, but King Dingsbums has had four regnal years. For each change of reign, assuming the worst case scenario, we add ±2 years as an error factor. The error factors are cumulative.
4. A slightly different addition can be found in Donald B. Redford, *Egypt, Canaan, and Israel in Ancient Times* (Princeton: Princeton University Press, 1992), 258; but note the objections to this in K. A. Kitchen, review of Redford, *Egypt, Canaan, and Israel in Ancient Times*, in *Journal of Semitic Studies* 41, no. 1 (Spring 1996): 123. Redford in his effort to attack inerrantist Christianity (see Redford, *Egypt, Canaan, and Israel in Ancient Times*, 257–63, et passim) misses the point; if one does not take an inerrantist position—and while not identical, neither Redford's nor the Latter-day Saints' position is inerrantist—one can, and Redford does, still use the Bible as a reliable historical source. Manuscript variants should alert us to particular problems in the record; numbers are among the easiest of textual errors. Redford, in attacking those who try to fit Biblical chronology with the rest of the Near East, acts as though he has never read any of the attempts to make the various chronologies of the Near East fit each other. J. J. Bimson also argues that Biblical chronology dating Abraham from 2167 to 1992 BC fits with archaeological evidence; J. J. Bimson, "Archaeological Data

from 2012 to 1837 BC, while the high end would have been from 2328 to 2153 BC. Since correlation with such absolute dates is rarely achievable for archaeology or ancient history, it is easier to correlate Abraham with archaeological time periods. The high-end biblical dates would place Abraham's life during the Middle Bronze Age I, while the low-end dates would place Abraham in the Middle Bronze Age IIA. Indeed, Abraham's life is usually dated to either the Middle Bronze Age I (MB I; approximately 2100–2000 BC) or the Middle Bronze Age II (MB II; approximately 2000–1750 BC) by the other means of argument.[5]

Latter-day Saints, however, have other means of dating Abraham. The Book of Abraham describes how Abraham lived at a time when Egyptians held hegemony over his hometown. This happened at a very specific time in Egyptian history. The Egyptians recorded their military conquest of the area around Byblos during the reign of either Sesostris II or Sesostris III.[6] Their rule over the area lasted until the rule of Amenemhet IV. The record of astronomical observations during the reign of Sesostris III and Amenemhet III provides a chronological anchor to the dates putting year one of Amenemhet III as 1844 or 1843 BC.[7] This gives a maximal time of the Egyptian Middle Kingdom empire from about 1871 to 1788 BC.[8] Abraham

---

and the Dating of the Patriarchs," in *Essays on the Patriarchal Narratives*, ed. D. J. Wiseman and A. R. Millard (Winona Lake, IN: Eisenbrauns, 1983), 81–85.

5. For the generally accepted dates for Abraham, see John Bright, *A History of Israel*, 3rd ed. (Philadelphia: Westminster, 1981), 77–87 (Middle Bronze Age I [MB I]); Bimson, "Archaeological Data and the Dating of the Patriarchs," 59–92 (transition between MBI and Middle Bronze Age II [MB II]); Amihai Mazar, *Archaeology of the Land of the Bible 10,000–586 B.C.E.* (New York: Doubleday, 1990), 224–26 (MBII); K. A. Kitchen, *Ancient Orient and Old Testament* (Chicago: Intervarsity Press, 1966), 41–56 (twentieth to eighteenth centuries BC).

6. James P. Allen, "The Historical Inscription of Khnumhotep at Dahshur: Preliminary Report," *Bulleting of the American Schools of Oriental Research* 352 (2008): 29–39.

7. See Rolf Krauss, "Lunar Dates," in *Ancient Egyptian Chronology*, ed. Erik Hornung, Rolf Krauss, and David A. Warburton (Leiden: E. J. Brill, 2006), 427.

8. See Thomas Schneider, "The Relative Chronology of the Middle Kingdom and the Hyksos Period (Dyns. 12–17)," in Hornung, Krauss, and Warburton, *Ancient Egyptian Chronology*, 174.

chapter 1 will have had to have taken place at this time, which lowers the Ussherian approach by at least a hundred years.[9]

IN UR OF THE CHALDEES

Both the Bible and the Book of Abraham begin his story with him living in Ur of the Chaldees (Genesis 11:27–31; Abraham 1:1, 20). The Hebrew here uses the word *kasdîm* rather than Chaldeans, which may not be the same thing as the later tribe, the *kaldu*, which we now equate with the Chaldeans.[10] Based on the Akkadian cognate, we would expect the *kasdîm* to mean "the conquerors."[11] While the tendency has been to put Ur in the south of Mesopotamia, near the Persian Gulf,[12] a number of scholars have argued for a northern location.[13]

---

9. The Ussherian approach refers to biblical dating proposed by James Ussher in the 1600s. While Ussher followed a "creationism" dating for the antediluvian period, his dating of the historical sequences was surprisingly solid, as he used multiple comparative texts to determine the dating.
10. See also the Targum Jonathan Genesis 11:28, which does not use the term *Chaldeans.*
11. A. Leo Oppenheim, Erica Reiner, and Robert D. Biggs, *The Assyrian Dictionary of the Oriental Institute of the University of Chicago. Volume 8: K* (Chicago: Oriental Institute, 1971), 271–84, s.v. "kašādu"; Jeremy Black, Andrew George, and Nicholas Postgate, *A Concise Dictionary of Akkadian* (Wiesbaden: Harrassowitz, 2000), 152.
12. H. W. F. Saggs, "Ur of the Chaldees: A Problem of Identification," *Iraq* 22 (1960): 200–209.
13. See Douglas Frayne, "In Abraham's Footsteps," in *The World of the Aramaeans I: Biblical Studies in Honour of Paul-Eugène Dion*, ed. P. M. Michèle Daviau, John W. Weve, and Michael Weigl (Sheffield, UK: Sheffield Academic Press, 2001), 216: "A brief examination of connections between the proper names appearing in the patriarchal Abraham narrative in Genesis 11 with ancient northwestern Syrian toponyms suggests a close connection of the homeland of Abraham and his relatives with the city and countryside of Harran." See also Daniel E. Fleming, "Mari and the Possibilities of Biblical Memory," *Revue d'Assyriologie et d'archéologie orientale* 92, no. 1 (1998): 67: "The Genesis tradition of a north Syrian origin for Abraham and his family is both central to the narrative and difficult to explain in terms of peoples and regional political relations during the lives of the Israelite states, the exiles, or early Judaism." Finally,

The Book of Abraham places Ur of the Chaldees at the edge of a plain known as the plain of Olishem (Abraham 1:10), which we take as the general area compassed by two catch basins that are drained by two rivers: the Quoeiq and the Sajur, an area that straddles modern Turkey and Syria. There also appears to have been a city called Olishem, which was a major administrative center for the region in Abraham's day.[14] Its ruler bore a Hurrian name (Šennam) indicative of perhaps a Hurrian population,[15] though some Semitic names (Sin-malik) also appear—suggesting that the population was mixed.[16] The area was noted for its olive oil.[17]

The Book of Abraham suggests that Ur was not the city Olishem itself but instead associates Ur with a smaller location in the surrounding plain,[18] distinguished by a "hill called Potiphar's Hill" that was located "at the head of the plain of Olishem" (Abraham 1:10). Since the "head" of a river refers to its source (Genesis 2:10),[19] the head of the plain of Olishem probably also refers to the headwaters. Thus, Ur was likely at the northern edge of the plain given the hills, the association with Olishem rather than

---

Mark W. Chavalas, "Syria and Northern Mesopotamia to the End of the Third Millennium BCE," in *Mesopotamia and the Bible*, ed. Mark W. Chavalas and K. Lawson Younger Jr. (Sheffield, UK: Sheffield Academic Press, 2002), 126: "The writers of the Bible claimed that their ancestors originated in this area from Harran in the Upper Euphrates region."

14. Atilla Engin and Barbara Helwing, "The EBA-MBA Transition in the Kilis Plain," in *Looking North: The Socioeconomic Dynamics of the Northern Mesopotamian and Anatolian Religions during the Late Third and Early Second Millennium BC*, ed. Nicola Laneri, Peter Pfälzner, and Stefano Valentini (Wiesbaden: Harrassowitz, 2012), 99–100.

15. Klaas R. Veenhof, "Across the Euphrates," in *Anatolia and the Jazira during the Old Assyrian Period*, ed. J. G. Dercksen (Leiden: Nederlands Instituut voor het Nabije Oosten, 2008), 17; Gernot Wilhelm, *The Hurrians* (Warminster, PA: Aris & Phillips, 1989), 15.

16. ARM 14 31, in Maurice Birot, *Lettres de Yaqqim–Addu gouverneur de Sagarâtum* (Paris: Paul Geuthner, 1974), 66.

17. AbB 2 143, in R. Frankena, *Briefe aus den Britischen Museum* (Leiden: E. J. Brill, 1966), 92–95.

18. Engin and Helwing, "The EBA–MBA Transition in the Kilis Plain," 99–100.

19. The usage of the "head" of a valley in Isaiah 28:1, 4 is, unfortunately, unclear. The "head of Lebanon" in Jeremiah 22:6 appears to refer to the highlands.

Aleppo, and the general pattern of drainage. Given the standard population estimate of one hundred people per hectare[20] and sites ranging from one to ten hectares, Abraham's Ur probably would not have had more than a thousand inhabitants. Given that Ur had an Egyptian priest (Abraham 1:7–8, 20), it would probably have been one of the larger settlements (at least four hectares per four hundred people), but the priest was a priest for multiple deities (Abraham 1:7), so the place was not so large that it could have supported a large and specialized group of priests.

Abraham shows concern with his father's house and the god of his fathers. The family or "house of the father" (*bīt abim*) was the "basic nucleus" of Babylonian society[21] and the standard term for a household.[22] Individuals were defined by their relationship to the head of the family.[23] While the father lived, he was "the head of the family, he was their spokesman in court and took part in the sessions of the city elders—if the family enjoyed sufficient social standing to have a representative among the elders."[24] The city elders were more involved in legal affairs in the south and military affairs in the north.[25] Solidarity with the family was expected.[26] To leave the house of one's father would be to leave oneself at the mercy of strangers from whom one otherwise had no protection.[27]

---

20. William G. Dever, *The Lives of Ordinary People in Ancient Israel: Where Archaeology and the Bible Intersect* (Grand Rapids, MI: William B. Eerdmans, 2012), 71–72; Mazar, *Archaeology of the Land of the Bible*, 112; William G. Dever, *Beyond the Texts: An Archaeological Portrait of Ancient Israel and Judah* (Atlanta: Society of Biblical Literature, 2017), 168.
21. Karel van der Toorn, *Family Religion in Babylonia, Syria and Israel: Continuity and Change in Forms of Religious Life* (Leiden: E. J. Brill, 1996), 20.
22. Ignace J. Gelb, "Household and Family in Early Mesopotamia," in *State and Temple Economy in the Ancient Near East*, ed. Edward Lipinski (Leuven: Departement Oriëntalistiek, 1979), 1:8.
23. Gelb, "Household and Family in Early Mesopotamia," 29–56.
24. van der Toorn, *Family Religion in Babylonia, Syria and Israel*, 21.
25. Andrea Seri, *Local Power in Old Babylonian Mesopotamia* (Sheffield, UK: Equinox, 2006), 97–137.
26. van der Toorn, *Family Religion in Babylonia, Syria and Israel*, 23–24.
27. van der Toorn, *Family Religion in Babylonia, Syria and Israel*, 22.

One of the challenges Abraham had in Ur was the fact that his father worshipped other deities. The family often had particular deities associated with them, referred to as "the gods of the fathers."[28] Sources indicate that one could be an official priest of one particular deity but have a different personal god.[29] The family deity would have been "passed on from father to son and from son to grandson. He [the deity] was part of the heritage, so to speak, and as such the god of the patrilineal family."[30] Some contemporary sources suggest that the god of the fathers could have acted as a mediator between the immediate family and the primary deities. For instance, a letter addressed by Apil-Adad to "the god of my father" reads: "Why have you neglected me? Who could offer to you like I do? Write to Marduk who loves you so that he may release me from my sins. Let me see your face. Let me kiss your feet. Look after my family, young and old. Have mercy on me because of them. May your help reach me."[31]

FAMINE IN THE LAND

A challenge for anyone in this time period was the prospect of famine, which unfortunately appears to have been pretty common (Genesis 12:10; Abraham 1:29–30; 2:1–5, 17–21). As one scholar put it, famine "should not be viewed as an abnormal and temporary deviation of the usual state of well-being but rather as a dramatic, albeit recurrent, worsening of endemic conditions of poverty and need."[32] Abraham certainly experienced his share of famines. One in Ur forced him to move to Haran (Abraham 1:29–2:4), while another forced him to go down to Egypt (Genesis 12:10;

---

28. AbB 11 15 20–23, in M. Stol, *Letters from Collections in Philadelphia, Chicago and Berkeley* (Leiden: E. J. Brill, 1986), 10–11; van der Toorn, *Family Religion in Babylonia, Syria and Israel*, 74–75.
29. van der Toorn, *Family Religion in Babylonia, Syria and Israel*, 67.
30. van der Toorn, *Family Religion in Babylonia, Syria and Israel*, 72.
31. AbB 9 141, in M. Stol, *Letters from Yale* (Leiden: E. J. Brill, 1981), 88–91; Henry Frederick Lutz, *Early Babylonian Letters from Larsa* (New Haven, CT: Yale University Press, 1917), pl. L. Read tu-uš-ta-ṭà-a-am in line 4. Line 10 has i-ḫ̮i-i[l-x-x-x]. Marduk was the primary deity of Babylon.
32. Carlo Zaccagnini, "War and Famine at Emar," *Orientalia*, n.s., 64, no. 2 (1995): 93.

Abraham 2:17–21). Certainly, changes in weather and climate would have had immediate and striking consequences,[33] but climate wasn't the only cause of famine; military crises, drought, or insect invasions had devastating consequences to one's food supply.[34] Of course, famine also affected not just one's immediate situation but also the future. Food storage systems were generally only designed to store food for the coming year. Harvest rates were generally sixfold at best, and so a sixth of the crop would have to be reserved for the next year's seed-corn.[35] One bad harvest could obliterate even a wealthy family's reserves.[36]

A letter roughly contemporary with Abraham describes the problem that the city of Qaṭṭunân faced in famine. The governor of the city, Zakira-Hammu, writes to Zimri-Lim: "This fortress did not harvest grain this year. The (seed)grain has been eaten and the powerful man who has grain has remained while the poor commoner who does not have grain has gone to the river."[37] It is no wonder that Abraham, after seeing "a fulfilment of those things which were said unto [him] concerning the land of Chaldea, that there should be a famine in the land" (Abraham 1:29), followed the instructions of the Lord to leave his father's house, his kindred, and his country and travel to Haran (1:1–4).

---

33. Zaccagnini, "War and Famine at Emar," 93: "Unfavorable climatic situations could have a dramatic impact of the cereal yields, especially in dry-farming areas; therefore we can easily understand why people often fell into debts, pledged or sold their children, relatives, houses and fields and eventually became serfs as an alternative to leaving the country and running away."

34. Seth Richardson, "Obedient Bellies: Hunger and Food Security in Ancient Mesopotamia," *Journal of the Economic and Social History of the Orient* 59, no. 5 (2016): 755–56.

35. G. E. Rickman, "The Grain Trade under the Roman Empire," *Memoires of the American Academy in Rome* 36 (1980): 261. Though based on Roman data, it is hard to imagine that the situation could have been appreciably better in Abraham's day.

36. James P. Allen, *The Heqanakht Papyri* (New York: Metropolitan Museum of Art, 2002), 170–71.

37. ARM 27 25 10–14, in Maurice Birot, *Correspondance des gouverneurs de Qaṭṭunân* (Paris: Editions Recherche sur les Civilisations, 1993), 73; Wolfgang Heimpel, *Letters to the King of Mari* (Winona Lake, IN: Eisenbrauns, 2003), 419.

HARAN

Abraham arrived in Haran with his wife Sarai; his brother Nahor; his brother's wife, Milcah; his father, Terah; and his brother's son, Lot, along with Lot's wife (Abraham 2:1–4). Biblical Haran is one of the few towns mentioned in the Ebla archives that can actually be identified with an archaeological site (referred to as Harran).[38] Located on the eastern side of a wadi feeding the Balikh River via the Cullab River,[39] Harran was not only an "area with optimal dry-farming conditions"[40] but also a major stop along the trade routes as one of the crossings of the Balikh.[41] The site of Harran lies at the center of the Harran plain.[42] The Harran plain is bordered on the east by the Tektek mountains and on the west by a series of low hills.[43] Harran is a massive site of some 125 or 150 hectares,[44] which would mean that it had a population of about 12,500 to 15,000 inhabitants. This city dominated the other fifty sites on the plain,[45] most of which did not exceed twenty hectares (two thousand inhabitants).[46] Such a large city, much bigger than Ur or even the district capital of Olishem, would have made a more or less ideal place for a fugitive like Abraham to disappear into.

---

38. Walther Sallberger, "History and Philology," in *Jezirah*, ed. Marc Lebeau (Turnhout: Brepolis, 2011), 328.
39. Andrew T. Creekmore III, "Landscape and Settlement in the Harran Plain, Turkey: The Context of Third-Millennium Urbanization," *American Journal of Archaeology* 122, no. 2 (2018): 177; Nurettin Yardımcı, *Archaeological Survey in the Harran Plain* (Istanbul: A Grafik ve Matbaacılık San, 2004), 1:14.
40. Creekmore, "Landscape and Settlement in the Harran Plain," 177.
41. YBC 4490 32, in William W. Hallo, "The Road to Emar," *Journal of Cuneiform Studies* 18, no. 3 (1964): 60, 64; Creekmore, "Landscape and Settlement in Harran," 188.
42. Yardımcı, *Archaeological Survey in the Harran Plain*, 1:24.
43. Yardımcı, *Archaeological Survey in the Harran Plain*, 1:14.
44. For the lower figure, see Yardımcı, *Archaeological Survey in the Harran Plain*, 1:23; for the higher figure, see Stefano Anastasio, Marc Lebeau, and Martin Sauvage, *Atlas of Preclassical Upper Mesopotamia*, Subartu XIII (Turnhout: Brepolis, 2004), 154.
45. Creekmore, "Landscape and Settlement in the Harran Plain," 178, 193.
46. Creekmore, "Landscape and Settlement in the Harran Plain," 180.

For Abraham's purposes, Haran had a major advantage over Ur. Being on the eastern side of the Euphrates, Ur was out of the area dominated by the Egyptians. Crossing the Euphrates required boats or being at one of the few fords,[47] a feat the Egyptians would not accomplish until a few hundred years later.[48] The Euphrates marked a political and cultural boundary, not just a geographic one.[49] According to Abraham 2:5, it is while Abraham is in Haran that he becomes associated with the herding of "flocks." While one may reasonably assume that "flocks" refers to sheep, it is possible that it included other animals and could consist of cattle (GU$_4$), sheep (UDU), goats (MÁŠ), donkeys (ANŠE), and horses (ANŠE.KUR.RA).[50] As for the size of a herd, herds of up to eleven hundred sheep are known.[51] Cattle tend to be found in smaller numbers, such as a herd of twelve,[52] twenty-four,[53] or sixty-five.[54]

How long Abraham was in Haran is unclear, but we do know that when he left he took all the property he acquired (*kāl-rᵉkûšām ʾašer rākāšû*) there (Genesis 12:5). The term *rᵉkûšām* is only used a handful of times in the Hebrew Bible, all in Genesis (12:5; 31:18; 36:6; 46:6). It usually refers to cattle and herds but can also refer to the household (36:6; 46:6). The Hebrew word seems to be a loanword from an Akkadian verb (*rakāsu*) meaning *to bind*,[55] and the derived noun (*riksu*) which is a term for a

47. Veenhof, "Across the Euphrates," 3–18.
48. Annals of Thutmosis III V 19–22, in Kurt Sethe, *Urkunden der 18. Dynastie* (Leipzig: J. C. Hinrichs, 1907), 3:697–98.
49. Veenhof, "Across the Euphrates," 3, 16–18.
50. Jean Bottéro, *Textes économiques et administratifs* (Paris: Imprimerie Nationale, 1957), 246–51; compare Marcel Sigrist, *Drehem* (Bethesda, MD: CDL Press, 1992), 22–43.
51. ARM 7 224, in Bottéro, *Textes économiques et administratifs*, 114–15. For a herd of one hundred, see ARM 7 137, in Bottéro, *Textes économiques et administratifs*, 54. For a herd of two hundred, see ARM 7 227, in Bottéro, *Textes économiques et administratifs*, 119–20.
52. ARM 7 91, in Bottéro, *Textes économiques et administratifs*, 31.
53. ARM 7 263, in Bottéro, *Textes économiques et administratifs*, 140–41.
54. ARM 7 272, in Bottéro, *Textes économiques et administratifs*, 149.
55. Black, George, and Postgate, *Concise Dictionary of Akkadian*, 296.

"knot" or "band" but also for a "treaty," "agreement," or "covenant."[56] The phrase thus indicates that Abraham took all those whom "they had bound to them" with them when they left Haran. The Book of Abraham expresses it as follows: "All our substance that we had gathered, and the souls that we had won in Haran" (Abraham 2:15).

JOURNEY TO CANAAN

The second half of Abraham's life, the time he spent in Canaan, was spent dwelling in a tent (Genesis 12:8; 13:3, 5, 12, 18; 18:1–2, 6, 9–10; 24:67), living the life of a pastoral nomad, a "mobile lifestyle [that] leaves few archaeological traces."[57] When Abraham left Haran, he traveled to Canaan. The area of Canaan in Abraham's day encompassed the entire Levantine littoral. This entire area had been under Egyptian influence, but with the collapse of the Egyptian empire at the end of the Twelfth Dynasty, the Egyptian influence had lessened. The northern end of Canaan was dominated by narrow coastal plains lying between the sea, the Lebanon range, and the Syrian hinterland.[58] The hinterland was dominated by the major cities along the Quoeiq River (Aleppo, Ebla, and Tell Tuqan)[59] or along the Orontes River (Alalakh, Hama, and Qatna),[60] though many of these cities were on the decline.

When Abraham first entered Canaan, he went "through the land unto the place of Sechem; it was situated in the plains of Moreh, and we had already come into the borders of the land of the Canaanites" (Abraham 2:18).

---

56. Black, George, and Postgate, *Concise Dictionary of Akkadian*, 304.
57. Peter M. M. G. Akkermans and Glenn M. Schwartz, *The Archaeology of Syria: From Complex Hunter-Gatherers to Early Urban Societies (ca. 16,000–300 BC)* (Cambridge: Cambridge University Press, 2003), 206.
58. Hélène Sader, *The History and Archaeology of Phoenicia* (Atlanta: SBL Press, 2019), 8–12.
59. Francesca Baffi and Luca Peyronel, "Tell Tuqan and the Matkh Basin in a Regional Perspective," in *Tell Tuqan Excavations and Regional Perspective: Cultural Developments in Inner Syria from the Early Bronze Age to the Persian/Hellenistic Period*, ed. Francesca Baffi, Roberto Fiorentino, and Luca Peyronel (Salento: Congedo Editore, 2014), 14–15.
60. Akkermans and Schwartz, *Archaeology of Syria*, 288–94.

Unfortunately, nothing more is said about this. Shechem's location near running water may have been a reason for Abraham stopping there.[61] After Shechem, Abraham "removed from thence unto a mountain on the east of Bethel, and pitched [his] tent there, Bethel on the west, and Hai on the east" (Abraham 2:20; Genesis 12:8). In the Middle Bronze II B-C period, Bethel was a fortified city,[62] with walls built of large semi-dressed limestone fitted together,[63] atop a glacis.[64] The town was destroyed by fire[65] at least twice during the Middle Bronze Age, suggesting that the city was strategically important to the powers that be.[66] The text, however, says that Abraham did not dwell there, but rather outside the city (Genesis 13:3). The site of Ai (et-Tell), if identified correctly,[67] had been an impressive military installation during the Early Bronze Age (ca. 3300–2300 BC). Anatolian-style stone axes[68] and Egyptian stone vessels were found there,[69] indicating both widespread trade networks and warfare. At the end of the Early Bronze Age, Ai was destroyed by an earthquake[70] when it was at the peak of its

---

61. Mazar, *Archaeology of the Land of the Bible*, 4.
62. James L. Kelso, *The Excavation of Bethel (1934-1960)* (Cambridge: American Schools of Oriental Research, 1968), 10; Mazar, *Archaeology of the Land of the Bible*, 197, 225.
63. Kelso, *Excavation of Bethel*, 10.
64. Kelso, *Excavations of Bethel*, 10.
65. Kelso, *Excavations of Bethel*, 24–25.
66. Kelso, *Excavations of Bethel*, 27.
67. The site of Khirbet Khudriya has also been proposed: see Joseph A. Callaway and G. Herbert Livingston, "The 1968–1969 'Ai (et–Tell) Excavations," *Bulletin of the American Schools of Oriental Research* 198 (1970): 10. For the problem in general, see Kenneth A. Kitchen, *On the Reliability of the Old Testament* (Grand Rapids, MI: William B. Eerdmans, 2003), 188–89.
68. Mazar, *Archaeology of the Land of the Bible*, 138.
69. Mazar, *Archaeology of the Land of the Bible*, 136.
70. Joseph A. Callaway and Kermit Schoonover, "The Early Bronze Age Citadel at Ai (Et-Tell)," *Bulletin of the American Schools of Oriental Research* 207 (1972): 53; Joseph A. Callaway, Dorothea Harvey, Kermit Schoonover, James M. Ward, Kenneth Vine, and G. Herbert Livingston, "The 1966 'Ai (Et–Tell) Excavations," *Bulletin of the American Schools of Oriental Research* 196 (1969): 11.

urban development,[71] but its ruins were exposed for centuries.[72] The biblical text only indicates the place as a geographic referent; it does not say that anyone actually lived there when Abraham was in the area. This is reinforced by the ancient name itself, *ʿaî*, which means "ruins."[73] While all of these sites are mentioned, there is nothing more that can really be said about their importance to the Abrahamic narrative, though they do highlight an interesting insight that will be reinforced later in the narrative, namely that Abraham seems to have preferred to live in areas outside settlements and near ruins rather than in an urban environment.

SOJOURN IN EGYPT

The area between Bethel and Ai was subject to occasional droughts. So when "there was a continuation of a famine in the land . . . I, Abraham, concluded to go down into Egypt, to sojourn there, for the famine became very grievous" (Abraham 2:21). By the time that Abraham arrived in Egypt, the Twelfth Dynasty, which had given him so much trouble in Ur, had gone the way of all the earth and had been replaced by another dynasty. There is some disagreement on which dynasty replaced the Twelfth Dynasty. Some think it was the Thirteenth Dynasty,[74] and others claim it was replaced by the Fourteenth Dynasty in the Nile Delta and the Thirteenth Dynasty in the Nile Valley.[75] The reason this may be significant is that the Fourteenth Dynasty was not native Egyptian: "The names of the royal house and of the treasurers of the Fourteenth Dynasty are mainly of foreign origin. . . .

71. Mazar, *Archaeology of the Land of the Bible*, 141.
72. Mazar, *Archaeology of the Land of the Bible*, 144.
73. Kitchen, *On the Reliability of the Old Testament*, 188; Ludwig Koehler and Walter Baugartner, *The Hebrew and Aramaic Lexicon of the Old Testament* (Leiden: E. J. Brill, 2001), 1:815–16.
74. Daphna Ben–Tor, Susan J. Allen, and James P. Allen, "Seals and Kings," *Bulletin of the American Schools of Oriental Research* 315 (1999): 47–74.
75. K. S. B. Ryholt, *The Political Situation in Egypt during the Second Intermediate Period c. 1800–1550 B.C.* (Copenhagen: The Carsten Niebuhr Institute of Near Eastern Studies, 1997), 75–78.

Notably, most of the cognates are West Semitic."[76] Archaeologically, there are no signs of an invasion, but starting in Phase E/2 of Tell el-Dab ʿa, found in the Nile delta, both Egyptian and Canaanite artifacts appear.[77] If Abraham went to the Egyptian capital, he would have gone through Tell el-Dab ʿa, anciently known as Avaris.

SARAH AS WIFE OR SISTER

Following a commandment of God (Abraham 2:22–25), Abraham instructed his wife Sarah to say that she was Abraham's sister. Although many have thought that Abraham was asking Sarah to lie,[78] that is not the case. In the Egyptian of Abraham's day, there are two words for *wife*. One (*ḥmt*) means only "wife";[79] the other (*snt*) means principally "sister"[80] but can also mean "wife."[81] So by using an ambiguous term, Abraham was not saying something that was false. Egyptian kings, at all time periods from the Old Kingdom through the Roman period, at least had the reputation of being able to seize and marry any woman whom they desired.[82] Rather

---

76. Ryholt, *The Political Situation in Egypt during the Second Intermediate Period*, 99.

77. Bettina Bader, *Tell el-Dab ʿa XIX: Auaris und Memphis im Mittleren Reich und in der Hyksoszeit: Vergleichsanalyse der Materiellen Kultur* (Vienna: Österreichischen Akademie der Wissenschaften, 2009), 40.

78. For example, see Gershon Hepner, "Abraham's Incestuous Marriage with Sarah: A Violation of the Holiness Code," *Vetus Testamentum* 53, no. 2 (2003): 143–45; Reuven Firestone, "Prophethood, Marriageable Consanguinity, and Text: The Problem of Abraham and Sarah's Kinship Relationship and the Response of Jewish and Islamic Exegesis," *The Jewish Quarterly Review* 83 (1993): 332–36.

79. Rainer Hannig, *Ägyptisches Wörterbuch II: Mittleres Reich und Zweite Zwischenzeit* (Mainz am Rhein: Philipp von Zabern, 2006), 2:1669–78.

80. Hannig, *Ägyptisches Wörterbuch II*, 2:2247–52.

81. For example, see München ÄS 33: *Wsḫ-iw mꜣʿ-ḫrw ms.n Snt snt=f Ḥtpt* "Wesekh-iu, justified, born of Senet, and his wife, Hetepet."

82. Pyramid Text 317 §510, in Kurt Sethe, *Die altaegyptischen Pyramidentexte* (Leipzig: J. C. Hinrichs, 1908–10), 1:261; James P. Allen, *The Egyptian Coffin Texts. Volume 8* (Chicago: The Oriental Institute, 2006), 293; R. O. Faulkner, *The Ancient Egyptian Pyramid Texts* (Oxford: Oxford University Press, 1969), 99; Miriam Lichtheim, *Ancient Egyptian Literature* (Berkeley: University of

than kill Abraham, Pharaoh pays a bride price of sheep, cattle, donkeys, cattle, and male and female servants (Genesis 12:16). A bride price was typically paid to the family for the intention to marry,[83] though this was typically less than the purchase price for a slave.[84] In this case, two striking things appear in the account: the bride price was much higher than typical,[85] and Pharaoh did not ask for the return of the bride price.[86] For taking Sarah into his household, Pharaoh's house is smitten with plagues (*negāʿîm*; Genesis 12:17), using a term associated with death (Exodus 11:1) and disease (Leviticus 13:2–6).[87]

BACK TO CANAAN

After his sojourn in Egypt, Abraham went back to the place between Bethel and Hai (Genesis 13:3). Abraham's herdsmen and his nephew Lot's herdsmen did not get along because there was insufficient pasturage

California Press, 1973–80), 1:40; P. D'Orbiney 11/2–12/8, in Alan H. Gardiner, *Late-Egyptian Stories* (Brussels: Fondation Égyptologique Reine Élisabeth, 1932), 20–22; Lichtheim, *Ancient Egyptian Literature*, 2:207–8; Bentresh Stele 5–6, in Adriaan de Buck, *Egyptian Readingbook* (Leiden: Nederlands Instituut voor het Nabije Oosten, 1963), 106; Orell Witthuhn, et al., *Die Bentresch-Stele: Ein Quellen- und Lesebuch* (Göttingen: Seminar für Ägyptologie und Koptologie der Georg-August-Universität, 2015); Lichtheim, *Ancient Egyptian Literature*, 3:91; John Gee, "The Cult of Chespisichis," in *Egypt in Transition: Social and Religious Development of Egypt in the First Millennium BCE*, ed. Ladislav Bareš, Filip Coppens, and Květa Smoláriková (Prague: Czech Institute of Egyptology, 2010), 137.

83. Raymond Westbrook, *Old Babylonian Marriage Law* (Horn, AT: Ferdinand Berger & Söhne, 1988), 6.
84. Westbrook, *Old Babylonian Marriage Law*, 55–56, 59–60, 99–101.
85. For an exception bride price (*terḫatum*) that included a slave and two-thirds a mina of silver, see VAS 8 4–5, in Westbrook, *Old Babylonian Marriage Law*, 134.
86. Westbrook, *Old Babylonian Marriage Law*, 99–100.
87. At least one Mesopotamian text discusses a type of disease associated with this situation: "If the blood vessels of his temples, his hands, and his feet on right and left are continually stiff and shift, they are bound, and he can lift them, and he continually sees his body, it is the hand of Šamaš because of a man's wife." DPS 4 116–17, in JoAnn Scurlock, *Sourcebook for Ancient Mesopotamian Medicine* (Atlanta: Society of Biblical Literature, 2014), 32.

there (13:6–9). The normal offer to friends and family is to pasture the flocks together: "Let my sheep and your sheep pasture together. Pasturage is plentiful here."[88] The eventual agreement between Abraham and Lot may have reflected typical arrangements. An Assyrian text describes just an agreement: "Puli-ila holds wadis while Barḫalanum holds the steppe. Between them is a stela. There is no Barḫalanum entitlement to the wadis."[89] Abraham and Lot are following a pattern known from their day.

WAR

Perhaps one of the more intriguing international elements of the Abrahamic narrative was the military alliance described in Genesis 14. According to 14:1, four kings are listed in an alliance that attacked where Lot lived: Amraphel, king of Shinar; Arioch, king of Eliasar; Chedorlaomer, king of Elam; and Tidal, king of nations (Genesis 14:1).

The elements of the name Amraphel (Amur-pi-el) are well attested in Abraham's day in names like Amer-kakka,[90] Amur-Ašur,[91] Amurru-ellati,[92] Amurru-naṣir,[93] Amud-pi-el,[94] and Ibal-pi-el.[95] The name of Amud-

---

88. ARM 5 15 9–11, in Geroge Dossin, *Correspondance de Iasmaḫ-Addu*, (Paris: Imprimerie Nationale, 1950), 30; Jack M. Sasson, *From the Mari Archives: An Anthology of Old Babylonian Letters* (Winona Lake, IN: Eisenbrauns, 2015), 105.
89. A. 3592, cited in Jean-Marie Durand, "Réalités amorrites et traditions bibliques," *Revue d'Assyriologie et d'archéologie orientale* 92 (1998): 32; translation in Sasson, *From the Mari Archives*, 258n69.
90. ARM 13 1 v 20, in G. Dossin, et al., *Textes Divers* (Paris: Firmi–Didot, 1964), 5.
91. ARM 4 76 35, in Georges Dossin, *Correspondance de Šamši–Addu et de ses Fils* (Paris: Imprimerie Nationale, 1951), 108.
92. ARM 13 1 xiv 40, in Dossin, et al., *Textes Divers*, 13.
93. ARM 13 1 xi 37, in Dossin, et al., *Textes Divers*, 12.
94. ARM 7 87 5, in Bottéro, *Textes économiques et administratifs*, 29; ARM 14 112 10, in Maurice Birot, *Lettres de Yaqqim-Addu gouverneur de Sagarâtum* (Paris: Paul Geuthner, 1974), 188.
95. For example, see ARM 14 112 8, in Birot, *Lettres de Yaqqim–Addu gouverneur de Sagarâtum*, 188.

pi-el is intriguing because it could easily become Amraphel in Hebrew.[96] It is also known that Amud-pi-el, the king of Qatna, had an alliance with Elam at this time.[97] The land of Shinar encompassed Babylon, Uruk, Akkad, Calneh, Nineveh, Rehoboth, Calah, and Resen (Genesis 10:10–12). Babylon and Uruk are in southern Mesopotamia, while Nineveh and Calah are in northern Mesopotamia. Qatna (Tell el-Mishrifeh) is located about 20 kilometers northeast of Homs and 155 kilometers south of Aleppo. Qatna seems somewhat distant to be considered part of Shinar.[98] Finds from the palace during the Middle Bronze Age are known,[99] but the tablets recovered from Qatna date to a later time period.[100] There is an

---

96. The cuneiform name is written with the signs A.MU.UD.BI.AN. These can be read as A–mu–ud–pí–el, which would be transcribed into Hebrew as *ʾmdpl*. In Hebrew, the graphic confusion between *r* and *d* is pervasive in all periods; see P. Kyle McCarter Jr., *Textual Criticism: Recovering the Text of the Hebrew Bible* (Philadelphia: Fortress Press, 1986), 45–46. Thus, a misinterpretation of *ʾmdpl* as *ʾmrpl* is well within the range of possibility. See also the discussion Kitchen, *On the Reliability of the Old Testament*, 568n21.

97. A.266, in Jean–Marie Durand, "La cité–état d'Imar à l'époque des rois de Mari," *Mari Annales de Recherches Interdisciplinaires* 6 (1990): 40n7; Heimpel, *Letters to the King of Mari*, 506: "Thus says your servant, Hammi–Šagiš, to my lord: An Elamite messenger, when he went to Halab, sent 3 of his young men from Imar [to Qaṭna]. Hammu–Rapi (of Halab) heard these things and dispatched [. . .] to his border. They seized those men when they returned. And they asked them for news, and they spoke as follows: The Qatanean sent us thus: The land is given to your hand. Rise up! If you rise up, you will not be attacked. Those people are concealed in a village. And that Qatanean has just dispatched two messengers of his, [. . .] having taken before them. My lord must give strict orders. And he must write to the Babylonian, and [those] men must not be allowed to leave."

98. It has also been suggested that this refers to Šangar, the area around the Gebel Sinjar in Syria; William F. Albright, "Shinar–Šanḡar and Its Monarch Amraphel," *The American Journal of Semitic Languages and Literature* 40, no. 2 (1924): 125–33. While this proposal is phonetically possible, it does not seem to match the biblical usage.

99. Thomas Richter and Sarah Lange, *Das Archiv des Idadda* (Wiesbaden: Harrassowitz, 2012), 2.

100. Richter and Lange, *Das Archiv des Idadda*.

Arriyuk attested at the right time,[101] but he is not king of Cyprus. Chedorlaomer, the Elamite king, has a known Elamite name: Kudur-Lagamar.[102] Tidal (Tidʿal) is the Hebrew version of the Hittite Tudhaliya. A Hittite king Tudhaliya dating before the founding of the Hittite Old Kingdom is known from an account of his military exploits from a manuscript dated to the Hittite Old Kingdom.[103]

The text does not describe an occupation of Sodom and Gomorrah. Instead the military campaign appears to reflect a quick raid, which was a common military tactic at the time, with the taking of hostages. The hostages would be held until they were redeemed by the immediate family, or, if the family could not afford the hostage price, by a temple or the palace of the affected town.[104]

COVENANT

Central to the Abrahamic narrative are the covenants that Abraham makes with both God and others. The form of the covenant that God makes with Abraham follows the pattern of treaties of the first half of the second millennium BC.[105] In the earliest references to the Hebrew term translated as "covenant" (*berît*), it refers to a specific obligation that a vassal owes to

---

101. ARM 2 63–64, in Jean, *Lettres Diverse*, 124–26; Kitchen, *Ancient Orient and Old Testament*, 43.

102. Ron Zadok, *The Elamite Onomasticon* (Naples: Istituto Universitario Orientale, 1984), 24–26. Though the name elements are attested, the name itself is not attested outside the Bible.

103. KBo 1.11 (CTH 7), in Gary Beckman, "The Siege of Uršu Text (*CTH* 7) and Old Hittite Historiography," *Journal of Cuneiform Studies* 47 (1995): 23–34.

104. Codex Hammurapi §32, in E. Bergmann, *Codex Ḫammurabi Textus Primigenius* (Rome: Pontificium Institutum Biblicum, 1953), 8; Martha T. Roth, *Law Collections from Mesopotamia and Asia Minor*, 2nd ed. (Atlanta: Scholars Press, 1995), 87; Kitchen and Lawrence, *Treaty, Law and Covenant*, 1:122–23.

105. John Gee, *An Introduction to the Book of Abraham* (Provo, UT: Religious Studies Center, Brigham Young University, 2017), 107–13; Kitchen and Lawrence, *Treaty, Law and Covenant*, 3:69–74.

his sovereign.[106] A covenant expresses an agreement in which an individual agrees to become subject to a master, which is expressed in familial terms.[107] These agreements were accompanied by specific ceremonies or rituals, some of which are mentioned in the context of one of Abraham's covenants with God (Genesis 15:1–21). Yasim-El provides a contemporary eyewitness account of one of these ceremonies:

> All of them got together at Ṣidqum. They began to discuss matters between them (*bi-ri-šu-nu*); then they sacrificed a donkey-stallion. Before killing the donkey-stallion while they were talking, in front of the representatives from Babylon, Ešnunna, the Turukku-tribes, and the seven kings standing before him, and before all his allied armies, all of them, Atamrum set the following right when he said, "Aside from Zimri-Lim, our father, our brother, and our chief, there is no other king." As Atamrum was setting this right, the messengers of Babylon and Ešnunna stood and withdrew to the side. Although I was secretly sick, two men were holding me up; I stood opposite the kings to hear the stipulations (*ṣi-im-da-tím*). Just then, Marduk-nišu, a palace attendant (LÚ.GÌR.SIG$_5$.GA) and messenger of the Babylonian king, who had withdrawn to the side, [objected]. . . . Before the donkey-stallion was slaughtered, Atamrum summoned Asqur-Adad and told him the following, "You are my son. Stay that way. Let me speak with Ḫaqba-ḫammu and the elders of Numḫa." He then summoned Ḫaqba-ḫammu and the elders of Numḫa, and took up the matter with them as follows, "Before the donkey-stallion is slaughtered and the oath of these gods is sworn, take some time and tell me what there is for me to contribute to you." When he said this thing to them, they claimed a cultivated field. . . . They were satisfied. Aside from this field, they did not claim anything else between them (*bi-ri-šu-nu*). So, by their donkey-stallion (sacrifice) and their discussion, the king was bound

106. Black, George, and Postgate, *Concise Dictionary of Akkadian*, 43. Further evidence on this topic will be published by Stephan Wimmer.

107. Scott W. Hahn, *Kinship by Covenant: A Canonical Approach to the Fulfillment of God's Saving Promises* (New Haven, CT: Yale University Press, 2009), 37–48.

> by covenant (*ra-ki-is*) for the whole land. . . . When they agreed, after they consented to their plan (*ṭe$_4$-em-šu-nu*), and were bound to their agreement (*ri-ik-sa-[tim ir-ku-s]ú-ma*), the donkey-stallion was sacrificed. Brother made brother swear an oath of god and sat down to drink. When they got together and drank, brother gave gifts to brother. Asqur-Adad arose to his land and Atamrum arose into Andarig.[108]

This account provides a view into a number of facets about Abraham's covenants (though the list is not exhaustive). (1) The covenant does not deal with equals but creates a situation where an inferior enters into a relationship with a superior. (2) A covenant deals with family relationships, either through birth (Genesis 15:2–4) or adoption (Abraham 2:9–10). The superior is the "father," and the subordinate is the "son." Two subordinates are in the relationship of "brother." (3) The covenant involves exclusive loyalty (faith)[109] on the part of those entering into the covenant (Genesis 15:6; 17:7–8). Those who were not willing to pledge that loyalty were excused from the covenant. (4) Though the subject party can ask for terms, ultimately it is the superior party that sets the terms of the covenant (15:2–5; 18:23–32). (5) A grant of land to the inferior party is part of the covenant (15:18–21; 17:8). (6) An oath is invoked (22:16–18). (7) A sacrifice is also involved (12:8; 15:9–10; 22:2, 13). (8) The same vocabulary (*rakāsu*) is used for making covenants as is used when Abraham amassed flocks and followers in Haran. The land grant is important because there were two types of land grants; some land (*niḫlatum*) was given irrevocably and unconditionally while other land was only given on conditions that each

---

108. ARM 26 404 11–26, 33–41, 48–51, 60–65, in Dominique Charpin, Francis Joannès, Sylvie Lackenbacher, and Bertrand Lafont, *Archives épistolaires de Mari I/2* (Paris: Éditions Recherche sur les Civilisations, 1988), 259–60; Sasson, *From the Mari Archives*, 93–95; Heimpel, *Letters to the King of Mari*, 343–46.

109. For a discussion of the relationship between loyalty and faith, see John Gee, *Saving Faith* (Provo, UT: Religious Studies Center, Brigham Young University, 2020), 294–96.

succeeding generation covenanted their loyalty (*kullu*).[110] Service and loyalty to the sovereign was expected of recipients of land grants.[111]

POLYGAMY

Another element of the narrative that may be hard for a modern audience to understand is Abraham's multiple wives. Because of barrenness, Sarah offers Abraham one of her handmaidens (*šipḥāh*), Hagar,[112] as a wife (Genesis 16:1–2). Polygamy was known[113] but not commonly practiced. It was usually under conditions of childlessness, sickness, or misconduct, and with the consent of the first wife.[114] Old Assyrian merchants would have a wife (*aššutum*) at home and a second wife (*amtum*) at his second base of operation.[115] With Abraham and Sarah we have two of the conditions that apply that are specifically mentioned in the text: childlessness and not just the consent but the instigation of the first wife (Genesis 16:2).

---

110. Jacob Lauinger, *Following the Man of Yamhad: Settlement and Territory in Old Babylonian Alalah* (Leiden: E. J. Brill, 2015), 155–61, 189–92.
111. Lauinger, *Following the Man of Yamhad*, 187.
112. The name means "hireling" from Akkadian *agru*; Black, George, and Postgate, *Concise Dictionary of Akkadian*, 6. It is attested in Neo-Assyrian sources; Simo Parpola, *The Prosopography of the Neo-Assyrian Empire* (Helsinki: The Neo-Assyrian Text Corpus Project, 1998), 1/1:55–56. It is also attested in Neo-Babylonian sources: John P. Nielsen, *Personal Names in Early Neo-Babylonian Legal and Administrative Tables, 747–626 B.C.E.* (Winona Lake, IN: Eisenbrauns, 2015), 9. The name Hagar is attested epigraphically in a fifth or fourth century BC seal from Jericho. See Philip C. Hammond, "A Note on Seal Impression from Tell es-Sulṭân," *Bulletin of the American Schools of Oriental Research* 147 (1957): 38–39. It is also known from the third century BC bust from Palmyra. See Wilhelm Eilers, "Eine Büste mit Inschrift aus Palmyra," *Archiv für Orientforschung* 16 (1952–1953): 311–13. By the Ptolemaic Period, it was synonymous with "Arab"; see Wolja Erichsen, *Demotisches Glossar* (Copenhagen: Ejnar Munksgaard, 1954), 281.
113. Gelb, "Household and Family in Early Mesopotamia," 66.
114. Westbrook, *Old Babylonian Marriage Law*, 107–9.
115. Mogens Trolle Larsen, *The Aššur-nādā Archive* (Leiden: Nederlands Instituut voor het Nabije Oosten, 2002), xxv–xxvi.

After her marriage while she is pregnant, Hagar demeans (*tēqal*) Sarah (Genesis 16:4). Legally, Sarah, as the first wife, takes precedence over the second wife and has power over her.[116] A roughly contemporaneous legal document spells out the situation this way: "Buneneabi and Belissunu have bought Šamašnuri, daughter of Ibišaan from Ibišaan, her father. To Buneneabi she will be a wife and to Belissunu she will be a servant. The day that Šamašnuri says to Belissunu, 'You are not my owner' she will shave her and sell her."[117] The text says that Sarah first oppressed or humbled (*tᵉʿannehā*) Hagar (Genesis 16:6). Hagar ran away but returned at the command of an angel (Genesis 16:7–15). Fugitive slaves were a serious matter; harboring them carried the death penalty.[118] Later, Sarah's expulsion of Hagar and her son after provocation (*meṣaḥēq*; Genesis 21:9–21) was according to standard legal practice of the time but was actually more lenient since Hagar and Ishmael were not sold but set free and sent away.

SACRIFICE

Abraham's last trials were the offering of his son, Isaac, and the death of his beloved Sarah. While sojourning in Beersheba, the Lord commanded Abraham to travel to Moriah to sacrifice Isaac. Traditionally, Moriah is associated with Jerusalem (2 Chronicles 3:1),[119] but this traditional

---

116. Westbrook, *Old Babylonian Marriage Law*, 110–11.

117. CT 8 22 b, in *Cuneiform Texts from Babylonian Tablets, &c., in the British Museum. Part VIII.* (London: British Museum, 1899), pl. 22; Westbrook, *Old Babylonian Marriage Law*, 119.

118. Codex Hammurapi §§15–20, in Bergmann, *Codex Ḫammurabi Textus Primigenius*, 6; Roth, *Law Collections from Mesopotamia and Asia Minor*, 84–85; Kitchen and Lawrence, *Treaty, Law and Covenant*, 1:118–21.

119. "The significance of the event grows exponentially over the course of the Second Temple and rabbinic Judaism. The name Moriah is an early example, for the only other appearance of that word in the Hebrew Bible occurs in Chronicles, a late book, where it is the name of the mountain on which King Solomon builds his temple in Jerusalem. The implication is clear: the Aqedah has become a foundation legend for the Jerusalem Temple." Jon D. Levenson, *Inheriting Abraham: The Legacy of the Patriarch in Judaism, Christianity, and Islam* (Princeton: Princeton University Press, 2012), 89.

identification, which is largely identified as such based on typology, may not be accurate. Jerusalem was a fortified city in Abraham's day[120] and stood at the top of the hill. It is unlikely that Moriah was at Jerusalem. Moriah was, however, some distance from the area in the Negev where Abraham lived (Genesis 22:2–4). Throughout the Book of Abraham, the emphasis is on obedience.[121] Being asked to sacrifice his son, when he himself had almost been sacrificed (Abraham 1:5–20), was the supreme test of obedience for Abraham. Human sacrifice was known elsewhere in the ancient world[122] but was rejected by later biblical authors.[123] In the end, God provided Abraham with another sacrifice so that he did not have to sacrifice his son.

After the binding of Isaac, Abraham returned to Hebron (Genesis 23:2). There Sarah died (23:1–2). Abraham sought a burial place for Sarah. In the area where Abraham grew up, it was customary to bury individuals under the foundation of a house,[124] but Abraham did not live in a permanent structure, but in a tent (12:8; 13:3; 18:1–2, 6, 9–10; 24:67). So he had to negotiate the purchase of a burial plot (23:3–20). At four hundred shekels of silver (23:15), the price seems very high. Other plots of land purchase from the same time were for 9 shekels of silver,[125] 10 shekels of

---

120. Mazar, *Archaeology of the Land of the Bible*, 197, 225.

121. Abraham 1:2; 2:13; 3:25; 4:10, 12, 18, 21, 25, 31; Gee, *Introduction to the Book of Abraham*, 47.

122. Constantine N 57–59, in Karel Jongeling, *Handbook of Neo-Punic Inscriptions* (Tübingen: Mohr Siebeck, 2008), 216–28; Jean-Pierre Albert and Béatrix Midant-Reynes, *Le sacrifice humain en Égypte ancienne et ailleurs* (Paris: Édition Soleb, 2005); Jon D. Levenson, *The Death and Resurrection of the Beloved Son* (New Haven, CT: Yale University Press, 1993); Kerry Muhlestein, *Violence in the Service of Order: The Religious Framework for Sanctioned Killing in Ancient Egypt* (Oxford: Archeopress, 2011).

123. See Jeremiah 19:5–6; Ezekiel 20:25–26; Micah 6:6–7; Levenson, *The Death and Resurrection of the Beloved Son*, 3–11; Ziony Zevit, *The Religions of Ancient Israel* (London: Continuum, 2001), 578–79.

124. Engin and Helwing, "The EBA-MBA Transition in the Kilis Plain," 97; Akkermans and Schwarz, *The Archaeology of Syria*, 299, 308, 312.

125. ARM 8 4, in Georges Boyer, *Testes juridiques* (Paris: Imprimerie Nationale, 1958), 10–12.

silver,[126] 11 5/6 shekels of silver,[127] 26 shekels of silver,[128] and 200 shekels of silver.[129] Even though 200 shekels of silver is the mode (most common price), it is still half the price that Abraham paid.

Something of importance lies behind this short episode. A substantial amount of narrative space is taken on the negotiation of a land transaction. Keeping track of land transactions, however, was very important because legal documents were needed to prove ownership, otherwise squatters could just claim land. People kept track of these legal documents (they are some of the earliest documents we have from Mesopotamia)[130] because they were important. Archives were built around them. They thus provide written sources for history. The fact that this narrative was kept argues that it is derived from legal documents that Abraham had, and his family had preserved and shows that the Genesis narrative was built from written sources that arguably derive from Abraham himself.

MISSION BACK TO HARAN

Camels have long been considered an anachronism in the patriarchal narratives,[131] though this was generally based on an argument from silence

---

126. ARM 8 5, in Boyer, *Testes juridiques*, 12–14; ARM 8 14, in Boyer, *Testes juridiques*, 28–30.
127. ARM 8 13, in Boyer, *Testes juridiques*, 26–28.
128. That is 1/3 mana + 6 shekels; ARM 8 2, in Boyer, *Testes juridiques*, 8.
129. ARM 8 8, in Boyer, *Testes juridiques*, 18–20; ARM 8 11, in Boyer, *Testes juridiques*, 22–24; ARM 8 12 in Boyer, *Testes juridiques*, 26.
130. J. N. Postgate, *Early Mesopotamia: Society and Economy at the Dawn of History* (London: Routledge, 1992), 67.
131. Mazar, *Archaeology of the Land of the Bible*, 225; Michael Ripnsky, "Camel Ancestry and Domestication in Egypt and the Sahara," *Archaeology* 36, no. 3 (1983): 23; Michael Ripinsky, "The Camel in Dynastic Egypt," *Journal of Egyptian Archaeology* 71 (1985): 134; Ludovic Orlando, "Back to the Roots and Routes of Dromedary Domestication," *Proceedings of the National Academy of Sciences of the United States of America* 113, no. 24 (2016): 6588; Steven A. Rosen and Benjamin A. Saidel, "The Camel and the Tent: An Exploration of Technological Change among Early Pastoralists," *Journal of Near Eastern Studies* 69, no. 1 (2010): 63–64, 74; Joseph P. Free, "Abraham's Camels," *Journal of Near Eastern Studies* 3, no. 3 (1944): 187–88.

(which is a logical fallacy) and on looking at Assyrian reliefs where the camel first appears in the reign of Shalmaeser III (858–824 BC).[132] Camels were spread across the Levant, the Arabian peninsula, and North Africa already in the Pleistocene.[133] Camels are attested in the Nile Delta by the First Dynasty of Egypt and were already depicted carrying loads.[134] Domesticated camels appear already in the Early Bronze Age.[135] Camel hair ropes are attested in Egypt during the Third or Fourth Dynasty[136] and were depicted as being led by the Sixth Dynasty.[137] Textual evidence listing the camel among domesticated animals is known from the Old Babylonian period in Mesopotamia.[138] An Old Syrian–style cylinder seal from the eighteenth century BC depicts a camel with a rider.[139] From the Middle Bronze Age, camel bones have been found in the Fayum in Egypt[140] and at Tell el-Far'ah North in Israel.[141] Camels provide a huge advantage over other pack animals because they can be ridden for sixty to ninety kilometers a day for extended periods and can go for days without drinking.[142]

The purpose of the mission was to secure a bride for Abraham's son, Isaac. This narrative has been read as a betrothal type-scene,[143] but it

132. T. C. Mitchell, "Camels in the Assyrian Bas-Reliefs," *Iraq* 62 (2000): 187–94.

133. Michael Ripinsky, "The Camel in Dynastic Egypt," *Journal of Egyptian Archaeology* 71 (1985): 134.

134. Ripinsky, "Camel in Dynastic Egypt," 136–37.

135. Rémi Berthon and Marjan Mashkour, "Animal Remains from Tilbeşar Excavations, Southeast Anatolia, Turkey," *Anatolia Antiqua* 16 (2008): 30, 35.

136. Ripinsky, "Camel in Dynastic Egypt," 138.

137. Ripinsky, "Camel in Dynastic Egypt," 138.

138. W. G. Lambert, "The Domesticated Camel in the Second Millennium—Evidence from Alalakh and Ugarit," *Bulletin of the American Schools of Oriental Research* 160 (1960): 42–43.

139. D. T. Potts, "Camel Hybridization and the Role of *Camelus Bactrianus* in the Ancient Near East," *Journal of the Economic and Social History of the Orient* 47, no. 2 (2004): 150, 161; Free, "Abraham's Camels," 191.

140. Kitchen, *On the Reliability of the Old Testament*, 339; Ripinsky, "Camel in Dynastic Egypt," 138.

141. Kitchen, *On the Reliability of the Old Testament*, 339.

142. Rosen and Saidel, "The Camel and the Tent," 72.

143. Robert Alter, *The Art of Biblical Narrative* (New York: Basic Books, 1981), 52–54.

also fits in with what we know from contemporary bridal negotiations. Abraham sends his servant with gifts (*migdānōt*; Genesis 24:22, 47, 53), which comprise the bride price (*terḫatum*): the gifts paid to the bride's family for the bride.[144] Rebekah is given a gold nose ring[145] of a half shekel of weight and two gold bracelets made of ten shekels of gold each (24:22). Contemporary documents show that in negotiating a bride price (*terḫatum*), the bride's family was given four talents of silver, and the bride was given a nose ring and a bracelet weighing together 470 shekels of silver.[146] Although it would seem to modern Western society that such arranged marriages were oppressive to the women, we actually have a case of a political marriage that the bride was eager to enter into. Inib-šarri wrote to her sister Šunuḫruḫalu: "About the news that I sent you, I am sending with this the bride-price (*ti-ir-ḫa-tum*) to my father the king," and urges her sister to "argue my case forcefully" to her father.[147]

CONCLUSIONS

Abraham was a real ancient person. He lived in a real ancient milieu. We have ancient records of his life. These are comparable with both written and archaeological sources from his day. Though coming from a dysfunctional family, Abraham built his own family where he cared for his wife and his children. Though his own fathers were faithless, he became the father of the faithful. He made and kept his covenants, and all his descendants have the opportunity to renew those covenents for themselves. Abraham thus becomes a real example to his descendants because he was a real person. He is not just a myth that we can deconstruct or diminish

144. Westbrook, *Old Babylonian Marriage Law*, 6.

145. See Genesis 24:47, where it is specifically stated in the Hebrew that the ring was placed on her nose (*ʿal-ʾappāh*).

146. ARM 1 46, in Georges Dossin, *Correspondance de Šamši-Addu et de ses fils*, 100–2; Sasson, *From the Mari Archives*, 104.

147. ARM 10 75, in Georges Dossin, *Correspondance feminine* (Paris: Paul Geuthner, 1978), 114–16; John Gee, "Love and Marriage in the Ancient World: An Historical Corrective," *Journal of the Society for the Study of Egyptian Antiquities* 35 (2008): 88–89.

by philosophizing or theologizing him away. If we can see how he met his challenges within the constraints of his day, he can better become a model for us as we demonstrate our faith and loyalty to God so that it too might be accounted to us for righteousness (Genesis 15:6).

— 9 —

ABRAHAM

A MAN OF RELATIONSHIPS

AVRAM R. SHANNON

Two chapters on Abraham may seem excessive, but the importance of Abraham's narrative to the Old Testament, indeed to the entire Latter-day Saint canon, suggests that even two may not be enough. In the last section, Gee reviewed the journeys described with the Abrahamic narrative. In this chapter, Shannon explores the narratives themselves, giving particular attention to the relationships depicted therein, and, in so doing, presents a perspective by which Abraham may be understood as a true disciple of God. —DB and AS

The story of Abraham is one of the central stories in Genesis and in the Old Testament/Hebrew Bible overall.[1] The scriptures themselves call Abraham "the Friend of God" (James 2:23, deriving from Isaiah 41:8), and Abraham gives his name to one of the central covenants in the Church and the gospel. The narratives surrounding Abraham, his family, and his wives provide plenty of space for discussion and investigation, as well for some intriguing dialogue about some difficult topics. Fundamentally, as presented in the scriptures, Abraham's life is one of relationships. Elliot Rabin, in his study of the concept of a biblical hero, highlights Abraham's "loyalty and concern for others."[2] Even the statements in James and Isaiah characterize Abraham based on his relationship to the Lord. Throughout the stories recorded in Genesis, we find Abraham interacting in relationships with Sarah, Hagar, Lot, Isaac, and God himself. These stories highlight his compassion and concern for others and his obedient relationship to the Lord. Relationships with God and his fellow human beings are central to the life and story of Abraham, and we should hold them central if we are to understand what Abraham's story means to us today, especially as heirs of the Abrahamic covenant.[3] Abraham's example helps us understand our own relationships with God and our fellow human beings.

---

1. Both Latter-day Saint and general scholarly literature on Abraham is immense. The following sources were especially useful in the preparation of this chapter: Dianne Bergant, *Genesis: In the Beginning* (Minneapolis: Liturgical Press, 2013); Joseph Blenkinsopp, *Abraham: The Story of a Life* (Grand Rapids, MI: Eerdmans, 2015); Elliot Rabin, *The Biblical Hero: Portraits in Nobility and Fallibility* (Philadelphia: The Jewish Publication Society, 2020); E. A. Speiser, *Genesis* (Garden City, NY: Doubleday, 1964), Richard Neitzel Holzapfel, Dana M. Pike, and David Rolph Seely, *Jehovah and the World of the Old Testament* (Salt Lake City: Deseret Book, 2009).
2. Rabin, *Biblical Hero*, 121.
3. David L. Peterson, "Genesis and Family Values," *Journal of Biblical Literature* 124, no. 1 (2005): 5–23. Peterson suggests that Genesis is *very* concerned with family and family values, although those values do not necessarily accord with twenty-first century notions about family.

METHODOLOGICAL CONSIDERATIONS

As we begin our discussion of Abraham, Sarah, and the various aspects of their life and story, there are a few points that need to be considered from the outset. The first is one of names and terminology. Abraham was born with the name Abram, and Sarah with the name Sarai. As part of the continual unfolding of the Lord's covenant, he changes their names in Genesis 17. This means that within the Bible itself, for much of the narrative surrounding them, Abraham and Sarah are referred to as Abram and Sarai. This is not, however, how we tend to refer to them in English, where we usually use their covenant names. Although I will be discussing and analyzing parts of the text that happen before the names are changed, I will refer to them as Abraham and Sarah for the sake of convenience and readability.

The other consideration is the relationship between the narratives and story of Abraham in the book of Genesis and the contributions to our knowledge about Abraham's life in the Book of Abraham, one of the distinctive books of scripture revealed by Joseph Smith as part of the Restoration.[4] It is difficult to determine the exact relationship between the Book of Abraham and the book of Genesis.[5] There are, however, a few observations that can be made that will be useful to the present discussion. The first is that the Book of Abraham is a relatively short book and that it adds only a few aspects to the broader narrative of Abraham as found in Genesis. Much of our present Book of Abraham is centered on Abraham's cosmic visions, including a discussion of the Creation in chapters 4 and 5. This essay is focused on the narrative of Abraham's life, and so, those

---

4. For a useful and approachable introduction to the Book of Abraham, see John Gee, *An Introduction to the Book of Abraham* (Provo: UT: Religious Studies Center, Brigham Young University; Salt Lake City: Deseret Book, 2017). Gee's book is especially useful because of his annotated bibliography at the end of each chapter.

5. This is in contradistinction with the Book of Moses, which, as an extract from the Joseph Smith Translation, is explicitly an inspired revision of the King James Version of the Bible. See Kent P. Jackson, *The Book of Moses and the Joseph Smith Translation Manuscripts* (Provo, UT: Religious Studies Center, Brigham Young University, 2005), 1.

cosmological aspects are not emphasized in this paper.[6] Instead, this paper instead focuses primarily on the portrayal of Abraham's life as found in Genesis, but in those places where the Book of Abraham provides insight I will incorporate those insights into my discussion.

This essay is arranged canonically, which is to say that the material in Abraham and Sarah's story is analyzed roughly in the order that it appears in the current biblical text. Biblical scholars have discussed various sources that were later compiled together in order to produce the Book of Genesis and other parts of the first five books of the Bible, much the way that Mormon compiled various sources in the production of the Book of Mormon.[7] Although I acknowledge many of the complexities of this scholarship, generally speaking, what are called "source critical" arguments are not addressed in this chapter. In general, the stories are examined and explored canonically in the way that they have come down in the received biblical text.

6. Readers interested in the cosmographic and cosmological aspects of the Book of Abraham should look at John Gee and Brian Hauglid, eds., *Astronomy, Papyrus, and Covenant* (Provo, UT: Foundation for Ancient Research and Mormon Studies, 2005). This book provides a number of essays looking at various aspects of the Book of Abraham and its relationship to ancient and modern astronomy. See also Kerry M. Muhlestein, "Encircling Astronomy and the Egyptians: An Approach to Abraham 3," *Religious Educator* 10 (2009): 33–50; Gee, *Introduction to the Book of Abraham*, 115–20.
7. For a Latter-day Saint discussion about issues regarding sources and interactions generally, see Daniel L. Belnap, "The Law of Moses: An Overview," in *New Testament: History, Culture, and Society*, ed. Lincoln H. Blumell (Salt Lake City: Deseret Book; Provo, UT: Religious Studies Center, Brigham Young University, 2019), 19–34. For a more in-depth discussion, see David Rolph Seely, "We Believe the Bible As Far As It Is Translated Correctly: Latter-day Saints and Historical Biblical Criticism," *Studies in Bible and Antiquity* 8 (2016): 64–87. For an accessible discussion of the various arguments in favor of understanding the processes in producing the first five books of the Bible from a literary perspective, see Joel S. Baden, *The Composition of the Pentateuch: Renewing the Documentary Hypothesis* (New Haven, CT: Yale University, 2012).

GOD'S CALL

The story of Abraham in the Bible begins with him living in a place identified in the King James Version (KJV) as Ur of the Chaldees (Hebrew *'or kasdim*) (Genesis 12:1). The traditional reading of this toponym places Abraham in a famous city on the banks of the Euphrates in Mesopotamia.[8] There is some scholarship that instead places this city in northwestern Syria rather than in Mesopotamia.[9] Recent scholarship has continued to study and adduce a plausible historical context for the milieu of Abraham and his family.[10]

The heart of Abraham's story really begins when the Lord tells Abraham to get up and leave his land.[11] There are places in Restoration scripture—and especially in the immense extrabiblical literature surrounding Abraham—that discuss Abraham's early life and offers valuable insights into Abraham's background, but this is not the focus of the Bible.[12] In the Bible, the story of Abraham really starts when he receives this command from the Lord: "Get thee out of thy country, and from thy kindred, and from thy father's house, unto a land that I will shew thee" (Genesis 12:1). From a relational perspective, Jehovah's command to Abraham is to leave not only where he lives but also his "kindred" and his "father's house." Biblical scholar Dianne Bergant notes, "In traditional societies such as ancient Israel, one's identity, livelihood, security, and future were all rooted in one's status in the household, which was the center of religious, social, and economic life. Such a household consisted of several

---

8. Blenkinsopp suggests that the Mesopotamian connections here indicate an exilic gloss on the original "land of the fathers." Blenkinsopp, *Abraham*, 26.
9. Paul Y. Hoskinson, "Research and Perspectives: Where was Ur of Abraham?" *Ensign*, July 1991. Because of the Egyptian influence visible in the Book of Abraham, that particular book of scripture is very suggestive of placing Abraham's Ur in what is now modern-day Syria.
10. See, for example, John Gee's chapter on Abraham in this volume.
11. Rabin, *Biblical Hero*, 123–24.
12. There is a useful collection of many of these traditions in John A. Tvedtnes, Brian M. Hauglid, and John Gee, *Traditions about the Early Life of Abraham* (Provo, UT: Foundation for Ancient Research and Mormon Studies, 2001). The material in the Book of Abraham is found in Abraham 1:5–20. Rabin discusses some of the rabbinic background in Rabin, *Biblical Hero*, 127–28.

generations of a family—grandparents, aunts and uncles, and cousins. Abram is told to leave all this, to sever the most intimate bonds imaginable, and to migrate to a foreign land."[13]

The Lord is calling Abraham to leave his old relationships and to build a new covenant relationship with the Lord, which would positively affect this extended family in the coming decades and become the backbone of the development of the ancestral family of Jacob/Israel.

Thus, the Lord promises to Abraham to give him blessings and to give him the ability to bless the whole world: "And I will make of thee a great nation, and I will bless thee, and make thy name great; and thou shalt be a blessing: And I will bless them that bless thee, and curse him that curseth thee: and in thee shall all families of the earth be blessed" (Genesis 12:2–3). Note here that at this point the specific promises of the Abrahamic covenant are not revealed to Abraham—only a statement of God's blessing over Abraham and of Abraham's ability to share that blessing with others,[14] including his own extended family. Indeed, this clearly shows that the Abrahamic covenant is fundamentally not just about Abraham receiving blessings for himself. At its core, the Abrahamic covenant is centered on its ability to bless others, and this is clearly mapped out very early here in the stories of Abraham.[15] This serves as another reminder that as the recipient of the covenant, Abraham is required to interact and relate with others to bless them.[16]

---

13. Bergant, *Genesis*, 42.
14. Blekinsopp, *Abraham*, 27.
15. The longer version of the Abrahamic covenant that Latter-day Saints are most familiar with is found in the Book of Abraham, which characteristically for that book, introduces ideas of priesthood blessings into the core idea of the covenant. According to the narrative timeline of the Book of Abraham, this happens right around the same time this shorter version is given in Genesis 12. For a discussion of the Book of Abraham's version of the Abrahamic covenant, see Monte S. Nyman, "The Covenant of Abraham," in *The Pearl of Great Price: Revelations from God*, ed. H. Donl Peterson and Charles D. Tate Jr. (Provo, UT: Religious Studies Center, Brigham Young University, 1989), 155–70. See also Shon Hopkin's chapter in this volume.
16. Again, this is explicitly laid out in Abraham 2:9–11, but it is perhaps implied in the ambiguous phrasing in Genesis 12:5, which talks about the "souls they had gotten in Haran." Jewish tradition understands this as bringing souls to

The Abrahamic covenant is not possible without Sarah. The Lord's promises are fundamentally centered around descent and posterity, which means that they are blessings that come through men and women. It is no mistake that when Jacob gives to Joseph the promises of these blessings, Jacob blesses Joseph with "blessings of the breasts, and of the womb" (Genesis 49:25). According to the Doctrine and Covenants, the highest degree of the celestial kingdom and the full blessings of the Abrahamic covenant are limited to men and women together (Doctrine and Covenants 131:1–3).[17] The blessings of Abraham are fundamentally the blessings of Sarah.[18]

One of the first things that Abraham does when he comes into the land of Canaan is to build an altar at Shechem (Genesis 12:6). In fact, Abraham's itinerary through the land of Canaan is characterized by his building of altars, many of which become holy places or other important locations in later Israelite history. The altars at places like Shechem (12:6), Beth-el (13:3–4), Hebron (13:8), and the Temple Mount (22:14) define and delineate the land for his descendants.[19] These altars mark places of divine promise and interaction, showing places where Abraham interacts with his family, God, and others. Through the course of Abraham's life, he travels up and down the land of Canaan, in preparation for the divine

---

the worship of Jehovah. The early Midrashic collection of Genesis Rabbah suggested that Abraham would convert the men, and Sarah would convert the women. See Genesis Rabbah 39:14. This is a convenient English translation: Harry Freedman, trans., *Genesis Rabbah* (London: Soncino Press, 1983).

17. "Abrahamic Covenant," a Gospel Topics essay at ChurchofJesusChrist.org, says that "Abraham made covenants with God when he received the gospel, when he was ordained a high priest, and when he entered into celestial marriage."

18. And, as we shall see, they are fundamentally the blessings of Hagar and Keturah.

19. Shechem is the first capital of the northern kingdom of Israel (see 1 Kings 12:1). Bethel was one of the earliest resting places of the ark of the covenant when the Israelites entered the land (Judges 20:27), and when the Israelite king builds his two national shrines, he places one at Bethel (1 Kings 12:29–39). Hebron was the first capital of David's kingdom before the capture of Jerusalem (2 Samuel 2:1–3). The significance of the Temple Mount in Jerusalem is well known. For a discussion of the relationship between the life of Abraham and later notions of place and space, see Koog P. Hong, "Abraham, Genesis 20–22, and the Northern Elohist," *Biblica* 94, no. 3 (2013): 321–39.

promises to inherit it for him and for his descendants (13:14–17). As biblical scholar Elliot Rabin notes, "Whereas for Cain, being forced to wander is a punishment, for Abraham, it is a sign of God's favor."[20] As Abraham travels throughout the land, he interacts with variety of kings and nobles. Sometimes, as with Melchizedek, these are sources of blessings. Sometimes, as in the interactions with Pharaoh or Abimelech, these are sources of confusion and difficulty, but we see God's delivering hand throughout the narratives.

SARAH AND THE SISTER-WIFE THEME

In many ways the narrative around Abraham is pushed forward by Sarah because the desire for a son and for posterity is understood in Genesis as deriving from her infertility. This makes Sarah's quest for a child in some ways even more poignant and helps explain her decision to allow Abraham to marry her enslaved handmaid, Hagar, as discussed below. The significance of Sarah to the covenant and story of Abraham cannot be overstated. She is part and parcel with the Abrahamic covenant, her desire for children pushes the interactions with Hagar and the birth of Ishmael, and her reputed beauty causes conflict with others around her and her husband.

There is a repeated story in Genesis, which some biblical scholars call the "sister-wife theme."[21] This is one of the first parts of the story of Sarah and Abraham in Genesis, and it bears unpacking because it is not exclusive to the Abraham narrative. In this theme, the matriarch and the patriarch (Sarah and Abraham in Genesis 12:10–20 and 20:1–18; Rebekah and Isaac in 26:1–16) pretend to be sister and brother in order to preserve the life of the husband, since they are afraid that the king of the land will kill the husband in order to marry the wife. The wife is protected from the king by miraculous means, and the patriarch usually ends up enriched by the process.

This theme presents some difficulties to latter-day readers of the Hebrew Bible/Old Testament. It can be uncomfortable to think of Abraham,

---

20. Rabin, *Biblical Hero*, 122.
21. Holzapfel, Pike, and Seely, *Jehovah and the World of the Old Testament*, 52.

Sarah, Isaac, and Rebekah lying to save their own skins.[22] It can also be difficult because these stories look so similar to one another, leading to questions of their role in the narrative and in Israelite history. Holzapfel, Pike, and Seely note that these stories "raise a variety of difficult questions and have been interpreted in various ways."[23]

On one level, these difficulties illustrate to us one of the great reasons to read the stories of these important figures in the Old Testament. The Old Testament is willing to show us the complexities of men and women like Abraham and Sarah, which in turn helps to remind us that fundamentally, the human story is one of redemption (2 Nephi 2:4–7). Like all of the children of our first parents, Sarah and Abraham inherit a fallen nature, which needs to be overcome through repentance and reliance on Jesus Christ (Mosiah 3:16–19). Some of the discomfort in the examples of Abraham, Sarah, Isaac, and Rebekah lying can help us to see places where the patriarchs and matriarchs may have struggled, but we know from modern revelation that they have entered into their exaltation (Doctrine and Covenants 132:37). The reminder that we do not need to see the patriarchs and matriarchs as always acting perfectly does not mean that we should ascribe to them gross unrighteousness. It simply means that we can acknowledge that as fallen human beings, they could sometimes make less than perfect choices.

The Book of Abraham adds a distinctive element to at least the first example of this theme. In Abraham 2:22–25, it is the Lord who commands

---

22. His interaction with Sarah in these circumstances both in the initial lie in Genesis 12:20 and in the rationalization that Sarah is his sister are two of the three places where Medieval Jewish commentator Nahmanides ascribed sin to Abraham. The third is the treatment of Hagar, discussed below. See the discussion in David Berger, "On the Morality of the Patriarchs in Jewish Polemic and Exegesis," *Modern Scholarship in the Study of Torah: Contributions and Limitations*, ed. Shalom Carmy (Northvale, NJ: Jason Aronson, 1996), 131–46. For a Latter-day Saint reading of the story that largely exonerates Abraham based on the Book of Abraham and its affinities with other ancient texts, see Thomas W. Mackay, "Abraham in Egypt: A Collation of Evidence for the Case of the Missing Wife," *BYU Studies Quarterly* 10, no. 4 (Summer 1970): 429–40.

23. Holzapfel, Pike, and Seely, *Jehovah and the Old Testament*, 52. In this section (containing page 52), they provide a useful summary of some of the literary problems and suggest solutions.

Abraham to lie and say that Sarah is his sister so that "[his] soul shall live" (Abraham 2:24).[24] This solves some problems but raises others—raising the question as to why God is commanding Abraham to lie. In a sermon given on August 27, 1842, Joseph Smith taught, "That which is wrong under one circumstance, may be, and often is, right under another. God said, 'Thou shalt not kill'; at another time he said, 'Thou shalt utterly destroy.' This is the principle on which the government of heaven is conducted, by revelation adapted to the circumstances in which the children of the Kingdom are placed. Whatever God requires is right, no matter what it is, although we may not see the reason thereof till long after the events transpire."[25] This teaching by Joseph Smith reminds us that the primary reason that we obey commandments is because of our relationship with God, who commanded them. Under this understanding, Abraham's lying about his relationship with Sarah becomes a test of his willingness to obey God no matter what he commands, a foreshadowing of the testing that the Lord will command when he asks Abraham to sacrifice his son Isaac.

ABRAHAM AND LOT

As noted, the story of Abraham plays out in Abraham's family relationships. This is certainly true of Abraham and his nephew, Lot. Although Lot's most prominent role in the stories in Genesis is in the destruction of Sodom and Gomorrah in Genesis 19, Lot is interwoven into the life and story of Abraham. There are fruitful lessons for us to learn from the interactions between Abraham and Lot.[26]

---

24. It is, perhaps, intriguing to note that the Joseph Smith Translation does not make the same change to the story, such that Abraham is still the originator of the idea in JST Genesis. See "Old Testament Revision 1," p. 29, The Joseph Smith Papers.

25. "History, 1838–1856, volume D-1 [1 August 1842–1 July 1843] [addenda]," p. 3 [addenda], The Joseph Smith Papers.

26. Larry R. Helyer, "The Separation of Abram and Lot: Its Significance in the Patriarchal Narratives," *Journal for the Study of the Old Testament* 26 (1983): 77–88.

According to Genesis 12:4, Lot was part of Abraham's travels from the very beginning, traveling with him as he left his "kindred" and his "father's house" (Genesis 12:1).[27] As Abraham and Lot begin to grow in wealth, tensions began to arise between their herders. It is worth remembering that, for Abraham and Lot, much of their wealth was in livestock. The Bible informs us that Abraham was "very rich in cattle" (13:2) and that Lot had "flocks, and herds, and tents" (13:5). Because livestock need land to pasture, as their wealth grew, Abraham and Lot were no longer able to live in close proximity. Thus, the biblical narrator informs us that "the land was not able to bear them, that they might dwell together: for their substance was great, so that they could not dwell together" (13:6). The tension is so great, in fact, that "there was a strife between the herdmen of Abram's cattle and the herdmen of Lot's cattle" (13:7). This seems to have been a quarrel over pastureland.

According to Genesis, Abraham goes to Lot and says, "Let there be no strife, I pray thee, between me and thee, and between my herdmen and thy herdmen; for we be brethren" (Genesis 13:8). Abraham is attempting to nip potential struggles between himself and Lot in the bud by addressing the concern head-on, and he does so by invoking their family relationship. "Brethren" in Genesis 13:8 clearly refers to general kinship rather than to a specific relationship as brothers. Abraham then makes Lot a very generous offer: "Is not the whole land before thee? separate thyself, I pray thee, from me: if thou wilt take the left hand, then I will go to the right; or if thou depart to the right hand, then I will go to the left" (13:9). Although Abraham is the elder of the two, and so would be able to claim any part of the land for himself, he offers the choice to Lot to pick whatever part he wants, and Abraham then will honor that choice. One of the things that characterizes Abraham is his generosity in his interpersonal relationships.

Lot chooses the "plain of Jordan," which the biblical narrator informs us was "well watered every where, before the Lord destroyed Sodom and Gomorrah" (Genesis 13:10). This choice will, of course, have disastrous consequences for Lot and his family, leading not just to his being captured

27. Raymond Hariri, "Abraham's Nephew Lot: A Biblical Portrayal," *Tradition: A Journal of Jewish Orthodox Thought* 25 (1989): 31–41, especially 31–32.

in battle but also to the loss of his wife and some of his children.[28] Biblical scholar Joseph Blenkinsopp suggests that Lot is "voluntarily taking himself out of contention as the heir presumptive of Abraham by choosing to live not only outside the land of promise but also among people of bad repute," thus preparing the way for the birth of Isaac and the passing of the covenant through Abraham's descendants.[29] Abraham allows Lot to choose where to go. Abraham does not focus on his right but instead extends to Lot the privilege of choice.

Part of what is intriguing about this story is that it leads to further communication and blessings from the Lord. After Abraham and Lot part ways, Abraham receives this communication from God:

> And the Lord said unto Abram, after that Lot was separated from him, Lift up now thine eyes, and look from the place where thou art northward, and southward, and eastward, and westward:
>
> For all the land which thou seest, to thee will I give it, and to thy seed for ever.
>
> And I will make thy seed as the dust of the earth: so that if a man can number the dust of the earth, then shall thy seed also be numbered.
>
> Arise, walk through the land in the length of it and in the breadth of it; for I will give it unto thee. (Genesis 13:14–17)

Having given up some of the more fertile parts of the land in a generous gesture to preserve the good feelings in the relationship between Lot and him, Abraham receives a promise of even more land and, more importantly to Abraham, a promise of numerous descendants. The Lord commands Abraham to look around him and explore in all directions because that will be a gift to him and, especially, to later Israel. In being willing to sacrifice his temporal blessings in favor of his connection to his nephew, Abraham showed the kind of person that he is. This passage in Genesis 13 is the first full articulation of the Abrahamic covenant in the

28. Hariri, "Lot: A Biblical Portrayal," 34–35.

29. Blenkinsopp, *Abraham*, 32.

Bible, and it is no mistake that it is given after Abraham's show of generosity.[30] His care for Lot leads him to to rescue Lot, but that in turn leads to Abraham's meeting with Melchizedek, a biblically mysterious figure.

ABRAHAM AND MELCHIZEDEK

Lot's decision to "[pitch] his tent toward Sodom" (Genesis 13:12) led to difficulties for himself and his family. According to Genesis 14, there was a war between a coalition of kings from places east of the land of Canaan and kings from the area surrounding the Dead Sea, including Sodom and Gomorrah.[31] Lot appears to have moved from his seminomadic experience to living within the border of Sodom (Genesis 14:12). Because of this, when the city of Sodom fell to the coalition of kings, Lot and his family and property are part of the spoils of war.

Abraham hears about Lot and his family needing rescue and gathers together 318 of those who were born in Abraham's household who were trained for combat. This number is suggestive both of Abraham's wealth—as his household was large enough to muster 318 individuals for combat—as well as the relative size of the conflict between the two coalitions, since Abraham's relatively small force is able to rout the invading armies. We do not know how much strength Abraham's allies Mamre, Eschol, and Aner brought to the conflict, but it is clear that this was a small, guerrilla-type action, since they attacked by night (Genesis 14:15).[32] The attack is successful, and Lot and his family are saved.

---

30. Speiser, *Genesis*, 98. Helyer lists numerous commentaries on Genesis that adduce this lesson from Abraham and Genesis. See Helyer, "Separation of Abram and Lot," 86n3.
31. Shinar is the biblical name for Mesopotamia generally. Elam was a kingdom in what is now Iran. Neither Ellasar nor "the nations" can be securely connected to any specific place. The five "cities of the plain" were destroyed in the destruction of Sodom and Gomorrah, and biblical scholarship has been unable to connect them to any specific place, with the notable exception of Zoar. See Willem C. van Hattem, "Once Again: Sodom and Gomorrah," *Biblical Archaeologist* 44 (1981): 87–92.
32. Rabin connects this to the idea that God fights the battles for his people because the odds are stacked against the Israelites. Rabin, *Biblical Hero*, 249. On that

This experience leads to an interlude where Abraham meets with the kings of Sodom that he saved but also with Melchizedek, the king of righteousness. Melchizedek is a mysterious figure in the Old Testament who appears only here and in Psalm 110. Because of the mysterious nature of his appearance in the book of Genesis (he appears without preamble and disappears without explanation), Melchizedek has attracted a large amount of discussion and interpretation in both Judaism and Christianity.[33] Because Melchizedek looms so large in Latter-day Saint readings and understandings of priesthood organization, he figures prominently in Latter-day Saint discourse, although his prominence in the priesthood discussion in Alma 13 was the forerunner for this.[34] Alma 13 expands on Melchizedek's narrative significantly, adding information such as Melchizedek being a king under his father, Melchizedek ruling over a wicked people, to whom he was preaching, how the people repented, and how Melchizedek set up a

---

idea from a Restoration perspective, see Kerry Muhlstein, "A Savior With a Sword: The Power of a Fuller Scriptural Picture of Christ," *Religious Educator* 20, no. 3 (2019): 114–21.

33. See J. Reiling, "Melchizedek" in *Dictionary of Deities and Demons in the Bible*, ed. Karel van der Toorn, Bob Becking, and Pieter W. van der Horst, 2nd ed. (Leiden: Brill; Grand Rapids, MI: Eerdmans, 1999), 560–62; Moshe Reiss, "The Melchizedek Traditions," *Scandinavian Journal of the Old Testament* 26 (2012): 259–65; Ioan Chirila, Stelian Pasca-Tusa, and Elena Onetiu, "Reconstruction of Melchizedek's History in Rabbinic and Christian Traditions," *Journal for the Study of Religions and Ideologies* 48 (2017): 3–15; Ann N. Madsen, "Melchizedek at Qumran and Nag Hammadi," in *Apocryphal Writings and the Latter-day Saints*, ed. C. Wilfred Griggs (Provo, UT: Religious Studies Center, Brigham Young University, 1986), 285–95.

34. Much of this discourse derives from Joseph Smith's use of the book of Hebrews in his explanation of the Latter-day priesthood order. See Frank F. Judd Jr. "Melchizedek: Seeing After the Zion of Enoch," in *Sperry Symposium Classics: The Old Testament*, ed. Paul Y. Hoskisson (Provo, UT: Religious Studies Center, Brigham Young University: Salt Lake City: Deseret Book, 2005), 69–82; John W. Welch, "The Melchizedek Material in Alma 13:13–19," in *By Study and Also by Faith*, ed. John M. Lundquist and Stephen D. Ricks (Salt Lake City: Deseret Book; Provo, UT: Foundation for Ancient Research and Mormon Studies, 1990), 2:238–72.

righteous civilization.[35] The Joseph Smith Translation (JST) contains a lengthy side narrative about Melchizedek that has some continuity with the account in Alma 13 but also has some differences. JST Genesis 14:26–30 talks about how Melchizedek performed miracles in his childhood and was an exemplary priesthood holder.[36] Regarding Abraham, Doctrine and Covenants 84:14 reveals that he received the priesthood from Melchizedek, although the scriptures do not specify whether Abraham received it before, during, or after the interactions between him and Melchizedek in Genesis 14.

None of the additional information about Melchizedek is in Genesis. Therein, Melchizedek is the king of Salem (traditionally associated with Jerusalem) and is the priest of the "most high God" (Hebrew *El-Elyon*).[37] Melchizedek brings bread and wine, blesses Abraham in the name of the most high God, and then blesses the most high God for aiding Abraham. Abraham then pays tithes "of all" to Melchizedek (Genesis 14:18–20). With

35. The immediate source for Alma's expanded Melchizedek narrative is not explicitly stated in the Book of Mormon. It does contain material that is not in Genesis, which is mostly concerned with Melchizedek's interactions with Abraham. The only clue to his source that Alma gives is when he says, "Now there were many before him, and also there were many afterwards, but none were greater; therefore, of him they have more particularly made mention" (Alma 13:19). Alma does not specify who "they" are, but he tells the people of Ammonihah that "the scriptures are before you" (13:20), suggesting that wherever this comes from, Alma views it as scriptural. See Judd, "Melchizedek," 69–72; Welch, "Melchizedek Material," 263–64.

36. Doctrine and Covenants 107:2–3 informs us that the higher priesthood was renamed the Melchizedek Priesthood "because Melchizedek was such a great high priest."

37. This is a name for God that is most common in the Psalms. Sometimes the element Elyon ("Highest") appears, as it does here, connected with God (Hebrew *Elohim*), sometimes it is used with Jehovah/YHWH (as in Psalm 7:17), but often it simply appears as a divine epithet by itself (numerous places in the Psalms, such as (9:2, 18:13, and 50:14). Some biblical scholars have suggested that El Elyon was originally a separate deity who has been conflated with the God of Israel, but the use of Elyon throughout the Hebrew Bible shows that this is not a necessary understanding. See Eric E. Elnes and Patrick D. Miller, "Elyon," in Toorn, Becking, and van der Hosrt, *Dictionary of Deities and Demons in the Bible*, 293–99; Judd, "Melchizedek," 69.

only this information in the Bible, it is no wonder that Melchizedek is such a mysterious figure.

We are blessed, however, to have the narrative additions from the Book of Mormon and Joseph Smith's New Translation because they add valuable information about Melchizedek's interactions with Abraham. First of all, both Alma and the JST make the point that Melchizedek is known as "prince of peace," which is a play on words in Hebrew with the name of Melchizedek's city of Salem (Alma 13:18; JST Genesis 14:33). This connects with Abraham 1:2, where Abraham says that he is looking to become a "prince of peace," which he says he received by becoming a "High Priest." Because Doctrine and Covenants 84:14 tells us that Abraham received priesthood from Melchizedek, we can make a connection between Abraham and Melchizedek's becoming princes of peace with their priesthood blessings.[38]

The New Translation also gives clarity to Abraham's paying tithing to Melchizedek. JST Genesis 14:37–38 says, "And he lifted up his voice, and he blessed Abram, being the high priest, and the keeper of the storehouse of God; Him whom God had appointed to receive tithes for the poor." This indicates that Melchizedek was the "keeper of the storehouse of God," thus one appointed to receive tithes. It also tells that the purpose of the tithing in this storehouse is "for the poor." In JST Genesis, Abraham specifically pays tithes because of his great economic blessings because "God had given him more than that which he had need" (JST Genesis 14:39).[39] Abraham's temporal blessings are more than what he needs to support himself, and thus he is willing to use those blessings to the economic benefit of others, which is just one other way in which the Abrahamic covenant becomes a blessing for "all the families of the earth."[40]

---

38. It is intriguing to connect these ideas to the prophecy in Isaiah that Jesus, as the Davidic Messiah, would be a "Prince of Peace" (Isaiah 9:6).

39. Judd connects this with the JST's connection of Melchizedek to Enoch in Judd, "Melchizedek," 79–80.

40. It also provides a valuable perspective on the relational aspect of the Abrahamic covenant, especially regarding who our "neighbor" is (in light of Jesus's teachings on the parable of the good Samaritan).

Abraham's willingness to put his life on the line for his nephew and his interactions with Melchizedek show the high premium that Abraham placed on family and the low premium he placed on the things of this world. This is underscored by his refusal of any of the spoils of the war, and shows that the king of Sodom could not say, "I have made [Abraham] rich" (Genesis 14:23). Abraham understood that it was the most high God who was the "possessor of heaven and earth" (14:19) and that he could give blessings far beyond any temporal treasure. In interpreting the narratives in Genesis, Hebrews 11:13–16 contains the beautiful teachings that Abraham and the rest of the patriarchs and matriarchs were "strangers and pilgrims" who were looking for a heavenly country. Abraham's covenant perspective was one that focused not on earthly things but on a "better country." This feeds into one of the great blessings of the Abrahamic covenant—eternal families and eternal relationships.[41]

Abraham's focus on eternal relationships with the Lord and with family did not mean that Abraham's life was without strife or trial, however. Sarah's continued infertility and the fraught relationship with her enslaved handmaid, Hagar, challenged all parties. These interactions are worth looking at in detail, and this will be our next point of investigation.

SARAH AND HAGAR

Some of the more difficult stories in Genesis relate to Abraham's interactions with his wives. Abraham and Sarah's quest for children is one of the driving forces behind many of the choices they made in their lives.[42] As noted above, this includes Sarah's decision to give her enslaved Egyptian maid Hagar to Abraham as a concubine.[43] The words *maid* and *concubine*

---

41. Kent P. Jackson, "The Abrahamic Covenant: A Blessing for All People," *Ensign*, February 1990.
42. Bergant, *Genesis*, 41.
43. For a discussion of the Latter-day Saint understanding and deployment of the Hagar stories, see Andrew C. Smith, "Hagar in LDS Scripture and Thought," *Interpreter: A Journal of Latter-day Saint Faith and Scholarship* 8 (2014): 87–137. Smith has a useful and in-depth examination of the Hagar passages in the Old Testament. See also Carol L. Meyers, "Hagar," in *The Oxford Companion to the*

had particular social connotations in the ancient world. According to Holzapfel, Pike, and Seely, a "concubine is a woman, usually a slave, [who is] married to a man, but who had less legal status terms of inheritance than a wife."[44] The word that the KJV translates as "maid" in Genesis 16:5 is used to "[translate] a Hebrew word that means slave—indicating that Hagar, Bilhah, and Zilpah were slaves to Sarah, Rachel, and Leah."[45]

It should be noted at the outset of this discussion that the laws regulating multiple wives were different in the ancient world than in the modern world of the Church of Jesus Christ of Latter-day Saints. During the Restoration, Joseph Smith received a revelation about why Abraham and his heirs had more than one wife. In the ancient world, men having multiple wives was an ordinary part of the ancient world.[46] It is clear from revelations received by Joseph Smith in this dispensation, however, that Abraham's multiple wives were not simply ordinary marriages from an ancient perspective but that they were celestial marriages that were approved and sealed in heaven (Doctrine and Covenants 132:34–35).

Just as with plural marriage in the early parts of this dispensation, divine approval did not make the actual marriages any easier. This was especially true in this case because the explicit reason for Sarah giving Hagar to Abraham as a wife was to have children.[47] Genesis 16:2 states, "And Sarai said unto Abram, Behold now, the Lord hath restrained me from bearing: I pray thee, go in unto my maid; it may be that I may obtain children by her." Note that because Hagar is Sarah's servant or slave, any children that Abraham had by Hagar would legally come from Sarah, at

---

Bible, ed. Bruce M. Metzger and Michael D. Coogan (Oxford: Oxford University Press, 1993), 266.

44. Holzapfel, Pike, and Seely, *Jehovah and the World of the Old Testament*, 64.

45. Holzapfel, Pike, and Seely, *Jehovah and the World of the Old Testament*, 66. Although not all of the modern connotations of the word *slave* are present in the biblical conception, it is important to be aware of the difference in social status between Sarah and Hagar.

46. Ze'ev Falk, *Hebrew Law in Biblical Times* (Provo, UT: Foundation for Ancient Research and Mormon Studies, 2001), 127–28; Petersen, "Genesis and Family Values," 15 argues that Genesis has an "expansive" view of what family means.

47. According to Jacob in the Book of Mormon, this is one of the primary reasons the Lord allows plural relationships. See Jacob 2:30.

least in theory.[48] E. A. Speiser connects this to Hurrian law, citing a case where "the husband may not marry again if his wife has children. But if the union proves to be childless, the wife is required to provide a concubine, but would then have all the legal rights to the offspring."[49] There are, however, some struggles between Hagar and Sarah, especially in terms of inheritance.

Some of this tension seems to come from Hagar. Genesis tells us that after Hagar conceives, "her mistress was despised in her eyes" (Genesis 16:4). The word translated as "despised" means to have contempt for someone. Sarah seems to feel that she has made a mistake on some level since she responds to being despised with a rejoinder to her husband, "*My wrong be upon thee*: I have given my maid into thy bosom; and when she saw that she had conceived, I was despised in her eyes: the Lord judge between me and thee" (16:5, emphasis added).[50] Abraham tells Sarah, "Thy maid is in thy hand; do to her as pleaseth thee" (16:6).[51] Genesis 16:6 goes on to say, "Sarai dealt hardly with her," eventually causing Hagar to flee the relative safety of Abraham's tent and the protection from the world that it represented.

This part of the narrative surrounding Abraham and his family deserves some unpacking. First, it is a reminder to us of one of the key reasons to read the Old Testament, in that it is not afraid to present its characters, even one as significant as Abraham, in all of their complexities. In spite of their covenant desire, there are still struggles in the relationship between Abraham and his wives, struggles that carry over into later parts of the biblical narrative and beyond. As we discussed in connection with Abraham lying about Sarah's status as his wife, one of the most useful parts of the Hebrew Bible/Old Testament is its willingness to share with later readers something of the actual difficulties that faced its people. The

48. Falk, *Hebrew Law*, 154.
49. Speiser, *Genesis*, 120–21.
50. Meyers, "Hagar," 266.
51. Although Abraham will ask the Lord for guidance in the later story in Genesis 21, the Bible gives no such indication that he does so here in Genesis 16. He might have done so, based on Genesis 21, but it is not explicit or implicit in Genesis 16.

stories of Abraham, Sarah, and Hagar in Genesis reminds us that these are real people, and like all people who have ever lived on this earth, they are people in need of redemption (Mosiah 3:19, Romans 3:23).

Because of the fundamental recognition that redemption is necessary for all of humanity, it is not necessary for us to try and justify or explain away actions in the scriptures that make us uncomfortable. When we see Abraham, Hagar, and Sarah acting in ways in their family that are not good, it gives us space to think about how we can work through our own family environments. Relationships can be very difficult, but difficult relationships do not ruin everything for us. Hagar's taking advantage of her mistress's infertility for self-aggrandizement, Sarah's dealing harshly with Hagar, and Abraham's unwillingness to intervene in the struggles between his wives are very human responses to the struggles in these individuals' lives. Yet, for all the difficulties, the family of Abraham is still remembered by the Lord, and each member still seeks the Lord.

Note, for example, the care that the Lord has for Hagar, Sarah's slave. According to Genesis 16:7, because of the struggles between these two women, Hagar flees into the desert.[52] While in the wilderness, an angel appears to her, bringing her a message from Jehovah. She is first told to return and submit to her mistress (Genesis 16:9). This is not the end of the statement, however. The Lord tells her, "I will multiply thy seed exceedingly, that it shall not be numbered for multitude" (16:10). The wording of this promise makes it very clear that Hagar's descendants are part and parcel with the promises of what we call the Abrahamic covenant, and although there will still be struggles, the Lord remembers her and her sacrifices for its fulfillment.[53] Indeed, Hagar is then informed that she will have a son and is commanded to name him Ishmael, "because the Lord hath heard thy affliction" (16:11). The name Ishmael means "God will hear"

52. Dozeman, "Wilderness and Salvation History in the Hagar Story," 24, especially notes 4 and 5.

53. The Bible tends to present Ishmael in a positive light, and there are numerous individuals in later Israelite history (including the Book of Mormon) who are named Ishmael. See Michael D. Coogan, "Ishmael," in *The Oxford Companion to the Bible*, 329.

in Hebrew, such that Ishmael bears the mark of the Lord's care for his mother in his very name.

The Lord's care for Hagar continues in the story of her being kicked out after the birth of Sarah and Abraham's son, Isaac.[54] After the birth of Isaac, Ishmael is "mocking" (Genesis 21:9).[55] This leads to Sarah requesting Hagar and her son be sent away, because "the son of this bondwoman shall not be heir with my son" (21:10). Abraham does not want to send them away, but he does so after the Lord tells him to (21:12). After Hagar leaves and their water runs out, she "cast[s] the child under one of the shrubs" (21:15).

Yet the Lord's care for Hagar is still evident in this chapter. Even before she is cast out, the Lord tells Abraham that he will also make Ishmael into "a nation, because he is [Abraham's] seed" (Genesis 21:13). The Lord reiterates this promise to Hagar herself in Genesis 21:18. Hagar receives comfort and direction from God, reminding the reader once again that he is not a respecter of persons and that he loves all of his children, black and white, male and female, and, as is especially germane to this story, bond and free (2 Nephi 26:33).[56] Being enslaved does not put Hagar out of the notice of the Lord, and she has a role to play in fulfilling of the Abrahamic covenant. For Latter-day Saints, Doctrine and Covenants 132 implies that her relationship with Abraham is a celestial relationship, suggesting that, like

---

54. Some scholars have suggested that there are a few problems with the chronology in Genesis here, since they understand Ishmael to be an infant here. The early biblical scholar Hermann Gunkel argued that the two stories of Hagar and Ishmael fleeing were two versions of the same story. Gunkel, "The Two Accounts of Hagar (Genesis xvi. and xxi., 8–21)," *The Monist* 10 (1900): 321–42. T. D. Alexander, "The Hagar Traditions in Genesis XVI and XXI," *Vetus Testamentum Supplements* 41(1990): 131–48, argues that the two stories derive from different traditions. Blenkinsopp, *Abraham*, 53, observes, "We can make sense of the activity of the characters at this juncture only by ignoring Ishmael's 'schematic' age and thinking of him as a young child."
55. This is a wordplay on the name Isaac, since the verb translated as "mocking" has the same root as Isaac's name. It is actually probably better translated as "laughing" or "playing," but these translations would not explain Sarah's violent reaction. For a discussion of the various interpretive strands here, see Smith, "Hagar," 96n32.
56. Meyers, "Hagar," 266.

Abraham, she has received her exaltation, and she sits on a throne (Doctrine and Covenants 132:29).[57] Indeed, being enslaved did not put her out of the notice of the Lord because none of God's children are outside of his notice. Hagar illustrates a key part of the relational nature of the Abraham narrative, reminding us that the Abrahamic covenant is about how we relate to each other and how the Lord relates to us.

THE CHANGING OF NAMES AND COVENANT

As with other parts of Genesis, there are a number of symbolic names in the stories surrounding Sarah and Abraham, including divinely appointed name changes.[58] Abram and Sarai have their names changed or modified as part of their process of seeking the covenant. The name Abram comes from Hebrew words that mean something like "exalted father." As noted above, Abraham's life and his story in Genesis focuses on his family relationships, including his desire to have children and to therefore become a father.[59] This has strong resonances with Abraham 1:1–5, which states that Abraham was searching for the "blessings of the fathers." Indeed, the idea of Abraham and fatherhood seems to be entwined through all of those first few verses in the Book of Abraham, with the word *father* or *fathers* appearing ten times in the first five verses.

Thus, it comes as no surprise that fatherhood remains part of the covenant that God makes with Abraham, and (although his name is changed from Abram to Abraham) the idea of fatherhood is still there. The Bible explains the name change as a transformation of Abraham into a "father of many nations" (Hebrew *ab hamon goyim*) (Genesis 17:5). Although this

57. Orson Hyde, an early Apostle of the Restoration, explicitly taught this point. In an address given in 1874, he said, "If you go right into Abraham's bosom there will be one side Sarah and on the other Hagar." See Orson Hyde, in *Journal of Discourses* (London: Latter-day Saints' Book Depot, 1875), 17:10. Smith, "Hagar," 108, argues that "the defense of polygamy is by far the most prevalent usage that Hagar has been put to [in early Latter-day Saint scriptural interpretation]."

58. On the importance of symbolic names in the Bible generally, see Gahl E. Sasson, "The Symbolic Meanings of Names as a Narrative Tool: Moses, Abraham, and David," *Storytelling, Self, Society* 11 (2015): 298–313.

59. See Sasson, "Symbolic Meanings of Names," 305.

explanation has elements of folk etymology to it (i.e., the name Abraham does not come from *ab hamon goyim*), the giving of the name symbolizes the covenant relationship between the Lord and Abraham.

Sarai's name is changed to Sarah. Unlike the change from Abram to Abraham, the Bible does not give a reason for this particular change. Although this change is probably not even a change in the root of the name, there is a still a symbolic element of receiving a new name as part of the new covenant identity. The new name represents a change from the old identity to a new covenant relationship with the Lord. Abraham and Sarah's new names are symbols of their covenant blessings and their covenant responsibilities to serve the Lord and to bless his children. This obligation to bless others stands at the center of Abraham's respect for the rules of hospitality, as shown when he met the three travelers.

ABRAHAM AND THE HOLY MEN

We have already noted that two of the major themes in the stories of Abraham are Abraham's generosity and his obedience. Both of those are displayed in his interactions with the three travelers as recorded in Genesis 18. Abraham was sitting in his tent when he saw three strangers and invited them into his hospitality. There is a little bit of incongruity in what Abraham offers the strangers and what he ends up giving them that serves to highlight Abraham's hospitality and generosity. In Genesis 18:4–5, when he invites the travelers in, Abraham offers them a "little water" and a "morsel of bread," which the travelers accept. He then tells Sarah to make cakes using three measures of the good flour. The KJV's "measures" are not the equivalent of modern cups. "Measure" translates an ancient measurement called a *seah*, meaning that Abraham's three measures of flour is the equivalent of roughly ninety-three cups of flour. Sarah would be able to make a lot of cakes with that much flour. Abraham also goes and kills a young calf and serves it the strangers with butter and milk.[60] The lengths that Abraham goes to in order to care for his guests is much more than he

60. This shows, incidentally, that the prohibition against eating milk and meat together was not yet on the table in this point in biblical history.

offered them at the outset. Rather than serving them a little bit of bread and water, Abraham throws a great feast for them.

Abraham's generous spirit is especially noteworthy in light of the ancient customs of hospitality. The ancient world could be a hostile place, and so there were cultural protections to protect and preserve travelers.[61] The book of Genesis portrays Abraham in such a way that highlights his concern for these protections—he wants to protect and preserve these travelers. This again highlights the importance of relationship in the Abraham story. Abraham is not only concerned with those with whom he is immediately connected, but he is also concerned with strangers who were passing by. This is a great example of what Rabin calls Abraham's "unwavering concern toward others, no matter whether they are family or stranger."[62] Abraham's willingness to extend love and protection to strangers is not limited to travelers and underscores a key interaction between him and Lord concerning the people in Sodom and Gomorrah, which we will explore next.

ABRAHAM AND PROPHETIC INTERCESSION

After the other two men leave, the third man, whom the scriptures present as Jehovah, lingers behind to speak with Abraham. He asks, "Shall I hide from Abraham that thing which I do; Seeing that Abraham shall surely become a great and mighty nation, and all the nations of the earth shall be blessed in him? For I know him, that he will command his children and his household after him, and they shall keep the way of the Lord, to do justice and judgment; that the Lord may bring upon Abraham that which he hath spoken of him" (Genesis 18:17–19).

---

61. Peter J. Sorenson has a very nice discussion of hospitality laws throughout history, including some discussion of how they might play out for modern Latter-day Saints. See Peter J. Sorenson, "The Lost Commandment: The Sacred Rites of Hospitality," *BYU Studies Quarterly* 44, no. 1 (2004): 1–29. For the biblical text specifically, see Peter Altmann, "Hospitality in the Hebrew Bible," *Bible Odyssey*, https://www.bibleodyssey.org:443/people/related-articles/hospitality-in-the-hebrew-bible.

62. Rabin, *Biblical Hero*, 130.

The Lord gives to Abraham quite the commendation here. Note that the Lord frames Abraham's righteousness as generational—many nations will be descended from him, and he will teach his children to keep the commandments and to do justice. The Lord takes the long view, and his relationship with Abraham reflects that view.

After this, the Lord tells Abraham that he is going to go down to Sodom to see whether they needed to be destroyed, "because the cry of Sodom and Gomorrah is great, and their sin is very grievous" (Genesis 18:20). Abraham then asks the Lord a famous question, "Wilt thou also destroy the righteous with the wicked?" (18:23). It is a difficult question to ask at the best of times. God is responsible for both life and death (1 Samuel 2:6), and his ways are not always knowable to humanity (Isaiah 55:8). Although Abraham surely has some sense of this, his relationship with Jehovah is sufficient that Abraham is willing and able to intercede with the Lord on behalf of the people of Sodom and Gomorrah. As it is recorded in Genesis, Abraham proceeds to continue to ask God to save the city for fewer and fewer people, until the Lord promises that he will not destroy the city of Sodom and Gomorrah if he found even ten righteous people (Genesis 18:32).

Abraham's willingness to stand between the Lord and the people of Sodom is what is known as "prophetic intercession," and Abraham is a distinctive example of this. Joshua M. Sears has discussed prophetic intercession by highlighting "the theological discomfort that may arise when modern readers study intercessory accounts in scripture."[63] It can be jarring for some to see the prophet seemingly protecting people from a presumably loving God. However, Sears points out that this seems to be a teaching tool on the part of the Lord. Sears notes,

> We may ask, if God were solely interested in prosecuting Israel, why bother holding conversations with the defense in the first place? God also serves as judge, and judgment would certainly be easier without the debate. But easier is not what he chooses. "Shall I hide

---

63. Joshua M. Sears, "'O Lord God, Forgive!': Prophetic Intercession in the Book of Amos," in *Prophets and Prophecies of the Old Testament*, ed. Aaron P. Schade, Brian M. Hauglid, and Kerry Muhlestein (Provo, UT: Religious Studies Center, Brigham Young University; Salt Lake City: Deseret Book, 2017), 194.

> from Abraham that thing which I do[?]" God asks, before deciding no (Genesis 18:17). He tells Abraham of his plans to destroy Sodom, Abraham balks, and the intercessory probing begins (see 18:20–33). One cannot help but sense that God had intended this all along. The invitation to be challenged hints that the prosecution has more in mind than winning. Furthermore, the fact that God the judge so often decides against God the prosecutor suggests that, despite all the talk of death and doom, God the judge really isn't rooting for God the prosecutor after all. The division between judge, prosecution, and defense begins to break down.[64]

This whole story serves as a good reminder that the occasional barriers that we put between God's justice and his mercy can be artificial, especially in an Old Testament context.[65]

In fact, Abraham's question at the outset of his interaction with God here is instructive in how it blurs the categories of justice and mercy: "That be far from thee to do after this manner, to slay the righteous with the wicked: and that the righteous should be as the wicked, that be far from thee: Shall not the Judge of all the earth do right?" (Genesis 18:25). Note that Abraham is pleading for mercy for the people of Sodom and Gomorrah, but he does so with an appeal to the Lord's justice and righteous judgment. This blurring of justice and mercy is characteristic of the Lord who serves as "judge, prosecution, and defense," but it also illustrates why relationships are so important in the stories surrounding the establishment of the covenant. Fundamentally, the purpose of the Abrahamic covenant is to help Abraham, Sarah, and their descendants to become "perfect," which means to be like God. By participating in God's twinned attributes of compassion and justice, Abraham learns something about what it means to be like God and what the kinds of relationships are that the Lord wants us to

---

64. Sears, "O Lord God Forgive," 194–5.

65. See Avram R. Shannon, "Law of God/God of Law: The Law of Moses in Alma's Teachings to Corianton," in *Give Ear to My Words: Text and Context of Alma 36–42*, ed. Kerry Hull, Nicholas J. Frederick, and Hank R. Smith (Provo, UT: Religious Studies Center, Brigham Young University; Salt Lake City: Deseret Book, 2019), 129–54.

build through covenant making with him and our fellow human beings.[66] That knowledge and those relationships will be tested by the Lord as part of the process of making Abraham holy. It is now to the great Abrahamic test that we turn next.

THE *AQEDAH*

After all of Abraham and Sarah's work and faithfulness in acquiring a son together comes one of the most difficult commandments recorded in scripture[67]: "And it came to pass after these things, that God did tempt Abraham, and said unto him, Abraham: and he said, Behold, here I am. And he said, Take now thy son, thine only son Isaac, whom thou lovest, and get thee into the land of Moriah; and offer him there for a burnt offering upon one of the mountains which I will tell thee of" (Genesis 22:1–2). This commandment tests Abraham's commitment to the covenant with the Lord, especially in light of the long-awaited birth of his son Isaac.[68]

Child sacrifice was not unknown in the ancient world and was seen as the ultimate of consecration, often done in great extremity.[69] It would not have been outside of the immediate religious world of Abraham. According to Restoration scripture (and some of the traditions that circulated in early Christianity and Judaism), Abraham had already had an experience with almost being sacrificed himself before his travel to the Holy Land (Abraham 1:11–12). The Near Eastern background of the Lord's command to Abraham makes this command even more remarkable and worthy of discussion. In later parts of the Hebrew Bible, human sacrifice is absolutely

---

66. Timothy D. Lytton, "'Shall Not the Judge of the Earth Deal Justly': Accountability, Compassion, and Judicial Authority in the Biblical Story of Sodom and Gomorrah," *Journal of Law and Religion* 18, no.1 (2002): 31–55.

67. Rabin, *Biblical Hero*, 145–48; Blenkinsopp, *Abraham*, 87–88.

68. For a Latter-day Saint discussion on this passage in view of learning about sacrifice, see Blair G. Van Dyke, "Elements of Sacrifice in Abraham's Time and Our Own," *Religious Educator* 10, no. 1 (2009): 51–69.

69. Blenkinsopp, *Abraham*, 84–86. For an in-depth discussion of the theological and historical ideas behind this see Jon D. Levenson, *The Death and Resurrection of the Beloved Son* (New Haven, CT: Yale University Press, 1993).

not associated with the God of Israel. In the Hebrew Bible, child sacrifice is often associated with the worship of the non-Israelite god Molech, who is worshipped through an act of "passing one's seed through the fire to Molech."[70] Some scholars have connected this ritual to the *Tophet*, a place of ritual burning condemned by the Israelite prophets, or to the Phoenician *molk* sacrifices, linking this practice to some form of Israelite or Canaanite human sacrifice.[71] The command given to Abraham to sacrifice his son would have felt both strange and familiar.

There are some elements from the Book of Abraham that add another element to this story and, on certain levels, make the command even more heart-wrenching. Abraham 1:10 references that the priest of Pharaoh would offer a "thank-offering of a child," which appears to be a reference to an attested practice in ancient Egypt.[72] What makes this episode particularly poignant is the addition of the information in Abraham 1:5–7 that Abraham's "fathers" had turned from the worship of the Lord and tried to have Abraham killed through ritual sacrifice, apparently for his

70. There is an overview of this worship in Geza Vermes, "Leviticus 18:21 in Ancient Jewish Bible Exegesis," in *Studies in Aggadah, Targum and Jewish Liturgy in Memory of Joseph Heinemann*, ed. Jakob J. Petuchowski and Ezra Fleischer (Jerusalem: Magnes Press, 1981), 109. See also Moshe Weinfeld and S. David Sperling, "Moloch, Cult of," in *Encyclopedia Judaica*, 2nd ed. (Detroit: Macmillan Reference USA, 2007), 14:427–29; George C. Heider, "Molech," in Toorn, Becking, and van der Horst, *Dictionary of Deities and Demons in the Bible*, 581–85; John Day, *Molech: A God of Human Sacrifice in the Old Testament* (Cambridge: Cambridge University Publications, 1985). Thomas Hieke does not even think that this worship has ritual connotations but, instead, refers to the avoidance of Persian military service. See Thomas Hieke, "Das Verbot der Übergabe von Nachkommen an den 'Molech' in Lev 18 und 20," *Die Velt des Orients* 41 (2011): 147–67.

71. First suggested in Otto Eissfeldt, *Molk als Opferbegriff im Punischen und Hebraïschen und das Ende des Gottes Moloch* (Halle [Saale], Germany: M. Niemeyer, 1935); Morton Smith defends the idea that this worship refers to the practice of human sacrifice. See Morton Smith, "A Note on Burning Babies," *Journal of the American Oriental Society* 95 (1975): 477–79.

72. For an Egyptological perspective on this particular element in the Book of Abraham, see John Gee and Kerry Muhlestein, "An Egyptian Context for the Sacrifice of Abraham," *Journal of Book of Mormon Studies* 20, no. 2 (2011): 72–77.

pushing against their idolatrous actions.[73] This means that the command to sacrifice his own son would have pushed against the horror of his own experiences on the altar, a fate that he was saved from only by the timely intervention of the Lord. This heightens the sense of what a difficult commandment this would have been for Abraham to fulfill.

Although the command to sacrifice Isaac is a striking one, it is one with important doctrinal significance to Latter-day Saints.[74] As already noted, this passage begins "And it came to pass . . . that God did tempt Abraham" (Genesis 22:1). The verb that the KJV translates as "tempt" is the Hebrew *nissah*, which is a verb that means to "try" or "prove." Rather than being tempted in the sense that the Lord is trying to get Abraham to do something wrong, this is testing whether or not Abraham will do anything that the Lord commands him to do.[75] This is confirmed later in the story of the binding, when the Lord tells Abraham, "Now I know that thou fearest God" (Genesis 22:12).[76] This test was fundamentally about whether Abraham loved God more than Abraham loved his son or his own self-image of himself as a "father of many nations." Given the amount of covenant and promise that has gone into the birth of Isaac, this is not an empty commandment—this is a real test of Abraham's love and loyalty to Jehovah. According to John Taylor, Joseph Smith taught the Quorum of the Twelve, "I heard the Prophet Joseph say, in speaking to the Twelve on one occasion: 'You will have all kinds of trials to pass through. And it

73. Gee and Muhlstein, "Egyptian Context," 75.

74. This is independent of the Christological significance that Christian readers have often placed on the story, a significance explicitly called out in the Book of Mormon by Jacob in Jacob 4:5. For the role that this story has played in Jewish, Christian, and Muslim discourse, see Jacques Doukhan, "The *Aqedah* at the 'Crossroad': Its Significance in the Jewish-Christian-Muslim Dialogue," *Andrews University Seminary Studies* 32 (1994): 29–40. See also Blenkinsopp, *Abraham*, 86–87.

75. According to Abraham 3:25, one of the primary points of the creation of the world was to provide a place for this kind of testing of obedience. See also Blenkinsopp, *Abraham*, 81.

76. On the connection between the test and the knowing, see Jean Louis Ska, "Genesis 22: What Question Should We Ask the Text?," *Biblica* 94 (2014): 257–67, especially 259–60.

is quite as necessary for you to be tried as it was for Abraham and other [people] of God, and (said he) God will feel after you, and He will take hold of you and wrench your very heart strings, and if you cannot stand it you will not be fit for an inheritance in the Celestial Kingdom of God.'"[77] In the Doctrine and Covenants, the Lord tells Joseph Smith that Abraham's obedience to this difficult testing is part of the "works of Abraham" (Doctrine and Covenants 132:32–36).

One of the compelling things about this part of Abraham's story is how laconic he is about the whole affair. We know from his prophetic intercession in the matter of Sodom and Gomorrah that Abraham is not afraid to intercede with God or even to argue when Abraham does not agree with something. Yet in this case, we do not see him protesting or pleading with God. He simply gets up and does what he is told. Genesis tells us, "And Abraham rose up early in the morning, and saddled his ass, and took two of his young men with him, and Isaac his son, and clave the wood for the burnt offering, and rose up, and went unto the place of which God had told him" (Genesis 22:3). Note Abraham's silent obedience here. Abraham's laconic response to the commandment is one of the features of this story. There could be many reasons behind this, but it speaks to Abraham's loyalty to the covenant that he made with Jehovah, as does everything in this story.

There is a beautiful and elegant structure to this narrative in Genesis 22. When the Lord first commands Abraham, he responds by saying, "Behold, here I am" (22:1). This is a translation of a Hebrew phrase that can be translated as something like, "Behold me," or "It is I." Although obscured by the translation in the KJV, when Isaac asks his question in 22:7, Abraham responds to him in the same way he did to the Lord. Abraham says the same thing again in Genesis 22:11, when the angel of Jehovah stops him from killing his son. This provides a nice symmetry between Abraham's relationship with Isaac and Abraham's relationship with the Lord. One of the characteristics of Abraham is his readiness to serve, and his exhortation of "Behold me." The binding of Isaac is fundamentally

77. Joseph Smith, as reported by John Taylor, in *Journal of Discourses* (London: Latter-day Saints' Book Depot, 1884), 24:197.

about Abraham's willingness, whatever the difficulty, to do what the Lord asks him.[78]

CONCLUSION

Abraham is sometimes described as "the father of the faithful." A close examination of his life and the lives of his family members shows that Abraham earned this title because of his willingness to be embedded in relationships—both with God and with his fellow human beings. Jesus Christ cited Deuteronomy 6 and Leviticus 19 to establish the two great commandments of loving God and your neighbor (Matthew 22:37–39). Abraham exemplifies the process of loving God through loving your neighbor. This is not to say that Abraham did not have his struggles in his life and his relationships, as his interactions with Hagar and Sarah clearly show. Sarah herself had her own struggles with becoming the "mother of the faith," but her own faith led her to becoming a biological mother long after any expectation of that happening. This did not free her from her struggles with Hagar, but the Lord was able to transform that into a great blessing for the descendants of Ishmael.

The Abrahamic covenant is about relationships, both with each other and the Lord, and in this life, sometimes these relationships are tested. This was true of Abraham and Lot and Sarah and Hagar. Sarah's trust in the Lord was tested by her long wait for motherhood. Abraham's relationship with the Lord was put to the greatest test with the Lord's command for Abraham to sacrifice Isaac, his beloved and covenant son. It is no mistake, however, that the test of Abraham's life was a test based on his relationships. Abraham, Sarah, and Hagar remind us that as we become the "seed of Abraham" (Doctrine and Covenants 84:34), we do so by entering into covenant relationships with the Lord and with others. As we do so, we are able to say, like Abraham, "Thy servant has sought thee earnestly; now I have found thee" (Abraham 2:12).

---

78. Jonathan Jacobs, "Willing Obedience with Doubts: Abraham at the Binding of Isaac," *Vetus Testamentum* 60 (2010): 546–59, especially 557–8.

LOT

LIKENED TO NOAH

ROSEANN BENSON

Among the many narratives of Genesis, one of the more difficult ones to read and understand is that of Lot. Although not many details are given about his early life, his relationship and journeys with Abraham suggest that there is much more to this individual than is often realized. Unfortunately, the text that does deal with Lot exclusively is problematic on a number of levels. Perhaps reflecting these difficulties, how we are to understand or interpret the character of Lot is not provided by the authors or redactors of the narrative. Yet a New Testament tradition exists in which Lot is understood as an example of a righteous man. This paper explores how this tradition may, in fact, be found in the Old Testament itself and how the Joseph Smith Translation provides insight into troubling aspects of the narrative of Lot. —DB and AS

The story of Lot as found in Genesis 11:26 to Genesis 13 and in Genesis 19 describes a complex and seemingly contradictory character. Readers are left with many unanswered questions about the nephew of Abraham and how to interpret the narratives associated with him.[1] On the one hand, Lot chose to move to the cities of the plain, which included Sodom—a city known throughout scripture for its wickedness. First, he pitched his tent facing the city and then moved his family into the city, buying or building a home. According to the Genesis account, when all the men of the city mobbed his home seeking "to know" his guests, he offered his virgin daughters to save the lives of the guests who were under the protection of his hospitality, procrastinated leaving the city when warned of impending destruction, and later, in his drunkenness, unknowingly impregnated his daughters (Genesis 13:10–12; 19:4–8, 15–16, 30–36). Some scholars view these points as illustrating literary forms of poetic justice and irony.[2] On the other hand, the narrative also relates that Lot accompanied Abraham, father of the faithful, from their native land of Haran and through Canaan and to Egypt. Lot was blessed with riches, miraculously rescued by his uncle from foreign servitude, offered hospitality to godly messengers, and then preserved by them from the destruction that devastated Sodom and Gomorrah.

These seeming contradictions in the narrative are evident in both ancient and modern exegesis, as well as in the Joseph Smith Translation. One scholar called these contradictions "fascinating interpretive maneuvers, omissions, inclusions,"[3] and speculations based on their culture and

---

1. James Kugel, *Traditions of the Bible: A Guide to the Bible as It Was at the Start of the Common Era* (Cambridge, MA: Harvard University Press, 1998), 328.
2. Laurence A. Turner, "Lot as Jekyll and Hyde: A Reading of Genesis 18–19," in *Bible in Three Dimensions: Essays in Celebration of Forty Years of Biblical Studies in the University of Sheffield*, ed. David J. A. Clines, Stephen E. Fowl, and Stanley E. Porter (Sheffield, UK: Sheffield Academic Press, 1990), 96; Jonathan Grossman, "'Associative Meanings' in the Character Evaluation of Lot's Daughters," *Catholic Biblical Quarterly* 76 (2014): 46; Berel Dov Lerner, "Lot's Failed Trial," *Jewish Bible Quarterly* 37, no. 3 (2009): 153–56.
3. Dan Rickett, "Creating an Unrighteous Outsider: The Separation of Abram and Lot in Early Scriptural Retellings," *Catholic Biblical Quarterly* 76 (2014): 611–33.

era, allowing the story to be reused and reshaped according to need.[4] What is clear is that by the New Testament era, despite negative associations, at least one tradition concerning Lot recognized his righteous character. Peter referred to Lot as a "righteous man" with a "righteous soul" and mentioned Lot's preservation in the same pericope as Noah—men both delivered out of temptation so that God could punish the unjust (2 Peter 2:7–9).

Lot has been used as a figure that demonstrates the importance of making correct choices.[5] Associated with the great sins of Sodom and Gomorrah, Lot is depicted as a man who desired to be both worldly and righteous. Specifically, his decision to point his tent toward these two cities and enter into their culture is cited as a notably poor choice.[6] These are useful examples for teaching important principles applicable to choices in life. In contrast, the Joseph Smith Translation and the Book of Abraham[7] provide significant insights about Lot that may support Peter's

4. Weston W. Fields, "The Sodom Tradition in Intertestamental and New Testament Literature," in *New Testament Essays in Honor of Homer A. Kent, Jr.* (Terra Haute, IN: Indiana State University, 1991), 35. For example, the Sodom tradition is found in the Apocrypha, Pseudepigrapha, Jewish legends, and New Testament.
5. Neal A. Maxwell, "The Tugs and Pulls of the World," *Ensign*, November 2000, 35.
6. Elder Maxwell also warned, "Brothers and sisters, we do not go many hours in our lives without having to decide again 'which way do we face' and whether we will pitch our tents facing Sodom or the holy temple (see Gen. 13:12; Mosiah 2:6)." Neal A. Maxwell, "How Choice a Seer!," *Ensign*, November 2003, 99–102. Elder L. Tom Perry noted, "Most of the problems that Lot later encountered in his life, and there were several, can be traced back to his early decision to position the door of his tent to look upon Sodom." L. Tom Perry, "The Power of Deliverance," *Ensign*, May 2012, 94–97.
7. In the summer of 1830, Joseph Smith began his translation work on the Old Testament, and included in this was an inspired translation that included Lot's story. Today, the inspired work on the Bible is called the Joseph Smith Translation (JST). The JST of Genesis follows the biblical storyline of Abram, Sarai, and Lot but has some significant changes. Interestingly, the Book of Abraham appears to present Abraham's life retrospectively, with Abraham always calling himself by that name, and contains only parts of the Genesis account. During the summer of 1835, Joseph Smith came into possession of Egyptian papyri, a copy of the events dating between approximately 150 and 200 BC, and began his translation of the Book of Abraham, which mentions Lot.

pronouncement of Lot as a righteous, godly, and just man who was comparable to Noah, "a preacher of righteousness" (2 Peter 2:5). Thus, we can find within the narrative of Lot a man who struggled with his place in the world, who made choices—good and bad—and yet who, at the core, was an individual who sought for and gained righteousness.

THE MISSION AND JOURNEY OF ABRAHAM AND LOT

Lot's narrative, in many instances, cannot be separated from that of his uncle Abraham, and often the events of their lives are interconnected. Perhaps unnecessarily at times, negative stigmas are attached to Lot that do not help people recognize the good within his life and the bigger picture of Abraham and Sarai's lives in general. Some scholars describe Lot as merely a comic foil to the greater Abrahamic narrative, a "tragic buffoon" to Abraham the hero.[8] A closer examination reveals more about the story of Lot, the orphan son of Haran, who is first briefly mentioned in Genesis 11 as part of a larger group that includes Abraham,[9] Lot's grandfather Terah, and Abraham's wife Sarai.[10] The Book of Abraham in the Pearl of Great Price adds little to this history, and what we do know is ultimately based on what is said about Abraham. Accordingly, it seems

---

8. George W. Coats, "Lot: A Foil in the Abraham Saga," in *Understanding the Word: Essays in Honor of Bernhard W. Anderson*, ed. J. T. Butler, E. W. Conrad, and B.C. Ollenburger (Sheffield, UK: Journal for the Study of the Old Testament Press, 1985), 113. See also K. Renato Lings, "Cultural Clash in Sodom: Patriarchal Tales of Heroes, Villains, and Manipulation," in *Patriarchs, Prophets and other Villains*, ed. Lisa Isherwood (London: Routledge, 2007), 183–207.

9. In the KJV Genesis account, the Joseph Smith Translation, and Josephus's *Antiquities of the Jews*, the name Abram is changed to Abraham. In the Pearl of Great Price, Abraham is the only name mentioned. To avoid confusion, Abraham is used in this paper except when direct quotations use Abram.

10. According to Jewish legend, Haran, the son of Terah and father of Lot, died when he was cast into a furnace with Abraham. Abraham was saved by the Lord, but Haran perished "because his heart was not perfect with the Lord." Louis Ginzberg, *The Legends of the Jews* (Philadelphia: The Jewish Publication Society of America, 1975), 1:216.

we can include Lot within the basic storyline who was, in some fashion, aligned with Abraham in the city of Ur, where idol worship was part of the inhabitants' rituals, and where Abraham faced stiff opposition for his religious convictions. At the command of God, Abraham leaves this society: "Now the Lord had said unto me: Abraham, get thee out of thy country, . . . and I took Lot, my brother's son, and his wife, and Sarai my wife; and also my father followed after me" (Abraham 2:3–4). Although Terah was the family patriarch, significantly, the Book of Abraham points out that Abraham was the patriarchal leader who received revelation and led his family, including taking Lot to Haran, in contrast to the biblical account (see Genesis 11:31). Thus, in the early narrative, we are presented with a Lot who accompanies his spiritual uncle. The small group, which included Lot, stayed for a time in Haran gathering flocks and, apparently, converts to God (see Abraham 2:15; Genesis 11:31–32).

In Abraham 2:6, we are presented with a sense of Lot's spiritual acumen: "But I, Abraham, and Lot, my brother's son, prayed unto the Lord."[11] Although only Abraham received the theophany, it is telling that Lot is included in the request for greater divine instruction. It may only be a small indication, but it suggests that Lot was more than simply a placeholder in the company; instead, he was an individual who recognized the import of what was happening for himself. This greater sense of purpose for Lot can also be found in God's instruction to Abraham: "Arise, and take Lot with thee; for I have purposed to take thee away out of Haran, and to make of thee a minister to bear my name in a strange land which I will give unto thy seed after thee for an everlasting possession, when they hearken to

11. The Jewish pseudepigraphical text *Jubilees* purports to give both the prayer of Abraham and God's response to it. It records that Abraham prayed, "My God, God Most High, Thou alone art my God, and Thee and Thy dominion have I chosen. And Thou hast created all things, and all things that are[,] are the work of Thy hands. Deliver me from the hands of evil spirits who have sway over the thoughts of men's hearts, And let them not lead me astray from Thee, my God. And [e]stablish Thou me and my seed for ever that we go not astray from henceforth and for evermore." *Jubilees* 12:19–20. It also records Abraham's question and God's answer: "Shall I return unto Ur of the Chaldees who seek my face that I may return to them, or am I to remain here in this place? The right path before Thee[,] prosper it in the hands of Thy servant that he may fulfil (it) and that I may not walk in the deceitfulness of my heart, O my God." *Jubilees* 12:20–21.

my voice" (Abraham 2:6; compare Genesis 12:1–3). Although the instruction appears to be specific to Abraham, the phrasing of God's response in Abraham 2 suggests something significant requiring the accompaniment of Lot and indicates that Jehovah had chosen Abraham and Lot for special purposes—one of which may have included Lot's bearing witness of God's name in a land that would become their covenant home.[12]

In obedience to the Lord God's direction, Lot left Haran with Abraham and Sarai along with the wealth they had accumulated and the souls they had gathered (Genesis 12:5; Abraham 2:14–15).[13] They traveled southward "by the way of Jershon to come to the land of Canaan" (Abraham 2:16). In a personal narrative, "I Abraham, built an altar in the land of Jershon to make offerings unto the Lord and prayed that the famine might be turned away from my father's house" (Abraham 2:17). From Jershon they continued south toward Sichem[14] and the plains of Moreh in Canaan. Here Abraham built another altar and "offered sacrifice and called on the Lord" because they were in an idolatrous land (Abraham 2:18). In answer to his prayers, the Lord appeared and told Abraham that this is the land his family will inherit. Abraham and his company continued southward to a mountain between "Beth-el on the west and Hai on the east" where he built a third altar unto the Lord, and called again upon the name of the Lord" (Abraham 2:20). It seems likely during this journey that Lot learned how to build an altar, make sacrifices, and call on the Lord for protection. Because of famine in Canaan, the family and those who came with them

---

12. The word *choose* is used frequently to designate people and places chosen by God. Although the word *choose* is not used in this case, the context makes clear that this is what the Lord's words are implying. Dana M. Pike, "Before Jeremiah Was: Divine Election in the Ancient Near East," in *A Witness for the Restoration: Essays in Honor of Robert J. Matthews*, ed. Kent P. Jackson and Andrew C. Skinner (Provo, UT: Religious Studies Center, Brigham Young University, 2007), 33–59.

13. "Souls" refers to converts to God. Abram had converted the men, and Sarah, the women. *Midrash Rabbah*, "Genesis" trans. Rabbi Dr. H. Freedman (London: Socino Press, 1939, 1951, 1961), 39:14, 324.

14. "Sichem" became "Shechem" and was located in the territory given to Manasseh, becoming the first capital of the northern kingdom of Israel.

continued to travel southward toward Egypt, a rich agricultural region due to the annual flooding of the Nile from the water in the highlands in Africa.

At this point, the Book of Abraham adds to our understanding of the company's activities in Egypt. Whereas the Genesis account describes the confrontational interaction between the Pharaoh with his princes and Abraham and Sarai, the Book of Abraham emphasizes Abraham's continuing efforts to teach and testify of God: "And the Lord said unto me: Abraham, I show these things unto thee before ye go into Egypt, that ye may declare all these words" (Abraham 3:15).[15] Facsimile 3 suggests that at some point a reconciliation took place between Abraham and the political elite of Egypt, who appear to be among those Egyptians who listened to Abraham's message. Lot is mentioned in none of this, but Genesis 13:1 makes known that upon Abraham's exit from Egypt, Lot was among the group leaving: "And Abram went up out of Egypt, he, and his wife, and all that he had, and Lot with him, into the south" (Genesis 13:1). Thus Lot may have engaged in the same teaching and testifying of God that Abraham did, a pattern of behavior that would indicate Lot was a righteous man like his uncle.

LOT'S SETTLEMENT IN SODOM AND GOMORRAH

After leaving Egypt, Abraham and Lot went back to the altar in Canaan that Abraham had built between Bethel and Hai, the altar being a sacred place for him to confer again with the Lord. It is at this point that the two narratives of Abraham and Lot separate. Over time, Abraham and Lot had collected a substantial number of "flocks, and herds, and tents" (Genesis 13:2, 5).[16] The hill country of Canaan could not support the numerous

---

15. Through a Urim and Thummim, God revealed to Abraham the hierarchy of the physical universe, a topic of great interest to the Egyptians, and likened it to the hierarchy of the spiritual universe so that Abraham could use it to also teach about God.

16. Abraham is also associated with gold and silver. Dan Rickett suggests this distinction was added to distinguish Abraham and Lot—Abraham's narrative being more important, and Abraham himself being more righteous (thus blessed with more). See Rickett, "Creating an Unrighteous Outsider," 611–33.

flocks, herds, and property of the two men and the native peoples. With a wide expanse of land before them, Abraham suggested they part ways, giving Lot the first choice of land and direction of travel. Lot looked toward the plain of Jordan and noted "it was well watered" and thought it comparable to the "garden of the Lord" and reminiscent of Egypt (Genesis 13:10). Apparently, this area had beautiful vistas and rich pastureland prior to its destruction.[17]

Regarding Lot's separation from Abraham, some scholars have speculated that it indicated not just geographical but also spiritual distance,[18] noting similarities between this separation and other biblical separations such as Jacob and Esau's;[19] Lot's choice of traveling eastward after separating from Abraham is also considered similar to Cain's traveling eastward after slaying his brother and separating from Adam and Eve.[20] Freitheim maintains, however, "Historically, quarreling among nomads over pastureland and water for their herds was common in that era and that the scriptural account does not lay blame on either man, nor does it regard the separation as unfortunate, but rather as a reasonable way to respond to the situation.[21]

The two men separated, Lot went eastward toward the cities of the Jordan plain—Sodom, Gomorrah, Admah, and Zoar—and Abraham

---

17. Jewish legend identifies the plain of Jordan as the "fruitful Vale of Siddim," the canals of which later formed the Dead Sea. Ginzberg, *Legends of the Jews*, 1:230. Scientists have compared the cellulose of ancient tamarix (tamarisk) trees used to construct the fortress at Masada to the same type of trees growing in the Masada area today and concluded that "the ancient trees enjoyed less arid environmental conditions during their growth compared to contemporary trees in this desert region," which indicates a "regional climatic change in desert areas." Dan Yakir, et al., "13C and 18O of Wood from the Roman Siege Rampart in Masada, Israel (AD 70–73): Evidence for a Less Arid Climate for the Region," *Geochimica et Comochimica Acta* 58, no. 16 (1994), 3535–39.

18. Sharon Pace Jeansonne, "The Characterization of Lot in Genesis," *Biblical Theology Bulletin* 18 (1988): 125.

19. Rickett, "Creating an Unrighteous Outsider," 620.

20. Rickett, "Creating an Unrighteous Outsider," 624; Jeansonne, "Characterization of Lot in Genesis," 125.

21. Fretheim, "Genesis," *New Interpreter's Bible* (Nashville: Abingdon Press, 1994), 1:433.

went northward to the plain of Mamre near Hebron.[22] The King James Version of the Genesis account reports that initially Lot pitched his tent "toward" the city of Sodom (Genesis 13:12), and, in seeming contrast, Abraham's tent was always near, if not actually facing the altars he built (Genesis 12:8; 13:18; Abraham 2:17, 20). Newer translations, however, emphasize the location rather than the orientation of Lot's tent.[23] The text does, however, make a definitive statement regarding the state of Sodom, declaring the community as "wicked and sinners before the LORD exceedingly" (Genesis 13:13). The Joseph Smith Translation clarifies the nature of society in Sodom: "But the men of Sodom *becoming* sinners, and exceedingly wicked before the Lord, *the Lord was angry with them*" (JST Genesis 13:11).[24] Both Old and New Testament prophets elaborated on the sins of Sodom and Gomorrah. The Lord, railing against false priests and prophets in Jerusalem in the days of Jeremiah, accusing them of adultery, lying, and helping the wicked, concludes his denunciation with this indictment: "They are all of them unto me as Sodom, and the inhabitants thereof as Gomorrah" (Jeremiah 23:14). Ezekiel identified some of the sins of Sodom as the people's pride, greed, idleness, failure to care for the poor and needy,

---

22. Hebron is a later designation. The area was earlier called Kiriath-arba.

23. For example: "pitched his tent close to Sodom" (Common English Bible), "moved his tent as far as Sodom" (Hebrew Bible in English), or "pitching his tents on the outskirts of Sodom" (New Jerusalem Bible). See also the Complete Jewish Bible, English Study Bible, Jewish Publication Society Bible, New American Standard Bible, New English Translation, New International Version, New Revised Version, etc. This is because the Hebrew preposition *ad*, rendered "toward" in the King James Version Genesis 13:12, is more correctly translated as "by," "near," or "unto." I am indebted to scholar Dana M. Pike for pointing me to the translation of this Hebrew preposition.

24. Josephus's assessment is similar to Joseph Smith's. At the time Lot chose Sodom, he stated, "which was then a fine city." Josephus also declared the city's later status: "The Sodomites grew proud, on account of their riches and great wealth; they became unjust towards men, and impious towards God, insomuch that they did not call to mind the advantages they received from him: they hated strangers, and abused themselves with Sodomitical practices." Josephus, *Antiquities of the Jews* 1, 11:1. Rabbinic traditions are also rife with stories about the immoral practices of the people living in these cities. Ginzberg, *Legends of the Jews*, 1:247–50.

arrogance, and sexual sins (Ezekiel 16:49–50). Jude deplored one of the sins of Sodom and Gomorrah and the nearby cities: their inhabitants were guilty of "giving themselves over to fornication, and going after strange flesh" (Jude 1:7).

As noted earlier, this choice to settle in these cities becomes one of the primary evidences that suggest Lot's weakness of character in later commentaries. In fact, as one rabbinic midrash stated: "He selected Sodom so he can do as they do" (Tanḥuma VaYera 12).[25] While it is possible that such was the case and that there may have been better places to reside to avoid such behavior, the text is silent as to the reasons for Lot's selection, and as some have pointed out, this silence may be taken either as an indictment or as a mere statement of fact. Indeed, at least one late tradition found in the Qur'an describes Lot as Allah's "trustworthy messenger" (Sura 26:160–73) who was sent to teach God's message and warn the cities of divine retribution should they ignore the message (26:208–9).[26] Although this tradition is not present in the biblical text, Joseph Smith, in an 1843 address, appears to have corroborated the Qur'an's assertion that prophets and messengers were sent and preached to Sodom and Gomorrah: "In consequence of rejecting the gospel of Jesus Christ and the Prophets whom God hath sent, the judgments of God have rested upon people, cities and nations in various ages of the world, which was the case with the cities of Sodom and Gomorrah, which were destroyed for rejecting the Prophets."[27] While this passage does not specifically state that Lot was one of those messengers, the story in Genesis shows Lot protecting such messengers and demonstrates that, at a minimum, he supported and facilitated their missions.

According to the biblical record, the region Lot chose to live in came under control of the kingdom of Elam for twelve years. In the thirteenth

---

25. For more on this, see Jonathan Grossman, "'Associative Meanings' in the Character Evaluation of Lot's Daughters," *Catholic Biblical Quarterly* 76 (2014): 40–57, specifically 45–46.

26. In at least one Islamic tradition, Abraham sent Lot as a prophet to the greatest cities of that day, those of the Jordan plains, where Lot lived for forty years preaching repentance to the inhabitants. W. M. Thackston Jr., trans., *The Tales of the Prophets of al-Kisa'i* (Boston: Twayne, 1978), 2:155.

27. "History of Joseph Smith," *Millennial Star* 20, no. 23 (July 10, 1858): 438.

year, however, the inhabitants of the cities of the Jordan plain rebelled against their Mesopotamian foreign overlord—presumably because the inhabitants had failed to pay the required yearly tribute. The attacking Mesopotamian kings were met by the kings and defenders of the cities of the Jordan plain, which included Sodom and Gomorrah. The victorious overlords invaded Sodom and Gomorrah, gathering all their food and riches, as well as capturing Lot and others. His inclusion as part of the spoils suggests that by this time, Lot had become associated with Sodom and Gomorrah on more than a superficial level.[28] Regardless, "when Abram, *the man of God,* heard that Lot, *his brother's son,* was taken captive, he armed his trained *men, and they which were* born in his own house to pursue northward" (JST Genesis 14:13). While the pursuit is often used to demonstrate the positive character traits of Abraham, it also says much about Lot's value to Abraham. Though nothing is recorded about the interactions between uncle and nephew following their separation on the plains of Jordan, Abraham's concern for his nephew is apparent by Abraham's attempt to rescue Lot. Continued contact between the two may be assumed by the fact that the escapee who tells of Lot's capture runs to Abraham directly (Genesis 14:13).[29]

The pursuit ends with a nighttime raid at Dan,[30] where Abraham recovered Lot, the women, and other prisoners, as well as all the substance that had been taken. The king of Sodom, the other surviving kings of the Jordan plain who were with him, and Melchizedek, the king of Salem,

---

28. Josephus states (whether historically accurate or not) that Lot joined in battle with the men of Sodom against Chedolaomer and four other kings who came to confront their vassals. Perhaps this is one reason that some have thought Lot was very involved in Sodom. Josephus, *Antiquities of the Jews* 1, 9:1.
29. See Turner, "Lot as Jekyll and Hyde," 88.
30. The ancient name for Dan was Laish. Dan was one of Abraham's great grandsons who received this territory along the Galilee as one of the sons of Jacob (Israel). The use of the name Dan in the text reflects a geographical connection of the day, representative of the event that took place in the then antiquated name of the location of Laish. Such interpolations in the Bible do not negate the historicity of the event, they simply reflect the sharing of the story over time and the superimposing of information to correspond to information of the respective present.

met Abraham and his army at the "valley of Shaveh, which is the king's dale," identified as the confluence of the three valleys southeast of Jerusalem (Genesis 14:17). At this point in the storyline, there are significant additions in Restoration scripture. The Joseph Smith Translation focuses on Melchizedek's missionary efforts in Salem,[31] and the biblical narrative becomes solely Abrahamic and concentrates on Melchizedek's blessing, an event that Lot may have been privy to.[32] This is followed by the Lord's own subsequent covenant with Abraham, the birth of Ishmael, and the promise of Isaac. The covenantal relationship between God and Abraham becomes integral in the Lot narrative because it introduces the judgments of God against Sodom and Gomorrah and Abraham's right to plead for mercy.

LOT'S HOSPITALITY

Perhaps the most crucial and difficult episode of the Lot narrative is that of the visitation by holy messengers to Lot in Sodom described in Genesis 18. The context of this episode begins in Genesis 17, with a divine visitation to Abraham. In both cases, hospitality lies at the heart of the narrative, and this ultimately may demonstrate the righteousness of Lot. According to Genesis 18, Abraham, resting in the shade one afternoon, looked up and saw three individuals approaching his tent. Running to meet them, he offered hospitality in the form of a meal, rest, and foot washing. Following the meal, the individuals arose and began walking in the direction of Sodom and Gomorrah.

At this point, the Joseph Smith Translation diverges from the biblical account and describes a conversation between Abraham and these individuals while they are journeying toward Sodom:

> *The angel of the Lord said unto* Abram, the Lord said *unto us*, Because the cry of Sodom and Gomorrah is great, and because

31. See JST Genesis 14.
32. The *New Interpreter's Bible* suggests that Lot was present and that Abraham by not accepting any of the spoils also refused to "take Lot's goods and use them (and that of others) for gaining hegemony in Lot's land." Because Abraham does not enrich himself with Lot's land he is not obligated to the king of Sodom. *New Interpreter's Bible*, 1:440, 442.

> their sin is grievous, *I will destroy them. And I will send you, and ye shall go down now, and see that their iniquities are rewarded unto them. And ye shall have all things done together according to the cry of it, which is come unto me. And if ye do it not, it shall be upon your heads; for I will destroy them, and you shall know that I will do it, for it shall be before your eyes. And the angels which were holy men, and were sent forth after the order of God* turned their faces from thence and went to Sodom. (JST Genesis 18:19–23)[33]

It is in this context that we find Abraham pleading to the Lord to spare the communities mentioned: Abram, "*remembering the things which had been told him*, . . . drew near *to Sodom*, and said *unto the Lord, calling upon his name*," asking if the righteous would be destroyed with the wicked and pleading: "*O God, may that be far from thee to do after this manner*" (JST Genesis 18:24–28; Genesis 18:23, 25).

Concerned that both the wicked and the righteous might be destroyed together, the Genesis account reveals that Abraham began to intercede with the Lord. Abraham was able to extract a promise from God that if ten righteous individuals inhabited Sodom and Gomorrah, then the cities would be spared destruction.[34] Satisfied with this promise, Abraham returned to his tent. Again, although Lot's name is not mentioned, his presence looms over Abraham's interaction with God. While it is possible that Abraham's concern for the cities merely reflects his generous and compassionate nature (as Genesis 19 demonstrates), by now, however, Lot was living in the city, and thus the destruction of Sodom would include him. This, in turn, suggests that Abraham's concern for the righteous to be

---

33. According to Jewish legend, Abraham was informed because the cities marked for destruction were part of Canaan, the land promised to Abraham. Ginzberg, *Legends of the Jews*, 1:250.

34. According to rabbinic tradition, Abraham did not ask for more when the Lord promised he would save the cities if ten righteous souls could be found, because even Noah and the seven other righteous family members were not sufficient to avert destruction by the flood. Abraham may have assumed that Lot's family with his daughters and sons-in-law would make the number ten and be enough to save the cities; however, though better than the rest of the people in the cities, Lot and his family were far from good. Ginzberg, *Legends of the Jews*, 1:252.

preserved would mean that he considered Lot to be one of those righteous individuals.

The scene then shifts to Sodom itself, where Lot sat at the city gate, drawing speculation about why he would be waiting there at that time. He invited the holy men into his home upon their arrival.[35] Though this may seem a minor detail, Lot's sitting at the gate may indicate the location of his home, his standing in the community as a compassionate individual, and the divine communication he received that instructed him to wait there. Later Israelite history associates the judgment of lesser individuals with taking place at the city gate.[36] Consequently, the one who invited a stranger to come in through the gate became the agent by which acceptance was provided.[37] Not surprisingly, considering its function as the place where the stranger became an honored guest, the gate or entrance also marked the place of offering hospitality. As a part of the hospitality process, the invitation to come in transformed the possibly dangerous stranger into an honored guest who was expected to observe the norms of behavior like those of the rest of the family.[38] Thus, like his uncle, Lot is depicted in a favorable setting: offering hospitality to the unknown strangers, including preparing a feast for them. Though some have tried to suggest that the

35. According to the JST, Lot is seated at the "*door of his house in the city of Sodom,*" not at the gate of the city (JST Genesis 19:1; compare with Genesis 19:1).

36. For instance, in the Ugaritic text of Aqhat, the hero's father, Danil, is described as one who "sat by the entrance to the gate. . . . He tried the case of the widow, he judged the cause of the orphan." *Keilalphabetische Texte aus Ugarit* (KTU) 1.17, v, lines 7–9.

37. See Carey Walsh, "Testing Entry: The Social Functions of City Gates in Biblical Memory," in *Memory and the City in Ancient Israel*, ed. Diana V. Edelman and Ehud Ben Zvi (Winona Lake, IN: Eisenbrauns, 2014), 43–60. See also Natalie M. May, "Gates and Their Functions in Mesopotamia and Ancient Israel," in *The Fabric of Cities: Aspects of Urbanism, Urban Topography and Society in Mesopotamia, Greece and Rome*, ed. Natalie M. May and Ulrike Steinert (Leiden: Brill, 2014), 77–121.

38. For more on the role of hospitality in the Old Testament, see T. R. Hobbs, "Hospitality in the First Testament and the 'Teleological Fallacy,'" in *Journal for the Study of the Old Testament* 26, no. 1 (2001): 3–30; Scott Morschauser, "'Hospitality,' Hostiles and Hostages: On the Legal Background to Genesis 19.1–9," *Journal for the Study of the Old Testament* 27, no. 4 (2003): 461–85.

hospitality of Lot is meant to contrast with the hospitality of Abraham,[39] nothing suggests that Lot's was less than that offered by the patriarch. In fact, if hospitality played as important a role in the life of patriarchs as the above suggests, then it is a primary symbol of Lot's righteousness and perhaps indicates his active role in establishing righteous behavior in the community. At the very least, his position at the gate may demonstrate the esteem his fellow citizens had for him.

The depiction of Lot as the righteous offerer of hospitality continues even as the very hospitality is threatened by apparently numerous men of Sodom, described as "both old and young, all the people from every quarter," who demand that the visitors be presented to them (Genesis 19:4). The men "called unto Lot, and said unto him, Where are the men which came in to thee this night? Bring them out unto us, that we may know them" (Genesis 19:5). According to the text, Lot, upon hearing this demand, steps outside and closes the door behind him, effectively making himself the barrier between the gathered mob and his guests. As such, he stands his ground even when they reject his entreaty to disperse and apparently physically attack him (Genesis 19:9). This unwillingness to cave to the mob while actively standing against their wishes is significant, for what follows is the most difficult part of the Genesis version. Lot pleads that the crowd would not disturb the guests because they are under his hospitality. In their place, he purportedly offers his two unmarried daughters to the mob and says, "Do ye to them as is good in your eyes" (Genesis 19:8).

The proffered exchange is difficult for two reasons. First, it is not exactly clear what the mob is asking for. Clearly, the norms of hospitality are to be broken, but the exact nature of their intent is only indicated by the phrase "to know" the guests. Traditionally, commentators have interpreted this as referring to sexual intent and misconduct since Sodom was associated with homosexual behavior. This seems to work in conjunction with the overall violation of the social norms of hospitality and the proper treatment of guests.[40] Additionally, as biblical scholar Scott Moreschouer

39. For example, see Jeansonne, "Characterization of Lot in Genesis," 126.

40. Robert Ignatius Letellier, *Day in Mamre, Night in Sodom: Abraham and Lot in Genesis 18 and 19*, Biblical Interpretation Series 10 (New York: Brill, 1995), 158: "The violation of social norms in the attack on Lot's house and the integrity

suggests, noting the juridical use of "to know" in treaties, the term may be referring to an illegal interrogation in which the inhabitants would rough up the guests.[41] Second, our modern sensibilities recoil at the proffered exchange: young daughters for strangers. Not surprisingly, this element has met with a variety of responses on the part of scholars, ranging from those who suggest this depicts the real Lot as cowardly and weak, while others suggest that it demonstrates the true sacrifices of hospitality.

These difficulties may be assuaged since the Joseph Smith Translation reveals a different view that highlights Lot's righteousness. According to the Joseph Smith Translation, the original demand by the mob included Lot's daughters: "*We will have the men, and thy daughters also; and we will do with them as seemeth us good. Now this was after the wickedness of Sodom*" (JST Genesis 19:11–12). Lot, as one would expect from any righteous father, pleads that the young women be excluded: "I have two daughters which have not known man; let me, I pray you, *plead with my brethren that I may not* bring them out unto you; and *ye shall not do unto them as seemeth good in your eyes; for God will not justify his servant in this thing*" (JST Genesis 19:13–14). In this narrative, Lot is not cowardly or selfish. Instead, he is presented as a man who willingly places himself between a wicked mob and those that are under his protection—his family and guests. Moreover, Lot does not bow to the mob members' demands but rebuffs them, engendering their anger. In fact, as both the Genesis and

---

of his guests (with the intended sexual violation, of course, inflaming the situation) is already a radical disruption of order in the social fabric. . . . The nature and limits of the rights of sojourners in the ancient Orient are still not well understood, but H. Brunner has pointed out by reference to ch. 22 of the Insinger Papyrus of the Ptolomaic period that these rights in Egypt could be frighteningly fragile. A sojourner could expect to be roughly received by the local populace, could be cursed, rejected and even subjected to the 'crime of women' (Egyp. *btw n shnt*) which means the crime of violating a man as if he was a woman (ie. sodomy) for which no redress was possible."

41. Moreschouer, "'Hospitality,' Hostiles and Hostages," 473: "While the term ['to know'] means here 'to interrogate' or 'to discover,' such an investigative procedure in the ancient world would have born little resemblance to modern Western concepts of 'legal rights.' Official questioning of individuals in the ancient Near East could often be brutal—accompanied by beatings, near-drowning and physical humiliation."

the Joseph Smith Translation demonstrate, Lot is saved only by the guests themselves who open the door and pull him inside to safety. This is the contrast in hospitality—Abraham and Lot in contradistinction to the men of Sodom. In this narrative tradition, Lot is no longer a passive individual in the shadow of his uncle but a heroic figure in his own right. Lot demonstrates that he also is a true patriarchal figure.

LOT AND HIS DAUGHTERS

Having reconciled this scene, another one immediately appears that is equally difficult to interpret and comprehend. Following the confrontation between Lot and the mob of Sodom, the holy men inquire if there are other family members in the city and warn Lot that the destruction of the city is imminent and that he must get his family out quickly. Lot's adherence to the directive to warn his family demonstrates his obedience, however, other family members do not believe him. The narrative relates that the sons-in-law think he is jesting, and they refuse to leave. At daybreak, Lot hesitates, perhaps hopeful more of his family will join him.[42] Miraculously, the holy men lead Lot, his wife, and two of their daughters to the outskirts of the city. Lot's wife, behind him, looks back on the city, even though she is expressly told not to, and dies in the conflagration. The result is the destruction of part of the family.

It may be tempting to view the apparent familial failures of Lot's family as an indication of Lot's spiritual inadequacies; however, Lot's family troubles fit within the parameters of other patriarchal narratives in which the

42. The KJV Genesis account is not clear whether Lot had two daughters who were married and two who were virgins or whether there were only two daughters who were virgins and betrothed to be married. E. A. Speiser states that the Hebrew can be interpreted in the past tense, they were married (see LXX), or future tense (see Vulgate), were due to marry. "The traditional translation presupposes that two older daughters had to be left behind with their husbands. . . . But the alterative interpretation is by no means improbable." E. A. Speiser, *Anchor Bible: Genesis* (Garden City, NY: Doubleday, 1962), 140. A rabbinic tradition maintains that Lot's wife, out of motherly love, looked back to see if her married daughters were following them out of the city. Ginzberg, *Legends of the Jews*, 1:255.

righteous father is not responsible for the behavior of family members. Both Abraham's son and grandson struggled with interfamily conflict, and Abraham himself dealt with the tension between his two sons and their mothers. As for Lot's unnamed wife, her demise reflects the complexity and difficulty of the overall narrative. While she does leave with Lot and the daughters, her unwillingness to obey completely leaves the family motherless.[43] And yet the disobedience may be understandable, as many commentators, ancient and modern, have noted that she left that appears to be at least two daughters in Sodom. These daughters are married and perhaps have children; thus, she may have also left behind grandchildren. In this light, Lot's wife's decision, while disobedient, is wholly a human one, and this ambiguity has been noted by others who see her demise as fundamentally different from the destruction of Sodom and Gomorrah.[44]

---

43. A *pillar* of salt would be a large amount of salt and, rather than acting as a preserving agent, would symbolize the destruction of something harmful. Also, since salt was an integral part of covenant making, perhaps the symbolism of Lot's wife becoming a pillar of salt represents both her contamination with the ideals of Sodom and the penalty for not keeping her covenants (the salt of her covenants raining down upon her and causing death). The valley in which Sodom and Gomorrah were located was later called the Valley of Salt—a great contrast to Lot's initial description of the land as Edenic. The ungodliness of the cities, demonstrated by their failure to heed the testimony of Lot, secured their destruction and made the land thenceforth unproductive. Additional scholarly comments in this area include the following: "In ancient treaty texts, salination of the earth is a symbol of judgment." J. Gerald Janzen, *International Theological Commentary: Genesis 12–50: Abraham and All the Families of the Earth* (Grand Rapids, MI: Eerdmans, 1993), 64. Salt can provoke "powerful images of death, desolation, and curse." Leland Ryken, James C. Wilhoit, and Tremper Longman III, eds., *Dictionary of Biblical Imagery* (Downers Grove, IL: InterVarsity, 1998), 752. When all is said and done, we do not have all the reasons for Lot's wife's behavior. We should leave open the possibility that she had good intentions in attempting to save the lives of her family.
44. Samuel Cheon, "Filling the Gap in the Story of Lot's Wife," *Asia Journal of Theology* 15, no. 1 (2001): 14–23: "The action of Lot's wife is qualitatively different from the wrongdoing of the Sodomites; the story does not intend to describe her as a wicked woman, but instead, to portray through her limitations of human abilities." Elder Holland appears to recognize the ambivalence here as well. "Apparently, what was wrong with Lot's wife was that she wasn't just *looking* back; in her heart she wanted to *go* back. It would appear that even before she was past

With all that has happened in the story, the final scene may be the most problematic and disconcerting. According to the narrative, following the death of his wife, Lot and the surviving daughters stay temporarily in a small village named Zoar, but they stay only briefly because Lot "feared to dwell in Zoar" (Genesis 19:30). Lot and his two young daughters continue into the hilly region surrounding the Jordan valley, where Lot finds a cave and establishes himself. At this point, it is worthwhile to note that all his flocks, herds, and wealth were gone, his home was destroyed, and many of his family members were dead, including his wife, at least some of his daughters, his sons-in-law, and possibly his grandchildren. All he has left are his two daughters hiding with him in a cave, and he is all the daughters have as well.

These points may be important to keep in mind to establish context for what follows. According to the text, at some point the older daughter states to the younger daughter that "there is not a man in the in the earth to come in unto us after the manner of all the earth" (Genesis 19:31) and that they need to "lie with him, that we may preserve alive (*n^ekhay^eh*) the seed of our father" (Genesis 19:32, translation by Dan Belnap). Over the course of two nights, the two daughters conceive and eventually bear two sons: Moab, whose name means "from my father," and Ben-Ammi, whose name means "son of my people." These two become the forebears of the Moabites and Ammonites.

It is possible to see the event as a necessary one, at least from the perspective of the young women. According to the text, they believe that they will never be able to be married and have children. This does not necessarily mean that the daughters are under the impression that they and their father are the only living humans on the earth, although that is what some scholars have suggested. Instead, it may indicate that they recognize the ability to be married and have children is gone. As noted above, Lot is now

---

the city limits, she was already missing what Sodom and Gomorrah had offered her. . . . It is possible that Lot's wife looked back with resentment toward the Lord for what He was asking her to leave behind. . . . So it isn't just that she looked back; she looked back *longingly.* In short, her attachment to the past outweighed her confidence in the future. That, apparently, was at least part of her sin." Jeffrey R. Holland, "The Best Is Yet to Be," *Ensign*, January 2010, 22, 27.

homeless and apparently lacking any possessions to make a dowry possible. The status that marriage and conceiving and bearing a child confers upon women is displayed throughout the Old Testament, as are the numerous inventive ways in which these women achieve the goal of bearing children. It is possible that the daughters recognize the immorality of their actions, but the extremity of the situation has forced the issue and justifies, in their minds, these actions. The text does not explain their motives, and we are left wondering and grappling for an answer to this unusual incident.

The Hebrew phraseology may provide another interpretation to this event. According to the text, the young women believe they need to lie with their father to *n*^{e}*khay*^{e}*h* the seed of their father. While the King James Version translates this verb as "preserve," the verb itself is a form of the verb "to live"; thus a more accurate translation could be "preserve the life of."[45] If it is translated in this manner, then the young women do this not because of their own losses but because they recognize the potential loss of the Lot's lineage, and therefore take it upon themselves to ensure the lineage of Lot is not erased. This possibility is also not unique in the Old Testament in that women are often depicted as the individuals who take upon themselves the responsibility to preserve the family lineage.[46]

For modern sensibilities, this scene is a difficult one to reconcile, and perhaps it was for ancient audiences as well. Incest was absolutely forbidden to ancient Israelites, who would be hearing the story with this perspective. Additionally, the daughters appear to recognize the moral morass that their acts represent, for the plan is to get their father so drunk that he is senseless and not able to recognize what they do. The plan anticipates that Lot would find their actions morally reprehensible and would not agree to it under any circumstance, thus proving the daughters' need to get him drunk. The moral reprehensibility of the act is clearly indicated by the Joseph Smith Translation, which states that the young women act "wickedly" (JST Genesis 19:37, 39). Although we never learn the why behind the behavior, the Joseph Smith Translation clarifies that the daughters'

45. "חיה" in Ludwig Koehler, Walter Baumgartner, and M. E. J. Richardon, eds., *The Hebrew and Aramaic Lexicon of the Old Testament* (Leiden: Brill, 2000).

46. See Camille Fronk Olson, "The Matriarchs: Administrators of God's Covenantal Blessings," in this volume.

actions are wicked, appearing to demonstrate that Lot is to be understood as innocent in these matters.

In attempting to give meaning to these later episodes, it seems one of the primary observations is that the account is etiological, meaning that one of its chief purposes is to give the origin to a territory or people.[47] In this case, the scene describes the origins of the Moabites and Ammonites, two peoples with whom the house of Israel will interact throughout its history. For example, in Deuteronomy 2, which recounts the journey of the Israelites through the wilderness, the reader learns that they were not to engage with the Moabites: "Distress not the Moabites, neither contend with them in battle: for I will not give thee of their land for a possession; because I have given Ar unto the children of Lot for a possession" (Deuteronomy 2:9). The same instruction is given concerning the Ammonites in 2:19. As is clear, the land of the Moabites and the Ammonites is to be respected because the Lord gave Lot these lands, just as he had promised specific territory to Abraham and his posterity. In fact, as one reviews all of Deuteronomy 2, the Israelites were to avoid conflict with all people in lands that had a direct connection to relatives of the patriarchs or to the secondary patriarchs, Esau and Lot. Yet Deuteronomy 23:3 dictates that no Ammonite or Moabite was to enter into the "congregation of the Lord" ever, perhaps reflecting their ambiguous status as outsiders who are nevertheless watched over by God. The enigmatic position that the Moabites and Ammonites have in relation to the Israelites is complicated further by a Moabite becoming what one can fairly say is a preeminent heroine in the Old Testament: Ruth.

Regardless, what the texts do seem to indicate is that Lot acts righteously in many instances and should not be judged according to the actions of his family. He is not complicit with his daughters' actions, and, as Deuteronomy 2 suggests, the offspring that result from these unions are blessed with land recognized by God as their own. Thus, the offspring stand as evidence of God's purposes, and perhaps of the righteousness of Lot, suggesting that his righteousness can offset the negative circumstances in which his sons would be born and alluding to the significant part they would play in the future.

---

47. Jonathan Grossman, "Association Meanings," 43–44.

CONCLUSION

As one reviews the Lot narrative, it is impossible not to recognize the ambiguities in the storyline. Clearly, it is set up against the greater narrative of Abraham, in which the latter reflects the ideal. The Lot narrative includes behaviors by Lot and his family that are difficult to reconcile. His choice to associate with the cities of Sodom and Gomorrah is questionable, unless as some traditions suggest, he was to be a messenger for God. His lingering in the city after being warned of imminent destruction perhaps reveals a man who recognizes what he must leave behind and regrets, to some degree, having to do so. Finally, Lot appears frozen in mind and spirit in the cave, not wanting to engage with the greater world and perhaps mentally and spiritually traumatized by the destruction of home and beloved family.[48] However, we also witness a man who engages in good, bolsters the ministry of Abraham and other righteous ministers, and works to ensure the safety of his family and the purposes of God. He has imperfections, but this does not qualify him as unrighteous, and we witness in many cases a man trying his best to accomplish great good.

Lot's narrative is powerful enough that Peter uses it as an example of God delivering the righteous from an evil world (2 Peter 2:7–9).[49] Latter-day revelation has fleshed out this side of Lot even further. The Book of Abraham notes his piety since he is shown praying for direction from the Lord alongside Abraham, and the Joseph Smith Translation notes Lot's bravery and courage by his willingness to place himself between the assembled mob and his family and guests. Both the Book of Abraham and Genesis suggest that Lot engaged in conveying God's message alongside Abraham in Egypt, and later traditions suggest that this might have been one of Lot's reasons for settling in Sodom. It is also telling that he is explicitly called a "just" and "righteous man" who suffered in mind and soul over the wickedness of the people that surrounded him (2 Peter 2:7–8). In this, Lot was comparable to Noah, another great patriarch. Lot's "vexation" over

---

48. Speiser, "Genesis," 142–43.

49. Tremper Longman III and David E. Garland, eds., *The Expositor's Bible Commentary: Hebrews–Revelation*, rev. ed. (Grand Rapids, MI: Zondervan, 2008), 279.

the wickedness of Sodom and Gomorrah may also remind the reader of Christ and Enoch, who both wept because of the wickedness and resulting misery of the people (2 Peter 2:7–8; Moses 7:28–29, 41).

Lot is clearly not Abraham, but Lot was worthy of God's attention and blessings. Lot's seed might not have been given *the* promised land, but they were given *a* promised land; and while his descendants might not have been the illustrious heroes of the Bible, they did include perhaps the greatest heroine, and they are counted in the lineage of Christ. Lot was not the great patriarch of the Bible, but he was a patriarch—an example of righteous behavior in the face of hostile opposition, great trials, suffering, and loss.

— 11 —

ISAAC AND JACOB

SUCCESSION NARRATIVES, BIRTHRIGHTS, AND BLESSINGS

AARON P. SCHADE

While the patriarch Isaac and his son Jacob continued the spiritual foundation laid down by Abraham and are thus fundamental characters to understanding not only the Old Testament but also the entirety of the Latter-day Saint canon, the narratives concerning them attaining their covenantal status can be difficult to follow and interpret. It is understandable if the reader grapples with some of the perceived measures taken to achieve and obtain the desired outcomes dealing with blessings of succession and birthright. In this chapter, Aaron Schade examines some of the complexities of these narratives, demonstrating that often our preconceived notions can affect the outcome of our perception of behavior and portrayed activities within scriptural texts. —DB and AS

Some of the Old Testament passages and stories that are more difficult to interpret are contained in the succession narratives pertaining to the lives of Isaac and Jacob. Within these chapters in the book of Genesis, we find notoriously problematic issues revolving around Ishmael's expulsion and Isaac's subsequent obtaining of the birthright, Esau's selling of his birthright to Jacob for a mess of pottage, and Jacob's procurement of the birthright from the aged Isaac in a manner that some deem as deceitful and others see as fulfilling the will of God at all costs (or some see it as a combination of both). For many of us, the narratives just don't make sense. We scratch our heads, wondering how deception runs so rampantly through these succession narratives, and puzzle over how we are supposed to reconcile them with our understanding of the nature of God and whom he chooses to bless, despite their dishonorable appearances and behaviors. The following statement illustrates this enigmatic topic:

> The single greatest theological issue that arises from this study is undoubtedly how to hold together the Hebrew Bible's descriptions of YHWH as deceptive and YHWH as trustworthy. The Hebrew Bible is adamant at several points that YWHW does not lie. Num 23:19 reads, "God is not a human being, that he should lie, or a mortal, that he should change his mind," and in 1 Sam 15:29[,] Samuel says, "the Glory of Israel will not deceive or change his mind, for he is not a mortal that he should change his mind." Compounding the potential difficulty, the Hebrew Bible also attests that YHWH is a God of truth, as in Ps 31:6, and of faithfulness, as in Deut 32:4. . . . How is one to address this very obvious tension? Or should one address it at all? The Hebrew Bible presents not only YHWH's subversive and sometimes ominous side but also YHWH's reliability, constancy, justice, and trustworthiness. Claus Westermann rightly acknowledges that "it is the task of a theology of the Old Testament to describe and view together what the Old Testament as a whole, in all its sections, says about God." How then are readers to address these seemingly incompatible witnesses?[1]

1. John E. Anderson, *Jacob and the Divine Trickster: A Theology of Deception and YHWH's Fidelity to the Ancestral Promise in the Jacob Cycle* (Winona Lake, IN: Eisenbrauns, 2011), 178.

While we must look at the Bible as a whole to construct a portrait of God, at times we set aside or overlook well-defined characteristics of God in favor of qualities we assign based on our inability to interpret admittedly difficult and solitary episodes occurring in the Bible. I will examine issues pertaining to these narratives that we may not sufficiently understand and show how presuppositions can influence how one interprets these episodes of succession. The bibliography on these topics is enormous and comes with an equally large number of diverse interpretations and explanations since authors have attempted to cope with and explain the respective perplexing issues. While many great insights may be found within this literature, I will inevitably provide my own interpretation (and at times speculation) based on my examination of the text, as well as use Restoration and modern prophetic materials found within the texts of The Church of Jesus Christ of Latter-day Saints to elucidate these disparate narratives. With that said, in some places I will simply state alternative possibilities in interpreting the passages, allowing readers to formulate their own ideas and to contemplate the diversity of possibilities that remain. Although this latter approach may seem less definitive to some readers, it is simply more academically responsible than to float unfounded results based on opinions and state them as fact and as conclusive.[2]

2. I wholeheartedly endorse the words of Elder D. Todd Christofferson, who taught, "'We believe all that God has revealed, all that He does now reveal, and we believe that He will yet reveal many great and important things pertaining to the Kingdom of God' (Articles of Faith 1:9). This is to say that while there is much we do not yet know, the truths and doctrine we have received have come and will continue to come by divine revelation. In some faith traditions, theologians claim equal teaching authority with the ecclesiastical hierarchy, and doctrinal matters may become a contest of opinions between them. Some rely on the ecumenical councils of the Middle Ages and their creeds. Others place primary emphasis on the reasoning of post-apostolic theologians or on biblical hermeneutics and exegesis. We value scholarship that enhances understanding, but in the Church today, just as anciently, establishing the doctrine of Christ or correcting doctrinal deviations is a matter of divine revelation to those the Lord endows with apostolic authority." D. Todd Christofferson, "The Doctrine of Christ," *Ensign*, May 2012, 86. This statement could not be clearer to me than it is after having gone through the process of researching and writing this paper. I have sifted through scholarly debates and provided statements by General Authorities to make some sense of these notoriously problematic issues.

THE SELECTION OF ISAAC

The first of these narratives—one that can leave us with disturbing questions and unsettled feelings—can be found in Genesis 21. In the narrative, Ishmael and his mother, Hagar, are driven out from Abraham's family and seemingly left to die in the wilderness. Following Sarah's instruction to "cast out this bondwoman and her son: for the son of this bondwoman shall not be heir with my son, even with Isaac" (Genesis 21:10), we read,

> And Abraham rose up early in the morning, and took bread, and a bottle of water, and gave it unto Hagar, putting it on her shoulder, and the child, and sent her away: and she departed, and wandered in the wilderness of Beer-sheba.
>
> And the water was spent in the bottle, and she cast the child under one of the shrubs.
>
> And she went, and sat her down over against him a good way off, as it were a bowshot: for she said, Let me not see the death of the child. And she sat over against him, and lift up her voice, and wept. (21:14–16)

The reader is left with the impression that Sarah is an embittered, spiteful soul who requests the expulsion of a young mother and her small infant child or toddler. Yet the text gives a few important temporal markers that may suggest otherwise. According to Genesis 21:5, "Abraham was an hundred years old, when his son Isaac was born unto him." Genesis 16:16 tells us that Ishmael was born when Abraham was eighty-six years old, making Ishmael around fourteen years old when Isaac was born. Thus, at the time Hagar and Ishmael wandered in the wilderness, Ishmael was not a helpless, unaccountable child, but a teenager. While this does not resolve all the potentially disturbing aspects of the narrative, it does at least expunge a reading of a mother and her helpless infant being driven into the wilderness to die. It also introduces an important concept inherent throughout the development of the narratives: accountability.

No doubt these events were difficult for everyone ("the thing was very grievous in Abraham's sight because of his son" [Genesis 21:11]), including Sarah, but they must have been especially difficult for Hagar and Ishmael, who had to endure the wilderness.[3] What we need to remember is that it appears that Abraham put his complete trust in God in following through with sending off his firstborn son, taking at face value the words of the Lord, who promised to protect Ishmael: "And God said unto Abraham, Let it not be grievous in thy sight because of the lad, and because of thy bondwoman; in all that Sarah hath said unto thee, hearken unto her voice; for in Isaac shall thy seed be called. And also of the son of the bondwoman will I make a nation, because he is thy seed" (21:12–13). Thus, although they may not have completely understood it, in the face of this difficult decision, Abraham and Sarah responded with faith and trust that Ishmael would grow to be blessed with a great nation stemming from his posterity and would not die in the wilderness.[4]

---

3. Some see in the geography of the events a diminished distance in the journey which would have ensured the survival of Hagar and Ishmael. They are also sent off early in the morning with provisions, in a planned and calculated manner. The two would thus have been able to get to safety before death ensued: "It seems more reasonable to assume that following the incident with Abimelech it was prudent for Abraham to somewhat distance himself from Gerar and perhaps dwell outside the city (Genesis 20:15). This situation appears attractive because the distance that Hagar would have had to walk in this case would be quite reasonable, Abraham probably had accommodations there, and Gerar belonged to the Muzrim to whom Hagar was related. Such an arrangement would have allowed Abraham convenient access to Hagar and Ishmael, yet [would have] ke[pt] them out of Sarah's sight and reach. When eventually Hagar and Ishmael decided to settle in the Desert of Paran they still were in the triangle Gerar-Beersheba-Paran where Abraham's cattle apparently roamed. Abraham would have had plenty of opportunity to be in contact with them. Thus, when Abraham dies Isaac does not have to send anyone to Ishmael, and Ishmael arrives in time to properly bury his father, as any son would do." Aron Pinker, "The Expulsion of Hagar and Ishmael (Gen 21:9–21)," *Women in Judaism: A Multidisciplinary Journal* 6, no. 1 (2009): 1–24.
4. Some may conclude that Sarah is calling the shots here and that Abraham is sitting on the sidelines as an insignificant player in the game. The fact of the matter is that the Lord is in charge. He assures Abraham that the Lord will protect Hagar and Ishmael and that Sarah's counsel is the proper route to take. Thus, the decision is reached by Sarah proposing a course of action, discussing the matter with Abraham, and the Lord confirming and approving it for both of them. Ellis T. Rasmussen, *A Latter-day Saint Commentary on the Old Testament* (Salt Lake City: Deseret Book, 1993), 50, states, "Abraham was naturally grieved

Concerning the motivations for the expulsion, the text gives clues about the emotional nature of this episode that may help resolve some of the apparent difficulties existing in the story. Genesis paints a picture of the religiosity of this family and portrays them as covenant makers and keepers, beginning with circumcision. Genesis 21:4 tells us that Abraham circumcised Isaac at eight days of age, just as the Lord had commanded him. Circumcision was a sacred part of the worship of this family. Despite the fact that other cultures and peoples were practicing circumcision before Abraham was commanded to, the act represented a token of a specific covenant for Abraham and his family.[5] The following passage is taken from the Joseph Smith Translation of Genesis and is unique in its depiction of the ordinance of baptism in the patriarchal age and additionally highlights an apostasy that was prevalent in that day, setting the stage for the necessity of the ordinance:

> And *it came to pass, that* Abram fell on his face, *and called upon the name of the Lord.*

---

by Sarah's demand that Hagar and her son be sent away, and only after receiving a revelation concerning Ishmael's destiny and Isaac's calling and responsibility did he let her be sent away." This was not an isolated decision; it was a decision made between Sarah, Abraham, and God. That all were involved in the process is important, and who received what first is less important to the conversation than the unanimous outcome. Subsequently, Abraham had already learned of Ishmael's fate a few chapters earlier. Sarah's counsel may have been the impetus for effectively pursing a path Abraham was already aware of but potentially hoped he would somehow be able to avoid it.

5. A famous Egyptian tomb painting from the sixth dynasty (2350–2000 BC) in Saqqara depicts circumcision. However, the practice did not hold the same symbolism and token of the covenant for the Egyptians as it did for Abraham and his family. See J. M. Sasson, "Circumcision in the Ancient Near East," *Journal of Biblical Literature* 85 (1966): 473–76; P. J. King, "Circumcision: Who Did it, Who Didn't, and Why," *Biblical Archaeology Review* 32, no. 4 (2006): 48–55; John H. Walton, *Genesis*, Zondervan Illustrated Bible Backgrounds Commentary (Grand Rapids, MI: Zondervan Academic, 2013), loc. 3464 of 10396, Kindle; John H. Walton, Victor H. Matthews, and Mark W. Chavalas, *The IVP Bible Background Commentary: Old Testament* (Downer's Grove, IN: InterVarsity Press, 2000), 49 of 812, Kindle.

> And God talked with him, saying, *My people have gone astray from my precepts, and have not kept mine ordinances, which I gave unto their fathers;*
>
> *And they have not observed mine anointing, and the burial, or baptism wherewith I commanded them;*
>
> *But have turned from the commandment, and taken unto themselves the washing of children, and the blood of sprinkling;*
>
> *And have said that the blood of the righteous Abel was shed for sins; and have not known wherein they are accountable before me.* (JST Genesis 17:3–7)

For Abraham, the head of this new dispensation, circumcision was implemented to reintroduce the teachings, ordinances, and covenants of the Lord. This revelation reestablished correct worship, which manifested itself in the form of circumcision at eight days, a reminder to them to continue taking upon them *all* the other ordinances of the gospel of the dispensation of Abraham, including baptism at eight years of age. This is highlighted in the revelations given to the Prophet Joseph Smith:

> And I will establish *a covenant of circumcision with thee, and it shall be* my covenant between me and thee, and thy seed after thee, in their generations; *that thou mayest know forever that children are not accountable before me until they are eight years old.*
>
> *And thou shalt observe to keep* ***all my covenants*** *wherein I covenanted with thy fathers; and thou shalt keep the commandments which I have given thee with mine own mouth, and I will be a God unto thee and thy seed after thee* (JST Genesis 17:11–12; emphasis added).

Circumcision was thus a sacred form of worship and reflected the principle of other ancient Near Eastern contracts, which were accompanied by the cutting of a covenant and binding unto death.[6] This worship

6. The Hebrew reads "cut a covenant" (כרת ברית). The covenantal process included two parties or individuals coming together to form a contract and consisted of declared stipulations, responsibilities, blessings, and curses, as well as the killing of a sacrificial animal, representing that one would keep the contract unto death, or one's life would be as the animal whose blood was shed. The covenant

helps to paint a picture of the religiosity and covenant-keeping nature of this family, and Ishmael, when he was thirteen years old, had also been circumcised as part of this covenant (Genesis 17:25). We do not have record as to whether or not he was also baptized as prescribed in the token of circumcision; however, in Genesis 17 when Abraham is told that Sarah would bear Isaac and that the covenant would be established through *him* and *his seed* (verse 19) and not Ishmael's, we get a foreshadowing that something is going to happen with Ishmael.[7] When the Lord

---

constituted obedience at all costs; even death was preferred to breaking it. This cutting of a covenant is reflected in Genesis 15:18, where the Lord cuts a covenant with Abraham and promises him the land, implying a contract of obligation on Abraham's part to receive the promised blessing. In similar fashion, the cutting of the foreskin in circumcision "assumes the structure of a treaty covenant, with mutual rights and obligations rather than a grant covenant," and it became a token for Abraham and his family that they would keep the Lord's covenant. Barry L. Bandstra, *Reading the Old Testament: An Introduction to the Hebrew Bible*, 2nd ed. (Belmont, WA: Wadsworth, 1999), 99–101. "Performed on infants, it is more a ritual scarring than something done for health reasons. The fact that blood is shed also signifies that this is a sacrificial *ritual. . . . Circumcision can be seen as one of many cases where God transforms a common practice to a new (though not necessarily unrelated) purpose in revealing himself and relating to his people." Walton, Matthews, and Chavalas, *IVP Bible*, 49–50.

7. Mark E. Petersen, *Abraham: Friend of God* (Salt Lake City: Deseret Book, 1979), 117, seems to imply that Ishmael was not baptized and certainly highlights that Ishmael's not receiving the covenant blessings had something to do with his attitude and behavior: "They would not have been refused baptism into the kingdom in those days any more than now, if they had but obeyed. They both were of Abraham's house, one a wife, one a son. So it was attitude, revealed in their obedience or disobedience that actually drew the line between Isaac and Ishmael. God had no prejudice against Ishmael. The scripture says that he loved the lad (Gen. 21:20). He also had due regard for the boy's mother." The episodes that follow are thus not about prejudice; they appear to be about choice. The covenants made in the course of circumcision seemed to have been neglected, the result of which may be foreshadowed in these events. In relation to the circumcision given to Abraham and his descendants, "his responsibilities are also clear from the collocation using 'keep' (*šmr*) with 'covenant' (*bĕrît*) in v. 9, and again in v. 10 to urge faithfulness (cf. Exod 19:5) . . . . Accordingly, circumcision is now instituted as the sign of the covenant for all Abraham's descendants, whether house-born or purchased slaves (vv. 12–13). . . . Indeed,

tells Abraham that Sarah will be the mother of the covenant, Abraham declares his concern and hopeful aspirations for Ishmael: "And Abraham said unto God, O that Ishmael might live before thee!" (verse 18). The Lord acknowledged Abraham's concerns and displayed his omniscience and foreknowledge that the covenant would be perpetuated through Isaac but also said that Ishmael would be blessed (verses 20–21). At this point in the story, we do not know why it will be such, but God does reassure Abraham that because of Ishmael, he has heard Abraham ("hearing" being a play on the meaning of Ishmael's name—"God shall hear/hears") and will bless him with posterity for Abraham's sake, as well as bless the entire family according to the covenant.[8]

After these divine announcements (Genesis 17:22), an event took place years later that caused Sarah to request Ishmael's sending away. This occurred when something happened when Isaac was a young boy and the family had gathered together at a feast: "And the child grew, and was weaned: and Abraham made a great feast the same day that Isaac was weaned. And Sarah saw the son of Hagar the Egyptian, which she had born unto Abraham, mocking. Wherefore she said unto Abraham, Cast out this bondwoman and her son: for the son of this bondwoman shall not be heir with my son, even with Isaac" (Genesis 21:8–10).

Although it is unclear how old Isaac is at his weaning, the event appears to be significant in that it is demarcated by a feast.[9] It is within this

---

'every male' (v. 10) must be circumcised or he has forfeited his membership in Israel's covenant community by neglect (v. 14). God's covenant 'in your flesh' (v. 13) is both the sign of the covenant and the covenant itself." Bill T. Arnold, *Genesis* (Cambridge: Cambridge University Press, 2009), 171. In relation to Ishmael, "Although tragic in the familial and the personal conflict surrounding Ishmael's abandonment, the text is not disparaging of him or his descendants, rather there is only the promise of a bright future as a descendant of Abraham (vv. 13, 18)." Arnold, *Genesis*, 195–96.

8. This does not imply that descendants of Ishmael could not embrace the covenant made with Abraham. Abraham himself did not receive blessings from his father and had to go to Melchizedek to get them. Those opportunities may have been extended to Ishmael's posterity if they so desired.

9. Estimates on weaning range from three years in Assyria and Second Temple Judaism to two to five years in rabbinic literature. Nahum M. Sarna, *The JPS Torah Commentary: Genesis* (Philadelphia: Jewish Publication Society, 1989), 46.

setting, when Ishmael is at least a teenager, that he comes "mocking." What exactly is meant by "mocking" is unclear; however, the biblical account seems to carry negative connotations, and the "mocking" appears to pose some sort of a threat to the family and their beliefs.[10] As a result of this, the Bible portrays Sarah as being genuinely concerned over the incident, and

---

Weaning is also mentioned in Egyptian literature as lasting three years. Miriam Lichtheim, *Ancient Egyptian Literature*, vol 2: *The Old and Middle Kingdoms* (Los Angeles: University of California Press, 1975), 141. Some estimates as to Ishmael's age at the time of the incident range from fifteen to seventeen. The text seems to imply that some time had elapsed between Isaac's circumcision (Genesis 21:4) and when "the child grew, and was weaned" (Genesis 21:8).

10. E. A. Speiser believed the traditional interpretation of "mocking" here requires a (*b*) preposition, which is lacking in the text. E. A. Speiser, *The Anchor Bible: Genesis* (New York: Doubleday, 1964), 155. Joseph Agar Beet explains the episode of mocking with an interpretation based on New Testament passages, "And this idea was taken up by Jewish tradition. This ridicule from Ishmael [that] Paul describes, in order to place the Christians of his day in line with Isaac, by the word persecuted, which recalls the many persecutions aroused against Christians by Jews: cp. 1 Thessalonians 2:14; Acts 13:50; 14:5, 19." Joseph Agar Beet, *A Commentary on St. Paul's Epistle to the Galatians* (London: Hodder and Stoughton, 1885), 137. Galatians 4:29 calls the incident persecuting, and Paul uses these events between Ishmael and Isaac as an "allegory" (Galatians 4:24; ἀλληγορέω [*allēgoreō*]) to highlight the differences between the bondage of the flesh and the liberating freedom of the gospel of Christ. Paul then invites his listeners to remain "born after the Spirit" (4:29) and "the children of the promise" (4:28) by enduring persecutions (mocking), as Isaac did of Ishmael. The piel (intensive) form of צחק used here in Genesis for "mocking" occurs elsewhere with negative overtones of mockery (Genesis 19:21; Exodus 32:6; Judges 16:25). Gordon J. Wenham, *Word Biblical Commentary*, vol. 2: *Genesis 16–50* (Nashville: Thomas Nelson, 1987), 82. Midrash Rabbah LIII 10 states that God was present on the occasion of weaning, and Midrash Rabbah LIII 11 accuses Ishmael of anything from sexual misconduct to idolatry. H. Freedman, trans., *Rabbah: Genesis* (New York: Soncino Press, 1983), 468. Islamic tradition views things in a different light. "Al-Tha'labi (d. 1036 CE) interprets the events of Genesis 21 on the authority of several sources, where Ishmael and Isaac compete in the presence of Abraham[,] and Ishmael wins. Abraham then suggests that Ishmael should be the primary inheritor. Sarah is furious at this turn of events, and when she sees the two boys fighting 'with one another as young boys tend to do,' . . . 'Sarah got angry with Hagar and said, "You will not live with me in the same place!" She commanded Abraham to dismiss Hagar. God then gave Abraham a revelation that he bring Hagar and her son to Mecca.' Firestone,

this spills over into the relationship between Hagar and Ishmael, affecting the covenantal status of the family.

As a prelude to these events, Hagar had been bound to the family to raise up seed and perpetuate the covenant given to Abraham and Sarah. The marriage union with Hagar was a sacred one with covenantal responsibilities, one which would affect the children in the family.[11]

> Hagar enjoyed many of the same aspects of the Abrahamic covenant that Sarah and Abraham did. Although the Lord in Genesis 17 states that he would establish his covenant with Isaac (v. 21), Hagar and her descendants occupy a position that denotes some sort of covenantal relationship with the Lord as well. Like Abraham and Sarah, Hagar obeyed the commandments of the Lord, was deemed righteous by Him, and shared in the same blessings of the Abrahamic covenant: a great posterity, a land of inheritance for her children, and the companionship of the Lord.[12]

The concept of marriage and covenant was no light matter to this family, and Hagar's son Ishmael is now threateningly portrayed as "mocking" it. We don't know all of the details of the present circumstance, nor what Hagar was thinking through all of this, but there is a history leading up to this event between Ishmael and Isaac that had also occurred between Hagar and Sarah, possibly reflecting the tension felt here in the narrative. Years earlier, upon entering into this sacred marriage at the consent

---

p. 67." David J. Zucker, "What Sarah Saw: Envisioning Genesis 21:9–10," *Jewish Bible Quarterly* 36, no. 1 (2008): 62.

11. "In ancient sources, it appears that the covenant referred to in Genesis and the [B]ook of Abraham was made between Abraham, Sarah, and the Lord, a covenant among three people. Likewise, Hagar becomes part of this covenant to some extent, although from the text that we have, her involvement is harder to ascertain." Janet C. Hovorka, "Sarah and Hagar: Ancient Women of the Abrahamic Covenant," in *Astronomy, Papyrus, and Covenant*, ed. John Gee and Brian M. Hauglid (Provo, UT: Brigham Young University, 2006), 2. See Doctrine and Covenants 132:65 for some clarification on the matter, as well as for the covenantal nature of this marriage for all parties involved and for who were following the commandments of the Lord.

12. Hovorka, "Sarah and Hagar," 10.

of Sarah, Hagar had despised the childless Sarah when Ishmael was conceived: "And he went in unto Hagar, and she conceived: and when she saw that she had conceived, her mistress was despised in her eyes. And Sarai said unto Abram, My wrong be upon thee: I have given my maid into thy bosom [see Doctrine and Covenants 132:65]; and when she saw that she had conceived, I was despised in her eyes: the Lord judge between me and thee" (Genesis 16:4–5).[13]

---

13. We witness a similar chiding between Peninnah and the childless Hannah (1 Samuel 1). Petersen, *Abraham*, 2, 115, saw a connection between the attitudes of Hagar and Ishmael: "Hagar had hated Sarah for fourteen years. Would not this motherly antagonism have rubbed off on Ishmael, leading to his mocking Isaac? . . . Her attitude was reflected in the behavior of Ishmael, who mocked Isaac." The text does not explicitly state that this was the case for so many years, just that at some point Hagar did feel this way (and thus this offers a possible explanation for a tension to have existed for so long). "The Hebrew implies that Hagar now considered Sarai less significant or no longer needed ('her mistress was lowered in her esteem')." Arnold, *Genesis*, 163. Janzen translated Hagar's behavior toward Sarah as "belittling" (*qll* also meaning "to curse" or "to look upon with contempt"), and he discusses the play on the word עָנָה that is used throughout the episode to describe both Sarah's and Hagar's behavior (the word carries a semantic domain that includes "dealing harshly," "submitting," and "affliction") J. Gerald Janzen, *Genesis 12–50: Abraham and All the Families of the Earth* (Grand Rapids, MI: Eerdmans, 1993), 42–45. Subsequently, the verb עָנָה also carries the meaning of "to answer" and may foreshadow the need for Hagar to be accountable for the behavior that has resulted in "belittling, dealing harshly, affliction" and, now, the need to "submit" to Sarah. When Hagar fled, she was met by a messenger of God and told to return (a possible reference to repent, a play on the verb שׁוּב, meaning "to return back") to her mistress and restore things in the form of submitting to her (שׁוּבִי אֶל־גְּבִרְתֵּךְ וְהִתְעַנִּי תַּחַת יָדֶיהָ)—a recognition that Sarah was in charge and that it was she who had been wronged. Concerning Hagar, "Yahweh finds her alone in the desert, tenderly addresses her with rhetorical questions, leading her along and directing her to return to the safety of her mistress's supervision, and even extends the ancestral promises to her and her son. This surprising turn of events confirms how deeply Yahweh is committed to the covenant promises to Abram's offspring." Arnold, *Genesis*, 164. Again, we do not have all the pieces of the puzzle provided for us in the text, and we struggle to make sense of these difficult episodes in the Bible. Nothing in this paper is intended to be ethnically insensitive; I am attempting to interpret these events in light of the biblical text's portrayal of the

This family had endured difficult times to maintain and claim the blessings of the covenant, particularly the described emotional trauma aroused by Hagar's actions toward the childless Sarah, and now Ishmael's "mocking" was more than Sarah could bear.[14] Yet the removal of Hagar and Ishmael would not have been easy for Sarah, as she had lived with and probably helped raise Ishmael through his youth and teenage years. In fact, Josephus stated that Sarah "loved Ishmael, who was born of her own handmaid Hagar, with an affection not inferior to that of her own Son."[15] Genesis 16:2 states that Hagar made it possible for Sarah to "obtain children by her," and she possibly assisted and had maternal responsibilities in raising him. Ishmael and Hagar were family, and this was a gut-wrenching, emotional experience. But it was a decision deemed necessary for the well-being of the covenant.

---

occurrences while acknowledging that various religions and streams provide different interpretations.

14. Ishmael's behavior may not constitute a onetime event but, in the eyes of Sarah, a cumulative demonstration of spiritually troubling behavior. Petersen, *Abraham*, 115, stated and then asked, "Abraham knew that all faithful people will be received by the Lord. Had he suffered from some previous difficulties with Ishmael's boyish attitude?" The text is not explicit, and we must try to piece things together. Petersen, *Abraham*, 114–15, continued, "Here the Lord makes a clear distinction between Isaac and Ishmael. Was he unjust? What was the nature of the covenant, and why did it distinguish between the two boys? What was the problem with Ishmael? We must acknowledge that the original choice of a covenant people related to [the] premortal existence. But Ishmael could have had the blessings of the gospel here on earth had he possessed a different attitude. . . . If he had caressed the child instead of mocking him, would not Abraham, the friend of God, have seen to his salvation?" Again, my intent is not to villainize Ishmael, and some writings have, but something has happened here that portrays Ishmael's behavior in a negative light (whatever it was). Ishmael will later show disregard for the covenant, but perhaps the focus of the sending away of Ishmael is more a concentration of the dissolution of the sacred marriage with Hagar than it is on a portrayal of Ishmael as an "evil" person. Again, something (a "mocking") appears to have happened. We are just unclear on what it was, but it was disconcerting enough for Sarah to suggest (and be sanctioned by the Lord and Abraham) the sending away of Hagar and Ishmael.
15. Flavius Josephus, *Jewish Antiquities*, 1.12.3, in *The Works of Josephus*, trans. William Whiston (Peabody, MA: Hendrickson, 1996), 42.

As for the expulsion itself, biblical scholar Nahum Sarna believed that Sarah was asking Abraham to grant Hagar, a slave, her freedom, thus forfeiting her rights in the marriage contract.[16] Gordon Wenham also wrote of the incident, "'Send her off' (piel שלח) is a softer term than 'drive out' (cf. 18:16; 19:22; 3:23). It is used of divorce (e.g., Deut 22:19; 24:1, 3) and the release of slaves with a generous provision (Exod 11:1–2; Deut 15:13). It may be that Abraham blessed his wife and sons before they left or gave them other gifts."[17]

These events may have led to a separation of Ishmael and Hagar from the plural or eternal marriage covenant originally entered into, but Abraham continued to love Ishmael, and Ishmael continued to be blessed in numerous ways under the covenant given to his father.[18] Abraham consented to sending Ishmael away because the Lord promised him that he would preserve, protect, and bless Ishmael and his posterity (Genesis 21:12–13) according to the Lord's omniscience within the framework of an eternal perspective. The episode is thus heartfelt, not heartless, and reflects obedience rather than malice.

---

16. Sarna, *Genesis*, 147. See also Walton, Matthews, and Chavalas, *IVP Bible*, 52.
17. Wenham, *Genesis 16–50*, 84. Hovorka also discusses the variant usages of terms describing Hagar's relationship to Abraham and Sarah throughout this incident and highlights that a more demeaning term is used for Hagar to separate her from Abraham at this juncture (i.e., her status had changed from "wife" to "maidservant"). Hovorka, "Sarah and Hagar," 13. See also Bruce K. Waltke and Cathi J. Fredricks, *Genesis: A Commentary* (Grand Rapids, MI: Zondervan, 2001), 294, who differentiate the terms applied to Hagar: "The former identifies Hagar as married to Abraham; the latter, as a possession and laborer for Sarah."
18. "The Lord covenanted through Isaac and not through Ishmael; but in fairness to him, Ishmael was promised nations, princes, and kings, even as was Isaac. God is fair to all [people]. He is just and no respecter of persons. To each he gives what is best suited for [the person], and he can judge this because he was well acquainted with us in our pre-earth life. . . . Although the Lord made covenants with Isaac, any child of Ishmael may have as many blessings in the Church or in eternity as any child of Isaac—if [the person] will but serve Almighty God and keep his commandments. Also, any child of Isaac, regardless of heritage, may lose those blessings if [the child] fails to keep the commandments of the Lord." Petersen, *Abraham*, 108–9.

This promised divine protection was revealed almost immediately after Hagar and Ishmael departed, when, after having finished the water provided them, Hagar had a personal encounter with God:

> And God heard the voice of the lad; and the angel of God called to Hagar out of heaven, and said unto her, What aileth thee, Hagar? fear not; for God hath heard the voice of the lad where he is.
>
> Arise, lift up the lad, and hold him in thine hand; for I will make him a great nation.
>
> And God opened her eyes, and she saw a well of water; and she went, and filled the bottle with water, and gave the lad drink.[19]
>
> And God was with the lad; and he grew, and dwelt in the wilderness, and became an archer.
>
> And he dwelt in the wilderness of Paran: and his mother took him a wife out of the land of Egypt. (Genesis 21:17–21)[20]

---

19. In the Islamic literature called "Prophetic Tales," the Zam-zam spring located in Mecca next to the Ka'bah is where God brought Ishmael after his and Hagar's expulsion and thus has become a holy site. Reuven Firestone, *An Introduction to Islam for Jews* (Philadelphia: The Jewish Publication Society, 2008), 20.

20. Of the sacred encounters experienced by Hagar, and the protection she received at the hand of God due to the promises made to Abraham, as well as the love the Lord had toward her, we read, "Teubal writes that these theophanies were singular in the scriptures. She states, 'Notwithstanding, the Hagar episodes record the only time in the bible that God is given a name, and the name is given by a woman. Hagar's god is a god who knows her, who addresses her in familiar terms: "What troubles you Hagar?" he asks with the tender concern of a loving relative.' McKenna also notes that the visions were affirmations of an impartial God. He is seen 'taking note of her, just a maid, a pregnant slave, and an Egyptian, not even a Jew! God cares about everyone.' In sum, Hagar, like Abraham and Sarah, enjoyed the threefold blessings of the Covenant—great posterity, a land for her descendants' inheritance, and the companionship of the Lord." Hovorka, "Sarah and Hagar," 12–13. As the Lord had been with Hagar before being sent off (as this quote describes), he was also going to protect her and Ishmael during their time of need after they were sent away from the family. Though the covenant would not go directly through Ishmael, he was still an important part of the covenant. Some may suggest that as a result of the close contact, God continues to maintain his efforts to bless Hagar and Ishmael, which constitutes a reason to assume that Ishmael never did anything to merit being driven away and that he continued to be a covenant keeper. However,

The text does not state that Ishmael was a bad person, nor that there was a long-lasting tension between Ishmael and Isaac in subsequent years. In fact, in the end, both Isaac and Ishmael would work together to bury their father and console the family at Abraham's passing (Genesis 25:9). The Lord's omniscience in the matter seems to have led to the greatest good for all parties involved, and we are not required to force conclusions that necessitate us to view these events in a negative light. The text itself suggests a loving God seeking to bless the entire family throughout the episode and to make the most of the situation at hand.[21]

JACOB: ENIGMATIC STORIES OF SUCCESSION AND BLESSINGS

Through the years, Isaac would prove valiant, and, in similitude of the Son of God, he would willingly allow himself to be offered as a sacrifice at the hand of his father (Genesis 22), marry (Genesis 24), and eventually be blessed with posterity, fulfilling the wish of the family (24:60). His son Jacob would become the presiding leader in the family; however, the portrayal of this succession story comes with no lack of perceived controversy. The story in Genesis 27 of Jacob dressing up as a hairy man to imitate his brother Esau, deceiving the aged Isaac, and tricking him into bestowing blessings upon Jacob instead of upon Esau, the firstborn son, has been one of the most diversely interpreted episodes in all of the Bible.

At the heart of this narrative is the unexpected, seemingly devious behavior of Jacob, Rebekah, and even God himself. Many people grapple with the narrative by assuming the reading reflects a disconnected

---

this view appears to ignore everything that the text seems to present to us. The biblical passages suggest a reason for all these events transpiring.

21. Russell M. Nelson, "Blessed Are the Peacemakers," *Ensign*, November 2002, 39, declared, "Father Abraham was uniquely called a 'Friend of God.' Peace was one of Abraham's highest priorities. He sought to be a 'prince of peace.' His influence could loom large in our present pursuit of peace. His sons, Ishmael and Isaac, though born of different mothers, overcame their differences when engaged in a common cause. After their father died, they worked together to bury the mortal remains of their exalted father. Their descendants could well follow that pattern." We could all follow that pattern.

historical context between ancient participants and the contemporary audience, resulting in a disconnection that ancient hearers may not have experienced but that causes difficulties for us to understand today. The result may lead us to take matters into our own hands to place meaning that is not there or to suppose that bad should not be a part of the Bible. For instance, as one scholar suggested in his study:

> Some of these methods may appear unpalatable to contemporary readers, yet the conclusions of this study raise an important issue: perhaps what Eric Seibert has called "disturbing divine behavior" is only disturbing to our contemporary sensibilities and has very little to do with the actual portrait of God gleaned from the Hebrew Bible. I have sought in this book to advance a descriptive theology of the book of Genesis, outlining not what I wish the text said—in conformity with my own ethical sensibilities and *more*—but, rather, what the text communicates and how it does so.[22]

While it is true that we should not wish for the text to say what we want it to say—and ignore it when it doesn't—it is also possible that the text can be misinterpreted, leading to methodological problems where we base assumptions and interpretations on faulty premises.

> We should freely admit that biblical portrayals of God have the capacity to both reveal and distort God's character, recognizing that while some portrayals help us see God clearly, others do not. Old Testament portrayals that do not reflect the true character of God should be identified as such and handled carefully. When God is portrayed behaving in ways that do not correspond to the character of God Jesus reveals, we should not shrink from saying that these portrayals fundamentally misrepresent God's true nature. We must do this if we hope to use the Bible to think rightly about God. . . . Some may feel compelled to defend God's behavior simply because it is in the Bible. But doing so is dangerous. It not only inhibits our ability to think rightly about God but actively supports and perpetuates false views of God. If we wish to deal responsibly with

22. Anderson, *Jacob and the Divine Trickster*, 175.

> disturbing divine behavior in the Old Testament, we must refuse to defend problematic portrayals that do not correspond to the true character of God.[23]

John Anderson writes of the challenges of reading such difficult stories:

> Reading the Bible should not be an easy enterprise. Readers of the Bible are invited to participate in the conversation occurring across time within its pages. This conversation should be unsettling at points. It should raise questions. It should prompt self-reflection. It should press us to think "outside the box," to reevaluate who we are and who God is. Eryl Davies offers a worthwhile caution on this point: "Besides, if we read the Hebrew Bible simply in order to take issue with its more unsavoury aspects, while appealing to its more positive, life-enhancing statements to confirm and corroborate values we already hold anyway, why bother reading the Bible at all?"[24]

As one can see, the scholarship is not settled as to how the text should be read, and, instead of avoiding the narrative, any confusion as to the exact meaning suggests that we should be engaging with it and attempting to find meaning. The recognition that God is a God of order rather than of mischievous confusion suggests that there is more to this narrative than costuming. Indeed, the narrative is not isolated but reflects a pattern

---

23. Eric A. Seibert, *Disturbing Divine Behavior: Troubling Old Testament Images of God* (Minneapolis: Fortress Press, 2009), 225, 227–28. Admittedly, this approach requires a subjective view to interpretation as we bring preconceived notions to the text as to how we believe God should or should not act. The point here is that most of those notions in Genesis 27 tend to cast a negative light on God or Jacob, while statistically larger portions of the scriptures do not. That is not to say that people can't make mistakes and that Jacob was perfect, though the text says he was (Genesis 25:27), and God certainly is. I just think we need to be cautious in how and where we assign blame. Ascertaining what is, what might be, or what shouldn't or couldn't be, when it exists in the text, is all part of the juggling act performed by biblical exegetes in attempting to explain difficult passages in the Bible.
24. Anderson, *Jacob and the Divine Trickster*, 175, in Eryl W. Davies, *The Immoral Bible: Approaches to Biblical Ethics* (London: T. & T. Clark, 2010), 132.

of divine intention and personal agency that began with the birth of the twins and is reflected in their conflict over the mess of pottage. [25]

REBEKAH'S REVELATION

As an introduction to the events portrayed in Genesis 27, before the birth of Jacob and Esau, their mother Rebekah received personal revelation that she would give birth to twins; there was no ultrasound and no other way of finding this out save it be through divine communication. She learned something at variance from the norm in birthright inheritances: the older would serve the younger:[26]

> And Isaac entreated the Lord for his wife, because she was barren: and the Lord was entreated of him, and Rebekah his wife conceived.
>
> And the children struggled together within her; and she said, If it be so, why am I thus? And she went to inquire of the Lord.
>
> And the Lord said unto her, Two nations are in thy womb, and two manner of people shall be separated from thy bowels; and the one people shall be stronger than the other people; and the elder shall serve the younger.
>
> And when her days to be delivered were fulfilled, behold, there were twins in her womb. (Genesis 25:21–24)

---

25. It may be tempting to read the Jacob stories with a grin and think, "This is great irony and builds the story; Jacob goes from trickster to the tricked." Such a view must also seemingly admit, in between laughs, that God is a trickster too. I, personally, am not convinced that these episodes are included in the Bible for us to get a good laugh or to revel in the irony as patriarchs and God are painted as incompetent and inconsistent and as swindlers, cheats, and tricksters. There must be some plausible purpose for their inclusion in the text beyond this! If they were included for this purpose, would they not already be theologically tainted?

26. "The privilege of the firstborn in inheritance is referred to as primogeniture. Primogeniture was not universally practiced in the ancient world, but it was a sort of default position. Sufficient numbers of examples exist of either a younger son having the privileges or oxf the estate being equally divided to demonstrate that a variety of arrangements was possible." Walton, *Genesis*, loc. 3928 of 10396, Kindle.

As is clear, Rebekah receives a revelation that something unique will happen with her two twin sons and that the younger was meant to have authority over the elder. Subsequently, many may see this revelation given to Rebekah as the source of the justification for encouraging Jacob to later deceive or trick his father into giving him the blessing apparently intended for Esau. Yet it is not altogether clear that the text refers only to the older serving the younger. The LXX portrays an ambiguous syntactic construction and could read as either (1) the greater/older shall serve the lesser/younger, or (2) the lesser shall serve the greater.[27] The birthright would ultimately be received based upon worthiness, not upon age.[28] While this does not explain Rebekah's place in the narrative per se, it does begin to suggest that the brothers' agency will play a major role in their respective experiences with the covenant.

JACOB AND ESAU: THE POTTAGE AND THE BIRTHRIGHT

At the outset of the story, we learn an important detail that is imperative in evaluating this birthright narrative: "And the boys grew: and Esau was a cunning hunter, a man of the field; and Jacob was a plain man, dwelling in tents" (Genesis 25:27). At times in the scriptures, the "hunter" is portrayed

---

27. See Joseph A. Fitzmyer, *The Anchor Bible: Romans* (New York: Doubleday, 1993), 563.

28. See Genesis 49, where Reuben loses his birthright through transgression, and it is passed on to Joseph—the first son of the next wife. When discussing the events surrounding Jacob and Esau, there is something we should remember: "God did not say that Jacob should be saved in the kingdom of God, and Esau be doomed to eternal hell, without any regard to their deeds; but He simply said that two distinct nations, widely differing, should spring from them, and one should be stronger than the other, and the elder should serve the younger." Parley P. Pratt, in *Journal of Discourses* (London: Latter-day Saints' Book Depot, 1854–86), 1:258. The text does not say that Esau becomes perdition (though he does become the personification of indifference to sacred things), nor does it say that all his ancestors are to be equated as such. There would be subsequent struggles between Israel and Edom, but we should be careful with applying blanket stereotypes.

in a negative light and here may foreshadow events and the indifferent character of Esau.[29] Furthermore, in the KJV, Jacob is described as "a plain man." The Hebrew words *'š tm* (אש תם) connote a "whole, complete, or perfect man." This designation is attached to very few people in the Bible (for example, to Noah and Job). This puts Jacob in outstanding company, and his impeccable character should be kept in mind as we work through these stories, particularly since the Hebrew words imply that there is no deceptive intent on the part of Jacob.[30]

After describing the two sons, the narrative mentions their differing relationships with their parents, after which the incident of the pottage occurs.

> And Isaac loved Esau, because he did eat of his venison: but Rebekah loved Jacob.[31]

---

29. See Waltke and Fredricks, *Genesis: A Commentary*, 362.

30. It is easy to slight this description of Jacob's character when viewing what follows. Some may see the emphasis on Jacob's character as an exaggeration, especially because of his actions that follow. However, and this is the point, perhaps we are supposed to read the story through the lens of a righteous Jacob and not diminish him by interpreting the story from back to front with the bias his subsequent behavior seems to produce. The contrast between the boys in the introduction of their lives in the text seems deliberate and intentional, and, rather than judge Jacob based on the perceived scandalous behavior that ensues, perhaps his description as a "perfect," or "complete" individual should drive our perception of him in what follows (and not vice versa). Susan Niditch writes of the polarized interpretations of these events: "Not all scholars would recognize the scene in [Genesis] 25:29–34 as a trickster episode. The interpretation depends on the understanding of verses 31–33. Does this scene portray an honest deal—pottage for the birthright—or extortion by a clever con artist, Jacob?" Susan Niditch, *Underdogs and Tricksters* (San Francisco: Harper & Row, 1987), 101. I take the stance of an honest Jacob.

31. This line seems a bit awkward in describing the parents and marks a transition from an old to a new paragraph. The text is about the birth of the boys, the pottage incident is about Jacob and Esau, and the parents don't really factor into what takes place—though this description of them establishes a polarity between Isaac and Rebekah that we will again encounter in Genesis 27. Undoubtedly, both parents loved their boys (we just see Isaac's motivation for the love of Esau revolving around a secular object that Esau had to offer him, while the unstated reason behind Rebekah's love of Jacob seems to be implied in

> And Jacob sod pottage: and Esau came from the field, and he was faint:
>
> And Esau said to Jacob, Feed me, I pray thee, with that same red pottage; for I am faint: therefore was his name called Edom.
>
> And Jacob said, Sell me this day thy birthright.
>
> And Esau said, Behold, I am at the point to die: and what profit shall this birthright do to me?
>
> And Jacob said, Swear to me this day; and he sware unto him: and he sold his birthright unto Jacob.
>
> Then Jacob gave Esau bread and pottage of lentiles; and he did eat and drink, and rose up, and went his way: thus Esau despised his birthright. (Genesis 25:28–34)

Although it may seem from our contemporary reading that Jacob unfairly wrests the birthright from Esau in a moment of extremity, the narrative ends placing the wrongdoing squarely on Esau: "thus Esau despised his birthright."[32] The word *despise* is used in the scriptures and other Greek texts to describe slighting, abhorring, or holding sacred things cheap, and its presence here suggests that Esau, by his own volition or agency, treats lightly or doesn't want the sacred covenant responsibilities

---

the spiritual manifestations she received while she was pregnant). The description of "venison" may thus highlight the worldly, or secular, nature behind what ensues with Esau and what he has been willing to offer his father, and the description may draw us to see Jacob in a "spiritual" light in seeking more "spiritual" things. Furthermore, Esau was just described as a hunter, and if anything, this line serves to tell us that Esau was perfectly capable of obtaining his own food for himself, as well as for others.

32. Gordon J. Wenham, *Story as Torah: Reading Old Testament Narratives Ethically* (Grand Rapids, MI: Baker, 2000), 94, 99, writes, "Esau's 'Let me eat some of that red pottage' (25:30) could be taken as abruptly uncouth, but his use of *na'* usually translated 'please' and a high-flown term for 'eat' could suggest that he is not quite at death's door, and that he therefore had no excuse for selling his birthright. . . . As we already noted, it is not all that obvious that Esau was at death's door, rather hunger made him exaggerate. Yet he says 'Of what use is the birthright to me?' So for some lentil stew Esau gave away his birthright, a move clearly disapproved of by the author who simply observes: 'Thus Esau despised his birthright' (25:32–34). These two stories suggest that though food is to be enjoyed, appetite must not overrule principle."

that are supposed to be his.[33] Such a reading is strengthened by the wordplay between "red pottage" and "Esau/Edom." The "red pottage" comes from the root אדם (*'dm*):

> The narrative depends upon the contrast of *pottage* and *birthright.* "Pottage" here is an unusual word. Its only biblical use is in this story. It is part of a dexterous play on words. "Pottage" translates the Hebrew *'ādôm*. It is modified by the adjective "red," also *'ādôm*. The latter is the same word used to describe the redness of Esau at birth (v. 27). Both words, "pottage" and "red," consist in the Hebrew letters 'dm, the same letters in "Edom," the same people embodied in Esau (cf. Gen. 36:16–43). Thus the word play of "Edom/red/pottage" cleverly asserts that Esau is a man (and the Edomites a people) peculiarly destined for pottage and not more.[34]

This wordplay continues on another level by virtue of the fact that the same letters אדם (*'dm*) can mean "people," or "land," as used later by Isaiah

---

33. The way the word *despised* is used in the Hebrew text and in the Septuagint includes the following instances that have been related to slighting sacred things: Genesis 25:34 (despised birthright), Numbers 15:31 (in tabernacle, despised the word of the Lord), 2 Samuel 12:9 (despised commandment), Malachi 1:6 (priests despise sacrifices), 2 Chronicles 36:16 (despised God and prophets), Ezekiel 16:59; 17:16, 18, 19 (despise oath and covenant), Ezekiel 22:8 (despise holy things), 1 Samuel 2:30 (despise the Lord), Proverbs 19:16 (despise commandments). The word is defined in Francis Brown, S. R. Driver, and Charles Briggs, *The Brown-Driver-Briggs Hebrew and English Lexicon* (Peabody, MA: Hendrickson Publishers, 1999), 102, as follows: בזה (*bā·zā*[*h*]): (compare بَزَا [*bazā*], *raise the head loftily and disdainfully*)—; *despise, regard with contempt*. In other Greek texts the word *despised* (φαυλίζω, f. Att. ιῶ, [φαῦλος]) means "*to hold cheap, to depreciate, disparage*."
34. Walter Brueggemann, *Genesis*, Interpretation: A Commentary for Teaching and Preaching (Louisville, KY: Westminster John Knox Press, 2010), 218, הלעיטני. Esau's plea to "let me taste/eat" is also a *hapax legomenon* (a word used only once in the Bible). See Joseph H. Prouser, "Seeing Red: On Translating Esau's Request for Soup," *Conservative Judaism* 56, no. 2 (2004): 14. The language of these verses is difficult and highly ambiguous, contributing to the difficulty in interpreting the story.

and other prophets to refer to the "world."[35] Esau and his desire for "red pottage" versus Jacob and his concern for the birthright may represent two contrasting values: concern for worldly values and concern for the eternal covenant and all that it represented (a representation of the "lesser shall serve the greater").[36] Regardless, what is clear is that Jacob did not

---

35. Edom/Idumea is later associated with the things of the world (Doctrine and Covenants 1:36). Writing about Isaiah 34:6, Victor L. Ludlow states, "The term 'Edom' has a double meaning here. In addition to denoting the country located east of the Dead Sea, it means 'the world' and especially 'the wicked world.' This second definition can be supported by modern revelation (D&C 1:36) and a linguistic evaluation of the term. The Hebrew word Edom also means 'red' or 'earth' and is the root for the words *Adam* and *man*. Therefore, it often connotes human or worldly qualities. As one scholar defines it, 'Edom is always figurative of the natural state of man in his antagonism against God' (Vine, *Isaiah*, p. 84; see also Mosiah 3:19)." Victor L. Ludlow, *Isaiah: Prophet, Seer, and Poet* (Salt Lake City: Deseret Book, 1982), 308–9. The appellation of Edom as attached to Esau after this incident seems to be drawing us into the worldly nature of the story (in contrast to the spiritual pursuits of Jacob). It should also be noted that Esau does not receive the name "Edom" (reflecting red) at the time of his birth, where he is described as red, but only receives it after this incident with "red pottage." The designation is thus not about a physical characteristic he possesses but a character feature ("pottage boy," or "worldly boy") that seems to label him in a secular fashion.
36. There is some room to question whether there was a literal mess of pottage involved in the story, or whether it simply represented a concept of worldliness. Without definitively answering that question, it is used proverbially in Church conference addresses. The following are illustrative: "Oh, my brethren, don't sell your birthright—your Priesthood birthright—for a mess of pottage (Gen. 25:29–34)." J. Reuben Clark Jr., in Conference Report, October 1951, 169–72. Or, "Because they loved worldliness more than they loved spirituality, they sold their birthright for a mess of pottage (Gen. 25:34)." Mark E. Petersen, in Conference Report, October 1948, 133. "Be honest with yourselves. Live up to the best that is in you. Do not sell your birthright for a mess of pottage (Gen. 25:34). Be true to the faith and God will be true to you no matter what the future may hold." Mark E. Petersen, in Conference Report, October 1960, 78–83. Brueggeman, *Genesis*, 219–20, states, "In Hebrews 11:20–21, Jacob is named among those who believed in the promise. (Note that Esau is also mentioned as having a blessing.) In Heb. 12:12–17, Esau is used as an illustration of those who do not believe the promise. The primary call of the letter to the Hebrews is for disciplined obedience in the face of persecution. The urging throughout is that waiting for and believing in the sure promises of God will lead to blessings of

trick Esau, but Esau willingly gave up the birthright because he despised it.[37] One may take issue with the text and claim that Esau was cheated in this endeavor; however, as will be seen below, the text just simply does not imply such an interpretation but does in fact state that Esau was an active, indifferent participant in these events.[38]

'rest' (Heb. 4:11) and inheritance (6:11–12). Those who do not believe promises and want more immediate satisfactions will no doubt compromise the faith for the sake of easier gains: pottage. Esau becomes a type for those who do not trust the promise and [who] accommodate themselves. The issue for the listening community is how to believe the promises seriously enough to withstand alternative forms of food, which are immediately available and within control. (Cf. Mark 8:15. Perhaps the 'leaven of the Pharisees' is another form of pottage.)" Perhaps the concept is that "man shall not live by bread alone" (Deuteronomy 8:3; Matthew 4:4).

37. "While Esau did not sense nor appreciate his condition and birthright; he did not respect it as he should have done, neither did be hearken to the counsels of his father and mother. On the contrary, he went his own way with a stubborn will, and followed his own passions and inclinations and took to wife one of the daughters of the Canaanites whom the Lord had not blessed; and he therefore rendered himself unacceptable to God and to his father and mother. He gave himself to wild pursuits—to hunting, and to following the ways of the Canaanites, and displeased the Lord and his parents, and was not worthy of this right of seniority. The Lord therefore saw fit to take it from him . . . [since] none can hold these rights of the Priesthood except in connection with the powers of heaven, and cannot be exercised only on the principles of righteousness; and all who fail to exercise these rights on the principles of righteousness and in connection with the powers of heaven subject to its counsels and directions and laws, forfeit their birthright, and the right passes to another." John Taylor, in *Journal of Discourses*, 21:371. It seems that Esau really did "despise" the birthright, and that is why it passed to Jacob. "We know the story of Jacob and Esau (Gen. 25:34). The birthright didn't seem to be so important to Esau, and so the birthright came to another." John H. Taylor, in Conference Report, October 1943, 53–55. Midrash Rabbah LXIII 11 implies Esau had lost his vision of eternity, declaring, "There is neither reward nor resurrection." H. Freedman, trans., *Rabbah: Genesis*, vol. 2 (London: Soncino Press, 1983), 566.

38. "The story of Esau's rejection of his birthright is purposefully attached to the end of the narrative that introduces the motif of the older brother's serving [of] the younger. It is a narrative example that God's choice of Jacob over Esau does not run contrary to the wishes of either brother. It is made clear from the narrative that Esau 'despises' his birthright. Jacob, however, is portrayed as one who will go to great lengths to gain it. . . . Esau, though he has the right of the

BIRTHRIGHT

Although the birthright is often thought of in terms of the double portion of family holdings (see Deuteronomy 21:7), the birthright appears to have also included cultic and priesthood responsibilities, attendant to the son with the birthright being officially dedicated to God (Exodus 22:28–29). As one scholar noted, "This special sanctity attaching to the first-born son originally accorded him a privileged position in the cult, although at a later time the Levitical tribe displaced the first-born in Israel and appropriated his cultic prerogatives."[39] Regarding Esau as firstborn, Sidney Sperry suggested, "According to ancient patriarchal customs, it appears that the eldest son in the family ordinarily fell heir to most of the material possessions of his father as well as to his spiritual calling. In the present instance, Esau would have been heir to his father's estate [and] to his patriarchal priesthood, something toward which Esau did not show much interest."[40] Jacob, on the other hand, as portrayed in the text, seems to recognize the significance and necessity of the birthright.

The priesthood component could of course, not be bought, but it could be forsaken, and the text seems to solidify the willing forsaking of the spiritual obligations of the birthright by Esau and the accepting and claiming of them by Jacob.[41] In fact, in the next chapter the Lord appears

---

firstborn, does not value it over a small bowl of soup. Thus when in God's plan Esau loses his birthright and consequently his blessing, there is no injustice dealt him. The narrative has shown that he did not care about the birthright." John H. Sailhamer, *Genesis*, The Expositor's Bible Commentary (Grand Rapids, MI: Zondervan Academic, 2008), locs. 7564–72 of 10676, Kindle.

39. Nahum M. Sarna, *Understanding Genesis* (New York: McGraw-Hill, 1966), 184. See also Numbers 3:5–13; 8:5–19. A Midrash stated that the right of the first-born included the sacrificial service provided by priests. H. Freedman, *Rabbah: Genesis*, 569.

40. Sidney B. Sperry, *The Spirit of the Old Testament* (Salt Lake City: LDS Department of Education, 1940), 38. See also Wenham, *Genesis 16–50*, 178.

41. When one reads the story, there is an inclination to lean heavily toward the physical exchange of a legal document transferring the birthright from Esau to Jacob. Other ancient Near Eastern texts demonstrate that heirs were able to sell off some of their future inheritances. See Sarna, *The JPS Torah Commentary: Genesis*, 181. "The inheritance was divided into the number of sons plus one.

The eldest son then received a double share. This was a customary practice throughout the ancient Near East. The stew buys from Esau that additional share (probably not his entire inheritance). There are no examples in the known literature from the ancient Near East of such a deal being made. The closest is in the legal materials from *Nuzi, where one brother sells some already inherited property to one of his brothers." Walton, *IVP Bible*, 58. These instances entailed transfers of physical property, not priesthood authority or leadership. So the comparisons are similar but not the same. Despite bearing some resemblances to such a formal exchange, the encounter here differs significantly from such legal contracts. For example, there is no previously arranged agreement leading up to the would-be covenantal meal. In this connection, the meal is already made before Esau arrives, and he simply asks for it. Jacob subsequently does not partake of the meal with him. Furthermore, there is no "swearing" of the oath between them. The text simply states that Esau swore, not Jacob, and then forsook his birthright. These differences may indicate the incident is symbolic, but they at least seem to demonstrate that this is not a "legal" type of exchange in a sacrificial setting, which would have been necessary for such a literal transfer of the birthright (see Genesis 26:28–31 for the swearing of an oath between two parties). Others see differences in the account as well: "Our sympathy with Esau is somewhat dissipated when the Narrator describes his inner feelings. Having finished the broth, Esau does not quarrel with Jacob but goes indifferently about his business, with no apparent regard for the sacred institution of the first-born. On the other hand, it is highly significant that the text only mentions Esau's sale of the birthright but does not state that Jacob bought it. This is contrary to the usual biblical legal style as, for instance, in the case of Abraham's purchase of the Cave of Machpelah, Jacob's acquisition of a field, and David's buying the threshing floor from Araunah. The omission in the present story is another way of dissociating Jacob's eventual ascendancy from the means he adopted." Sarna, *Genesis*, 182. Perhaps the exclusion of Jacob's "purchase" is intentional, as this is about Esau giving up the blessing, not Jacob's seizing of it in a scandalous manner. It should be stated that many rabbinic and Islamic interpretations view the story as based on a legal exchange, and thus the incident is based on real events—though the lens through which we see them in the story may not be crystal clear: "Abraham passed the garments to his son Isaac and he to his eldest son Esau. . . . Having obtained the garment, Esau either buried it or sold it to Jacob along with his birthright. Numbers Rabbah relates that Jacob desired to offer sacrifice but could not because he was not the firstborn and did not have the birthright, part of which consisted of Adam's garment. It was for this reason that Jacob bought the birthright from Esau, who said, 'There is no afterlife, death ends everything, and the inheritance will do me no good,' and willingly let Jacob have the garment, along with his birthright. Immediately Jacob built an altar and offered sacrifice. Here, again, Muslim and Jewish traditions overlap.

to Jacob, offers him instruction on how to preserve his family, and reiterates the blessings offered to Abraham that would now fall upon him. The chapter ends with a lament after Esau chooses to marry a Hittite and give up the blessings of the Abrahamic covenant his father and grandfather had sacrificed so dearly to preserve: "And Esau was forty years old when he took to wife Judith the daughter of Beeri the Hittite, and Bashemath the daughter of Elon the Hittite: which were a grief of mind unto Isaac and to Rebekah" (Genesis 26:34–35).[42] No matter how hard one tries to cast blame on Jacob, the text emphasizes that this is really about Esau's behavior. When it comes to receiving the blessings of the covenant, one must be willing to remain faithful to it. Elder Dallin H. Oaks has taught,

> The contrast between the spiritual and the temporal is also illustrated by the twins Esau and Jacob and their different attitudes toward their birthright. The firstborn, Esau, "despised his birthright" (Gen. 25:34). Jacob, the second twin, desired it. Jacob valued the spiritual, while Esau sought the things of this world. When he was hungry, Esau sold his birthright for a mess of pottage. "Behold," he explained, "I am at the point to die: and what profit shall this birthright do to me?" (Gen. 25:32). Many Esaus have given up something of eternal value in order to satisfy a momentary hunger for the things of the world.[43]

In the Rasa'il Ikhwan al-Safa, Esau's sale of the birthright to Jacob was symbolized by the transfer of the sacred garment. Again, according to bin Gorion, 'Esau's garment in which Rebekah clothed him, namely those made by God for Adam and Eve, had now rightfully become Jacob's, and Isaac recognized their paradisiacal fragrance' [this last reference is to the events in Genesis 27]." Donald W. Parry, "Ritual and Symbolism," in *Temples of the Ancient World*, ed. Donald W. Parry (Salt Lake City: Deseret Book, 1994), 713.

42. Jon D. Levenson, "Genesis," in *The Jewish Study Bible*, ed. Adele Berlin and Marc Brettler (Oxford: Oxford University Press, 2004), 55, attributes Esau's intermarriage as an explicit sign of his forsaking of the covenant, "Esau's intermarriages are in jarring contrast to Abraham's strenuous effort to find a wife for Isaac from within the clan (chap. 24) and demonstrate Esau's unworthiness to serve as the next figure in the patriarchal line."
43. Dallin H. Oaks, "Spirituality," *Ensign*, November 1985, 61.

JACOB MASQUERADES AS ESAU: WHAT REALLY HAPPENS IN THE STORY?

With the history of Esau and Jacob in place we can now address, what is at times, perceived to be one of the most scandalous episodes in scripture: Jacob dressing up as Esau to get their father's blessing. In Genesis 27 we encounter the perceived fiasco of Jacob's deceit, where he and Rebekah blatantly attempt to deceive Isaac into bestowing the more significant priesthood blessing on Jacob instead of Esau (Genesis 27). To do so, Jacob must dress up like Esau to fool their aged and apparently dying father, offering him a meal while in disguise. The chapter is admittedly a difficult one to interpret, and in the following quotation one may hear the tones of question that arise from the story but also the removal of any scandal that many seem to hold over Jacob throughout the remainder of his life:

> How could Jacob get a different patriarchal blessing through deceit and it be legitimate? . . . We wish we had a more complete account of what really happened. We do not get additional help from the Joseph Smith Translation in this instance. I'll add a comment by President Joseph Fielding Smith on the subject of patriarchal blessings. Among other things, President Smith said: "I am here today to stand in the defense of Jacob. I don't like these statements that are made so frequently about Jacob being a thief, a robber in stealing his brother's blessing. He didn't steal his brother's blessing. . . . When he went to get his blessing, he got the blessing the Lord gave him and had for him, and he didn't steal anything from Esau. The Lord would not have permitted it. Furthermore, the Lord gave him the same blessing, or much of the same blessing on another occasion.[44] . . . There is a difference between the words of a blessing and the actual realization and reception of the promises stated in the blessing. The Lord would not have been obligated to fulfill the

44. As will be discussed below, if the blessing in Genesis 27 can be distinguished from the birthright blessing, then the chapter is not about possessions associated with the birthright, rights to which Esau had already forfeited as described in the pottage incident. In Genesis 27:36, Esau distinguished between the birthright (presumably the mess of pottage) and now, here, "my blessing."

> words of Isaac if Jacob and Esau didn't get the blessing they each deserved.[45] . . . So in answer to the question, How can Jacob get a legitimate, different patriarchal blessing through deceit? I would answer, he can't, and he didn't."[46]

The subsequent portion of this chapter will explore some elements of the story that will hopefully cause us to pause and reconsider options of interpretation, rather than accept as authoritative certain lines of reasoning that simply at times fail to supply ample reason to accept them, although we usually do so in frustration as we digest such interpretations with a grain of salt.

INTERPRETATIONS OF THE CHAPTER

As noted, there are several elements that make understanding and interpreting this chapter difficult, a difficulty that has led to a multifarious range of approaches in effort to supply a proper interpretation to the story. I will discuss a number of these below, attempting to formulate a plausible scenario from these perspectives, and then look at the chapter to see what it can tell us. One such approach sees this narrative as completely independent of the birthright scene: "All the action and the dialogue is directed toward the dominant, recurring theme of the entire episode: the father's final blessing. The Hebrew noun *berakhah* occurs seven times and its verbal form exactly twenty-one times. *The birthright is not an issue here*, and its relationship to the blessing is unclear. Apparently, they were separate institutions. Nothing is said about the disposition of property, and

45. In some scholarly studies on this subject, Isaac is portrayed in an unfavorable light. The following is representative of this: "We have already been told that 'Isaac loved Esau for his hunting,' so when he says 'Make me a tasty stew that I love,' we realize that Isaac's sensuality is more powerful than his theology. Outside this chapter (vv 7, 9, 14, 17, 31) 'tasty stew' only occurs in Prov 23:3, 6. Note the qualifying phrase, 'that I love,' suggesting the old man's bondage to his appetite." Wenham, *Genesis 16–50*, 206.
46. Robert J. Matthews, *Selected Writings of Robert J. Matthews*, Gospel Scholars Series (Salt Lake City: Deseret Book, 1999), 155–56.

it is striking that Esau expected to receive the blessing even though he admitted to having lost the birthright."[47]

Under this interpretation, the blessing, and therefore the entire purpose of the deception, is not on the inherited property but concerns a "materialistic blessing"[48] associated with the future, regardless of worthiness. From the perspective of Isaac, this distinguishing between the two types of blessings makes sense, and he was not attempting to tamper with the birthright but seems to have had a fatherly blessing in mind. In fact, the two boys are given similar temporal blessings, "the dew of heaven, and the fatness of the earth, and plenty of corn and wine" (Genesis 27:28) for Jacob, and "the fatness of the earth, and of the dew of heaven from above" (27:39) for Esau—perhaps the exclusion of "corn and wine" in Esau's blessing stems from the fact that he is a hunter. There is an affirmation that Esau would serve Jacob, but Esau is promised that, "when thou shalt have the dominion, that thou shalt break his yoke from off thy neck" (27:40)—a possible reference to the more temporal aspects of their existence in relatively close proximity, a proximity of which Esau is a beneficiary by the end of the story. While this does not address the deception per se, it does provide a context by which later historical contact between the descendants of Esau and Jacob is set out (both become prosperous). The confusion over the nature of the blessing also seems to be significant.

Others have attempted to situate this chapter within a ritual context, claiming that the scene is similar to other ancient Near Eastern appeals for blessings within the context of a feast, or meal.[49] This comparative

---

47. Sarna, *Genesis*, 189.

48. See Joseph Rackman, "Was Isaac Deceived?," *Judaism* (1997): 38. "The blessing that Isaac bestows on Jacob (whom he mistakes for Esau) grants him fertility of the ground, dominion over other nations, including those descended from siblings, and a boomerang effect for curses and blessings. These are typical elements for the patriarchal blessing and have no relationship to either material inheritance or to the *covenant, though some of these features are also present in the covenant benefits that the Lord promises to Israel. They constitute the foundational elements of survival and prosperity." Walton, *IVP Bible*, 59.

49. See David E. Bokovoy, "From the Hand of Jacob: A Ritual Analysis of Genesis 27," *Studies in the Bible and Antiquity* (2009): 35–50, and the bibliography found there. Such studies are generally not focused on attempting to offer an in-depth

approach does have value as there are some general similarities between these rituals and Genesis 27, although interpreters must sift through the data to figure out how this context may have bearing on the story, especially if we disassociate the birthright from the blessing found within the chapter. Esau does indeed distinguish between the two blessings in that Jacob "took away my [Esau's] birthright; and, behold, now he hath taken away my [Esau's] blessing" (27:36). Such ritual foci seem productive in attempting to understand the story, and despite potential roots in a ritual setting, I personally don't think the current text is preoccupied with a ritual dinner in this scenario but that Isaac is probably attempting to give Esau a fatherly blessing before Isaac's assumed imminent and ensuing death, something that may not have been contingent solely upon receiving a meal.[50]

---

explanation concerning the motivations, behavior, and resultant actions of Jacob and Rebekah.

50. Dean Andrew Nicholas, *The Trickster Revisited: Deception as a Motif in the Pentateuch* (New York: Peter Lang, 2009), 54, states, "Folklorists have long commented on the apparent cultic basis for this act. In the present narrative, however, it only functions as a disguise for the trickster; its original cultic context is now subverted by the surface structure of the text." This statement seems to imply that there is an undergirding of the story based on ritual but also that the text in its current form has been changed to craft a tale of trickery. Although I am not going to spend significant time on the theory, it should be stated that it is possible that Genesis 27 constitutes some redaction activity. If we look at Genesis 26 and 28, it is as if Genesis 27 has been picked up and dropped into an otherwise smoothly flowing narrative. Source critics have long recognized variations in the text at this juncture and that Genesis 27 can be attributed to another author or later redactor. In sum, it would not surprise me if we did not have all the details in the story as they really unfolded. Below I will attempt to explain what we do have and focus on what the text says and how it says it. Concerning the distinguishing between types of blessings, Elder Dallin H. Oaks cites Genesis 27:28–29, 39–40 as examples of priesthood blessings. As far as I can tell, he is not equating these verses with the "birthright" blessing: "Worthy Melchizedek Priesthood holders can give blessings to their posterity. The scriptures record many such blessings, including Adam's (see D&C 107:53–57), Isaac's (see Genesis 27:28–29, 39–40; 28:3–4; Hebrews 11:20), Jacob's (see Genesis 48:9–22; 49; Hebrews 11:21), and Lehi's (see 2 Nephi 1:28–32; 2 Nephi 4)." Dallin H. Oaks, "Priesthood Blessings," *Ensign*, May 1987, 37.

Other interpretations are more subjective and based on opinions that may not offer solid foundations for understanding these stories. For example, the concept that while deception is generally bad, this particular deception is good because of the circumstances—that is, the inability of Jacob to receive the blessing in any other way justified the means—which is not a solid foundation upon which to base an interpretation. Similarly, the concept that the only problem with the text is our modern sensibilities compared to ancient ones is also not foundationally solid: "Jacob's methods of obtaining the blessings would not be looked upon as sinful or unethical. From the point of view of the ancient writer, Jacob was justified in being shrewd in obtaining his blessings, since God had promised them to him."[51] While it is true that we must find ancient layers and mentalities within the original framework and that through time our judgments tend to be shaped by our personal experiences, we can probably do better than dismissing the problematic texts with "They thought it was OK." In fact, as will be seen below, Jacob strenuously objects to the behavior in which he will engage.

Two other perspectives suggest that the narrative's difficulties reflect the nature of God: one suggests that the events highlight the principle that God can do whatever he wants under any circumstance, and he and it are right; while the other suggests that the depiction of God in this narrative is best understood as a trickster, similar to other divine tricksters in mythology. One such explanation that shows the latter's perspective is as follows:

> YHWH functions throughout the Jacob cycle as a trickster par excellence. Through participation in and with Jacob's many deceptions, an underappreciated theological portrait of God emerges, one in which YHWH's cunning matches and at times exceeds that of the patriarch. This divine unscrupulousness, while not entirely benign, is the mechanism by which YHWH tenaciously works toward the divine purpose. By means of deception, YHWH makes advances toward the "great nation" that will become Israel, toward blessing[s] for the entire cosmos through Israel, and toward a return to the promised land. In the Jacob cycle, therefore, one

51. Sperry, *Spirit of the Old Testament*, 31.

> observes not an aberrant, devious God but a divine trickster who will go to any lengths for the sake of the ancestral promise. In the Jacob cycle, one may discern a true theology of deception.[52]

In my opinion, these explanations and justifications are unsatisfactory because they suggest that God himself is not bound by moral and ethical constraints so far as he is meeting his theological purposes. In our efforts to take the blame off the actual participants in the story, we somehow think the burden can be shifted to God, something not stated in the text, and that his divinity justifies any type of behavior. Below, I will offer some possible interpretations that are less focused on God as being the driving force behind some of the questionable decisions and that are more focused on the individuals who made those decisions, with a concentration on a few subtle nuances in the text that may help us view the story in a less "scandalous" light for all parties involved. This is not because I don't want unethical behavior to be a part of this story, but because I am not sure the text is telling us that it is unethical—at least, not on the part of God.

Genesis 27 begins,

> And it came to pass, that when Isaac was old, and his eyes were dim, so that he could not see, he called Esau his eldest son, and said unto him, My son: and he said unto him, Behold, here am I.
>
> And he said, Behold now, *I am old, I know not the day of my death*:
>
> Now therefore take, I pray thee, thy weapons, thy quiver and thy bow, and go out to the field, and take me some venison;
>
> And make me savoury meat, such as I love, and bring it to me, that I may eat; that my soul may bless thee before I die (Genesis 27:1–4; emphasis mine).

It is within this context that this deception occurs—when the patriarch Isaac, who is perceived as in danger of death (he was not sure when)—asks for meat.[53] If these chapters form a sequential chronological order,

52. Anderson, *Jacob and the Divine Trickster,* 188.

53. Isaac is portrayed here as old and having dim eyes, and one gets the impression that he is on his deathbed. Genesis 25:26 states that Isaac is sixty years old when

then we must conclude that Isaac was so seriously ill, or at least felt so old and stricken with poor eyesight, to have convinced himself and those around him that he was indeed in danger of dying—although he would live eight decades longer. In this condition, Isaac does call upon Esau to prepare a meal and offers the reason: "That my soul may bless thee before I die" (Genesis 27:4). Interpretations surrounding the events sometimes portray Isaac in shady tones, creating a polarization in the text that is not crystal clear:

> "So that my soul may bless you before I die." Isaac does not say simply, "So that I may bless you." The use of "my soul" rather than "I" seems to express Isaac's strong desire to bless Esau (cf. Deut 12:20; 14:26; Ps 84:3[2]; Cant 1:7; 3:1–4). He is quite deliberately prepared to overlook Esau's misdemeanors and the God-given oracle. Isaac's will is pitted against God's and Rebekah's.[54] Thus the stakes are high. Though [the fact that] "Esau" went out into the country to hunt game sounds very matter-of-fact, it is a dramatic exit to those who

---

Jacob and Esau are born. Genesis 26:34 informs us that Esau is forty when he marries a Hittite wife. This would make Isaac one hundred years old when he is depicted as old and concerned about dying in the first few verses of Genesis 27. Isaac subsequently goes on to live another eighty years before he dies at the age of 180 (Genesis 35:28–29). I do find it interesting that at the end of the "deception," out of nowhere we again find the real accusation against Esau as to why he forfeited his birthright: he chose to marry a Hittite wife, "And Rebekah said to Isaac, I am weary of my life because of the daughters of Heth: if Jacob take a wife of the daughters of Heth, such as these which are of the daughters of the land, what good shall my life do me?" (Genesis 27:46). This is conspicuously similar to the last verses, just prior to the beginning of the deception of chapter 27: "And Esau was forty years old when he took to wife Judith the daughter of Beeri the Hittite, and Bashemath the daughter of Elon the Hittite: Which were a grief of mind unto Isaac and to Rebekah" (Genesis 26:34–35). Chapter 28 begins with Isaac completely and clearly in control, instructing Jacob to go to Padan-aram, not to flee Esau but to find a daughter of Laban so Jacob could marry in the covenant. Perhaps the text is coherent, and this is just a coincidence within a chronological difficulty and idiosyncrasy, but it is interesting nonetheless.

54. This conception of a God-given oracle is a huge question mark for me. What is the oracle, and where is it given? This common element of the story seems self-imposed by us as readers as we attempt to interpret the story with preconceived notions as we suppose Isaac is pitted against God and Rebekah.

> are aware of the issues at stake. Will Isaac and Esau triumph or Rebekah and Jacob, as the LORD had promised?[55]

While it does seem clear that Isaac genuinely loves Esau and wants to leave him a blessing before Isaac's supposed death, the text gives no indication that Isaac is attempting to oppose God or intentionally disregard a divine injunction. Isaac simply asks Esau for a meal that Isaac loves so much and, in return, as a bearer of the priesthood and as a father who loves and is concerned for his son, wants to provide a blessing for Esau.[56] It is at this stage that something interesting happens at a juncture that leads us down questionable avenues of interpretation: "And Rebekah heard when Isaac spake to Esau his son. And Esau went to the field to hunt *for* venison, *and* to bring *it.* And Rebekah spake unto Jacob her son, saying, Behold, I heard thy father speak unto Esau thy brother, saying, Bring me venison, and make me savoury meat, that I may eat, and bless thee before the Lord before my death. Now therefore, my son, obey my voice according to that which I command thee" (Genesis 27:5–8).

Significantly, what Isaac says and what Rebekah hears and then repeats to Jacob are a bit different (at least as reported in the text). Some see her report to Jacob as intentionally altered in order to try and convince him to participate in her scheme (something the text never states):

> Rebekah, perhaps surmising that Jacob will need a little persuading to undertake her potentially dangerous scheme, modifies Isaac's words to Esau. Isaac said, "Take your weapons . . . so that my soul may bless you before I die" (vs 3–4). Rebekah omits all the remarks about hunting, which might have put Jacob off, then continues "that I may bless you in the Lord's presence before I die." By changing "my soul" to "I," Rebekah seems to be playing down the strength of Isaac's desire to bless Esau, while by adding "in the Lord's presence," she is emphasizing the importance of what Isaac proposes to do. Through this reporting of Isaac's remarks, she seems to be

55. Gordon J. Wenham, *Genesis 16–50*, 206.
56. Second Nephi 4:5–12 describes Lehi leaving such patriarchal blessings upon his posterity before his death.

> insinuating the importance of Jacob acquiring the blessing while minimizing Isaac's determination to bless Esau.[57]

The only thing that is certain about the interpretation of this incident is its uncertainty. We have no unequivocal statement in the text that Isaac is mentally incapacitated, that he is disregarding the edict of God, nor that Rebekah is more divinely inspired than Isaac, thus offering us a solution as to what is driving the incident: what seems clear is that Rebekah's understanding of Isaac's intentions is unclear. The language of the text does not argue in favor of associating the blessing with the birthright, and Rebekah's actions may have been motivated by good intentions but were based on a misunderstanding of what she thought Isaac meant: some type of blessing "before the Lord" (verse 7), which she perceived belonged to Jacob and which he would now not receive (possibly confusing this blessing with the birthright)—intentions that Isaac may have never had but that would trigger the events that follow.[58]

With what ensues, both Rebekah and Jacob seem to know it is not the proper way to go about things:

> My father peradventure will feel me, and I shall seem to him as a deceiver; and I shall bring a curse upon me, and not a blessing.[59]
>
> And his mother said unto him, Upon me *be* thy curse, my son: only obey my voice, and go fetch me *them*.

---

57. Wenham, *Genesis 16–50*, 206–7.
58. I understand that in the end, my speculations about this incident continue to be speculations. What I am hoping they will accomplish is that they will open new ways of interpreting this difficult story in the Bible. In relation to this particular story, it seems that the norm of interpretation has become so conditioned on negatively portraying either God, Isaac, or Jacob—an interpretation that is not clearly depicted in the text—that we accept as authoritative stances that are not particularly well grounded nor that are explicitly stated in the biblical account.
59. Here, Jacob is worrying about losing a blessing because of his behavior rather than worrying about what he can gain from his actions. This concern may further accentuate and highlight the earlier episode where Esau sold his birthright in the form of behavior constituting its loss.

> And he went, and fetched, and brought them to his mother: and his mother made savoury meat, such as his father loved. (Genesis 27:12–14)

The text does not tell us that Rebekah was inspired in her actions, and rather than finding deception in God at this stage of things, perhaps it is here we best see his divine hand at work to overcome human foibles (both Rebekah's and Jacob's, who participate).[60] Although Isaac will later fear when he discovers he has laid his hands on Jacob rather than Esau, the blessing intended for Jacob proceeded forth from his mouth: true inspiration prevailed in the midst of human misguiding. Through divine guidance, Isaac blesses everyone according to the will of the Lord.[61] This line

---

60. There have been others who have absolutely seen Rebekah as the inspired one in this episode. See, for example, Robert L. Millet, *Selected Writings of Robert L. Millet* (Salt Lake City: Deseret Book, 2000), 283; John Taylor, in *Journal of Discourses*, 21:370–71. However, nowhere in the text is this expressly stated. Rebekah's inspiration is something we just tend to assume, and she herself declares the effects of the deception and wishes any curse resulting in such a course to come upon her. In the process of such assumptions, Isaac, Jacob, and God are all portrayed as tricksters and deceivers and as dishonest or incompetent, while somehow Rebekah remains inspired and is expunged from the guilt now to be borne by Jacob. My intentions are not to convict and defame Rebekah—her desperate actions may have been based upon an honest misunderstanding. At the end of this episode, she sends away Jacob and laments, "Why should I be deprived also of you both in one day?" (Genesis 27:45). She seems fully aware that what she has done will lose the trust of Esau and, potentially, his desire to be her son. An interesting occurrence may arise when interpreting Rebekah's actions as inspired. This equates the blessing here with the birthright—a potential irony that may highlight Rebekah's misunderstanding and the foundation on which her decision is based.
61. Ultimately, some have questioned Isaac's intentions and capacity in this story; however, a fundamental principle seems to prevail, "It is a very sacred responsibility for a Melchizedek Priesthood holder to speak for the Lord in giving a priesthood blessing. As the Lord has told us in modern revelation, 'My word . . . shall all be fulfilled, whether by mine own voice or by the voice of my servants, it is the same' (D&C 1:38). If a servant of the Lord speaks as he is moved upon by the Holy Ghost, his words are 'the will of the Lord . . . the mind of the Lord . . . the word of the Lord . . . [and] the voice of the Lord' (D&C 68:4). But if the words of a blessing only represent the priesthood holder's own desires and opinions, uninspired by the Holy Ghost, then the blessing is conditioned

of thinking at least offers a possible alternative interpretation to the story based on what the language of the text says.

In an enigmatic turn of events, when we move to Genesis 28, we get an entirely different picture. Isaac is no longer on his death bed (or at least does not appear to be), and he is getting ready to live another eighty years. He is in complete control, and he blesses Jacob.[62] Following the lament in Genesis 27:46 over Esau marrying a Hittite and the hope that Jacob will not follow that path, Genesis 28:1 has Isaac blessing Jacob and charging him, "Thou shalt not take a wife of the daughters of Canaan," highlighting the contrast between him and his brother Esau. Isaac further commands Jacob when attempting to help him to secure the blessings of the covenant:

---

on whether it represents the will of the Lord. Worthy Melchizedek Priesthood holders can give blessings to their posterity. The scriptures record many such blessings, including Adam's (see D&C 107:53–57), Isaac's (see Genesis 27:28–29, 39–40; 28:3–4; Hebrews 11:20), Jacob's (see Genesis 48:9–22; 49; Hebrews 11:21), and Lehi's (see 2 Nephi 1:28–32; 4)." Oaks, "Priesthood Blessings," 37.

62. Subsequently, there is no direct mention of the motivations for Isaac sending Jacob off to marry as a result of what happened in the previous chapter (contrast Rebekah's motivations as expressed in Genesis 27:43–46) and thus they may be unrelated chronologically. Again, if the chapters are sequentially connected, the dust seems to have settled, and Isaac had given Jacob clear instructions, along with the blessing of Abraham, a blessing not associated with those mentioned in Genesis 27. In this connection Rackman, "*Deceived?*," 38, writes, "It is the third blessing which reveals that Isaac truly understood the difference between his two sons, and intended that Jacob be his spiritual heir. The scene opens after Esau has received his blessing, but is furious that Jacob had sneaked in ahead of him to steal the blessing (Genesis 27:41). Thereafter, in Chapter 28, *for the first time,* Jacob appears before Isaac with Isaac knowing that it is Jacob before him, and Isaac's blessing is for him to 'become an assembly of peoples. He [God] will grant Abraham's blessing to you and your descendants, so that you will take over the land which God gave to Abraham' (Genesis 28:3–4). Here, what is transmitted for the first time, is Isaac's *spiritual* legacy from Abraham, now clearly intended for Jacob." It is this type of awkwardness in the text that causes source critics to look for clues of redaction in the story and leaves us wondering how chapter 27 fits into the grand scheme of things.

> Arise, go to Padan-aram, to the house of Bethuel thy mother's father; and take thee a wife from thence of the daughters of Laban thy mother's brother.
>
> And God Almighty bless thee, and make thee fruitful, and multiply thee, that thou mayest be a multitude of people;
>
> And give thee the blessing of Abraham, to thee, and to thy seed with thee; that thou mayest inherit the land wherein thou art a stranger, which God gave unto Abraham.
>
> And Isaac sent away Jacob: and he went to Padan-aram unto Laban, son of Bethuel the Syrian, the brother of Rebekah, Jacob's and Esau's mother.
>
> When Esau saw that Isaac had blessed Jacob, and sent him away to Padan-aram, to take him a wife from thence; and that as he blessed him he gave him a charge, saying, Thou shalt not take a wife of the daughters of Canaan;
>
> And that Jacob obeyed his father and his mother, and was gone to Padan-aram;
>
> And Esau seeing that the daughters of Canaan pleased not Isaac his father;
>
> Then went Esau unto Ishmael, and took unto the wives which he had Mahalath the daughter of Ishmael Abraham's son, the sister of Nebajoth, to be his wife. (Genesis 28:2–9)

Jacob is to go to adherents of the covenant and find a wife to ensure the claiming of that covenant. He is offered "the blessing of Abraham, to thee, and to thy seed with thee," foreshadowing being faithful, multiplying, and inheriting the land (Genesis 28:3–4). To summarize this event, the blessings associated with the covenant appear to have been intended for Jacob—not for Esau—and were not to be gained by deceit.

> It is not at all clear even to the careful reader precisely what it is that Esau "lost" and Jacob "gained" as a result of the deception. Particularly when before Jacob leaves home we read: *And Isaac blessed Jacob and said, "May God give you the blessing of Abraham"* (28:4). This would indicate that the "blessing of Abraham" which designates who is to be the successor to the Abrahamic covenant, and

> was the only spiritually significant element possibly involved in either the *bechora* or the *bracha,* was never contemplated by Isaac as something to be given to Esau. Therefore, both events may well have been cases of "much ado about nothing."[63]

This segment ends with another stark contrast between Jacob and Esau: "Jacob obeyed his father and his mother" (Genesis 28:7), and Esau fully recognized that marrying outside of the covenant "pleased not Isaac" (28:8). As a result of Jacob's obedience, Genesis 28:10–22 highlights that during Jacob's quest to obey his father and claim the blessings of the covenant, Jacob enjoys one of the most sacred experiences recorded in scripture: the Jacob's ladder dream (a dream describing the covenants he would have to make in order to obtain the presence of God, a temple-like experience that would become a defining moment in his life).[64]

Yet the narrative doesn't end there. We are also presented with Jacob and Esau's reunion years later, where there appears to be no hard feelings or ill will on the part of either of them, despite Jacob's recognition for the potential concerns:

---

63. Shubert Spero, "Jacob and Esau: The Relationship Reconsidered," *Jewish Bible Quarterly* 32, no. 4 (2004): 247. Spero further states, "The text does not make it clear as to precisely what privileges or benefits the 'birthright' confers, or in what sense it could be 'sold.' Nor does it describe the nature of the coveted 'blessing' that Isaac confers on the disguised Jacob or what value a 'blessing' could have [had] when given under false pretenses" (247). All these items must be considered together to formulate a big picture of what happened in these interconnected events, rather than just viewing them as separate or in isolation.
64. See Marion G. Romney, "Temples—The Gates to Heaven," *Ensign*, March 1971, 16; Andrew C. Skinner, "Jacob: Keeper of Covenants," *Ensign*, March 1998, 51. "The ladder or stairway that Jacob sees in his dream is the passageway between heaven and earth. The comparable word in *Akkadian is used in Mesopotamian mythology to describe what the messenger of the gods uses when he wants to pass from one realm to another. It is this mythological stairway that the Babylonians sought to represent in the architecture of the ziggurats. These had been built to provide a way for the deity to descend to the temple and the town. Jacob's background would have given him familiarity with this concept, and thus he would conclude that he was in a sacred spot where there was a portal opened between worlds." Walton, *IVP Bible*, 60.

> And Jacob lifted up his eyes, and looked, and, behold, Esau came, and with him four hundred men. And he divided the children unto Leah, and unto Rachel, and unto the two handmaids.
>
> And he put the handmaids and their children foremost, and Leah and her children after, and Rachel and Joseph hindermost.
>
> And he passed over before them, and bowed himself to the ground seven times, until he came near to his brother.
>
> And Esau ran to meet him, and embraced him, and fell on his neck, and kissed him: and they wept.
>
> And he lifted up his eyes, and saw the women and the children; and said, Who are those with thee? And he said, The children which God hath graciously given thy servant.
>
> Then the handmaidens came near, they and their children, and they bowed themselves.
>
> And Leah also with her children came near, and bowed themselves: and after came Joseph near and Rachel, and they bowed themselves.
>
> And he said, What meanest thou by all this drove which I met? And he said, These are to find grace in the sight of my lord.
>
> And Esau said, I have enough, my brother; keep that thou hast unto thyself. (Genesis 33:1–9)

It appears that Isaac's blessing upon Esau had come to pass and that he enjoyed an abundance of material possessions. Concerning the terms upon which they had departed, as presented in chapter 27 (again chapter 28 paints a much different picture), Jacob was obviously concerned with how Esau might react after so many years (approximately twenty years later). To mend any potentially injured feelings or perceptions of monetary loss and deprivation, when Jacob finally does meet Esau, he offers him what he could to alleviate any possible grudges: physical possessions (Genesis 33:9–11). It turns out there were not any permanent hard feelings. Perhaps the events described in chapter 27 do not tend to accurately portray the events, or the language is so confusing that it makes comprehension difficult. Perhaps this is precisely the point and thus highlights the confusion all the participants experienced within the story. It may be tempting to revert to claims that Esau was innocent and maligned through all these events, and his forgiving nature here suggests it. However, it is fruitless to attempt to depict Esau as the hero and the wronged of these stories. The biblical text just does not portray him that way, and we are left trying to fill in the missing pieces of the puzzle that help make up the narrative. What is clear is that at the end of the story, these two brothers eventually joined together to bury their father upon his death, and that whatever had happened in the past, it was no longer a part of their present.

JACOB AND ESAU—A COMEDY?

Sometimes the stories of Jacob and Esau are viewed in terms of a larger comedic narrative, and future episodes are interpreted in terms of irony and comedy in the Bible. Within this framework, the switching of Laban's daughter at marriage and the changing of Jacob's wages are interpreted as just recompense for Jacob as he goes from being the trickster (in the Esau story) to being tricked:

> Disguise and deception are common characteristics of comedy; indeed, as Frye puts it, "craft or fraud is the animating spirit of comic form. Moreover, a classic comic triad of trickster, dupe, and innocent victim appears, with the two sons and their senile father playing roles and the shrewd, scheming mother performing backstage as a "co-trickster" in collusion with her favorite son. Apropos of the plot-line of comedy, the two brothers will become at least temporally reconciled by the end of the story, but all this is to anticipate the rest of this comic tale of twins and tricksters . . . [in relation to Genesis 29:26 where Laban switches Rachel for Leah at Jacob's wedding, where we read that this is] . . . a painfully ironic rebuttal to Jacob who had once cheated his elder brother. But turn-about is fair play, and there is a kind of poetic justice in Jacob's world, as the trickster is tricked.[65]

65. J. William Whedbee, *The Bible and the Comic Vision* (Cambridge: Cambridge University Press, 1998), 97, 99, 102. See also Richard Elliot Friedman, "The Cycle of Deception in the Jacob Tradition," in *Approaches to the Bible: The Best of Bible Review*, vol 2., *A Multitude of Perspectives*, ed. Harvey Minkoff (Washington, DC: Biblical Archaeology Society, 1995), 227–36.

This line of reasoning seems to read Jacob's experiences from back to front, and the later stories are used to formulate a negative opinion of Jacob that is used to influence the interpretation of the earlier episodes of his life. However, rather than including this portion of the text in the Bible so that we could all get a good laugh and marvel at the poetic justice behind the supposed deceptive events, perhaps we are to see Jacob, described from the beginning as a righteous man, as one who is subjected to trials and hardships but endures them nobly due to the sacred, spiritual experiences he has had in witnessing dreams and seeing God (Genesis 28:12ff).[66] God promised Jacob at the beginning of his journey that he would "keep thee in all places whither thou goest, and will bring thee again into this land; for I will not leave thee, until I have done that which I have spoken to thee of" (Genesis 28:15). Perhaps God is tenderly promising Jacob to help bring him the promises of the covenant now that things have become difficult. It takes twenty years for the Lord to send instruction to Jacob that he must finally return home (Genesis 31:3), a duration of time none could have foreseen, and it occurs only after Jacob has experienced great blessings of family but also great hardship and maltreatment. The text never states that such trials come as a result of divine retribution because of Jacob's deceitful past. Rather than chuckle at Jacob through those trials, perhaps we are supposed to empathize with and marvel at him.[67] Jacob puts enduring his trials in perspective in his conversations with Rachel and Leah: "Your father hath deceived me, and changed my wages ten times; but God suffered him not to hurt me" (Genesis 31:7). Jacob seems to epitomize the phrase "come what may, and love it," as through his trials, optimism, and

---

66. If these chapters in the Bible were written for comedy, then we are dealing with a genre that already exhibits a tainted theology, reflecting the intent to amuse—although a theology based on some actual event or moral issue. The account we read in the text then may have skewed actual events or painted characters in a different light than may be entirely true to form. If this is the case, then the result of a final shaping of the text can leave some theological black holes, and we do our best to make sense of things.

67. Several studies have attempted to demonstrate that many of Jacob's interactions with Laban constituted trickery, but there are just too many other ways to interpret those passages to categorically label Jacob in this manner. For a recent example, see Anderson, *Jacob and the Divine Trickster*.

love enable them to seem "unto him but a few days, for the love he had to her" (Genesis 29:20, meaning Rachel and how his love for her helped him to endure the challenges he faced in his life).[68] Such characteristics do not appear to reflect a liar and a cheat.

Throughout the hardships and challenges faced by Jacob and his family during this long absence from home, when Jacob finally receives instruction to leave, he takes his family and flees without telling Laban. Laban accuses him of "foolishly" doing so (Genesis 31:28) and threatens him (verse 29). Jacob's actions may not have been the best choice, a scenario that landed him in Laban's grasp in the first place, but given past experiences, perhaps he feared Laban would take his family by force (verse 31). Jacob eventually cries out, "What is my trespass? what is my sin, that thou hast so hotly pursued after me?" (verse 36). In a fortunate turn of events, Laban receives a dream from God forbidding him to harm Jacob (verse 24), and Laban refrains and reconciles with Jacob. Rather than the trickster Jacob is so commonly portrayed to be, these verses can be read as depicting him as the epitome of endurance and longsuffering through situations that were not necessarily or entirely his fault. These stories may also constitute situations resulting from decisions that were made that may not have been God-given but that reflected imperfect people trying to do their best but not always succeeding. Perhaps we should see God's deliverance of Jacob not through the lens of sustaining a trickster but of upholding a righteous sufferer. Jacob declared to Laban, "God hath seen mine affliction and the labour of my hands, and rebuked thee yesternight" (verse 42). Therefore, taking this as a comedy may not be the only way to interpret Jacob's later life, and perhaps the theological perspective of endurance and trust in God are really at the heart of this message.

CONCLUDING OBSERVATIONS

The result of this essay is, I hope, to forward an approach of caution, not skepticism, when dealing with these difficult passages in the Old Testament

68. Joseph B. Wirthlin, "Come What May, and Love It," *Ensign*, November 2008, 26–28.

and to encourage a search for answers when they may not always be clearly available. The biblical text, when examined closely in relation to the Jacob and Esau stories, seems to expunge Jacob from the scandal commonly attached to him, placing more emphasis on Esau's behavior and lack of regard for his birthright as an explanation as to how the succession passes on to Jacob. The interpretation of Jacob and Esau's initial conflict over a mess of pottage, where Esau is portrayed in a worldly fashion, in contrast to Jacob's spiritual mannerisms, appears to have been one accepted by Malachi almost fourteen hundred years after the event and used as a central thematic thread throughout the entire prophetic book. The book of Malachi begins with a direct allusion to Esau and Jacob as Malachi speaks to the Levitical priests in the postexilic community in Jerusalem: "I have loved you, saith the Lord. Yet ye say, Wherein hast thou loved us? *Was* not Esau Jacob's brother? saith the Lord: yet I loved Jacob, and I hated Esau, and laid his mountains and his heritage waste for the dragons of the wilderness" (Malachi 1:2–3).

As noted by Andrew Hill, this opening statement, following the trauma of the Babylonian exile, established that the Lord's selection and continued support of the Israelites began with his initial selection of Jacob over Esau: "For this reason, Yahweh's love for Israel constitutes the central argument of the opening disputation; the restoration community's *identity crisis* could be overcome only by the affirmation and experience of [a] covenant relationship with the God of Abraham, Isaac, and Jacob."[69] The Israelites had thus been loved and blessed through the priesthood and the covenant. Yet Malachi's intended audience does not appear to be the Israelites in general but to the priests and Levites. It is to their negligence or in those "that despise my name" (Malachi 1:6) that Malachi admonishes.[70]

69. Andrew E. Hill, *The Anchor Bible: Malachi* (New York: Doubleday, 1998), 163. "Indeed it is the individual characters of Jacob and Esau that infuse the symbols of Israel and Edom with explicit theological content" (164).

70. Subsequently, when Malachi has the Lord stating that he has "hated" Esau, this seems to have reference to the breaking of the covenant, not a whimsical desire of passion. "Yahweh admits his 'hate' for Esau and vows never to 'love' them again on account of all their evil (Hos 9:15; cf. Andersen and Freedman [1980:545] on 'hate' describing the hostility of a broken covenant relationship)." Hill, *Malachi*, 167. "Wallis suggests that the book of Deuteronomy was

Despise is the same word we find in the Genesis account relating to Esau "despising" his birthright.

> Bluntly, Malachi points out how the people fail time and again to live up to YHWH's commandments (e.g. Mal. 1.6–8; 3.6–7a), while in the same breath, a call for repentance is uttered on behalf of YHWH (e.g. Mal. 1.9; 3.7a). Calling the people "Israel" (Mal. 1.1) and addressing them in the second person plural (v. 2a) before having them paralleled with Jacob (v. 2b), Malachi indicates the representative use of Jacob and Esau. It is this Jacob-Israel the book addresses in its opening statement (Mal. 1.2–5) which lays out the line of the argument to be pursued throughout the three chapters.[71]

The prophet goes on to chastise the priests for defiling their offerings (Malachi 1:6–7), as well as marrying foreign wives (2:11), two practices for which Esau was also guilty. Thus, it appears that Malachi appropriated the Jacob-Esau narrative to highlight the priestly wrongdoing of his day, suggesting that their indifference was parallel to Esau's willing neglect.

---

especially intended to educate Israel in 'her duty to reciprocate God's love, not in the original sense of emotion, but in the form of genuine obedience and pure devotion.'" G. Johannes Botterweck, Helmer Ringgren, and Heinz-Josef Fabry, eds., *Theological Dictionary of the Old Testament*, vol. 1 (Grand Rapids, MI: Eerdmans, 2011), 1:115. "The prophet Malachi sought to perpetuate that pedagogical legacy by calling postexilic Yehud to 'take seriously' her relationship with Yahweh (2:2); especially the priests who had perverted religious instruction) by offering 'righteous worship' (3:3) and obeying God's commandments (3:14)." Hill, *Malachi*, 165.

71. Joachim J. Krause, "Tradition, History, and Our Story: Some Observations on Jacob and Esau in the Books of Obadiah and Malachi," *Journal for the Study of the Old Testament* 32 (2008): 482. "Malachi's message served as a much-needed corrective to wrong thinking about covenant relationship with Yahweh (so Fischer [1972: 318–19]; Mallone [1981: 26–27])." Hill, *Malachi*, 162. The crafting of the story with the selling of the birthright in Genesis may reflect what we see and read about in the Book of Mormon and the Old Testament: "Yea, for thus saith the Lord: Have I put thee away, or have I cast thee off forever? For thus saith the Lord: Where is the bill of your mother's divorcement? To whom have I put thee away, or to which of my creditors have I sold you? Yea, to whom have I sold you? Behold, for your iniquities have ye sold yourselves, and for your transgressions is your mother put away" (2 Nephi 7:1/Isaiah 50:1).

Though less explicit than Malachi, Paul, almost five centuries later, also seems to have understood the Jacob-Esau narrative as one that was meant to highlight Esau's covenantal disregard. In Romans 9:11–13, Paul—drawing upon the references in Malachi chapter 1: "As it is written, Jacob have I loved, but Esau have I hated"—used the narrative to define the difference between foreordination and predestination. "Here in particular it should be remembered that Paul's aim is to prick the bubble of Israel's presumptuousness as the elect, not to affirm Esau's rejection. Paul's argument, in fact, is an attack on the only dogma of predestination then current, and constitutes a standing warning against any attempt to define or rationalize a doctrine of election."[72]

---

72. James D. G. Dunn, *Word Biblical Commentary: Romans 9–16*, vol. 38b (Nashville: Thomas Nelson, 1988), 545. This statement should be clarified with Paul's warning against rationalizing foreordination as inherent and not earned. The Prophet Joseph Smith, speaking of Romans chapter 9, taught, "The whole of the chapter had reference to the Priesthood and the house of Israel; and unconditional election of individuals to eternal life was not taught by the Apostles. God did elect or predestinate, that all those who would be saved, should be saved in Christ Jesus, and through obedience to the Gospel; but He passes over no man's sins, but visits them with correction, and if His children will not repent of their sins He will discard them." "Discourse, 16 May 1841, as Reported by *Times and Seasons*," p. 430, The Joseph Smith Papers. D. Kelly Ogden and Andrew C. Skinner, *Verse by Verse Acts through Revelation* (Salt Lake City: Deseret Book, 1998), 180–181, state in relation to Romans 9:13, "'Hated' is used here to translate a Greek verb that also means 'displeased with' or 'rejected.' Jacob and Esau are used here as a hyperbolic contrast, for, of course, the Lord did not hate Esau. Rather, the Lord's preferential regard for one over the other is based on their righteousness in premortal life (see McConkie, *Doctrinal New Testament Commentary*, 2:277)." Premortal foreordinations can certainly explain Jacob's inheriting of the birthright, but it is also apparent that actions taken during mortality afford the mechanism to bring such foreordinations to fruition. In "At Times, Blessing Goes to Younger, Faithful Son," *Church News*, January 22, 1994, we read, "In The Way to Perfection, Elder Joseph Fielding Smith wrote: 'We may not know all the circumstances concerning the call of Jacob over Esau, and just why the Lord chose the younger to inherit the rights of priesthood and appointed the older to serve the younger. We may say in truth, that Jacob was more faithful and gave better heed to the commandments of the Lord. This would entitle him to the blessings, for let it be remembered that all blessings are predicated on faithfulness, and this according to a law "irrevocably decreed in heaven before the foundations of the world, . . . and when we obtain any

Elsewhere, Esau is portrayed as a secular, neglectful man, indifferent to things of eternal consequences; a seeker after the pleasures of the world.[73] Between the usage of these episodes of Malachi and Paul, it seems that the clearest interpretation of the story includes a focus rooted in priesthood responsibility and authority (which is also reflected in Rabbinic literature) and on righteously claiming the blessings one can obtain through the covenant (blessings that could be lost through negligence but that could not be purchased with a mess of pottage).

In the course of this essay, I have attempted to demonstrate the need to explore what the text says rather than what we assume it says (and that things are not always as they seem). Through the difficulties of interpretation, we do not need to fret or become frustrated with the lack of answers, but perhaps we need to ask more questions. Despite the fact that what we see in these succession stories may remain nebulous in relation to what God intends us to see, the words of President Wilford Woodruff ring true: "We should be men and women of faith, valiant for the truth as it has been revealed and committed into our hand. We should be men and women of

---

blessing from God, it is by obedience to that law upon which it is predicated." On this ground, then, Jacob was entitled to supplant Esau, if there was any such thing as a supplanting. Our history of those events informs us that Jacob was called before he was born to inherit these blessings.'"

73. Some commentators on the book of Hebrews describe the New Testament view that Esau was an "apostate," who became a secular person over a godly person and thus rejected the covenant. William L. Lane, *Word Biblical Commentary*, vol. 47b: *Hebrews 9–13* (Nashville: Thomas Nelson, 1991), 451, 457. "It describes the persons who are prepared to turn their backs on that which is holy in order to focus their attention on that which is immediately present. Esau thus typifies the godless person who relinquishes the rights conferred upon [the person] by the covenant for the sake of momentary relief. He is 'the prototype of all who throw away the heavenly reality for the sake of the earthly one' (Thompson, *Beginning of Christian Philosophy*, 43). . . . Esau's willingness to give up all that was his as the firstborn son reflected a contempt for the covenant by which his rights were warranted. By descriptive analogy, he is representative of apostate persons who are ready to turn their backs on God and the divine promises, in reckless disregard of the covenant blessings secured by the sacrificial death of Jesus." Lane, *Hebrews 9–13*, 455. Most Jewish and Christian literature view Esau as representing an individual who rejected God. See David Noel Freedman, ed. *The Anchor Bible Dictionary*, vol. 2 (New York: Doubleday, 1992), 575.

integrity to God, and to his Holy Priesthood, true to him and true to one another."[74] Our struggle in life really is reflected in the succession narratives of Isaac and Jacob, and our efforts to make decisions will enable us to qualify for the eternal rewards that God has offered to each of us as we endure whatever trials may come to us in our lives (and in whatever form they may appear). What we see in the lives of Isaac, Rebekah, and Jacob (or even God from this perspective) remains our challenge as we read and attempt to interpret these stories.

74. Wilford Woodruff, in *Journal of Discourses*, 22:233.

— 12 —

THE MATRIARCHS

ADMINISTRATORS OF GOD'S COVENANTAL BLESSINGS

CAMILLE FRONK OLSON

In recent years, biblical scholarship has recognized the value of discovering different voices as found in the text. One such approach has sought to rediscover female voices and perspectives, which are often overlooked in light of the bigger, more prominent emphases placed on male figures within the biblical text. This feminist approach is of great value to Latter-day Saints, especially since a greater understanding and recognition of the role of women within the plan of salvation has emerged over the past few years. Yet one of the challenges of engaging in this approach is that it is often used in what may be described as a "hermeneutic of doubt" when an author is suspicious of the claims being made in the given narrative, especially concerning the female voice. In light of this challenge, Camille Fronk Olson's chapter is doubly of value. Not only does it provide insight into the often-overlooked voices of the matriarchs, it frames it within a "hermeneutic of faith," meaning that the voices of the women found within the patriarchal narratives are not found at the expense of devaluing the patriarchs themselves. Instead, the narratives highlight the unique and shared experiences of the matriarchs and the men in their lives and, in so doing, demonstrate the vital role both women and men play in each other's salvation. —DB and AS

Beginning with Abraham, patriarchs were called of God to preside over extended families, administer priesthood ordinances, and perpetuate God's covenant. Matriarchs were also called of God to perform his work. Generation after generation, matriarchs are described as performing challenging and essential roles to safeguard families and ensure that God's foreordained sons were appointed to receive Jehovah's blessing to establish the covenant in their generation. Restoration scripture provides an important contribution to our understanding of the matriarchal role during the formative generations of the house of Israel. Through Joseph Smith, the Lord spoke of Sarah, "who administered unto Abraham" (Doctrine and Covenants 132:65). This chapter will consider matriarchs who were central characters during the patriarchal era, paying attention to their administrative words and actions in connection with God's covenant that complemented, reinforced, and refined their husbands' inspiration and leadership. Each of these women served as a catalyst to discover the worth God sees in all individuals, not just in those who received the birthright or presiding priesthood responsibility.

Sarah, Hagar, Rebekah, Leah, Rachel, Tamar, and Zipporah are pivotal in telling the story of how "the children of Abraham" became distinguished as a peculiar people to establish God's covenant and prepare for the coming Messiah. The focus of their stories is therefore on inheritance and continuity of the genealogy through a prepared lineage.[1] Whenever details are

1. Tammi J. Schneider, *Mothers of Promise: Women in the Book of Genesis* (Grand Rapids, MI: Baker, 2008), 15–17; Tikva Frymer-Kensky, *Reading Women of the Bible: A New Interpretation of Their Stories* (New York: Schocken Books, 2002): 5; Nelly Furman, "His Story Versus Her Story: Male Genealogy and Female Strategy in the Jacob Cycle," in *Women in the Hebrew Bible*, ed. Alice Bach (New

given in the scriptural text for determining the next steward of the covenant or recipient of the birthright blessings, the mother often played a significant role in God's plan for the next generation. God directed Abraham to "hearken" to Sarah's voice to remind him of the Lord's promise that Isaac was to be the heir (Genesis 21:12); Hagar received the witness of the angel of the Lord concerning the important role of her unborn son (Genesis 16:7–16); God revealed to Rebekah before her twins were born that her older child would "serve the younger" (Genesis 25:21–23); despite recurring tensions between the sisters Leah and Rachel, they were united in their counsel to their husband Jacob to follow God's command, knowing that their children's future—and the twelve tribes of Israel—would be shaped by it (Genesis 31:3–16); Tamar saved Judah's lineage in spite of his attempts to merge with the Canaanites (Genesis 38); and Zipporah circumcised her son, thereby rescuing Moses from divine punishment (JST Exodus 4:25–26). In concert with their husbands' divinely appointed assignments, God trusted these matriarchs with revelations and abilities to establish a people who would pledge allegiance to the God of Abraham and keep their deity's influence alive in an ancient polytheistic world.

Abraham learned that Jehovah's everlasting covenant was available to Abraham and his seed through which Jehovah would be their eternal God: "I will establish my covenant between me and thee and thy seed after thee in their generations for an everlasting covenant, to be a God unto thee, and to thy seed after thee" (Genesis 17:7). A millennium later, the prophet Isaiah clarified that Sarah the matriarch was also foundational to the covenant: "Ye that follow after righteousness . . . look unto the rock whence ye are hewn. . . . Look unto Abraham your father, and unto Sarah that bare you" (Isaiah 51:1–4; 2 Nephi 8:1–4). Importantly, multiple scriptural passages reinforce the concept that reverence for and obedience to the God of Abraham and Sarah constitute their seed rather than biological descent

York: Routledge, 1999), 119–26; Esther Fuchs, "The Literary Characterization of Mothers and Sexual Politics in the Hebrew Bible," in Bach, *Women in the Hebrew Bible*, 127–39; Naomi Steinberg, *Kinship and Marriage in Genesis* (Minneapolis: Fortress Press, 1993), 5; Rachel Havrelock, "The Myth of Birthing the Hero: Heroic Barrenness in the Hebrew Bible, *Biblical Interpretation* 16 (2008): 154–78; Terry J. Prewitt, "Kinship Structures and the Genesis Genealogies," *Journal of Near Eastern Studies* 40, no. 2 (1981): 87–98.

or birth order.[2] Even in these formative years, the covenant seed spread to include multiple branches of Abraham's descendants and some of the surrounding people.[3]

This chapter will explore evidence from the Bible, latter-day scripture, and extracanonical texts from ancient societies where domestic customs and laws parallel the biblical narrative in order to appreciate the societal opportunities and expectations for women of that day. Specifically in this chapter, I will analyze the efforts of the matriarchs to nurture and promote life by administering divine directives pertaining to the covenant among those numbered among the seed of Abraham.

CULTURAL CONTEXT

Evidence from contemporary peoples provides added insight into the possible lifestyle of the matriarchs. Extrabiblical texts from the Middle Bronze Age (2000–1500 BC), such as those from Nuzi and Middle Assyrian literature, report similar social and legal conditions that existed among the patriarchal communities.[4] Additionally, archaeologists have used material culture from the Late Bronze Age (1500–1200 BC) in Canaan to describe patriarchal families because these findings show that people continued to

---

2. See also Abraham 2:10: "As many as receive this Gospel shall be called after thy [Abraham's] name"; Galatians 3:7–9, 29: "They which are of faith, the same are the children of Abraham," and "if ye be Christ's, then are ye Abraham's seed, and heirs according to the promise"; Romans 4:11, 16: Abraham is the "father of all them that believe"; 2 Nephi 30:2: "As many . . . as will repent are the covenant people of the Lord"; Doctrine and Covenants 84:33–34: "Those who are "faithful" and "sanctified by the Spirit" are those who are "the seed of Abraham."
3. Cynthia R. Chapman discusses kinship that is defined by being nursed by the same woman rather than through blood, as in Song of Solomon 8:1: "'Oh that you were like a brother to me, one who had nursed at my mother's breast:' Breast Milk as a Kinship-Forging Substance," *Journal of Hebrew Scriptures* 12, no. 7 (2012): 1–41.
4. John Bright, *A History of Israel*, 4th ed. (Louisville: Westminster John Knox Press, 2000), 70; William G. Denver, "Patriarchal Traditions: Palestine in the Second Millennium BCE: The Archaeological Picture," *Israelite and Judean History*, ed. John H. Hayes and J. Maxwell Miller (Philadelphia: S.C.M. Press; Trinity Press International, 1977), 92–102.

reside in multigenerational households and multifamily clans.[5] Matriarchs were part of an agrarian society where men's and women's roles were integrally related, where there was no division between public and domestic spheres, and where women's contributions were as essential to societal survival as were those made by men.[6] The home, rather than a commercial center, was the hub of these ancient pastoral clans. The Genesis narrative assumes communities made up of numerous households related to an extended family and led by a "king," chieftain, or family head.[7] At one time Abraham is reported to have owned 318 servants who were available to join him in battle (Genesis 14:14), suggesting a community as large as two thousand people.[8]

In such ancient societies, the shared intent to strengthen the entire household or clan was more important than individual rights. Each member of the community received responsibilities for the progress and welfare of the whole, thereby creating gender interdependence wherein "gender hierarchy in work roles [would have been] virtually nonexistent."[9] Women's roles were pivotal in society where large families were valued to support extensive labor needs and regeneration of the community.[10] Women were responsible for the domestic sphere, especially for the care

5. Carol Meyers, *Discovering Eve: Ancient Israelite Women in Context* (New York: Oxford University Press, 1988), 138; Carol Meyers, "Women and the Domestic Economy of Ancient Israel," in Bach, *Women in the Hebrew Bible*, 33–43.
6. Meyers, "Women and the Domestic Economy of Ancient Israel," 36; Meyers, *Discovering Eve*, 168–73; Carol Meyers, "Double Vision: Textual and Archaeological Images of Women," *Hebrew Bible and Ancient Israel* 5, no. 2 (2016): 126–27; Henry Jackson Flanders, Robert Wilson Crapps, and David Anthony Smith, *People of the Covenant*, 4th ed. (New York: Oxford, 1996), 163.
7. See Genesis 14:1–2, 18; 20:2; 23:10; 32:6; 46:5–7; Meyers, *Discovering Eve*, 73.
8. Ze'ev W. Falk, *Hebrew Law in Biblical Times*, 24; Bright, *History of Israel*, 76, 96. Some seventy men were included in Jacob's clan at one time, indicating that subsequent smaller clans were created when numbers of members became sufficiently large (Genesis 46:27).
9. Meyers, *Discovering Eve*, 173; Flanders, Crapps, and Smith, *People of the Covenant*, 165.
10. Meyers, "Domestic Economy," 35, notes that "the apparent hierarchical control of men over women may have been functionally far less powerful than might be expected."

and teaching of children as well as for food preparation and the management of resources. It is estimated that half a woman's life span was devoted to maternity and motherhood.[11] Women and children worked in the fields and with the livestock alongside the men, which required the women to be physically strong and able to work long hours every day. When men were away fighting during military conflicts, women and children maintained the farming operations, further underscoring the women's significant economic roles.[12] Chief women, or the senior women in a multifamily compound such as the matriarchs in Genesis, would have assumed increased authority and management status as the numbers in the community increased.[13] Their shared authority with the male chiefs is evidenced by the joint greeting of visitors to their community (Genesis 18:1–8). In short, family households were the main focus and source of strength for society in the Israel's ancestral era. Each of the matriarchs in Genesis reflects aspects of the physical and intellectual strength needed to survive in her day. These women also demonstrate the spiritual acumen needed to administer their divine roles to their husbands and on behalf of those who received the gospel and covenant of Abraham.

SARAH AND HAGAR

Sarah's importance to the covenant is not immediately obvious in Genesis. Her husband, Abraham, received the revelation from Jehovah to move away from his father, Terah, and take Sarah, his nephew Lot, and "the souls that [they] had won in Haran" (Abraham 2:15) to Canaan, a land south of Haran, which was to be their land of inheritance (Genesis 12:4–7). When a famine hit Canaan, Abraham and Sarah relocated to Egypt for

---

11. Meyers, *Discovering Eve*, 167; Meyers, "Double Vision," 128.

12. Meyers, "Domestic Economy," 37–38.

13. Margaret English de Alminana, "A Biblical Investigation of Matriarchal Structures in Ancient Semitic Life," *Journal of Pentecostal Theology* 25, no. 1 (2016): 58–73; C. Meyers, "Domestic Economy," 39; *Discovering Eve,* 186.

relief, receiving a subsequent mission from Jehovah "that ye may declare [my] words" (Genesis 12:10; Abraham 3:15).[14]

Jehovah spoke to Abraham again just before they arrived in Egypt to warn him that his life would be threatened if Sarah did not tell the Egyptians that she was his sister rather than his wife (Genesis 12:11–13; Abraham 2:22–25). Asking Sarah to pose as her husband's sister in order to save his life must have made sense in their culture, but it strains the modern reader's understanding without additional details. As a childless woman, she was limited in bargaining power and at risk of being replaced by a wife who could give Abraham an heir. It is of no question that these events were terrifying and required both Sarah and Abraham to trust in the Lord's counsel. Fortunately, at this point in the narrative, the Lord intervened to save Sarah by sending a plague to afflict the Pharaoh and his household, thereby indicating that she was essential to reestablishing the Lord's covenant among the humankind (Genesis 12:17–19). Sarah provides a foreshadowing, or type, of the people of Israel who, in a later generation, would also be released from Egyptian bondage because of plagues that afflicted the pharaoh and his household (Exodus 8–12). After these events, when Sarah and Abraham had again settled in Canaan, another threat to God's promise to bring their descendants and others to know of and receive his gospel became apparent. Sarah continued to bear no child. She concluded that she was barren and that Jehovah had "restrained" her from bearing a child. According to the Genesis text, Sarah therefore inaugurated an alternative plan to obtain a child: she thought to give her handmaid Hagar to Abraham as a surrogate wife in order to secure an heir for Abraham and thereby preserve the covenant (Genesis 16:1–4).

The idea to give Hagar to Abraham, however, was likely not Sarah's alone. Extrabiblical sources support the idea that both Sarah and Abraham acted

---

14. Drawing on traditions handed down to his day, Flavius Josephus, the Jewish historian who lived some two thousand years after the patriarchs and matriarchs, recorded a divinely assigned mission for Abraham similar to one Joseph Smith received by revelation in the Book of Abraham. Josephus explained that while in Egypt, Abraham was to hear the Egyptian priests' views concerning their gods and "to convert them into a better way, if his own notions proved the truest." Josephus, *Antiquities of the Jews*, in *The Works of Josephus*, trans. William Whiston (Peabody, MA: Hendrickson, 1996), 1.8.1–2.

in obedience to God in this matter. The Lord revealed to Joseph Smith that "God commanded Abraham, and Sarah gave Hagar to Abraham to wife. And why did she do it? Because this was the law," and "[Sarah] administered unto Abraham according to the law when I commanded Abraham to take Hagar to wife" (Doctrine and Covenants 132:34, 65), indicating that the Lord revealed the plan to Sarah and Abraham. Some modern scholars have also read Sarah's solution and subsequent actions as evidence that she believed "the Israelite Deity was the one who control[led] her destiny" and that her "plan [would] meet with divine sanction."[15] Some two thousand years after Sarah and Abraham's time, Jewish tradition indicates that Jews believed that God directed Sarah to give Hagar to Abraham. For example, Josephus chronicled that "Sarah, at God's command, brought to Abraham's bed one of her handmaidens, a woman of Egyptian descent, in order to obtain children by her."[16] Rabbinic literature also connotes a divine command given to Abraham to accept Sarah's plan: "Taught and bred by Sarah, [Hagar] walked in the same path of righteousness as her mistress, and thus was a suitable companion for Abraham, and, instructed by the holy spirit, he acceded to Sarah's proposal."[17]

In regard to familial and childbearing practices in the ancient Near East, a similar custom was followed in Mesopotamia during this period. The Nuzi texts, written by the Hurrians in the mid-second millennium BC include laws involving adoption, polygamy, and voluntary slave status among the common people in the ancient Near East. A law that relates to Sarah's predicament cites the case of a man named Shennima, who marries a woman named Kelim-ninu. If Kelim-ninu bears him children, the law instructs, he "shall not take another wife; but if [she] does not bear, [she] shall acquire a woman of the land of Lullu as a wife for [her husband], and [Kelim-ninu] may not send the offspring away."[18] In other words, according

15. Schneider, *Mothers of Promise*, 27–28; Steinberg, *Kinship and Marriage in Genesis*, 61.

16. Josephus, *Antiquities of the Jews*, 1.10.4.

17. Ginzberg, *The Legends of the Jews*, 7 vols., trans. Henrietta Szold (Baltimore: Johns Hopkins University Press, 1998), 1.237.

18. Jonathan Paradise, "Marriage Contracts of Free Persons at Nuzi," *Journal of Cuneiform Studies* 39, no. 1 (1987): 1–36, especially 28–29; M. J. Selman

to Nuzi law, the barren wife bore the responsibility to choose a second wife for her husband in the event of infertility, and if the second wife bore him a child, the first wife was not to reject that child but should treat the child as family. Thus Sarah may have also selected the woman who would bear Abraham a child in her place, but whatever the case, the Genesis account seems to follow a practice witnessed elsewhere in the region. In response to this plan, the narrator of Genesis simply reports that "[Abraham] hearkened to the voice of [Sarah]" (Genesis 16:2).[19]

As the story progresses, however positive the relationship between Sarah and Hagar was before Hagar conceived, it quickly dissipated, for "when [Hagar] saw that she had conceived, her mistress was despised in her eyes" (Genesis 16:4), or Sarah was "lowered in her esteem."[20] A similar circumstance and corresponding law appears in an ancient Babylonian law code, the Code of Hammurabi (ca. 1850–1550 BC), and rescinds freedom and status should an enslaved pregnant woman assume equality with her mistress. The regulation reads, "If a man has married a temple-woman and she has given a slave-girl to her husband and she has born sons, but afterwards that slave-girl takes over the position of her mistress because she has born sons, her mistress may not sell her for silver. She shall put on her the marker of slavery and she shall be treated as a slave girl."[21] This custom may echo Sarah's response to Hagar by "[dealing hardly with her]" (Genesis 16:5–6), perhaps treating her like a regular enslaved servant rather than as part of the family, reinforcing the custom that gave

---

translates "land of Lullu" as a "Nullu woman" or a slave girl. M. J. Selman, "The Social Environment of the Patriarchs," *Tyndale Bulletin* 27 (1976): 128.

19. Anna Fisk explores the story through Hagar's eyes as a parallel to African-American slavery in "Sisterhood in the Wilderness: Biblical Paradigms and Feminist Identity Politics in Readings of Hagar and Sarah," *Looking Through a Glass Bible*, ed. A. K. M. Adam and Samuel Tongue (Leiden: Brill, 2014), 115–21.

20. Schneider, *Mothers of Promise*, 30.

21. Law code no. 146, in M. E. J. Richardson, *Hammurabi's Laws: Text, Translation, and Glossary* (Sheffield: Sheffield Academic Press, 2000), 87. The Akkadian term translated here as "temple-woman" is *nadītu*, which refers to a female devotee or priestess, thus a high-ranking female (241); see also Martha T. Roth, *Law Collections from Mesopotamia and Asia Minor* (Atlanta, GA: Scholars Press, 1997), 109, for an alternate translation of the law.

free tribal women latitude to determine the kinship status of their slaves.[22] The parallels between the ancient Babylonian law and the Genesis narrative further underscore the Bible's cultural authenticity with the Middle Bronze Age.

In response to Sarah's harsh treatment, rather than submit, the pregnant Hagar fled into the wilderness of Shur (Genesis 16:6–7). Hagar's importance to God is attested in the Genesis text. An angel from the Lord found Hagar where she had fled and instructed her to return and submit—not to her husband—but to Sarah, her mistress (Genesis 16:7–9). Most likely, Hagar as a bondwoman did not have the legal right to walk away from her mistress. But the angel's intervention likely carried a spiritual reason for her return to Sarah as well. In essence, the angel instructed Hagar to voluntarily return and confront the source of her pain and degradation—in this case, Sarah—rather than run from it. In return, the Lord would give her a large posterity, beginning with a son, who should be named Ishmael according to the angel's instructions, and the Lord would hear her afflictions (Genesis 16:10–11). Hagar's ordeal finds a type with what the Lord prophesied to Abraham: his posterity would live in a strange land where they would be afflicted (Genesis 15:13).[23] The foreigner Hagar was told by God's messenger to return to a strange land, and the Lord would be with her throughout her afflictions. By submitting to the Lord's counsel, Hagar would eventually recognize that God's mission for her exceeded giving birth alone in the wilderness.

Hagar's involvement in the community was important for years after Ishmael was born.[24] Her obedience to this revelation to return and submit to Sarah put her and her son Ishmael in Abraham and Sarah's community when, thirteen years later, God established his covenant with the family

---

22. Jo Ann Hacket, "Rehabilitating Hagar: Fragments of an Epic Pattern," in *Gender and Difference in Ancient Israel*, ed. Peggy L. Day (Minneapolis: Fortress Press, 1989), 12–27; de Alminana, "Matriarchal Structures," 66–68. See also Aaron Schade's chapter on Isaac and Jacob in this volume.

23. Tikya Frymer-Kensky, "Hagar," in *Women in Scripture: A Dictionary of Named and Unnamed Women in the Bible, Apocryphal/Deuterocanonical Books, and the New Testament*, ed. Carol Meyers (Grand Rapids, MI: Eerdmans, 2000), 87; Meyers, *Women in Scripture*, 87.

24. Fisk, "Sisterhood in the Wilderness," 121–37.

of Abraham. Because Hagar faithfully returned, Ishmael was included in the covenant, as was evidenced by him being circumcised (Genesis 17:23–26). Restoration scripture reports the importance, especially to God, of her lineage through Ishmael as a further way of "fulfilling, among other things, the promises" of God (Doctrine and Covenants 132:34). As further evidence that the blessings of the priesthood and the covenant were not restricted to Isaac's lineage but were indeed efficacious among other branches of the family is the later lineage of Midian, another of Abraham's sons by a third wife named Keturah (Genesis 25:1–2; Doctrine and Covenants 84:6). The clearest example of God's power being exercised in an alternate branch of the family is when Jethro, a descendant of Midian, ordained Moses to the priesthood (Doctrine and Covenants 84:6–17).

Miraculously, Sarah eventually conceived a child at the age of ninety (Genesis 21:1–5). Jehovah had told Abraham that he would indeed "be a father of many nations" and also that Sarah would be "a mother of nations" (Genesis 17:4, 16).[25] The New Testament attributes the miracle to Sarah's faith, her assurance of things hoped for even when the evidence is yet unseen (JST Hebrews 11:1, 11), though Abraham is also lauded for his faith in the miracle: "And being not weak in faith, [Abraham] considered not his own body now dead, when he was about an hundred years old, neither yet the deadness of Sara's womb" (Romans 4:19). The birth of Isaac brought great reason to rejoice and celebrate. However, at some point Isaac's teenage half-brother Ishmael was found "mocking" (Genesis 21:9). Modern scholars have debated what Ishmael was actually doing, ranging from innocently playing with Isaac to molesting him.[26] The Apostle Paul

25. In setting up the covenant with Abraham, God also gave new names to the couple—Abram became Abraham, and Sarai became Sarah. The assignment of new names likely underscores God's promises to them and their posterity by establishing this covenant; Abraham and Sarah would become a father and mother of many nations. See Flanders, Crapps, and Smith, *People of the Covenant*, 160.

26. For example, the LXX Greek is often translated as "sporting." E. A. Speiser, *Genesis* (New York: Doubleday, 1962), 155; Robert Alter, *Genesis: Translation and Commentary* (New York: Norton, 1996), 98, acknowledges attempts to portray Ishmael as a child molester but prefers to translate Ishmael's interaction with young Isaac as "playing"; C. F. Keil and F. Delitzsch imagine Isaac being the object of "profane sport" because Ishmael was full of "unbelief, envy, [and]

attributed harmful motives in Ishmael, who "persecuted" Isaac (Galatians 4:29). In his history of the Jewish people, Josephus claimed that Sarah loved Ishmael "with an affection not inferior to that of her own son" until she feared that, due to the significant difference in the two boys' ages, Ishmael should "do [Isaac] injuries when their father should be dead."[27] As chief wife, Sarah was responsible for the safety of the entire clan, not just Isaac. Whatever occurred between the boys, she concluded that the interaction was not helpful and that the boys needed to be separated. Assuming that Isaac would have been about three or four at his weaning and that Ishmael was thirteen when he was circumcised before Isaac's birth, Ishmael would have been close to seventeen years old and Isaac would have been a toddler when these problems were reported.[28] Considering the blessings that followed both boys, I would argue that Sarah acted out of desires to provide each son with opportunities best adapted to prepare them for their future God-given assignments.

Readings of the Genesis narrative often portray Sarah as an angry and selfish mother when she directed Abraham to "cast out this bondwoman [Hagar] and her son [Ishmael]: for the son of this bondwoman shall not be heir with my son, even with Isaac" (Genesis 21:10).[29] But when Abraham approached the Lord, saddened with this seemingly insensitive request, Abraham is told, "In all that Sarah hath said unto thee, hearken unto her voice; for in Isaac shall thy seed be called" (21:11–12). This suggests that

---

pride of carnal superiority." C. F. Keil and F. Delitzsch, *Commentary on the Old Testament*, (Peabody, MA: Hendrickson, 1996), 1:156, while Steinberg, *Kinship and Marriage in Genesis*, 80, considers sexual perversion in Ishmael's actions.

27. Josephus, *Antiquities of the Jews*, 1.123.

28. Ambiguity in the wording of Genesis 21:1–5 makes it unclear who nursed Isaac. Chapman suggests that Hagar may have been a wet nurse to Isaac, which strengthens kinship ties and also could explain why only then did Sarah wish to dismiss Hagar and Ishmael from the clan. Chapman, "Breast Milk as Kinship-Forging," 26–30.

29. Others have perceived more selfish motives in Sarah. For example, see John Van Seters, "The Problem of Childlessness in Near Eastern Law and the Patriarchs of Israel," *Journal of Biblical Literature* 87, no. 4 (1968): 401–8, who posits that Sarah's objective in banishing Hagar and Ishmael was to keep the inheritance intact for Isaac alone rather than splitting it between the sons.

Sarah's request was more than a vindictive response to perceived slights against her son but was, in fact, divine will. The Lord was working through Sarah who *administered* the needed reminder to her husband. Moreover, the inclusion of the last clause, "through Isaac shall thy seed be called," indicates what may have prompted Sarah's concern—namely, that the birthright may go to the wrong child.

As far as the fate of Hagar is concerned, the language of the text seems to imply that she left as a free woman. Leaving with this free status perhaps parallels another ancient Near Eastern legal code that explains that if the father of sons by a maidservant calls them "my sons," then when he dies, "the slave-girl's sons shall not share the treasures in the father's house with the first wife's sons after the father has passed to his destiny. An emancipation shall be arranged for the slave-girl and her sons. The first wife's sons shall have no rights of slavery over the slave-girl's sons."[30] Regardless, the text does make clear that Hagar is worthy enough to receive divine revelation herself, having her eyes opened while in the wilderness and being promised that God would be "with" Ishmael as he grew to manhood, making him "a great nation" (Genesis 21:18, 20).

Perhaps reflecting her free status, Hagar would eventually choose a woman from her homeland to be the wife of Ishmael (Genesis 21:21)—who would be directed to safety through God's intervention—and like Jacob and his twelve sons, Hagar would become the matriarch of the twelve tribes of Ishmael, a posterity divinely destined to bless the earth as part of God's promises (Doctrine and Covenants 132:34). Centuries later, the Apostle Paul drew on this symbolism by using Hagar and her descendants as representatives of the law of Moses, while Sarah's descendants symbolized the full law of the gospel. Ishmael's descendants would need to come to Isaac's descendants to receive the gospel of Abraham, the power of God, and the promise of exaltation (Galatians 4:21–31; Abraham 2:9–11). Ishmael's descendants would, however, have these divine promises fully available to them just like Jacob's descendants—but only when they embraced the gospel of Abraham.

30. Hammurabi Law no. 171a, in Richardson, *Hammurabi's Laws*, 95; Roth, *Law Collections*, 114.

The stories of Sarah and Hagar reinforce that the value God places on an individual is not attached to birthrights. Isaac received a greater responsibility as Abraham's heir, but that did not make him better or more loved by God than Ishmael was, nor did it make Sarah superior in God's eyes to Hagar. Sarah *administered* to Abraham as a second witness to God's revelation that through the son she bore in her old age, Abraham would establish his covenant (Genesis 17:19–21; 21:12). To Abraham and separately to Hagar, God promised his love and support for Ishmael and that his descendants would be "a great nation" blessed by the name of Abraham (Genesis 21:13, 18–20), underscoring the availability of the covenant blessings to all those who receive the gospel of Abraham (Abraham 2:10). In both cases, the women were necessarily attuned to receive God's word for their families and played pivotal roles to highlight individual worth in every son or daughter of God.[31] The pattern continued in the next generation when Sarah's daughter-in-law received divine direction for her children even before they were born.

REBEKAH

In the narrative recounting the succeeding generation, Rebekah's individuality and vitality among the covenant people is striking in stories of her becoming as Isaac's wife, receiving revelation from God for their sons, and ensuring the bestowal of the birthright on the younger child, as God intended. Rebekah becomes an agent of change in all the stories in which she appears, free to decide and act in ways that fit her perception of what is best for her and her family.[32]

---

31. Michelle A. Clifton-Soderstrom, "Beyond the Blessed/Cursed Dichotomy: The Barren Matriarchs as Oracles of Hope," *Covenant Quarterly* 69, nos. 1–2 (February–May 2011): 51–53.

32. According to Jack M. Sasson, Rebekah "proves to be the most determined of Israel's matriarchs" in "The Servant's Tale: How Rebekah Found a Spouse," *Journal of Near Eastern Studies* 65, no. 4 (2006): 265. In Schneider, *Mothers of Promise*, 50–59, Schneider consistently describes Rebekah as "decisive" and "willing to act without hesitation." Fuchs concluded that Rebekah is more "active, assertive, and talkative" than other females in the Bible. Esther Fuchs, "Structure and Patriarchal Functions in the Biblical Betrothal Type-Scenes," in

When Isaac came of age, Abraham sent his servant to find a wife for Isaac rather than sending Isaac himself (Genesis 24:1–9). After offering a prayer for assistance to identify God's choice for Isaac's wife, Abraham's servant selected Rebekah because she "hasted" to give him drink, volunteered to water all his camels, and then "hasted" and "ran" to complete the task (24:18–20)—an answer to a prayer he had previously offered that would manifest the proper woman for Isaac's wife. Rebekah's energy, discipline, and work ethic matched the servant's list of characteristics for which he sought and prayed. Indeed, her actions more than qualified for the servant's stipulation that she offer to "give thy camels drink also" (24:14). Although she is identified as the "daughter of Bethuel," Rebekah ran to "her mother's house" with news of the stranger's gifts, which is possible evidence of a matriarchate (24:24, 28).[33] When Rebekah's family preferred her to remain with them a little longer before departing with the servant, Rebekah answered, "I will go" (24:58). In their response, her family honored her opinion and wishes.[34] Here, Rebekah demonstrates that women had a voice within this ancient culture. Again, the Nuzi texts from the same general region report that although betrothals were arranged by

---

Bach, *Women in the Hebrew Bible*, 47. Frymer-Kensky posits that Rebekah devoted her life to God's covenantal promise as his "divine helper." Fyrmer-Kensky, *Reading Women of the Bible*, 19, 22. In Steinberg, *Kinship and Marriage in Genesis*, 91, 96–97, Steinberg argues for a more selfish Rebekah who chooses to act in ways that will secure her best interests in the future, such as favoring Jacob who would then favor her when he rises to power. See also Clifton-Soderstrom, "Beyond the Blessed," 53–54.

33. Cynthia Ruth Chapman, "The Biblical 'House of the Mother' and the Brokering of Marriage: Economic Reciprocity Among Natal Siblings," in *In the Wake of Tikva Frymer-Kensky*, ed. S. Holloway, J. Scurlock, R. Beal, (Piscataway, NJ: Gorgias Press, 2009): 143–69; de Alminana, "Matriarchal Structures," 58–73.

34. E. Hamori observes that Rebekah's initiative in this circumstance is key to appreciating her strategy for obtaining the birthright blessing for Jacob in Genesis 27, and her subsequent confidence to tell Jacob to obey her three times underscores this exercise of her agency to leave her homeland with Abraham's servant in *Women's Divination in Biblical Literature: Prophecy, Necromancy, and Other Arts of Knowledge* (New Haven, CT: Yale University Press, 2015): 44–45; see also Sasson, "The Servant's Tale," 261–63.

others, the bride had the option to either reject or accept the proposal.[35] Later, we, the readers, will also be asked to trust her when she crafts a plan to secure blessings for Jacob.

As the narrative progresses, it would be another twenty years after her marriage to Isaac before Rebekah gave birth to her two sons. The biblical text reports that "Isaac entreated the Lord for his wife, because she was barren" (Genesis 25:21). God heard Isaac's prayers, and Rebekah conceived.[36] When she experienced unusual discomfort in her pregnancy,[37] Rebekah spoke of her concerns directly to God, and he responded directly to her (25:22–23): she sought divine wisdom and received it. Of note, her communication with the Divine occurred during her pregnancy and not after her children were born, an indication that her individual worth to God was not dependent on giving birth. The fact that she recognized God's multifaceted revelation also suggests that communication with God was

35. See Paradise, "Marriage Contracts," 34–35; see also Cyrus H. Gordon, "The Status of Woman Reflected in the Nuzi Tablets," *Zeitschrift fur Assyriologie und Vorderasiatische Archaologie* 43, nos. 1–4 (1936): 159; Speiser, *Genesis*, 184–85, interprets the Nuzi passage as the woman's "declaration of concurrence" with the marriage proposal and by saying "[I do this] of my own free will." Selman refutes claims that the Nuzi tablets specifically describe the Hurrian culture and are therefore the best source for explaining the patriarchal era in the Bible because additional ancient Mesopotamian texts could also be cited for similar customs. He therefore concludes that people of Nuzi as well as Hurrians and the patriarchs were influenced by the larger Mesopotamian society from which they may have each adopted certain laws and customs. Selman, "The Social Environment of the Patriarchs," *Tyndale Bulletin* 27 (1976): 114–36.

36. Others translate Genesis 25:21 as follows: "Yahweh responded to [Isaac's] plea, and his wife Rebekah conceived" (Speiser, *Genesis*, 193); or "The Lord granted his plea" (Alter, *Genesis*, 126); whereas the King James Version translates the first part as follows: "And the Lord was entreated of him," which may not communicate as clearly as later translations do that God heard and answered Isaac's prayer.

37. Hamori, *Women's Divination*, 52, suggests that Rebekah feared her pregnancy may be ending because she argues for a better translation than "struggled" for what Rebekah felt between her unborn offspring when they "crushed one another within her," noting that the same Hebrew word is used to describe the skull of Abimelech being crushed by a millstone dropped from a tower (Judges 9:53) or people being crushed with oppression (Amos 4:1; Hosea 5:11).

not a novelty for Rebekah. She had likely already nurtured a relationship with her Lord and thus had developed the spiritual sensitivities necessary for clear communication.

In response to her prayer, Rebekah learned three prophetic truths: she would give birth to twin boys, each son would be a leader of a nation, and the secondborn would lead the firstborn (Genesis 25:23). In time, all three prophecies were fulfilled. The Apostle Paul referred to Rebekah's revelation about her two sons as evidence for the doctrine of election, God's practice of choosing specific missions for individuals and peoples before their mortal births (Romans 9:11).

At the time of the inheritance blessing for passing on the stewardship of the covenant to the next generation, Isaac was nearly incapacitated, described as "old, and his eyes were dim, so that he could not see" (Genesis 27:1). He was unable to distinguish his sons from each other and considered his mortal life nearly at its end (27:2). Yet he still had the divine responsibility to pronounce God's blessings upon his children, including accountability for the covenant. Isaac "loved Esau, because he did eat of his venison" and announced that he would give his firstborn his blessing after he brought back some venison for him to eat (25:28; 27:3–4). Like Abraham, who showed acceptance for Ishmael as heir, Isaac appears satisfied to give Esau the blessing.

The reader is not told whether or not God revealed to Isaac what Rebekah knew about the boys or even whether Rebekah had relayed the answer to her prayer to him. Ready to accept whatever "curse" may befall her for orchestrating a plan that sounded deceptive even to Jacob, she directed the events that followed. God had prepared a matriarch to *administer* to her husband to endorse or reconfirm that Jacob was to be the birthright son.[38] As soon as Esau departed to hunt for his father's favorite

38. In Schneider, *Mothers of Promise*, 51, Schneider interprets Rebekah's actions as motivated by her desire to see that promise be given to the one identified by God; Hamori, *Women's Divination*, 59–60, concludes that Rebekah took "independent and decisive action in family matters" because of her ability to inquire of God to understand and then to interpret the outcome; David Zucher hypothesized that Isaac understood that Jacob was the God-selected heir because neither Rebekah nor Jacob were even chastised for what they did and because Isaac took Rebekah's counsel to immediately send Jacob to her brother's home and

meat, Rebekah directed Jacob to fetch meat from the flock of goats near at hand so that she could prepare it before Esau returned (Genesis 27:5–10). Her preparation also included covering Jacob in Esau's "goodly raiment" and putting animal skin over Jacob's skin (27:15) so that he would more closely resemble his older brother.[39]

The deceptive nature of this scene can be difficult to reconcile. Her leadership in engineering the setting is undeniable and seemingly manipulative by modern standards. Yet this type of approach is not unique in the Old Testament. Several other examples of women applied what we can call trickery that was not in and of itself unethical, especially when a more direct approach did not work.[40] For example, Michal used a pillow in bed to trick Saul's hit man into thinking that David was sick in bed, thereby giving David time to escape (1 Samuel 19:11–18); the midwives Shiphrah and Puah tricked Pharaoh into thinking that Hebrew women delivered babies so quickly that no midwife was needed in childbirth, thereby saving many male babies (Exodus 1:16–20); and Jael deceived Sisera by promising hospitality when, in fact, she killed him in his sleep (Judges 4:18–22). In each case, lives were spared and God's blessings spread. Whatever the nature of Rebekah's actions, they produced an effect that she perceived

---

furthermore blessed him in their plan. David Zucher, "The Deceiver Deceived: Rereading Genesis 27," *Jewish Bible Quarterly* 39, no. 1 (2011): 46–58.

39. According to a Jewish midrash, Esau's "wonderful garments . . . were the high-priestly raiment in which God had clothed Adam," which had been handed down to Noah, Shem, Abraham, Isaac, and finally to Esau, as Isaac's firstborn. Ginzberg, *Legends of the Jews*, 1.332. The Lord clothed Adam and Eve with "coats of skins" (Genesis 3:21; Moses 4:27), and Joseph was given a covering by his father that his older brothers envied (Genesis 37:3–4). Later in the Hebrew Bible, the prophet Zechariah warned against false prophets who wear "a rough garment to deceive" (Zechariah 13:4). The resultant image is that of the true covenant son is covered with the skins of a sacrificed animal in preparation of inheriting stewardship over the covenant people.

40. Frymer-Kensky argues that trickery is often the best recourse for influencing circumstances for good, particularly by the "powerless"; their wit is often underestimated by those in power, thereby they are able to level the playing field and bring about God's plan. Frymer-Kensky, *Reading the Women of the Bible*, 19.

was necessary to the fulfilling of God's purposes—namely, the blessing placed upon Jacob instead of Esau.[41]

Isaac's subsequent blessing to Jacob (when Isaac thought the recipient was Esau) echoed the revelation that Rebekah received before the twins' birth as well as portions of the Abrahamic covenant (Genesis 27:28–29; 28:4). When Isaac discovered what had happened, he did not rescind the blessing but instead blessed Esau with "the fatness of the earth, and the dew of heaven from above," then reiterated what Rebekah learned before he was born, that "[Esau] . . . shalt serve [his] brother" (27:39–40). Having proper authority to pronounce inspired blessings, it was later written that "by faith Isaac blessed Jacob and Esau concerning things to come," implying that Isaac was directed by the Spirit (Hebrews 11:20). Whatever the impetus was behind this unusual incident, in 1880, President John Taylor defended both Rebekah and Jacob in their action on this occasion: "There was neither unrighteousness in Rebekah nor in Jacob in this matter; but on the contrary, there was the wisdom of the Almighty, showing forth his providences in guiding them in such a manner as to bring about his purposes . . . that He might ratify and confirm [the birthright] upon the head of Jacob."[42]

Whatever one's personal interpretation of Rebekah's plan to deceive Isaac in order to create an environment where God's will could be enacted,

---

41. See John E. Anderson, *Jacob and the Divine Trickster: A Theology of Deception and YHWH's Fidelity to the Ancestral Promise in the Jacob Cycle* (Winona Lake, IN: Eisenbrauns, 2011), 73–75; Speiser, *Genesis*, 195; Frymer-Kensky, *Reading the Women in the Bible*, 18. In an 1841 essay to The Church of Jesus Christ of Latter-day Saints, Apostles Brigham Young and Willard Richards suggested that God was prescient that Esau would lose his birthright so instigated a plan to preserve the blessing: "Through unbelief, hardness of heart, and hunger, [Esau] sold his birthright to his younger brother, Jacob, and God knowing beforehand that [Esau] would do this of his own free will and choice, or acting upon that agency which God has delegated to all [people], said to his mother, the elder shall serve the younger." Brigham Young and Willard Richards, "Election and Reprobation," *Millennial Star* 9, no. 1 (January 1841): 222. We do not learn the details of how this will happen, nor does the story tell us that Rebekah learn such details, but we know that Jacob is to become the birthright son.
42. John Taylor, in *Journal of Discourses* (London: Latter-day Saints' Book Depot, 1881), 21:370–71.

she prioritized her actions in order to please God and help her sons. She is never shown to turn her back on Esau, neither when he married the daughters of Hittites (Genesis 26:34–35) nor when he threatened to slay Jacob for "[taking] away [his] birthright" (27:36, 41). Juxtaposed with the scene where Sarah sent Ishmael away and kept Isaac at home, Rebekah sent Jacob away and kept Esau at home so she could watch over him.[43] In order to properly perpetuate the covenant blessings to the next generation, Jacob needed to secure the birthright blessing from his father and to secure a wife from an approved lineage, or a community of apparent believers—not from among the local women as his brother had done. The matriarch's concern for both her sons is captured in her words to Jacob, "Arise, flee thou to Laban my brother to Haran . . . until thy brother's anger turn away from thee, and he forget that which thou hast done to him: then I will send, and fetch thee from thence: why should I be deprived also of you both in one day?" (27:43–45).

The narrative hints that Esau did indeed change while his brother was away. After Jacob's departure, Esau noted his parents' pleasure when his younger brother "obeyed his father and his mother" in pursuing a wife from an acceptable lineage and how Esau had hurt them when he married two Hittite women (Genesis 26:34–35; 28:6–8). So Esau visited Ishmael and married one of his daughters (28:6–9). This passage may imply that Isaac and Ishmael had remained in contact through the years (25:9). It also allows for the interpretation that Esau may have tried to repair his relationship with his mother when he married into a family more closely related to their immediate ancestors. Another possible indication that Esau may have changed is that Esau's anger toward Jacob had evaporated by the time the brothers met again some twenty years later (33:1–15). Remarkably, it was Esau and not Jacob who initiated their reunion, and Esau who "ran to meet [Jacob], and fell on his neck and kissed him" (32:6–8; 33:4). A final amicable encounter is recorded when the brothers met to bury their dead father (35:29).

43. Speiser, *Genesis*, 211, reads Rebekah's intent and her plan's consequences for Jacob differently than I do; he sees Rebekah in a negative light in her scheme to get Jacob the blessing and that Jacob therefore paid the price of a "strong-willed mother" with "twenty years of exile."

Rebekah was unflinching in her desire to ensure that the divinely chosen son would receive the birthright, and she was confident when she *administered* to Isaac as he confirmed the promises to both sons. Far from colorless and helpless in what one would expect in a patriarchal culture, Rebekah's emotions, leadership, and willingness to act make her real to the modern reader. Through all, she retained a relationship with God. The narrative also provides a reminder that all that Rebekah and Isaac contributed to the future greatness of the covenant people came through the power of God and the covenant, despite their personal shortcomings. In the millennia that followed, distrust and war frequently defined the relationship between Esau and Jacob's descendants. The same, however, could not be said in Rebekah's day. As with other matriarchs in the patriarchal era, Rebekah was a key player in encouraging the healing of family breaches and accepting divine directives for establishing the covenant.

LEAH AND RACHEL

After receiving the birthright blessing from his father and threats on his life from his brother, Jacob escaped to his mother's homeland in hopes of finding a God-fearing wife and thereby establishing the covenant for another generation. In Haran he found just such individuals in Leah and Rachel, daughters of Laban (Rebekah's brother). As pawns in their father's strategy to exploit Jacob's favor with God, Leah and Rachel found themselves married to the same man. The biblical text reports Jacob's anger and dismay when he discovered that he had been deceived into marrying Leah instead of his beloved Rachel, but no mention is made of the women's response (Genesis 29:25). Regardless of their initial feelings, Leah and Rachel competed for a place of honor in Jacob's lineage while being equally appropriate wives for Jacob.[44] In their generation as matriarchs, the question of inheritance would not be contested between only two sons because all twelve sons received covenant responsibilities as the twelve tribes of Israel.

---

44. Leah and Rachel's struggles to gain acceptance as the chief wife are often marginalized as petty jealousy without accounting for a mother's responsibility to ensure a secure future both for her children and for herself.

In addition to being used as a mere bargaining chip for her father's financial gain, Leah felt the sting of knowing her husband had a particular affinity for Rachel, whom he had originally sought in marriage (Genesis 29:31). Leah's family members may not have been sensitive to her feelings of inferiority, but she believed that God certainly was. As reported in Genesis, the author offers glimpses of Leah's life after her marriage to suggest God's compensatory blessings to this faithful woman: "When the Lord saw that Leah was hated, he opened her womb . . . and Leah conceived, and bare a son, . . . and she conceived again, and bare a son; . . . and she conceived again, and bare a son; . . . and she conceived again, and bare a son" (29:31–35).

Leah's voice is also recorded as she named her first four sons in a manner that may reflect her growing realization that the Lord's grace and enduring love for her personally was compensation for any feelings of heartbreak or inferiority she may have felt or experienced due to her circumstances in marriage. After giving birth to Reuben, she said, "Surely the Lord hath looked upon my affliction; now therefore my husband will love me" (Genesis 29:32). When her second son was born, she called him Simeon "because the Lord hath heard that I was hated, he hath therefore given me this son also" (29:33). After her third son, Levi, was born, she said, "Now this time will my husband be joined unto me, because I have born him three sons" (29:34). And with the birth of Judah, she exclaimed, "Now will I praise the Lord" (29:35). Like the other matriarchs, she "encoded" her exclamations of gratitude and struggles into the names of her children.[45] In all, Leah bore six sons and one daughter.

On the other hand, the beautiful Rachel was fortunate to receive Jacob's adoring love but was deprived of bearing children, the cultural and visual evidence that gave women value in her society.[46] Her cry "Give me

45. The name Reuben comes from "Look, a son"; Simeon, from "Hearing"; Levi, from "Joined"; Judah, from "Praise"; Issachar, from "Recompense"; and Zebulon, from "Endued" or "Exalted." Alter, *Genesis*, 156, observes that the etymologies of these names are Leah's "ad hoc improvisations" and are a "midrashic play on the sounds of the names." See Havrelock, "Myth of Birthing the Hero," 154.

46. In the ancient world, being barren was an "acutely painful predicament." Alter, *Genesis*, 128; Meyers, "Women and the Domestic Economy of Early Israel," 37–38; Susan Niditch, "The Wronged Woman Righted: An Analysis of Genesis

children, or else I die" gives painful reality to the void in her life (Genesis 30:1). Her husband's love and visible gifts did not provide an escape from serious disappointment and trials of faith. As he did for Leah, God would also lead Rachel to where only he could help her. Jacob's response to Rachel concerning the predicament, "Am I in God's stead, who hath withheld from thee the fruit of the womb?" indicates his realization of the same truth (30:2).

Throughout the generations of Abraham, Isaac, and Jacob, all but one of the matriarchs faced trial and refinement through a period of barrenness. For a significant length of time, all except Leah feared that they might never bear a child. In addition to contributing to the strength of society, a son for these matriarchs was the assurance of the continuation of God's covenant with Abraham. As we've seen, even after giving birth, the matriarchs were responsible to ensure that the son that God had elected inherited the birthright, that he married an appropriate woman, and that the covenant was properly perpetuated through a worthy heir. In light of this, the trial of barrenness may be understood as a uniquely tailored trial that demonstrate the spiritual capacity of these women, highlighting their faith in their God.[47] From this perspective, Rachel's plea "Give me children, or else I die" was more than an instinctive maternal yearning. It was a profound longing to fulfill her God-given responsibility to continue the Abrahamic covenant through future generations. It may also highlight a stark reality. Women of the time lived on average only thirty years because of complications associated with childbirth in comparison to men, who could expect to live to at least forty, even allowing for military involvement.[48] Rachel was probably representative of more women than are noted in the Bible in that she died shortly after giving birth to her second son, Benjamin (Genesis 35:17–18).

Despite the expanding size of his son-in-law's family and their greater use of his land for over twenty years, Laban was loath to see Jacob's large

---

38," *Harvard Theological Review* 72, nos. 1–2 (January–April 1979): 143–49; Van Seters, "The Problem of Childlessness," 401–8.

47. Havrelock, "Myth of Birthing the Hero," 160; Clifton-Soderstrom, "Beyond the Blessed," 47–64.

48. Meyers, *Discovering Eve*, 112; Meyers, "Double Vision," 126.

family depart. Jacob, Leah, Rachel, and their servants were a significant workforce to him and collectively contributed incredible wealth. Clearly, the Lord had blessed Laban's clan since Jacob's coming (Genesis 30:30). Should they depart, Laban's holdings and potential for expansion would be dramatically reduced. Laban's insistence that Jacob had no right to take away his wives and their children from their family home indicates a coexisting and competing system of marriage in that era. Rather than bring a wife into the husband's father's clan, the system that Laban assumed echoes Adam's instruction, "Therefore shall a man leave his father and his mother, and shall cleave unto his wife" (Genesis 2:24). Arguably, Laban was legally protected in his demands to keep his daughters' families at their maternal home.[49]

After Rachel gave birth to Joseph, her first son and Jacob's eleventh, and after Laban changed his payment agreement with Jacob for the tenth time, the Lord directed Jacob to return to his homeland in Canaan (Genesis 31:3). Rachel and Leah also found dishonesty in their father's dealings with them. Rather than providing each with a dowry, derived at least in part from the bride price paid to the bride's family, Laban had "quite devoured" it (31:15). The dowry was compensation for a daughter's separation from the family property and was a critical part of establishing a new household, including what she contributed toward an inheritance for the next generation and her security should she become widowed or divorced.[50] Thus, Leah and Rachel were angry with Laban because he failed to give them their dowries or bride wealth earned from the fourteen years Jacob worked for them (31:14–16).

Betrayed by their earthly father, Leah and Rachel could have been tempted to distrust others close to them. But here, the sisters appear at their best. Their finest moment in scripture occurs when their voices

---

49. de Alminana, "Matriarchal Structures," 61–65.

50. See the following laws dealing with a father's obligation to pay a dowry from the Code of Hammurabi: #138 as security if her husband divorces her, #163–64 as security if she cannot bear children, and #183–84 as security whether or not her father dies before she marries. Ze'ev W. Falk notes that the father's dowry to his daughters at marriage finally gives them independence from their father in *Hebrew Law in Biblical Times*, 2nd ed. (Provo, UT: Brigham Young University Press; Winona Lake, IN: Eisenbrauns, 2001), 143.

combine to give inspired counsel to their husband. The Lord commanded Jacob to depart from Haran, but before acting upon the command, Jacob counseled with Leah and Rachel (Genesis 31:4). Despite the fact that their departure would be in obedience to God, leaving under such circumstances would damage the relationship between the women and their father. The decision to leave therefore required partnership. Surrounded by a flock of sheep in their father's fields, Rachel and Leah were united and grounded in their reverence for God's word as they counseled Jacob, "Whatsoever God hath said unto thee, do" (31:16). Different from Sarah and Hagar, Leah and Rachel eventually overcame their rivalry and united in their family's best interest.[51] The two matriarchs contributed inspired support to Jacob's revelation considering that their children's futures would be shaped by this decision.

In the short time that Laban needed to organize his pursuit of Jacob's clan, Laban must have surveyed the security of his greatest valuables only to find that his *teraphim* were missing.[52] Scripture reports that "Rachel had stolen the images that were her father's" just before they secretly departed (Genesis 31:19). Because no explanation is given for the significance of the "images" or for Rachel's motive for taking them, a plethora of varied justifications have been proposed. For example, Josephus posited that she took them as a form of collateral to barter for their freedom should her father try to stop them.[53] Rabbinic literature depicts Rachel as trying to break Laban from his reliance on idolatry by removing the figurines from his home.[54] Because *teraphim* were used for divination in other biblical accounts (1 Samuel 15:22–23; 2 Kings 23:24; Ezekiel 21:26; Zecheriah

51. Alice Ogden Bellis, "A Sister Is a Forever Friend: Reflections on the Story of Rachel and Leah," *Journal of Religious Thought* 55–56, nos. 1–2 (1999): 109–15.

52. The Hebrew term is of uncertain etymology but may reflect a custom in Aram where figurines were used as deities that represented household gods or ancestors believed to hold some special power or influence in the clan. See Edward M. Curtis, "Idol, Idolatry," in *Anchor Bible Dictionary*, 6 vols., ed. David Noel Freedman (New York: Doubleday, 1992); 3:378–79.

53. Josephus, *Antiquities of the Jews*, 1.19.8.

54. Ginzberg, *Legends of the Jews*, 1:374.

10:2), she may have feared her father could detect their whereabouts if he had them.[55]

Again, the Nuzi texts may provide insight since modern scholars have considered them as a source to suggest that possession of the household gods determined inheritance or paterfamilias.[56] Others suggest that *teraphim* were believed to invite their ancestor or a divine presence to protect their households from harm[57] or guarantee "them a place in the family's heritage"[58] or bestow upon them divine gifts, including childbirth.[59] Each of these explanations is worthy of consideration, although no one of them has been overwhelmingly accepted in the absence of further evidence. One's preferred explanation is likely based on how one perceives Rachel. Did she look to figurines for answers and protection, or did she trust in Jacob's God for these blessings? Considering her important role as a matriarch of the covenant, I can't help but assign her a God-fearing motive in light of the dearth of details.

---

55. Rabbinic literature assigns fears in Rachel that her father would use the teraphim to learn about their "flight" and where to find them, so she stole them. Ginzberg, *Legends of the Jews*, 1:371–72.

56. *Ancient Near Eastern Texts*, 219; see, for example, Cyrus H. Gordon, who cites the Nuzi texts to show Rachel's attempt to make Jacob the head of the family after Laban died, "Biblical Customs and the Nuzu Tablets," *Biblical Archaeology* 3 (1940): 1–12, and Anne E. Draftkorn, who cites both family leadership and inheritance as justification for Rachel taking the images in "Ilani/Elohim," *Journal of Biblical Literature* 76 (1957): 216–24, as does Alter, *Genesis*, 169.

57. Frymer-Kensky, "Rachel," in *Women in Scripture: A Dictionary of Named and Unnamed Women in the Bible, Apocryphal/Deuterocanonical Books, and the New Testament*, edited by Carol Meyers (Grand Rapids, MI: Eerdmans, 2000), page 139. Ktziah Spanier argues, "Rachel stole her father's teraphim in order to enhance her position in the family and to secure Joseph's position among his brothers," thus setting the stage for the future rivalry between the House of Joseph and the House of Judah in "Rachel's Theft of the Teraphim: Her Struggle for Family Primacy," *Vestus Testamentum* 42, no. 3 (1992): 404–12.

58. Flanders, Crapps, and Smith, *People of the Covenant*, 152.

59. Moshe Greenburg, "Another Look at Rachel's Theft of the Teraphim," *Journal of Biblical Literature* 81, no. 3 (1962): 239–48. In Bright, *History of Israel*, 79, Bright considers the Nuzi texts "especially illuminating" for explaining the Laban-Jacob stories but acknowledges that any explanation may be disputed.

Whatever Rachel's motives or the significance of the "images," she did not tell Jacob what she had done (Genesis 31:32). She also succeeded in sending her father home without them, although she may not have kept them either. In preparing his family to enter their new homeland and make an offering to God at Bethel, Jacob required them all to "put away the strange gods that are among you, and be clean, and change your garments" (35:2), suggesting that others in the traveling group brought similar artifacts of idolatry. The narrator reports that "they gave unto Jacob all the strange gods which were in their hand, and all their earrings which were in their ears; and Jacob hid them under the oak which was by Shechem" (35:4). If Laban's *teraphim* were indeed household gods, Rachel did not keep them but instead buried them in the ground along with other "strange gods" that others in the company had carried with them.

Leah and Rachel's individual responses to God in the midst of their unexpected trials helped to shape the foundation of God's covenant people. Centuries after the patriarchal era, community leaders in Bethlehem would bless a new bride named Ruth, praying that she would be a woman "like Rachel and like Leah, which two did build the house of Israel" (Ruth 4:11). The Hebrew word translated here as "build" appears frequently in the Old Testament and is used to describe literal and figurative construction, be it men constructing a physical edifice (Genesis 8:20; 1 Kings 6:1) or women creating an individual, family, or nation through childbirth (Genesis 16:2; 30:3). Genesis also uses this verb in conjunction with God's works: God "built" woman from a rib (2:22).[60]

Different in appearance from each other as well as in their challenges, Rachel and Leah are known best by what they accomplished together. Along with their maids Zilpah and Bilhah, Leah and Rachel are the mothers of the twelve tribes of Israel. Rachel became the ancestor of many of the Israelites' leaders from the time of the conquest of Canaan, including Joshua; the judges Gideon, Deborah, Jephthah, and Samuel; and Saul, the first king of Israel. One of her two sons, Joseph, also received the

60. The same Hebrew word בנה *(banah)* is translated in the KJV as "made" (a woman) in Genesis 2:2, "obtain" (children) in Genesis 16:2, and "have" (children) in Genesis 30:3 but most often "build/builded" when describing physical construction of edifices.

birthright blessing, which includes important responsibilities in the latter days (2 Nephi 3). Leah's posterity was every bit as impressive. She was the ancestor of Moses and Aaron and the other administrators of the Levitical priesthood down to John the Baptist. Most notably, through her son Judah, Leah was an ancestor of the kings of Israel and Judah from David until Jesus Christ. Recognizing that all of Abraham's children and all of the tribes of Israel are invited to receive the Lord's choicest blessings, Leah and Rachel remind us that our specific lineage is not as critical as what we do with the opportunities gleaned through the covenant. That truth is magnified in the next generation through the unique approach of a matriarch connected to Judah's family.

TAMAR

A lesser-known matriarch in Genesis is Tamar, the daughter-in-law of Judah and mother of two of his children. Her story can provide another example of *administering* when the continuity of Judah's lineage was threatened. Although some within Judah's clan at the time may have found Tamar's application of wit and wisdom shameful in securing an heir, her reaction to Judah's deceit fit the acceptable customs of the day and established his lineage among the other tribes of Israel.

A comparison of Judah's character before Tamar's influence on him and after it, with his portrayal in later Genesis chapters, reveals a dramatic transformation. Judah concocted the plan to sell Joseph, Rachel's firstborn and the chosen heir, to the Ishmaelites/Midianites, because "what profit is it if we slay our brother, and conceal his blood?" (Genesis 37:26–33). When this portrayal of Judah's jealous and mercenary attitudes is contrasted with his mature actions years later when he believed that his youngest brother Benjamin was in mortal danger, a significant change of heart is evident. Judah offered himself as a slave in place of Benjamin, who had replaced the seemingly dead Joseph in their father's heart (44:18–34). Judah, the betrayer, offered his own life to redeem his victim's successor. The only story included in the Genesis narrative to possibly explain Judah's transformation is the story of Tamar.

In the ancient Near East, a woman's marital obligation was to her husband's family, which obligation continued for as long as her husband's brothers or her father-in-law lived. Since there was no welfare, life insurance, or social security in ancient Israel and since a woman's security in old age was dependent upon her sons, the law of the *levir* (Latin for "husband's brother") stated that a widow of childbearing age was entitled to bear children through a male in-law acting as proxy for her dead husband (Deuteronomy 25:5–6). The men in the family could refuse, but in so doing would be shamed in a public ritual, probably similar to that described in the later law of Moses, where the widow is instructed to remove a shoe of the unwilling man and spit in his face (25:7–9). The levirate duty both honored the dead brother by continuing his family line and reaffirmed the young widow's inclusion in the family of her dead husband.[61] According to a Middle Assyrian law from the fourteenth century BC, a widow's father-in-law was obliged to arrange a levirate marriage for her if she had not borne a son. The same law stipulated that if a father-in-law had no other son over the age of ten years, he himself could be the *levir* for a widowed daughter-in-law.[62] This ancient law also declared that a woman was only truly a widow when her husband and father-in-law were both dead and she had no son. According to these ancient laws, Judah was a legal proxy for Tamar's deceased husband. Yet Judah is depicted as not fulfilling his duties, instead leaving Tamar without a spouse and therefore without the legitimate means to continue her husband's line, which, as we shall see, is the impetus to recognizing Tamar's willingness to do what she can to secure the blessing of posterity.

The narrative begins with Judah selecting Tamar as a wife for Er, his eldest son. As a result of Er's wickedness, "the Lord slew him," and Judah gave Tamar to his second son, Onan, to marry "and raise up seed to

---

61. Niditch, "Wronged Woman Righted," 145–46.

62. Middle Assyrian Law 33: "If a woman is residing in her own father's house, her husband is dead, and she has sons . . . , or [if he so pleases], he shall give her into the protection of the household of her father-in-law. If her husband and her father-in-law are both dead, and she has not son, she is indeed a widow; she shall go wherever she pleases." Roth, *Law Collections*, 165; *Ancient Near Eastern Texts*, 182.

[Er]," as allowed by the law of the *levir* (Genesis 38:7–8). Because Onan's actions also "displeased the Lord . . . he slew him also," leaving Judah with only one remaining son, Shelah (38:10). The scriptures report that Judah instructed Tamar to "remain a widow at thy father's house, till Shelah my son be grown, . . . lest peradventure he die also, as his brethren did" (38:11). Though the text suggests that the reason for Tamar remaining a widow is because of the young age of Judah's third son, Shelah, Judah's concern that Shelah would die like his brothers suggests that he may have feared that the environment surrounding Shelah could lead to him being as wicked as his brothers or that Tamar herself was the reason behind the brothers' premature deaths.[63] What is clear is that Judah's concern here was clearly for Shelah and not for Tamar. Yet, after marrying into Judah's family, she no longer belonged to her father's family.[64] Thus, the incident highlights Tamar's precarious and anomalous position in her society because, by marrying, she was no longer a legitimate member of her father's clan, and without producing an heir for Judah's family, she was not yet a full member of Judah's clan.[65]

Tamar had done all that she was asked as a member of Judah's family, but she was once again in the vulnerable position of being without any legal ties to family support and honor. Her only other option was to risk death if she illegally went outside Judah's family in order to procure the security that only a son could provide her. To make matters worse, Judah appears to have avoided visiting her or allowing her to see Shelah, thus placing her in a position where she could not fulfill her marital responsibilities. In this predicament, Tamar takes matters into her own hands, demonstrating again the seriousness to which these women sought to fulfil their responsibilities. When she heard that Judah would be traveling nearby on his way to shear sheep, she set out to meet him and, in so doing,

---

63. Mordecai Friedman assumes that Judah blamed Tamar for his sons' deaths in "Tamar, A Symbol of Life: The 'Killer Wife' Superstition in the Bible and Jewish Tradition," *Association for Jewish Studies Review* 15 (1990): 23–61; see also Alter, *Genesis*, 219.

64. Niditch, "Wronged Woman Righted," 146; Alter, *Genesis*, 219, points out the social disgrace that would have attended Tamar by having to return to her father's house "after having been twice married."

65. Niditch, "Wronged Woman Righted," 144–46.

saw that Shelah was with Judah and noted that "Shelah was grown, and she was not given unto him to wife" (Genesis 38:13–14).

The narrator does not explain Tamar's intent when she intercepted her father-in-law in his travels, nor does the text state she was right or wrong in what follows. The Genesis account only tells us that she removed any indication of her widowhood, covered herself with a veil so as not to be recognized, and sat in an open place to await Judah's arrival along the road (38:14). Wearing a veil did not in and of itself signify that a woman was a prostitute.[66] On the contrary, veils most often indicated respectability. Rebekah donned a veil before meeting Isaac (Genesis 24:65). Leah was probably veiled for her wedding to Jacob to disguise the fact that she was not Rachel (29:23–25). By contrast, harlots were expected to reveal their faces to clearly communicate who and what they were, as indicated by a Middle Assyrian law that banned prostitutes from wearing veils on penalty of punishment to prevent them from being mistaken as honorable women.[67]

Although the reader is not told Tamar's initial intention, Judah's intent is clear; he solicited a solitary woman whom he assumed to be easy game.[68] Judah saw what he wanted to see, whether the woman was veiled or not. Stated another way, the text does not call Tamar a harlot—Judah did (Genesis 38:15). With that said, Tamar does establish whereby Judah's response may have been expected, and in so doing, she shamed him into performing his proper responsibilities. "And [Judah] turned unto her by

---

66. Victor P. Hamilton suggested, "Tamar's wearing of the veil was not to make Judah think she was a prostitute. Rather, it was intended to prevent him from recognizing her. It is not the veil but Tamar's positioning herself [alone on an open road] that made her appear to be a prostitute" in *Book of Genesis: Chapters 18–50*, New International Commentary on the Old Testament Series, (Grand Rapids, MI: Eerdmans, 1995), 442–43.

67. Middle Assyrian Law #40: "Wives of a man, or [widows], or any [Assyrian] women who go out into the main thoroughfare [shall not have] their heads [bare]. . . . A concubine who goes about in the main thoroughfare with her mistress is to be veiled. A prostitute shall not be veiled, her head shall be bare. Whoever sees a veiled prostitute shall seize her, secure witnesses, and bring her to the palace entrance. . . . They shall strike her 50 blows with rods; they shall pour hot pitch over her head." Roth, *Law Collections*, 167–68.

68. Schneider, *Mothers of Promise*, 153–56.

the way, and said, Go to, I pray thee, let me come in unto thee; (for he knew not that she was his daughter in law)" (38:16). Tamar accepted his proposition with a request for some form of collateral from him until he could send payment. The fact that a woman thought to be a harlot was not condemned or chastised suggests that prostitution was an occurring line of work for marginalized women who lived outside the family unit and beyond society's boundaries.[69] If Judah wanted to treat his neglected daughter-in-law as a prostitute, she could play the role to ensure that her legal family rights were met.

Tamar wanted something that would clearly prove that the man who slept with her was Judah. She requested as security "[Judah's] signet, and [his] bracelets, and [his] staff which is in [his] hand" (Genesis 38:18), thus securing items that would have clearly identified Judah as the father if she succeeded in conceiving.[70] When Judah's Canaanite friend returned with a kid goat for payment to "the harlot," no woman by such a description could be found. So Judah decided to forfeit his pledge and avoid public ridicule, saying to his friend, "Let her take it to her, lest we be shamed" (38:23), or, in other words, "Let her keep the things, or we shall become a laughingstock."[71] These details seem to suggest that there was some sort of moral concern running throughout the logistics of the story and the appearance behind the unfolding events.

Three months after his encounter with "the harlot," Judah was informed that his "daughter in law hath played the harlot" because she was pregnant (Genesis 38:24). Even though she lived with her own father, by law Tamar was still responsible to Judah, the head of her husband's family. Knowing that Shelah had not been near her, Judah assumed that Tamar had acted outside his family. As head of Er's clan and protector of the family's honor, Judah therefore sentenced Tamar to be burned. As Tamar was being led to her death, she publicly announced, "By the man, whose these are, am I with child. . . . Discern, I pray thee" (38:25). The

---

69. Niditch, "Wronged Woman Righted," 147.

70. In *Genesis*, 298, Speiser explains that Judah gave Tamar his "seal on the cord," which was a cylinder seal used for legal identification, and that his staff would have also contained personalized markings. See also Alter, *Genesis*, 221.

71. Alter, *Genesis*, 222; Frymer-Kensky, *Women in Scripture*, 162.

collateral she collected from Judah now vindicated her. Upon realizing his role in Tamar's pregnancy, Judah honestly owned up to his fault and declared, "She hath been more righteous than I" (38:26). He admitted that he had behaved unjustly toward his daughter-in-law, absolved her of any guilt in her unconventional act, and acknowledged that she had assumed greater responsibility for guaranteeing the continuity of the family than he had done.[72] Her extreme example humiliated him and helped to awaken him to repent.

Tamar's solution to her impossible situation is difficult to square with moral standards of today. She used deception to obtain what was rightfully hers. We would never advise a young woman to try a similar stunt to achieve her dream of motherhood. But like some of the former matriarchal stories, such behavior ends up playing a major part in an individual's ability to obtain blessings that result in God's plan moving forward. Sarah agrees to claim she is Abraham's sister rather than his wife, Rebekah disguises Jacob to appear like Esau, and Leah barters with Rachel to spend a night with Jacob. Through Tamar's unusual yet courageous actions, Judah reawakened his loyalty to the covenant family. If she had remained docile and obedient to Judah's commands by living without hope in her father's house, Judah would have likely remained separate from his father and siblings. Because Tamar led him to face his own deceit, Judah learned that to act shamefully before the Lord will bring heartache in return. After losing his wife, two sons, and almost his last son, Judah experienced a change of heart to sense a greater concern for what God thought of him than for what his neighbors thought of him. The Genesis narrative of Judah's future encounters with his family, including Joseph, indicates that this change of heart was profound and permanent (Genesis 43:8–9; 44:18–34). While we witness human imperfections and difficult decisions that are made within these stories (which are not always extolled or credited to God's direct involvement or directives), we see that God works with well-intentioned individuals who are trying their best to act for the greater good and with a desire to accomplish the works of God for their families. Within these unconventional stories, we also see that God is concerned for the destitute

72. Steinberg, *Kinship and Marriage in Genesis*, 127; Speiser, *Genesis*, 300; Alter, *Genesis*, 223.

and enables people to change and receive their greatest righteous desires, especially through the most difficult of circumstances.

Tamar eventually bore Judah twin sons, Pharez and Zarah (Genesis 38:27–30). These boys secured their mother's place in Judah's family and support for her in her old age. But, more importantly for religious history, they were sons of Judah who were chosen to prepare a royal lineage that began with King David and culminated with the Savior's birth. Centuries after she joined with Jacob's clan, Tamar's descendants noted her lasting contribution to set aright Judah and his family. On Boaz and Ruth's wedding day, the community at Bethlehem pronounced a blessing on them: "Let thy house be like the house of Pharez, whom Tamar bare unto Judah" (Ruth 4:12). Obed, the son of Ruth and Boaz, was a progenitor of David and of Jesus. Matthew recognized the magnitude of these events when he noted them in the Savior's genealogy, "And Judas begat Phares and Zara of Thamar" (Matthew 1:3). Tamar is one of only four women named in the genealogy that introduces the reader to Mary, the mother of Jesus. The other three are Rahab, Ruth, and Bathsheba. A plausible explanation for this unusual inclusion is that each of these four women combine two elements that make them types of Mary, the mother of Jesus: (1) they experienced an irregular marital history that could be misjudged as scandalous by outsiders and (2) each woman showed initiative in carrying out God's plan and thereby continued the chosen lineage of the Son of God.[73]

ZIPPORAH

God's power and authority for the miraculous deliverance of the Israelites centers on Moses and his older brother, Aaron. Several women also played prominent roles that exemplified unshakable benevolence and established

73. Raymond E. Brown, *Mary in the New Testament* (Philadelphia: Fortress Press, 1978): 82. If Matthew's intent in the genealogy of Jesus was to dissuade Jews of his day from discounting Mary's divine role because of questions surrounding the paternity of her son, Matthew may have listed these four women, who were considered heroines in his day but were wrongfully judged by some at the time over these irregular episodes, which would have made this theory very attractive.

a foundation from which a God-fearing people could develop—chief among such people being Zipporah (Exodus 2:16–21).

Zipporah, we are told, was the eldest daughter of Jethro, who himself was a descendant of Midian, one of six sons born to Abraham and his third wife Keturah (Genesis 25:2). It was Jethro who later taught Moses about delegating responsibility when the weight of governing the children of Israel in the wilderness became especially onerous (Exodus 18:13–27). From Restoration scripture, we learn that it was also from Jethro that Moses received the Melchizedek Priesthood, Jethro having received the higher priesthood by the laying on of hands as it had been handed down to each generation beginning with Adam (Doctrine and Covenants 84:6–17). Knowing that Jethro held legitimate priesthood authority provides the needed connection for the appropriateness of Zipporah as a wife for Moses, who would be Jehovah's elected deliverer and leader of the Israelites (Exodus 2:21). Without clarification from this modern revelation, Zipporah is easily imagined as an outsider from the faith and covenant of Abraham.[74]

While not much is said about Zipporah, one account demonstrates her matriarchal qualities to act in order for the covenant to be established. According to Exodus 4, on their way back to Egypt, having received his prophetic commission at Sinai, "the Lord met [Moses], and sought to kill him" (Exodus 4:24). The circumstances behind this meeting are not given in the text, but according to the account, in response to the divine death threat, "Zipporah took a sharp stone, and cut off the foreskin of her son,

74. Edith Deen, *All the Women in the Bible* (San Francisco: Harper and Row, 1988), 54–56, describes Zipporah as "prejudiced and rebellious," as indicated by Deen's conjecture that Midianites and Hebrews had such different religious views, so Zipporah refused to allow their sons to be circumcised. In Siegfried Herrmann, *A History of Israel in Old Testament Times*, 2nd ed. (Philadelphia: Fortress Press, 1981), 75, Herrmann maintains that nothing in the text supports suggestions that Jethro and the Midianites followed Jehovah worship either previous to Moses's residence with them or as a result of his residence with them. In Bright, *History of Israel*, 127, Bright acknowledges that one might read Exodus 18 to mean that Jethro was already a worshipper of Jehovah before Moses came but that "many scholars" argue against such an interpretation. Restoration clarifies that Jethro was indeed a worshipper before and ordained Moses to the higher priesthood; see Doctrine and Covenants 84:6–7.

and cast it at his [Moses'] feet, and said, Surely a bloody husband art thou to me. So he [the Lord] let him go: then she said, A bloody husband thou art, because of the circumcision" (Exodus 4:25–26).

This passage has been recognized as one of the most difficult in the Old Testament to decipher and understand because so much appears to be missing.[75] Some have suggested that the blood of Moses's firstborn son vicariously functioned to save him, foreshadowing the use of blood to save the Israelites from the destroying angel and the destruction of the firstborn as recorded in Exodus 12:12–14, 43–48. In this analysis, the rite of circumcision is subsumed into the larger ritual of vicarious purification for sin to enjoy the blessings of salvation.[76]

Bernard P. Robinson explains God's anger against Moses to be the result of Moses's reticence to obey God in the important task at hand: confronting Pharaoh with the potential death of his son if he refused to free the Israelites (Exodus 4:21–23). Robinson argues for "son-in-law" as a better translation than "husband" or "bridegroom" for the Hebrew *ḥātān* in Zipporah's statement in Exodus 4:25–26 because they were no longer newlyweds (Zipporah had borne two sons), and in the absence of her father, Zipporah became a surrogate father-in-law to perform circumcision, which was considered "a male role." Like William Propp, Robinson concludes that "if Israel is to survive the wrath of YHWH, it must, our text implies, be by virtue of the spilling of atoning blood. . . . Gershom's blood saves Moses, just as the blood of the Passover lamb will save the Israelites." Therefore, Zipporah should be praised, Robinson argues, as a "foreign woman who puts Israelites to shame and earns the right to be held up as a model for imitation."[77]

---

75. William H. Propp, "That Bloody Bridegroom (Exodus IV 24–6)," *Vestus Testamentum* 43, no. 4 (1993): 495–519; Bernard P. Robinson, "Zipporah to the Rescue: A Contextual Study of Exodus IV 24–6," *Vestus Testamentum* 36, no. 4 (1986), 447–61; Godfrey W. Ashby, "The Bloody Bridegroom: The Interpretation of Exodus 4:24–26," *Expository Times* 106 (1995): 203–5.

76. Propp, "That Bloody Bridegroom," 495–519.

77. Robinson, "Zipporah to the Rescue," 447–61; Susan Ackerman goes so far as to call Zipporah a priestess because she assumed the male role of a priest or spiritual leader during a transitional time for Moses, see Susan Ackerman, "Why

Godfrey Ashby assigned God's anger against Moses to his omission of "liturgical conformity," or failure to heed the requirement of ordinances in his obedience to God, though this was made right by Zipporah's obedience. Ashby argues for the importance of circumcision and blood in the story as "a token sacrifice for the whole person" and by extension the sacrificial offering of the firstborn son to God. Ashby further connects blood with the power of holiness in the way Paul used it in Colossians 1:15–20 to describe Jesus as the firstborn who redeemed humankind with his own blood. To Ashby, "Bridegroom of blood" or "bloody husband" is evidence of Zipporah's triumphant administrations that finally qualified Moses completely to lead the covenant people of God. Similar to others, Ashby sees the episode as a type of the Passover and as the Israelites' deliverance occurring on condition of their "willingness to serve" God.[78]

Finally, Christopher B. Hays suggests that the blood of Zipporah's son is a type or echo of the blood of the lamb and that Zipporah's actions represent "its vicarious sacrificial value." Hays explores whose feet Zipporah touched with her son's blood because the wording is vague (Zipporah "cut off the foreskin of her son, and cast it at his feet"). The feet could belong to any male present: Moses, their son, or Jehovah. Hays opines that she touched Jehovah's feet with the blood to signify her claims to divine kinship in the covenant Jehovah made with Abraham.[79] In all four arguments, Zipporah's actions are depicted as positive acts that save the lives of both her husband and son, acts that are even prophetic in that they seem to foreshadow the same divine protection for all of the Israelites in their attempt to escape Egypt.

Latter-day revelation provides even greater understanding to the narrative, with the Joseph Smith Translation underscoring Zipporah's role as Moses's rescuer and a believer. First, the JST specifies the reason for the Lord's ire: "The Lord was angry with Moses, and his hand was about to fall upon him, to kill him; for he had not circumcised his son" (JST Exodus

---

Is Miriam Also among the Prophets? (And Is Zipporah among the Priests?)," *Journal of Biblical Literature* 121, no. 1 (2002): 47-80, specifically 71–75.

78. Ashby, "The Bloody Bridegroom," 203–5.

79. Christopher B. Hays, "'Lest Ye Perish in the Way': Ritual and Kinship in Exodus 4:24–26," *Hebrew Studies* 48 (2007): 39–54.

4:24). No explanation is given in the JST for why Moses had failed to honor God's directive to circumcise his son, but God's displeasure is obvious. So Zipporah *administered* the required token of the covenant, satisfying the Lord and saving her husband's life: "And the Lord spared Moses and let him go, because Zipporah, his wife, circumcised the child. And she said, Thou art a bloody husband [unto me]. And Moses was ashamed, and hid his face from the Lord, and said, I have sinned before the Lord" (JST Exodus 4:25–26). As the JST makes clear, Moses had not fulfilled his patriarchal duty (for whatever reasons) and had therefore instigated divine retribution. This lack of information is important because it makes Zipporah's quick and immediate action the significant act in the narrative. Her immediate obedience becomes the center of the story at this pivotal moment in the history of the Israelites' deliverance. Moreover, it appears that her actions caused Moses to feel guilty, thus bringing him back into a state of repentance whereby God could again trust in Moses, his servant. Thus, like the matriarchs before her, Zipporah not only ensured the future of her posterity but also made it possible for her husband to fully become what the Lord needed him to be.

CONCLUSION

The patriarchs in the pre-Exodus stories of the Bible are portrayed as having God's authority and power to pronounce God's blessings on the next generation and to act as heads of their extended families. A close reading of the text supplies sufficient evidence to argue that God also allotted the matriarchs significant positions to act and actively influence the well-being of their families and to help shape an environment where life can progress and achieve God's divine plan. Each woman also illustrates how her struggles surrounding motherhood were essential to forming a personal relationship between herself and God. The roles of men assigned as patriarchs and protectors of these ancient societies were not diminished but rather magnified by the complementary authority exercised by the matriarchs. The text reinforces the reality that women and men need each other to fulfill their divine missions and that both need to establish a personal relationship with God.

The lives of the matriarchs bespeak their good intentions and the powerful effects they had on their families. Their lives demonstrate courage and a desire to fulfill the purposes of God. The result of the joint efforts between these husbands and wives, patriarchs and matriarchs, are described in a revelation relating to the eternal nature of the marriage covenant and may be summarized as follows: when this covenant is sealed by "the Holy Spirit of promise," the Lord taught that "Abraham received concubines, and they bore him children; and it was accounted unto him for righteousness, because they were given unto him, and he abode in my law; as Isaac also and Jacob did none other things than that which they were commanded; and because they did none other things than that which they were commanded, they have entered into their exaltation, according to the promises, and sit upon thrones, *and are not angels but are gods*" (Doctrine and Covenants 132:37; emphasis added). Exaltation is not awarded to a patriarch alone; modern scripture teaches that in order to obtain this highest eternal reward, "a man must enter into . . . the new and everlasting covenant of marriage" (Doctrine and Covenants 131:2). Together, the patriarchs and matriarchs performed their divine roles to establish and spread God's covenant blessings that continue to strengthen us today.

In summary, by considering the biblical text in light of Restoration scripture and teachings, we may appreciate four truths about the leading women of Israel's ancestral era. First, the matriarchs are as interesting and capable as their male counterparts. The matriarchs acted with divine insight, desired to accomplish the purposes of God, and took initiative to do their best to fulfill his purposes. Second, the matriarchs and patriarchs need to work together through difficult environments to ensure the perpetuation of the covenant. Whatever the circumstance, matriarchs and patriarchs need divine direction to decipher the best responses. Third, the matriarchs were as much the recipients God's love and concern as were the patriarchs. God spoke directly to these women to accomplish his plan and promises to their families.

Finally, evidence of women and men receiving God's power in their weakness is palpable during the ancestral era. These leaders were human and often responded in ways that appear unusual to us. As some have observed, the men and women of the ancestral era show that God was "working not with angels or puppets, but with believable human persons, male and female, whose lives reflect the conflicting dimensions of free personhood."[80] Despite some of the challenging and unique circumstances they encountered in their lives and despite some of the unusual solutions that were enacted to address these situations, in every case, the narratives of these imperfect women highlight their awareness of God's purposes and plans for the men, women, and children in their lives, while at the same time demonstrating that women themselves could have deep, individualized relationships with God.

The biblical story of establishing the Abrahamic covenant commences with men and women teaching each other, supporting each other, and depending on each other to do much more than survive. Unmistakably, the Bible teaches us today that women and men still need each other to succeed in God's plan to save them. Indeed, this early biblical era underscores that salvation is both an individual and a community endeavor. This era also highlights that in nothing did the covenant people succeed without God's enabling power.

80. Flanders, Crapps, and Smith, *People of the Covenant*, 164.

— 13 —

CLOTHES AND CUPS

THE TANGIBLE WORLD OF JOSEPH

JOHN GEE

The story of Joseph is a colorful one, to say the least. Perhaps one of the more interesting aspects of the narrative is the role of objects to perpetuate the narrative, specifically the role of clothing and the cup Joseph used in his reconciliation with his family. In other words, it isn't just what the objects were that is significant; it is also what the objects meant within the culture. In this chapter, John Gee examines these two objects from the perspective of their cultural relevance, which, in turn, may provide readers with a new methodological approach to objects in other scriptural texts. —DB and AS

The events narrated in the Bible were not the interactions of ethereal essences but the stories of mortals with physical bodies using material objects in specific geographical locations. Part of the mortal existence for both us and the individuals spoken of in the Bible is the physical dimension of our mortal lives. If one were to name the physical item most associated with the biblical Joseph, it would probably be his clothing. When a Broadway musical retold the story of Joseph, the plot may have concentrated on the dreams, but the title mentioned his coat. Another key physical object associated with Joseph are cups. The cups may not be as prominent as the clothes, but they still play an important and telling role in the story. Both these physical artifacts point to a tangible reality behind the account of Joseph that emphasizes that the story of Joseph is based in fact rather than fiction. In the brief space that we have here, we will examine the role that these two types of objects play in the Joseph narrative. While there are many other facets of Joseph's history, we will not deal with those here.

PART 1: CLOTHES

While the old adage that "clothes make the man" may be overstating the situation, clothing serves a number of different functions. It provides protection from heat, cold, and the elements. It also signals status. Clothes, or the lack thereof, can communicate wealth or status, or the lack thereof, ethnicity, and a wide variety of other things. In Joseph's day, one could tell whether one was a master or a slave, a local or a foreigner, wealthy or poor, simply by the clothing one was wearing. Three millennia, however, of fashions and fads lie between the modern reader and Joseph's day, so what was obvious in Joseph's day is opaque in ours.

GIVEN

The garment that Joseph is most remembered for is the one that he is given, the so-called "coat of many colors" (Genesis 37:3 KJV).[1] The Hebrew term for this, *k^{e}tonet passim*, is rare; it is used only in this passage (Genesis 37:3,

1. Unless otherwise noted, all translations are my own.

23, 32) and in the description of the clothes of Tamar, the daughter of King David (2 Samuel 13:18–19). In Tamar's case, the garment is said to be something that "virgin daughters of the king used to wear" (13:18). Tamar rent this set of clothes when her status involuntarily changed (13:19), and though it may not have meant the same thing in Joseph's own day, when this story was told in the time of Solomon, it would have signaled to the audiences why Joseph might have wanted to resist the advances of Potiphar's wife.

The term *k*^{e}*tonet* is straightforward. It is a tunic,[2] basically a large T-shirt. In the times of the Israelite monarchy, these tunics are typically depicted as having sleeves that go halfway down the upper arm and extending halfway down the thigh or halfway down the calf on the leg.[3] The use of such garments is known to go back a thousand years earlier, though in earlier times the garment often went over only one shoulder.[4] For ancient Israelites, this was a standard garment.

The term *passim* is harder to understand. In Aramaic it means something like the "palm of the hand" or "sole of the feet."[5] In some Semitic languages, it means something like a "piece" of something,[6] and possibly comes from Egyptian *psš*, meaning "division, portion."[7] In Ugartic, *psm* means "veil" or "gauze."[8] Though such a definition would explain Tamar's garment, it makes less sense for Joseph's. In Akkadian, *passu* means either

---

2. Ludwig Koehler, Walter Baumgartner, et al., *The Hebrew and Aramaic Lexicon of the Old Testament* (Leiden: Brill, 2001), 1:505 (hereafter, *HALOT*).
3. Paul Collins, *Assyrian Palace Sculptures* (London: British Museum Press, 2008), 92–95; R. D. Barnett, *Assyrian Palace Reliefs* (London: Batchworth Press, n.d.), 44–49; T. C. Mitchell, *The Bible in the British Museum* (London: British Museum Press, 2004), 68–69, 71.
4. Percy E. Newberry, *Beni Hasan, Part I* (London: Kegan Paul, Trench, Trübner, & Co., 1893), pl. XXXI.
5. *HALOT*, 2:946.
6. *HALOT*, 2:946.
7. R. O. Faulkner, *Concise Dictionary of Middle Egyptian* (Oxford: Griffith Institute, 1962), 94; Adolf Erman and Hermann Grapow, *Wörterbuch der aegyptischen Sprache* (Leipzig: J. C. Hinrichs, 1926-1931) 1:554.
8. Gregorio del Olmo Lete and Joaquín Sanmartín, *A Dictionary of the Ugaritic Language in the Alphabetic Tradition* (Leiden: Brill, 2015), 2:675.

a "gaming piece" or a kind of reed,[9] but *pasāmu* means "to cover" or "to veil,"[10] *pussumu* means "covered up,"[11] and *pusummu* is a "veil."[12] The Septuagint translated it with the word *poikilon* in Genesis and *karpōntos* in Samuel. The term *poikilos* originally meant something "dappled," referring to animal skins, but came to mean "intricate," or "embroidered" and "colorful."[13] The term *karpōntos* meant "fruitful"[14] or "offering."[15] The Aramaic translation uses the same term *pasê*,[16] but it means "strips."[17] The garment that Jacob gave to Joseph seems to have been a special garment, but what distinguished it is now obscure to us.

Joseph's garment, as well as his aggrandizing dreams and his father's favor, made his brothers "jealous of him" (Genesis 37:11). It was clearly a mark of his status as his father's favorite. In the time of the Israelite monarchy, the garment, along with the deliberate narrative juxtaposition of Joseph's brother's infidelities (Genesis 34, 38), would have signaled Joseph's chastity to Israelite readers and listeners. Joseph's brothers initially set out to kill him (37:20) but soon decided to sell him for profit (*beṣa*ʿ) instead (37:26). It was not uncommon for families in debt to sell family members into slavery to pay off debts,[18] nor for slaves to come from captives of war.

---

9. Jeremy Black, Andrew George, and Nicholas Postgate, *A Concise Dictionary of Akkadian* (Wiesbaden: Harrassowitz, 2000), 268 (hereafter *CDA*); Simo Parpola, *Assyrian-English-Assyrian Dictionary* (Helsinki: The Neo-Assyrian Text Corpus Project, 2007), 81.
10. *CDA*, 268.
11. *CDA*, 279.
12. *CDA*, 280.
13. Henry George Liddell and Robert Scott, *A Greek-English Lexicon* (Oxford: Clarendon Press, 1968), 1430 (hereafter *LSJ*); T. Muraoka, *A Greek-English Lexicon of the Septuagint* (Leuven: Peeters, 2009), 571.
14. *LSJ*, 880.
15. Muraoka, *Greek-English Lexicon of the Septuagint*, 364.
16. Targum Onkelos Genesis 37:3, in Alexander Sperber, *The Bible in Aramaic* (Leiden: E. J. Brill, 2004), 1178.
17. Marcus Jastrow, *A Dictionary of the Targumim, the Talmud Babli and Yerushalmi, and the Midrashic Literature* (New York: Traditional Press, n.d.), 1191.
18. J. N. Postgate, *Early Mesopotamia: Society and Economy at the Dawn of History* (London: Routledge, 1992), 195–96; Sumerian Laws Handbook viii 11–15 (§R),

The Midianites to whom his brothers sold Joseph might have assumed that he fit into one of these categories. Joseph enters Egypt at a time that today is classified as either the end of the Middle Kingdom or the Second Intermediate Period (different scholars place the dividing line in different places), when there were a considerable number of slaves from the Levant entering Egypt. Lists of Egyptian slaves at the time show that fifty-seven percent were from that area,[19] and about two in five of those were renamed, being given an Egyptian name instead of a Semitic one.[20] Joseph being given an Egyptian name,[21] Zaphnath-paaneah (41:45), would not have been unusual.

Joseph's brothers take his garment, dip it in blood, and show it to their father, Jacob (Genesis 37:31–32). In response, Jacob (and earlier, Reuben) rend (*yiqra'*) their clothes (37:29, 34). Since the point is to make it look like Joseph has been killed by wild beasts, the garment must have been torn as well. The Hebrew term for a *tear* or a *rent* is also used for a torn piece of cloth (1 Kings 11:30–31; 2 Kings 2:12; Proverbs 23:21). This term is used in the Book of Mormon when Captain Moroni waves a rent (that is, a torn piece of cloth) in the air.[22] Moroni specifically states that the rent was to remind the Nephites of "our God, our religion, and freedom, and our peace, our wives, and our children" (Alma 46:12). These were things

---

in Martha T. Roth, *Law Collections from Mesopotamia and Asia Minor* (Atlanta: Scholars Press, 1997), 53; Kenneth A. Kitchen and Paul J. N. Lawrence, *Treaty, Law and Covenant in the Ancient Near East* (Wiesbaden: Harrassowitz, 2012), 1:90–91.

19. William C. Hayes, *A Papyrus of the Late Middle Kingdom in the Brooklyn Museum* (Brooklyn: The Brooklyn Museum, 1955), 87–94.

20. Hayes, *A Papyrus of the Late Middle Kingdom*, 92.

21. For a list of possible Egyptian interpretations, see James K. Hoffmeier, *Israel in Egypt: The Evidence for the Authenticity of the Exodus Tradition* (Oxford: Oxford University Press, 1996), 85–87.

22. Alma 46:19; see the commentary in Royal Skousen, *Analysis of Textual Variants of the Book of Mormon, Part 4* (Provo, UT: Foundation for Ancient Research and Mormon Studies, 2007), 2541–42; Royal Skousen, *The History of the Text of the Book of Mormon, Part Three: The Nature of the Original Language* (Provo, UT: Foundation for Ancient Research and Mormon Studies, 2018), 162.

taken away from Joseph when his garment was rent and which he recovered later. Thus, Joseph's garment has a long significance.

TAKEN

The second garment associated with Joseph is the one he leaves behind in his haste to flee Potiphar's wife (Genesis 39:12–13). This is simply termed a "garment" (*beged*), which is a generic word for a piece of clothing.[23] What sort of clothing would Joseph have been wearing? The climate in Egypt is different from the place where Joseph grew up, and the clothing is also different. Egypt is warmer, and rain is rare. The clothing Joseph wore would also be different in ways that figure into the story.

Potiphar was a captain of the guard (*śar haṭṭabbāḥîm*), which seems to be the equivalent of the Egyptian title translated as "controller of guards" (*sḥḏ šmsw*).[24] This is not an elite position but probably the equivalent of upper middle class. One example of someone who held this position is Iby-iaw, the younger son of a commander of the crew of the ruler (*ꜣṯw n ṯt ḥqꜣ*);[25] his father was high ranking enough to get him a comfortable position, but, as a younger son, he was unable to rise to the same rank as his father. Thus, Iby-iaw is mentioned on his father's stele but does not have the rank, status, or resources to have one of his own. Potiphar was wealthy enough to own a few slaves, including Joseph and some others whose presence is only mentioned.

While Joseph was a slave he rose to the position of overseer of the house (*ʿal-bêt*, Genesis 39:4–5), which may be the equivalent of an

---

23. *HALOT*, 1:108.

24. Danijela Stefanovič, *The Holders of Regular Military Titles in the Period of the Middle Kingdom: Dossiers* (London: Golden House Publications, 2006), 156–69; William A. Ward, *Index of Egyptian Administrative and Religious Titles of the Middle Kingdom* (Beirut: American University of Beirut, 1982), 155.

25. Svetlana Hodjash and Oleg Berlev, *The Egyptian Reliefs and Stelae in the Pushkin Museum of Fine Arts, Moscow* (Leningrad: Aurora Art Publishers, 1982), 85n38; compare Stefanovič, *The Holders of Regular Military Titles in the Period of the Middle Kingdom*, 90; Ward, *Index of Egyptian Administrative and Religious Titles*, 7–8.

Egyptian title normally translated "chamberlain" or "steward" (*imy-rꜣ-pr*).[26] The exact duties of this position are not clear, but a supervisory role is indicated. Household staff might range from a few people[27] to a dozen or more.[28] The presence of other slaves in the house seems to have been typical (39:11). The narrative laconically lays out the background information that we need spelled out more.

It has long been known that there are parallels between Joseph's story and the Tale of Two Brothers recorded on Papyrus D'Orbiney (BM EA 10183),[29] which dates about two or three hundred years after Joseph lived. In both stories, the wife of the householder seeks to seduce one of the men attached to the house: Joseph in the case of the Bible (Genesis 39:2–20), Bata in the case of Papyrus D'Orbiney.[30] The man rebuffs her advances. She accuses him of seduction to the householder. The man is expelled from the house: in one case to prison, in the other case to exile. He is nevertheless favored by deity and eventually rises to the top of the government in Egypt. In Joseph's case, he rises to be Pharaoh's right-hand man (Genesis 40:37–46). In Bata's case, he rises to become the Pharaoh himself and reigns for thirty years.[31]

Besides the general thematic parallels (which gloss over some significant differences in the stories), the description of the seduction scenes parallel each other in the way that they are narrated. This may not be a case

---

26. Ward, *Index of Egyptian Administrative and Religious Titles*, 21; compare James K. Hoffmeier, *Israel in Egypt* (Oxford: Oxford University Press, 1996), 84.
27. UC 32167, in Mark Collier and Stephen Quirke, *The UCL Lahun Papyri: Religious, Literary, Legal, Mathematical and Medical* (Oxford: Archaeopress, 2004), 118–19.
28. UC 32166, in Collier and Quirke, *The UCL Lahun Papyri: Religious, Literary, Legal, Mathematical and Medical*, 116.
29. Victor H. Matthews and Don C. Benjamin, *Old Testament Parallels: Laws and Stories from the Ancient Near East* (New York: Paulist Press, 1991), 41–45; Susan Tower Hollis, *The Ancient Egyptian "Tale of Two Brothers": A Mythological, Religious, Literary, and Historico-Political Study* (Oakville, CT: Bannerstone Press, 2008), 12–13, 107–11.
30. P. D'Orbiney (BM EA 10183) 2/9–4/2, in Alan H. Gardiner, *Late-Egyptian Stories* (Brussels: Fondation Égyptologique Reine Élisabeth, 1932), 11–13.
31. P. D'Orbiney 18/10–19/6, in Gardiner, *Late-Egyptian Stories*, 28–29.

of direct literary dependence as much as what Robert Alter called type scenes,[32] a convention about how a story is told. The use of a formula for writing history may seem strange in modern times, but most ancient historical sources and most ancient historical writing was formulaic.[33] While Joseph's story is historical, it is told following a particular formula that the fictional Bata story also uses. This allowed ancient audiences to appreciate aspects of the story that were similar to other accounts and to situations that they might potentially face, as well as the differences that indicated whether the story were fictional or historical. The differences also help them recognize that while the situations that they encounter might follow a type, there would also be differences. For example, Joseph's case differs from Bata's because Bata faces the temptation only once, while Joseph faces it repeatedly. Bata's was a fictional case, but in a real-life situation like Joseph's, the temptation is likely not to be an isolated affair that need only be resisted but once. Comparing and contrasting the two stories illustrates how the same type scene may be used in narrating both historical and fictional situations.

THE ERRAND IN THE HOUSE

In both instances, the protagonist is doing his errands about the house. Doing his job as he is supposed to be doing it sets the stage for him to face temptation. We will look first at the less-familiar fictional case of Bata:

---

32. Robert Alter, *The Art of Biblical Narrative* (New York: Basic Books, 1981), 47–62.

33. Anthony John Spalinger, *Aspects of Military Documents of the Ancient Egyptians* (New Haven, CT: Yale University Press, 1982), 1–33; Donald B. Redford, *Pharaonic King-Lists, Annals and Day-Books: A Contribution to the Study of the Egyptian Sense of History* (Mississauga, ON: Benben, 1986), 1–230; Marcel Sigrist, *Drehem* (Bethesda, MD: CDL Press, 1992), 19–21, 44–90; Roberto B. Gozzoli, *The Writing of History in Ancient Egypt during the First Millennium BC (ca. 1070–180 BC): Trends and Perspectives* (London: Golden House Publications, 2006), 1–8; Maynard Paul Maidman, *Nuzi Texts and Their Uses as Historical Evidence* (Atlanta: Society of Biblical Literature, 2010), 1–8; Nicholas Postgate, *Bronze Age Bureaucracy: Writing and the Practice of Government in Assyria* (Cambridge: Cambridge University Press, 2013), 47–85; Shalom E. Holz, *Neo-Babylonian Trial Records* (Atlanta: Society of Biblical Literature, 2014), 3–9; Mario Liverani, *Assyria: The Imperial Mission* (Winona Lake, IN: Eisenbrauns, 2017).

> And after many days, while they were in the field, they ran out of seed-corn. He sent his younger brother saying: Hurry and bring us seed-corn from the town. His younger brother found the wife of his older brother sitting braiding her hair. He said to her: "Get up so that you can give me seed[34] so I can hurry back to the field, for my older brother is waiting for me. Do not delay." She said to him: "Go! Open the storehouse and fetch for yourself what you desire. Do not make me leave my braids on the road." The lad entered into his stable and fetched a big pot (*ḥnw*) since he wanted to take a lot of seed-corn. He loaded it with barley and wheat and came out carrying them. She said to him: "How much is on your shoulders?" He said to her: "Three sacks of wheat and two sacks of barley for a total of five is what is on my shoulders." So he said to her.[35]

That a *sack* was a measure of grain is obscured over the passage of time and change in culture. A sack (*ẖꜣr*) held 76.88 liters.[36] Thus, the young man, Bata, was carrying about 670 pounds (303.7 kilograms) of grain on his shoulders. The unrealistic amount of grain is an indication that the story was seen as fictional. The unnamed seductress of this story had paid Bata no attention until he came out with rippling muscles. The fantastic exaggeration of the Bata story contrasts with the sober, restrained, and commonplace nature of the Joseph story.

---

34. The scribe apparently placed a stroke in the wrong place, resulting in switching the pronouns (see Gardiner, *Late-Egyptian Stories*, 11a) so that the manuscript actually reads: "Get up so that I can give you seed." The term for *seed*, *prt*, means both *seed-corn* and *descendants*, and so it does have the sexual connotation whether it is emended or not. For the term, see Rainer Hannig, *Ägyptisches Wörterbuch I: Altes Reich and Erste Zwischenzeit* (Mainz am Rhein: Philipp von Zabern, 2003), 467; Rainer Hannig, *Ägyptisches Wörterbuch II: Mittleres Reich and Zweite Zwischenzeit* (Mainz am Rhein: Philipp von Zabern, 2006) 1:926–27; R. O. Faulkner, *Concise Dictionary of Middle Egyptian* (Oxford: Griffith Institute, 1962), 91; Adolf Erham and Hermann Grapow, *Wörterbuch der Aegyptischen Sprache* (Leipzig: J. C. Hinrichs, 1926), 1:530–31. This term is also borrowed into Hebrew.
35. P. D'Orbiney 2/7–3/6, in Gardiner, *Late-Egyptian Stories*, 11–12.
36. Jac. J. Janssen, *Commodity Prices from the Ramessid Period* (Leiden: E. J. Brill, 1975), 109.

The biblical account starts with a general statement: "And Joseph was very handsome and good-looking" (Genesis 39:6). Later the account tells of a specific instance: "And it came to pass about this time, he went into the house to do his business but there was no man among the men of the house there in the house" (39:11). In both cases, the young man is alone at the house with the wife of the householder. In Bata's case, his sister-in-law is sitting in front of the house and sends him to the storage to get the seed-corn. Bata's request is straightforward but happens to contain a double entendre about providing seed, which the audience would recognize, though Bata plainly does not. In Joseph's case, he is actually inside the house. An upper middle-class house was typically designed for privacy.[37] A blank facade on the street opened to a long hall leading to a central courtyard. The courtyard might have a small pool and trees,[38] and among the wealthy the courtyard would be peristyle, surrounded by pillars. This allowed for some cooling in the house. The remainder of the house branched off this central area. The archaeological evidence from ancient Egypt coincides with the biblical account in indicating the secluded nature of the encounter.

THE TEMPTATION

In the Egyptian account of Bata, the wife reacts when she finally notices her young brother-in-law whom she has previously considered a child: "She [spoke with] him, saying: 'There is great strength in you. I see your manliness daily.' She desired to know him as a man. She stood up and grabbed him, saying to him: 'Come that we may spend an hour sleeping. This will be good for you. I will make good clothes for you.'"[39]

Earlier in the Egyptian account, the protagonist had been noted for making his own clothing,[40] which in ancient Egypt was generally done by

37. For examples, see W. M. Flinders Petrie, *Kahun, Gurob, and Hawara* (London: Kegan Paul, Trench, Trübner, and Co., 1890), pl. XV; W. Stevenson Smith and William Kelly Simpson, *The Art and Architecture of Ancient Egypt* (New Haven, CT: Yale University Press, 1998), 93.

38. MMA 20.3.13, in William C. Hayes, *The Scepter of Egypt* (New York: Metropolitan Museum of Art, 1953), 1:262–63.

39. P. D'Orbiney 3/6–7, in Gardiner, *Late-Egyptian Stories*, 12.

40. P. D'Orbiney 1/2 , in Gardiner, *Late-Egyptian Stories*, 9.

women.[41] Clothing, for women, served as a source of wealth as is reflected in marriage contracts where most of the wealth that the woman brought to the marriage was in the form of either clothing or jewelry.[42] In the biblical account, the wife also notices Joseph: "And it came to pass after these things the wife of his master lifted up her eyes on Joseph and said, 'Sleep with me'" (Genesis 39:7). Later she takes things a step further, although the proposition itself is still the exact same words. "And she caught his garment saying, 'Sleep with me'" (Genesis 39:12). In both cases the woman's actual proposition is fairly brief. In the Egyptian story, possible benefits are mentioned. These are missing from the biblical version. Though the biblical narrative may tell a particular type story, it does not elaborate it. Everything is kept to the bare essentials. The reader is not meant to be titillated or enticed by the encounter. The brazen bluntness of the proposal is not meant to be attractive.

THE REFUTATION

In the Egyptian story, Bata declines, citing his reasons for doing so:

> The lad became like a southern panther in his anger at the evil report. She said to him and she was exceedingly frightened. He spoke with her saying: "Look, you are like a mother to me and your husband is like a father to me. He is older than me. He raised me. What is this great crime that you have proposed to me? Do not speak it to me again. I will not mention it to anyone. I will never let it go forth out of my mouth to any person." He picked up his load and went to the field.[43]

In the biblical account, Joseph also has a long refutation listing his reasons for declining the offer:

---

41. Gillian M. Vogelsang-Eastwood, "Weaving, Looms, and Textiles," in *The Oxford Encyclopedia of Ancient Egypt*, ed. Donald B. Redford (Oxford: Oxford University Press, 2001), 3:491.
42. Erich Lüddeckens, *Ägyptische Eheverträge* (Wiesbaden: Otto Harrassowitz, 1960); P. W. Pestman, *Marriage and Matrimonial Property in Ancient Egypt* (Leiden: E. J. Brill, 1961), 91–102.
43. P. D'Orbiney 3/7–4/2, in Gardiner, *Late-Egyptian Stories*, 12–13.

> And he refused and said to his master's wife: "My master does not know what is with me in the house, although he has given everything he has into my hand. There is no one greater in this house than I and he has withheld nothing from me except you because you are his wife and how can I do this great evil and sin against God? And it came to pass when she spoke to Joseph day by day, he did not listen to her to sleep with her or to be with her. (Genesis 39:8–10)

In both cases the woman's proposition is brutally blunt and short. The man's response is comparatively long and reasoned. Both men reference their respective positions in the household. Both state that what they are asked to do is a crime or a sin. Of the responses, however, only Joseph's invokes God. In Bata's case, he becomes angry and fierce, like a wild animal. While the Egyptian account features ferocity, the biblical account promotes piety.

In both stories, a garment appears prominently but differently. In Bata's case, the garment is offered. In Joseph's case, it is seized. In the first mention of the temptation, Joseph speaks. The second time the temptation comes around, Joseph acts: "And he left his garment in her hand, and fled, and got out" (Genesis 39:12). Manual laborers are typically depicted[44] as wearing either a plain skirt or kilt of some sort, either short[45] or long,[46] or wearing a loincloth.[47] The kilt "consisted of a rectangular piece of linen

44. Janssen, *Commodity Prices from the Ramessid Period*, 250–51.

45. MMA 09.180.13ab, in William C. Hayes, *The Scepter of Egypt* (New York: Metropolitan Museum of Art, 1953), 1:186; MMA 22.1.200, in Hayes, *Scepter of Egypt*, 1:206; MMA 24.1.45, in Hayes, *The Scepter of Egypt*, 1:208; MMA 30.8.76, in Hayes, *Scepter of Egypt*, 1:214; MMA 20.3.12, in Hayes, *Scepter of Egypt*, 1:263; MMA 20.3.12, in Hayes, *Scepter of Egypt*, 1:264; MMA 36.5, in Hayes, *The Scepter of Egypt*, 1:266; MMA 20.3.6, in Hayes, *Scepter of Egypt*, 1:269; MMA 20.3.4, in Hayes, *Scepter of Egypt*, 1:270; MMA 12.184, in Hayes, *Scepter of Egypt*, 1:298; Smith and Simpson, *The Art and Architecture of Ancient Egypt*, 111; JE 45625, in Francesco Tiradritti, *Egyptian Treasures from the Egyptian Museum in Cairo* (New York: Harry N. Abrams, 1999), 124–25.

46. MMA 07.228.180, in Hayes, *Scepter of Egypt*, 1:211; MMA 20.3.1, 3, in Hayes, *Scepter of Egypt*, 1:268; MMA 12.183.4, in Hayes, *Scepter of Egypt*, 1:273.

47. MMA 10.176.57, 58, 59, 60, in Hayes, *Scepter of Egypt*, 1:212.

wrapped around the body and tied at the waist with a knot or fastened with a sort of buckle."[48] Whether he left a kilt or a loincloth with Potiphar's wife, Joseph left an incriminating piece of evidence behind, which was enough to convict him circumstantially.

After the temptation, both women accuse the spurned lover of trying to seduce them, resulting in the husband attempting vengeance on the men. While Bata voluntarily goes into exile, Joseph is cast into prison. Adultery was not condoned in ancient Egypt and could be punished by throwing the adulterer or adulteress to the crocodiles,[49] setting them on fire,[50] killing them,[51] beating them up,[52] or fining them. The historical accounts indicate less severe punishments.[53] Egyptian investigations normally included interrogation, beatings, threats, and torture.[54] Joseph's punishment for a crime he did not commit was comparatively mild.

PART 2: CUPS

After Joseph was cast into prison, the emphasis on material objects shifts from clothes to cups. The change in state is accompanied by a change

---

48. Lyn Green, "Clothing and Personal Adornment," in Redford, *The Oxford Encyclopedia of Ancient Egypt*, 1:275.
49. P. Westcar 2/2–4/17, in A. M. Blackman, *The Story of King Kheops and the Magicians* (Reading: J. V. Books, 1988), 1–5; Stephen Quirke, *Egyptian Literature 1800 BC* (London: Golden House Publications, 2004), 77–81.
50. P. Westcar 4/9–10, in Blackman, *The Story of King Kheops and the Magicians*, 4; Quirke, *Egyptian Literature 1800 BC*, 80–81.
51. P. D'Orbiney 8/7–8, 9/5, 9, in Gardiner, *Late Egyptian Stories*, 18–19.
52. P. BM EA 10416, in John Gee, "Notes on Egyptian Marriage: P. BM 10416 Reconsidered," *Bulletin of the Egyptological Seminar* 15 (2001): 17, 19–20.
53. Sandra Lippert, *Einführung in die altägyptische Rechtsgeschichte* (Berlin: LIT Verlag, 2012), 66.
54. P. Amherst 3/6, in T. Eric Peet, *The Great Tomb-Robberies of the Twentieth Egyptian Dynasty* (Oxford: Clarendon, 1930), 2:pl. V; P. BM EA 10052 1/13, in Peet, *The Great Tomb-Robberies*, 2:pl. XXV; P. BM EA 10054 v 1/4, in Peet, *The Great Tomb-Robberies*, 2:pl. VII; P. BM EA 10403 3/1, in Peet, *The Great Tomb-Robberies*, 2:pl. XXXVII; Lippert, *Einführung in die altägyptische Rechtsgeschichte*, 66, 79–82.

in object. But one thing that does not change is Joseph's abilities. These abilities were recognized by prison officials. While he could not leave the prison, he had charge of all the prisoners (Genesis 39:21–23) and apparently visited them and took them their rations. Few Egyptian records detail much information about Egyptian prisons. One account details the attempted arrest of an official[55] who is set free by the governor.[56] Other individuals were cast into prison pending trial or investigation.[57] We have other records of a man who was thrown into prison and "an agent, a staff bearer, a man of the household staff of Pharaoh was assigned to him, and it came to pass that his rations used to be brought in daily from Pharaoh's palace in Memphis."[58] Joseph would have served this role to the other prisoners. The only record we have indicates that the palace was responsible for providing provisions for the prison. At the time of Joseph, provisioning the palace was a complex operation because the provisions were divided into three areas: the outer palace (*ẖnty*) staffed with officials (*srw*), the inner palace (*kꜣp*) with the royal family, and the auxiliaries (*šnꜥ*) and their serving staff (*ꜥqyw ꜥšꜣ*).[59] All of these people needed to be fed daily.[60] The palace provisions consisted mainly of bread, beer, dates, and vegetables.[61] How many of the dates and vegetables made it to the lower classes is unknown. Joseph was cast into the same prison as royal officials who had fallen out of favor, which turned to his advantage.

HANDED

During Joseph's time in prison, both the butler and the baker are also thrown into prison (Genesis 40:1–3). While there, each had a dream (40:5).

55. P. 2/63–64, in Gardiner, *Late Egyptian Stories*, 73.
56. P. 2/70–73, in Gardiner, *Late Egyptian Stories*, 74.
57. P. Amherst 4/2–4, in Peet, *The Great Tomb-Robberies*, 2:pl. V.
58. P. Onch. 4/6–8, in S. R. K. Glanville, *The Instructions of ꜥOnchsheshonqy* (London: British Museum, 1955), pl. 4; Friedhelm Hoffmann and Joachim Freidrich Quack, *Anthologie der demotischen Literatur* (Berlin: LIT, 2007), 279.
59. Stephen Quirke, *The Administration of Egypt in the Late Middle Kingdom* (Surrey, UK: Sia Publishing, 1990), 44.
60. Quirke, *The Administration of Egypt in the Late Middle Kingdom*, 42.
61. Quirke, *The Administration of Egypt in the Late Middle Kingdom*, 111.

Being in prison, they were cut off from society including those who served as dream interpreters. Dream interpreters consulted manuals, a number of which are known from ancient Egypt.[62] We know that the owner of the earliest one of these was Qenherkhopeshef,[63] who was a scribe of the tomb.[64] The prisoners do not seem to have been able to have access to scribes. In Egyptian manuals for interpreting dreams the situation in the dream is described, classified as either good or bad, and is then interpreted as a sign of what will happen in the future. For example, "if a man sees himself in a dream reading from a papyrus roll (*šfdt*), it is good because the man will be established in his house,"[65] but "if a man sees himself in a dream writing a papyrus roll (*šfdt*), it is bad because his crimes will be reckoned by his god."[66] Accurately predicting the result of dreams was not necessarily intuitive. This was not the method that Joseph used to interpret dreams but the manuals tell us how Egyptians would have interpreted them and give us an idea of what might have made sense to them.

The butler's dream centers around cups. He told Joseph about three vines. "And the cup (*kôs*) of Pharaoh was in my hand. And I took the grapes and pressed them on the cup of Pharaoh and I placed the cup on the palm of Pharaoh" (Genesis 40:11). The same term (*ks*) is inscribed on a bowl 15.2 cm in diameter and 4.2 cm deep.[67] The description of the handling of the cup is paralleled in roughly contemporary Egyptian

---

62. P. Chester Beatty III, in Alan H. Gardiner, *Chester Beatty Gift* (London: British Museum, 1935), 9–22, 2:pl. 5–12a; P. Carlsberg XIII and P. Carlsberg XIV verso, in Aksel Volten, *Demotische Traumdeutung* (Copenhagen: Einar Munksgaard, 1942).

63. P. W. Pestman, "Who Were the Owners, in the 'Community of Workmen', of the Chester Beatty Papyri," in *Gleanings from Deir el-Medîna*, ed. R. J. Demarée and Jac. J. Janssen (Leiden: Nederlands Instituut voor het Nabije Oosten, 1982), 155–72.

64. Benedict G. Davies, *Who's Who at Deir el-Medina: A Prosopographic Study of the Royal Workmen's Community* (Leiden: Nederlands Instituut voor het Nabije Oosten, 1999), 84–86.

65. P. Chester Beatty III r 5/9, in Gardiner, *Chester Beatty Gift*, 2:pl. 6.

66. P. Chester Beatty III r 7/21, in Gardiner, *Chester Beatty Gift*, 2:pl. 7.

67. Manfried Dietich, Oswald Loretz, and Joaqín Sanmartin, *Die keilslphabetischen Texte aus Ugarit, Ras Ibn Hani und anderen Orten* (Münster: Ugarit-Verlag, 2013), 634.

tomb scenes, where cups[68]—particularly containers holding grapes[69]—are shown resting on the palms of the hand, rather than in the hands. The Joseph story thus reflects a Middle Kingdom reality and historical setting. Egyptian accounts also refer to "placing the bowl of beer on your hand (*dit n=k wꜥ ṯbw n ḥnqt ḥr ḏrt=k*)."[70] The Egyptian dream manual says that "if a man sees himself in a dream drinking wine, it is good because it means living in righteousness."[71] It also claims that "if a man sees himself in a dream eating grapes, it is good because his own things will be given to him."[72] In this case, Joseph's interpretation aligns with the ancient Egyptian interpretations of similar dreams. It would have seemed like a reasonable interpretation to the butler and would have been comforting in both its content and style of presentation. From the interpretation, the butler would be able to view Joseph as being divinely inspired.

The baker also had a dream, but Joseph's interpretation of it differed from the ancient Egyptian interpretation of similar dreams. The baker dreamt that he had "three baskets of white bread (*ḥorî*) on my head and in the top basket were all of the foods of Pharaoh made by the baker, and the birds ate them from the basket on my head" (Genesis 40:16–7). The dream manual has a similar case: "If a man sees himself in a dream and white bread (*t ḥḏ*) is given to him, it is good because it means that things will cheer him up (*ḥḏ ḥr=f*)."[73] The baker was looking to be cheered up, because he saw that the previous "interpretation was good" (40:16). But Joseph's interpretation of the baker's dream was not good, and it did not turn out well for the baker. Joseph's interpretations from the Lord did not necessarily match those that Egyptian sages gave because while God is willing to speak to individuals so that they might come to understanding (Doctrine

68. Abdel Ghaffar Shedid, *The Tomb of Nakht: The Art and History of an Eighteenth Dynastie Official's Tomb at Western Thebes* (Mainz: Philipp von Zabern, 1996), 42.
69. Shedid, *The Tomb of Nakht*, 56–57, 65, 76–78.
70. P. D'Orbiney 8/6, in Gardiner, *Late Egyptian Stories*, 18.
71. P. Chester Beatty III r 3/5, in Gardiner, *Chester Beatty Gift*, 2:pl. 5.
72. P. Chester Beatty III r 6/8, in Gardiner, *Chester Beatty Gift*, 2:pl. 6.
73. P. Chester Beatty III r 3/4, in Gardiner, *Chester Beatty Gift*, 2:pl. 5.

and Covenants 1:24), there would be no need for divine intervention if God only told us what our culture or our own desires already told us.

Joseph's ability to interpret the butler's dreams later gives him the opportunity to interpret Pharaoh's dreams (Genesis 41:9–14). Pharaoh's dreams would have perplexed the Egyptian priests because a connection with a cow was seen as good,[74] while measuring barley was seen as bad.[75] Joseph, however, does not interpret the dream the way that the Egyptian dream interpretation manuals would have, even if he had used Egyptian symbols in a way that might have made sense to the Egyptians. For example, the hieratic sign for grain looks like the hieratic sign for year at the time of Joseph.[76] Thus, interpreting seven stalks of grain as years would have made sense to literate Egyptians. Joseph's coherent interpretation of the dream along with his pragmatic advice about how to use the information in the dream to benefit both Pharaoh and his people showed the Pharaoh that Joseph was someone who could use divine inspiration for the benefit of all, an ability that his other advisers lacked.

DIVINING

As a result of his interpretation, Joseph is given the king's seal ring (Genesis 41:41–42) and fine linen clothing. Only the highest-ranking officials (*ẖmty-bity*) were allowed to use the king's seal[77] and act in the king's stead, making Joseph truly one who was "over all the land of Egypt" (41:43) and granting him an immense amount of power. The linen garments (*bigdê-šēš*, 41:42) also marked Joseph's rank, as the Hebrew term for linen is a loanword from Egyptian,[78] denoting "royal linen" (*sšr-nsw*), the best type of

74. P. Chester Beatty III r 5/16, in Gardiner, *Chester Beatty Gift*, 2:pl. 6.
75. P. Chester Beatty III r 7/20, in Gardiner, *Chester Beatty Gift*, 2:pl. 7.
76. Compare Georg Möller, *Hieratische Paläographie* (Leipzig: J. C. Hinrichs, 1909), 1:26 (#270) with 1:1:28 (#293).
77. John Gee, "On the Practice of Sealing in the Book of the Dead and the Coffin Texts," *Journal of the Society for the Study of Egyptian Antiquities* 35 (2008): 108–17.
78. Benjamin J. Noonan, *Non-Semitic Loanwords in the Hebrew Bible* (University Park, PA: Eisenbrauns, 2019), 215.

cloth.[79] Joseph's case follows the traditional pattern since clothing was normally given by higher ranking officials to lower ranking ones.[80]

After a number of years have passed, Joseph finally meets his family. At this meeting, Joseph fulfills the earlier dreams he had (Genesis 37:7, 9) since he was now a ruler—a high government official—and they are peasants, literally bowing at his feet (Genesis 41:6). When Joseph finally meets his brothers again, he hides his drinking bowl (*gᵉbîaʿ*) in Benjamin's sack as an excuse to bring his brothers back (Genesis 44:2). The term for the bowl is thought to have an Egyptian origin,[81] but the vessel described is not a drinking vessel but a pouring vessel,[82] and the phonetic shifts proposed are otherwise unattested.[83] This cup is made of silver and is explicitly said to be for both drinking and divination (*naḥēš*, Genesis 44:5). Examples of cups and bowls of silver and other metals are known,[84] though many more in faience are known,[85] the meaning and use of which is speculative and disputed.

---

79. The others being (in descending order of quality): *šmꜥ nfr* "fine thin cloth," *šmꜥ* "thin cloth," and *nꜥꜥ* "smooth cloth." Janssen, *Commodity Prices from the Ramessid Period*, 256.

80. Denise M. Doxey, *Egyptian Non-Royal Epithets in the Middle Kingdom* (Leiden: E. J. Brill, 1998), 184, 198.

81. *HALOT* 1:173; Noonan, *Non-Semitic Loanwords in the Hebrew Bible*, 79–80.

82. Hannig, *Ägyptisches Wörterbuch II: Mittleres Reich und Zweite Zwischenzeit*, 2:2513; Janssen, *Commodity Prices from the Ramessid Period*, 433.

83. Specifically, it would require a shift between Egyptian *q* and Semitic *g* and Egyptian *ḥ* and Semitic ʿ. But while Egyptian *q* can go to Semitic *g*, Egyptian *ḥ* only goes to Semitic *ḥ* or *ḫ*. Semitic ʿ can only derive from Egyptian ꜥ. See James E. Hoch, *Semitic Words in Egyptian Texts of the New Kingdom and Third Intermediate Period* (Princeton: Princeton University Press, 1994), 431–37; Yoshiyuki Muchiki, *Egyptian Proper Names and Loanwords in North-West Semitic* (Atlanta: Society of Biblical Literature, 1999), 260–61, 267.

84. Geraldine Pinch, *Votive Offerings to Hathor* (Oxford: Griffith Institute, 1993), 313; A. F. Shore, "A Silver Libation Bowl from Egypt," *The British Museum Quarterly* 29, nos. 1–2 (1964–65): 21–25.

85. Pinch, *Votive Offerings to Hathor*, 308–15; *Gifts of the Nile: Ancient Egyptian Faience*, ed. Florence Dunn Friedman (London: Thames and Hudson, 1998), 112–13.

From the Egyptian perspective, using a cup for divination is a known technique. The normal term for a drinking cup in the Middle Kingdom is *ḥnw*,[86] which in Joseph's time can refer to a shallow bowl,[87] but is normally used for a generic container. This, however, is precisely the term used in texts describing divination using cups (*ḥnw*).[88] Egyptian texts describing divination through cups reveal a variety of procedures[89] and date long after Joseph's time. Most of these cups, though, are said to be copper[90] or pottery,[91] not silver, but that probably reflects the impoverished times in which these late accounts were written. These practices are thought to be much older than the texts describing them. The individual dressed in clean clothes[92] would have "his face bent over the vessel,"[93] which was filled with oil,[94] his eyes closed while praying.[95] Upon opening his eyes, he would see a light,[96] in which the gods would appear and answer questions.[97] In the Egyptian divinatory use, the cup, often given to a young boy, is a means to open the eyes of the user to reveal things otherwise invisible to the eyes.

---

86. Janine Bourriau and Stephen Quirke, "The Late Middle Kingdom Ceramic Repertoire in Words and Objects," in *Lahun Studies*, ed. Stephen Quirke (Reigate, Surrey: Sia Publishing, 1998), 81.
87. Bourriau and Quirke, "The Late Middle Kingdom Ceramic Repertoire in Words and Objects," 64.
88. For example, see P. Mag. 9/1, in F. Ll. Griffith and Herbert Thompson, *The Demotic Magical Papyrus of London and Leiden* (London: H. Grevel & Co., 1905), 2:pl. IX.
89. P. Mag. 1/1–3/35; 9/1–10/22; 14/1–33; 18/7–33; 21/1–9; 28/1–15; verso 22/1–20; 26/1–9.
90. P. Mag. 10/10; 28/4–5.
91. P. Mag. 10/11.
92. P. Mag. 3/13, in Griffith and Thompson, *The Demotic Magical Papyrus*, 2:pl. III.
93. P. Mag. 1/8, 3/14, in Griffith and Thompson, *The Demotic Magical Papyrus*, 2:pl. I, III.
94. P. Mag. 3/9–10, in Griffith and Thompson, *The Demotic Magical Papyrus*, 2:pl. III.
95. P. Mag. 3/14–15, in Griffith and Thompson, *The Demotic Magical Papyrus*, 2:pl. III.
96. P. Mag. 2/1, in Griffith and Thompson, *The Demotic Magical Papyrus*, 2:pl. II.
97. P. Mag. 2/15, 28–3/5, in Griffith and Thompson, *The Demotic Magical Papyrus*, 2:pl. II–III.

Similarly, the cup in Joseph's story, given to the youngest brother, functions as a device used to open the eyes of the brothers to reveal what they, of themselves, could not see.

GARMENTS AGAIN

DISGUISE

While both of Joseph's more famous garments are notable for being taken from him, when Joseph was in power, he put on his own disguise to test his brothers when they came into Egypt. He could have punished them on the spot, but he might have followed the Egyptian proverb that "self-restraint will control his [your enemy's] excess."[98] "Joseph saw his brothers and recognized them (*wayyakkirēm*) but disguised himself (*wayyitnakkēr ʾalêhem*) from them" (Genesis 42:7). The Hebrew text expresses the event with a play off the same verbal root. Why did Joseph's brothers not recognize him? While Semites tended to grow beards,[99] Egyptians would shave,[100] and Joseph is specifically said to have shaved (Genesis 41:14). Both men and women would also wear wigs and makeup.[101] He was also called by a different name (Genesis 41:45) and used an interpreter as though he could not understand them (Genesis 42:23).

Joseph was seen by later writers as an example of forgiveness. He does forgive his brothers, but not at first. They had tried to kill him and instead had sold him into slavery and made a profit on him. He needed to be certain that they would not do so to him or others again. He needed to see fruits meet for repentance—that is, evidence of their repentance.

When his brothers initially appear before him, Joseph sees neither his full brother Benjamin, nor his father. Have his brothers killed those most dear to him? He accuses them of being spies (Genesis 42:9) as a way

98. P. Prisse 5/12–13, in E. Prisse d'Avennes, *Fac-simile d'un papyrus égyptien en caractères hiératiques. Trouvé à Thebes* (Paris, 1847; repr., Wiesbaden: LTR-Verlag, 1982), pl. V.
99. Newberry, *Beni Hasan, Part I*, pl. XXXI.
100. Ann Macy Roth, *Egyptian Phyles in the Old Kingdom: The Evolution of a System of Social Organization* (Chicago: Oriental Institute, 1991), 66–68.
101. Hayes, *Scepter of Egypt*, 1:240–47.

of finding out about his family. In this he followed the Egyptian proverb about dealing with an enemy who is a poor man: "Do vent your feelings to the one who is opposing you. . . . Protect yourself with the hostility of the officials."[102] When they claimed that their younger brother was still alive, he demanded to see him first (verses 15–20) and took his brother Simeon hostage (verse 24). Joseph also tested their honesty by returning their money in the grain sacks to see whether they would keep the money (verse 25). According to the Egyptian proverb current in Joseph's day, "If you wish your conduct to be good and save yourself from all evil, guard against the occasion of greed."[103] Joseph would know by their actions whether they had repented. In Egyptian wisdom literature, it was important to "make for yourself dependents who are trustworthy and be trustworthy."[104] Joseph requests his brothers to return with Benjamin.

When they return with Benjamin, Joseph treats them well but puts his cup into Benjamin's sack to allow a means of accusing Benjamin of theft so that Joseph can test his brothers and see whether their attitudes toward his mother's children have changed or whether they will abandon Benjamin to prison or death the way that they had abandoned Joseph. Judah, the one who had first proposed selling Joseph into slavery (Genesis 37:26) is the one who intercedes for Benjamin (Genesis 44:18). Judah's response indicates that he has changed. Only then does Joseph reveal who he is to his brothers (Genesis 45:1–3). His brothers, who have not seen him for years since they sold him into slavery and thought he was dead, do not believe it.

Thus, Joseph forgives his brothers but only after he has given them a chance to prove that they have actually repented. They had to demonstrate that they had changed first. The Egyptian proverb was "If you are merciful for a past occurrence, favor a man for his virtue; forgive him and do not remember it."[105] Then Joseph showed that he forgave them. The first sign that Joseph had forgiven his brothers is by dismissing his staff and leaving himself alone with ten men who had previously tried to kill him (Genesis

102. P. Prisse 6/2–3, in Prisse d'Avennes, *Fac-simile d'un papyrus égyptien*, pl. VI.

103. P. Prisse 9/13–10/1, in Prisse d'Avennes, *Fac-simile d'un papyrus égyptien*, pl. IX–X.

104. P. Prisse 8/6–7, in Prisse d'Avennes, *Fac-simile d'un papyrus égyptien*, pl. VIII.

105. P. Prisse 13/4–5, in Prisse d'Avennes, *Fac-simile d'un papyrus égyptien*, pl. XIII.

45:1). He gathers his family together, sending for his father and his brothers' families, and provides food and places to live. The second sign that Joseph had forgiven his brothers happened after his father died and was buried: Joseph reassures his brothers that he has forgiven them (Genesis 50:15–21).

CONCLUSION

Two physical types of artifacts in the history of Joseph serve as tangible metaphors in his history. Although archeologists may be familiar with many of these elements, most have not been explored in connection with Joseph's history. Many of them are also particular to Joseph's time and change at later times, indicating that Joseph's story is based in historical events.

The cup that individuals drink from is given to them: some may find the cup sweet, and some bitter, but Joseph's use of the cup extends to revelation—both seeing the future and seeing into the hearts of those around him.

Joseph's garment represents a favored status given to him. The garment and the status are forcibly taken from him, and he wears a slave's raiment. Even that is taken from him when he is falsely accused. But, over time, he is awarded with a new garment fit for one who has proven himself faithful, a garment of surpassing status that even his own family does not recognize. In the book of Revelation, white garments are given to those who overcome (Revelation 3:5). It is probably not a coincidence that the same word used in the Septuagint to describe the garment that Pharoah gave to Joseph (*stolēn*)[106] is also used to describe those who gave their all for the testimony of God (Revelation 6:9–11). The use of the same vocabulary demonstrates that using Joseph as a model for our behavior provides hope for a similar reward.

106. Genesis 41:42 LXX.

"WHAT I WILL DO TO PHARAOH"

THE PLAGUES VIEWED AS A DIVINE CONFRONTATION WITH PHARAOH

KERRY MUHLESTEIN

If the Creation narrative is the most read biblical narrative, one can argue that the Exodus narrative, with its place in popular culture, is the most well-known Old Testament narrative. Certainly, within the Old Testament itself, this account is alluded to repeatedly throughout the biblical literature and is central to the heilsgeschichte (literally "salvation history"), or God's redemptive plan for the Israelites, which runs throughout the Old Testament. In this chapter, Kerry Muhlestein approaches this narrative from the perspective of a conflict concerning kingship—pharaonic kingship versus the divine kingship of Jehovah—noting the relationships between the titles of warrior, creator, and redeemer that God holds. —DB and AS

The story of the Exodus is one of the centerpieces of the Hebrew Bible. Accordingly, this narrative has been the subject of a great deal of commentary and study. Because we can always learn more of what the biblical text is trying to teach us when we better understand its original context and because the plagues narrative is set in Egypt, it behooves us to see what we can learn from this storyline in light of its Egyptian setting.[1] There are a number of complex factors that must be taken into account in order to compare the Plagues narrative with Egyptian cultural ideas. Not everyone will be interested in a discussion of those factors. For the reader who is not interested in discussions regarding how and when the narrative came together, or the era of Egyptian kingship that may be challenged by the plagues, it may be profitable to skip to the section entitled "Plagues, Gods, and Kings." I hope, however, that the historical circumstances of the story will enhance our study of the theological implications presented in the narrative.

THE PLAGUES NARRATIVE

The plagues portion of the Exodus story has been the recipient of a variety of approaches. It cannot be considered without bearing in mind the various approaches taken to the Exodus narrative as a whole. Source critics have generally thought a number of sources have contributed to this narrative,[2] with P (the "Priestly" source) being especially prevalent.[3] Others have

---

1. I am grateful to William Schniedewind, who gave me input on this paper about twenty years ago, and to Jacob Murphy, Aaron Schade, and Daniel Belnap for their aid as well.
2. Typically, this is seen as a composite of J, E, and P. See S. R. Driver, *Introduction to the Literature of the Old Testament* (Cambridge: Cambridge University Press, 1913), 24–29. See also Joel S. Baden, "From Joseph to Moses: The Narratives of Exodus 1–2," *Vetus Testamentum* 62 (2012): 133–58; Joel S. Baden, *Composition of the Pentateuch: Renewing the Documentary Hypothesis* (New Haven, CT: Yale University Press, 2012). My gratitude to Jacob Murphy, my student research assistant, for bringing this and several other sources to my attention.
3. See Konrad Schmid, "Distinguishing the World of the Exodus Narrative from the World of the Narrators: The Question of the Priestly Exodus Account in Its Historical Setting," in *Israel's Exodus in Transdisciplinary Perspective: Text,*

disagreed with this idea for a number of reasons.[4] The dizzying array of ideas put forth by scholars as to the origin of the narrative, coupled with its complexity and unity of theme and style, have led scholars like Thomas Thompson to say that the plagues pericope is a "complex-chain narrative"[5] and James K. Hoffmeier to write that if the literary unity of the narrative is the process of a redactor, "it might be asked if it is possible any longer to isolate the threads that have been so thoroughly reworked."[6] While there are certainly various sources and redactions behind the Bible as we now have it, at least in this case it seems completely impractical and impossible

---

Archaeology, Culture, and Geoscience, ed. Thomas E. Levy, Thomas Schneider, and William H. C. Propp (New York: Springer International Publishing, 2013), 331–44.

4. Martin Noth, *Exodus: A Commentary* (Philadelphia: Westminster Press, 1962), 9–18, believed that there was a JE source, which P added to. Ronald E. Clements, *Exodus* (Cambridge: Cambridge University Press, 1972), 4–5, believed that the Deuteronomist was the redactor. John Van Seters, *The Life of Moses: The Yahwist as Historian in Exodus–Numbers* (Philadelphia: Westminster Press, 1994), 77–105, rejected an independent E source and believed that J and P were present. See also Gary A. Rendsburg, *Redaction of Genesis* (Ann Arbor, MI: American Oriental Society, 1986); Christoph Berner, "The Exodus Narrative Between History and Literary Fiction: The Portrayal of the Egyptian Burden as a Test Case," in Levy, Schneider, and Propp, *Israel's Exodus in Transdisciplinary Perspective*, 285–92.

5. Thomas Thompson, *The Origin Tradition of Ancient Israel*, vol. 1: *The Literary Formation of Genesis and Exodus 1–23* (Sheffield, UK: Journal for the Study of the Old Testament Press, 1987), 155. Others have said of the entire Exodus narrative that it is only possible to study it as if it were a story, such as Baruch Halpern, "Fracturing the Exodus, as Told by Edward Everett Horton," in Levy, Schneider, and Propp, *Israel's Exodus in Transdisciplinary Perspective*, 293–304.

6. James K. Hoffmeier, "Egypt, Plagues In," in *The Anchor Bible Dictionary*, ed. David Noel Freedman (New York: Doubleday, 1992), 374. Elsewhere, James K. Hoffmeier, *Israel in Egypt, the Evidence for the Authenticity of the Exodus Tradition* (New York: Oxford University Press, 1996), 146–48, Hoffmeier has convincingly demonstrated a cyclical unity to the narrative. Hoffmeier further writes in "Egypt, Plagues," 374, that "the emphasis has shifted from the micro to the macro structure of pericopes."

to attempt to identify them with even a modicum of confidence. Accordingly, this study will examine the plagues narrative as a whole.[7]

Approaches to examining the plagues narrative as a whole have differed markedly. Many have endeavored to explain the plagues as natural disasters, not atypical of other events in the ancient Near East.[8] Others have felt that they are wholly literary creations, merely conveying theological or ideological reasons.[9] Some have approached it from the point of view of looking for parallels between Egyptian literature and the biblical narrative.[10] One approach has been to examine the plagues narrative in the light cast by its Egyptian setting. Many have taken the phrase "I will bring judgment against all the gods of Egypt, I am Jehovah" (Exodus 12:12; author's translation) to mean that each plague was purposefully aimed at showing Jehovah's power over a specific deity of Egypt.[11] These attempts

---

7. Many have taken such an approach. For an example of examining the Exodus narrative as a whole, see Gary A. Rendsburg, "Moses the Magician," in Levy, Schneider, and Propp, *Israel's Exodus in Transdisciplinary Perspective*, 243–58. Later, Gary A. Rendsburg, "The Literary Unity of the Exodus Narrative," in *"Did I Not Bring Israel Out of Egypt?" Biblical, Archaeological, and Egyptological Perspectives on the Exodus Narratives*, ed. James K. Hoffmeier, Alan R. Millard, and Gary A. Rendsburg (Winona Lake, IN: Eisenbrauns, 2016), 113-132, argues most convincingly for the unity of the narrative, especially the plagues pericope.
8. The most well-known and detailed attempt is Greta Hort, "The Plagues of Egypt," *Zeitschrift fur die alttestamentliche Wissenschaft* 69 (1957), 84-103. See also R. Steiglitz, "Ancient Records and the Exodus Plagues," *Biblical Archaeology Review* 13, no. 6 (1987): 46–49.
9. For an example of the former, see G. A. F. Knight, *Theology as Narration* (Grand Rapids, MI: Eerdmans, 1976); for the latter, see D. Irvin and T. L. Thompson, "The Joseph and Moses Narratives," in *Israelite and Judean History*, ed. J. H. Hayes and J. M. Miller (Philadelphia: Westminster Press, 1977); John Van Seters, "The Plagues of Egypt: Ancient Tradition or Literary Invention?," *Zeitschrift für die alttestamentliche Wissenschaft* 98 (1986).
10. Brad C. Sparks, "Egyptian Texts Relating to the Exodus: Discussions of Exodus Parallels in the Egyptology Literature," in Levy, Schneider, and Propp, *Israel's Exodus in Transdisciplinary Perspective*, 259–81, provides an excellent summary of various comparative efforts.
11. In Numbers 33:4 and in Exodus 18:11, Jethro believes that the deliverance has demonstrated that Jehovah is greater than all the gods. For examples of this kind of study, see John D. Currid, *Ancient Egypt and the Old Testament* (Grand

have been executed with varying degrees of success but, as Hoffmeier has noted, may be missing the true confrontation being played out in the narrative.[12] In his *Anchor Bible Dictionary* entry on the subject, Hoffmeier called for further examination of the plagues as they affected the office of pharaoh.[13] Hoffmeier partially met this challenge himself in a small section of his 1996 monograph, but it was not the intent of his book to answer it fully.[14] This article will be an attempt to go a step further in answering that call.

Examining the plagues narrative in the light of Egyptian kingship begs two crucial questions: When was the narrative composed, and at the time of its composition was there substantial enough contact between Egypt and the Israelite kingdoms for an Israelite writer to know anything of Egyptian kingship? The current study will partially answer the latter question, and thus it will be left until the conclusion for consideration. The former question is deserving of greater space than can be allowed here, but it must be addressed sufficiently for us to know where in Egyptian history we should extract the model of kingship that the plagues narrative is challenging.

Despite the fact that there are probably various redactional stages, here we are looking for the period in which the text as we now have it came together in something close to the form we now have it. While it is quite impossible to set an exact date for the composition of the plagues

---

Rapids, MI: Baker Books, 1997), 109–13; C. Aling, *Egypt and Bible History* (Grand Rapids, MI: Baker Books, 1981), 103–10; Knight, *Theology as Narration*, 62–79. Action serving as a symbol is not uncommon in the Hebrew Bible. See Donald W. Parry, "Symbolic Action as Prophecy in the Old Testament," in *Thy People Shall Be My People, and Thy God My God*, ed. Paul Y. Hoskisson (Salt Lake City: Deseret Book, 1994); J. C. L. Gibson, *Language and Imagery in the Old Testament* (Peabody, MA: Hendrickson, 1998), 10.

12. See Hoffmeier, *Plagues*, 376; Hoffmeier, *Israel*, 151.

13. Hoffmeier, "Egypt, Plagues," 376. Hoffmeier has also called for further involvement of Egyptologists in studying the Exodus, which call this also hopefully satisfies. See James K. Hoffmeier, "Egyptologists and the Israelite Exodus from Egypt," in Levy, Schneider, and Propp, *Israel's Exodus in Transdisciplinary Perspective*, 206.

14. Hoffmeier, *Israel*, 151–55.

narrative, we can set some limits to it. The purported setting for the narrative seems to be during the late Eighteenth or early Nineteenth Dynasty (roughly the thirteenth century). This, then, confines the very earliest possible date for our text. Opinions about the latest possible date for the initial construction of the text vary widely, and any attempt at setting such a date is sure to draw criticism from one ideological camp or another.[15] However, we do have some clues that can be used to come to a reasonable conclusion. The initial weaving together of different threads into the narrative we now have likely occurred in the first half of the first millennium (Iron Age), during the Twenty-fifth or Twenty-sixth Dynasties, and toward the end of Egypt's Third Intermediate Period.[16] One important piece of evidence is the composition commonly known as the Song of the Sea, the great piece of poetry recorded in Exodus 15. This is generally viewed as one of the earliest compositions in the Hebrew Bible and purports to be the actual song sung at the time of the event.[17] Yet the prose of the narrative seems to be in later Hebrew than the Song of the Sea, somewhat similar to how the prose introduction to a Shakespeare play will be written in

15. By *construction*, one may mean either its initial writing or its weaving together of several sources into something similar to the narrative we now have. See Schmid, "Distinguishing the World of the Exodus Narrative," 334.

16. For an excellent treatment of this period, see Kenneth A. Kitchen, *The Third Intermediate Period in Egypt* (Warminster, UK: Aris & Phillips, 1986).

17. Frank Moore Cross Jr. and David Noel Freedman, *Studies in Ancient Yahwistic Poetry* (Grand Rapids, MI: Eerdmans, 1975), 31–33. Diana Vikander Edelman, "The Creation of Exodus 14–15," *Jerusalem Studies in Egyptology*, ed. Irene Shirun-Grumach (Wiesbaden: Harrassowitz Verlag, 1998), 137–58, believes that only a portion of Exodus 15 is this old, relying upon the idea that a song by a woman (Miriam) is the oldest tradition. But even by Shirun-Grumach's standard, part of the Exodus tradition is very old. Additionally, Yair Hoffman, "The Exodus: Tradition and Reality. The Status of the Exodus Tradition in Ancient Israel," in Shirun-Grumach, *Jerusalem Studies in Egyptology*, 196, dates the Song of the Sea to the inauguration of the First Temple because he sees it as politically expedient at that time. Both Hoffman and Edelman fail to address the authentically archaic Hebrew elements of Exodus 15, the very elements that have led scholars to believe that this is an archaic composition. See also A. Klein, "Hymn and History in Ex. 15: Observations on the Relationship between Temple Theology and Exodus Narrative in the Song of the Sea," *Zeitschrift für die alttestamentliche Wissenschaft* 124 (2012): 516–27.

a later English than will the play itself. This later (though still classical) Hebrew introduction suggests that the narrative we now have was composed sometime after the events it described. Additionally, eighth-century prophets Amos and Hosea place enough emphasis on the Exodus motif to demonstrate that it must have been an important and entrenched story by their time.[18] Thus, we can conclude that at least the substantial storyline of the Exodus was in existence by the eighth century. It therefore seems likely that the story came to life in the form in which we now know it sometime between the Nineteenth and Twenty-sixth Dynasties or, in other words, sometime during the decline of the New Kingdom and the Third Intermediate Period.[19]

TIMING AND THE CONCEPT OF KINGSHIP IN ANCIENT EGYPT

At the outset, then, it would seem that we have two periods to examine: one, the purported setting of the story and two, the time of the composition. However, a closer analysis will help to narrow our investigation. In

---

18. See Shmuel Ahituv, "The Exodus: Survey of the Theories of the Last Fifty Years," in Shirun-Grumach, *Jerusalem Studies in Egyptology*, 132. Even Hoffman, "The Exodus: Tradition and Reality," 197, sees the established use of the tradition in Hosea, though Hoffman fails to note it in Isaiah. By Hoffman's own admission, the tradition was older than the period of the United Monarchy (196).
19. There are many who would posit a later date for the composition of the plagues narrative. See, for example, Schmid, "Distinguishing the World of the Exodus Narrative," who posits the Persian Period. See also Donald B. Redford, "An Egyptological Perspective on the Exodus Narrative," *Egypt, Israel, Sinai*, ed. Anson F. Rainey (Tel Aviv: Tel Aviv University, 1987), 150. Disagreeing with many of his points is Manfred Bietak, "Comments on the 'Exodus,'" in Rainey, *Egypt, Israel, Sinai*. Redford's arguments are also systematically refuted by Sarah I. Groll, "The Egyptian Background of the Exodus and the Crossing of the Reed Sea: A New Reading of Papyrus Anastasi VIII," in Shirun-Grumach, *Jerusalem Studies in Egyptology*, 189–92. Frank J. Yurco, "Merenptah's Canaanite Campaign and Israel's Origins," *Exodus: the Egyptian Evidence*, ed. Ernest S. Frerichs and Leonard H. Lesko (Winona Lake, IN: Eisenbrauns, 1997), 50, using the Merenptah Stela, Exodus 15, Judges 5, and "the mileiu of Ramesses II's Egypt," dates "the root of the Exodus story to the Ramesside era."

the late Nineteenth and Twentieth Dynasties, as well as in the Third Intermediate Period, the concept of kingship that Egypt's kings were trying to resuscitate was the concept that had existed under the great pharaohs of the New Kingdom. These later kings were very aware of their predecessors and the glorious kingship that they had wielded. While there were some practical differences in their political potency,[20] many of these later pharaohs went so far as to write of their success in returning to a "traditional" kingship[21] or to intentionally mimic accounts of earlier kings as they made their own.[22] There can be little doubt that whatever their royal power was in reality, the image these kings desired to portray to subjects and foreigners was that of the Eighteenth and early Nineteenth Dynasties; thus, it is

---

20. See John Baines, "Kingship, Definition of Culture, and Legitimation," *Ancient Egyptian Kingship*, ed. David O'Connor and David P. Silverman (New York: Brill, 1995), 36–43. See also Peter Der Manuelian, *Living in the Past: Studies in Archaism of the Egyptian Twenty-sixth Dynasty* (New York: Keagan Paul International, 1994); Anthony Spalinger, "The Concept of Monarchy during the Saite Epoch: An Essay of Synthesis," *Orientalia* 47 (1978). It is important to note, as mentioned above, that the narrative seems to be written before the Twenty-sixth Dynasty because a crucial shift in the decorum of the presentation of the king began during that dynasty. See Antonio Loprieno, "Le Pharaon recostruit. La figure du roi dans la littérature égyptienne au Ier millénaire avant J.C.," *Bulletin De La Société Française d'égyptologie*, no. 142 (June 1998). While it was at this period that the decorum of royal presentation changed, it was also then that intentional "archaizing" reached its peak; see Der Manuelian, *Living in the Past*, 387. We see during this period "incentives to 'bypass' recent history in favor of linking contemporary (Saite) times with the past." Der Manuelian, *Living in the Past*, 409.
21. Baines, "Kingship," 36.
22. Baines, "Kingship," 38. See also Erik Hornung, *History of Ancient Egypt: An Introduction*, trans. David Lorton (Ithaca, NY: Cornell University Press, 1999), 126, where he writes of the new dynasties carefully continuing Ramesside traditions. Cyril Aldred, *The Egyptians* (London: Thames and Hudson, 1998), 188, writes of a religious shift during this period that lessened the king's worship, but Hornung also writes of the "weight of traditional thought" that continued to be attached to the kingship and its official theology. Der Manuelian (summarized in *Living in the Past*, 403–404) carefully outlines a retrogression in the language of royal stelae from "Late Egyptianisms" to classical Egyptian and even the Egyptian of the Old Kingdom.

that period to which we should look to find the concept of kingship that the plagues narrative is challenging.

The idea of kingship in Egypt is complex, and different genres of the ancient texts will paint a different picture of the institution.[23] An investigation of the history of Egyptian kingship is well outside of the scope of this paper. However, because many of the sources I will cite were written a thousand years before the purported setting of the text we are studying here, with an even greater gap until the core of the written form we now have took shape, a comment on the sources' relevance is requisite. While many of the details of kingship would surely have changed between the times of the Old Kingdom and the New Kingdom,[24] or the Third Intermediate Period, the *concept* of kingship really changed very little over the three thousand years of Egyptian history.[25] In fact, kingship in the Eighteenth Dynasty was intentionally modeled on the Twelfth Dynasty,[26] which in turn was an attempt to restore the kingship of the Old Kingdom. As was mentioned above, the kingship of the Third Intermediate Period was modeled after the New Kingdom.

This continual return to the kingship of the past creates a type of spiraling unity in the ideology of Egyptian kingship. While some of the details of the Pyramid Texts[27] may have been mostly lost by the New Kingdom,

---

23. David P. Silverman, "The Nature of Kingship," in O'Connor and Silverman, *Ancient Egyptian Kingship*, 50. For example, see the discussion on how kings had to portray their violence differently depending upon whether it was personal or institutional in Kerry Muhlestein, *Violence in the Service of Order: The Religious Framework for Sanctioned Killing in Ancient Egypt* (Oxford, UK: British Archaeological Reports, 2011), 77–80.

24. For example, in the New Kingdom the kings lost some of their cosmic role, but in the Eighteenth Dynasty it was somewhat regained as the king and the creator god received a new convergence. See Baines, "Kingship," 24, 26.

25. See Donald B. Redford, "The Concept of Kingship during the Eighteenth Dynasty," in O'Connor and Silverman, *Ancient Egyptian Kingship*, 181; Baines, "Kingship," 21–31.

26. Redford, "Concept of Kingship," 159–61.

27. In this article, citations of ancient sources will typically be referred to by English publications readily available to the lay reader. In the case of the Pyramid Texts (abbreviated PT in citations herein, except when a more detailed part is referred to, in which case we will use the "pyr" designation), it is assumed that

the interrelationship of the Pyramid Texts and the Coffin Texts,[28] combined with the clear continuity between the Coffin Texts and the Book of the Dead,[29] coupled with the interdependence of many temple liturgies of the New Kingdom and later periods with the Pyramid Texts,[30] suggests that a general knowledge of this earlier corpus was had at least among the elite. In this study, when the Pyramid Texts are cited in connection with so minute a detail that it may not have formed part of the New Kingdom milieu, it will be observed in the notes. Still, as Rendsburg has demonstrated, "An educated Israelite and his well-informed Israelite audience would have been familiar with the Egyptian cultural context which motivated a good portion of the dramatic narrative of Exodus 1–15."[31] On the whole we may safely assume that the concepts of kingship being addressed in this paper were predominantly constant throughout the history of ancient Egypt.[32]

---

the abundance of online and print versions of the Pyramid Texts makes it such that a simple PT citation along with the number of the PT will be sufficient. Similarly, Book of the Dead references will simply be listed as BD along with the spell number.

28. Bernard Mathieu, "La distinction entre Textes des Pyramides et Textes des Sarcophages est-elle légitime?," in *Textes des pyramides et textes des sarcophages: D'un monde à l'autre*, ed. Susanne Bickel and Bernard Mathieu (Cairo: Institut Français d'Archéologie Orientale, 2008), 247–62. My gratitude to John Gee for bringing this source to my attention.

29. See John Gee, "The Book of the Dead as Canon," *British Museum Studies in Ancient Egypt and Sudan* 15 (2010): 30–31.

30. See Jan Assman, "Egyptian Mortuary Liturgies," *Studies in Egyptology, Presented to Miriam Lichtheim*, ed. Sarah Israelit-Groll (Jerusalem: The Magnes Press, Hebrew University, 1990), 1:1–45.

31. Rendsburg, "Moses the Magician," 256.

32. Rendsburg, "Moses the Magician," 219, argues persuasively that there is no point during which this narrative may have been composed in which the contact with Egypt was not strong enough to have ideas of Egyptian culture not be taken into account.

PLAGUES, GODS, AND KINGS

Drawing a distinction between a confrontation with Egyptian deities and Egypt's king is somewhat an artificially created modern division. In the cultural mindset of ancient Egypt, such a division would not have been conceived. Indeed, the similarities between the king and the gods "point toward a comprehensive and fundamental kinship that links the king with all deities."[33] According to many ancient sources, the Egyptians viewed Re[34] or Osiris[35] as the first king of Egypt. The current king was seen as the successor of both. Additionally, the current king was the successor to the creator god in whatever form the creator god was manifest.[36] In a Western impossibility, the king was both Re and Re's son and successor from the Fourth Dynasty onward.[37] To add to the conundrum, the king was also

---

33. Erik Hornung, *Conceptions of God in Ancient Egypt, the One and the Many*, trans. John Baines (Ithaca, NY: Cornell University Press, 1971), 139.

34. See John A. Wilson, trans., "Deliverance of Mankind from Destruction," in *The Ancient Near East*, vol. 1: *An Anthology of Texts and Pictures*, ed. James B. Pritchard (Princeton: Princeton University Press, 1958), 3–5; Herodotus, *The Histories*, 2.144; Turin Cannon; Henri Frankfort, *Kingship and the Gods: A Study of Ancient Near Eastern Religion as the Integration of Society and Nature* (Chicago: The University of Chicago Press, 1948), 148–49.

35. Papyrus Chester Beatty; George Hart, *A Dictionary of Egyptian Gods and Goddesses* (New York: Routledge, 1996), 155.

36. Frankfort, *Kingship and the Gods*, 148. Re is a creator god but so is Atum, Khnum, and Ptah, as well as others. See also Lanny Bell, "The New Kingdom 'Divine' Temple: The Example of Luxor," in *Temples of Ancient Egypt*, ed. Byron E. Shafer (Ithaca, NY: Cornell University Press, 1997), 138, who writes that "the reigning pharaoh was the physical son of the universal sun god, the Creator." In note 46 Bell shares three depictions of New Kingdom monarchs as they are conceived by divinity.

37. Bell, "The New Kingdom 'Divine' Temple," 138. Hornung, *Conceptions*, 138–39, speaks of the king as being both the prime son and the image of the creator god. See Useratet to Amenophis II, in R. A. Caminos, "The Shrines and Rock Inscriptions of Ibrim," *Archaeological Survey of Egypt* 32 (1968), wherein New Kingdom officials cry out to the king "you are Re." Ramses II is called the "Son of Re" in his Kadesh Battle Inscriptions; see Miriam Lichtheim, *Ancient Egyptian Literature*, vol. 2: *The New Kingdom* (Los Angeles: University of California Press, 1976), 63. Redford, *Concept of Kingship*, 123, demonstrates that during the Eighteenth Dynasty, Canaanites knew that the king was both Re and the son of

Horus, Orsiris's son.[38] In fact, the Pyramid Texts associate the king with Atum,[39] an unspecified creator,[40] Osiris,[41] and Horus,[42] to name a few of the more important deities.[43] The texts also ascribe to the king a divinity of his own. It is impossible to entirely separate Pharaoh from the pantheon of which he was an integral part and for which he served as the earthly representative.

There is another aspect that must be considered as we think of the contest between God and Pharaoh. In Exodus 4:16 and 7:1, God tells Moses that when he appears before Pharaoh, Moses will be as a God and Aaron will serve as his prophet, thus mimicking the relationship that Moses and Jehovah shared. Because Pharaoh was viewed as divine (or semidivine), any normal meeting between Moses and Pharaoh would have

---

Re. This relationship was true of Re in his various syncretistic forms, especially of Amun, or Amun-Re. See Kadesh Battle Inscriptions, 69; Baines, "Kingship," 18; William J. Murnane, "The Kingship of the Nineteenth Dynasty: A Study in the Resilience of an Institution," in O'Connor and Silverman, *Ancient Egyptian Kingship* (New York: Brill, 1995), 187–90.

38. See "A Cycle of Hymns to King Sesostris III," in Miriam Lichtheim, *Ancient Egyptian Literature*, vol. 1 (Los Angeles: University of California Press, 1975), 198. See also Hart, *Dictionary of Egyptian Gods and Goddesses*, 169; Jeremy Naydler, *Temple of the Cosmos: The Ancient Egyptian Experience of the Sacred* (Rochester, VT: Inner Traditions, 1996), 104, who writes that "although the king was Horus incarnate, the kingly prototype was always Ra, the creator god." Horus was also seen as a god who was king of Egypt, following in the footsteps of his father. See Herodotus, *Histories*, 2.144; Papyrus Chester Beatty.

39. PT 215. This, as with the next four references, is just one of the many available examples from the Pyramid Texts. While the Pyramid Texts were well over a thousand years old by this time, they were known and reused in Egypt even into the Ptolemaic period. See Erhart Graefe, "Über die Verarbeitung von Pyramidentexten in den späten Tempeln," in *Religion und Philosophie im Alten Ägypten, Festabe für Philippe Derchain*, ed. Ursula Verhoeven and Erhart Graefe (Leuven: Uitgeveru Peeters, 1991), 129–48.

40. PT 222.

41. PT 535.

42. PT 20.

43. The Pyramid Texts and later sources associate the king with a great number of gods. See David P. Silverman, "The Nature of Egyptian Kingship," in O'Connor and Silverman, *Ancient Egyptian Kingship*, 62.

been between unequals. By designating Moses as being similar to a god with an attendant prophet, Jehovah made it so that Moses and Pharaoh were equal.[44] This innately lifted Jehovah above Pharaoh, because Jehovah was still greater than Moses, who was now Pharaoh's equal. Thus, even in the way Jehovah labeled his representatives, he was challenging Pharaoh.

It was appropriate that Moses dealt with the king, for the king was the mediator between the gods and humans, and the only way in which the gods could be approached.[45] Thus, Moses, the intermediary of Jehovah, dealt with Pharaoh, the intermediary of the Egyptian gods. However, it must be remembered that Pharaoh was divine himself; he simultaneously *was* Re, Atum, Osiris, Horus,[46] *and* their representative on earth, while Moses was just a man. Thus, the confrontation takes the form of a contest between Jehovah and Pharaoh.

This semidivinity is what made it so important for God to set up a contest with Pharaoh. The Israelites had been influenced by Egyptian idolatry and were struggling with idolatrous practices. By setting up such a contest, Jehovah would make it clear to the Israelites that he alone was divine; not Pharaoh, not the gods Pharaoh was one of or interacted with, but only Jehovah. This was part of the purpose of the contest. It would also be important that other nations recognize the power of Jehovah. In fact, as the Israelites exited Egypt and came into the promised land, the fame of God's contest with Egypt's king had reached those lands and made them less willing to attack the Israelites (Joshua 2:10). Further, it should help

---

44. Rendsburg, "Moses as Equal to Pharaoh," argues this point eloquently. I wrote the current article as a paper presented at a meeting of the 2001 Pacific Region Society of Biblical Literature. Between then and now, Rendsuburg has written two articles, both already cited, arguing various aspects of Jehovah being in a contest with Pharaoh. We arrived at our ideas independently, and while there is overlap between the ideas we present, there is also much that is unique about each approach.
45. Dimitri Meeks and Christine Favard-Meeks, *Daily Life of the Egyptian Gods*, trans. G. M. Goshgarian (Ithaca, NY: Cornell University Press, 1993), 120.
46. On the Egyptian concept of being more than one kind of being at once and on identifying with deity, see Kerry Muhlestein, "Empty Threats? How Egyptians' Self-Ontology Should Affect the Way We Read Many Texts," *Journal of the Society for the Study of Egyptian Antiquities* 34 (2007): 115–30.

convince readers for time immemorial of the true nature and sovereignty of Jehovah. In our day we do not often think of the sovereignty of our God, but it seems he intends for us to recognize it.

There is textual evidence for the idea of the plagues being a contest between God and Pharaoh. As mentioned above, Jehovah says that he will mete out punishments on the gods of Egypt, but as the confrontation begins, he instructs Moses to see "that which I will do to Pharaoh" (Exodus 6:1), and at the end Jehovah affirms he will "get glory through Pharaoh" (Exodus 14:4). In Exodus 9:16 Jehovah informs Pharaoh that Jehovah has raised him up specifically for the cause of showing his power via the monarch. The Song of the Sea (Exodus 15) is specific in stating that it is Pharaoh that Jehovah has triumphed over.[47]

Furthermore, some have seen the juxtaposed use by Jehovah and Pharaoh of "Thus says" phrases as an intentional comparison and contest between the two beings, demonstrating which of the two could actually bring about that which he said.[48] Hoffmeier has shown that the Exodus narrative's expressions concerning the arm of Jehovah are "Hebrew derivations or counterparts to Egyptian expressions that symbolized Egyptian royal power."[49] The language that creates these images of Jehovah's arm seems to be employed specifically to invoke the image of Pharaoh's might and Jehovah's ability to overcome that might. Additionally, the Hebrew Bible paints the picture of Jehovah as the true king of Israel.[50] It is fitting that when the king of Israel does battle with Egypt, it would be with its king. Since the battle took place on earth, it should be viewed as taking place with the Egyptian gods' representative on earth, the king. Thus, the

---

47. See, for example, Exodus 15:3–4, 18–19. See also Thomas B. Dozeman, *God at War: Power in the Exodus Tradition* (New York: Oxford University Press, 1996), 15.

48. Currid, *Ancient Egypt*, 83–84.

49. James K. Hoffmeier, "The Arm of God Versus the Arm of Pharaoh in the Exodus Narratives," *Biblica* 67, no. 3 (1986): 387; see also David R. Seely, "The Image of the Hand of God in the Exodus Traditions" (PhD diss., University of Michigan, 1990).

50. Gibson, *Language and Imagery in the Old Testament*, 21; Marc Brettler, *God Is King: Understanding an Israelite Metaphor* (Sheffield, UK: JSOT Press, 1989).

proper lens through which we should view the conflict acted out in the plagues pericope is that of Jehovah's triumph over Pharaoh.

To properly appropriate this lens, we will first briefly look at each individual plague and its relationship with Egyptian kingship, and then we will examine the concept of plagues as a whole and their effect on royal efficacy and theology.

THE PLAGUES

While the turning of Moses's rod into a snake[51] is not traditionally considered a plague, some have viewed it in this light,[52] and it is certainly the beginning of the contest between Jehovah and Pharaoh. We will briefly examine this contest because the snake was so much a symbol of Pharaoh and his power. The Pyramid Texts describe the king as being a snake.[53] Other Egyptian literature informs us that Horus would trample snakes to protect the king[54] and that Re would drive them away for the same

51. When Moses is atop Sinai, the rod turns into a snake. In Pharaoh's court, the word likely used actually means "crocodile." It is difficult to know whether the use of *crocodile* represents a later change or whether it was the original word used. See Rendsburg, "Moses the Magician," 245–46; Gary A. Rendsburg, "Moses as Equal to Pharaoh," in *Text, Artifact, and Image: Revealing Ancient Israelite Religion*, ed. Gary Beckman and Theodore J. Lewis (Providence, RI: Brown Judaic Studies, 2006), 209–10. Rendsburg points out that both animals are associated with the king and that the Horus myth was also associated with the king. Because the text predicts that Moses will turn his staff into a snake, and then at the time it was turned into a crocodile (if the text was not amended), it seems that the text certainly wants us to associate the snake with the event in Pharaoh's court, even if it was a crocodile then (see PT 317 for an example of the king being associated with the crocodile). Because of this, and because of the very real possibility that the text originally read "snake," we will here speak of a snake. The crocodile has royal and chaos associations that are very similar to that of the snake, so there is no effective difference. Rendsburg, "The Literary Unity of the Exodus Narrative," 128–29, argues that the crocodile serves as an upgrade in Moses's miraculous powers.

52. See Currid, *Ancient Egypt*, 85–103; D. J. McCarthy, "Moses' Dealings with Pharaoh," *Catholic Biblical Quarterly* 27 (1965): 336–47.

53. PT 318.

54. PT 378.

purpose.[55] Moreover, the king wore the *Uraeus*, a snake-shaped crownlet, which was charged with power and "spat fire at the king's enemies," embodying "protective power and aggressive intent towards the forces of disorder."[56] The *Uraeus* was the embodiment of the cobra goddess who was to protect the king and imbue him with divine power.[57] This aspect was so intertwined with kingship that it was a part of the king's titulary, manifest in the "Two Ladies" name of the king. The Cobra Goddess was the second of the two goddesses that gave rise to the "Two Ladies" name that every king received. Further, staffs that appear to be snakes are ubiquitous in Egyptian art, including many that depict the king herding calves with a snake staff.[58] Rendsburg has pointed out that when Moses or Aaron picked the snake up by the tail, which is not how snakes are typically handled, it imitated many depictions of Horus (who was strongly associated with the king) holding a snake by the tail. Depictions of the king herding calves typically show the king holding his snake staff by the tail.[59] As we will see below, there is more to this contest than is immediately apparent, but what is clear at the outset is that the king is closely associated with snakes.

The next challenge came when Moses and Aaron turned the Nile and all of Egypt's water to blood, making it unfit for drinking. In a way, Jehovah had usurped the king's abilities since the king is listed as the one

55. BD 85.

56. Toby A. H. Wilkinson, *Early Dynastic Egypt* (New York: Routledge, 1999), 191–92; Currid, *Ancient Egypt*, 89–90. See also "The Annals of the Battle at Megiddo by Tuthmose III," in Lichtheim, *Ancient Egyptian Literature*, 2:36, wherein Amun-Re says, "My serpent on your brow consumed them [the enemy]"; Ramses II's Kadesh inscriptions, in Lichtheim, 2:70, which says, "The serpent on my brow felled my foes." The idea of protecting against disorder becomes particularly important when it is realized that the plagues represent disorder. See the discussion provided later in this paper.

57. PT 220–21. Herein, the king addresses the "fiery serpent" and asks it to give him its dread, fear, and acclaim, as well as its protection. See also a depiction in the tomb of Thutmosis III, wherein a five-headed serpent protects the king's body within its coils.

58. Rendsburg, "Moses the Magician," 210–13.

59. Rendsburg, "Moses the Magician," 213–15.

who brings about "reddening."[60] This challenge to Pharaoh is more properly understood when we know a little more of Pharaoh's identity with the Nile. The Pyramid Texts assert that the king becomes the god Sobek, and in this form cares for Egypt's water.[61] Elsewhere we are informed that the king is "in charge of the Nile."[62] Thuthmosis III is described as having the Nile in his service, by which he gives life to Egypt.[63] One pharaoh was told that "the water in the river is drunk when you wish."[64] From the earliest times the king was seen as having the ability to dominate and further the processes of nature, especially those concerned with the Nile.[65] The Admonitions of Ipuwer tell us that when there is a weak king, or no king, the "river is blood, as one drinks of it one shrinks from people and thirsts for

---

60. PT 273–74. Lichtheim, *Ancient Egyptian Literature*, 1:37, disagrees with this translation, as does Samuel A. B. Mercer, *The Pyramid Texts*, vol. 2 (New York: Longmans, Green and Co., 1952), 1:187. These seem to be the only two published dissensions in translating this difficult passage. The word *tr* is used for red ink, and since Teti I's Pyramid Texts include a scribal determinative after the word, there can be little doubt that it referred to red ink, and thus it must have something to do with the color red. In any case, this detail is obscure enough that it may have provided no reference for New Kingdom kingship; though the color may have been familiar to them as an attribute of the king since the king caused the flood, which looked red as it turned muddy. This annual event may have continually carried the impression that the king was the "reddener" of water.
61. PT 317.
62. PT 217.
63. This description is from the translation of a scarab in Frankfort, *Kingship and the Gods*, 195. See also Frankfort, *Kingship and the Gods*, 57; Naydler, *Temple of the Cosmos*, 167, where Frankfort and Naydler speak of the Nile "respecting" the king and of rituals enacted in order to ensure that this took place, concepts that are known because of translations from the instructions of King Amenemhet I.
64. "Tale of Sinuhe," translated in Lichtheim, *Ancient Egyptian Literature*, 1:231.
65. Frankfort, *Kingship and the Gods*, 58; Wilkinson, *Early Dynastic Egypt*, 183. See also A. Erman, "Hymn on the Accession of King Merenptah," in *The Ancient Egyptians: A Sourcebook of Their Writings* (New York: Harper Torchbooks, 1966), 279, wherein the king is credited with the fact that "the water standeth and faileth not, the Nile carrieth a high flood."

water."[66] In contaminating the Nile, Jehovah had shown his superiority in an area that was an integral part of the king's powers.

The next three plagues are problematic to the current approach, or to any approach that tries to tie them in with the king or deity. There simply are not substantial references to anything having to do with these plagues in Egyptian literature. Some attempts have been made to tie the god Khnum in with the plague of frogs since he is associated with reptiles, among other living things.[67] This does have some bearing because Khnum is one of the creator gods, and, as discussed above, the king is associated with all creator gods. The argument becomes a little more appropriate when coupled with the idea that Khnum's consort is Heket, a frog-headed goddess whose job, among other things, was to control the multiplication of frogs by protecting frog-eating crocodiles.[68] Overpowering the domain of the creator's consort can be seen as an indirect challenge of the king.[69] However, the nature of this challenge to the king is probably better seen in light of the overall challenge to *ma'at* that will be presented below.[70]

Understanding the two plagues following the plague of frogs is even more difficult because of the question of translating the words used to designate the creatures of which these plagues consist. These terms have been taken to mean gnats, flies, lice, mosquitos, dog flies, maggots, and beetles.[71] The only one of these translations that could be connected with the king,

66. Papyrus Leiden 344, translation from Lichtheim, *Ancient Egyptian Literature*, 1:151.

67. Currid, *Ancient Egypt*, 53.

68. Currid, *Ancient Egypt*, 110; Knight, *Theology as Narration*, 6; Hart, *Dictionary of Egyptian Gods and Goddesses*, 83–84. This connection is even stronger if Moses and Aaron were dealing with staffs turning into crocodiles. The destruction of Pharaoh's crocodiles in that story (if they were crocodiles) would tie into the sudden multiplication of frogs.

69. Hoffmeier, *Israel*, 150, calls the Heket connection into question. Indeed, both Currid and Knight are unconvincing and show little evidence for their conclusions.

70. Bruce Wells, *Exodus*, Zondervan Illustrated Bible Backgrounds Commentary (Grand Rapids, MI: Zondervan Academic, 206), 1709, also discusses this idea of maintaining *ma'at*.

71. See Hoffmeier, *Plagues*, 375; Currid, *Ancient Egypt*, 110–11; Knight, *Theology as Narration*, 63.

that of "beetle," is a dubious translation.[72] It would be convenient for those who desire to see a direct challenge to Egypt's gods or king in the plagues if these two plagues could be dismissed. However, they are among the shorter lists of plagues provided in Psalms 78 and 105, lending even more weight to their traditional place among the plagues. This forces the author to admit a weakness in the current approach. However, the challenge that these plagues present will be incorporated into this study in a later section. Indeed, little can be said about these plagues except to refer the reader to the section below about the king and the maintenance of order.

The plague on domesticated animals resumes the direct connections that can be made with the king. It assails two of the oldest and most basic ideas behind Egyptian kingship, that of Pharaoh's role as shepherd and his identity as a bull.[73] There is a tremendous amount of evidence supporting the idea of Pharaoh as a shepherd or herder, including iconography spanning from Early Dynastic to New Kingdom times, etymological ties, passages from wisdom texts, and Egyptological opinions.[74] The king is often depicted as a herder, especially in an important ritual having to do with driving calves.[75] Among the strong animal husbandry connections[76] are the two most prevalent trappings of kingship, the crook and flail; both stem from the image of the king as a herder.[77] This tradition seems to have continued throughout the institution of Egyptian kingship. I add to these arguments the passage from the Book of the Dead that informs us that the creator god was a herder.[78] Though the Bible informs us that "all shepherds are abhorrent to Egyptians" (Genesis 46:34), it is apparent that the royal ideology included the idea of caring for the livestock of Egypt.

---

72. Knight does not supply any evidence as to how he arrived at the translation of "beetle."
73. Hoffmeier, *Israel*, 154, sees this plague as at least partially a battle between Moses's shepherd's rod and the king's shepherd's crook.
74. Hoffmeier, *Israel*, 154–55.
75. Rendsburg, "Moses the Magician," 211–13.
76. Wilkinson, *Early Dynastic Egypt*, 188–89.
77. Wilkinson, *Early Dynastic Egypt*, 190.
78. BD 15.

The king and the gods he represented were also seen to be some of the very animals that were being afflicted by Jehovah. Pharaoh was the Ram of Eternity[79] and the bull.[80] The king's coronation involved an "inheritance of the bull,"[81] and a host of iconography associated with kingship shows the king wearing a bull's tail. Additionally, Pharaoh's kingship was reproclaimed at the Feast of Min, a feast associated with a bull.[82] Iconography often drew the king as a bull.[83] In the New Kingdom, kings adopted titles such as "Strong Bull."[84] This became part of the king's titulary as the "Horus Name" became it was listed as "Horus, Strong (or victorious) Bull." "Indeed, the bull appears to have been the animal most closely associated with the king."[85] The ideas of the king as both a shepherd and bull, when coupled together, present the plague upon Egyptian livestock as being fraught with implications for the potency of the king.

The plague of boils was also a direct challenge to the king's ability to carry out his royal duties in the face of Jehovah's intervention. Osiris, with whom the king was associated, is described as one who did not let anything putrefy or swell up.[86] We learn that "well-being" and "health" actually share the throne with the sun god,[87] who was simultaneously both the king and the king's father. Horus, who was the king, was a doctor, as was his mother Isis.[88] Clearly the king should have been able to prevent boils

79. BD 18.
80. BD 82. See also PT 246, which lists the king as a ram and a bull.
81. Meeks and Favard-Meeks, *Daily Life of the Egyptian Gods*, 190–91.
82. Frankfort, *Kingship and the Gods*, 189–90.
83. Wilkinson, *Early Dynastic Egypt*, 190. This iconography is extremely early.
84. Wilkinson, *Early Dynastic Egypt*, 191. This title is very appropriate for this study because the New Kingdom is the purported setting of the plagues narrative. See "Coronation Decree of Tuthmose I" in Kurt Sethe, *Urkunden des aegyptischen Altertums IV: der 18. Dynastie* (Leipzig, 1906), 79-81; Alan Gardiner, *Egyptian Grammar, Being and Introduction to the Study of Hieroglyphs* (London: Oxford University Press, 1982), 458, who refers to it as a "victorious bull" epithet.
85. Wilkinson, *Early Dynastic Egypt*, 191.
86. BD 58.
87. PT 517. This idea continues throughout Egyptian kingship.
88. Meeks and Favard-Meeks, *Daily Life of the Egyptian Gods*, 106. This is from a New Kingdom setting.

from coming upon his people. But the narrative demonstrates that he was unable to exercise his divine abilities contrary to Jehovah's will. This plague does not seem to have come upon the Israelites, demonstrating that Jehovah was able to protect his people. This was also true of the plague upon the cattle of Egypt, which did not come upon the Israelites' cattle.

There are two aspects to the plague of hail. One is involved with the hail itself and its fiery manifestation. The second is that of the corresponding damage to crops. As to the former, the king had both the ability to cause such happenings and to stop them. Again, Jehovah was usurping the king's ability, which was to manifest himself as a storm of both flame and lightening[89] or storm clouds[90] or to perform the errand of the storm.[91] Instead, these qualities are applied to Jehovah and his powers. At the same time, the king was supposed to be the one who protected his people from the storm[92] and would not let them be given over to the flame of the gods.[93] Here we see again that Jehovah protected his people from storms and flames, while Pharaoh could not. It is plain that the king was unable to live up to his purported abilities in the face of Jehovah's onslaught. It was not Pharaoh who caused or was manifest in the flaming storm, and he could not quench it nor avoid being given over to it. He was once again vanquished in his royal abilities. The greater power of Jehovah and his representative is ironically highlighted when *Moses* stopped Egypt from being given over to the storm or flame by the simple supplicating gesture of spreading out his hands before Jehovah.[94]

---

89. PT 261.
90. PT 254. This idea of the king being a storming flame continues, tied up with the Uraeus, into the New Kingdom.
91. PT 261.
92. "Cycle of Hymns to King Sesostris III," Lichtheim 1:200. Additionally, in Papyrus Leiden 344, we are informed that one of the results of weak or nonexistent kingship is that "storm sweeps the land."
93. PT 260.
94. Mayer I. Gruber, *Aspects of Nonverbal Communication in the Ancient Near East*, vol. 1 (Rome: Biblical Institute Press, 1980), 25–60, discusses this gesture of supplication. See also Kerry M. Muhlestein, "The Use of the Palm of the Hand in the Rituals of the Tabernacle and Temple of Solomon" (master's thesis, Brigham Young University, 1997), 75–80.

The damage done to the crops by the hail is compounded by the damage wrought thereafter by the locusts. Hence, we should consider this damage as a single aspect of two plagues and investigate the phenomenon accordingly. Again, we see that Jehovah was exercising pharaonic ability by striking the fields of the Egyptians, for it was the king who had the ability to damage the crops, and it was he whom the fields feared.[95] More apropos to the contest motif, the king was supposed to be able to ensure a good harvest and prevent such calamities. Egyptian literature consistently and abundantly describes the king's ability to bring forth crops abundantly and to stop the agricultural calamities that follow in the wake of a weak or nonexistent king.[96] This is a common motif of propagandist writings, showing that the kings themselves promoted the idea. It was the king's responsibility to ensure the benefits of nature's abundance for his society.[97] According to the Admonitions of Ipuwer, the lack of a strong king led to bare storehouses and a lack of grain.[98] The Pyramid Texts, unaccounted for in the earlier studies I have cited thus far, liberally supply us with information such as the king being divinely ensured of having "barley, emmer, bread, and beer."[99] Furthermore, these texts say that "if the King flourishes, Want cannot take his meal."[100] Elsewhere in these texts, we read that the king has the ability to give food to whomever he wants and that he has the ability to protect himself against those who would take his food away from him.[101] However, this all became an empty boast in the face of Jehovah's destructive elements. As the story continued, Jehovah would be the one to display these kingly abilities. In this divine conflict, Pharaoh failed in his task to protect his people's crops against outside forces. Jehovah succeeded in bringing about the destruction that was supposedly the prerogative of the pharaoh.

---

95. PT 254. This small point may not have been well known in the New Kingdom.
96. Hoffmeier, *Israel*, 152–53.
97. Frankfort, *Kingship and the Gods*, 189.
98. Papyrus Leiden 344.
99. PT 205.
100. PT 209.
101. PT 254.

The darkening of the sun may be the most direct attack against Pharaoh's ability to fulfill his royal duties in the face of Jehovah's power. The sun was among the greatest objects of Egyptian worship and was integrally tied to Re and his various syncretistic manifestations. The king was intimately caught up in this association, being both the son of Re and Re himself. Rendsburg and Cassuto have shown that Re was a favorite target in the writings of the Pentateuch, frequently involving a wordplay on rʿâ, especially in the plagues pericope.[102] The king was seen as being directly responsible for Egypt receiving sunlight or for illuminating the two lands.[103] It is the king who covers the horizon, and the sun rises at his pleasure.[104] The king is described as being the Sun of the Two Shores[105] and is responsible for dawn[106] or for shining anew each day in the east.[107] The sun shines because of his love for the king.[108] Netherworld books such as the Amduat and the Book of Gates demonstrate how integral the king was to the sun's daily journey or rebirth. The presence of the sun was a mainstay of Egyptian theological stability and royal ideology. Thus, Jehovah's power over the sun was monumental. It was incontrovertible evidence that the king had been bested.

---

102. U. Cassuto, *A Commentary on the Book of Exodus*, trans. Israel Abrahams (Jerusalem: Magnes Press, 1967), 129; G. A. Rendsburg, "The Egyptian Sun-God Ra in the Pentateuch," *Henoch* 10 (1988); Hoffmeier, *Plagues*, 376.

103. "Instructions of Sehetepibre," in Erman, *Ancient Egyptians*, 84–85; Hoffmeier, *Plagues*, 377.

104. "Tale of Sinuhe," Lichtheim, *Ancient Egyptian Literature*, 1:231.

105. "Stela of Amenhotep III," translated in Lichtheim, *Ancient Egyptian Literature*, 2:46.

106. PT 217.

107. PT 257. See also Papyrus Anastasi 2.5.6, translated in Erman, *Ancient Egyptians*, 280, wherein the king is described as "thou rising sun, that illumines the Two Lands with its beauty! Thou sun of mankind that banishes darkness from Egypt!"

108. "Poetical Stela of Thutmose III," translated in Lichtheim, *Ancient Egyptian Literature*, 2:36. See also Bell, *Divine Temple*, 129, who notes texts in which the king's accession is likened to the sun's rising. In note 9 Bell discusses iconography that denotes that the king is one with the sun, especially when he was manifest in the Window of Appearance.

The king's titulary was also tied up with this plague, since one of his names was the "Son of Re." It is interesting to note that aspects of three of the five names of the king—the "Two Ladies" name, the "Horus, Strong Bull" name, and the "Son of Re" name—are affected by the plagues. Clearly, much of what was integral to the king's nature and ability was being challenged.

The final plague, the smiting of the firstborn of the Egyptians, was in some ways less monumental, though it certainly struck the individual Egyptian more personally. Additionally, the Exodus account makes it plain that the plague was brought specifically upon *Pharaoh*, as well as upon all of Egypt (Exodus 11:1).[109] It also affected the pharaonic facade. In a somewhat difficult translation of the Pyramid Texts, it is the king who claims to eat the firstborn males and females of the Egyptians, thus acquiring their power.[110] We are also told that the king will cause to live those whom he wishes to live, and those whom he wishes to die will surely die.[111] It is implied that the king had the ability to protect his children.[112] In a set of hymns for Senusret III, he is ascribed the power of protecting the youths that they may slumber and of making it possible for the Egyptians to raise their youths.[113] Again, we see that Jehovah had demonstrated an ability to exercise that which was kingly privilege and that Pharaoh could not

---

109. See also Dozeman, *God at War*, 19.

110. PT 273–74. See also CT 163 and 178. Lichtheim, *Ancient Egyptian Literature* 1:37, poses a translation that can be read this way. R. O. Faulkner, *The Ancient Egyptian Pyramid Texts* (Oxford: Oxford University Press, 1969), 81–82, presents a translation that cannot. See also Mercer, *Pyramid Texts*, 2:189, who believes that this refers to old men and women, as in those most advanced in age. However, the term *smsw* refers to a relative age, not a static one. It means the oldest, or eldest, in terms of someone else. The term *i3w* would be used for those who are old. Clearly *smsw* refers to the first born. I am indebted to Antonio Loprieno for help in understanding this term, though the responsibility for the translation is mine. See also Mordechai Gilula, "The Smiting of the First Born: An Egyptian Myth?," *Tel Aviv* 4 (1977): 95.

111. PT 217.

112. PT 224.

113. "Hymns to Sesostris III," Lichtheim, 1:199.

exercise *his* powers in opposition to Jehovah, who was in complete control over these royal prerogative elements throughout the story.

THE CONCEPT OF KINGSHIP IN CHALLENGE

An analysis of each plague as it bears upon the abilities of Egypt's gods and king may at first seem to be somewhat methodologically problematic. One could argue that the whole concept is undermined by the idea that almost every aspect of nature was tied to some god and the king. As a result, it would be difficult to conceive of a natural plague that was not in some way connected with an ability of the king. While at the onset, this notion does seem to compromise the idea of methodologically demonstrating a contest with Pharaoh, a closer examination reveals that, instead, it is exactly the point. Jehovah may have been challenging particular aspects of kingship, but primarily it was the concept of Egypt's divine king as a whole that was being debunked.

We must first understand the Egyptian concept of the created world, though that can only be presented briefly here. The world was created, or organized, out of chaos, or disorganization.[114] The concept of the correct organization of both natural beings and processes as well as social order was summed up in the term *ma'at*.[115] "*Maat* reveals itself as the foundation of all order in the created world."[116] In Egyptian thought, ma'at was in

---

114. See PT 600. For brief outlines of Egyptian cosmogony, see James P. Allen, "The Celestial Realm," in *Ancient Egypt*, ed. David P. Silverman (New York: Oxford University Press, 1997), 120–21; Meeks and Favard-Meeks, *Daily Life of the Egyptian Gods*, 13–17; Erik Hornung, *Idea into Image: Essays on Ancient Egyptian Thought*, trans. Elizabeth Bredeck (Princeton: Princeton University Press, 1992), 39–45; Leonard H. Lesko, "Ancient Egyptian Cosmogonies and Cosmology," *Religion in Ancient Egypt*, ed. Byron E. Shafer (Ithaca, NY: Cornell University Press, 1991.

115. Of course, this is an oversimplification of the concept. See Hornung, *Idea*, 131–46; Jan Assmann, *Ma'at: Gerechtigkeit und Unsterblichkeit im alten Ägypten* (Munich: C. H. Beck, 1969); Stephen Quirke, "Translating Ma'at," *Journal of Egptian Archaeology* 80 (1994): 219–31; Terence DuQuesne, "I Know Ma'et: Counted, Complete, Enduring," *Discussions in Egyptolgy* 22 (1992): 79–89.

116. Hornung, *Idea*, 134. Hornung presents this idea in light of one of ma'at's symbols, the type of beveled pedestal on which the throne of gods and the king rested.

constant danger of being overcome by disorder, or chaos.[117] "The conception of the universe as a fragile entity that was perpetually threatened with oblivion gave to the Egyptian cult of the gods an urgency."[118] Chaos (*Isfet*) had to be destroyed in order to uphold order. [119]

The being who was responsible for maintaining ma'at, which necessarily included the destruction of isfet, was the king.[120] This is *the* primary concept of kingship in Egypt. Texts from virtually every period of Egyptian history that bear on this study express this. For example, a Pyramid Text states that the king "put Ma'at in the place of Isfet."[121] Similarly, a New Kingdom religious text states that "Re has put the king on the land of the living for eternity and infinity so that he may judge [hu]mankind, so that he may satisfy the gods, so that he may bring about Ma'at, so that he may destroy Isfet."[122] Amenemhet I claimed to have appeared "as Atum himself, setting in order that which he found decaying."[123] Thutmosis III was described as one who "transforms Egypt into the condition of the past, as when Re was king,"[124] which was a condition of ma'at. Speaking of what a strong king will cause to happen, the prophecies of Neferti state, "Ma'at

117. See Muhlestein, *Violence in the Service of Order*, 2–7, 94–96.

118. Stephen Quirke, *Ancient Egyptian Religion* (New York: Dover Publications, 1992), 70. Hornung, *Idea*, 135, writes that "passively adapting to a preexisting order, following it and respecting it, will not suffice; rather, this order must be established and actively realized time and again." See also the Admonitions of Ipuwer, in Papyrus Leiden 344, wherein it is presented that only the presence of a strong king will maintain ma'at.

119. Besides the passages already quoted and those cited below, see Harry Smith, "Ma'et and Isfet," *Bulletin of the Australian Centre for Egyptology* 5 (1994): 67–88; Assman devotes much of the second section of chapter 7 in *Ma'at* to this idea.

120. See Naydler, *Temple of the Cosmos*, 96; Frankfort, *Kingship and the Gods*, 51–52; Siegfried Morenz, *Egyptian Religion* (London: Methuen, 1973), 113; Donald B. Redford, *Pharaonic King Lists: Annals and Day Books* (Mississauga, ON: Benben Publications, 1986), 259–75. Bell, "Divine Temple," 128, writes of the king's royal name being equated with ma'at.

121. PT 256, translation mine.

122. "The King as Sun Priest," as in Jan Assmann, *Der König als Sonnenpriester* (Glückstadt: J. J. Augustin, 1970), 19, translation mine.

123. *Urk.* 7, 27, translation mine.

124. *Urk.* 4, 1246, translation mine.

will return to its seat, Isfet is driven out."[125] A host of other texts could be cited to further demonstrate this.[126]

One particularly important aspect of kingship was the ability to destroy chaos (isfet) in order to restore order (ma'at). This is also stressed in many texts. For example, it was spoken of Amenemhet I that "his majesty came to drive out Isfet . . . since he loves Ma'at so much."[127] Tutankhamun was said to have "driven Isfet out of both lands, and fixed Ma'at in its place."[128] It was said of Taharqa that "Ma'at is spread throughout the land, Isfet is transfixed to the ground."[129] Clearly the king had to be able to destroy chaos if he was going to uphold order. This was a foundational principle of kingship.[130]

Many other Egyptologists have commented on the crucial role of the king in the establishment and maintenance of ma'at. A small sampling of comments will help illustrate how central this role was to kingship. "Maat represented . . . qualities which precisely embodied the responsibility of the king's role."[131] Wilkinson writes, "The king's primary duty: to safeguard created order by attacking the forces of disorder."[132] It has been said that

---

125. P. Leningrad 1116B, 69, as in Wolfgang Helck, *Die Prophezeihung des Nfr.tj* (Wiesbaden: Otto Harrassowitz, 1970), 57.

126. For example, Pyr. 1774–76, "the King put Ma'at in the place of Isfe"; Eloquent Peasant B1.272, the king should "bring about Ma'at"; translations mine.

127. *Urk.* 7:27, translation mine.

128. *Urk.* 4:2026, translation mine.

129. Stela of Taharqa year 6, lines 3–5 (Kawa version), as in M. F. Laming Macadam, *The Temples of Kawa I* (London: Oxford University Press, 1949), translation mine.

130. See Kerry Muhlestein, *Violence in the Service of Order: The Religious Framework for Sanctioned Killing in Ancient Egypt*, British Archaeological Reports International Series 2299 (Oxford: Archaeopress, 2011), 96–98.

131. Richard H. Wilkinson, *The Complete Temples of Ancient Egypt* (New York: Thames and Hudson, 2000), 88.

132. Wilkinson, *Early Dynastic Egypt*, 197. Hornung, *Idea*, 142, agrees with this principle, writing that the king presents the *wedjet* eye and ma'at to the gods, symbolizing both an upholding of ma'at and an eradication of the forces of chaos. The idea of the king presenting ma'at to the gods is depicted frequently in temples and elsewhere. It is one of the most common motifs depicted when the king approaches deity. See also PT 255.

"the king was, ultimately, the source of the well-being of the whole country, not only causing human society to flourish but also causing natural processes such as the succession of seasons, the Nile's flood, the growth of crops, and so on to take place in an orderly and beneficial way."[133] Frankfort asserts that the king is the champion of order.[134] Hornung explains that all the elements of ma'at converge in the king, who is responsible for maintaining ma'at and providing it for both the gods and humans.[135]

It is significant to note that it is the king, not the gods, who is responsible for maintaining ma'at. Indeed, much of the iconography of the king was tied up with his maintenance of ma'at: it seems that all of the offerings which the king gave to the gods were tokens of offering ma'at;[136] all of the scenes of the king smiting enemies, conquering in battle, hunting hippopotamus or netting wild birds are symbolic of his conquering chaos.[137] Much more could be said, but the point is well enough made for our

---

133. Naydler, *Temple of the Cosmos*, 103. See also Frankfort, *Kingship and the Gods*, 58.

134. Frankfort, *Kingship and the Gods*, 149. It was the avowed policy of each king to "make Egypt flourish as in the First Time, in the condition of maat," see *Urkunden*, 4.1725.5, words of Amenophis III. The king lived on ma'at and fed the gods on it, enabling him to say, "I have made bright maat which Re loves, I know that he lives by it; it is my bread too, I eat of its brightness." See "Inscription of Sepos Artemidos," in J.H. Breasted, *Ancient Records* (New York: Russell and Russell, 1962), 2.299; Naydler, *Temple of the Cosmos*, 96.

135. Hornung, *Idea*, 138. See also PT 627. Vincent Arieh Tobin, *Theological Principles of Egyptian Religion* (New York: Peter Lang, 1989), 82–83, writes that ma'at experienced "embodiment in the person of the Pharaoh" and that this aspect of the pharaoh "transformed the land into a type of Messianic kingdom on earth."

136. Representations and inscriptions of the king presenting ma'at are identical to food and wine presentations, and in some cases the wine jars are labeled as "presentation of ma'at." See Emily Teeter, *The Presentation of Maat: Ritual and Legitimacy in Ancient Egypt* (Chicago: Oriental Institute of the University of Chicago, 1997); Wilkinson, *Complete Temples*, 88.

137. Wilkinson, *Complete Temples*, 89. See also Byron E. Shafer, "Temples, Priests, and Rituals: An Overview," *Temples of Ancient Egypt*, ed. Byron E. Shafer (Ithaca, NY: Cornell University Press, 1997) 25, who writes that the extremely common scene of the king hunting and in battle symbolized his conquering the forces of disorder.

purposes.[138] The first (and really only) test of kingship was to maintain ma'at and destroy isfet. In our narrative this is precisely the test that the plagues put the king to and found him wanting. Currid has correlated the plagues with the creative sequence of Genesis, postulating that the plagues were seen as a type of decreation.[139] This adds to the idea of chaos overcoming ma'at, the essence of creation.

During the setting of the Eighteenth and Nineteenth Dynasties, it was certainly understood that the king had a human nature. But it was also acknowledged that when performing divinely appointed duties, especially upholding and defending ma'at, he could transcend his human nature and become divine.[140] Of the many possible examples of this, we need examine only the Kadesh Battle inscriptions, where we see that as Ramses II is battling Egypt's enemies, or forces of disorder, he transcends his human nature and becomes a divine warrior.[141] It was also during this same time period that the depiction of the king as the result of divine conception was

---

138. Quirke, *Ancient Egyptian Religion*, 70, writes that the king represented the sun god as he controlled the damage chaos does to creation. Currid, *Ancient Egypt*, 119, writes that the primary job of the king is to confirm and consolidate ma'at. Hornung, *Conceptions*, 139–41, writes that the king carries out the role of the creator god by preserving the order of the world. Upon the accession of Merneptah it was written, "Water is plentiful; and the Nile carries a high flood. The days are long, the nights have hours, and the months come in due order;" Papyrus Sallier, 1.8.9, translation from A. Blackman in *The Ancient Egyptians: A Sourcebook of Their Writings*, ed. A. Ermand (New York: Harper Torchbooks, 1966), 278–79.

139. Currid, *Ancient Egypt*, 113–17.

140. Silverman, "Nature of Egyptian Kingship," 52. On page 66, Silverman points out that ritual was one of the primary tools that enabled the king to perform these duties. See also, Shafer, "An Overview," 22, who writes that ritual shifted the king from "humanity" to "divinity." Bell, "Divine Temple," 128, writes of the king being the only person capable of offering ma'at because of his simultaneously mortal and divine nature. His cultic acts enabled him to "renew and perpetuate the creation by maintaining the divinely ordained cosmic order—*ma'at*." Elsewhere, Lanny Bell, "Luxor Temple and the Cult of the Royal *Ka*," *Journal of Near Eastern Studies* 44 (1985): 283–85, notes that ritual allowed the king to assume the role of the creator god or to enact a union with him, which allowed him to re-create.

141. See Kadesh Battle Inscriptions; see also Naydler, *Temple of the Cosmos*, 112–18.

reaching new heights.[142] During this era there was an acute sense, and a feeling of crucial need, that as the forces of disorder arose, the king's divine nature would respond, and the king would be victorious in reestablishing ma'at.

Rendsburg has demonstrated that the birth story of Moses pushes him into being identified with Horus. Thus, when Moses contends with Pharaoh, it transforms Pharaoh into the role of Seth while contending with Horus. In their contest, because Horus represents order and Seth represents chaos, we see that this idea of order and chaos being turned upside down is furthered.[143]

The confrontation between Moses and Pharaoh is initially set up as a contest between chaos and order. This is because Moses represents a group of foreigners, and foreigners often fulfilled the prototypical role of chaos.[144] As will be discussed, one of the king's roles was to conquer and control chaos in its role as foreigners. The request of foreigners to escape the control of the king was a request to allow chaos to not be overcome by order.

As the contest between Jehovah and Pharaoh begins, we are presented with the defeat of Pharaoh's snakes, a symbolic enactment of the loss of Pharaoh's divinely granted ability—given him by his uraei—to defeat disorder. As the narrative then moves into the plagues scenario, the reader sees that the plagues are integrally tied up with the same idea. Contaminated water, too many frogs, various insect infestations, disease among humans and animals, storms, loss of crops, the sun being darkened, and loss of human life are all elements of disorder that touch on *every* aspect of Egyptian life. These calamities as individual catastrophes were just the sort of thing that the king was supposed to prevent, but their arrival in an unrelenting sequence could be seen as nothing short of chaos triumphing over order.

Pharaoh both failed to maintain order *and* failed to destroy its enemies—his two main duties. Viewed in this light, the plagues of frogs,

142. Silverman, "Nature of Egyptian Kingship," 72. On page 87, Silverman demonstrates that this was particularly true during the reign of Ramses II.

143. Rendsburg, "Moses the Magician," 215.

144. See Muhlestein, *Violence in the Service of Order*, 83–85.

lice, and flies are much more understandable.[145] They represent familiar elements of the known world, and it is the whole of the known world, down to the most minute elements, that seems to be rising up against the king and Egypt in a chaotic manner. Further, being infested with bugs and boils rendered the priests ritually unclean and thus unable to perform the rituals that could have perhaps aided the king in trying to restore order.[146] Thus, Jehovah both brought chaos into Egypt and prevented the king from restoring order.

Ironically, Jehovah asked Pharaoh to avert this chaos through Moses and Aaron. It was not what Jehovah wanted. Pharaoh's court also pleaded with him to acquiesce to Jehovah and end the chaos. Yet in his arrogance, Pharaoh refused to comply with Jehovah's request, and thus Pharaoh created the scenario that highlighted his impotence before God. This ultimately created chaos, the antitheses of everything Pharaoh was supposed to create but was powerless to do so when in conflict with the desires and decrees of Jehovah.

Especially apropos to the chaos-versus-order conflict are the plagues affecting the Nile, crops,[147] herds, the sun, and the firstborn. All of these were symbolic of the crucial cycle of rebirth. Rebirth and the reestablishment of ma'at were essentially the same thing, and the continuation of this cycle, which ensured Egypt's existence and stability, was the primary role of the king.

As noted, the king was considered responsible for ensuring the regular and healthy flow of the Nile. Disruption to this was seen as a sign of chaos. Particularly pertinent to the Nile's plague is a text that appears to predate the Exodus, but the copy of which we have is from the Nineteenth Dynasty, roughly contemporary with the Exodus. This text speaks of a time of chaos

---

145. James P. Allen, *Middle Egyptian, an Introduction to the Language and Culture of Hieroglyphs* (Cambridge: Cambridge University Press, 2000), 126, notes that snakes and frogs were tied up with creation. This is made apparent in drawings found in Medinet Habu.

146. Rendsburg, "Moses the Magician," 247–48.

147. Irene Shirun-Grumach, "Remarks on the Goddess Maat," *Pharaonic Egypt: The Bible and Christianity*, ed. Sarah Israelit-Groll (Jerusalem: The Magnes Press, the Hebrew University, 1985), 174, notes that ma'at has an "association with the fertility of the land."

in which the river turned to blood and foreigners were in the land.[148] This plague was not only part of the unending wave of chaos, but the plague took a form that was specifically associated with chaos, while disrupting the all-important rebirth cycle that could have reestablished order.[149]

Particularly important in the rebirth cycle was the daily circuit of the sun god, Re. A consistent theme in the afterlife literature created by the Egyptians, and even in the art depicted on the walls of the tombs of the pharaohs, was that each night, the sun, accompanied by the king and others, underwent a dangerous journey. Often the sun is depicted as being protected by a snake, but usually the most dangerous element the sun faced was a large snake named Apophis, who was chaos incarnate.[150] In the books of the netherworld, the king played a crucial role in assisting Re in his triumph. His nightly triumph over Apophis, or disorder, allowed Re his daily reappearance or re-creation. It is critical to understand that one of the major symbols for chaos was a snake. It is also important to note that another strong symbol for chaos was foreigners.[151] Thus, a foreigner

148. P. Leiden 344, col. 2 line 10 and col. 3 line 1. See Rendsburg, "Moses the Magician," 246. For an excellent critical translation as well as comments on the striking parallel between this text and the plague in Exodus, see Roland Enmarch, *A World Upturned: Commentary on and Analysis of The Dialogue of Ipuwer and the Lord of All* (Oxford: Oxford University Press, 2009), 28.

149. J. Black, *The Literature of Ancient Sumer* (Oxford: Oxford Univ. Press, 2004), 197–204. The myth is also known as Inanna and the Gardener; see S. N. Kramer, *History Begins at Sumer*, 3rd ed. (Philadelphia: University of Pennsylvania, 1981), 73. This source talks of a plague of a bloody river in Mesopotamia, though the reason for it is a bit unsavory and as a result of rape.

150. For example, see the tombs of Seti I and Thutmosis III. See also Bojan Mojsov, "The Ancient Egyptian Underworld in the Tomb of Sety I: Sacred Books of Eternal Life," *Massachussetts Review* 42, no. 4 (2001/2002): 489–506.

151. See G. Belova, "The Egyptians' Ideas of Hostile Encirclement," in *Proceedings of the Seventh International Congress of Egyptologists*, ed. C. J. Eyre, Orientalia Lovaniensia Analecta (Leuven: Uitgeverij Peeters, 1998), 145; Edda Bresciani, "Foreigners," in *The Egyptians*, ed. Sergio Donadoni (Chicago: University of Chicago Press, 1997), 222; Antonio Loprieno, *Topos und Mimesis. Zum Ausländer in der ägyptischen Literatur*, Ägyptologische Abhandlungen 48 (Wiesbaden: Otto Harrosowitz, 1988); Kerry Muhlestein, *Violence in the Service of Order: The Religious Framework for Sanctioned Killing in Ancient Egypt* (Oxford: Archaeopress, 2011), 83–85. There has been a small recent movement

casting a snake down before Pharaoh would have been seen as a reenactment of the battle between chaotic and protecting snakes, a battle that the king was to be a part of in the afterlife. With all this ideology, Jehovah dared to show his power via a snake and came away from the battle as the *victor*. Pharaoh's magicians were unable to overcome Jehovah's messenger.[152] It would seem that in this journey, Apophis was triumphant, an unthinkable event. To those with a knowledge of Pharaoh's ties with snakes, this must have been viewed as a direct challenge to Pharaoh's power.

This same idea of the crucial nature of the sun's nightly journey to be born again in the morning plays out in the plague of darkening the sun. Both the contest with snakes and the darkened sun seem to draw on a host of literature about the journey of the sun and point to the failure of the king to ensure that ma'at would continue to be reborn. Thus, the sun not shining is poignantly demonstrative of chaos's triumph over ma'at. Such a darkening of the sun was already associated with chaos and foreigners in Egyptian texts.[153] Still, the individual identifications of the plagues with

---

to say that foreigners should not be equated with chaos. This was presented in the 2019 annual meeting of the American Research Center in Egypt by Jonathan Winnerman, "Maat and the Orientalist Apology," and Niv Allon, "War and Order in New Kingdom Egypt." While these two presenters had very interesting ideas, they are counter to the communis opinio and thus far have not sufficiently demonstrated arguments to overturn the general opnion. I look forward to hearing more of their arguments so that the process of scholarly debate can come to a clearer picture of this topic.

152. The meaning and etymology of the term *arummîm*, usually translated as "magician," is complex and debated. Some believe that the word is of Egyptian origin, and others believe that it is of Akkadian origin. Among those who think that the word comes from Egyptian, there is no degree of agreement as to which word it is related to. See Hans Goedicke, "*arummîm*," *Orientalia* 65 (1996); Jan Quaegebeur, "On the Egyptian Equivalent of Biblical *arummîm*," in Israelit-Groll, *Pharaonic Egypt: The Bible and Christianity*; Currid, *Ancient Egypt*, 94. I am grateful to Dr. Kasia Szpakowska for help in researching this word. The term could have been employed in order to give a "foreign feel" to the story. See Gary Rendsburg, "Linguistic Variation and the 'Foreign' Factor in the Hebrew Bible," in *Israel Oriental Studies: Language and Culture in the Near East*, ed. Shlomo Izre'el and Rina Drory (Leiden: Brill, 1995).

153. St. Petersburg 1116B, lines 25 and 32–33. Rendsburg, "Moses the Magician," 248, also noticed this connection.

aspects of the king only add irony to the true challenge, the challenge to Pharaoh's ability to keep the cosmos in accord with ma'at.

This premise is strengthened when we examine the continuation of the narrative after the conclusion of the plagues pericope. Throughout Egypt's history, but especially in the New Kingdom, one of the primary ways in which the king maintained ma'at was by defeating Egypt's enemies in battle, a manifestation of his ability to destroy chaos in his campaign to replace it with order.[154] In the Exodus story, after the king's abject failure to maintain order throughout his kingdom in the face of the plagues, he turns to his last resort. He arrays Egypt's formidable army against the Israelites. A victory would have symbolically demonstrated not only Pharaoh's ability to defeat this disorderly people and their god but also, by extension, his ability to conquer chaos in general. A victory would have shown that, in the end, after all the incursions of chaos his people had experienced, the king could defeat the ever uprising forces of disorder. But the battle scene again shows the king's inability to defeat chaos.

As the king attempted to attack the Israelites, he was suddenly forced to deal with the sea. In Egyptian thought, the sea was the embodiment of chaos. Jehovah's division of the sea to provide dry ground for the Israelites is reminiscent of Egyptian creation concepts, in which creation began with the emergence of dry land from watery chaos. In Israelite thought, Jehovah brought about creation, or the original establishment of pristine ma'at, by dividing the sea and thus creating dry ground. Thus, he again demonstrated the ability to perform that which was Pharaoh's prerogative. However, for Pharaoh, the sea did not stay divided. As the armies of Egypt attempted to cross on the dry ground, they were overcome by the water. Creation or ma'at ceased to exist for them, and they were engulfed by chaos. It is interesting to note that at the point of the division of the waters, the sea is the direct object of Jehovah's actions. However, as Pharaoh's armies are covered, the sea is the subject of the action.[155] This seems to indicate that Jehovah can defeat disorder and establish ma'at but that Pharaoh is

154. See the annals of the Battle at Megiddo by Tuthmose III; the Qadesh Battle Inscriptions; Naydler, *Temple of the Cosmos*, 108–12; Frankfort, *Kingship and the Gods*, 9.

155. Dozeman, *God at War*, 21, points this out.

unable to control the forces of chaos in a similar manner, enabling them to run their natural course and overcome Egypt's armies.[156] It is the perfect symbol for Pharaoh's utter defeat at the hands of chaos. He is shown as being completely unable to execute the primary function of his office. He cannot discharge his divine duties.

An additional element that stems from the episode of dividing the waters at the sea is that it demonstrates Jehovah's creative abilities. Thus, it was clear that he was not just a god of destructive powers. He was, in fact, the great Creator. As the Israelites left Egypt and began to construct the tabernacle with its Creation motifs and symbols, they would play all the more powerfully in the Israelites' minds after having just seen a dramatic testimony of Jehovah's creative powers. Truly he was the God of all things, the true king of Creation!

A fervent knowledge of the divine kingship of Jehovah, so forcefully demonstrated throughout the plagues narrative, would play another important role soon thereafter. As the Israelites gathered at Sinai to make a covenant with God, they were in essence acknowledging him as their king and were accepting the terms of being his people. The covenant was more meaningful and powerful as they recognized the full power of their sovereign. God's covenant promises to protect them and provide a land for them meant all the more when those promises followed on the heels of God's stunning and intentional victory over the greatest worldly power of the day.

The plagues, followed by the events at the sea, represent the perfect challenge to Pharaoh's kingship and, by way of contrast, the perfect testament of Jehovah's divine sovereignty. As such, the biblical account of the plagues was seemingly written with this in mind. We are left with the conclusion that the writer of this narrative had mastered a sound understanding of Egyptian religious thought and the place that the king occupied within this belief system, both in the details and in the larger concepts that loomed behind them. This was no mere guess as to how the plagues were a

156. This is in contrast to an older tale in which the king had a priest divide water in a lake to find an attendant's last jewelry. Now, Jehovah divides the sea to save his people, but it becomes an agent of chaos when it comes to Pharaoh. See Rendsburg, "Moses the Magician," 251–52.

challenge to Pharaoh. The contest is skillfully presented by someone who had experienced enough contact with Egypt to understand the cultural context of the time that was being portrayed.

The Egyptian milieu of this challenge seems to be part of the point of the Exodus account of the plagues. According to Egyptian history, the pharaohs had always maintained ma'at and vanquished Egypt's enemies. This became a profound lesson that Israelite prophets would draw on for generations. This lesson struck fear in the hearts of those that the Israelites were about to encounter. And it continues to teach a powerful lesson today as we find ourselves threatened by the powers of the world. When this happens, and we feel as if we are metaphorically in bondage to the great power of Egypt or are surrounded by its insurmountable army, we would do well to remember the lesson taught by the plagues and Exodus narrative. Via methods that an Egyptian and those familiar with Egypt would have understood as touching upon the very core of kingship, the narrative showed that Pharaoh was not able to execute his divine abilities in opposition to Jehovah's powers; and in this way, Jehovah, the true king of the world, obtained glory over Pharaoh, as Jehovah always will. Such knowledge would be a guiding principle for the ancient Israelites in the days and years thereafter and should continue to be so today.

— 15 —

THE PROMISE AND THE PROVOCATION

THE SINAI NARRATIVE

DANIEL L. BELNAP

ANDREW C. SKINNER

Following the deliverance from the Red Sea, the Israelites encamped at Sinai, where events would take place that defined them from that period on, such as receiving the law of Moses and the rites associated with the tabernacle. For Latter-day Saints, perhaps even more significant is the event of the provocation, an event that is alluded to in Restoration scripture and that addresses the most profound of religious experiences: entering into the presence of God. Dan Belnap and Andrew Skinner explore the ramifications of the Sinai narrative in this chapter, noting in particular that the promises made to the Israelites then still apply to covenant Israel today. —DB and AS

Set free from Egyptian bondage, the great family of Israel—some six hundred thousand men plus women and children—embarked on their epic wilderness sojourn called the Exodus (Exodus 12:37). In the third month of this religious pilgrimage, they arrived at Mount Sinai (or Horeb) and set up camp. They would stay there for the next eleven months—a period of unprecedented revelation recorded in the rest of the book of Exodus, all of Leviticus, and the first third of Numbers (1:1–10:10). These passages of scripture also happen to be some of the most dense and difficult passages in the Old Testament. Much of the text consists of the law given to the Israelites during their Sinai sojourn as recorded in the three law codes, but these will be discussed elsewhere in this volume. Of significance here is the revelatory experience, comprising Exodus 19–34, that was the foundation of their stay at Sinai. This paper will explore this narrative, in particular, the supernal promise given to the Israelites and conditioned on their obedience, the aftermath of their refusal, and the reinstitution of the covenant.

THE PROMISE

At some point during the third month of their exodus, the Israelites arrived at Sinai, whereupon almost immediately, or so it seems, Moses went up "unto God, and the Lord called unto him out of the mountain" (Exodus 19:3). This event begins what is known in biblical scholarship as the Sinai pericope or Sinai narrative, which comprises Exodus 19–34. It is fronted by Moses's first meeting and is ended by the reception of the second set of tablets. The challenge of this section is that it appears to have been worked and reworked by unknown redactors.[1] This appears to have muddied the account as to what happened.

1. See Joseph Blenkinsopp, "Structure and Meaning in the Sinai-Horeb Narrative (Exodus 19–34)," in *A Biblical Itinerary: In Search of Method, Form, and Content: Essays in Honor of George W. Coats*, ed. Eugene E. Carpenter (Sheffield, UK: Sheffield Academic Press, 1997), 109–25, who referred to this section as "this most complex section of the Penteteuch" (111). See also T. B. Dozeman, *God on the Mountain: A Study of Redaction, Theology, and Canon in Exodus 19–24* (Atlanta: Scholars Press, 1989); T. D. Alexander, "The Composition of the Sinai Narrative in Exodus XIX 1–XXIV 11," in *Vetus Testamentum* 49, no. 1 (1999):

The pericope begins with Moses's interaction with God on Sinai, as described in Exodus 19:1–13. Having ascended Sinai, Moses heard the voice of God, who instructed, "Thus shalt thou say to the house of Jacob, and tell the children of Israel; Ye have seen what I did unto the Egyptians, and how I bare you on eagles' wings, and brought you unto myself. Now therefore, if ye will obey my voice indeed, and keep my covenant, then ye shall be a peculiar treasure unto me above all people: for all the earth is mine: And ye shall be unto me a kingdom of priests, and an holy nation. These are the words which thou shalt speak unto the children of Israel" (Exodus 19:3–6).

While the overall meaning seems clear—namely, that God was offering the Israelites an opportunity unlike any experienced by any other people or nation—what exactly that offer means is a question that many have. The promise begins with God reminding the Israelites of what he had done up to this point. The first reminder is that they saw "what [he] did unto the Egyptians." While it would be tempting to think this may have alluded to the destruction of the Egyptian army described in the chapters preceding, the remainder of the verse suggests another focus: "how I bare you on eagles' wings, and brought you unto myself" (19:4). The divine metaphor of the Israelites being borne "on eagles' wings" may suggest the swiftness

---

2–20, who quotes John I. Durham: "Though many helpful observations may be harvested from the critical work of more than a century, the sum total of that work is a clear assertion that no literary solution to this complex narrative has been found, with more than a hint that none is likely to be found." John I. Durham, *Exodus* (Waco, TX: Word Books, 1984), 259. Speaking of Exodus 19 specifically, Marc Z. Brettler has pronounced the chapter to be "one of the most intractable chapter[s] in the entirety of the Pentateuch in terms of source-critical analysis." Marc Zvi Brettler, "The Many Faces of God in Exodus 19," in *Jews, Christians, and the Theology of the Hebrew Scriptures*, ed. Alice Ogden Bellis and Joel S. Kaminsky (Atlanta: Scholars Press for the Society of Biblical Literature, 2000), 353–67, specifically 354. See also Benjamin D. Sommer, "The Source Critic and the Religious Interpreter," in *Interpretation* 60, no. 1 (2006): 9–20, who discusses the confusion of Exodus 19–20 and examines the supposed role of a later redactor: "In many cases, I am not at all sure that the reactors intended to bury the older voice or to create a unified text. This is very clearly the case in Exodus 19–20, for this text—even in its redacted form—repeatedly presents material ambiguously" (12).

and power by which the children of Israel had been brought to this point, but some suggested that the imagery is not so much one of the power of an eagle but the nurturing nature of such, the terminology reflecting the image of the eagles' protective wings.[2] Regardless whether the imagery is meant to remind the Israelites of God's martial deliverance or his nurturing gathering, the point of the reminder is to note how God was explicitly involved in their coming to him. What is emphasized are the Israelites' relationship with God himself and, more importantly, God's own desire to bring them to him.

The purpose of the reminder, though, is not just to remind the Israelites of God's beneficence but to lay the groundwork for his promise: "Now, therefore, if ye will obey my voice indeed, and keep my covenant, then ye shall be a peculiar treasure unto me above all people: for all the earth is mine" (Exodus 19:5). As the grammar suggests, the promise relies on the Israelites' remembrance of God's prior actions so that the people may know that the following will happen because of what has already happened. In other words, the children of Israel can trust that their acceptance of the terms will result in them being a "peculiar treasure" because they already know what God has done for them in the past. Their faith and trust in God can be confirmed regarding what he will do because of what he has already done. The protasis of the oath is simple: if they will obey God's voice and obey his covenant; it is the apodosis of the oath—that they would be a peculiar treasure—that requires them to understand a bit more. The English phrase "peculiar treasure" derives from the Latin *peculium*, meaning "private property"[3] and is translated from the Hebrew word *s^{e}ḡŭllâ*, meaning "private, acquired treasure."[4] These terms suggest that the Israelites, via the covenant, were to be understood as God's highly valued personal treasure.

---

2. C. F. Keil and F. Delitzsch, *Biblical Commentary on the Old Testament*, vol. 2, *The Pentateuch* (Grand Rapids, MI: Eerdmans, n.d.), 96.
3. John C. Traupman, *The New College Latin and English Dictionary* (New York: Bantam Books, 1981), 215.
4. Edward Lipiński, "*s^{e}ḡŭllâ*," in *Theological Dictionary of the Old Testament* (hereafter, *TDOT*) (Grand Rapids, MI: Eerdmans, 1974–2021), 10:144–48. As with its Akkadian cognate, *sikiltum*, the term *segullah* denotes the exclusive right of ownership.

Further explanation as to what was meant by "peculiar treasure" is given in the next verse: "Ye shall be unto me a kingdom of priests, and an holy nation" (Exodus 19:6). The first of these clauses, a kingdom of priests (or *mamleket kohanîm*) is unique to the Hebrew Bible, and, while the roots of each term is clear, an exact translation of the terms together is more difficult.[5] The first term, *mamleket*, is the nominative derivative of *mlk*, or "king"; thus, *mamleket* is often rendered as "kingdom," and since the clause itself is possessive, the resulting translation is "kingdom of priests." But *mamleket*'s position in the clause, as well as the clause's ending, suggests that the term could also be in a constructive clause, meaning that the term serves an adjectival function. In this case, the translation would be "royal priesthood." This is the manner in which the Septuagint understood the clause.[6] Finally, some early Jewish texts suggest that the two terms represented independent nouns, thus providing a reading of "kings and priests."[7]

Complicating the translation, at least for some scholars, is whether or not the phrase is to be understood as a literal promise—that Israel would be a nation of priests and kings or a kingdom in which all could be priests—or if the phrase was meant metaphorically—that Israel would be a nation distinct from others because of its privileged status to God. And even if the phrase were to be taken literally, some scholars question whether or not it was meant for all of the Israelites or whether it was specifically designating only the soon-to-be priestly and royal lineages.[8] Biblical scholars Nahum

5. Arie Van Der Kooij, "A Kingdom of Priests: Comment on Exodus 19:6," in *The Interpretation of Exodus: Studies in Honor of Cornelis Houtman*, ed. Riemer Roukema (Leuven: Peeters, 2006), 171–79; see also John A. Davies, *A Royal Priesthood: Literary and Intertextual Perspectives on an Image of Israel in Exodus 19:6* (London: T&T Clark, 2004)

6. βασίλειον ἱεράτευμα. The adjectival reading by the Septuagint of Exodus 19:6 is reflected in 1 Peter 2:9: "But ye are a chosen generation, a royal priesthood, an holy nation, a peculiar people." See also Ralph Allan Smith, "The Royal Priesthood in Exodus 19:6," in *The Glory of Kings: A Festschrift in Honor of James B. Jordan*, ed. Peter J. Leithart and John Barach (Eugene, OR: Pickwick Publications, 2011), 93–111.

7. Kooij, "Kingdom of Priests," 174–75.

8. This last question is particularly vexing for those who try to figure out the different sources that supposedly make up the chapter. The emphasis on priestly

Sarna assumed the promise referred specifically to the priests, asserting that "the priest's place and function within society must serve as the ideal model for Israel's self-understanding of its role among the nations. The priest is set apart by a distinctive way of life, . . . dedicated to ministering to the needs of the people."[9] Of the passage in Exodus, J. C. Rylaarsdam wrote, "The covenant was between Yahweh and his servants," but then, in a somewhat muddled statement, Rylaarsdam goes on to say, "The covenant is with the people, not with its leaders or priesthood. Just as in Israel the priests had access to the altar and the Levites rejoiced in the service of God, . . . so Israel will fulfill the role of priest in the world. It will be a holy nation, i.e., set apart for a peculiar task. Israel was to be the church."[10] Unfortunately, as noted, the unique usage of the clause means that there is no other reference in the Bible by which one can compare and get a sense of the manner in which the Bible writers understood it (did it refer to kings and priests, royal priesthood, or kingdom of priests, or did it refer to all the Israelites or only specific classes?), and somewhat surprisingly, Joseph Smith had little to say about this particular phrase.

Regardless of the exact meaning, it is clear that the Israelites were promised a transformation that would make them unique among all nations. Yet the fulfillment of the promise was contingent on the Israelites' acceptance of the agreement, their obedience to the covenant that would beget the promise. The acceptance would be a twofold process: first, the Israelites had to verbally accept the terms, and, second, some recognized physical act by which both parties demonstrated that the new relationship was now in force must be enacted. The first element is recorded in Exodus 19:7–8 as Moses calls the assembly and asks whether they agree to the conditions. With their approval, Moses then ascends Mount Sinai again, formally notifying God of the community's acceptance. The second element

---

individuals suggests P, or the Priestly writer, while the holy nation is a phrase found throughout D, or the writings of Deuteronomy.

9. Nahum Sarna, *The JPS Commentary: Exodus* (New York: The Jewish Publication Society, 1991), 104.

10. J. C. Rylaarsdam, "Exodus," in George A. Buttrick, ed., *The Interpreter's Bible* (Nashville: Abingdon, 1978), 1:972–73. Here we see a modern term, *church*, applied to an ancient religious structure. It carries a different connotation from the way we envision it today.

of the process, the physical act by which the new relationship is ratified, makes up the next set of instructions from God: "And the Lord said unto Moses, Go unto the people and sanctify them to day and to morrow, and let them wash their clothes, and be ready against the third day: for the third day the Lord will come down in the sight of all the people on mount Sinai" (literally, "YHWH will descend before/to the eyes of all the people"; Exodus 19:10–11). As the instructions suggest, the ratifying event appears to be a visual manifestation of God himself, with preparatory acts to be performed—the washing of clothes and sexual abstinence—for the ratifying act to take place.

Further instruction is given in which Moses is told to set up a boundary around the base of the mountain to prevent anyone from unauthorized ascents, which would lead to death. The boundary was to be in effect until the third day, and the promised manifestation is noted by the end of the instruction: "There shall not an hand touch it, . . . whether it be beast or man, it shall not live: when the trumpet soundeth long, they shall come up to the mount" (Exodus 19:13). With the instruction given, Moses then descends again and prepares his people, sanctifying them for the upcoming theophany. Not surprisingly, there are questions concerning the exact nature of the event, yet the instruction seems pretty straightforward. The ratifying of the new relationship would take place with the children of Israel seeing God in his glory. In sum, Moses's second trip up Mount Sinai entailed receiving instructions from the Lord on preparing the people to enter his divine presence. The people were to become sanctified (cleansed inwardly and outwardly), were not to treat sacred space casually (but were to show extreme reverence for it, upon penalty of death), and were to refrain from sexual thoughts or actions (which would detract from the absolute sanctity and utter holiness of the experience).

Three days later, the theophanic elements associated with God's presence took place: the text mentioning the thunder and lightning, the cloud, and most importantly, the "voice" of the trumpet, which, according to the earlier instructions was to mark the time that the Israelites could now ascend the mountain.[11] The people already had, and would yet have, sig-

11. The source of the trumpet, whether human or heavenly, is not made clear. In ancient Israel the trumpet, or *shofar*, could be blown for several reasons: to

nificant experience with the cloud of the Lord. It was, up to that point, the great symbol of God's divine presence and protection: it had led the children of Israel during their pilgrimage (Exodus 13:21). Yet the narrative now presents a paradox; though the Israelites are at the "nether part of the mount" and ready to ascend, according to Exodus 19:20, only Moses is called up the mountain, and he is told to "go down, charge the people, lest they break through unto the Lord to gaze, and many of them perish" (Exodus 19:21). Having been told that that the Lord would come "before the eyes" of the people, now the selfsame are told that they are not to see God. No reason is given as to why the instructions have changed. The apparent contradiction seems to have troubled the ancient compilers as well.[12] In Exodus 19:23, Moses reiterates the boundary injunction sans the temporary marker, thereby implying that the Lord is unaware of what is going on or that he needs an excuse as to the recusal of invitation, which interrupts the flow of the narrative and reads as a later insertion in an attempt to reconcile the contradiction.

The narrative becomes even more complicated in Exodus 20. The chapter itself opens with Moses's reception of the Ten Commandments, the implied setting being the same as the end of chapter 19—namely, Moses's third ascent. Yet the commandments are followed by another

---

call to war (Numbers 10:9; Judges 3:27; 6:34; 1 Samuel 13:3), to warn of an approaching enemy (Hosea 5:8; Ezekiel 33:3), to scare the enemy (Judges 7:19–22), to announce a ceasefire or peace (2 Samuel 18:16), to declare rebellion (2 Samuel 20:1), to celebrate the coronation of the king (1 Kings 1:34, 39), and to praise the Lord (Psalm 98:1–6). The New Testament attests to the sounding of a heavenly trumpet by which God announces his presence or his coming, as 1 Thessalonians 4:16 asserts: "For the Lord himself shall descend from heaven with a shout, with the voice of the archangel, and with the trump of God." See also Matthew 24:31; 1 Corinthians 15:52. This passage in 1 Thessalonians certainly fits well with the theophany described in Exodus 19, as does Psalm 98. The Lord's presence was being heralded, and it should be praised. For more on the role of the *shofar* in ancient Israel, see Filip Vukosavovic, ed., *Sound the Shofar: A Witness to History* (Jerusalem: Bible Lands Museum Jerusalem, 2011), 28.

12. See Sommer, "The Source Critic and the Religious Interpreter," 13–15. "In Judaism of both the Talmudic era and the Middle Ages we can note a debate concerning the essential nature of revelation at Sinai" (14).

descriptive scene of the theophany: "And all the people saw the thunderings and the lightnings, and the noise of the trumpet, and the mountain smoking" (Exodus 20:18). As with the beginning of the chapter, the implied timing of this scene is one that follows the initial theophany—that is, that it describes events of the ongoing divine presence. Yet the remainder of the scene suggests this is not a continuation but is a variant to the theophany as presented in Exodus 19. Following the descriptive elements in Exodus 20:18, the text states, "And when the people saw it [the theophanic elements], they removed, and stood afar off. And they said unto Moses, Speak thou with us, and we will hear: but let not God speak with us, lest we die, . . . and the people stood afar off, and Moses drew near unto the thick darkness where God was" (20:18–21). As the last set of clauses suggests, this supposedly later event happened before Moses ascended the third time. Moreover, it presents an Israelite community that is not seeking to enter into the presence of God but presents one that is actively engaged in removing itself from God's presence.[13] Thus, this second narrative is not describing a divine recension of the invitation but is showing the Israelites' rejection of the invitation.

Nowhere in the text is there an explicit rejection of the narratives, yet later references suggest that, at least for some, the second narrative was understood as the correct one. In Deuteronomy 5, Moses recounts the Sinaitic narrative, noting that God made a covenant with the Israelites in Sinai when "the Lord talked with [the Israelites] face to face in the mount out of the midst of fire" (5:4). Yet this is immediately followed by this statement: "I stood between the Lord and you at that time, to show you the word of the Lord for ye were afraid by reason of the fire, and went not up into the mount" (5:5). Both verses suggest that the children of Israel were to come before God "face to face," as the text states, but they did not, instead sending Moses in their stead, with the mention that they refused

13. Sommer, "The Source Critic and the Religious Interpreter," 13, suggests that the ambiguous relationship of this scene with the earlier scenes in chapter 19 is the result of later redactors deliberately confusing the scene: "The final form of this text wants the audience to be perplexed. . . . The relative places of God, Moses, and Israel at the most important moment of Israel's history are a matter of dispute in the final form of Exodus—aggressively, insistently so."

to go up, a clear allusion to the Exodus 20 narrative.[14] Deuteronomy 18 also alludes to the Exodus 20 version as part of the Mosaic prophecy, comprising Deuteronomy 18:15–19. Verse 16 describes the new prophet in terms of the Sinaitic Moses, whom "thou desiredst of the Lord thy God in Horeb [Sinai] in the day of the assembly, saying, Let me not hear again the voice of the Lord my God, neither let me see this great fire any more, that I die not." As in the earlier Deuteronomic reference, it is the Israelites' refusal to experience God's presence that is mentioned, not the supposed contradictory instruction.

Psalm 95 appears to allude to the event and introduces language that will be later associated with the event: "Harden not your heart, as in the provocation, and as in the day of temptation in the wilderness: when your fathers tempted me, proved me, and saw my work. Forty years long was I grieved with this generation, and said, It is a people that do err in their heart, and they have not known my ways: unto whom I sware in my wrath that they should not enter into my rest" (Psalm 95:8–11). Though Sinai is not mentioned, the psalmist notes an event that can be referred to as "the provocation." This term is a translation of the Hebrew word *mᵉrîbā*, which

14. Moshe Weinfeld, *Deuteronomy 1–11*, Anchor Bible Commentary 5 (New York: Doubleday, 1991), 241: "In v 4 it was said that God spoke on the mountain out of the fire. The glossator comes to harmonize this with the old tradition. In agreement with Exod 20:15 that 'the people fell back and stood at a distance', the glossator adds here that the people did not ascend the mountain out of fear. According to another tradition (J?), the people were prohibited from ascending the mountain (Exod 19:12, 21, 24; cf. 34:3) in order to prevent their 'seeing' the Deity, but this is not in line with Deuteronomy, which never speaks of 'seeing' God, but only of 'hearing' him." The actual terminology in verse 4 is "*pānîm bᵉpānîm*" (literally "face in face"). The more common form of the phrase is "*pānîm ʾel pānîm*" ("face to face"). While most agree that technically the terminology suggests direct visual interaction, most assume that it should be understood as metaphorical, since the Israelites never did see God. See Jeffrey J. Tigay, *The JPS Torah Commentary–Deuteronomy* (Philadelphia: Jewish Publication Society, 1996), 61. Weinfeld suggests that the unique phrasing reflects a deliberate change from *pānîm ʾel pānîm* to *pānîm bᵉpānîm* to harmonize with the later, Deuteronomic principle mentioned above—namely, that no one can see God (239–40). In any case, it appears that the later tradition understood that the Israelites were supposed to have had direct interactions with God in some manner.

is often associated with a particular event—namely, the Israelites' provoking of the Lord for water at the site that would eventually be called Meribah. Yet the term's relationship in Psalm 95 with the "day of temptation in the wilderness" means that it could be used to describe any number of events in which the children of Israel provoked God, including one that will be discussed later in this study—namely, the construction of the golden calf.[15] Yet the term appears to also allude directly to the Sinai variant in Exodus 20, since the verb *nasah* is used in the psalm ("when your fathers *tempted* me," Psalm 95:9; emphasis added) and in Exodus 20:20 ("fear not: for God is come *to prove* you"; emphasis added). Found some thirty-six times in the Hebrew Bible, the term is also used in Exodus 20:19 after the assembly's declaration that they wished for Moses to go up the mountain for them, "lest [they] die." Moses responds to their request, stating, "Fear not. In order to test (*nasah*) you he comes; his "fear" will be on your faces so that you do not sin" (Exodus 20:20, author's translation).[16]

Perhaps the most intriguing addition to the narrative, though, is the last verse of Psalm 95, which notes that the "provocation" (verse 8) led the Lord to "sware in [his] wrath" that the Israelites would not enter into God's "rest" (verse 11). What is meant by God's rest is not clear from the context, the psalm assuming that the reader grasps the meaning. The concept of "rest" is associated with the Sinai and wilderness narratives. In Exodus 33:14, as part of his promise to Moses concerning the future state of the Israelites, God promises, "My presence [literally, 'my face'] will walk [presumably with the Israelites], and I will cause you to have rest" (author's translation). In this instance, "rest" is associated with the future settlement of the children of Israel after their wandering in the wilderness

---

15. Catherine M. Thomas, "The Provocation in the Wilderness and the Rejection of Grace" in *Sperry Symposium Classics: The Old Testament*, ed. Paul Y. Hoskisson (Provo, UT: Religious Studies Center, Brigham Young University; Salt Lake City: Deseret Book, 2005), 165: "The Provocation refers not only to the specific incident at Meribah but to a persistent behavior of the children of Israel that greatly reduced their spiritual knowledge. . . . After a succession of provocations, the Israelites in time rejected and lost the knowledge of . . . the great plan of grace inherent in the doctrine of the Father and the Son."

16. Moshe Greenberg, "נסה in Exodus 20.20 and the Purpose of the Sinaitic Theophany," *Journal of Biblical Literature* 76 (1960): 273–76.

or the reception of their "inheritance." This is the same way in which "rest" is used in various other scriptures (Numbers 14:23; Deuteronomy 3:20; 12:9,10; 25:19). In these instances, "rest" is understood as the cessation of conflict with Israelites' neighbors that will accompany the Israelites' settlement into the promised land. The same meaning is associated with "rest" in Joshua, and both references discuss the rest given to the Israelites. Yet the rest in Psalm 95 is God's rest. In other words, Psalm 95 suggests that the children of Israel could have entered into God's own rest.

Divine rest is often associated with the Creation narrative, with divine rest marking not the cessation of conflict but the cessation of creative organization. Outside of the Creation accounts, divine rest is also associated with the presence of God in his temple. Psalm 132:8 invites God to arise and come into his rest, along with the ark, while in verses 13–14, the reader is told that God chose Zion for his "habitation," saying, "This is my rest for ever: here will I dwell; for I have desired it." In a similar manner, in Isaiah 18:4, God's rest is associated with his dwelling place, whereas in Isaiah 66, God's resting place is paralleled with his house. The verbal form is also associated with the immanence of God's presence with both the cloud and God's spirit resting at certain places and on certain individuals. If this rest is what was meant in Psalm 95, then the provocation, in which the Israelites rejected God's invitation to enter his presence led to a divine decree that they would not enter into his rest, presumably in the foreseeable future.

Outside of these references, the Sinai narrative is not alluded to in the Old Testament. Yet intriguingly, Psalm 95 is alluded to in Hebrews 3–4. Noting that Christians could enter the Lord's rest if they held "fast the confidence and the rejoicing of the hope firm unto the end," the writer of Hebrews then cited Psalm 95: "Wherefore (as the Holy Ghost saith: To day if ye will hear his voice, Harden not your hearts, as in the provocation, in the day of temptation in the wilderness: When your fathers tempted me, proved me, and saw my works forty years. Wherefore I was grieved with that generation, and said, they do always err in their heart and they have not known my ways. So I sware in my wrath, they should not enter into my rest)" (Hebrew 3:6–11).

Though not an exact quote, being couched in first person rather than third person, this Hebrews passage is clearly an allusion to Psalm 95. As for the allusion, it appears that the writer of Hebrews believed that the invitation associated with the narrative, to enter into God's presence, was in effect for the early Christian community as shown in Hebrews 4, which opens with a warning: "Let us therefore fear, lest, a promise being left us of entering his rest, any of you should seem to come short of it" (4:1). This concern is repeated a few verses later, where having demonstrated that there must be a rest that one could enter, the Hebrews writer exhorts: "Let us labour therefore to enter into that rest, lest any man fall after the same example of unbelief" (4:11). As to what that rest is, or what entering into that rest may mean, the remainder of the chapter establishes the preeminence of Christ as high priest, who made it possible for all that believe to "come boldly unto the throne of grace" (4:16); thus, the implication of the Lord's rest is having his presence in the temple.

As for the Sinai narrative, it too is alluded to in Hebrews. Beginning in Hebrews 12:18, the Christian is told that "ye are not come unto the mount that might be touched, and that burned with fire, nor unto blackness, and darkness, and tempest, and the sound of the trumpet, and the voice of words; which voice they that heard entreated that the word should not be spoken to them any more (for they could not endure that which was commanded)" (Hebrews 12:18–20). The allusions are clear: the theophanic elements, the trumpet sound, the entreaty to Moses that he meet with God, and so forth, all point to Exodus 20. Yet, significantly, the believer is told that this was not to be the experience. Instead, the ideal experience was one in which one would "come unto mount Sion, and unto the city of the living God, the heavenly Jerusalem, and to an innumerable company of angels, to the general assembly of the church of the firstborn, . . . and to God the Judge of all, and to the spirits of just men made perfect, and to Jesus the Mediator of the new covenant" (Hebrews 12:22–24).

The excerpt concludes with the injunction "see that ye refuse not him that speaketh, . . . for our God is a consuming fire" (Hebrews 12:25, 29). As the final exhortation makes clear, this later Christian interpretation of the narrative appears to have assumed that the events of Exodus 20 described the Israelites' refusal of God's invitation to enter into his presence and engage with the divine community.

This understanding of the Sinai narrative is reinforced by Restoration scripture. Jacob alludes to the provocation while defending the ministerial work of himself and the other ecclesiastical leaders. Using language first used by his older brother Nephi, Jacob stated, "We labored diligently among our people, that we might persuade them to come unto Christ, and partake of the goodness of God, that they might enter into his rest, lest by any means he should swear in his wrath they should not enter in, as in the provocation in the days of temptation while the children of Israel were in the wilderness" (Jacob 1:7). Though the similar phrase "to come unto him [Christ] and partake of his goodness" can be found earlier in 2 Nephi 26:23, the use of language similar to Psalm 95 suggests that Jacob is comparing himself and the others to Moses, who, presumably, also taught his people to come unto God and partake of his goodness. Doing so, according to Jacob, would allow one to enter into the rest of God—Jacob's declaration implying that this is precisely what the Israelites did not do, again suggesting that the Exodus 20 narrative and its portrayal of the Israelites rejecting God is the correct interpretation.[17]

The entering into God's rest takes on a cosmic perspective in Alma 12, where provocation and Sinai narrative language are both used, but in the context of the Garden of Eden narrative and the plan of salvation as a whole. Beginning in verse 32, Alma the Younger explains that, following the Fall of Adam and Eve, a second set of commandments were given since the first set given in the Garden of Eden could no longer be met: "But God did call on men, in the name of his Son (this being the plan of redemption which was laid) saying: If ye will repent, and harden not your hearts, then will I have mercy upon you, through mine Only Begotten Son; therefore whosoever repenteth, and hardeneth not his heart, he shall have claim

17. The similarity between Jacob 1:7 and Psalm 95:8 may suggest that at least some of the psalms were a part of the brass plates. See John Hilton III, "Old Testament Psalms in the Book of Mormon," in *Ascending the Mountain of the Lord: Temple, Praise, and Worship in the Old Testament* ed. David Rolph Seely, Jeffrey R. Chadwick, and Matthew J. Grey (Provo, UT: Religious Studies Center, Brigham Young University; Salt Lake City; Deseret Book, 2013), 291-311.

through mine Only Begotten Son, unto a remission of his sins; and these shall enter into my rest. And whosoever will harden his heart, and will do iniquity, behold, I swear in my wrath that he shall not enter into my rest" (Alma 12:33–35). In this instance, the promise associated with the Sinai narrative becomes the promise associated with the plan of salvation: the invitation defining all humankind following the Fall. Alma continues his theological usage of the provocation, observing,

> My brethren, behold, I say unto you, that if ye will harden your hearts ye shall not enter into the rest of the Lord; therefore your iniquity provoketh him that he sendeth down his wrath upon you as in the first provocation, yea, according to his word in the last provocation as well as the first, to the everlasting destruction of your souls. . . . Seeing we know these things, and they are true, let us repent, and harden not our hearts, that we provoke not the Lord our God to pull down his wrath upon us in these his second commandments which he has given unto us; but let us enter into the rest of God. (Alma 12:36–37)

As in the verses prior, Alma appears to have equated the Fall as a provocation, even the first provocation, which brought about the second commandments; his second provocation apparently being the mortal experience overall.

Christ himself alludes explicitly to God's rest—associating it directly with the Exodus 19 event—in his discourse on the gospel as recorded in 3 Nephi 27. In verse 19, Christ posits that "no unclean thing can enter into [God's] kingdom; therefore nothing entereth into his rest save it be those who have washed their garments in my blood." The context is of a cosmic event rather than the event of entering God's presence at Sinai, yet the requirements to entering into this rest by having one's garments washed in the blood of Christ is similar to the original Sinaitic instruction to wash one's clothes in preparation for the theophany that would take place three days later.

Yet Doctrine and Covenants 84 contains perhaps the most explicit Latter-day Saint text alluding to the events in Exodus 19 and 20. Received in 1832, the revelation addressed the nature of the priesthood, noting that the "greater priesthood administereth the gospel and holdeth the keys of the mysteries of the kingdom" and that one of those keys referred to is "the key of the knowledge of God" (Doctrine and Covenants 84:19). The next verse suggests that it is the priesthood ordinances, or physical acts, by which this knowledge could be acquired. With both the ordinances and priesthood authority, one could "see the face of God . . . and live" (verse 22). Having established this principle, Joseph was then told, "Now this Moses plainly taught to the children of Israel in the wilderness, and sought diligently to sanctify his people that they might behold the face of God; But they hardened their hearts and could not endure his presence; therefore, the Lord in his wrath, for his anger was kindled against them, swore that they should not enter into his rest while in the wilderness, which rest is the fulness of his glory" (verses 23–24).

While this passage contains similar terminology to phrases found in Psalm 95 ("harden not your heart," "his wrath," "not enter into his rest"), the event itself—the Israelites' refusal to enter into God's presence—is clearly the Exodus 19–20 narrative.[18] As for the nature of God's rest, it appears that it indicates entering into the direct presence of God.

THE TABERNACLE

Yet, even as the Israelites rejected this great blessing, the revealed law to Moses provided another avenue by which they could enter into the presence of God—the tabernacle. Here we must turn to latter-day revelation

18. As noted later, Joseph placed God's injunction to the Israelites concerning his rest at the end of the golden calf narrative, thus there appears to be a possible discrepancy between the placement of the injunction. The confusion may be alleviated by noting that in the JST text of Exodus 34:1–2, when God references the injunction, it is implied that it had already taken place: "But I will give unto them the law as at the first, but it shall be after the law of a carnal commandment; for I *have sworn* in my wrath, that they shall not enter into my presence, into my rest" (emphasis added). Thus, the two versions may be reconciled with the Exodus 34 version referring to an earlier event, which is not mentioned by name. It should also be noted that the JST injunction version was received sometime in 1830–31, while Doctrine and Covenants 84 was received in 1832, thus it may reflect a later, amended understanding of the overall narrative.

in order to comprehend the full purpose of the tabernacle as Jehovah originally planned. To Joseph Smith the Lord offered this profound insight: "And again, verily I say unto you, how shall your washings be acceptable unto me, except ye perform them in a house which you have built to my name? For, for this cause I commanded Moses that he should build a tabernacle, that they should bear it with them in the wilderness, and to build a house in the land of promise, that those ordinances might be revealed which had been hid from before the world was" (Doctrine and Covenants 124:37–38). Joseph associated these ordinances with our temple rites today. In August of 1843, while discussing the "3 grand orders of the priesthood," the Prophet noted that the law governing the Melchizedek Priesthood had been taught to Moses was "a perfect law of Theocracy," which Joseph Smith associated with becoming a king and priest.[19]

Unfortunately, this insight is not as clear cut in the biblical text itself. Following the reception of the "social" law, which comprises Exodus 20–23, Exodus 24 records an event in which "Moses wrote all the words of the Lord" (24:4), built an altar, erected twelve pillars (each one representing one of the tribes of Israel), and offered sacrifices wherein the blood of the sacrifices were splashed on the altar and the people. As will be discussed later, these rites initiated the Israelites into a covenant relationship with God. Following this, Moses, Aaron, Aaron's sons, and seventy of the elders of Israel ascended the mountain, where they "saw the God of Israel" (24:10–11). Verse 12 then records Moses being called up the mountain (again) to be given "tables of stone and a law, and commandments."

At first blush, the event appears to contradict the events recorded in Exodus 19–20—namely, that no one but Moses can see God. As with the earlier sequence, this may reflect different versions of the entire Sinai narrative.[20] Yet Joseph suggested another possibility. In May of 1843, he

19. "History, 1838–1856, volume E-1 [1 July 1843–30 April 1844]," p. 1708, The Joseph Smith Papers.

20. Alexander, "Composition of the Sinai Narrative," 7: "It should be noted that previous attempts to uncover the sources underlying this section [Ex. Xxic 1–11] have not proved particularly satisfactory." For more, see Walter A. Maier, "The Analysis of Exodus 24, According to Modern Literary, Form, and Redactional Critical Methodology," in *Springfielder* 37, no. 1 (1973): 35–52; see also E. W.

delivered a sermon in which he noted a difference between seeing God and engaging directly with him: "It is one thing to be on the Mount and hear the excellent voice &c &c and another to hear the voice declare to you, you have a part and lot in the kingdom."[21] In light of the quote, it is possible that what was being recorded was the two different types of divine experiences: the event in Exodus 19–20 offering direct interaction with God to all of the Israelites and the lesser event in Exodus 24 in which one saw God. In any case, following the visual experience, Moses is again called up to the mountain and receives the next set of instructions concerning Aaron and the construction, dedication, and sanctification of the tabernacle.

These plans comprise chapters 25–31 of Exodus, while the report of the actual construction is found in chapters 35–40 and the dedication and initiation takes place in Leviticus 8–9. As to the tabernacle's intended function, the Lord's own words reiterate his plan to dwell among the people, mentoring them and guiding them to become the holy nation and kingdom of priests that he had proposed in the very beginning of their encampment at Sinai. To Moses the Lord declared, "And let them make me a sanctuary; that I may dwell among them" (Exodus 25:8).

Though verse 8 suggests that the tabernacle was meant to house God, another term commonly used for the tabernacle throughout the Pentateuch is *ʾohel môēd*, or the tent of meeting/the congregation. In light of this, it may be more accurate to view the tabernacle as more of a temporary meeting place rather than as a permanent dwelling place of God. Recognizing the tabernacle as a meeting place suggests that the purpose of the tabernacle was to facilitate the interaction between the visiting parties, God and humankind. Thus, the tabernacle space represented a place that was neither in the mortal world nor in the divine world, but a liminal

---

Nicholson, "The Antiquity of the Tradition in Exodus XXIV 9–11," *Vetus Testamentum* 25, no. 1 (1976): 69–79.

21. "History, 1838–1856, volume D-1 [1 August 1842–1 July 1843]," p. 1557, The Joseph Smith Papers.

space that was specifically designed for interaction by parties from both worlds.[22]

Just as with today's temples, many aspects of the tabernacle, both functional and symbolic, highlighted its liminal nature, though not always in an obvious way. For instance, all of the entrances associated with the tabernacle, such as the gate, the entrance into the tabernacle proper, and the veil separating the Holy Place from the Holy of Holies, were distinguished from the surrounding cloth by their coloration, having been dyed in blue, scarlet, and purple. Any explicit meaning behind this selection of colors is unknown because the text gives no indication of their significance, but they clearly distinguished these spaces from other spaces in the tabernacle. Besides the colors, these spaces also shared a similar function—to mark where one could enter and leave. The color pattern set these spaces apart and highlighted their unique function.[23]

---

22. Such spaces, neither fully in one state nor another but straddling both, are known as liminalities, or liminal spaces, so named from the Latin *limen*, meaning "doorway" or "threshold." Significantly, these spaces are not meant to be permanent but are merely transition points where individuals can interact in ways not possible in regular spaces because of physical or social limitations, or where individuals can prepare one to move from one social state to another. Though the term *liminality* may be new to readers, if they are temple-attending Latter-day Saints, they are quite familiar with the concept. When a Saint speaks of attending the temple as leaving the world temporarily in order to commune with God and reemerging stronger and more powerful than before, such language reflects the liminal nature of the temple, both in practice and in space.

23. While there is no explicit explanation to these colors provided in the text, they do appear elsewhere in the Bible. All three are noted as colors associated with clothing worn by well-to-do individuals, including royalty. They are also incorporated in cloth assigned to cover the items of the tabernacle when the camp of Israel was moving. According to Numbers 4, the ark was to be covered by the veil, then a layer of badger skin, then a cloth of blue; the table of shewbread was covered in blue, then scarlet cloth, then badger skin. The menorah, the altar of incense, and the other items used in the sanctuary itself were covered in blue cloth, followed by a layer of badger cloth. The altar of burnt offering was to be covered in purple cloth, then badger skin. Unfortunately, while it is clear what the Israelites were expected to do, why they were to do it in this manner or what the symbolism meant in doing it this way is not clear. It is intriguing that of the colors themselves, two of them, the red and the blue are primary colors, while the purple is a blend of both, but while it is fun to speculate on

Blue, scarlet, and purple were also dominant in the clothing worn by the priest. The association of the priest with these colors suggests that the priest was a liminal figure, one who moved between the different states and whose purpose was to facilitate such movement, which in fact, is exactly what the priest did. The same colors also appeared on the innermost linen layer of the tabernacle, which was also embroidered with gold filament in the image of cherubim (Exodus 26:31). The presence of the same color scheme that was, as previously shown, associated with liminality, suggests that the rooms surrounded by this material were liminal spaces that differed from the reality outside of the tent—spaces specifically dedicated to direct interaction between God and mortals.

Besides the color scheme, the types and functions of items found within the sanctuary may also have emphasized the liminal nature of the tabernacle proper. The sanctuary itself was divided into two rooms by the veil, of which the larger of the two possessed only three items: the menorah, the table of the bread of the presence, and the altar of incense—all three either made of pure gold or covered in gold (Exodus 26:33–35);[24] and while all three may have had cosmic significance, it is also noteworthy that each served a mundane, domestic function. Thus, while the menorah may have represented the cosmic tree, functionally its purpose was to provide

---

the theological nature of this relationship, to do so would simply be surmise. For more on the role of visualization in the Israelite tabernacle/temple system, see Daniel L. Belnap, "'Let the Beauty of the Lord our God Be upon Us': The Importance of an Aesthetic in the Ritualized Visualizations of the Israelite Cult," *The Temple: Ancient and Restored, Proceedings of the Second Interpreter Matthew B. Brown Memorial Conference "The Temple on Mount Zion," 25 October 2014*, ed. Stephen D. Ricks, Donald W. Parry (Orem, UT: The Interpreter Foundation; Salt Lake City: Eborn Books, 2016), 125-144.

24. Philip Peter Jenson, *Graded Holiness: A Key to the Priestly Conception of the World*, Journal for the Study of the Old Testament Supplement Series 106 (Sheffield, UK: Sheffield Academic Press, 1992), 103: "The predominance of gold in the Tabernacle can be related to its valued physical properties and great social significance. This is the basis for the analogies which are made between the human and divine spheres, and a close connection between gold, divinity, and holiness is evident throughout the ancient Near East. Gold is rare, desirable, and very costly, and fittingly represents the dignity and power of those who are able to possess it, to a pre-eminent degree, God."

light within the room like any other lamp.[25] Similarly, the table of the presence, so named for the bread that was placed on the table and replaced every Sabbath, was, functionally, simply a table with food on it. Even the incense altar appears to have had a domestic analogue, as both texts and archaeological evidence suggest that private households used incense.[26]

---

25. Carol L. Meyers, *The Tabernacle Menorah: A Synthetic Study of a Symbol from the Biblical Cult*, American Society of Oriental Research Dissertation Series 2 (Missoula, MT: Scholars Press, 1976), explores both the symbolic and functional aspects of the menorah.
26. While the burning of incense within domestic spaces may have had religious implications, it also appears that it burned to make the home a more pleasing place to be. See Seymour Gitin, "The Four-Horned Altar and Sacred Space: An Archaeological Perspective," in *Sacred Time, Sacred Space*, 95–123 (108 specifically). See also C. Houtman, "On the Function of the Holy Incense (Exodus XXX 34–8) and the Sacred Anointing Oil (Exodus XXX 22–33)," *Vetus Testamentum* 42, no. 4 (1992): 458–65: "As incense was burnt in the houses of the well-to-do to create a pleasant atmosphere, and as the purity of the aromatics and the exquisite character of the fragrance indicated the status of their residents, so the incense of the sanctuary also was a symbol of status" (463). The burning of incense was also associated with hospitality. See Béatrice Caseau, "Eudoia: The Use and Meaning of Fragrances in the Ancient World and Their Christianization (100–900 AD)" (PhD diss., Princeton University, 1994), which may be a useful worldview to understand the role of the tabernacle. See Robert Ignatius Letellier, *Day in Mamre, Night in Sodom: Abraham and Lot in Genesis 18 and 19*, Biblical Interpretation Series 10 (Leiden: Brill, 1995), 155: "In nomadic societies of the ancient Middle East hospitality to a stranger was a sacred obligation, a manifestation of social graciousness that touches the deepest values. . . . The guest is sacred and it is an honour to provide for [the guest]." For more on ancient Near Eastern hospitality, see Andrew Arterbury, *Entertaining Angels: Early Christian Hospitality in its Mediterranean Setting* (Sheffield, UK: Sheffield Phoenix Press, 2005); Jean-Jacques Glassner, "L'hospitalité en Mésopotamie ancienne: aspect de la question de l'étranger," in *Zeitschrift fur Assyriologie und vorderasiatische Archologie* 80, no. 1 (1990): 60–75; Michael Herzfeld, "'As in Your Own House': Hospitality, Ethnography, and the Stereotype of Mediterranean Society," in *Honor and Shame and the Unity of the Mediterranean*, ed. David D. Gilmore (Washington, DC: American Anthropological Association, 1987), 75–89; Robert C. Stallman, "Divine Hospitality in the Pentateuch: A Metaphorical Perspective on God as Host" (PhD diss., Westminster Theological Seminary, 1999).

The principle of liminality continued as one moved beyond the Holy Place to the veil, which separated the Holy Place from the Holy of Holies. The veil was similar to the other cloth items, being made of fine linen embroidered with purple, scarlet, and blue thread. Yet, unlike the other cloth items associated with ingress and egress (the other "doors"), the veil also included images of cherubim similar to those on the innermost roof covering. Thus, when in the holy room, cherubim images could be seen on the ceiling and on the eastern "wall." While we are not told specifically why the cherubim were to be incorporated into these demarcations of space, cherubim are found elsewhere in the Old Testament, and their functions within these other texts may provide insight into their presence in the tabernacle. Their first function in these texts is to guard selected space. In Genesis, cherubim are placed before the tree of life to keep Adam and Eve from eating of the fruit. Thus, the presence of the cherubim demarcates the garden into at least two sections: the part that possesses the tree of life and the part with the rest of the garden.

Another function associated with the cherubim is that of movement. First Samuel 4:4 is the first reference to speak of God as sitting between cherubim, a concept repeated a number of times in the Old Testament, culminating in the writings of Ezekiel, where the cherubim are depicted not only as beings that surround God but also as beings that bear him from place to place.[27] Not only did the cherubim serve to mark the space in which one could interact with God, but their presence also signified that the space was not permanent. Thus, the embroidered cherubim images on the veil would have indicated that liminal nature of the veil. The verb used to describe the function of the veil itself, *hibdil*, appears to be a specialized term used almost exclusively in the priestly literature to describe the separating or the ordering of the different elements of the Creation—light from dark, upper waters from lower waters, day from night—which in turn reflected the creation of the social cosmos (the separation of man and

27. For more on the function of the cherubim, see T. N. D. Mettinger, "cherubim," in *Dictionary of Deities and Demons in the Bible*, ed. Karel Van Der Toorn, Bob Becking, and Pieter W. Van Der Horst (Leiden: Eerdmans, 1999), 189–92.

woman, the separation of child from parent, the establishment of marriage, and the ability to discern or categorize between good and evil).[28]

The final element associated with liminality was the Holy of Holies itself. As in the Holy Place, the roof—which draped over the northern, southern, and western sides—was made of blue, scarlet, and purple cloth with cherubim embroidery, as was the eastern wall, or veil. Thus, the Holy of Holies was completely surrounded by cloth marked with liminal symbolism, suggesting that the space within, the room itself, was wholly liminal space. In terms of furniture, the room possessed only the ark of the covenant (also known as the ark of the testimony), and the lid for the ark, or the mercy seat. The ark was a wooden box encased in gold, about two and a half feet in length and one and a half feet in both width and height. It contained the two tablets of stone upon which was written by God himself the law of God, as well as a pot of manna.[29] The mercy seat consisted of two cherubim with wings that touched each other, thus creating an open-air enclosure on top of the ark.[30]

---

28. *bdl*, in *TDOT*, 2:1–3: "*bdl* is used in a typical way in the Priestly account of creation (Gen. 1:4, 6, 7, 14, 18): the individual phases in creation are depicted as a separation of the different elements form one another. . . . The author uses the word *bdl* in order to emphasize a major idea in the Priestly account of creation, viz., that the creator-God is a God of order rather than a mythological procreator" (2). The use of the verb suggests that the veil may have also represented the ongoing nature of the creation, as well as the distinction between mortal and divine spheres. Elsewhere in the scriptures, God's heavenly abode is described as a tent, with the "curtains stretched out still" suggesting that the cosmos was architecturally represented by the tabernacle (Moses 7:30; see also Psalm 104:2–3; Isaiah 40:22, 42:5; Jeremiah 10:12). Yet the irony of this separation is that as the cosmos was divided, it became more and more possible for humanity and God to interact more fully. Thus, the separation of the Holy Place and the Holy of Holies by the veil, a representation of the order and organization of the cosmos, also represents the coming together of the divine and mortal worlds.
29. Numbers 17:10–11 notes that Aaron's blossoming rod, the indicator of his chosen status as high priest, was also placed in the ark. The rod is also mentioned in Hebrews 9:4, along with the tablets and a pot of manna.
30. Parallels from other ancient descriptions of royal thrones indicate that the divine cherubim themselves formed the throne of Jehovah. For example, a carved relief on the stone coffin of Ahiram, king of Byblos, a Phoenician city

As mentioned, one of the designations for the ark is the ark of the testimony. The Hebrew term translated as "testimony" in this case indicates the establishment of a relationship between two parties.[31] The two items—the stone tablets given to Moses and the pot of manna—placed in the ark emphasize this function in that they represent two items that God himself provided to facilitate the relationship between him and the Israelites. The tablets of stone contained the moral or ethical precepts by which the Israelites could be made holy and therefore enter into his presence, while the manna represented the means by which God interacted directly in the people's livelihood. The presence of the manna and the stone tablets—representing God's contribution to the God-Israel relationship—coupled with the presence of the cherubim—representing the liminal nature of the space in the tabernacle—lead us to the supernal reason given as to why the Israelites should have a tabernacle: so that God could dwell among them. God's express desire to be among his people demonstrates a mortal-divine relationship that did not exist in other religions of the ancient Near East.[32]

---

in the late second millennium BC, depicts the king "sitting on a throne whose sides are winged sphinxes, like the cherubim that formed part of Yahweh's throne. The kings' feet rest on a footstool, recalling the designation of the ark of the covenant as the footstool of Yahweh." See Michael D. Coogan, *The Old Testament: A Historical and Literary Introduction to the Hebrew Scriptures* (New York: Oxford University Press, 2006), 127, caption to figure 8.3.

31. *ya'ad*, *TDOT*, 6:135–44. This is also the root for *mo'ed*, the term translated as tent of "meeting."

32. For the Mesopotamian perspective, see Jean Bottéro, *Religion in Ancient Mesopotamia*, trans. Teresa Lavender Fagan (Chicago: University of Chicago Press, 2001): "The divinity was never the object of an anxious, enthusiastic pursuit: 'to seek out *(še'u)* a god,' as was sometimes said, was out of a need for his protection, his assistance. It was not inspired by a desire to be close to him, to be in his presence, to have the peace or happiness of finding oneself in his company. Hymns professing a bottomless desire for a god's presence indicate admiration (as in the case of the moon god, the splendid lamp of the night) and not an impatience to get closer to him. . . . One submitted to them, one feared them, one bowed down and trembled before them: one did not 'love' or 'like' them. . . . [Temples] were not only to shelter them but to isolate them in peace and allow them to lead, separately and among themselves, a peaceful and refined existence in a magnificent solemn place where their subjects knew they could be found and admire them, take care of them, and request their benevolent

There, in the ultimate liminal space of the Holy of Holies, one confronted tangible symbols of God's effort and desire to be among his people. The entire tabernacle structure and attendant items culminated in the revelation that God himself desired interaction with them, while the emphasis on liminality highlighted the reality of mortal-divine relationships, which in turn elucidated the true worth of God and humans.

"TO MAKE ATONEMENT"

This relationship was also expressed in the primary actions associated with the tabernacle and was alluded to in the instructions—sacrifice and anointing, both of which were performed in Exodus 24 and in the dedication event. The instructions of these ritual actions make up sizable portions of Exodus, Leviticus, and Numbers and can be difficult to follow and appreciate. The first of three primary forms of offerings was the burnt offering, or the *ʿolāh* offering (derived from the Hebrew *ʿalah*, meaning "to ascend"); the Hebrew designation reflects the nature by which this offering ascends into the divine realm, and the English designation reflects that the entire animal or offering is burnt. The instructions concerning the

---

aid" (37, 115). For the Egyptian perspective, see Erik Hornung, *Conceptions of God in Ancient Egypt: The One and the Many*, trans. John Bains (Ithaca, NY: Cornell University Press, 1982), 197–8, 205, 207: "The first emotion that grips an Egyptian who encounters a deity or the image of a god is fear, mixed with wonder and exultation. . . . The gods created the world and ensure[d] that not only [hu]mankind but all beings can live and grow in it. But to what end? What made the creator god call the world and all its creatures into being and keep them in being? No Egyptian text is known which gives direct, unambiguous answers to questions of this sort: the Egyptians evidently did not consider these to be serious issues. . . . The Egyptians believed that by performing the cult and presenting themselves before the god they were at least increasing his existence and presence, while also keeping his negative, dangerous side at a distance. Cult actions do not coerce but they do encourage the gods to show their gracious side—for the converse of a god's love on [hu]mankind his violent aspect, which is always present beneath the surface and must be assuaged by means of appropriate cult services. . . . The Egyptians evidently never experience a longing for union with the deity. They keep their distance from the gods, whom no one can approach too closely without being punished."

performance of the burnt offering in Leviticus 1 begins with the requirements for the offering itself. The ideal offering was a male without blemish. The offering had to be offered voluntarily, meaning that the offerer willingly chose to be a part of the ritual process and was not forced to participate. That the offerer was a willing participant in the ritual process is significant and suggests that the efficacy of the rite was tied to the willingness of all participants. Upon presentation at the tabernacle, the offerer placed a hand on the head of the animal, an act repeated in each ritual offering, at which point the reader was told: "and it shall be accepted for him to make atonement for him" (Leviticus 1:4). Following the placement of the hand, the animal's blood could be used to make an atonement. The animal was slaughtered and divided into sections, and some parts were immediately put on the altar (the head and the fat), while others were first washed. The blood was collected and splashed around the base of the altar.

The second type of offering was the sin offering, and its performance closely resembled that of the burnt offering, except instead of the blood being poured at the base of the altar, some of the blood of the sin offering was to be smeared on certain objects of the tabernacles. When performing this rite on behalf of the whole Israelite congregation, the priest splashed the blood seven times before the veil separating the Holy Place from the inner Holy of Holies. The priest then took the blood and smeared it on the horns or corners of the altar of incense in the Holy Place that stood before the veil, pouring the remaining blood at the base of the altar of burnt offerings outside. The placing of the hand on the forehead would suggest that the animal was not a substitute but represented the individual, and thus its blood could be used to effect what atonement was necessary in a positive manner for the participant. Like the burnt offering, the sin offering was also used to "make atonement."

The term *atonement* was first used in a theological sense by William Tyndale.[33] Literally meaning "at one with," the term was used to describe the reconciliation between God and humans. In the Old Testament, "to

33. See David Rolph Seely, "William Tyndale and the Language of At-one-ment," in *The King James Bible and the Restoration*, ed. Kent P. Jackson (Provo, UT: Religious Studies Center, Brigham Young University; Salt Lake City: Deseret Book, 2011), 25–42.

make an atonement" is the translation of the verb *kpr*, a term that is difficult to translate correctly. Noting the similarities between this verb and the Akkadian verb *kuppuru*, which means to cleanse by wiping off, many have suggested that the verb is expiatory in meaning.[34] This does appear to be the case when the term is associated with the sin offering, which is offered when offense or uncleanliness has been experienced. Yet "to make atonement" is also one of the purposes behind the burnt offering, which is not offered as a direct result of sin or wrongdoing. Thus, two types of atonement appear to be associated with the sacrificial rituals: (1) the atonement that is associated with the forgiveness of sins, reflected in the sin offering, and (2) the atonement enacted not for sin or wrongdoing at all, such as in the case of the burnt offering.

So what are we to make of these acts effecting atonement? First, the acts presuppose an already existing relationship between the Israelites and God. In other words, these acts do not highlight the entering into of a relationship with God; instead, their purpose was to reconcile or renew an already existing relationship. Second, as those that required an item coming into contact with the altar demonstrated, we see the primary purpose of atonement was to make one holy and, therefore, like God. Third, in all cases, the atoning acts were performed by mortals to bring themselves into a state where they could interact with God and receive his beneficence. This last point cannot be stressed enough. From the biblical texts, it appears that atonement required the actions of two parties, God and mortals, in which the latter was responsible to create a situation that allowed God to engage with them. Thus, in the liminal space of the tabernacle, acts of atonement made it possible for humans and God to interact directly, each one willing and desirous to engage with the other.

It is not hard to see the Christological symbolism inherent within each of these sacrificial acts, not the least of which is in the importance of the blood to enact atonement.[35] In the Book of Mormon, Lehi explained

---

34. *kipper, kappōret, kōper, kippurîm*, in *TDOT*, 7:290.

35. Leviticus 17:10–14: "And whatsoever man there be of the house of Israel, or of the strangers that sojourn among you, that eateth any manner of blood; I will even set my face against that soul that eateth blood, and will cut him off from among his people. For the life of the flesh is in the blood: and I have given it

the relationship between the Christ's atoning act and sacrifice, calling Christ's act a "sacrifice for sin," or, in other words, a sin offering (2 Nephi 2:7). Christ's sacrifice is certainly reflected in the sin offering, the explicit purpose of which is to bring on forgiveness through the individual's offering. Just as the blood of the sin offering covers certain items of the tabernacle, thereby reconciling to God the individual represented by the offering, Christ's blood covers us, reconciling us to his Father. Similarly, the burnt offering represents all that he offered to bring about reconciliation, as well as what we are expected to offer for this reconciliation.[36]

---

to you upon the altar to make an atonement for your souls: for it is the blood that maketh an atonement for the soul. Therefore I said unto the children of Israel, No soul of you shall eat blood, neither shall any stranger that sojourneth among you eat blood. . . . For the life of all flesh is the blood thereof." As the verses above indicate, blood represented the concept of life—the dynamic element that made living things alive—and was, by virtue of that significance, a divine possession used by God to effect atonement. For more, see William K. Gilders, *Blood Ritual in the Hebrew Bible: Meaning and Power* (Baltimore: Johns Hopkins University Press, 2004).

36. The astute reader will have noted that this study has only addressed two of the three primary sacrificial forms. The third sacrificial form is the šᵉ*lāmîm*, or peace offering, and may be distinguished from the others by the consumption of the animal by the offerer. Unlike the *ʿolāh* and *hattʾāt*/ ʾāshām sacrifices, once the priest has offered the portion of the animal dedicated to God (namely, the blood and some of the internal viscera such as the fat), the offerer then takes the rest of the animal to consume at home. There is a time restriction to the consumption: the animal has to be consumed within one or two days, depending on whether it is a thanksgiving or vow offering (Leviticus 7:15–17). Nothing may be preserved or saved; thus, the *šᵉlāmîm* offering was a shared experienced with friends, family, or neighbors, who often helped in the consumption of the sacrifice. Of the three sacrificial forms, the peace offering is perhaps the most intriguing because it is not intended to overcome a negative condition. Instead, it acts to enhance a positive event, whether that was the completion of a project (i.e., the construction of the temple) or the fulfilling of a vow. The communal nature of this sacrificial form, in light of its function, suggests that the peace offering was the highest offering that could be offered. "To make atonement" is not mentioned as a function of the third form of animal sacrifice, the "peace offering." This may be because the peace offering is not offered to overcome a deficit or division between God and his people but instead to commemorate the fulfillment of a vow, or other blessed event, in which God's hand is recognized.

But, perhaps most importantly, Christ and the agency he expressed in performing the atoning sacrifice is an example to us that we, too, can have a direct relationship with the Father. Just as he offered up a sacrifice of a broken heart and a contrite spirit, so he has encouraged us to do the same, showing that it is possible for us to achieve our ultimate goal of oneness with the Father. Through their ritual performance, the Israelites expressed their desire to be reconciled in their covenant relationship with God—a relationship that emphasized their divine nature and potential to become holy (just as God himself was), a relationship that is the very essence of worship.[37]

"FOR THE ANOINTING OF THE LORD IS UPON YOU"

As important as the atonement rites were to the Israelites' worship, another category of rites may have been equally as important—those performed when making the relationships in the first place. Such was the purpose of the rite described in Exodus 24 and the anointing of the tabernacle and the priests as described in Exodus 40 and Leviticus 8, respectively.[38] Like the rites of reconciliation, while each rite of induction or inclusion differed from one another at points, there does seem to have been a common element that defined these rites as part of their own classification, that

---

In other words, there is no need for atonement to be made because the peace offering recognizes that atonement, or reconciliation, is already present.

37. Biblical scholar Jonathan Klawans considers this in his article "Pure Violence: Sacrifice and Defilement in Ancient Israel," *Harvard Theological Review* 94, no. 2 (2001): 135–57: "Jon D. Levenson . . . has argued that the biblical narrative of tabernacle (and temple) construction take on a cosmic significance. . . . In so doing, Levenson demonstrates that the priestly traditions understand tabernacle and temple construction as an act of *imitatio Dei*. If the building of the temple can be understood as an act of *imitatio Dei*, and if the process of preparation for the rituals that will take place there can be understood likewise, can this concept help us to better understand at least some aspects of ancient Israelite animal sacrifice?" (145).

38. As was the reintroduction of the leper described in Leviticus 14.

element being the placement of blood, water, or oil on the individual being introduced or reintroduced into the society.

The ritual sequence in Exodus 24 was used to note Israel's acceptance of the law as described in Exodus 24:3, "And Moses came and told the people all the words of the Lord, and all the judgments: and all the people answered with one voice, and said, All the words which the Lord hath said will we do." According to the text, Moses then copied the law down onto another medium, rose up the next morning, built an altar, and erected twelve pillars representing the twelve tribes of Israel. Since priests had not been ordained yet, Moses had young men of Israel offer both burnt and peace offerings, both of which included the splashing of blood against the sides of the altar.[39]

But in this account, only half of the blood was used against the sides of the altar, unlike the practice in later burnt and peace offerings. The other half was splashed on the people following the reading of the law and the people's declaration that they would obey the precepts within: "And he [Moses] took the book of the covenant, and read in the audience of the people: and they said, All that the Lord hath said will we do, and be obedient. And Moses took the blood, and sprinkled it on the people, and said, Behold the blood of the covenant, which the Lord hath made with you concerning all these words" (Exodus 24:7–8). In this case, the blood became the tangible symbol of the covenant made between God and the Israelites, and the splashing of blood upon the altar perhaps suggested that the altar stood as a symbol for God.[40] In other words, blood was splashed on the altar, which represented God, just as blood was splashed on the

---

39. The use of the young men in the ritual process highlights that the Israelite priestly system had not been established yet, nor had the election of the Levites taken place. In light of this, it is possible that the young men were firstborn. Numbers 8 recounts the substitution of the Levites for the firstborn of the Israelites, suggesting that the firstborn generally could have had priestly or cultic functions, which were now subsumed into the Aaronic and Levitical families.

40. The concept of inanimate objects representing God is found elsewhere in the Old Testament. For instance, the ark of the covenant represented God when taken into battle against the Philistines. Likewise, both the Book of Mormon and New Testament Saints understood that the bronze serpent represented Christ.

people—both parties were bound by blood and partook of the covenant experience.[41]

In a similar manner were the tabernacle and Aaron and his sons to be initiated, using both the special anointing oil and the blood of a particular offering known as the consecration offering. Unlike other oil the anointing oil was a scented oil, made according to a specific formula, to be used solely to sanctify the items within the tabernacle: "And thou shalt anoint the tabernacle of the congregation therewith, and the ark of the testimony, and the table and all his vessels, and the candlestick and his vessels, and the altar of incense, and the altar of burnt offering with all his vessels, and the laver and his foot. And thou shalt sanctify them, that they may be most holy: whatsoever toucheth them shall be holy. And thou shalt anoint Aaron and his sons, and consecrate them, that they may minister unto me in the priest's office" (Exodus 30:26–30).

Beginning in the Holy of Holies and moving outward until reaching the wash laver in the tabernacle courtyard, Moses anointed the tabernacle furniture. After that, Aaron and his sons were brought forward and washed. Moses then clothed Aaron and anointed him by pouring the oil over his head. The ram of consecration was then slaughtered, but instead of splashing all of the blood on the sides of the altar, some of it was daubed on the right earlobe, the right thumb, and the right big toe of Aaron and his sons. The final rite of the sanctification process was to take the blood on the altar, which had mingled with the anointing oil, and splash it onto Aaron, and his sons, rendering him "hallowed, and his garments, and his sons, and his sons' garments" (Exodus 29:21). As with the splashing of the blood onto the whole of Israel in Exodus 24, the splashing of the blood

---

41. Tzvi Abusch, "Blood in Israel and Mesopotamia," in *Emanuel: Studies in Hebrew Bible, Septuagint and Dead Sea Scrolls in Honor of Emanuel Tov*, ed. Shalom M. Paul et al. (Leiden: Brill, 2003), 675–84: "Blood sacrifice, in and [of] itself, actually stands in opposition to the natural relationship created at birth. It creates relations between [people], and places these artificial relationships on a higher level than the natural relationship of mother and child created in the blood of birth. . . . Blood served many purposes in the Israelite cult. Surely one of them was that of creating and maintaining bonds of kinship which were defined in terms of covenant" (678, 684).

and oil onto Aaron ritually established the relationship between Aaron and God.[42]

Unlike the atonement rites, the induction rites used to establish the initial relationship with God were not repeated. In other words, whereas all the atoning rituals were repeated often, the act of being anointed or splashed with the blood or oil, once done, was never performed again. Moreover, in the case of the tabernacle's dedication, the process of anointing began from the inside out, from the Holy of Holies to the laver outside. The direction from which the anointing began, with the oil specifically designated as God's own, and the single performance of the act each suggest that the act was to be understood as if God himself were doing it. Just as individuals prepared themselves to enter into the presence of God, the anointing process seems to have suggested that God did not just wait, but he prepared the space and items so that such interaction was possible. In other words, just as mortals sanctified themselves and the space around them to reconcile themselves with God, so God participated in preparing the space and the individual so that reconciliation could happen.

Unlike the acts of the mortal, however, which had to be repeated often, God's anointing act needed to be done only once to transform the individual or item into a state of holiness. This transformation by God

---

42. C. Houtman, "On the Function of the Holy Incense (Exodus XXX 34–38) and the Sacred Anointing Oil (Exodus XXX 22–33)," *Vetus Testamentum* 42, no. 4 (1992): 465: "Emphatically, [God] forbids [the oil's use] as a cosmetic. Also sprinkling it on unqualified persons is not permitted by him (Ex. xxx 32–33). The fragrance, which is spread abroad by the anointing oil, is determined by its composition. By claiming the exclusive right to the composition of the sacred anointing oil, YHWH reserves its special fragrance for himself. By anointing[,] 'his' fragrance is transmitted to his dwelling and its inventory (Ex. xxx 26–29) and to the priests, devoted to his service (Ex. xxx 30). So YHWH's fragrance becomes attached to his house and his attendants. So they are marked by his personality. Their exclusive belonging to YHWH is expressed for an organ of sense in a perceptible way. Because YHWH's aroma envelopes them, by nose they can be known as YHWH's representatives." Interestingly, according to the great medieval rabbinic commentator Rashi, the command to wash Aaron and his sons with water (Exodus 29:4) actually meant immersion of the whole body. Abraham Cohen, ed., *The Soncino Chumash* (New York: The Soncino Press, 1997), 527n4.

is expressed throughout Leviticus. Leviticus 21:10–12 reveals that the high priest is not allowed to act like the rest of society during the mourning process because "the crown of the anointing oil of his God is upon him." The same concept can be found earlier in chapter 10, where, after the deaths of Nadab and Abihu, Aaron and the remaining sons are told to "not let the hair of your heads hang loose, and do not tear your clothes, lest you die, and wrath come upon all the congregation; . . . and do not go outside the entrance of the tent of meeting, lest you die, for the anointing oil of the Lord is upon you" (Leviticus 10:6–7 English Standard Version). As the two passages suggest, the oil belonged to God himself, transforming that which touched it and making those items representative of him or able to interact with him. Aaron, having been anointed, is not allowed to engage in normal, "profane" behavior. The anointing allows Aaron to interact with the divine—the anointing being a divine act and creating an environment that allows mortal acts to have efficacy.[43]

What is particularly pleasing about this rite of induction is that in many ways it is the complement to the atonement rites. Both sets of rituals present the performer, either divine or mortal, as one who wants to have a relationship with the other. In the case of the atonement rites, the rituals emphasize an individual's right to have a relationship with God, even the inherent right to become like God, while the initiation rites demonstrate God's continuing work in bringing that result about.

43. That Moses is performing the rite instead of God is not a hindrance, since Moses is more than a priest—he acts in the stead of God. For more on the association of Moses with God, see W. A. Meeks, "Moses as God and King," in *Religions in Antiquity: Essays in Memory of Erwin Ramsdell Goodenough*, ed. J. Neusner, Numen Supplemental 14 (Leiden: Brill, 1968), 353–59; see also Crispin Fletcher-Louis, "4Q374: A Discourse on the Sinai Tradition: The Deification of Moses and Early Christology," in *Dead Sea Discoveries* 3, no. 3 (Leiden: Brill, 1996): 236–52. This principle is of course found in Restoration scripture: "And I will lay my hand upon you by the hand of my servant Sidney Rigdon" (Doctrine and Covenants 36:2).

THE GOLDEN CALF

As Moses was receiving the instructions for the tabernacle and its dedication at the top of Sinai, the Israelites at the mountain's base feared that Moses would not return. They requested of Aaron the crafting of "gods, which shall go before us" (Exodus 32:1). The result of this was a golden calf, which was to be "thy gods, O Israel, which brought thee up out of the land of Egypt" (verse 4), commemorated by a dedicatory feast "to the Lord" (literally, "to Yahweh"). Like the other scenes of the Sinai narrative, the golden calf narrative in its final form demonstrates inconsistencies that suggest multiple texts were used in its construction.[44] Perhaps the biggest challenge is the presumed ignorance of the Israelites concerning God's

44. See Cornelis Houtman, *Exodus*, vol. 3: *Chapters 20–40* (Leuven: Peeters, 2000), 617, 619. Nowhere is this more obvious than in the outcome of Aaron. The Hebrew text of Exodus 32:22–25 is clear that Aaron tried to excuse himself to Moses for making the golden calf by vilifying the people to Moses. But Aaron bore responsibility for letting the people get out of control: "And Aaron said, Let not the anger of my lord wax hot: thou knowest the people, that they are set on mischief. For they said unto me, Make us gods, which shall go before us: for as for this Moses, the man that brought us up out of the land of Egypt, we wot not what is become of him. And I said unto them, Whosoever hath any gold, let them break it off. So they gave it to me: then I cast it into the fire, and thre came out this calf. And when Moses saw that the people were naked; (for Aaron had made them naked unto their shame among their enemies:) Yet, when Moses called for the righteous Levites to slay the three thousand rebels (Exodus 32:26–28), Aaron was not destroyed. He lived to the ripe old age of 123 and died on Mount Hor (Numbers 20:22–29; 33:38–39). Apparently, Aaron's repentance was real and accepted by the Lord. Some have suggested that the confusion concerning Aaron and his role reflects two versions of this narrative, a northern, Israelite narrative and a southern, Judahite narrative. See Frank Moore Cross, *Canaanite Myth and Hebrew Epic: Essays in the History of the Religion of Israel* (Cambridge, MA: Harvard University Press, 1973, 195–216; see also Matthew Robert Rasure, "Priests Like Moses: Earliest Divisions in the Priesthood of Ancient Israel" (PhD diss., Harvard University, 2019). The relationship between Exodus 32 and Deuteronomy 9–10 has also been noted by many; for instance, see Christine E. Hayes, "Golden Calf Stories: The Relationship of Exodus 32 and Deuteronomy 9–10," in *Idea of Biblical Interpretation: Essays in Honor of James L. Kugel*, ed. H. Najman (Leiden: Brill, 2003), 45–93, who assumes the Exodus tradition came before the Deuteronomic one; see also John Van Seters, "Law and the Wilderness Rebellion Tradition: Ex 32," in *Society of Biblical*

hand in their deliverance. As many have noted, even as the narrative states that the calf was to represent the gods that led the children of Israel out of Egypt, Aaron declares that the day of the calf's dedication would be a feast to Yahweh.[45] Two questions thus arise. First, what exactly did the calf represent, and second, was there one idol or many?

The function of the idol seems relatively clear. As the text states, Moses's absence has led the Israelites to fear that their connection with the divine has been broken in some fashion; thus, the idol was needed for access. As to what they wished to access, some have suggested, based on the image of a calf, that the deity expressed represented someone other than Yahweh. In most major cultures of the ancient Near East, the bull (and in some cases the cow as well) represented a major deity of that culture (which is why figurines of these animals have been found by archaeologists). "The depiction of a god in the form of a bull was widespread throughout the entire ancient Near East [and] . . . was a symbol of lordship, strength, vital energy, and fertility"—all sovereign attributes.[46] In light of the Israelites' history in Egypt, some have suggested that the golden calf represented the bull-god Apis: "Deification of a live, 'sacred' bull was initiated during the First Egyptian Dynasty and continued throughout ancient Egypt's long history. Bull cults of the Nile delta, which existed at the same time and location as the Israelites' sojourn in Egypt, were dedicated to Horus, the 'god of heaven.'"[47] But this would presuppose that the Israelites expected an Egyptian deity to deliver them from Egypt, which hardly seems correct. Others have suggested that the calf represented the Mesopotamian deity Sin, from

---

Literature Seminar Papers 29, ed. David J. Lull (1990): 583–91, who argues that the Exodus tradition is secondary.

45. It should be noted that some scholars believe this to be a later gloss in order to rehabilitate the image of Aaron, from whom will emerge the prominent priestly line during the Davidic monarchy and beyond. See Cross, *Canaanite Myth and Hebrew Epic*, 195–207; see also Lloyd R. Bailey, "The Golden Calf," *Hebrew Union College Annual* 42 (1971): 99.

46. Nahum Sarna, *Exploring Exodus*, 218.

47. "Cultural and Historical Notes, The Golden Calf," in Duane Garrett and Walter C. Kaiser Jr., *NIV Archaeological Study Bible* (Grand Rapids, MI: Zondervan, 2005), 143.

the Israelites' historical attachment to Harran.[48] Yet, outside of this one supposed instance, the deity Sin does not seem to play any particular role elsewhere in Israelite religious practice. Furthermore, closer culturally and linguistically, both the Ugaritic deities El and Baal were depicted in bovine imagery.[49] Having said all this, it is more likely that the idol was meant to represent Yahweh, who could be found to be represented by the bull as well.[50]

Though not common at all in the Old Testament, there are a few references that associate Yahweh with a bull—more specifically, the power and vitality of the bull. A portion of Israel's blessing to his son Joseph is translated in the King James Version as "the arms of his hands were made strong by the hands of the mighty *God* of Jacob" (Genesis 49:24; italics in original). However, the word *God* appears in italics, meaning that the literal word in the Hebrew text was not God. Rather, it is *'avir*—which means "bull" or "bull-like."[51] That is also the case in Psalm 132:2, "God" is translated from *'avir*. Though it is unclear what exactly the symbolism from the

48. Jack M. Sasson, "Bovine Symbolism in the Exodus Narrative," *Vetus Testamentum* 18 (1968): 380–87; see also Bailey, "Golden Calf," 97–15.

49. See Mark S. Smith, *The Origins of Biblical Monotheism: Israel's Polytheistic Background and the Ugaritic Texts* (Oxford: Oxford University Press, 2001), 32; see also Marjo A. Korpel, *A Rift in the Clouds: Ugaritic and Hebrew Descriptions of the Divine*, Ugaritisch-Biblische Literatur 8 (Münster, Germany: Ugarit-Verlag, 1990), 524–28, 532–34; see also Glenn S. Holland, *Gods in the Desert: Religions of the Ancient Near East* (Lanham, MD: Rowman and Littlefield, 2010), 144.

50. Michael B. Hundley, "What Is the Golden Calf?," *Catholic Biblical Quarterly* 79 (2017): 568: "To this point in Exodus, Yhwh has demonstrated his power by leading the people out of Egypt, and Yhwh/Elohim has been the only god directly referenced. Indeed, nothing in the text to this point indicates that any deity other than Yhwh is in view."

51. John N. Oswalt, "Golden Calves and the 'Bull of Jacob': The Impact on Israel of Its Religious Environment," in *Israel's Apostasy and Restoration: Essays in Honor of Roland K. Harrison*, ed. Avraham Gileadi (Grand Rapids, MI: Baker Book House, 1988), 12: " *'abbîr* refers to the characteristics of the bull, in particular, its might. Thus, especially in Hebrew poetry, it may be used of the bull itself (Ps 50:13). More frequently, however, it refers to 'mighty (bullish) ones,' either divine (Ps 68:30) or human (Isa 34:7). The term *abir*, if indeed it is a cognate of *abbir*, is removed from bull one step further and concentrates solely on the

Old Testament is, the bronze sea constructed for Solomon's Temple rested on twelve oxen. Archaeologists have found representations of small male calves, cast in metal, among the material remains of cultures surrounding the Israelites', while an ostracon from Samaria was found with the name ʿglyw ("Yahweh-Calf," "Yahweh is the Calf," or "Calf of Yahweh").[52]

It has also been argued that figurines or images of animals such as the bull were used as pedestals of a god. Thus, the golden calf would have served as the pedestal for Jehovah—a symbol of his presence.[53] In support of this notion, scholars point to parallels in other cultures. For example, a stela from the eighth century BC shows the storm god Adad (also known as Hadad and Baal) standing on the back of a bull, with lightning bolts in each hand.[54] In such a scenario, Aaron may have had it in his mind that he was making a graphic visual aid to help the people refocus on Jehovah. Thus, it is likely that the Israelites substituted the intercessory role of Moses with an idol that would function the same way.[55]

As to whether there was one or more idols, though *calf* is singular, the narrative is consistent in the use of the plural, particularly the verbal forms, when referring to the idol. In light of the plural, some have suggested that the calf narrative reflects the cultic innovations made by Jeroboam.[56]

---

attribute of might. . . . Its biblical usage makes it plain that the phrase no longer has any reference to the concrete bull but has become solely descriptive."

52. For more on the figurines, see Amihai Mazar, "The Bull Site: An Iron Age 1 Open Cult Place," *Bulletin for the American Society of Oriental Research* 247 (1982), 27–42; see also "Cultural and Historical Notes, The Golden Calf," 143. For more on the ostracon, see Graham I. Davies, *Ancient Hebrew Inscriptions: Corpus and Concordance* (Cambridge: Cambridge University Press, 1991–2004), 3.3.041. See further K. Koenen, "Der Name ᶜGLYW auf Samaria-Ostrakon nr. 41," *Vetus Testamentum* 44 (1994): 396–400.
53. Coogan, *Old Testament*, 131; Sarna, *Exploring Exodus*, 218.
54. See the photograph in Coogan, *Old Testament*, 132.
55. It is possible that this explains why the idol was to be made out of the earrings. This jewelry was associated with the organs of hearing and thus the reception of God's will since the Israelites had refused to see or talk with Yahweh directly.
56. The relationship between 1 Kings 12 and Exodus 32 has been the subject of much discussion. Some believe that the Exodus 32 narrative was written based on Jeroboam's innovations. See John Van Seters, "Law and the Wilderness Rebellion Tradition: Exodus 32," in *Society of Biblical Literature Seminar Papers*

According to 1 Kings 12, to forestall the travel of Israelites to Jerusalem to worship at the temple (and therefore potentially placing themselves under Solomonic hegemony), Jeroboam installed two calves, one at Bethel and one at Dan, declaring at their installation: "It is too much for you to go up to Jerusalem: behold thy gods, O Israel, which brought thee up out of the land of Egypt" (12:28). Unfortunately, if the Exodus narrative is influenced by the 1 Kings narrative, then the argument is circular, for it is clear that the Jeroboam narrative is dependent on the Sinai scene.[57] Interestingly, a reference in Nehemiah suggests that the original Exodus narrative may have had the singular: "Yea, when they had made them a [golden] molten

---

29 (1990): 583–91; see also Marvin A. Sweeney, "The Wilderness Traditions of the Pentateuch: A Reassessment of Their Function and Intent in Relation to Exodus 32–34," *Society of Biblical Literature Seminar Papers* 26 (1989): 291–99, though others believe that the final form of Exodus 32 contains both an original narrative and a later editorial gloss in which the influence of Jeroboam's narrative can be seen. See Moses Aberbach and Leivy Smolar, "Aaron, Jeroboam, and the Golden Calves," *Journal of Biblical Literature* 86 (1967): 129–40; see also Gary N. Knoppers, "Aaron's Calf and Jeroboam's Calves," in *Fortunate the Eyes That See: Essays in Honor of David Noel Freedman in Celebration of His Seventieth Birthday*, ed. Astrid B. Beck et al. (Grand Rapids, MI: Eerdmans, 1995), 92–104. In her study, Christine E. Hayes suggests that Exodus 32, in its current form, was used to construct 1 Kings 12. See Christine E. Hayes, "Golden Calf Stories: The Relationship of Exodus 32 and Deuteronomy 9–10," in *Idea of Biblical Interpretation: Essays in Honor of James L. Kugel*, ed. H. Najman (Leiden: Brill, 2003), 4593.

57. While some have suggested that the golden calf narrative is dependent upon 1 Kings 12 (see previous note), the consensus is that the Exodus account reflects at the very least an early tradition. This appears to be the sense in the 1 Kings 12 narrative, as Jeroboam suggests his innovations are really a reform, returning the Israelites to an older worship tradition, rather than a divergence from established orthopraxy. For instance, see Nicholas Wyatt, "Of Calves and Kings: The Canaanite Dimension in the Religion of Israel," *Scandinavian Journal of the Old Testament* 6, no. 1 (1992): 68–91, who believes that it is a return to El worship. What has gone unnoticed is that the 1 Kings narrative hearkens back not only to Exodus 32 but also to Exodus 19. Among the reforms, was the institution of a priesthood that was to be made up of "the lowest of the people, which were not of the sons of Levi" (1 Kings 12:31). This new priesthood, not dependent upon lineage, would accord with the original promise God made in Exodus 19—namely, that all of Israel could be a "royal priesthood/kingdom of priests/kings and priests."

calf, and said, This is thy God that brought thee up out of Egypt" (Nehemiah 9:18).

Yet even if the golden calf was made to represent Yahweh, the reader is to understand the image fell under the parameter of an idol, and thus the Israelites had quickly broken the explicit commandments concerning the worshipping of idols and other gods.[58] As the Israelites' perfidy unfolded and Jehovah reported their treachery to Moses, Jehovah created a circumstance that tested and then demonstrated the prophet's exceptional integrity and character. The Lord proposed to Moses that the Israelites should be destroyed and that he (Moses) should be raised up as the father of a great replacement nation. Instead of seizing the opportunity to exalt himself, his name, and his posterity, Moses interceded on behalf of Jacob's posterity, pled for their continued existence, and reasoned with the Lord for another chance for them to repent. The superior reading of the Joseph Smith Translation demonstrates Moses's intercessory compassion: "And Moses besought the Lord his God, and said, Lord, why doth thy wrath wax hot against thy people, which thou hast brought forth out of the land of Egypt with great power, and with a mighty hand? Wherefore should the Egyptians speak, and say, For mischief did he bring them out, to slay them in the mountains, and to consume them from the face of the earth? Turn from thy fierce wrath. *Thy people will repent of this evil; therefore come thou not out against them*" (JST Exodus 32:11–12, emphasis added).[59]

---

58. Hundley, "What Is the Golden Calf?," 578: "Worshiping the deity in an unapproved way—in this case through a calf image—even in a dire situation is unacceptable and subject to extreme censure. It lies in the category of heterodox worship, which leads to the worship of other gods and the rejection of YHWH. The use of the grammatically plural: *elohim* in a singular context is the storyteller's way of making his displeasure clear."

59. This specific episode immediately causes one to reflect on the scene depicted in modern revelation wherein Jesus Christ, the Great Intercessor, continually stands before God the Father and pleads the cause of the entire human family (see Doctrine and Covenants 45:3–5). Thus, the meekness and intercessory roles of both Moses and Jesus Christ are highlighted in scripture across the ages. Ironically, as Moses returned from the mountain to the camp of Israel to witness firsthand the Israelites' apostasy, his own "anger waxed hot, and he cast the tables out of his hands, and brake them beneath the mount" (Exodus 32:19).

The making of the golden calf appears to have been a manifestation of the fear and unabating spiritual immaturity that the Israelites exhibited when Jehovah first manifested his glory and power to them. The practical effect of the golden calf was for the Israelites to signal that they had finally rejected Jehovah's offer to make of them a holy nation and a kingdom of priests. At first, the Israelites had committed to do all that Jehovah desired, to comply with all he was attempting to accomplish. But they rejected the proffered blessings. Now, many weeks later, they were not just rejecting the Lord's proposal, they were committing an act of open rebellion. Sadly, they forfeited the glory and power and blessings of the true and living God in exchange for a worthless, lifeless figurine. As the psalmist recorded, "They made a calf in Horeb, and worshipped the molten image. Thus they changed their glory into the similitude of an ox that eateth grass. They forgat God their saviour, which had done great things in Egypt" (Psalm 106:19–21).

Thereby hangs the tale. The Israelites gave up the promise of sanctification and exaltation for a lesser order of things. The nullification of Jehovah's highest promises to the children of Israel was graphically and symbolically communicated by Moses in his breaking the tablets when he came down from Mount Sinai. In the ancient Near East, to "break a tablet" could signify the invalidating of a treaty. In the Akkadian legal terminology of Hammurabi's era, for example, the phrase *tuppam hepu* ("break the tablet") meant to break an agreement, to invalidate or repudiate a document.[60] Thus, the terms of Jehovah's original agreement with the Israelites (Exodus 19:5–8) were no longer in force. Broken tablets reflected the rejected promise.

The result of this provocation was the giving of a new set of tablets, which included a set of commandments that emphasized and built upon the earlier injunctions against worshipping other gods and engaging in idol worship.[61] Joseph Smith revealed that the new instructions also reflected

60. James Pritchard, *Ancient Near Eastern Texts Relating to the Old Testament* (Princeton: Princeton University Press, 1955), 167, section 37.

61. This second set of instructions is often referred to as the "ritual decalogue" because of its focus on worship performances. Some have suggested that it is a "J" version of the covenant law. For more, see Coogan, *Old Testament*, 115.

the loss of the Melchizedek Priesthood and the saving ordinances associated with the higher priesthood, as noted in his translation:

> And the Lord said unto Moses, Hew thee two other tables of stone, like unto the first, and I will write upon *them also*, the words *of the law, according as they* were *written at* the first *on the* tables which thou brakest; *but it shall not be according to the first, for I will take away the priesthood out of their midst; therefore my holy order, and the ordinances thereof, shall not go before them; for my presence shall not go up in their midst, lest I destroy them.*
>
> *But I will give unto them the law as at the first, but it shall be after the law of a carnal commandment; for I have sworn in my wrath, that they shall not enter into my presence, into my rest, in the days of their pilgrimage. Therefore do as I have commanded thee*, and be ready in the morning, and come up in the morning unto mount Sinai, and present thyself there to me, in the top of the mount. (JST Exodus 34:1–2)

As the additional revelation make clear, the first set of instructions, at least in terms of worship, included ordinances associated with the Melchizedek Priesthood. The Israelites, having rejected the first promise to enter into the Lord's presence at Sinai, had now, through the golden calf, rejected the Melchizedek Priesthood. Only a select few, including the prophets, held the higher priesthood, the holy order of the Son of God. In fact, in practical terms, only one-twelfth of the tribes of Israel held any priesthood at all—the Levites. This meant that the opportunity for the community of Israel to see God was curtailed. Instead of a kingdom of priests of the Most High, the Israelites (the Levites) became a kingdom of Aaronic priests.

Instead of a holy nation, where all individuals could represent themselves directly to God, the priests began to act as intermediaries and represented the people before God. The Mosaic law replaced the higher law. Instead of the opportunity and privilege of becoming sanctified through individually administered temple ordinances, the Israelites as a whole came to live under the corporate structures administered by the lesser priesthood. Brigham Young stated, "If they [the Israelites] had been sanctified and holy, the children of Israel would not have travelled one year with Moses before they would have received their endowments and the Melchisedec Priesthood."[62]

The children of Israel lost much that would not be restored until the Messiah came in the meridian of time. Yet, even at this lowest point, God did not abandon them. Even as the instructions restricted the blessings that the Israelites could experience on a large scale, the instructions still formally established a covenant relationship in which God promised to "do marvels, such as have not been done in all the earth, nor in any nation" (Exodus 34:10), before the people of Israel, which in turn, would be the means by which others would see the wonderful things of God. The tabernacle itself was to still act as a meeting place.

Intriguingly, one set of instructions stayed the same between the original and the secondary tablets—namely, that all Israelites were to come to the tabernacle three times a year. The King James Version of Exodus 23:17 reads, "Three times in the year all thy males shall appear [Hebrew, *yērā'eh*] before the Lord God." It has been argued that before the Masoretes vocalized the consonants of the text of Exodus 23:17, specifically the Hebrew verb *yod-resh-he*, *yērā'eh* was originally intended to be read as *yir*ᵉ*'eh*—the Qal active form rather than the now extant Niphal passive form, thus providing a reading of "three times in the year all thy males shall see the Lord God" rather than "three times in the year all thy males shall be seen/present themselves ("appear before") before the Lord God."[63] The Samaritan Bible supports this emended reading and better harmonizes with Jehovah's intended purpose for the Israelites. If this emended reading is correct, the commandment to go to the tabernacle three times per year, reflected in both sets of tablets, potentially carried with it the great promise to see the face of God.

Whether such a reading is correct, the new law still emphasized the election of the children of Israel and the important role they played in the salvation history for all humankind. Ideally, the Israelites would act, as Paul described it, as a "schoolmaster," preparing those who practiced it

---

62. Brigham Young, in *Journal of Discourses* (London: Latter-day Saints' Book Depot, 1859), 6:100.

63. Margaret Barker, *Temple Themes in Christian Worship* (London: T & T Clark, 2010), 146.

sincerely a means by which they would remember God and their duty to him (Galatians 3:24). Again, Restoration scripture gives us a better appreciation of this law, Nephi in particular noting that the law functioned to direct one to "look forward with steadfastness unto Christ" (2 Nephi 25:24). Perhaps even more intriguing is Nephi's declaration that one of the purposes of the law was to teach one "that life . . . is in Christ, and know for what end the law was given" (25:27). Nephi's words imply that even as the law itself did not allow for salvation, it was meant to teach one a life in Christ and the original promise given to the Israelites. Thus, the narrative concludes on a hopeful note. Even as the children of Israel failed to enter into God's rest at Sinai, Christ gave the instructions necessary and appropriate for their spiritual state in order to better themselves, increase their faith, and ultimately avail themselves of the promise offered in the first place.

— 16 —

"I WILL GIVE JUDGMENT UNTO HIM IN WRITING"

THE THREE LAW CODES OF THE PENTATEUCH

MATTHEW L. BOWEN

For many, it is hard to fully appreciate the law of Moses. Often understood as a punishment, the technical and detailed elements of the law can be confusing. Moreover, because of the fulfillment of the law in the Atonement of Jesus Christ, some may feel that there is no real need to understand the precepts that make up this law. Yet, for all its challenges, the law of Moses is still a law sent from God to his prophet and, as such, reflects the correct relationship and responsibilities between God and human beings and human beings and each other. This understanding of the law lies behind Matt Bowen's chapter, within which he introduces the versions of the law as found in the Pentateuch, outlines the specific legal expectations associated with each, and, in so doing, demonstrates that the law was meant to produce holy individuals and communities built

Regarding Moses, his life, and his roles, Egyptologist and biblical scholar Kenneth Kitchen has observed that "a large amount of inconclusive discussion by biblical scholars in almost two hundred years has established next to nothing with any surety, and has vacillated all the way between extreme conservatism ('Moses wrote all the Pentateuch') and total nihilism ('There was no Moses, and he left nothing')."[1] The Prophet Joseph Smith's reported statement regarding the imperfection of the diachronic transmission and translation of the Bible alleviates Latter-day Saints of the need to embrace an extreme conservative position. He said, "I believe the bible as it read when it came from the pen of the original writers; ignorant translators, careless transcribers, or designing and corrupt priests have committed many errors."[2]

On the other hand, the appearance of Jesus and other biblical figures—including Moses himself—to the Prophet Joseph Smith on April 3, 1836, in the Kirtland Temple also means that Latter-day Saints do not embrace a nihilist or minimalist position either. Moses did live. He was a prophet, and he did leave a record—that is, he wrote books (see, especially, Moses 1:23, 40–42). Not only did Moses write, but a prophecy preserved in the Book of Mormon confirms that he was foreordained to receive divine law written by God himself. As mentioned by Lehi to his son Joseph (as recorded by Nephi), the Lord foretold the birth, life, and ministry of Moses to Joseph in Egypt: "I will raise up a Moses; and I will give power unto him in a rod; and *I will give judgment unto him in writing*. Yet I will not loose his tongue, that he shall speak much, for I will not make him mighty in speaking. But I will write unto him my law, by the finger of mine own hand; and I will make a spokesman for him" (2 Nephi 3:17; see also JST Genesis 50:35; emphasis added). Elsewhere, Nephi refers to "the five books of Moses" (1 Nephi 5:11) that Lehi found on the plates of brass, indicating that by his time—the late seventh and early sixth centuries BC—there was already a fivefold

1. Kenneth A. Kitchen, *On the Reliability of the Old Testament* (Grand Rapids, MI: Eerdmans, 2003), 299. Here he also notes, "As for the role of a Moses, there is no factual evidence to exclude such a person at this period, or his having played the roles implied in Exodus and Genesis."

2. "History, 1838–1856, volume E-1 [1 July 1843–30 April 1844]," p. 1755, The Joseph Smith Papers.

division of the texts ascribed to Mosaic authorship or derivation (1 Nephi 5:11). What those five books—the Pentateuch—looked like in the sixth century BC vis-à-vis the Pentateuch in its present form is unknowable.

Biblical scholars generally recognize three law codes within the Pentateuch. In this chapter, I will describe the law codes and the implications of their legislation for Latter-day Saints living in the twenty-first century. In many instances, "in the reading of the old testament" (including its law codes), it is the "vail upon [our own] heart[s]" that needs to be "taken away" or "done away in Christ" (2 Corinthians 3:14–16). Although we typically understand the law of Moses as having been "fulfilled"[3] or "done away"[4] in Christ, the eternal doctrinal principles of the gospel of Jesus Christ constitute the underpinnings of these law codes as a whole.

In their present canonical context, the three law codes can be viewed as follows. First, the Covenant Code (Exodus 20:22–23:33) legislation constitutes an ethos for the establishment of the Israelites in the wilderness as a covenant people—and holding them together as such—with a view of their eventual entry into the land of promise. Second, the Holiness Code's (Leviticus 17–26) framing of Yahweh's commandments to Moses in terms of holiness, ritual purity, and priestly instruction can be seen as preparing the Israelites to become a temple-worthy people (i.e., worthy of the temple in their midst and of the land itself as a kind of temple) and to partake of Yahweh's holiness (Atonement). Third, the largest law code, the Deuteronomic Code (Deuteronomy 12–26), reiterates the Lord's covenant expectations for the Israelites in the context of their exclusive relationship with him and their imminent inheritance of the land of promise. The Israelites' relationship with the land will be unique, and the Deuteronomic Code's statutes have the long-range view of preparing and enabling the Israelites to maintain their inheritance of the land. Taken together, the three law codes articulate Yahweh's purpose for the children of Israel: to

3. Matthew 5:17–19; JST Matthew 5:21; JST Luke 16:20; Luke 24:44; Alma 25:15; 30:3; 34:13; 2 Nephi 25:24–30; 3 Nephi 1:25; 9:17; 12:17–18, 46; 15:5; Ether 12:11; Doctrine and Covenants 74:1–7; compare Romans 8:4; 13:8–10; Galatians 5:14; 6:2; James 2:8.

4. Second Corinthians 3:11–14; 2 Nephi 25:27; 3 Nephi 9:20–21; 12:47; Doctrine and Covenants 22:1–4; 76:4–5.

"purify unto himself a peculiar people" (Titus 2:14) who would become and remain "partakers of his holiness" (Hebrews 12:10).

TORAH: THE LEGAL BACKDROP FOR THE THREE LAW CODES

When one encounters the word *law* in the King James Version of the Bible (KJV), the underlying term in the Hebrew Bible is almost always *tôrâ*. Formed from the verbal root *yry*/*yrh* (III) meaning "instruct, teach"[5] (originally from the idea of "stretching out the finger, or the hand, to point out a route"),[6] the noun *tôrâ*, more precisely than "law," denotes "direction, [or] instruction."[7]

The Hebrew word *tôrâ* almost certainly represents a cognate of the Akkadian *têrtu*(*m*) "instruction," "commission," "directive," "omen," "liver" (of an animal)[8] from the verb *wâru*(*m*) = "instruct, govern,"[9] although it is not clear whether *tôrâ* was appropriated from Akkadian as a loanword, as some who argue for a late date of the Pentateuch often assume. *Tôrâ* seems, rather, to have been formed in accordance with the normal patterns for Hebrew noun formation. Nevertheless, the overlap between "instruction" and "direction"/"directive" in the semantic ranges of *tôrâ* and *têrtu*(*m*) is clear, which is to be expected if "a great deal of continuity

5. Ludwig Koehler and Walter Baumgartner, *The Hebrew and Aramaic Lexicon of the Old Testament* (Leiden, Netherlands: Brill, 2001), 436–37 (hereafter, *HALOT*).

6. *HALOT*, 1710.

7. *HALOT*, 1710–11. This general sense of *tôrâ* ("law") as "instruction" is evident in Lehi's fatherly paranesis to Jacob, whose days were to be spent as a priest (2 Nephi 5:26; Jacob 1:18) in the "service of [his] God" (2 Nephi 2:3) in the then-future Nephite temple—and thus whose responsibility it would be to "instruct" the Nephites (2 Nephi 2:7, 13). On the priestly responsibility to "instruct" in ancient Israel, see 2 Kings 12:3; Ezekiel 44:23; 2 Chronicles 15:3.

8. Jeremy Black, Andrew George, and Nicolas Postgate, eds., *A Concise Dictionary of Akkadian*, Arbeiten und Untersuchungen zur Keilschriftkunde 5 (Wiesbaden, Germany: Harrassowitz, 2000), 405 (hereafter, *CDA*).

9. *CDA*, 435.

exists between biblical and cuneiform law."[10] As Hebrew scholar Hector Avalos notes, other *tôrâ*-related Hebrew legal terms—for example, *ḥōq* ("statute," "decree"), *miṣwâ* ("commandment," "precept"), *mišpaṭ* ("judgment," "justice"), and *ṣĕdāqâ* ("righteousness," "justice")—"apply to rules of conduct said to be prescribed by God (Exodus 18:16), kings (1 Kings 2:43), Canaanites (Leviticus 18:3), or even unjust judges."[11]

Although often referring to "direction" or "instruction" in general, *tôrâ* came to have an almost overriding technical reference to the body of legal material ascribed to Moses, with the Pentateuch standing at the head of the biblical corpus (Genesis, Exodus, Leviticus, Numbers, and Deuteronomy). The phrase "law of Moses"—*tôrat mōšeh*—was already in use before the time of the Babylonian exile, as evidenced by five passages widely ascribed to the editorship or authorship of the Deuteronomistic Historian (Joshua 8:31–32; 23:6; 1 Kings 2:3; 2 Kings 14:6; 23:25). This expression remains a feature of postexilic Jewish discourse (Ezra 3:2; 7:6; Daniel 9:11–13; Malachi 4:4; 2 Chronicles 23:18; 30:16). The phrase "law of the Lord" (*tôrat yhwh*) came to have a synonymous technical reference to the same body of material.[12]

Even as a technical expression, we must allow for some uncertainty and ambiguity in the phrase "law of Moses." As Douglas H. Parker and Ze'ev W. Falk have stated, "A narrow definition would confine the Law of Moses to a body of prohibitions and commands set forth in separate, unrelated literary units within the first five books of the Bible."[13] And yet, as they note, "this view makes it difficult to speak of 'biblical law,' since these provisions are not drawn together as a unity by the Torah itself."[14]

10. See, for example, Bruce Wells, "The Covenant Code and Near Eastern Legal Traditions: A Response to David P. Wright," *Maarav* 13, no. 1 (2006): 118.

11. Hector Avalos," Legal and Social Institutions in Canaan and Ancient Israel," in *Civilizations of the Ancient Near East*, ed. Jack M. Sasson (Peabody, MA: Hendrickson, 1995), 617.

12. See, for example, 2 Kings 10:31; Psalm 1:2; Ezra 7:10; Nehemiah 9:3; 1 Chronicles 16:40; 22:12; 2 Chronicles 12:1; 17:9; 31:3–4, 14; 35:26. Compare Amos 2:4; Isaiah 30:9; Psalms 1:2; 19:7; 119:1.

13. Douglas H. Parker and Ze'ev W. Falk, "Law of Moses," in *Encyclopedia of Mormonism*, ed. Daniel H. Ludlow (New York: Macmillan, 1992), 2:811.

14. Parker and Falk, "Law of Moses," 2:811.

Moreover, the content of the Pentateuch and its law codes changed over time. Thus we cannot say with any exactness what constituted an original text. Despite an overabundance of source critical studies from the Graf-Wellhausen Documentary Hypothesis[15] in the nineteenth century to the present, we find ourselves none the nearer to an original text or confirmation of its presumed sources (unless we countenance some of the restorative aspects of Joseph Smith's inspired revision). Without earlier witnesses to the Pentateuchal texts (and its law codes), we are left to make do with the text and textual witnesses as we have them.

Our oldest witnesses of the Pentateuch and its "law codes" come from the Hellenistic period (although it surely did exist as authoritative scripture long before that time). Those who translated sacred biblical texts from Hebrew into Greek—a collection that eventually came to be known as the Septuagint (LXX)—rendered Hebrew *tôrâ* into Greek with the term *nomos* ("custom"). At least to some degree, the ancient Israelite idea of *tôrâ* accumulated the Hellenistic cultural baggage of *nomos*.

Similarly, centuries later when these texts were translated into Latin by Jerome (the Vulgate) and others (e.g., the earlier Old Latin [*Vetus Latina*]), *nomos* was translated using the word *lex* (genitive, *legis*). Thus, the original Israelite idea of *tôrâ* in its Hellenistic representation as *nomos* was further suffused with Roman legal connotations as *lex* ("law," legal "enactment," "motion," "bill").[16] All these scriptural terms have been traditionally translated into English as "law," which derives from Old English *lagu* (from Old Norse *lag*) but which is also a cognate with the word *lay*—that is, "law" is something that is "laid down or fixed" (compare Alma 30:23; Helaman

15. See Karl Heinrich Graf, *Die geschichtlichen Bücher des Alten Testaments: Zwei historisch-kritische Untersuchungen* (Leipzig: Weigel, 1866); Karl Heinrich Graf, "Die sogenannte Grundschrift des Pentateuchs," *Archiv für wissenschaftlich Erforschung des Alten Testaments* 1 (1869): 466–77 (repr. *Theologische Studien und Kritiken* 45 [1872]: 287–303); Julius Wellhausen, *Prolegomena to the History of Ancient Israel* (Edinburgh: Black, 1885).

16. Originally, "a set form of words," *lex* (*legis*) also came to denote "a proposition made by a magistrate to the people." See J. R. Marchant and Joseph F. Charles, *Cassell's Latin Dictionary* (London: Cassell, 1897), 316.

11:22).[17] Biblical scholar Dennis T. Olson has observed that this lexical layering has "led to Christian misunderstandings that the Torah meant legalism."[18]

It should be remembered that much of the Torah (that is, the Pentateuch) is actually narrative rather than legal material. The narrative material often provides context within which to understand the legal material. The "law codes" and other legal materials themselves exhibit two main forms: apodictic and casuistic. The former term has been adapted from the Greek verb *apodeiknunai* and its cognate adjective *apodeiktos* ("demonstrable," that is, true or applicable under all conditions). The latter derives from the Latin word *casus* ("fall") and refers to "case law."

Apodictic laws are most often familiar to readers of the King James Version of the Bible in the form of "thou shalt" or "ye shall" commandments, reflecting the deontic modality of the verbs (that is, verbs having the force of "you must . . .") in the underlying Hebrew text. There are some exceptions to this tendency: for example, "And he that curseth his father, or his mother, shall surely be put to death" (Exodus 21:17). Another example is the commandment to "remember the Sabbath day, to keep it holy," which employs a Hebrew infinitive absolute with imperative force: *zākôr*—"remember" (Exodus 20:8). Apodictic laws are moreover characterized by their unconditionality—they prescribe what is to be done in all situations. Casuistic laws or statutes, on the other hand, are commandments that govern behavior on a case-by-case basis. These statutes are worded as conditional sentences and often begin with the word "if." Casuistic and apodictic laws primarily constitute the material found within the three law codes.

---

17. Alma 30:23: "Now the high priest's name was Giddonah. And Korihor said unto him: Because I do not teach the foolish traditions of your fathers, and because I do not teach this people to bind themselves down under the foolish ordinances and performances *which are laid down by ancient priests*, to usurp power and authority over them, to keep them in ignorance, that they may not lift up their heads, but be brought down according to thy words"; Helaman 11:22: "And also they had peace in the seventy and eighth year, save it were a few contentions concerning the points of doctrine which had been laid down by the prophets."
18. Dennis T. Olsen, "Torah," in *Dictionary of Ethics and Scripture*, ed. Joel B. Green (Grand Rapids, MI: Baker, 2011), 788.

"I WILL GIVE JUDGMENT[S] TO HIM IN WRITING": THE COVENANT CODE OR BOOK OF THE COVENANT (EXODUS 20:22–23:33)

The legislative material in Exodus begins with Yahweh's giving of the Ten Commandments, or Decalogue, to Moses at Mount Sinai (Exodus 20:1–17). The first four commandments define and protect the Israelites' covenant relationship with Yahweh (Exodus 20:1–11). These four commandments can be distilled down to what Jesus described as "the first and great commandment" (that is, to "love the Lord thy God"; Matthew 22:37–38, citing Deuteronomy 6:5). In other words, these first four commandments pertain to the Israelites' relationship with God. The next six commandments pertain to their inner relationships within the covenant (Exodus 20:12–17). These six commandments may be thought of as Jesus's second great commandment (that is, loving those around us; Matthew 22:39, citing Leviticus 19:8). The location of the Decalogue at the head of the three law codes that follow in the Pentateuch—Deuteronomy 5, in fact, recapitulates it ahead of the Deuteronomic legislation—helps us appreciate and understand the social/relational nature of all the legislation that follows.

The first major law code in the Pentateuch, immediately after the giving of the Decalogue, is the Covenant Code (Exodus 20:22–23:33), for which the Decalogue serves as a kind of prologue. The description of the legislation as the Covenant Code is appropriate, given its framing as a "covenant" (Hebrew *bĕrît*) on both ends. The opening frame attaches the promise to covenant obedience: "*if ye will obey* [truly hear] my voice *indeed*, and keep *my covenant* [*bĕrîtî*], then ye shall be a *peculiar treasure* [*sĕgullâ* = a marked or sealed possession][19] unto me above all people" (Exodus 19:5; see further below). Similarly, the Covenant Code legislation is punctuated with an enumeration of the covenant promises predicated upon covenant

19. Compare Akkadian *sikiltu(m)* = "acquisition(s), (hoarded) property" (see CDA, 322) and *sakālu(m)* = "to acquire, hoard" (i.e., treasure up); "acquire possessions" (CDA, 312). Compare also Ugaritic *sglt* = "treasure; property." A. Murtonen, *Hebrew in Its West Semitic Setting, Part 1: A Comparative Lexicon* (Leiden, Netherlands: Brill, 1990), 296.

obedience, Moses's writing "all the words of the Lord" (Exodus 24:4) in the "book of the covenant" (24:7), and Moses's ratifying the covenant by applying "the blood of the covenant" to the people (24:8; compare Mosiah 4:2).[20]

Biblical scholars have frequently compared the Covenant Code to other law codes in the ancient Near East, especially the Code of Hammurabi. Although they possess similar content, direct textual dependency remains unclear at best.[21] In any case, the content of the Covenant Code is framed as a direct revelation from God to which the people would bind themselves by covenant: "And the Lord said unto Moses, Thus thou shalt say unto the children of Israel, Ye have seen that *I have talked with you from heaven*" (Exodus 20:22; compare 20:18–22); "And Moses came and told the people all *the words of the* Lord, *and all the judgments*: and all the people answered *with one voice*, and said, *All the words which the* Lord *hath said* will we do" (Exodus 24:3; compare 24:4, 7–8; emphasis added).[22] The dispensing of this covenant in the wilderness and its ratification mark the foundation of Israel as a community. The following constitute some

20. This has led many scholars to suggest that the foregoing legislation constitutes the book of the covenant mentioned in Exodus 24:7: "And he took the book of the covenant, and read in the audience of the people: and they said, All that the Lord hath said will we do, and be obedient." In other words, the Book of the Covenant is the Covenant code. Perhaps a more important point is that here the text insists that Moses *wrote*. Thus, it may be of this "Book of the Covenant" or "Covenant Code" that the Lord prophesied to Joseph in Egypt (as preserved on the brass plates, mentioned by Lehi, and recorded by Nephi): "I will raise up a Moses; and I will give power unto him in a rod; and I will give judgment [cf. Hebrew *mišpaṭ*] unto him in writing" (2 Nephi 3:17; compare Moses 1; emphasis mine). The "Covenant Code" largely consists of the "judgments" (*ham-mišpāṭîm*)—apodictic and casuistic laws—which are both civil and religious in character.

21. See, for example, Wells, "Covenant Code," 85–188; Bruce Wells, "Review of D. P. Wright, Inventing God's Law: How the Covenant Code of the Bible Used and Revised the Laws of Hammurabi," *Journal of Religion* 90 (2010): 558–60; contrary to David P. Wright, "The Laws of Hammurabi as a Source for the Covenant Collection (Exodus 20:23–23:19)," *Maarav* (2003): 11–87; David P. Wright, *Inventing God's Law: How the Covenant Code of the Bible Used and Revised the Laws of Hammurabi* (New York: Oxford University Press, 2009).

22. In the Book of Mormon, covenant renewals were often made with "one voice." See, for example, Mosiah 4:2; 5:2; Alma 43:49; 3 Nephi 4:30; 3 Nephi 20:9.

laws pertaining to Israelite sociality and property that helped accomplish this ideal. The blessings for obedience to the Covenant Code are also adumbrated.

LAWS GOVERNING ISRAELITE "SOCIALITY" (EXODUS 22:15–23:9)

Though it is the shortest of the three law codes, and presumably the earliest, the Covenant Code sets up the primary focus of the law given to the Israelites—namely, the social standards that they were to observe in relation to God and each other. This legislation again forbids worshipping or tolerating other gods (Exodus 22:19). It strictly forbids mistreatment of society's weakest members, exemplified here by the foreign migrant ("stranger"), the widow, the orphan, and the poor (Exodus 22:19–26; 23:6; see further below). The reminder that the Israelites had themselves lived as marginalized, enslaved, and displaced "strangers" in Egypt helped them to recognize their obligation to care for their society's weakest members and to do so with sympathy ("thou shalt not oppress a stranger: for ye know the heart of a stranger, seeing ye were strangers in the land of Egypt," Exodus 23:9; compare 22:1). The Israelites had collectively been "the stranger," "the widow," and "the orphan" (as it were) in times past, and they could not become Yahweh's "special possession" or "sealed people"[23] if they treated others unethically and abused the weakest among them.

The Joseph Smith Translation makes some noteworthy alterations to the text here. Exodus 22:18 (MT 22:17) mandates, "Thou shalt not suffer a witch [Hebrew *mĕkaššēpâ*][24] to live." The JST renders this text: "Thou shalt not suffer *a murderer* to live" (JST Exodus 22:18; emphasis added). This alteration reflects the notion, consistent elsewhere in the Mosaic legislation, that murder constitutes a capital crime. Apparently, witchcraft—though a grievous sin—is conceivably forgivable (compare Deuteronomy 18:10–12).

23. Hugh W. Nibley, "On the Sacred and the Symbolic," in *Temples of the Ancient World*, ed. Donald W. Parry (Salt Lake City: Deseret Book and Foundation for Ancient Research and Mormon Studies, 1994), 559.

24. Compare Akkadian *kišpu* = "witchcraft."

The King James Version of Exodus 22:28 (MT 22:27) reads, "Thou shalt not revile the gods, nor curse the ruler of thy people." The JST renders this statute "Thou shalt not revile *against God*, nor curse the ruler of thy people" (JST Exodus 22:28; emphasis added). The Mosaic legislation places considerable emphasis on the exclusivity of worshipping Yahweh and Yahweh alone. Here most other English translations, like the JST, render Hebrew *ʾĕlōhîm* in the singular, as "God" rather than plural "gods" (the KJV follows the Greek Septuagint [LXX], which renders *ʾĕlōhîm* plural: *theous*). Here, too, the social or relational dimension of the Covenant Code is evident: this statute requires recognition and respect for God's authority (rather than reviling him) from every Israelite. It also stipulated respect for authority within the community, because rejection of communal religious and political authority would have imperiled the Israelites' existence. Today, Latter-day Saints readily recognize the need to avoid taking the name of God in vain (compare Doctrine and Covenants 63:61) and any blasphemy in general, but some are considerably less reticent when it comes to speaking evil of or "lift[ing] up the heal against [the Lord's] anointed" (Doctrine and Covenants 121:16).[25]

Lastly, Exodus 23:3 stipulates, "Neither shalt thou countenance [favor] a poor man in his cause." The JST rendering of the statute in Exodus 23:3 reads, "Neither shalt thou countenance a *wicked* man in his cause" (emphasis added). While on one hand, it might seem appropriate to legislate impartiality in all judicial cases, this juxtaposition of "poor" in Exodus 23:3 with "poor" in Exodus 23:6 that forbids "wrest[ing] the judgment [*mišpaṭ*, or justice] of thy poor in his cause" seems strange. The Mosaic legislation elsewhere—particularly in the Deuteronomic Code (see below)—in fact, provides certain protections and perhaps even some privileges to the poor. The JST alteration of "poor" to "wicked" here accords with both Deuteronomy and the Zion theology articulated in JST Genesis (Moses 7:18). Indeed, the impartiality mandated for the Israelites in Exodus 23:1–2, 6 should produce the ethic of fairness and equality necessary for the establishment of a "Zion" people (Moses 7:18).

---

25. For more on this subject, see Dallin H. Oaks, "Criticism," *Ensign*, February 1987, 68–70.

PERSONAL INJURY STATUTES AND LAWS ON COMPENSATING FOR PROPERTY DAMAGE AND LOSS (EXODUS 21:12–22:14)

That these "judgments" establish (or at least intend) a higher ethic for the Israelites is further evident in the details of the casuistic laws in Exodus 21:12–32, which govern personal injuries and reparations. Deliberate murder constituted an unambiguous capital offense (Exodus 21:12, 14), but the legislation made provision for those who had unintentionally killed (Exodus 21:13), holding divine justice and mercy in balance (Alma 34:10–26). These places of refuge are described in greater detail in Numbers and in the Deuteronomic Code. Violence and imprecatory oaths against one's parents, as well as kidnapping, also amounted to capital offenses (Exodus 21:15–17). This legislation thus taught the ancient Israelites to value the lives of those around them as they would their very own.

Higher valuation of human life is evident in the legislation that immediately follows in Exodus 21:22–25, wherein we find the first articulation of the so-called *lex talionis*. Biblical scholar Pamela Barmash suggests that the "Lex talionis . . . expresses a principle of legal symmetry, of repaying in kind."[26] In other words, "those guilty of physical assault are made to suffer the exact same harm they inflicted on others. This is in sharp contrast to fines, a fixed amount to be paid in particular circumstances. In the case of killing a person, *lex talionis* means the killer is killed. The act of the punishment must be similar to the offense in aspects in which the original act was wrong."[27]

For his part, Jesus later attempted to move his disciples, all of Israel, and indeed the entire world back to a "more excellent"[28] standard in which we commit all personal vengeance or justice into his hands: "Ye have heard that it hath been said, An eye for an eye, and a tooth for a tooth: But I say

26. Pamela Barmash, *Homicide in the Biblical World* (Cambridge: Cambridge University Press, 2005), 157–58. Nephite law seemed to operate on this principle. Compare, for example, Alma 1:1–19 [see especially 1:17–18]; 11:2; 30:10. There are perhaps additional echoes of the eternal law of restoration as formulated by Alma to his son Corianton, who struggled with the idea of divine justice (see especially Alma 41:12–15).

27. Barmash, *Homicide in the Biblical World*, 158.

28. Compare 1 Corinthians 12:31; Ether 12:11; Hebrews 8:6.

unto you, That ye resist not evil: but whosoever shall smite thee on thy right cheek, turn to him the other also. And if any man will sue thee at the law, and take away thy coat, let him have thy cloak also. And whosoever shall compel thee to go a mile, go with him twain" (Matthew 5:38–40).[29] Perhaps Jesus did not so much intend to institute a new ethic as to restore the true ethic underlying the Mosaic legislation and the true *telos* to which that legislation had been given: that "they [may] be called the children of God"; "that ye may be the children of your Father" (Matthew 5:9, 45; compare Exodus 19:5–6; 22:31).

In the context of the Exodus, the Israelites' journey through the wilderness and the establishment of a covenant people, the laws or statutes in Exodus 21:33–23:9 can be broadly viewed as rules necessary to holding a community together—that is, establishing a community ethos. These rules helped the Israelites to maintain and protect personal relationships. The establishment of basic rules governing property and the loss or damage of property helped hold the Israelites together as a community. The casuistic statutes of Exodus 21:33–22:14 ensured the forthcoming of some form of restitution (*yĕšallēm*, "he shall restore/make restitution")[30] when property was lost or damaged. In other words, restitution ensured the *šālôm*—peace, integrity—of the community.

COVENANT RECIPROCITY: BLESSINGS FOR COVENANT OBEDIENCE (EXODUS 23:20–33)

The Covenant Code closes with an enumeration of blessings (Exodus 23:20–33). To receive these blessings, the Israelites must obey the "Angel" (*malʾāk*) that he is sending before the Israelites "to keep [them] in the way" (or, on the covenant path)[31] and "to bring [them] into the place which [Yahweh has] prepared" (Exodus 23:20). Disobedience will result in

29. The covenant conduct of the Anti-Nephi-Lehies constitutes one of best recorded examples of living a principle that Jesus later taught (Alma 24:17–19).

30. Saul M. Olyan, "Hăšālôm: Some Literary Considerations of 2 Kings 9," *Catholic Biblical Quarterly* 46 (1984) 661, asserts that the Piel form of *šlm* "describes a process only necessary when the state of *šālôm* ["peace"] is absent."

31. Compare the phrase "to keep them in the right way," as used in Moroni 6:4.

catastrophe, the Lord asserts, because "my name is in him [*šĕmî bĕqirbô*]"—that is, "he has my authority."[32]

The blessings for covenant obedience enumerated here include the promise to the Israelites that the Lord himself "be an enemy unto thine enemies, and an adversary unto thine adversaries" (Exodus 23:22). The Angel will destroy the Israelites' Canaanite adversaries, who will flee before the Israelites and the hornets that the Lord will send (23:23, 27–30); the Lord will bless the Israelites with the blessings of safe food and water, absence of disease and illness, fertility, healthy birth, and long life (23:25–26); and the Israelites will have expansive borders (23:31).

However, all of it is predicated on obedience or "hearing" (Exodus 23:21–22), which should cause us to recall what is taught in Doctrine and Covenants 130:20–21: "There is a law, irrevocably decreed in heaven before the foundations of this world, upon which all blessings are predicated—and when we obtain any blessing from God, it is by obedience to that law upon which it is predicated." In Doctrine and Covenants 82:10, the Lord formulates it thus: "I, the Lord, am bound when ye do what I say; but when ye do not what I say, ye have no promise." These two statements are perhaps the clearest and most concise articulations of the principle of covenant obedience in the scriptures, and they summarize the point of Exodus 23:20–33. All covenant blessings are predicated upon obedience: "If ye will obey my voice indeed, and keep my covenant [the Covenant Code], then ye shall be [become] a peculiar treasure [*ʿam sĕgullâ*] unto me above all people: for all the earth is mine" (Exodus 19:5; compare 22:31). By divine design, the Israelites' sociality was to be one characterized by unity or *oneness* (see also Psalm 133:1), oneness with Yahweh and with each other—to be sealed "his." The Holiness Code provided further instruction that enabled that "at-one-ment."

32. The identity of this theophanic "Angel"—in Exodus 23:20, he is called "my Angel" (*malʾākî*)—has elicited no small amount of discussion and speculation. The description *malʾākî* draws our attention forward to the book of Malachi ("my angel/messenger") and the Lord's promise that he would again send "my messenger" (*malʾākî*) to "prepare the way before me: and the Lord, whom ye seek, shall suddenly come to his temple, even the messenger of the covenant" (Malachi 3:1). That promise identifies "the Lord" himself as "the messenger of the covenant." Perhaps it is the same here: the Angel is the Lord himself.

"SPEAK UNTO AARON . . . THIS IS THE THING WHICH THE LORD HATH COMMANDED": THE HOLINESS CODE (LEVITICUS 17–26)

Yahweh sought not only an ethically pure but also a ritually pure, ultimately sanctified people. Accordingly, the second large law code in the Pentateuch is the Holiness Code, so called by biblical scholars since 1877, when A. Klostermann identified Leviticus 17–26 as a distinct unit within the Pentateuch, denominating it the *Heiligkeitsgesetz* (Holiness Code).[33] As biblical scholar Peter R. Ackroyd puts it, "Much of the material of the section is concerned with the problem of the holiness, the fitness in both cultic and ethical and ways, of the people before their God."[34] Moreover, the Holiness Code can be viewed as the "instruction" (*tôrâ*)—or that part of the law of Moses that has been given a specific priestly orientation for the priests to instruct or teach the Israelites how to become holy like Yahweh himself.

We may surmise that if, as Exodus 19:6 indicates, Yahweh wished to have a "kingdom of priests [*mamleket kōhănîm*] and an holy nation [*gôy qādôš*]," one major reason the Holiness Code lays such stress on the ritual and ethical purity of priests (e.g., Leviticus 21) is that such priestly holiness would necessarily serve as a kind of beachhead for the broader hallowing (or sanctification) of the entire community. The priest was to be a representation of Yahweh's "holiness" before the people (compare "angels"). The high priest was to be a representation of Yahweh himself—the "Holy One of Israel" (*qĕdôš yiśrāʾēl*).

In fact, an important term for understanding Leviticus and its legislation generally is the Semitic/Hebrew root *qdš*, adjectival forms of which are often translated as "holy." The basic sense of *qdš* is usually thought

33. A. Klostermann, "Beiträge zur Entstehungsgeschichte des Pentateuchs," *Zeitschrift für lutherische Theologie und Kirche* 33 (1877): 401–45; A. Klostermann, *Der Pentateuch: Beiträge zu seinem Verständnis und seiner Entstehungsgeschichte* (Leipzig: Deichert, 1893), 368–418.

34. Peter R. Ackroyd, *Exile and Restoration: A Study of Hebrew Thought of the Sixth Century B.C.*, Old Testament Library (Louisville: Westminster/John Knox, 1968), 87.

to be "set apart"[35] but may, in fact, have more specific reference to "that which belongs to the sphere of God's being or activity."[36] The designation of the Holiness Code for Leviticus 17–26 is apt because, as Coogan notes, cognate forms of *qdš* "occur more than twice as many times in the ten chapters of the Holiness Code as in the other seventeen chapters of the book of Leviticus."[37]

For the Israelites, "holiness"—the state of being *qdš*—is extrinsic rather than intrinsic because it has its ultimate source in Yahweh. Yahweh commanded all of the Israelites to become "holy," beginning with the priests. Significantly, then, the Holiness Code is framed as instruction to Aaron and his sons—that is, as priestly instruction (*tôrâ*) to the Israelites: "And the Lord spake unto Moses, saying, Speak unto Aaron, and unto his sons, and unto all the children of Israel, and say unto them; This is the thing which the Lord hath commanded" (Leviticus 17:1–2). The role of Aaron as the "spokesman" provided for Moses the prophet to the Israelites (Exodus 4:16; 2 Nephi 3:17–18) continues in Aaron's priesthood descendants who speak to the Israelites on the Lord's and the prophets' behalf (their authority is subordinate to the latter).

The closing frame reasserts the origin and authority of the foregoing "statutes and judgments": "These are the statutes and judgments and laws, which the Lord made between him and the children of Israel in mount Sinai by the hand of Moses" (Leviticus 26:46). This priestly formulation of "the statutes and judgments and laws" aims to prepare the Israelites to

35. See *HALOT*, p. 1072, where it is noted that *qdš* as "an original verb . . . can only with difficulty be traced back to a root קד [*qd*]; if this is the case, the basic meaning of קדש would be 'to set apart.'"

36. Philip Peter Jensen, *Graded Holiness: A Key to the Priestly Conception of the World* (Sheffield, UK: JSOT Press, 1992), 48. David J. A. Clines, "The Holy and the Clean: Category Confusion in Semitic?" (paper presented at the Society for Biblical Literature annual meeting in Atlanta on Monday, November 23, 2015), points out that in 2 Samuel 11:4 *qdš* has the definite sense of "purify" (rather than "sanctify") and describes Bathsheba's ritual purification (not sanctification). He also argues that in other Semitic contexts *qdš* has the sense, contra expectation, of "make clean, purify."

37. Michael D. Coogan, *The Old Testament: A Historical and Literary Introduction to the Hebrew Scriptures* (Oxford: Oxford University Press, 2011), 151.

become worthy of the land they will be inheriting—temple worthy, one might say—and to partake of Yahweh's holiness. Since Yahweh's holiness could not be compromised, this would require the Israelites and its priests to become not only ethically pure but *ritually* pure as well.

MAKING ATONEMENT: THE SANCTIFYING CHARACTER OF BLOOD (LEVITICUS 17)

The first part of the Holiness Code emphasizes the sanctifying character of blood (compare Moses 6:60). In fact, Leviticus 17:10–14 helps us to understand why blood is so closely associated with covenant and holiness:[38]

> And whatsoever man there be of the house of Israel, or of the strangers that sojourn among you, that eateth any manner of blood; I will even set my face against that soul that eateth blood, and will cut him off from among his people.
>
> For *the life of the flesh is in the blood: and I have given it to you upon the altar to make an atonement for your souls: for it is the blood that maketh an atonement for the soul.*
>
> Therefore I said unto the children of Israel, No soul of you shall eat blood, neither shall any stranger that sojourneth among you eat blood.
>
> And whatsoever man there be of the children of Israel, or of the strangers that sojourn among you, which hunteth and catcheth any beast or fowl that may be eaten; he shall even pour out the blood thereof, and cover it with dust.
>
> For it is the life of all flesh; the blood of it is for the life thereof: therefore I said unto the children of Israel, Ye shall eat the blood of no manner of flesh: *for the life of all flesh is the blood thereof*: whosoever eateth it shall be cut off. (Leviticus 17:10–14)

In the ancient world, including in ancient Israel, blood was recognized as the seat of life (compare Genesis 9:4–5; Deuteronomy 12:23; John 6:53–54). Blood was thus sacred and not to be consumed. To this day, kosher

38. The sacred character of blood is especially evident in Moroni's description of the covenant that subsumes all other covenants and in the role of Christ's blood in that effectuation of that covenant (Moroni 10:32–33).

meat in Judaism (via *shechitah*) and halal meat in Islam must be from animals slaughtered in the appropriate way—that is, their throats must be cut and their blood, drained. Even in early Christianity, when Gentile converts were exempted from the requirements of the law of Moses, the prohibition against eating meat with blood in it remained (Acts 15:20, 29; 21:25).

Here, however, we see the additional typology of atoning blood: that Yahweh had given blood to "make an atonement [*yěkappēr*] for the soul." In other words, the sacralizing character of blood of a living thing designated as *qdš*[39] enabled it to effect *kpr*, or "atonement." The apparent root meaning of *kpr* is to "rub"[40] and hence, as scholar and theologian Michael L. Brown summarizes it, "to rub off" and "to efface," "wipe way," but also "to rub on" (or wipe on, smear on) and thus "to cover."[41] Anthropologist and Leviticus scholar Mary Douglas suggests that *kpr* came to mean "cover"[42] in the sense of "recover, cover again, to repair a hole, cure a sickness, mend a rift, make good a torn or broken covering."[43] The Piel stem of the root *kpr* can take on the sense of reintegrating or making intact something that

---

39. If Yahweh, the Holy One of Israel, is the source of holiness (*qdš*), the sacrificial system, with its animals designated as *qdš*, and the blood of those sacrifices must ultimately point to him and the giving of his own blood (compare Alma 34:10–14). The author of Hebrews, commenting on the meaning of the Mosaic sacrificial system, points out that apart from Jesus's sacrifice, "it is not possible that the blood of bulls and of goats should take away sins" (Hebrews 10:4). Regarding the priests who offered the sacrifices, the same author avers, "And every priest standeth daily ministering and offering oftentimes the same sacrifices, which can never take away sins" (10:11).

40. Benno Landsberger, *The Date Palm and Its By-Products according to the Cuneiform Sources* (Graz, Austria: Weidner, 1967), 32; Jacob Milgrom, *Leviticus 1–16: A New Translation with Introduction and Commentary* (New York: Doubleday, 1991), 1079–84 (especially 1080).

41. Michael L. Brown, "*Kippēr* and Atonement in the Book of Isaiah," in *Ki Baruch Hu: Ancient Near Eastern, Biblical, and Judaic Studies in Honor of Baruch A. Levine*, ed. Robert Chazan, William W. Hallo, and Lawrence H. Schiffman (Winona Lake, IN: Eisenbrauns: 1999), 192–93.

42. See, especially, Mary Douglas, "Atonement in Leviticus," *Jewish Studies Quarterly* 1, no. 2 (1993): 109–30.

43. Margaret Barker, "Atonement: The Rite of Healing," http://www.marquette.edu/maqom/Atonement.pdf, 8.

has been disintegrated, pierced, broken, torn, and so forth. Thus, the *kpr* process was not only *cleansing*, but *reparative* and *rehabilitative*. As theologian and biblical scholar Margaret Barker further notes, "Atonement does not mean covering a sin so as to hide it from the sight of God; it means making good an outer layer which has rotted or been pierced."[44]

This conceptual framework helps us appreciate the Atonement implications of Jesus's paradoxical teaching: "Except ye eat the flesh of the Son of man, and drink his blood, ye have no life in you. Whoso eateth my flesh, and drinketh my blood, hath eternal life; and I will raise him up at the last day" (John 6:53–54). It also helps us understand Jesus's declaration about himself: "For God so loved the world, that he gave his only begotten Son, that whosoever believeth in him should not perish, but have everlasting life" (John 3:16). The blood that Yahweh himself "had given" to the Israelites by the will of God the Father and by his own will[45] "upon the altar to make an atonement" for their "atonement" was his own—the "blood of the covenant."[46] Jesus did this as both High Priest and sacrifice. Margaret Barker writes,

> When lesser offenses were *kpr*, the priest 'carried' the sin by virtue of eating the flesh of the animal whose life had effected the *kpr*. For the great *kpr*, the blood/life of the goat 'as the Lord' was a substitute for the blood/life of the high priest (also the Lord), who thus carried the sin of the people himself as he performed the act of *kpr* throughout the temple/creation. Thus, having collected the sins, he it was who was able to transfer them onto the goat who 'carried' them (*nś'*, Lev. 16.22) and he took them to the desert. The role of the high priest, the Lord, was to remove the damaging effect of

44. Barker, "Atonement," 8.
45. Jeffrey R. Holland, "Lord, I Believe," *Ensign*, May 2013, 94: "I know Jesus was His only perfect child, whose life was given lovingly by the will of both the Father and the Son for the redemption of all the rest of us who are not perfect."
46. See, for example, Exodus 24:8; Zechariah 9:11; Hebrews 10:20; 12:24; 13:20; Moroni 10:33.

> sin from the community and the creation, and thus to restore the bonds which held together the community and creation.[47]

Barker's description of the high priest's conceptual function within Israel's cult helps us to understand the importance of the purity of the high priests, the priests, and the people in general. Each in their own sphere was a representation of Yahweh himself: the high priest as Yahweh, the priests as his heavenly attendants/angels/messengers, and the Israelites themselves as his people/kin. They were all to become *qdš*—"holy," "belonging to the divine realm," "pure"—and to effect his "holiness" throughout the world/temple/creation (compare Jacob 5).

LAWS GOVERNING SEXUAL BEHAVIOR AND PRIESTLY HOLINESS (LEVITICUS 18–22:16)

The Israelites, as a covenant people, have always been composed of families. Perhaps nothing, then as now, threatens communal or family integrity and holiness as much as improper sexual relationships. Leviticus 18 contains apodictic injunctions against sexual relationships that would wreak havoc upon the Israelites' individual families and the community as a whole. The Lord had gathered the Israelites, as a people, in families. These sexual sins threatened then, as they do today, to undo family bonds—to scatter families from each other and from the Church.

This legislation strictly forbade sexual relationships between close relatives, by blood or by marriage (Leviticus 18:6–18); adultery (18:20); homosexuality (18:22);[48] and bestiality (18:23). The legislation also prohibited sexual relationships during a woman's menstrual period (18:19) and it also forbade so-called *MLK* offerings (often translated as "Molech" offerings)—that is, child sacrifices (18:21). The Lord declared the same penalty for the Israelites' failure to observe these commandments as he

---

47. Margaret Barker, *The Great High Priest: The Temple Roots of Christian Liturgy* (London: T&T Clark, 2003), 53.

48. It is frequently pointed out that Leviticus 18:22, strictly speaking, condemns only male homosexuality. However, this can probably be understood as a metonym for all homosexual relations; see especially Romans 1:26–27. First Corinthians 6:9 should also be understood as speaking metonymically regarding all homosexual relations.

had as for the Canaanites that had preceded them: "The land is defiled: therefore I do visit the iniquity thereof upon it, and the land itself vomiteth out her inhabitants; . . . ye shall therefore keep my statutes and my judgments, and shall not commit any of these abominations . . . that the land spue [spew] not you out also, when ye defile it, as it spued out the nations that were before you" (Leviticus 18:25–28). Improper sexual relationships constituted a formidable obstacle to the holiness that the Lord intended for the Israelites.

In Leviticus 19:2, Yahweh commands: "Ye shall be [become] holy: for I the LORD your God am holy." This commandment presupposes the human potential to ultimately become like divinity in the latter's defining characteristic: holiness (and all that holiness implies).[49] As noted, the high priest and the priests were representations of Yahweh and his holiness. Consequently, the Holiness Code contained numerous regulations governing priestly holiness. Priests were not allowed to become "defiled for the dead" (that is, to incur ritual/cultic impurity from dead bodies) except in the case of close relatives (Leviticus 21:1–4; for the Aaronic high priest the restrictions were even tighter, see 21:11). Priests were restricted in the way that they were allowed to mourn (21:5, 10). The high priest Caiaphas apparently violated Leviticus 21:10 when he tore his clothes during the illegal proceedings involving Jesus before his crucifixion (Mark 14:63; Matthew 26:65).[50]

---

49. This Holiness prescription was paraphrased by Jesus in the Sermon on the Mount, in Mathew 5:48, and again in another version of the sermon delivered at the temple in Bountiful when he reiterated this commandment following his own "perfection" (see especially Luke 13:32) at his resurrection, "Be ye therefore perfect, even as your Father which is in heaven is perfect," and again in 3 Nephi 12:48, "Therefore I would that ye should be perfect even as I, or your Father who is in heaven is perfect." Perhaps the best statement on holiness, perfection, the source of both in Yahweh, and on how all of this applies to us today comes from Moroni 10:33: "And again, if ye by the grace of God are perfect in Christ, and deny not his power, then are ye sanctified in Christ by the grace of God, through the shedding of the blood of Christ, which is in the covenant of the Father unto the remission of your sins, that ye become holy, without spot."

50. Compare D. Kelly Ogden and Andrew C. Skinner, *Verse by Verse: The Four Gospels* (Salt Lake City: Deseret Book, 2006), 615.

Like the sacrifices that they offered, priests had to be free of certain physical "blemishes" and impairments (Leviticus 21:18–21). Viewing this legislation christologically, the "unblemished" priest, like the "unblemished" sacrifice typifies Christ, who lived free of both physical and moral blemish—highlighting the sacred nature of their priestly service. Moreover, Leviticus 22:3–9 contains statutes for the maintenance of ceremonial purity. The legislation required that the Aaronic priests maintain ceremonial purity in order to officiate in the temple or sanctuary to avoid "bear[ing] sin and d[ying] therefore" (Leviticus 22:9)—all of this to the end that the priest and the high priest might maintain and partake of Yahweh's holiness (Leviticus 21:4, 6, 15, 22; 22:2).

Of the six verses in Leviticus to which the Prophet Joseph Smith made alterations, three are in the Holiness Code, all three in Leviticus 21–22. JST Leviticus 21:1 changes the prepositional phrase "for the dead" to "with the dead." This change may simply be an attempt at clarification: *for* could be mistakenly understood as "on behalf of"—the phrase "for the dead" in 1 Corinthians 15:29 had this sense, which came to have important connotations within Latter-day Saint discourse. *With*, on the other hand, more clearly conveys the instrumental idea of "by means of," which seems to be the sense of the Hebrew preposition in context. JST Leviticus 21:11 similarly clarifies that the phrase "go in unto any dead body" (KJV) means to "go in to touch any dead body." This clarification emphasizes that the priest must avoid physical contact with the corpse, not simply its presence. To the phrase "I the Lord do sanctify them" (Leviticus 22:9), JST Leviticus 22:9 adds the condition: "*if they profane not mine ordinances*, I the Lord will sanctify them." Here again we see the principle of divine reciprocity: the addition emphasizes that the blessing of sanctification is conditional upon obedience—a covenant principle as true then as it is now.

LAWS OF THE SABBATICAL YEAR, THE REDEMPTION OF PROPERTY, AND THE JUBILEE YEAR (LEVITICUS 25:1–22)

Like the Covenant Code (Exodus 23:10–12), the Holiness Code mandates a land Sabbath, or rest for the land. However, the latter extends the concept to include a jubilee year every seven Sabbath years (after forty-nine years): "And ye shall hallow the fiftieth year, and proclaim liberty throughout all the land unto all the inhabitants thereof: it shall be a jubilee unto you (Leviticus 25:10). The prophet Isaiah and Jesus himself alluded to the Jubilee year when they declared their missions "to proclaim liberty [preach deliverance] to the captives" and "proclaim [preach] the acceptable year of the Lord" (Isaiah 61:1–2; quoted by Jesus in Luke 4:18–19). This Jubilee was to be inaugurated on the Day of Atonement of the fiftieth year by "mak[ing] the trumpet sound throughout all your land" (Leviticus 25:9). Latter-day Saints will appreciate the latter image, a variation of which bestrides many of our temples, as a symbol of the proclamation or preaching of the gospel—true liberty—to every human being *on both sides of the veil* and of the Atonement of Jesus Christ having its full impact upon the human family (and creation).

The Lord commanded the Jubilee as a year of release or liberty for the land itself as well. The Jubilee statutes required that the Israelites only eat what the land produced on its own during this year (and to not cultivate the land per usual, Leviticus 25:12, 20–22). The legislation, moreover, envisioned a year in which all people could "return" to the land of their inheritance and family (25:10, 13)—another interesting concept for Latter-day Saints who perform work in the temple.

The institution of the Jubilee also allowed for the redemption of property that had been sold off on account of debt and poverty, and for a kinsman-redeemer (another christological type) to buy back the property. The legislation afforded the possibility of the land's redemption to the original owner, and during the jubilee year, the rights to the land reverted to that owner. The basis for all of the foregoing legislation is the truth that the land is ultimately Yahweh's (Leviticus 25:23; compare Psalm 24:1: "The earth is the Lord's, and the fulness thereof; the world, and they that dwell therein"). The Jubilee, like the rest of the foregoing legislation in the Holiness Code, aimed to prepare the Israelites, from its most important cultic functionaries (the priests and high priest) to its lowliest members, to become a ritually and ethically pure people—a people prepared to receive the realities of greater eternal blessings of which the Jubilee, atonement rites, and so forth served as emotive types and shadows. The Jubilee legislation regarding the Lord's land appropriately sets the stage for what Deuteronomy and the Deuteronomic Code required the Israelites to do in it.

"THESE ARE THE STATUTES AND JUDGMENTS WHICH YE SHALL . . . DO IN THE LAND": THE DEUTERONOMIC CODE (DEUTERONOMY 12–26)

The opening frame of the Deuteronomic Code contextualizes the legislation as: what Yahweh requires the Israelites to "do in the land"—that is, in the promised land—once they had entered and inherited it, and what Yahweh requires them to do to remain a distinct people in the land from the rest of the nations. "These are the statutes and judgments, *which ye shall observe to do in the land*, which the Lord God of thy fathers *giveth thee to possess it*, all the days that ye live upon the earth" (Deuteronomy 12:1). The content of Deuteronomy is a series of speeches given by Moses following the forty-year dwelling in the wilderness, after the less faithful generation had passed away and before he was taken to heaven. The instructions contained therein constitute Moses's passionate pleas to be obedient to the law of the Lord, become a holy people, and avoid death by claiming the blessings of eternity. The Deuteronomic code instructs the ancient Israelites on how to discern between false and true prophets and emphasizes obedience to the latter. Moreover, it provided rules for kingship and mandated the observance of "covenant economics."[51]

Aside from the legal designations ("statutes," "judgments") and the divine name, the key terms found in Deuteronomy here are *land/earth*: observance of this arrangement of statutes and judgments would enable the Israelites to not only inherit the promised land but also to stay worthy enough, even in the midst of idolatrous neighbors, to remain on the land.

The closing frame of the Deuteronomic Code invokes a variation of the opening formula "these are the statutes and judgments," creating an *inclusio*, or envelope figure around the entire body of legislation:

> This day the Lord thy God hath commanded thee to do these statutes and judgments: thou shalt therefore keep and do them with all thine heart, and with all thy soul.

51. For an extended treatment of this subject from a biblical ethics perspective, see Richard A. Horsley, *Covenant Economics: A Biblical Vision of Justice for All* (Louisville: Westminster/John Knox Press, 2009).

> Thou hast avouched the LORD this day to be thy God, and to walk in his ways, and to keep his statutes, and his commandments, and his judgments, and to *hearken unto his voice*:
>
> And the LORD hath avouched thee this day to be his peculiar people, as he hath promised thee, and that thou shouldest keep all his commandments.
>
> And to make thee high [most high] above all nations which he hath made, in praise, and in name, and in honour; and that thou mayest be an holy people unto the LORD thy God, as he hath spoken. (Deuteronomy 26:16–19; emphasis added)

This closing frame of the Deuteronomic Code, like the material prefacing the Covenant Code, stresses the importance of the Israelites becoming not only a "holy people" (compare the "Holiness Code") but a "peculiar people" (*ʿam sĕgullâ*)[52] (compare the Covenant Code, Exodus 19:6; 22:31). Latter-day Saints will further appreciate the term *sĕgullâ* as the term used by the Lord in his oft-cited words to Malachi: "in that day when I make up my jewels [*sĕgullâ* = "sealed possession"]; and I will spare them, as a man spareth his own son that serveth him."[53] The Lord intends to make all who are willing, to become his "sealed people"—or, he intends to "seal [us] his" (Mosiah 5:15).[54] The Deuteronomic Code's prohibitions against idolatry, war regulations, marriage laws and so forth were given to further Yahweh's purpose "in the land." This legislation additionally emphasized the Israelites' special relationship with "the land," of which the Jubilee, tithes and other cereal offerings, and so forth were signs or tokens.

---

52. This expression is found twice in the Deuteronomic Code (14:2; 26:18) and in one other instance in Deuteronomy (Deuteronomy 7:6) that describes the Israelites as the Lord's people.
53. Malachi 3:17; 3 Nephi 24:17; Doctrine and Covenants 60:4; 101:3.
54. See John Gee, "Book of Mormon Word Usage: 'Seal You His,'" *Insights* 22, no. 1 (2002): 4; see also Matthew L. Bowen, "Becoming Sons and Daughters at God's Right Hand: King Benjamin's Rhetorical Wordplay on His Own Name," *Journal of the Book of Mormon and Other Restoration Scripture* 21, no. 2 (2012): 2–13.

DISCERNING FALSE PROPHETS AND "A PROPHET . . . LIKE UNTO ME" (DEUTERONOMY 13; 18:15–22)

In addition to idolatry and foreign cults, perhaps nothing threatened communal integrity and survival as much as false prophets and illicit mantic activities. Deuteronomy 13:1–5 indicates that unauthorized mantic "prophet[s]" or "dreamer[s] of dreams" could, in fact, effect signs and wonders, not only for the purpose of pushing the Israelites away from Yahweh ("Let us go after other gods, which thou hast not known, and let us serve them," Deuteronomy 13:2 [MT 13:2]), but also, in the language of the Savior, to "deceive the very elect, who are the elect according to the covenant" (Joseph Smith—Matthew 1:22). The legislation helped the Israelites to understand that when this happens, "the LORD your God proveth you, to know whether ye love the Lord your God with all your heart and with all your soul" (Deuteronomy 13:3 [MT 13:4]). Mortal existence, after all, constitutes a "probationary state" and the Lord intends to "prove [us all] herewith, to see if [we] will do all things whatsoever the Lord their God shall command [us]" (Abraham 3:25) and whether we will "love God with all [our] might, mind, and strength" (Moroni 10:32, quoting Deuteronomy 6:5). The Israelites were to remain distinct from the nations by its faithful maintenance of its covenant relationship with Yahweh.

Amid the two iterations of the law of witnesses in Deuteronomy 17:6 and 19:15—and perhaps in direct connection to it—comes Moses's prophecy of a "raised up" (*yāqîm*) prophet "like unto Moses." This text constitutes, far and away, one of the most important texts in the present form of the Deuteronomic Code:

> The LORD thy God will *raise up* [*yāqîm*, or "establish"] unto thee a Prophet from the midst of thee, of thy brethren, like unto me; unto him ye shall hearken;
>
> According to all that thou desiredst of the LORD thy God in Horeb in the day of the assembly, saying, Let me not hear again the voice of the Lord my God, neither let me see this great fire any more, that I die not.
>
> And the LORD said unto me, They have well spoken that which they have spoken.

> *I will raise them up* [*ʾāqîm*] a Prophet from among their brethren, like unto thee, and will put my words in his mouth; and he shall speak unto them all that I shall command him.
>
> And it shall come to pass, that whosoever will not hearken unto my words which he shall speak in my name, I will require it of him. (Deuteronomy 18:15–19; emphasis added)

The Savior himself declared this prophecy fulfilled in himself in 3 Nephi 20:23. This text became foundational to the early understanding of Jesus's ministry. Peter declared this prophecy fulfilled in Jesus in Acts 2:22–23. Stephen cited this prophecy to the Sanhedrin in Acts 7:37.[55]

Because the Israelites' rejection of the immediate presence of God and a request for human intermediaries served as the basis for the giving of this prophecy (compare Exodus 20:18–19 [MT 16–17]; Deuteronomy 5:23–28 [MT 19–24]), many biblical scholars have understood it as an etiology (or causal explanation) for the existence of prophets—that is, prophets authorized or "raised up" by Yahweh—in ancient Israel. I have argued elsewhere that the Deuteronomistic Historian understood Samuel, in particular, as having fulfilled this prophecy.[56] The "raise[d]-up" language in Deuteronomy 18:15–19 echoes the language regarding the "choice seer" of whom Joseph in Egypt prophesied (2 Nephi 3; JST Genesis 50). Like Jesus and the Israelite prophets who preceded him, the Prophet Joseph Smith also represents a fulfillment of this prophecy, as do his successors. These raised-up prophets constitute, in a legal sense, witnesses, as Deuteronomy 18:19 makes clear: "Whosoever will not hearken unto my words which he shall speak in my name, I will require it of him," or, as the penalty is

---

55. Deuteronomy 18:15–19 was read messianically even before Jesus's time, as evident in Lehi's citation of it when prophesying of a coming Messiah and Savior (1 Nephi 10:4). Nephi, too, directly quoted Deuteronomy 18:15–19 in predicting its fulfillment in Jesus Christ (1 Nephi 22:20).

56. Matthew L. Bowen, *Rejective Requests and Deadly Disobedience: The Literary Utilization of Deut 18:15–17 in 1 Samuel and Its Function within the Deuteronomistic History* (master's thesis, Catholic University of America, 2009), 20–21; Matthew L. Bowen, "'According to All That You Demanded' (Deuteronomy 18:16): The Literary Use of Names and *Leitworte* as Antimonarchic Polemic in the Deuteronomistic History" (PhD diss., Catholic University of America, 2014), 34–69.

expressed elsewhere, "cut off from among the people"[57] or "destroyed from among the people."[58]

LAW OF THE KING (DEUTERONOMY (17:14–20)

Deuteronomy repeatedly warns the Israelites against becoming like the nations whose land they were dispossessing. All of the "de-Canaanization" and cult centralization legislation of Deuteronomy 12 is given to that end. This legislation obligated the Israelites to not seek after those nations' gods or cults. Child sacrifice arguably constituted the worst of those nations' abominations (Deuteronomy 12:30–31).[59]

Human kingship (in place of Yahweh's kingship) presented yet another way in which the ancient Israelites risked becoming like their idolatrous neighbors and put additional distance between themselves and the Lord. Recognizing monarchy's innate dangers, the Deuteronomic Code sought to drastically curb the power and prerogatives of the king. The Israelites' request or demand for kings mentioned above (1 Samuel 8) is anticipated already in this legislation ("I will set a king over me, like as all the nations that are about me," Deuteronomy 17:14). However, the Deuteronomic Code required that the king reign differently than the kings of the other nations. It forbade the multiplication of horses, wives, and silver and gold (Deuteronomy 17:16–17). It mandated, rather, that the king diligently "read" and "keep" the law (Deuteronomy 17:19–20). According to the Deuteronomistic historian, Hezekiah and Josiah of Judah represent the only truly outstanding representatives of this type of king vis-à-vis Solomon

---

57. See, for example, Exodus 30:33, 38; 31:14; Leviticus 7:20–27; 17:4, 9–10; 18:29; 19:8; 20:3–18; 23:29; Numbers 9:13; 15:30; 1 Nephi 22:20; 3 Nephi 20:23; 21:11, 20; Doctrine and Covenants 1:14; 133:63; Joseph Smith—Matthew 1:55; Joseph Smith—History 1:40. Compare also 1 Kings 9:7; Ezekiel 14:8; 27:7; 31:12.

58. Leviticus 23:20; Acts 3:23; compare 2 Nephi 30:10.

59. The subsequent Deuteronomistic History records that the king of Moab sacrifices his son in 2 Kings 3:27. The historian condemns Ahaz of Judah for this specific violation (2 Kings 16:3). Manasseh of Judah, whom the historian evaluates as the worst of the kings of Judah and Israel and whom he ultimately blames for the exile of Judah to Babylon, would similarly commit this abomination (2 Kings 21:6). The problem appears to have become particularly pervasive in Judah (Jeremiah 7:31) and was perpetuated by its monarchy (Jeremiah 19:5).

and most of his successors in both the north (e.g., Ahab) and the south (e.g., Manasseh). Kingship, by and large, brought about or exacerbated the apostasy and idolatry that the Deuteronomic Code legislated and warned against.

COVENANT ECONOMICS (DEUTERONOMY 14:22–29; 15:1–11; 24:10–15)

We see the Israelites' unique relationship to the land that Yahweh had granted on covenant conditions evident in the Deuteronomic Code's tithing requirement. This legislation mandated that Israelites set aside one-tenth of their agricultural produce (Deuteronomy 14:22). It further directed that the Israelites bring these tithes to the central sanctuary (Deuteronomy 14:23). The clear implication is that Yahweh gives the increase: "the Lord thy God hath blessed thee" (Deuteronomy 14:24). Provision was made for those who would have to travel great distances to exchange their tithing crops for money, which could then be used to purchase sacrificial goods for the use at the central sanctuary (Deuteronomy 14:24–26). The payment of tithes at the central sanctuary (temple) was to be a time of rejoicing (14:26). Every third year, the tithe (the "increase") belonged to the local community (14:28). These tithes contributed to the support of the Levites (14:27, 29), as well as that of the foreign migrant, the widow, and the orphan (14:29). How Israelites used their tithes for the benefit of their society's most vulnerable members served as an infallible indicator of their regard for Yahweh and the increase that he had so freely given them.

The Israelites' covenant with Yahweh meant a form of economics that differentiated them from their neighbors. What was beneficial to the land on which the Israelites resided would consequently benefit the poor and the vulnerable. Where the Sabbatical year in the Covenant Code emphasizes the land being given "rest" ("thou shalt let it rest [*tišmĕṭennâ*]," Exodus 23:11), the Deuteronomic Code, using the very same root, emphasizes that this sabbatical year was also a time for the remission or "release" (*šĕmiṭṭâ*) of debts: "At the end of every seven years thou shalt make a release. And this is the manner of the release: Every creditor that lendeth ought unto his neighbour shall release it; he shall not exact it of his neighbour, or of his brother; because it is called the Lord's release" (Deuteronomy 15:1–2).

Both the year of the land Sabbath and the year of the Lord's release provided for the poor (compare Exodus 23:11 with Deuteronomy 15:4). Deuteronomy 15:5–6 contains the promise of divine blessings upon the children of Israel if they will observe this principle (compare especially Malachi 3:8–12).

Moreover, the Deuteronomic Code strictly entailed care for the poor in Israel within the gates: "Thou shalt not harden thine heart, nor shut thine hand from thy poor brother" (Deuteronomy 15:7). That care was to be abundantly generous—"Thou shalt open thine hand wide unto him, and shalt surely lend him sufficient for his need, in that which he wanteth" (15:8)—and given with a willing heart: "Thou shalt surely give him, and thine heart shall not be grieved when thou givest unto him" (15:10). Contrary to some bad exegesis, the statement "for *the poor* shall never cease out of *the land*" (15:11) does not amount to a commandment or a prophecy but rather a sad statement of fact. Moses 7:18 implies that Zion cannot exist under this condition. Therefore, Yahweh commanded, "Thou shalt open thine hand wide unto thy brother, to thy poor, and to thy needy, *in thy land*" (Deuteronomy 15:11). Again, this legislation emphasizes the Israelites' unique relationship with the land and the moral obligations they owed to each other while upon it. Responsibility for the land's abundance belonged to Yahweh, who predicated that abundance upon the Israelites' obedience. The Israelites' care for the poor should have always evidenced recognition of that fact, not least because their poor depended so greatly upon the land to sustain an always difficult existence.

Furthermore, when the Israelites harvested the crops of their fields, olive orchards, and so forth, the legislation required them to leave behind a liberal amount for these disadvantaged classes to glean and thus to provide for themselves (compare Naomi and Ruth in Ruth 2). The principle that the Lord has given these "good things of the earth" to the whole human family "to be used, with judgment, not to excess, neither by extortion" (Doctrine and Covenants 59:16–20) underlies this legislation. Moreover, it reflects the Israelites' strong connection to the land of promise as the fulfillment of Yahweh's covenant with Abraham, Isaac, and Jacob. The poorest and most vulnerable especially needed the blessings afforded by the land.

In further recognition of the needy, Deuteronomy 23:24–25 allowed the Israelites to eat from, but not gather up, the grapes in their neighbors' vineyards and the grain in their neighbors vineyards as safeguards against hunger and as a protection of the poor. Jesus's disciples made use of this allowance when they ate the grain in the fields through which they passed (Matthew 12:1; Mark 2:23; Luke 6:1). All of this legislation reflects the economics of Yahweh's covenant regarding the land that the Israelites stood to inherit: both they and the land belonged to Yahweh. The Israelites' performance of this legislation would become a defining measure of its regard for Yahweh and his covenant.

Using a mix of casuistic and apodictic statutes, the Deuteronomic Code forbade practices that could easily lead to the oppression and extortion of vulnerable persons. The one making a loan could not take a pledge inside the house of the borrower (Deuteronomy 24:11). Clothing taken from poor people as pledges had to be returned before sundown (24:12–13). The code forbade Israelites from oppressing hired servants, whether native Israelite or migrant foreigners (24:14), and required employers to pay them for a day's labor by sundown (24:15).

Here, too, the Deuteronomic legislation reflects Yahweh's strong concern for the poor and the vulnerable, and proper treatment of the poor becomes a matter of covenant obedience The "widow and the fatherless [orphan]" becomes a metonymy throughout the Hebrew Bible for the most vulnerable members of its society, and the Israelites and Judahites repeatedly come under condemnation by prophets such Amos,[60] Isaiah,[61] Jeremiah,[62] Zechariah,[63] and Malachi[64] for their mistreatment of the poor and the aforementioned vulnerable members. James describes "pure religion . . . undefiled before God"[65] as meeting the needs of those whom Jesus

60. See, for example, Amos 2:4–6; 8:4–10.

61. See, for example, Isaiah 1:17, 23; 10:2.

62. Jeremiah 7:6; 22:3.

63. Zechariah 7:10.

64. Malachi 3:5.

65. James 1:27 says, "Pure religion and undefiled before God and the Father is this, To visit the fatherless and widows in their affliction, and to keep himself unspotted from the world."

characterizes as "the least of these," his brothers and sisters (*adelphōn*).[66] The treatment of a society's most vulnerable constitutes a kind of spiritual barometer.[67] A Zion society takes care of the needs of its most vulnerable (Moses 7:18).[68] To that end, modern revelation, like the Deuteronomic Code, establishes provisions for these members: "The storehouse shall be kept by the consecrations of the church; and widows and orphans shall be provided for, as also the poor" (Doctrine and Covenants 83:6). The Israelites could distinguish themselves from the nations by their care for their most vulnerable and could thereby keep their covenant with Yahweh.

In keeping that covenant, ancient Israel, like latter-day Israel,[69] was to live in thanksgiving and generosity one toward another. Deuteronomy 26:1–11 constituted the Israelites' formal, ritual acknowledgment that Yahweh was not only the giver of the land but the one who gave them increase and constituted a fundamental requirement of the Deuteronomic Code. In a sense, this rite functioned like the sacrament does for Latter-day Saints today, wherein we formally acknowledge ("witness") that we do and will remember the Lord Jesus Christ ("they do always remember him"), all that he does for us, and that we will remain faithful to our covenants with

---

66. Matthew 25:31–46.

67. This can be inferred not only from these biblical passages but from the Book of Mormon. Mormon himself described the Nephites' treatment of their widows in graphic terms in a letter to his son Moroni in the waning days of their civilization. Moroni 9:16 says, "And again, my son, there are many widows and their daughters who remain in Sherrizah; and that part of the provisions which the Lamanites did not carry away, behold, the army of Zenephi has carried away, and left them to wander whithersoever they can for food; and many old women do faint by the way and die." Moroni foresaw that we would face a similar moral crisis with respect to our society's most vulnerable members: "Yea, why do ye build up your secret abominations to get gain, and cause that widows should mourn before the Lord, and also orphans to mourn before the Lord, and also the blood of their fathers and their husbands to cry unto the Lord from the ground, for vengeance upon your heads?" (Mormon 8:40; compare Doctrine and Covenants 123:9).

68. See further Acts 2:44; 4:32; 3 Nephi 26:19; 4 Nephi 1:3.

69. The same principle that underlies Deuteronomy 26:1–11 underlies Doctrine and Covenants 59:7, 21: "Thou shalt thank the Lord thy God in all things. . . . And in nothing doth man offend God, or against none is his wrath kindled, save those who confess not his hand in all things, and obey not his commandments."

him ("keep his commandments which he hath given them"; Moroni 4–5; Doctrine and Covenants 20:77–79).

CONCLUSION

Although the present-day form of the Pentateuch has resulted from numerous diachronic processes, latter-day revelation confirms that Moses was a real person and a true prophet and that he wrote the judgment or law that the Lord gave unto him in revelation. The Covenant Code, Holiness Code, and Deuteronomic Code can be seen as three context-based expressions of these instructions. The Covenant Code constitutes a foundational ethos upon which to establish a covenant people in the wilderness. The Holiness Code represents a holiness or ritual purity-oriented instruction calibrated for priestly administration in order to prepare the Israelites to become a ritually pure and ethically pure (essentially a temple-worthy) people—so that the people can become worthy to inherit the land of promise and partake of Yahweh's holiness. Finally, the Deuteronomic Code iterates obedience to "the statutes and judgments" that are to be "observe[d] . . . in the land" to help the Israelites retain possession of the land of promise after inheriting it, all while maintaining its unique relationship with Yahweh and its uniqueness among the nations of the earth. The Israelites' observance of covenant economics would constitute a sure sign of the intactness of their covenant relationship with him.

All of this has relevance for Latter-day Saints as temples now "dot the earth," thus making "lands of promise" out of all the nations of the earth. We seek not only to become a people founded upon divine covenant principles and doctrine but also to receive preparatory Aaronic Priesthood ordinances[70] that enable atonement with the Lord. We thus become temple worthy—and not just in the temporal (mortal) sense, meaning worthy to receive the ordinances that enable us to see the face of God and live.[71] We seek to bring all into the covenant relationship that Yahweh offers the willing and, while so doing, to become worthy to enter and inherit the

70. See Doctrine and Covenants 84:26–28.

71. See Doctrine and Covenants 84:21–22.

true "far better land of promise" of which Alma spoke (Alma 37:45) and to retain an inheritance in that kingdom, "to go no more out" (Alma 7:25; 29:17; 34:36; Helaman 3:30; 3 Nephi 28:40; Revelation 3:17). The instructions God gave and will give to his people, then and now, will help accomplish these goals.

The author would like to thank Suzy Bowen, Daniel Belnap, Aaron Schade, Devan Jensen, and Meghan Rollins Wilson.

— 17 —

BALAAM IN THE BOOK OF NUMBERS

DANA M. PIKE

The latter portion of the book of Numbers recounts that the Israelites, toward the end of their forty years of dwelling in the wilderness, headed north along the eastern side of the Dead Sea before entering the promised land of Canaan. The biblical narrative relates a unique episode in the Old Testament when the Israelites finally encamped on the eastern side of the Jordan River: the story of Balaam. From a talking donkey to a prophesying non-Israelite, the fascinating account of Balaam is explored in this chapter in an attempt to make sense of this enigmatic episode that emphasizes God's delivering power against the backdrop of the Israelites traversing foreign, and often hostile, territory. The Balaam account highlights in dramatic fashion the fact that God's plans for the Israelites would not be thwarted, despite serious human efforts to the contrary. —DB and AS

The account of Balaam, the non-Israelite "prophet" who was commissioned by a Moabite king to curse the Israelites and whose donkey spoke to him, is one of the most entertaining and enigmatic episodes in the Hebrew Bible (the Christian Old Testament).[1] Numbers 22–24 narrates the experiences and pronouncements of Balaam. However, any consideration of this episode must also, of necessity, include an examination of its larger context: the book of Numbers itself. This paper briefly introduces the Book of Numbers, paying particular attention to its prominent themes, and then analyzes the account of Balaam (Numbers 22–24) for the purpose of making better sense of the context, content, and purpose of that fascinating episode.

OVERVIEW OF THE BOOK OF NUMBERS

The name of the fourth book of the Old Testament, "Numbers,"[2] is derived from the Septuagint and is based on the theme of numbering.[3] In chapters 1 and 26 the Israelite men capable of military action are numbered, and

---

1. I express my appreciation to Courtney Dotson, my former student assistant, for her help gathering materials that I used in preparing this paper. I also thank the editors of this volume, Aaron Schade and Daniel Belnap; the anonymous reviewers; and my wife, Jane Allis-Pike, for providing helpful feedback on earlier drafts of this paper.

2. For a somewhat more extended overview of the book of Numbers (with pictures), written for a Latter-day Saint audience, see Richard Neitzel Holzapfel, Dana M. Pike, and David Rolph Seely, *Jehovah and the World of the Old Testament* (Salt Lake City: Deseret Book, 2009), 124–35. For those desiring to study the book of Numbers in greater detail, the commentaries cited in the notes of this paper are a good starting point. The received Hebrew text of the book of Numbers is generally free from corruptions, so this paper focuses on the content of the book, without concerns about textual readings. Jacob Milgrom, *The JPS Torah Commentary: Numbers* (Philadelphia: Jewish Publication Society, 1989), xi, provides a concise assessment of this issue. See also Timothy R. Ashley, *The Book of Numbers*, NICOT (Grand Rapids, MI: Eerdmans, 1993), 11–12. These commentators and others provide observations on the relationship between the Masoretic Text of Numbers and how it reads in the Versions.

3. The Septuagint, abbreviated LXX, is the name given to the early translation of the Hebrew scriptures into Greek. This translation was produced by Jews living in Egypt in the third and second centuries BC.

the Levites are numbered in chapters 3–4 and 26. The traditional Hebrew title of the book is *bĕmidbar* ("In the Wilderness"), which is based on the opening verse, "The LORD spoke to Moses in the wilderness of Sinai" (Numbers 1:1), and nicely introduces the geographical context for the book's initial contents.[4]

Although the book of Numbers may initially sound like dry or boring reading to some people, it has been aptly described in this manner: "Humour, magic, prophecy, dramatic story, solemn ritual and practical laws are not what most readers would expect to find in a book entitled 'Numbers.' . . . Many readers give up at the census lists with which the book opens and thereby miss some of the most gripping stories in Scripture, its most ancient poetry and its rich theology. Narratives and laws which have inspired Jews and Christians down the centuries are overlooked and forgotten."[5]

The book of Numbers focuses on Israelite activities in three main locations: at Mount Sinai, near Kadesh, and at the plains of Moab.[6]

At Mount Sinai. The first of these locations is Mount Sinai, where the Lord had already revealed his law to the Israelites, where the Israelites had entered into a covenant relationship with him, and where they had then constructed the tabernacle according to divine design (Exodus

---

4. I have used the NRSV translation throughout, unless otherwise indicated, because it reads more smoothly and requires less commentary about the meaning and usage of words than does the KJV. "Jehovah" is the traditional English representation of the Tetragrammaton, the Hebrew divine name *yhwh*/YHWH, and is now generally vocalized as "Yahweh" by scholars. This name usually appears in the Bible with the substitute title "the LORD," with the second word in capital letters. For a discussion of the name YHWH/Yahweh and its forms, including *Jehovah*, see Dana M. Pike, "Biblical Hebrew Words You Already Know and Why They Are Important," *Religious Educator* 7, no. 3 (2006): 106–9; "The Name and Titles of God in the Old Testament," *Religious Educator* 11, no 1 (2010): 19–21.
5. Gordon J. Wenham, *Numbers* (Sheffield, UK: Sheffield, 1997), 11.
6. I focus on geographical progression, although a few commentators prefer to focus on generations as the primary organizer of the materials in Numbers: (1) the original generation of the Exodus, which died off in the wilderness (Numbers 1–25), and (2) the younger generation that would eventually go into Canaan (Numbers 26–36). See, for example, Ashley, *Book of Numbers*, 2–3.

18–40). Numbers 1:1–10:11 relates events during the Israelites' final weeks at Mount Sinai, including the numbering of Israelite fighting men "from twenty years old and upward" (Numbers 1:3), the dedication of the tabernacle (Numbers 7; compare Leviticus 8–9), and the first anniversary celebration of the Passover (Numbers 9; compare Exodus 12). Additionally, these chapters contain a variety of important laws and instructions, including the Nazirite vow and Aaronic priestly blessing (Numbers 6).

Not quite a year after arriving at Mount Sinai, the bright cloud—which represented the Lord's presence with the Israelites and which had appeared over the tabernacle—began to move. In response, the Israelites left Mount Sinai and began their journey toward Canaan (Exodus 19:1; Numbers 9:15–23; 10:11–12).

Near Kadesh.[7] As narrated in Numbers 10–20, Kadesh (also called Kadesh-barnea) was the second geographic area, after Mount Sinai, in which the Israelites spent considerable time (Numbers 13:26–20:22). It was to Kadesh that the twelve Israelite scouts who had reconnoitered the land of Canaan returned (chapter 13), and Kadesh was where Joshua and Caleb encouraged the disgruntled Israelites thusly: "Only, do not rebel against the LORD; and do not fear the people of the land [of Canaan]" (14:8–9). The adult Israelites' lack of faith in Jehovah's power to deliver them into the promised land resulted in the divine decree that they would die in the wilderness during the ensuing forty years (14:29–30, 38; 26:63–65).

The time spent at this second main location, Kadesh-barnea, in the book of Numbers thus functioned as a "spiritual incubator" in which the rising generation of the Israelites could mature. And it was during this interval that most of the adult generation of the Israelites who had left Egypt died. Numbers 10–20 also contain divine instructions and laws, including a purification ritual that involved ashes from a red cow (chapter

---

7. Numbers 33 relates an itinerary of the Israelites' journey and their stops in the wilderness. There is uncertainty about the location of many of the sites listed in chapter 33, and there is some confusion in the biblical account about where and for how long Israelites stayed "in the wilderness." They did not "break camp" every day. See a concise review of the situation in Dale W. Manor, "Kadesh, Kadesh-barnea," in *The New Interpreter's Dictionary of the Bible*, vol. 3, ed. Katharine Doob Sakenfeld et al. (Nashville: Abingdon, 2008), 479–80, Accordance version 1.2.

19), accounts of subsequent Israelite rebellions against Jehovah and Moses (chapters 16, 20), and the death of Miriam (20:1).

At the Plains of Moab. Numbers 20:28–36:13 constitutes the third and last major portion of the book, relating events during the final year or so of the Israelites' forty years in the wilderness. They traveled through the eastern Negev, northward on the east side of the Dead Sea, and then encamped in the "plains of Moab," on the northeast shoulder of the Dead Sea (22:1), until, under Joshua's direction, they crossed the Jordan River into Canaan, near Jericho (Joshua 1–4).[8] Events recounted on the way to the plains of Moab included the death of Aaron (Numbers 20:22–29), the Israelites' being bitten by snakes and Moses's subsequent raising of a bronze image of a snake to provide deliverance for them (21:4–9), and military victories against the Amorite king Sihon and against Og, the king over Bashan (21:21–35).

A main focus of this third time period is the five to six months that the Israelites spent in the last main location, the plains of Moab. This final, and large, portion of the book of Numbers includes the account of Balaam (Numbers 22–24; discussed below), the Israelites' false worship and immoral involvement with the Moabites (chapter 25), a second Israelite numbering (or census), now that the people of the Exodus generation were dead and their successors were on the doorstep of the promised land (chapter 26, see especially verses 64–65), the investiture of Joshua as Moses's successor (27:12–23), and arrangements for the tribes of Reuben, Gad, and half the tribe of Manasseh to settle in Transjordan, the region east of the Jordan River (chapter 32). But the end of the book of Numbers is not the real "end" of the Israelites' journey. This comes only after Moses's farewell (in Deuteronomy) and Joshua's leading them into Canaan (in Joshua).

---

8. Compare Numbers 22:1; 36:13; Deuteronomy 1:3; 2:13–15; 34:1. There is ambiguity as to the length of time it took the Israelites to travel between leaving Kadesh and arriving in the plains of Moab; see Numbers 20:28; 22:1.

MAJOR THEMES IN NUMBERS

The book of Numbers contains a distinctive mix of narrative, laws, and lists. In addition to such literary forms, there are several prominent themes in this book that deserve brief attention.

Geography/Land. The most obvious theme is movement toward a promised land (Numbers 10:29) with the purpose of occupying it. Actual geographical progression, as well as what it symbolically represents, is a major theme in the books of Genesis through Joshua. Thomas B. Dozeman, for example, has claimed that "geography plays a central role in the story line of the Pentateuch. Eden and Canaan frame the literature. In between these locations, travelogue weaves together innumerable cities, oases, itineraries, boundary lines, and kingdoms into a single story."[9] The physical journey recounted in Numbers plays a particularly prominent role in the greater context of the Pentateuch as Israelites moved toward claiming and settling in the land of Canaan promised centuries earlier by Yahweh/Jehovah to Abraham and Sarah and their posterity (e.g., Genesis 12:1, 7). Three additional themes are highlighted here.[10]

Posterity. The opening chapters of Numbers emphasize a theme that involves another aspect of promises made to Abraham and Sarah: posterity. In addition to determining the size of the Israelites' fighting force, the numbering of the Israelites in the book of Numbers emphasizes their great numerical growth. Abraham and Sarah had one son together: Isaac (Genesis 21:1–3). Exodus 1:5 recounts that a few generations later, the "total number of people born to Jacob [the son of Isaac] was seventy. Joseph was already in Egypt." Now, having recently left Egypt, this family of Israelites had swelled to over two million people, based, at least, on Numbers 1–4 (a reported count of 603,550 fighting men twenty years old and older, 22,000 Levites, all the unnumbered younger males, and all the females). There are reasons to question the literal accuracy of this extremely large

9. Thomas B. Dozeman, in *ASOR Newsletter* 49, no. 3 (Fall 1999): 16.

10. For further thoughts on themes in Numbers, see the comments of, for example, Milgrom, *Numbers*, xxxviii–xl; Ashley, *Book of Numbers*, 8–11.

number,[11] however, it functions in part to highlight the ongoing fulfillment of Jehovah's promise to Abraham and Sarah: "I will make your offspring as numerous as the stars of heaven and as the sand that is on the seashore" (Genesis 22:17; see 15:5).

Further emphasizing this theme of posterity, Numbers relates that whenever the Israelites ceased traveling and camped around the ark of the covenant, Moses would say, "Return, O Lord of the ten thousand thousands of Israel" (Numbers 10:36). Thus prominent themes in Numbers are the fulfillment of promises made to ancestral Patriarchs and Matriarchs, particularly promises of posterity and land (e.g., Genesis 17:7–8). Of course, undergirding the promises of land and numberless posterity was the concept of a formal relationship with Yahweh/Jehovah.

Covenant Obligations. Numbers also emphasizes the theme of obligations inherent in the Israelite covenant relationship with the Lord, fidelity to which brought Israelites great blessings, but in which faith*less*ness and rebellion brought curse-consequences. Although there are a few examples of Israelite "stumbles" recounted in Exodus and Leviticus (e.g., Exodus 32:15–29; Leviticus 10:1–11), most accounts narrated in Numbers 11–25 are painful in their portrayal of murmuring (chapters 11, 21), rebellion against Moses's leadership (chapters 12, 14, 16), and apostasy (chapter 25), as varying numbers of Israelites demonstrated a fateful lack of faith in and loyalty to Yahweh/Jehovah. Collectively, the Israelites learned many lessons "the hard way." Their spiritual experiences and covenants at Mount Sinai did not automatically ensure their faith and obedience as they moved toward Canaan.[12] The consequences meted out by the Lord in

11. Various explanations have been given for the exceptionally large numbers of Israelites in the book of Numbers (and elsewhere in the Bible). For a convenient summary of such suggestions, see Everett Fox, *The Five Books of Moses, A New Translation with Introductions, Commentary, and Notes* (New York: Schocken, 1995), 654; Holzapfel, Pike, and Seely, *Jehovah and the World of the Old Testament*, 126.

12. Holzapfel, Pike, and Seely, *Jehovah and the World of the Old Testament*, 124; see also Fox, *Five Books of Moses*, 649: "It becomes clear that nation-founding involves not only the giving of laws and the arranging of societal roles, but also the developing of the ability to cope with physical and spiritual challenges to survival."

the tragic accounts in Numbers can only be understood in the context of the covenant commitments the Israelites had made at Mount Sinai and the associated divine expectations.[13]

True Prophets. The last major theme that will be mentioned here deals with the nature of prophetic leadership and what constitutes a true prophet. The center portion of Numbers, in particular, highlights these related issues. In Numbers 11:14–15, Jehovah provided spiritual powers to seventy Israelite men to assist Moses, and they prophesied. The Spirit also rested on two men who had not gathered with Moses and the others at the tabernacle (Numbers 11:16–17, 24–26). This prompted Joshua to express concern for Moses's position, to which Moses replied, "Are you jealous for my sake? Would that all the LORD's people were prophets, and that the LORD would put his spirit on them!" (11:28–29). Thus, one indicator of a true prophet, by biblical standards, is having access to the spiritual gifts necessary to communicate and help bring about divine will.

Complaints against and challenges to Moses and his prophetic leadership were numerous, including complaints from Miriam and Aaron (Moses's older siblings; Numbers 12:2); the Israelite scouts' evaluation of the peoples in Canaan (14:2); and when Korah, Dothan, Abiram, and their followers gathered against Moses, and to a lesser extent, against Aaron (16:1–35). Much of the remainder of chapter 16 narrates another challenge against Moses and Aaron (16:41–50).[14]

Each of these challenges ended tragically for some Israelites, as the Lord reaffirmed Moses's position as the divinely sanctioned leader and as the Lord taught the Israelites that safety is found *with* the Lord's chosen leaders, not by fighting against them. Thus another indicator of a true prophet is being divinely chosen, which preempts presumptions

---

13. As Milgrom, *Numbers*, xvi, has observed, "The Book of Numbers . . . operates in the shadow of Sinai: Israel has accepted the suzerainty of its God and is bound to His law [Exodus 19–40]."

14. As is sometimes the case in various portions of the Bible, there is a difference between the chapter and verse division between the Hebrew Bible and the English translations most readers of this paper likely use. In this case, Numbers 16:36 in English corresponds to Numbers 17:1 in Hebrew. So 16:41–50 in English, as is cited in this paper, is 17:6–15 in the Hebrew Bible.

to leadership based on family connection, perceived ability, pride, and self-promotion.

These themes of geographic progression, the Israelites' numerical size, the Israelites' covenant relationship with Yahweh/Jehovah, and the nature of a true prophet are emphasized at certain points in the account of Balaam in Numbers 22–24. They provide a good context for considering the report of Balaam's activities and his role in the book of Numbers.

BALAAM IN NUMBERS 22–24

Balaam is the key figure in the narrative in Numbers 22–24. Balaam's name in Hebrew is *bilʿām*, the etymology of which is uncertain. However, the English vocalization of his name, typically pronounced "BAY-lum," is based on the Greek form of the name, which occurs in the Septuagint and the New Testament.

Although there are thematic ties between the rest of Numbers and the account of Balaam (Numbers 22–24), it is in several ways an odd and separate portion of this biblical book.[15] The Israelites, their activities, and even Moses are no longer the direct focus of attention. Ironically, the primary focus is Yahweh/Jehovah's use of the *non-Israelite* Balaam to announce divine decrees about the Israelites. As recounted in Numbers 22–24, the Israelites seem to have no awareness of Balaam's actions or his pronouncement of blessings on them.

BRIEF SUMMARY OF NUMBERS 22–24

Following the events narrated in Numbers 21, the Israelites journeyed to the "plains of Moab," the region just northeast of the Dead Sea, on the opposite side of the Jordan River from Jericho (which was in Canaan; see Numbers 22:1). Balak, king of the Moabites, was alarmed because a vast

15. Numbers 22–24 is considered by many commentators to have existed separately before it was incorporated into Numbers. See, for example, Milgrom, *Numbers*, 467: "Traditionists and moderns are in agreement that chapters 22–24 . . . constitute an independent work that was later inserted into the text of the Book of Numbers."

number of Israelites was now in his region (22:2–4; Moab was located east of the Dead Sea). The Israelites had not attacked the Moabites, but the Israelites' success in defeating the Amorite kings Sihon and Og (chapter 21) provided Balak ample reason for concern. To counteract this perceived threat, Balak sent messengers to hire Balaam to come curse the Israelites.

Balak's messengers carried his description of the encamped Israelites to Balaam, "They have spread over the face of the earth" (Numbers 22:5; see 22:12; 23:10). Balak's description is reminiscent of the large number of Israelites counted at the beginning of Numbers, which hearkens back to the promises made to the Patriarchs and Matriarchs in Genesis. Furthermore, besides displaying a great deal of confidence in Balaam's power, Balak's words contain an obvious play on the language of Jehovah's covenant with Abraham and Sarah. In Genesis 12:3, Jehovah declares to Abraham, "I will bless those who bless you, and the one who curses you I will curse" (see also Abraham 2:11). However, Balak seemingly puts Balaam in the place of Jehovah, requesting of Balaam, "Curse this people for me [Balak], since they are stronger than I, . . . for I know that whomever you [Balaam] bless is blessed, and whomever you curse is cursed" (22:6).

When Balaam asked Yahweh/Jehovah about Balak's request that he curse the Israelites, God responded, "You shall not curse the people, for they are blessed" (Numbers 22:7–12). The messengers returned to Balak, informing him of Balaam's refusal, so Balak sent "more numerous and more distinguished" messengers with an even better offer of reward to further encourage Balaam to come curse the Israelites (22:13–17). As before, Balaam asked Yahweh/Jehovah about accepting Balak's invitation, but this time Balaam appears to have received God's approval to go with the messengers, with the stipulation that Balaam "do only what I [God] tell you [Balaam] to do" (22:18–21).

Balaam started for Moab with Balak's messengers, but Yahweh was angry with Balaam (see discussion below) and sent an angel to confront him.[16] In one of the great ironies of scripture, Balaam's donkey could see Jehovah's angel, but Balaam could not. After mistreating his donkey and

16. In verse 32, the angel refers to himself as a *śāṭān*, "an adversary," which is the same Hebrew word that is transliterated as "Satan." See Pike, "Biblical Hebrew Words," 105–6, for a discussion of this word and its uses in the Bible.

angrily wishing her dead, "the LORD [*yhwh*/Yahweh] opened the mouth of the donkey." Surprisingly, Balaam did not appear startled to be conversing with his donkey. "Then the LORD opened the eyes of Balaam, and he saw the angel of the LORD standing in the road, with his drawn sword in his hand; and he bowed down, falling on his face" (22:21–31; there is no mention of Balaam's servants or Balak's messengers—the narrative focus stays on Balaam).

Following his interaction with this angel, Balaam was allowed to continue on his way, meeting Balak near Moab's northern border (Numbers 22:32–36). After exchanging pleasantries, "Balaam said to Balak, 'I have come to you now, but do I have power to say just anything? The word God puts in my mouth, that is what I must say'" (22:36–38). Balak appeared unphased by this qualification, and after offering sacrifices, he positioned Balaam where "he could see part of the people of Israel" (22:39–41). Then Balaam and Balak built altars and offered sacrifices. Following this, "God met Balaam" (23:1–4), and then Balaam uttered a poetically formatted prophetic oracle (or pronouncement)—the essential point of which was that God was going to bless his people and there was nothing Balak or Balaam could do to curse the Israelites (23:5–10).

After venting his frustration about this, Balak took Balaam to another spot, where they repeated the same procedure: they built altars, offered sacrifices, and Balaam consulted with Yahweh/Jehovah. The resulting poetic oracle repeated the same basic message, "The LORD their God is with them [Israelites]. . . . Surely there is . . . no divination [that will succeed] against Israel" (Numbers 23:11–24). In response to Balak's increasing dissatisfaction, Balaam replied, "Did I not tell you [Balak], 'Whatever the LORD says, that is what I [Balaam] must do'?" (23:25–26). Balak then took Balaam to a *third* observation point, and the same procedure of offerings on altars was repeated (there is an emphasis on the number three in the larger Balaam narrative). However, this time, "Balaam saw that it pleased the LORD to bless Israel, so he did not go, as at other times, to look for omens" (23:27–24:1). Looking over the encamped Israelites and imbued with God's spirit, Balaam poetically expressed a third prophetic pronouncement on the Israelites, blessing them and concluding with language reminiscent of the

Abrahamic covenant (mentioned above): "Blessed is everyone who blesses you [Israel], and cursed is everyone who curses you" (24:2–9).

At this point Balak angrily dismissed Balaam, who, in response, expressed a poetic oracle *against* Balak (Numbers 24:10–19; discussed below). Ironically, Balaam was hired by Balak to curse the Israelites, but Balaam ended up blessing them and cursing Balak. Following pronouncements of curses on the Amalekites, Kenites, and others, Balaam returned to his home (24:20–25).

As noted above, the Israelites are depicted as completely unaware of these actions and Balaam's pronouncements.[17] However, this account of Balaam and Barak was no doubt included in the book of Numbers to emphasize that Jehovah could and would fulfill his past promises to multiply the Israelites and to establish them in the land of Canaan, despite opposition from the Moabite king, Balak, and his efforts to have Balaam invoke magical curses on the Israelites.

QUESTIONS REGARDING BALAAM AND THE BALAAM NARRATIVE (NUMBERS 22-24)

From a literary standpoint, the account of Balaam in Numbers 22–24 is fascinating in its own right. However, when considered historically and theologically, a number of questions arise about Balaam and the narrative that cannot be easily answered. The space limitations of this paper do not allow exploration of all possible issues, but several of them are discussed here.

Was Balaam a prophet? The answer to this seemingly simple question is complex because of the differing indications of the roles in which Balaam is depicted in Numbers 22–24 and in later biblical passages (a few

17. For those who accept the events and pronouncements recounted in Numbers 22–24 as historical, this, of course, raises questions about this episode's literary history: who recorded this information, and how did it make its way into the biblical narrative? There are currently no answers to these questions. But it reinforces the idea that there is much that is still unknown about the early stages of the production of biblical texts (see discussion below on the Deir 'Alla inscription).

of these other biblical passages will be referenced in this section, and then they will be discussed below as a group).

When Balak sent messengers to hire Balaam, they brought with them "the fees for divination [*qĕsāmîm*]" (Numbers 22:7).[18] And in the King James translation of Joshua 13:22, Balaam is called a diviner or "soothsayer [*qōsēm*]." *Divination* is the attempt to discern divine will—typically by utilizing ritual activity—and to thus read the future through various manifestations in the natural world. Divination was practiced both formally and informally by peoples, including the Israelites, throughout the ancient Near East. While anyone could attempt to ascertain divine will (see, for example, Gideon with dew on and off his sheepskin in Judges 6:37–40), most cultures also had trained specialists who observed and catalogued unusual divine manifestations and their related consequences and who sought to track and predict signs of divine will. Methods of divination included necromancy (consulting the spirits of the dead), extispicy (inspecting the entrails of sacrificial animals for ominous abnormalities—a subset of which is hepatoscopy, the inspection of livers), observations of astral and weather phenomena, and the flight patterns of birds.[19] The casting of lots (cleromancy) was widespread in the ancient world and was an acceptable form of divination in Israelite culture; prophets, priests, and common people all used cleromancy, at least in some circumstances.[20] Ancient Near Eastern kings, including at least some Israelite kings, sought to divine the advisability of military maneuvers through various means

18. Although this is how this phrase is usually translated, there have been suggestions that an alternative is preferable. See, for example, Victor (Avigdor) Hurowitz, "The Expression *ûqsāmîm bĕyādām* (Numbers 22:7) in Light of Divinatory Practices from Mari," *Hebrew Studies* 33 (1992): 5–15.

19. On Mesopotamian divination, see for example, Ulla Susanne Koch, "Sheep and Sky: Systems of Divinatory Interpretation," and Francesca Rochberg, "Observing and Describing the World through Divination and Astronomy," in Karen Radner and Eleanor Robson, eds., *The Oxford Handbook of Cuneiform Culture* (New York: Oxford, 2011), 447–69 and 618–36, respectively.

20. See, for example, Numbers 26:52–56; Leviticus 16:8–10; 1 Nephi 3:11. For further discussion, see Holzapfel, Pike, and Seely, *Jehovah and the World of the Old Testament*, 157. Additionally, the Urim and Thummim—carried by the Aaronic high priest in his ephod (Exodus 28:30–35)—is often viewed as a legitimate Israelite divinatory instrument.

(e.g., 1 Kings 22:5–7). A few biblical texts condemn and ban divination in general among the Israelites, which indicates the prevalence of divination (e.g., Deuteronomy 18:10–12, including *qōsēm qĕsāmîm* in verse 10; 2 Kings 17:17).

Certain biblical passages depict Balaam as a trained diviner. And his requests for Balak to provide altars and sacrifices, Balaam's movement to elevated vantage points, and his efforts to "look for omens" (Numbers 24:1) can all be interpreted as part of his divinatory activities (e.g., 23:1–4). However, Balak did not want Balaam to merely divine the future of Israelite-Moabite relations. Balak wanted Balaam to curse the Israelites. This is made clear in several passages, beginning with Balak's initial request in 22:6: "Come now, curse this people for me, since they are stronger than I; perhaps I shall be able to defeat them and drive them from the land; for I know that . . . whomever you [Balaam] curse is cursed." Several similar requests occur in the Balaam narrative.[21]

Cursing is different from just divining the future; cursing involves manipulating the future against an adversary. But Balaam was unable to fulfill Balak's request to curse and thus harm the Israelites. Balaam could only pronounce blessings on them.[22] This is certainly the view expressed in Nehemiah 13:2, in which it is claimed that the Moabites "hired Balaam against them [the Israelites] to curse them—yet our God turned the curse into a blessing." And in this outcome, a great theological message is conveyed: "Surely there is no [successful] enchantment [*naḥaš*] against Jacob, no divination [*qesem*] against Israel" (Numbers 23:23). Based on the promise in Genesis 12:2–3, the Israelites' God did not permit others

21. See Numbers 22:6, 7, 11; 23:7, 8, 11, 13, 27; 24:10. The more frequently used Hebrew lexical root meaning "to curse" in these passages is *q-b-b*, but *ʾ-r-r* also occurs.

22. Commentators have much to say about this situation. Fox, *Five Books of Moses*, 774, for example, observes, "curse is turned to blessing, despite all the correct ritual preparations and previous promises of payment for services rendered. One almost has the impression of a séance gone wrong. And, professionally speaking, hired prophets are supposed to tell kings what they want to hear."

to curse them collectively (although he obviously allowed them to bring curses upon themselves).[23]

Numbers 22:6 and other verses thus strongly suggest that Balaam had a well-known reputation as a sorcerer (or else, why would Balak seek him out for such activity?) and that Balak presumed Balaam really could curse the Israelites to their detriment. But in Numbers 23–24 Balaam acted only as a diviner because he just obtained and communicated God's will to bless the Israelites. Whatever his initial intentions, Balaam did not and could not curse the Israelites.[24]

Why is it then that commentators often describe Balaam not only as a diviner but also as a prophet, especially since this title is never explicitly used in reference to him in Numbers 22–24? This designation is based in part on the fact that after failing twice to curse the Israelites, Balaam abandoned his previous actions, and "then the spirit of God came upon him, and he uttered his [third] oracle" (Numbers 24:2–3).[25] He then uttered a series of prophetic pronouncements against non-Israelite peoples, as reported in 24:14–24. But even prior to this, in his first two attempts to curse the Israelites, the biblical narrative claims that "the Lord put a word in Balaam's mouth," a figure of speech that is associated with prophecy (Numbers 23:5, 16; compare Numbers 22:38; Deuteronomy 18:18; Isaiah 51:16; Jeremiah 1:9). These instances and the witness of the Deir 'Alla inscription (discussed below) suggest a prophetic dimension to Balaam's activities.

---

23. For publications on curses and cursing, see, for example, J. K. Aitken, *The Semantics of Blessing and Cursing in Ancient Hebrew* (Louvain: Peeters, 2007); Timothy G. Crawford, *Blessing and Curse in Syro-Palestinian Inscriptions of the Iron Age* (New York: Peter Lang, 1992).

24. My thinking on this matter is analogous to, but independent from, Milgrom, *Numbers*, 471–73.

25. Modern translations, such as the NRSV (quoted here) and the NET, sometimes translate the Hebrew word *māšāl* as "oracle," meaning pronouncement, saying, or prophecy. Although *māšāl* is translated as "proverb" or "wise saying" in some contexts (e.g., 1 Kings 5:12; Ezekiel 12:22), including in the KJV (Numbers 24:3), several prophetic passages combine the verb *nāśā*ʾ ("to lift, raise, carry") and the noun *māšāl* to convey the sense of a mocking or taunting prophetic pronouncement against someone (e.g., Numbers 23:7, 18; 24:3, 15, 20, 23; Isaiah 14:4; Habakkuk 2:6).

Furthermore, in Balaam's final prophetic pronouncement about the Israelites, the Bible employs language associated with seership: "The oracle of one who hears the words of God, who sees the vision [*māḥăzēh*] of the Almighty, who falls down, but with eyes uncovered" (Numbers 24:4). At this point in the narrative, Balaam's claim to "see" the things of God comes as a significant development because earlier Balaam could *not* see the Lord's angel right in front of him, even when his donkey could (22:23–31).[26] An important inscription from Deir ʿAlla (reviewed below) parallels this dimension of Balaam's activity, describing him as a "seer of the gods" or "a divine seer [*ḥzh ʾlhn*]."[27]

Thus Balaam functions in overlapping roles as depicted in the biblical text: diviner, prophet, and seer. However, Balaam did not have a sorcerer's power over the Israelites, although Balak certainly expected that Balaam had such power. Nonetheless, Balaam is depicted as functioning prophetically. Of course, some other ancient Near Eastern peoples besides the Israelites believed in divine communication through prophets.[28] The real question is, What is the nature of Balaam's relationship with Yahweh/Jehovah?

---

26. In fact, seeing (and not seeing) is an important motif that occurs throughout the Balaam account. See, for example, the comments of Robert Alter, *The Hebrew Bible: A Translation with Commentary* (New York: W. W. Norton, 2019), 1:556, 560.
27. See, respectively, Shmuel Aḥituv, *Echoes from the Past* (Jerusalem: Carta, 2008), 435, 438; Baruch A. Levine, "The Deir ʿAlla Plaster Inscriptions (2.27)," in *Context of Scripture*, ed. William W. Hallo and K. Lawson Younger (Boston: Brill, 2000), 2:142.
28. Classic examples of types of non-Israelite prophetic activity are found in the Mari and the Neo-Assyrian texts, but other texts mention prophets as well. Relatively recent publications on this phenomenon include Martti Nissinen, *Ancient Prophecy: Near Eastern, Biblical, and Greek Perspectives* (New York: Oxford, 2018) and Jonathan Stökl, *Prophecy in the Ancient Near East, A Philological and Sociological Comparison* (Boston: Brill, 2012). See also James K. Mead, "The Biblical Prophets in Historiography," in *Ancient Israel's History, An Introduction to Issues and Sources*, ed. Bill T. Arnold and Richard S. Hess (Grand Rapids, MI: Baker Academic, 2014), 262–85, especially the review of ancient Near Eastern prophecy, 270–80.

Was Balaam a prophet of Yahweh/Jehovah? Since Balaam was a non-Israelite, the question naturally arises: Was Balaam a prophet of the Lord (*yhwh*/Yahweh) in the same sense that Moses and later Israelites prophets were? This is a challenging question. The answer depends in large part on how one approaches the biblical material.[29]

On the one hand, the Bible includes the positive account of the non-Israelite Jethro, Moses's Midianite father-in-law who Latter-day Saints believe held the Melchizedek Priesthood that he later conferred upon Moses (Doctrine and Covenants 84:6). So Latter-day Saints are open to understanding how Jehovah had worked through other non-Israelites in the eastern Mediterranean region. Furthermore, the general depiction in Numbers 23–24 of Balaam blessing the Israelites in accordance with God's will suggests he was representing their God (also emphasized in Micah 6:5). Passages such as Numbers 23:5, 16 ("The Lord put a word in Balaam's mouth") depict Balaam speaking for Jehovah. Balaam even refers to Jehovah as his God: "I [Balaam] could not go beyond the command of the Lord [*yhwh*] my God" (Numbers 22:18; compare Numbers 22:8, 13; 23:5, 12, 16; 24:11). Because of such biblical statements, some later Jewish authors described Balaam positively.[30]

However, despite this seemingly positive depiction of Balaam in Numbers 22–24, most other biblical and postbiblical traditions depict Balaam as an adversary to the Israelites (see discussion below). For example, Deuteronomy 23:5 provides a clear claim that Balaam's intention was to curse the Israelites: "The Lord your God refused to heed Balaam; the Lord your God turned the curse into a blessing for you" (see also the discussion below; Joshua 24:10; Nehemiah 13:2).

---

29. See, for example, Ed Noort, "Balaam the Villain: The History of Reception of the Balaam Narrative in the Pentateuch and the Former Prophets," in *The Prestige of the Pagan Prophet Balaam in Judaism, Early Christianity and Islam*, ed. George H. van Kooten and Jacques van Ruiten (Brill: Boston, 2008), 3: "On the one hand he [Balaam] is a stranger, foreign to Israel. On the other hand, he acts like an Israelite seer, even like a prophet bound to the word of YHWH." See Noort, "Balaam the Villain," 10–16, for review comments on biblical passages mentioning Balaam.

30. See Milgrom, *Numbers*, 470, for examples and citations.

Based on the conflicting aspects of various biblical traditions, some commentators traditionally describe Balaam as a once-legitimate "prophet of the true God" who fell from Jehovah's grace due to greed and pride.[31] These commentators posited that Balaam had originally been obedient to and blessed by Jehovah, but Balaam changed and thus lost his spiritual gifts over time.

A different and probably better assessment of the biblical and non-biblical evidence is that Balaam was a non-Israelite diviner for hire. He was someone who worshipped Jehovah when it served his purposes, but Balaam did not *exclusively* worship Jehovah and did not prophesy or divine *solely* under his influence. An established reputation as a successful diviner and sorcerer prior to the Israelites' arrival in the plains of Moab apparently lay behind Balak's efforts to hire Balaam to curse the Israelites. People presumably believed Balaam could connect with various deities in the world around him (see further the Deir ʿAlla inscription, below). Therefore, as David Noel Freedman stated in this wry observation, "This is a man who, as you know, makes his services available to the highest bidder. He is what I would call an amiable polytheist."[32]

Viewed this way, the Bible depicts only one aspect of a larger, multifaceted picture of Balaam: Yahweh/Jehovah choosing to speak to and work through Balaam to show his (Jehovah's) power to bring about his own purposes regarding the Israelites, *in spite of* Balak's intentions and Balaam's prior reputation, thus heightening the drama and impact of these blessing-pronouncements. As Victor Hurowitz has observed, "The Balaam story—even while claiming that YHWH, God of Israel, is the only true source of revelation—admits that he [Yahweh/Jehovah] can and does, when he so desires, answer non-Israelite divinatory queries, . . . he communicates his wishes to them in their divinatory mechanisms, . . .

31. For this quotation and perspective, see Adam Clarke, *A Commentary and Critical Notes on the Holy Bible*, "A New Edition with the Author's Final Corrections," vol. 3 (New York: Phillips & Hunt, 1830), s.v. Numbers 22:6. See also Milgrom, *Numbers*, 470, for examples from and citations to Jewish authors.

32. David Noel Freedman, "Yahweh of Samaria and his Asherah," *Biblical Archaeologist* 50, no. 4 (December 1987): 243.

he controls their divination."[33] In other words, one can imagine Jehovah speaking through Moses or any other Israelite to prophesy favorably about the Israelites. But Yahweh/Jehovah using a non-Israelite with a prior reputation of connections with other deities really adds ironic punch to the portrayal in Numbers 22–24. As such, various biblical passages and traditions depict Balaam as both in harmony *and* at odds with Jehovah.

Why was God angry with Balaam? When the second contingent of Balak's men came to hire Balaam, Numbers 22:20 reports, "That night God came to Balaam and said to him, 'If the men have come to summon you, get up and go with them; but do only what I tell you to do.'" Not surprisingly, readers are confused when only two verses later, "God's anger was kindled because he [Balaam] was going" with Balak's messengers (Numbers 22:22).

Commentators have long wrestled with this passage because in its received form it provides no good reason for this sudden shift in God's attitude. It has been suggested that God's anger arose simply because Balaam did not wait to be summoned by Balak's men, rather Balaam got up and set forth with no further prompting.[34] But if this is the reason for the divine displeasure, why, after the angel confronted Balaam, did the angel allow Balaam to proceed, even after he had offered to return to his home? (Numbers 22:34–35; see below for the discussion of Balaam outside Numbers 22–24). Thus a common current assumption is that this apparent incongruity of the text results from the insertion of a previously independent account (what now comprises 22:22–35) about Balaam, which interrupts the flow of an earlier narrative.[35]

---

33. Hurowitz, "The Expression *ûqsāmîm bĕyādām* (Numbers 22:7) in Light of Divinatory Practices from Mari," 14.

34. For example, Clarke cites this option almost two centuries ago in Clarke, *Commentary and Critical Notes*, s.v. Numbers 22:20.

35. See, for example, Ashley, *Book of Numbers*, 435, who states, "Thus it seems reasonable to conclude that 22:22–35 probably form an independent story about Balaam that has been brought into the present narrative about Balaam and Balak at some point in the stream of tradition, although how and when this happened is unclear." See, similarly, Hans Ausloos, "On an Obedient Prophet and a Fickle God, The Narrative of Balaam in Num 22–24," *Old Testament Essays* 20, no. 1 (2007): 92–95.

Alternatively, some earlier commentators saw evidence of a character flaw in Balaam. For example, some Jewish scholars in the early centuries of the Christian era suggested that God was frustrated due to Balaam's *intentions* but still allowed him to go because that was *Balaam's* desire (to get gain/money), even though it was not the Lord's desire.[36]

Latter-day Saints would generally accept that Jehovah knew Balaam's heart and was aware of his intentions. A JST revision at least partially echoes this latter sentiment: "And God came unto Balaam at night, and said unto him, If the men come to call thee, rise up, ~~and~~ if thou wilt[,] go with them; but yet the word which I shall say unto thee, that shalt thou ~~do~~ speak" (JST Numbers 22:20).[37] This reading places responsibility on Balaam to choose whether he would go and to consider his reasons for meeting with Balak. But, there is no way of knowing whether this JST revision is meant to restore the original text or whether it is a latter-day prophetic emendation to provide more clarity to a difficult passage.[38]

Despite whatever intentions he may have had, and whether they changed or not, Balaam is consistently depicted as acting in obedience to Yahweh/Jehovah in the received text of Numbers 22–24. Therefore, there is currently no explicit and compelling answer to the question of why God was angry with Balaam.

A Talking Donkey? Whatever the reason for God's anger against Balaam, the next episode involves Balaam, his donkey, and a divine messenger who stopped Balaam but then allowed him to continue his journey

---

36. See Milgrom, *Numbers*, 189, who cites passages to this effect in the Mishnah and in Numbers Rabbah. For a brief survey of the opinions of early Christian scholars on this issue, see Stephen K. Sherwood, *Leviticus, Numbers, Deuteronomy* (Collegeville, MN: Liturgical, 2002), 176–77. See also Robert Alter, *Hebrew Bible*, 1:558–59.

37. See Scott H. Faulring, Kent P. Jackson, and Robert J. Matthews, eds., *Joseph Smith's New Translation of the Bible: Original Manuscripts* (Provo, UT: Religious Studies Center, Brigham Young University, 2004), 707. As presented, the text with strike-throughs in the quotation was deleted in the JST, and underlined text was added in the JST. For some reason this JST revision is not included in the notes of the Latter-day Saint edition of the KJV.

38. See Faulring, Jackson, and Matthews, eds., *Joseph Smith's New Translation of the Bible*, 8–11, for a helpful overview of five possible categories of JST revisions.

with a warning similar to the divine instruction already given in verse 20: "Go with the men; but speak only what I tell you to speak" (Numbers 22:35).

The donkey's ability to speak to Balaam brings a comic dimension to an otherwise serious narrative account. This ability is attributed to divine power: "The Lord opened the mouth of the donkey" (Numbers 22:28).[39] Although Numbers 22 depicts this episode in a matter-of-fact way, as if it really happened, different understandings of this event derive from the perspectives that readers bring to this passage. Interpretations range from the literal (Jehovah had power to cause a donkey to speak, so the donkey really spoke, just as the text claims) to the figurative (the account is often said to be "folklore" or a "fable").[40] The only biblical passage that is remotely analogous to the account of Balaam's talking donkey is the report of a pre-Fall talking snake in the Garden of Eden (Genesis 3:1–5; Moses 4:5–11). Responses to this latter episode likewise range from the literal to the figurative.[41]

Whatever one's views of the account of Balaam's donkey speaking by divine power, a main and ironic point of this narrative is that the man who was hired because of his reputation for sorcery and "seeing" divine intent could not see God's angel. Indeed, the angel was right in front of Balaam, but it was his donkey that saw the angel three times and also spoke to

---

39. Many commentators mention the perceived humor in this account. See, for example, Mark W. Hamilton, *A Theological Introduction to the Old Testament* (New York: Oxford University Press, 2018), 78: "Again, this part of the story has a highly comic element. Talking donkeys and frustrated prophets are things to laugh at, and Numbers certainly intends the reader to laugh." See also Alter, *Hebrew Bible*, 1:473, 559–60.

40. See, for example, Thomas B. Dozeman, "The Book of Numbers," in *The New Interpreter's Bible* (Nashville: Abingdon, 1998), 2:183; Milgrom, *Numbers*, 468–69.

41. These are the only biblical accounts of creatures speaking human language. For further comments on these episodes, see G. Savran, "Beastly Speech: Intertextuality, Balaam's Ass and the Garden of Eden," *Journal for the Study of the Old Testament* 19, no. 64 (December 1994): 33–55. For Latter-day Saints, Moses 4:6–7 indicates that Satan "spake by the mouth of the serpent" in Eden. Second Peter 2:16, presumably relying on Numbers 22, reiterates that Balaam's donkey spoke to him.

Balaam, thereby saving Balaam's life (Numbers 22:22–33).[42] So this short account of Balaam, his donkey, and an angel serves to ridicule Balaam, suggesting that he was not really who he claimed to be. Rather, as some have said, he was "a fool, a caricature of a seer, one outwitted even by his dumb beast."[43]

Additionally, in this episode, "the LORD opened the mouth of the donkey" to speak to Balaam, and then "the LORD opened the eyes of Balaam" to see an angel with a sword (Numbers 22:28, 31). This experience serves as narrative preparation for when Jehovah later opened Balaam's mouth to pronounce blessings on the Israelites.[44] Through this sequence of events, as well as in previous incidents in Numbers, the biblical account emphasizes that Yahweh/Jehovah could speak through whatever and whomever he chose, whether through a donkey, a non-Israelite diviner, Moses (12:6–8), or potentially all of the covenant people (11:29: "Would that all the LORD's people were prophets, and that the LORD would put his spirit on them!"). The biblical Balaam episode reiterates that prophetic pronouncements come via divine not human inclination.

Where did Balaam live? Since Balak sent messengers to Balaam to hire his services to curse the Israelites, one important but seemingly background consideration in Numbers 22 is the location of Balaam's home. This question arises from challenges in the Hebrew text itself and is handled differently in different Bible translations. For example, in the KJV, Numbers 22:5 reads, "[Balak] sent messengers therefore unto Balaam the son of Beor to Pethor, which is by the river of the land of the children of his people." But the same passage in the NRSV reads, "[Balak] sent

---

42. Most commentators make the observation of the inherent irony. Additionally, E. R. Wendland, "Two Dumb Donkeys Declare the Word of the Lord: A Literary-Structural Analysis of Numbers 22–24," *Journal for Semitics* 21, no. 2 (2012): 173–75, sees a relational irony in "the tale of 'two donkeys', one bestial the other human [Balaam], both of which are compelled to pronounce the word of the LORD in the face of strong opposition" (174). See therein for further comments on the many literary and rhetorical features of Numbers 22–24.

43. Milgrom, *Numbers*, 469.

44. See the observation by Alter, *Hebrew Bible*, 1:473 that the donkey in this episode is to Balaam as Balaam, the one who God allows to see and speak, will later be to Balak.

messengers to Balaam son of Beor at Pethor, which is on the Euphrates, in the land of Amaw."

The identity of Pethor is a matter of question. Many scholars have suggested connecting Pethor with Pitru, a town named in an Assyrian source, apparently situated on the upper Euphrates River (the site itself has not been convincingly identified).[45] This would make sense in relation to passages such as Numbers 23:7, in which Balaam claims, "Balak has brought me from Aram," the biblical/ancient name for what is now Syria,[46] and Deuteronomy 23:4, "Balaam son of Beor, from Pethor of Mesopotamia [Hebrew, 23:5: *ʾăram nahărayîm*, "Aram of the two rivers"]."

The NRSV translation of Numbers 22:5 illustrates this presumed location of Pethor in northern Aram by representing the Hebrew word *nāhār* as "Euphrates [River]." Although the common noun *nāhār*, "river," is sometimes used to specifically designate the Euphrates (Genesis 31:21; Micah 7:12), it is often employed in the Bible to indicate other rivers, named and unnamed (e.g., Genesis 2:13; Numbers 24:6; Isaiah 19:5). *If* Balaam's Pethor was located in northern Aram/Syria near the Euphrates, which is not certain, it is amazing that Balak both knew about Balaam and his abilities and was able to persuade him to journey to Moab, a distance of about 350 miles.

For this reason, some scholars have suggested a home for Balaam closer to Moab, a home that makes the account of his donkey ride more realistic, accompanied as he was by only two servants with little or no preparation (Numbers 22:22) and with reference to fields and vineyards along the way (22:24–25). Indeed, one scholar, based on his reading of a tablet found at Deir ʿAlla, has suggested equating Pethor with Deir ʿAlla,

45. See for example, Noort, "Balaam the Villain," 21–22; Jo Ann Hackett, "Balaam," in *Anchor Bible Dictionary*, ed. David N. Freedman (New York: Doubleday, 1992), 1:571.

46. For a brief overview of Aram/Syria in the Bible, see Dana M. Pike, "Syria," in *Book of Mormon Reference Companion*, ed. Dennis L. Largey et al. (Salt Lake City: Deseret Book, 2003), 749–50; and the Latter-day Saint Bible Dictionary, s.v. "Syria."

which is located near the Zerqa (Jabbok) River, about 35 miles north of the Israelite encampment in the plains of Moab (see below).[47]

A related consideration is the meaning of the phrase, *ʾerṣ bĕnê- ʿammô*, in Numbers 22:5 in the traditional Hebrew Masoretic Text (MT), which the KJV renders quite literally as "the land of the children of his people." By contrast, the NRSV, the NET, and some other modern translations ignore the word *bĕnê* ("sons, children") and revocalize the MT form *ʿammô*, rendering this phrase as "the land of Amaw." This land of Amaw, however, is otherwise unknown. Thus, some have proposed that *ʿammô* is a corruption of *ʿammōn*, "Ammon," Moab's neighbor in Transjordan. The phrase *bĕnê ʿammōn*, "children of Ammon" occurs dozens of times in the Hebrew Bible (e.g., Numbers 21:24; Deuteronomy 2:19). This latter approach—emending *ʿammô* to *ʿammōn*—is supported by the Samaritan Pentateuch, the Syriac, and the Vulgate (ancient versions of the Hebrew scriptures), all of which read "the land of the Ammonites" in Numbers 22:5.[48]

A proposed Ammonite (or perhaps Gileadite), and thus more proximate, home for Balaam makes good sense in many ways. However, it is not in harmony with the biblical passages cited above that indicate Balaam's home was in northern Aram/Syria (Numbers 23:7; Deuteronomy 23:4). Thus, the question of Balaam's homeland remains unresolved, but a location closer to Moab seems more likely in the context of the story as we have it and finds additional support from the alternative reading of Numbers 22:5 in some ancient versions, from the tradition preserved in the Deir ʿAlla inscription, and from the account of Balaam's death (Numbers 31:8;

47. William H. Shea, "The Inscribed Tablets from Tell Deir ʿAlla, Part I," *Andrews University Seminary Studies* 27, no. 1 (Spring 1989): 29, 31; William H. Shea, "The Inscribed Tablets from Tell Deir ʿAlla, Part II," *Andrews University Seminary Studies* 27, no. 2 (Summer 1989): 97, 107.

48. See Alter, *Hebrew Bible*, 1:556. For the Samaritan Pentateuch, see Benyamim Tsedaka, *The Israelite Samaritan Version of the Torah* (Grand Rapids, MI: Eerdmans, 2013), 364. Of course, as Alter notes, one could argue that the ancient translators revised a challenging Hebrew text—"the land of the children of his people"—to make sense of it. A number of other scholars, however, have made the plausible connection between Balaam's residence and the region of Ammon or Gilead.

the latter two points are discussed below). Thus, a homeland for Balaam closer to Moab is currently preferred by many scholars.[49]

Why are Balaam's oracles in poetry? Once Balaam traveled to and met with Balak, Balaam uttered three different pronouncements on the Israelites, each of which were requested by Balak to be cursings. Although the KJV does not represent poetic passages as poetry, as most biblical translations now do, Balaam's three pronouncements on the Israelites are all in poetic form, as are his later pronouncements against Moabites and others. The three pronouncements thus read differently from the narrative prose in which the rest of this account is presented.

The Bible contains a great deal of poetry, since poetry was generally employed to present psalms, proverbs, prophecy, and prayers. Creating biblical poetic passages presumably required greater conscious effort on the part of biblical authors than did producing prose texts. And the reading and hearing of poetic passages would have generally required greater attention on the part of listening Israelites, since most ancient Israelites encountered biblical texts orally. The imagery, metaphors, rhythm, repetition of sounds and thoughts, and the multifaceted nature of Hebrew poetry invite and require greater focus to appreciate and comprehend, but these aspects of Hebrew poetry also tend to reward readers and hearers with greater insight and literary pleasure.

The poetry employed to express Balaam's utterances about Israel serves to emphsize and elevate Jehovah's words given through Balaam. While Balaam's first oracle (Numbers 23:7–10) draws on elements already presented in the preceding prose narrative, the oracle's poetic form conveys an impact unlike prose narration, especially when read aloud:

> For from the top of the crags I see him,
> from the hills I behold him . . .
> Who can count the dust of Jacob,
> or number the dust-cloud of Israel?
> Let me die the death of the upright,
> and let my end be like his! (23:9–10)

---

49. For further discussion of this issue, see for example, S. C. Layton, "Whence Comes Balaam? Num 22, 5 Revisited," *Biblica* 73, no. 1 (1992): 32–61.

Similarly, Balaam's second oracle (23:18–24) continues the declaration of Israel's blessed status but does so with an increased focus on God:

> God is not a human being, that he should lie,
> or a mortal, that he should change his mind.
> Has he promised, and will he not do it?
> Has he spoken, and will he not fulfill it?
> See, I [Balaam] received a command to bless;
> he has blessed, and I cannot revoke it. (23:19–20)

The prose narration preceding both of these pronouncements—"The LORD put a word in Balaam's mouth" (Numbers 23:5; similarly, verse 16)—is an allusion to prophecy (see above). Balaam uttered his third oracle (24:1–9) after "the spirit of God came upon him" (24:2; also mentioned above). The following few lines from the third oracle are included to further illustrate the poetic nature of these texts:

> How fair are your tents, O Jacob,
> your encampments, O Israel!
> Like palm groves that stretch far away,
> like gardens beside a river, . . .
> God who brings him [Israel] out of Egypt,
> is like the horns of a wild ox for him;
> he shall devour the nations that are his foes
> and break their bones. (24:5–6, 8)

As Milgrom has rightly observed, "This [third] oracle is the climactic one: In the first, only God determines blessing and curse (23:8); in the second, God's blessing cannot be revoked (23:20); in this, the third, those who bless or curse Israel will themselves be blessed or cursed [24:9]."[50]

Thus, the non-Israelite Balaam's pronouncements of Yahweh's protection of and intentions for the Israelites are expressed poetically. These oracles do not stand independent from the prose narrative in Numbers 22–24. However, their poetic form serves to portray their divine origin and to accentuate their significant content.

50. Milgrom, *Numbers*, 202.

A messianic prophecy in Numbers 24? Following Balaam's failure to curse Israel as Balak had requested, Balak angrily dismissed Balaam (Numbers 24:10–13). However, Balaam did not leave Moab before prophesying against it (24:14–19). The content of Balaam's prophetic pronouncement against Moab includes a passage that has long been interpreted by some Jews and Christians as messianic:

> I see him, but not now;
> I behold him, but not near—
>   a star shall come out of Jacob,
>   and a scepter shall rise out of Israel;
> it shall crush the borderlands of Moab,
>   and the territory of all the Shethites.
> Edom will become a possession,
>   Seir a possession of its enemies,
>   while Israel does valiantly.
> One out of Jacob shall rule,
>   and destroy the survivors of Ir. (24:17–19)

This poetic passage not only prophesies a future Israelite military domination of Moab and its southern neighbor Edom (also known as Seir in the Bible) but also indicates this domination will be accomplished when "a star comes out of Jacob, and a scepter shall rise out of Israel" (24:17).

Evidence exists from as early as the last few centuries BC that at least some Jews considered Numbers 24:17 to be a messianic passage. For example, members of the Dead Sea community at Qumran understood this passage as referring to the two eschatological messiahs, the priestly messiah (the "star") and the royal Davidic messiah (the "scepter").[51] A few

51. See Dana M. Pike, "The Book of Numbers at Qumran: Texts and Context," in *Current Research and Technological Developments on the Dead Sea Scrolls*, ed. Donald W. Parry and Stephen D. Ricks (New York: Brill, 1996), 182–85. For references to Jewish texts other than the Dead Sea Scrolls that also viewed Numbers 24:17 as messianic (and notice the title of the book!), see John J. Collins, *The Scepter and the Star, Messianism in Light of the Dead Sea Scrolls*, 2nd ed. (Grand Rapids, MI: Eerdmans, 2010), 71–73.

centuries later, some Jews, including the famed Rabbi Akiba,[52] referred to Simon bar Kosiba—leader of the unsuccessful second Jewish revolt against the Roman Empire (AD 132–135)—as Simon bar Kokhba ("son of the star"), presumably because some saw Simon as the messianic fulfillment of the passage in Numbers 24:17.[53] Christians have understood not only David as partial fulfillment of this prophecy (according to 2 Samuel 8:2, David defeated the Moabites) but ultimately Jesus Christ as the priestly *and* royal Messiah (Revelation 22:16).

Were there Midianites in Moab? Midianites are mentioned as living among the Moabites in Numbers 22 and 25.[54] This is another seemingly minor detail that is an important element in the biblical account, since Midianites are mentioned several times in Numbers 22–31. The Bible depicts the Midianites as the descendants of Midian, the fourth son of Abraham and his concubine Keturah (Genesis 25:1–2; 1 Chronicles 1:32). Although the Midianites were primarily located in northwestern Arabia, biblical accounts occasionally mention them in Moab and even in Canaan/Israel (e.g., Genesis 36:35; 37:28; Judges 6:1, 33). The Bible indicates that by the time of Moses, who himself fled Egypt to Midian and married a Midianite woman (Exodus 2:15–21), there were various Midianite clans, some of which lived in areas east and north of the Dead Sea and maintained shifting relationships with other peoples from those areas (e.g., Genesis

52. Akiba's name is additionally spelled in English as Akiva, Aqiba, and Aqiva. Many Bible dictionaries have an entry on Akiba.

53. See, for example, Collins, *The Scepter and the Star*, 72, 226–27. See also Stefan Beyerle, "'A Star Shall Come Out of Jacob': A Critical Evaluation of the Balaam Oracle in the Context of Jewish Revolts in Roman Times," in *Prestige of the Pagan Prophet Balaam*, 163–88.

54. Note also the interchange between these two names in Numbers 25:1, which recounts Israelite men having sexual relations with *Moabite* women at Baal Peor; in Numbers 25:9, 15, which report that a *Midianite* woman was involved in sinful activity with an Israelite at Baal Peor (probably cultic activity rather than merely sexual misconduct); and in Numbers 31:16, where Moses says that *Midianite* women "on Balaam's advice, made the Israelites act treacherously against the Lord in the affair of Peor." Although multiple textual traditions could be postulated, enough biblical passages place some Midianites in Moabite territory to accept that some mixing of peoples lies behind these variations.

25:6; Joshua 13:21; Judges 6–8). Thus, it is not surprising to read of Midianites in the region of Moab.

BALAAM MENTIONED IN OTHER SCRIPTURE

Following the account in Numbers 22–24, Balaam is occasionally cited elsewhere in the Bible.[55] Some of these other references have already been cited above. How these other passages are interpreted in relation to the main account of Balaam strongly influences one's ultimate perception of this fascinating character. In general, an "increasingly negative characterization of Balaam" is displayed in later biblical and postbiblical writings.[56]

Balaam's death is mentioned in passing in Numbers 31. Following a note that the Israelites defeated the Midianites in battle and killed their kings, the text then matter-of-factly reads, "They also killed Balaam son of Beor with the sword" (Numbers 31:8; compare Joshua 13:22).[57] This appears as a surprising report—the Israelites killing Balaam—since he had been depicted as acting on behalf of Yahweh/Jehovah by pronouncing blessings on the Israelites rather than the curses he was hired to invoke. However, Numbers 31:16 provides this further explanation: "These women here, *on Balaam's advice*, made the Israelites act treacherously against the LORD in the affair of Peor, so that the plague came among the congregation of the LORD" (31:16; emphasis added; for the full account see 31:1–20). The incident at Baal Peor is recounted in Numbers 25. After Balaam left Moab

55. An important recent study on the broader tradition history of Balaam, but one that was not available to me when this paper was originally written, is Jonathan Miles Robker, *Balaam in Text and Tradition* (Tübingen: Mohr Siebeck, 2019). See also the seven-part entry "Balaam," in *Encyclopedia of the Bible and Its Reception*, ed. Hans-Josef Klauck et al. (Boston: De Gruyter, 2011), 3:357–73, for a succinct overview of Balaam in biblical and postbiblical traditions.

56. Dennis T. Olson, "Balaam, I. Ancient Near East and Hebrew Bible/Old Testament," in *Encyclopedia of the Bible and Its Reception*, 3:358.

57. Various theories have been propounded to harmonize Numbers 24:25 ("Balaam got up and went back to his place, and Balak also went his way") with the slaying of Balaam when the Israelites later fought the Midianites (31:8). For the purposes herein, it is sufficient to observe that the received text is not clear on this matter.

to return to his home, "the [Israelites] began to have sexual relations with the women of Moab. These invited the [Israelites] to the sacrifices of [the Moabite] gods, and the [Israelites] ate and bowed down to [the Moabite] gods. Thus, Israel yoked itself to the [god] Baal of Peor, and the LORD's anger was kindled against Israel" (25:1–3).[58] The claim in Numbers 31:16, that Balaam had suggested that the Moabites could "defeat" the Israelites by getting them to sin and thus curse themselves is a major factor in the reversal of the generally positive depiction of Balaam given in Numbers 22–24 (except in the donkey episode).[59]

Deuteronomy 23:5 suggests that Balaam was actually trying to curse the Israelites but that Jehovah "refused to heed" him (see, similarly, Joshua 24:10; Nehemiah 13:2).[60] Joshua 13:22 echoes Numbers 31:8 in claiming that "the Israelites also put to the sword Balaam son of Beor" because he had "practiced divination" (Joshua 13:22).

A major exception to this negative recasting of Balaam is in Micah 6:5: "O my people, remember now what King Balak of Moab devised, what Balaam son of Beor answered him, . . . that you may know the saving acts of the LORD." Balaam here is depicted as a hero who had helped to overturn Balak's evil intentions to destroy the Israelites.

In the New Testament, 2 Peter 2:15 and Jude 1:11 both cite Balaam as illustrating that those who go astray from God do so because they love the gain of the world. And Revelation 2:14 blames Balaam for teaching "Balak to put a stumbling block before the people of Israel, so that they would eat food sacrificed to idols and practice fornication" (this passage draws

---

58. In Numbers 25:1 the women are designated as Moabite, but in 31:16 it sounds like they are Midianite. See the comments in note 54 on the occurrences of "Midianite" and "Moabite" in Numbers 22.

59. Some commentators prefer the option of multiple sources with differing perspectives on Balaam to explain these differences. Among Latter-day Saint authors, see, for example, Victor L. Ludlow, *Unlocking the Old Testament* (Salt Lake City: Deseret Book, 1981), 48–49.

60. It is not clear what the basis is for this biblical assessment, other than perhaps the fact that Balaam agreed to go with Balak's messengers. Perhaps other authors and editors had additional information not now found in Numbers 22–24 or they assumed that the text had not made Balaam's original intentions sufficiently clear.

on Numbers 25:1–3; 31:16).[61] Furthermore, as Milgrom has expressed, "[many] postbiblical [Jewish] texts exaggerate Balaam's vices to such a degree that he becomes an exemplar of villainy."[62]

Regarding this interpretive trend, Ashley has correctly observed, "The text of [Numbers] chs. 22–24 is not [explicitly] concerned to pronounce [judgment] on the matter [of Balaam's virtue]. Balaam's character is incidental to the story."[63] This is because from a literary and theological perspective, Balaam functions in Numbers 22–24 primarily as a foil to Balak and as the mouthpiece for Jehovah's will for the Israelites. Later biblical and related traditions derive lessons from Balaam's activities and perceived intentions that are not explicitly emphasized in Numbers 22–24, apart from in the donkey episode.[64] If all we knew about Balaam is what is related in Numbers 22–24 and Micah 6:5, his reputation in our minds might be much different. Overall, the Bible and post-biblical traditions present a complex and mixed picture of Balaam, one that becomes predominantly negative through later texts and time. There is currently no good evidence for the origins of these varied traditions.

BALAAM IN THE DEIR 'ALLA INSCRIPTION

Deir 'Alla is a site in the eastern Jordan River valley, about one mile north of where the biblical Jabbok River flows into the Jordan. In 1967 archaeologists discovered there the very fragmentary remains of a literary text written in ink on plaster. Originally thought to have lined a temple wall, the

---

61. For recent examinations of the New Testament's uses of Balaam, see Jan Willem van Henten, "Balaam in Revelation 2:14," and Tord Fornberg, "Balaam and 2 Peter 2:15: 'They Have Followed in the Steps of Balaam' (Jude 11)," in *The Prestige of the Pagan Prophet Balaam in Judaism, Early Christianity and Islam*, 247–63 and 265–74, respectively.
62. See Milgrom, *Numbers*, 471, for this quote and for supporting examples.
63. Ashley, *The Book of Numbers*, 435.
64. See, for example, Jacques T. A. G. M. van Ruiten, "The Rewriting of Numbers 22–24 in Pseudo-Philo, *Liber Antiquitatum Biblicarum* 18," and Johan Leemans, "'To Bless with a Mouth Bent on Cursing': Patristic Interpretations of Balaam (Num 24:17)," in *The Prestige of the Pagan Prophet Balaam in Judaism, Early Christianity and Islam*, 101–30 and 287–99, respectively.

room in which the fragments were found is now considered to have been "part of a manufacturing and distribution center located on the mound, where some religious activity may have [also] taken place." Some scholars now suggest that the plaster originally coated a large stela or other object, not a wall (compare Deuteronomy 27:2–3).[65] Dated to about 800 BC, most of the surviving text is primarily written in black ink, although some words are in red. Also evident is a line of red ink that frames columns of the text. Classifying the language of the Deir ʿAlla text is challenging; it is perhaps best described as a dialect demonstrating Aramaic and Ammonite, or at least Southern Canaanite, affinities.[66] Two fragmentary "combinations" of the Deir ʿAlla inscription (from what were two columns of writing) have been partially reconstructed.[67] This inscription has generated great interest because it mentions Balaam, previously known only from the Bible (and later traditions).

65. For the quote, see Levine, "The Deir ʿAlla Plaster Inscriptions (2.27)," 141. See pages 140–41 for a discussion of these and related issues. See also Christopher A. Rollston, *Writing and Literacy in the World of Ancient Israel: Epigraphic Evidence from the Iron Age* (Atlanta: Society of Biblical Literature, 2010), 61; Émile Puech, "Balaʿam and Deir ʿAlla," in *The Prestige of the Pagan Prophet Balaam in Judaism, Early Christianity and Islam*, 25–47; J. Hoftijzer and G. van der Kooij, eds., *The Balaam Text from Deir ʿAlla Re-Evaluated* (New York: Brill, 1991).

66. Similarly, Levine's assessment, "The Deir ʿAlla Plaster Inscriptions (2.27)," 141, reads: "In the first publication, the language of these inscriptions was simply identified as Aramaic, but subsequent analysis has altered scholarly opinion, favoring a local, or regional language bearing affinities to both the Aramaic and Canaanite groups, with opinion still divided on this question." Puech, "Balaʿam and Deir ʿAlla," 40–43, claims that Aramaic is not the language of the inscription but that it "is a local dialect close to the Canaanite of its time, . . . this dialect can be viewed as Gileadite or ʿAmmonite'" (43).

67. For a brief discussion of the Deir ʿAlla inscription, including a picture, see Holzapfel, Pike, and Seely, *Jehovah and the World of the Old Testament*, 134. For somewhat differing translations of the surviving text, with commentary, see Levine, "The Deir ʿAlla Plaster Inscriptions (2.27)," 142–45; Shmuel Aḥituv, *Echoes from the Past: Hebrew and Cognate Inscriptions from the Biblical Period*, trans. Anson F. Rainey (Jerusalem: Carta, 2008), 433–465. For an examination of religious perspectives at Deir ʿAlla and throughout the broader Transjordan, see Jeremy M. Hutton, "Southern, Northern and Transjordanian Perspectives," in *Religious Diversity in Ancient Israel and Judah*, ed. Francesca Stavrakopoulou and John Barton (New York: T&T Clark, 2010), 161–68.

The Deir ʿAlla inscription does *not* recount the events narrated in Numbers 22–24. However, there are fascinating similarities between the content of the two texts. Combination I of the inscription contains phrases such as "Balaam son of Beor" (I.2, 4; compare Numbers 22:5), identifying him as a "seer of the gods [*ḥzh ʾlhn*]" (I.1). "The gods [plural] came to him by night [compare Numbers 22:8–9, 20] and he saw a vision [*yḥz mḥzh*; compare Numbers 24:4, 16] like an oracle of ʾEl [*ʾl*]. Then they said to [Balaa]m, son of Beor . . ." (I.1–2).[68] The noun *ʾl* occurs several times in poetic passages in Numbers 23–24, where it is translated as "God" and is used in reference to Yahweh/Jehovah (e.g., 23:8, 19). This noun was also used anciently to designate the chief Canaanite god, El.[69]

This inscription further relates that Balaam wept and fasted after seeing his nighttime vision. "His people" inquired the reason for his behavior; Balaam related his experience, claiming, "I will tell you what the Shadda[yyin will do]. . . . Come see the work of the gods [*ʾlhyn*]" (I.3–5). Compare this line in the Deir ʿAlla inscription with Numbers 24:4, which reads, "The oracle of one [Balaam] who hears the words of God [*ʾēl*], who sees the vision of the Almighty [*šadday*]."

"Shaddayyin," a plural form thought to be related to the Hebrew singular Shadday/Shaddai (*šadday*), occurs in this inscription parallel to "gods"; the Shaddayyin are best understood as part of the divine council (see I.6, "the Shaddayyin took their places at the assembly").[70] Shadday (*šadday*) occurs several dozen times in the Bible, including in Numbers 24:4, 16, and has been traditionally translated as "Almighty."[71]

Revealed to Balaam in the Deir ʿAlla text was the divine plan of doom to "bolt up the heavens with a cloud; set darkness there forever instead of

68. The translation used here is based on Aḥituv, *Echoes from the Past*, 435, 438.

69. For a discussion of the forms and uses of *ʾēl* and *ʾĕlōhîm* in the Hebrew Bible, see Pike, "Name and Titles of God in the Old Testament," 21–25.

70. This possible connection between "shaddayyin" and Hebrew *šadday* is usually favored over a connection with Hebrew *šēdîm*, which is usually translated as "devils/demons" in Deuteronomy 32:17 and Psalm 106:37.

71. For a discussion of the use and meaning of this term in the Hebrew Bible, see Pike, "Name and Titles of God in the Old Testament," 26. Biblical occurrences of *šadday* are primarily in Job, with several in Genesis and occasional attestations in Ruth and elsewhere.

light" (I.6–7). The next lines are problematic, and are rendered somewhat differently by different scholars. "What follows is obscure, but it appears that Balaam thwarts this plan by offering a series of oracles and magical rituals."[72] None of the surviving text of this inscription portrays Balaam in a negative light, as do several biblical passages.

Discovered about thirty-five miles from where the Bible places Balak's employment of Balaam against the Israelites in the plains of Moab, the Deir ʿAlla inscription strikingly demonstrates that Balaam traditions existed in that region for quite some time.[73] And the fact that this ink inscription was created at all demonstrates the remarkable degree of reputation Balaam must have had in the region.

As mentioned, the location of this inscription plausibly supports a locale for Balaam's hometown in the vicinity, rather than in northern Aram/Syria. And as related in the Deir ʿAlla inscription, Balaam receives divine communication from deities other than Yahweh/Jehovah. Thus, in important ways, this inscription affects our understanding of the depiction of Balaam in the biblical account.

Although it is interesting to contemplate the extent to which Israelite influence may have informed the traditions behind this inscription, there is uncertainty regarding who produced the Deir ʿAlla text. According to the Bible, Israelites descended from the tribes of Gad and Manasseh, that settled east of the Jordan River at the time of Moses and Joshua (Numbers 32:1–5; Joshua 13:8–11, 24–31). Given the focus on Balaam in Numbers 22–24 and in this inscription, some scholars have naturally postulated Israelite authorship of the Deir ʿAlla inscription, although these would have been Israelites who differed from the prophetically approved religious orientation represented in the Bible.[74] Others caution that we cannot

72. Kenton L. Sparks, *Ancient Texts for the Study of the Hebrew Bible: A Guide to the Background Literature* (Peabody, MA: Hendrickson, 2005), 234.

73. Dating to about 800 BC, the inscription was produced about 400–450 years after the conventional dating of the Israelite encampment in the plains of Moab. Some scholars use the date of the inscription to support a later date of composition for the biblical text in Numbers 22–24.

74. Levine's claim in "The Deir ʿAlla Plaster Inscriptions (2.27)," 141, for example, is quite plausible: "Given what is known of the immediate region [around Deir ʿAlla] in the early to mid-eighth century BCE, it is likely that Israelites

yet tell whether Israelites or non-Israelites (presumably Ammonites) produced this text.[75] No matter who composed it, this inscription provides important information about a Balaam tradition relatively near the plains of Moab centuries after the traditional biblical portrayal in the book of Numbers.

BALAAM AND LATTER-DAY SAINTS

Two assertions are prominent in references Latter-day Saint authors and Church leaders have made to Balaam during the past fifty years: (1) Balaam had been a prophet of Jehovah, and (2) we are encouraged to learn lessons from Balaam's waywardness, lessons based on the predominantly negative biblical and postbiblical depictions of Balaam preserved after Numbers 22–24.

One oft-cited Latter-day Saint publication on Balaam is Elder Bruce R. McConkie's "The Story of a Prophet's Madness." The title of Elder McConkie's remarks and his opening line—"Let me tell you the story of a prophet, in some respects a very great prophet"—convey the idea that Elder McConkie considered Balaam to have been a legitimate prophet of Jehovah (as I've indicated above, I see the biblical depiction of Jehovah's use of Balaam to speak Jehovah's words as part of a larger complex of Balaam's activities as a diviner and sorcerer on behalf of a variety of gods). However, Elder McConkie's main purpose in relating Balaam's story was didactic (instructive). Employing the negative biblical evaluation of Balaam as preserved in the New Testament, Elder McConkie taught, "Balaam the prophet, inspired and mighty as he once was, lost his soul in

---

constituted the principal element in the Gileadite population. It has been argued that, indeed, the inscriptions speak for Gileadite Israelites who worshipped El, a regional deity."

75. See, for example, E. A. Knauf, "Shadday," in *Dictionary of Deities and Demons in the Bible*, 2nd ed., ed. Karel van der Toorn (Boston: Brill, 1999), 750, who refers to "the presumably Israelite . . . Deir 'Alla inscription"; and Aḥituv, *Echoes from the Past*, 435, who more pointedly claims that "conjectures about the ethnic/national affiliation of the inscription are futile."

the end because he set his heart on the things of this world rather than the riches of eternity."[76]

The terse entry in the Latter-day Saint Bible Dictionary is more straightforward, identifying Balaam only as a prophet: "A prophet from Pethor by the Euphrates, bribed by Balak, king of Moab, to curse the Israelites" (see the discussion above on the location of Pethor).[77] Commentary on Balaam and Numbers 22–24 by Latter-day Saint authors tends to be brief, follows the more traditional options, and generally highlights potential didactic dimensions of the passages outside Numbers 22–24.[78] Therefore, these commentators' positions do not always agree with the conclusions presented herein, including the more likely location of Balaam's hometown and especially Balaam's background and relationship with Yahweh/Jehovah.[79]

Interestingly, although several references were made regarding Balaam and his experiences by early Latter-day Saint Church leaders (again, usually for didactic purposes), Balaam was mentioned only *once* in a formal

---

76. Bruce R. McConkie, "The Story of a Prophet's Madness," *New Era*, April 1972, 7.
77. Latter-day Saint Bible Dictionary, s.v., "Balaam." The use of the term "bribed" in this entry has interesting and unfounded connotations. The Bible depicts the event in question as essentially a proposed business transaction.
78. See, for example, Ludlow, *Unlocking the Old Testament*, 48–49; Robert L. Millet, "Lessons in the Wilderness (Numbers)," in *Genesis to 2 Samuel*, ed. Kent P. Jackson and Robert L. Millet (Salt Lake City: Deseret Book, 1985), 200–202; Ellis T. Rasmussen, *A Latter-day Saint Commentary on the Old Testament* (Salt Lake City: Deseret Book, 1993), 160–61; Kerry Muhlestein, *The Essential Old Testament Companion* (American Fork, UT: Covenant Communications, 2013), 142–46; D. Kelly Ogden and Andrew C. Skinner, *Verse by Verse, The Old Testament* (Salt Lake City: Deseret Book, 2013), 1:289–92. Ludlow, Millet, and Ogden and Skinner all quote rather extensively from Elder McConkie's article.
79. As illustrations, Rasmussen, *A Latter-day Saint Commentary on the Old Testament*, 160, placed Balaam's hometown in northern Syria, near Haran (where remnants of Abraham and Sarah's ancestry and their culture "may have remained"), claiming, "in Pethor was a people who believed in the same God as the Israelites;" however, we do *not* know this from any biblical source. And Muhlestein, *The Essential Old Testament Companion*, 144, claims Balaam came from "eastern Aram, or Syria," and that he "worshipped and followed Jehovah," implying that this was Balaam's only connection with the divine. Again, I have presented differing interpretations above.

general conference address during the past one hundred years.[80] Elder Neal A. Maxwell employed the story of Balaam when he taught in October 2000, "Actually, discipleship may keep the honors of the world from us. As Balak told Balaam, 'I thought to promote thee unto great honour; but, lo, the Lord hath kept thee back from honour' (Numbers 24:11–12)."[81] Of course, Balaam's name appears in various Latter-day Saint lesson manuals, articles in Church magazines, and presentations by Church leaders. These occurrences usually involve teaching lessons based on what is said about Balaam in biblical passages outside Numbers 22–24.[82]

Certainly, there is value in these teachings, but they represent only one dimension of a complex figure and scriptural account. After all, as presented in the Bible, Balaam consistently claimed that he would only speak the words that Yahweh/Jehovah gave him to speak (e.g., Numbers 22:18, 38; 23:12), he was granted prophetic gifts because he would not be bought with gold or silver (chapters 23–24), *and yet* he is also vilified because he "practiced divination" (Joshua 13:22; the KJV renders this as "the soothsayer") and because he "loved the wages of doing wrong" (2 Peter 2:15).

---

80. Additionally, in the last century, only one conference speaker included a citation to Numbers 22–24, which was Numbers 23:19, a verse used to support the principle that God does not lie. See Brian K. Ashton, "The Father," *Ensign* November 2018, 96 n46. To determine the use of Numbers 22–24 in general conference addresses, see the online resource "LDS Scripture Citation Index" (http://scriptures.byu.edu). Other citations connected with Numbers 22–24 offered on this website refer to nineteenth-century Church leaders.

81. Neal A. Maxwell, "The Tugs and Pulls of the World," *Ensign*, November 2000, 60.

82. Two recent examples are the following: Dieter F. Uchtdorf, "What is Truth?" (Church Educational System address, January 2013); and H. Ross Workman, "Breaking the Chains of Sin," *Liahona*, July 2006, 38–39. Surprisingly, this latter article asserts that "Balaam was an *Israelite* prophet residing near the borders of Moab at the time [of] Moses" (emphasis added). From my comments above, it should be clear that the Bible does *not* depict Balaam as an Israelite, although I do agree that Balaam lived somewhere relatively close to Moab.

CONCLUDING THOUGHTS

Balaam, the non-Israelite who prophesied positively about the Israelites, remains an enigmatic biblical figure, at least in part, because we cannot fully or confidently answer several important questions about him. The account of Balaam in Numbers 22–24 is oddly unique and reads like an independent unit, but it connects in several ways with the content and themes of the rest of the book of Numbers. So, however this account developed and was incorporated into the book of Numbers, it can at least be appreciated as part of the organic whole of the book.

Although many of the details about Balaam's identity are sketchy, his historicity is further supported (beyond the biblical text) by the tradition preserved in the Deir ʿAlla inscription. As overviewed above, the biblical tradition provides a mixed evaluation of him at best. Presuming he was a historical figure, it is quite likely that traditions about Balaam the person developed through time. Certainly, the biblical traditions about Balaam appear to have become more negative in contexts outside of Numbers 22–24. Thus, his reputation among Latter-day Saints and other Bible readers generally remains unfavorable. Balaam and his life are thus regularly employed as a warning: "Woe to them . . . [who] abandon themselves to Balaam's error for the sake of gain" (Jude 1:11).

INDEX

A

B

C

F

G

H

M

N

Q

R

S

T

U

V

W

Y

Z